Scott Foresman • Addison Wesley

enVisionMATH™

Scott Foresman · Addison Wesley

enVisionMATH™

Texas

Authors

Randall I. Charles
Professor Emeritus
Department of Mathematics
San Jose State University
San Jose, California

Janet H. Caldwell
Professor of Mathematics
Rowan University
Glassboro, New Jersey

Mary Cavanagh
Mathematics Consultant
San Diego County Office of Education
San Diego, California

Dinah Chancellor
Mathematics Consultant with Carroll ISD
Southlake, Texas
Mathematics Specialist with Venus ISD
Venus, Texas

Juanita V. Copley
Professor
College of Education
University of Houston
Houston, Texas

Warren D. Crown
Associate Dean for Academic Affairs
Graduate School of Education
Rutgers University
New Brunswick, New Jersey

Francis (Skip) Fennell
Professor of Education
McDaniel College
Westminster, Maryland

Kay B. Sammons
Coordinator of Elementary Mathematics
Howard County Public Schools
Ellicott City, Maryland

Jane F. Schielack
Professor of Mathematics
Associate Dean for Assessment and
Pre K-12 Education, College of Science
Texas A&M University
College Station, Texas

William Tate
Edward Mallinckrodt Distinguished
University Professor in Arts & Sciences
Washington University
St. Louis, Missouri

John A. Van de Walle
Professor Emeritus, Mathematics Education
Virginia Commonwealth University
Richmond, Virginia

Consulting Mathematicians

Edward J. Barbeau
Professor of Mathematics
University of Toronto
Toronto, Canada

Sybilla Beckmann
Professor of Mathematics
Department of Mathematics
University of Georgia
Athens, Georgia

David Bressoud
DeWitt Wallace Professor of Mathematics
Macalester College
Saint Paul, Minnesota

Gary Lippman
Professor of Mathematics and Computer Science
California State University East Bay
Hayward, California

Editorial Offices: Glenview, Illinois • Parsippany, New Jersey • New York, New York
Sales Offices: Boston, Massachusetts • Duluth, Georgia • Glenview, Illinois
Coppell, Texas • Sacramento, California • Mesa, Arizona

Consulting Authors

Stuart J. Murphy
Visual Learning Specialist
Boston, Massachusetts

Jeanne Ramos
Secondary Mathematics Coordinator
Los Angeles Unified School District
Los Angeles, California

Verónica Galván Carlan
Private Consultant Mathematics
Harlingen, Texas

ELL Consultants/Reviewers

Jim Cummins
Professor
The University of Toronto
Toronto, Canada

Alma B. Ramirez
Sr. Research Associate
Math Pathways and Pitfalls WestEd
Oakland, California

Texas Reviewers

Norma Dorado Armijo
Math Coach
El Paso Independent School District

Jose Rafael Cantu
Teacher
Jose Antonio Navarro Elementary
McAllen ISD

Aimee M. Delaney
Teacher
Aldine ISD

Cassandra R. Fulton
Teacher
Lancaster ISD

Debra Gibson
Math Specialist
Lubbock ISD

Sherry M. Johnson
Teacher
Round Rock ISD

Nelda R. Lujan
Teacher
Frisco ISD

Kim Mayo
Math Specialist
Houston ISD

Kristine Quisenberry
Teacher
McKinney ISD

Courtney J. Ridlehuber
Teacher
Mansfield ISD

Paulette Savoie-Speyrer
Campus Lead Teacher
Katy ISD

Tricia Shaughnessy
Teacher
San Antonio ISD

Nancy Shock
Teacher
Conroe ISD

Rebecca Spikes
Teacher
Fort Worth ISD

Anne Turner
Teacher
Klein ISD

Christe Warner
Math Specialist
Alief ISD

Debbie Wells
Math Facilitator
Victoria ISD

Elba Armandina Williams –Alejandro
Mathematics Curriculum Coach
Austin ISD

ISBN-13: 978-0-328-27277-8
ISBN-10: 0-328-27277-9

2 3 4 5 6 7 8 9 10 V042 12 11 10 09 08

Topic Titles

Topic 1 **Numeration**

Topic 2 **Addition and Subtraction Number Sense**

Topic 3 **Multiplication Meanings and Facts**

Topic 4 **Division Meanings and Facts**

Topic 5 **Multiplication Number Sense**

Topic 6 **Multiplying by 1-Digit Numbers**

Topic 7 **Multiplying by 2-Digit Numbers**

Topic 8 **Division Number Sense**

Topic 9 **Dividing by 1-Digit Divisors**

Topic 10 **Fraction Concepts**

Topic 11 **Fractions and Decimals**

Topic 12 **Patterns and Expressions**

Topic 13 **Whole Numbers, Fractions, and Decimals on the Number Line**

Topic 14 **Lines, Angles, Shapes, and Solids**

Topic 15 **Transformations, Symmetry, and Congruence**

Topic 16 **Estimating and Measuring Length, Perimeter, and Area**

Topic 17 **Estimating and Measuring Volume, Capacity, Weight, and Mass**

Topic 18 **Converting Measurements**

Topic 19 **Time and Temperature**

Topic 20 **Probability and Statistics**

Table of Contents

TAKS OBJECTIVE COLORS

TAKS Objective 1	Number and Operations
TAKS Objective 2	Algebraic Thinking
TAKS Objective 3	Geometry
TAKS Objective 4	Measurement
TAKS Objective 5	Probability and Statistics
TAKS Objective 6	Problem Solving

Underlying Processes and Mathematical Tools, which includes problem solving, are infused throughout all lessons.

TAKS Objective 1

Topic 1 Numeration (TEKS 4.1A, 4.1B)

TAKS Objective 1

Topic 2 Addition and Subtraction Number Sense (TEKS 4.3A, 4.3B, 4.5A)

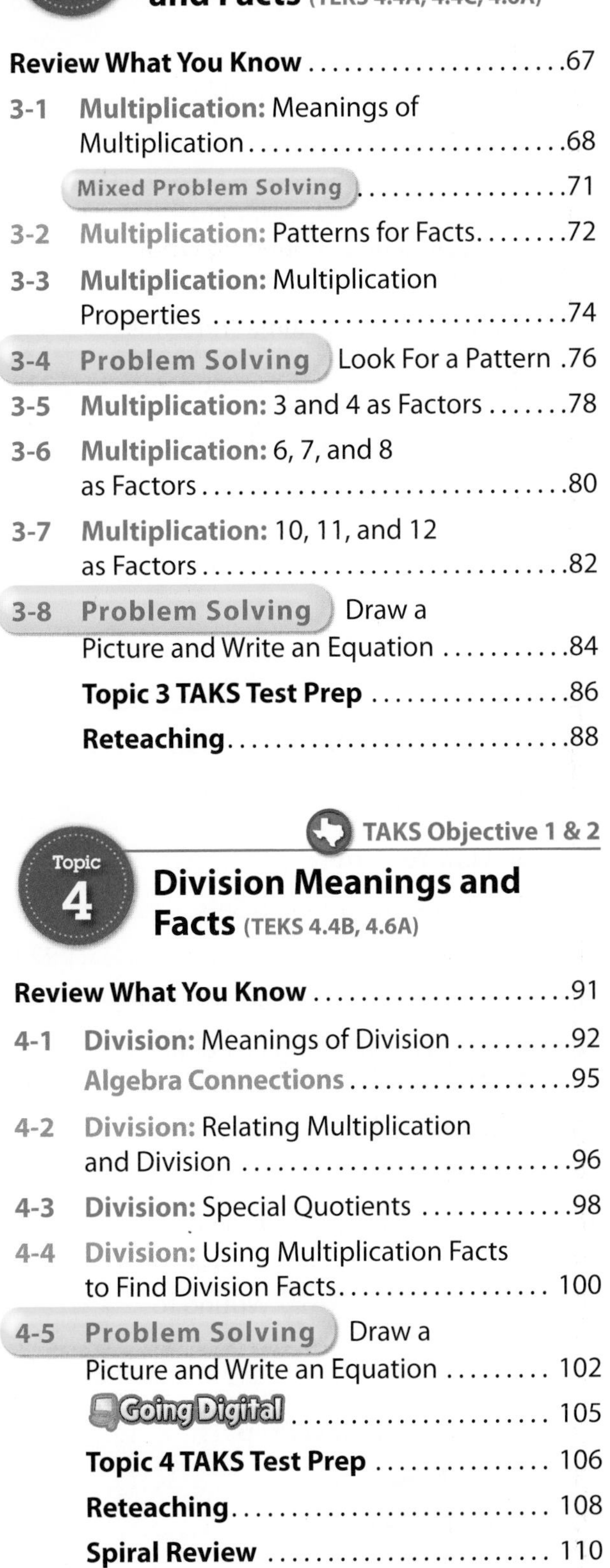

TAKS Objective 1 & 2

Topic 3 Multiplication Meanings and Facts (TEKS 4.4A, 4.4C, 4.6A)

TAKS Objective 1 & 2

Topic 4 Division Meanings and Facts (TEKS 4.4B, 4.6A)

TAKS Objective 1 & 2

Topic 5 Multiplication Number Sense (TEKS 4.4, 4.5B, 4.6B)

TAKS Objective 1

Topic 6 Multiplying by 1-Digit Numbers (TEKS 4.4A, 4.4D)

TAKS Objective 1

Topic 7

Multiplying by 2-Digit Numbers (TEKS 4.4A, 4.4D, 4.5B, 4.6B)

TAKS Objective 1

Topic 8

Division Number Sense (TEKS 4.4B, 4.4E, 4.5B)

TAKS Objective 1

Topic 9

Dividing by 1-Digit Divisors (TEKS 4.4B, 4.4E)

TAKS Objective 1

Topic 10

Fraction Concepts (TEKS 4.2, 4.2A)

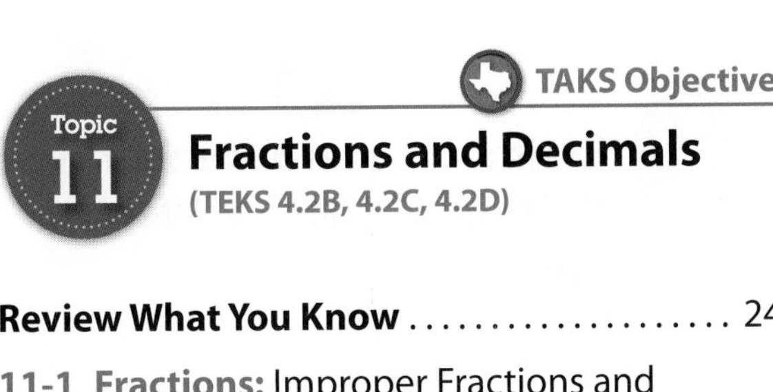

TAKS Objective 1

Topic 11 Fractions and Decimals
(TEKS 4.2B, 4.2C, 4.2D)

TAKS Objective 2

Topic 12 Patterns and Expressions
(TEKS 4.7)

TAKS Objective 3

Topic 13 Whole Numbers, Fractions, and Decimals on the Number Line
(TEKS 4.2C, 4.10)

TAKS Objective 3

Topic 14 Lines, Angles, Shapes, and Solids
(TEKS 4.8A, 4.8B, 4.8C)

TAKS Objective 3

Topic 15 Transformations, Symmetry, and Congruence (TEKS 4.9A, 4.9B, 4.9C)

TAKS Objective 4

Topic 16 Estimating and Measuring Length, Perimeter, and Area (TEKS 4.11A)

TAKS Objective 4

Topic 17 Estimating and Measuring Volume, Capacity, Weight and Mass (TEKS 4.11A, 4.11C, 4.11D, 4.11E)

TAKS Objective 4

Topic 18 Converting Measurements (TEKS 4.11B)

TAKS Objective 4

Topic 19

Time and Temperature (TEKS 4.12A, 4.12B)

TAKS Objective 5

Topic 20

Probability and Statistics (TEKS 4.13, 4.13A, 4.13B)

Student Resources

Problem-Solving Handbook

Use this Problem-Solving Handbook throughout the year to help you solve problems.

Don't give up!

Everybody can be a good problem solver!

There's almost always more than one way to solve a problem!

Don't trust key words.

Pictures help me understand!

Explaining helps me understand!

Problem-Solving Process

Read and Understand

What am I trying to find?
- Tell what the question is asking.

What do I know?
- Tell the problem in my own words.
- Identify key facts and details.

Plan and Solve

What strategy or strategies should I try?

Can I show the problem?
- Try drawing a picture.
- Try making a list, table, or graph.
- Try acting it out or using objects.

How will I solve the problem?

What is the answer?
- Tell the answer in a complete sentence.

Strategies

- Show What You Know
  - Draw a Picture
  - Make an Organized List
  - Make a Table
  - Make a Graph
  - Act It Out/ Use Objects
- Look for a Pattern
- Try, Check, Revise
- Write an Equation
- Use Reasoning
- Work Backward
- Solve a Simpler Problem

Look Back and Check

Did I check my work?
- Compare my work to the information in the problem.
- Be sure all calculations are correct.

Is my answer reasonable?
- Estimate to see if my answer makes sense.
- Make sure the question was answered.

Using Bar Diagrams

Use a bar diagram to show how what you know and what you want to find are related. Then choose an operation to solve the problem.

Problem 1

Carrie helps at the family flower store in the summer. She keeps a record of how many flower bouquets she sells. How many bouquets did she sell on Monday and Wednesday?

Carrie's Sales

Data

Days	Bouquets Sold
Monday	19
Tuesday	22
Wednesday	24
Thursday	33
Friday	41

Bar Diagram

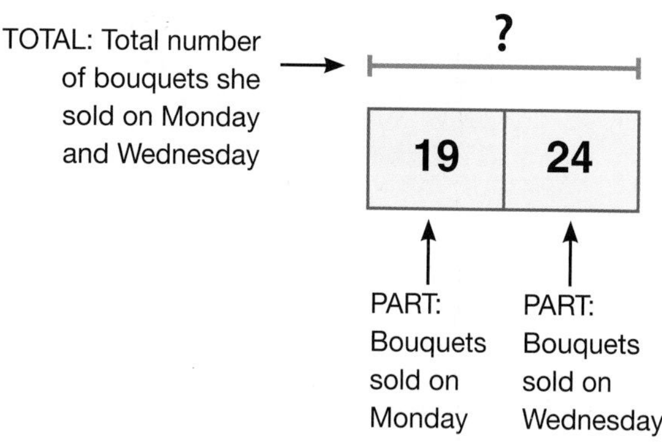

19 + 24 = ?

I can add to find the total.

Problem 2

Kim is saving to buy a sweatshirt for the college her brother attends. She has $18. How much more money does she need to buy the sweatshirt?

Bar Diagram

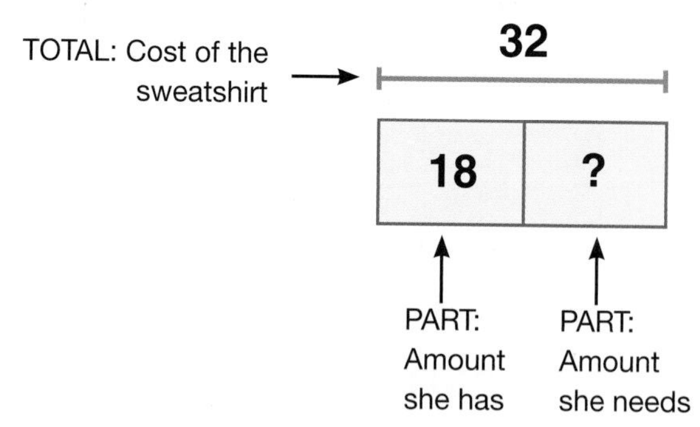

32 − 18 = ?

I can subtract to find the missing part.

Pictures help me understand!

Don't trust key words!

Problem 3

Tickets to a movie on Saturday cost only $5 each no matter what age you are. What is the cost of tickets for a family of four?

Bar Diagram

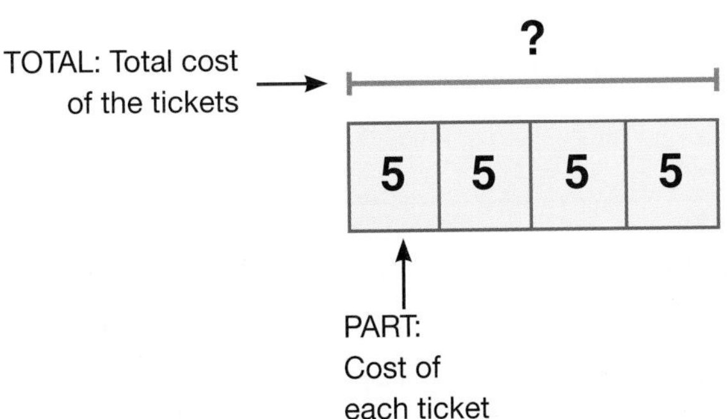

$$4 \times 5 = ?$$

I can multiply because the parts are equal.

Problem 4

Thirty students traveled in 3 vans to the zoo. The same numbers of students were in each van. How many students were in each van?

Bar Diagram

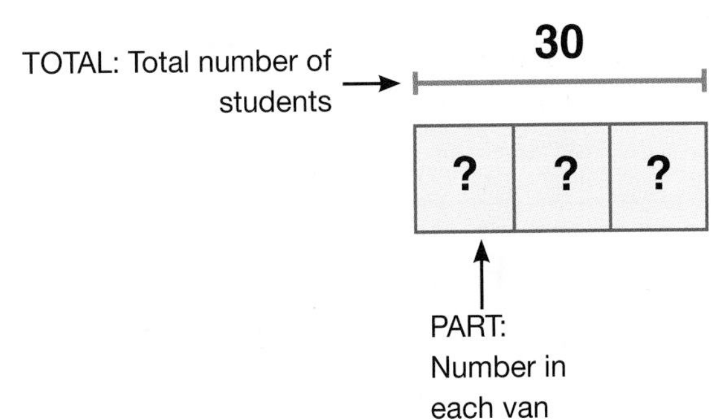

$$30 \div 3 = ?$$

I can divide to find how many are in each part.

Problem-Solving Strategies

Strategy	Example	When I Use It
Draw a Picture	The race was 5 kilometers. Markers were at the starting line and the finish line. Markers showed each kilometer of the race. Find the number of markers used. Start Line — Finish Line Start Line, 1 km, 2 km, 3 km, 4 km, Finish Line	Try drawing a picture when it helps you visualize the problem or when the relationships such as joining or separating are involved.
Make a Table	Phil and Marcy spent all day Saturday at the fair. Phil rode 3 rides each half hour and Marcy rode 2 rides each half hour. How many rides had Marcy ridden when Phil rode 24 rides?	Try making a table when: • there are 2 or more quantities, • amounts change using a pattern.
Look for a Pattern	The house numbers on Forest Road change in a planned way. Describe the pattern. Tell what the next two house numbers should be. 3, 6, 10, 15, ?, ?	Look for a pattern when something repeats in a predictable way.

Rides for Phil	3	6	9	12	15	18	21	24
Rides for Marcy	2	4	6	8	10	12	14	16

Everybody can be a good problem solver!

Strategy	Example	When I Use It
Make an Organized List	How many ways can you make change for a quarter using dimes and nickels? 1 quarter = 1 dime + 1 dime + 1 nickel 1 dime + 1 nickel + 1 nickel + 1 nickel 1 nickel + 1 nickel + 1 nickel + 1 nickel + 1 nickel	Make an organized list when asked to find combinations of two or more items.
Try, Check, Revise	Suzanne spent \$27, not including tax, on dog supplies. She bought two of one item and one of another item. What did she buy? $\$8 + \$8 + \$15 = \$31$ $\$7 + \$7 + \$12 = \$26$ $\$6 + \$6 + \$15 = \$27$	Use Try, Check, Revise when quantities are being combined to find a total, but you don't know which quantities. **Dog Supplies Sale!** Leash .... \$8 Collar .... \$6 Bowls .... \$7 Medium Beds .... \$15 Toys \$12
Write an Equation	Maria's new CD player can hold 6 discs at a time. If she has 204 CDs, how many times can the player be filled without repeating a CD? Find $204 \div 6 = n$.	Write an equation when the story describes a situation that uses an operation or operations.

Even More Strategies

Strategy	Example	When I Use It
Act It Out	How many ways can 3 students snake each other's hand?	Think about acting out a problem when the numbers are small and there is action in the problem you can do.
Use Reasoning	Beth collected some shells, rocks, and beach glass. **Beth's Collection** 2 rocks 3 times as many shells as rocks 12 objects in all How many of each object are in the collection?	Use reasoning when you can use known information to reason out unknown information.
Work Backward	Tracy has band practice at 10:15 A.M. It takes her 20 minutes to get from home to practice and 5 minutes to warm up. What time should she leave home to get to practice on time? Time Tracy leaves home ? ← 20 minutes ← Time warm up starts ← 5 minutes ← Time practice starts **10:15**	Try working backward when: • you know the end result of a series of steps, • you want to know what happened at the beginning.

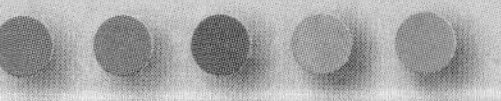

I can think about when to use each strategy.

Strategy	Example	When I Use It
Solve a Simpler Problem 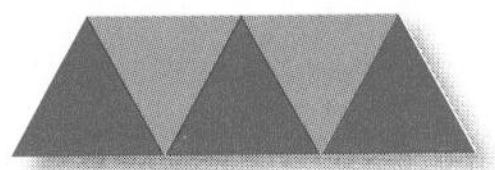	Each side of each triangle in the figure at the left is one centimeter. If there are 12 triangles in a row, what is the perimeter of the figure? I can look at 1 triangle, then 2 triangles, then 3 triangles. 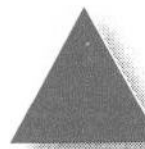 perimeter = 3 cm 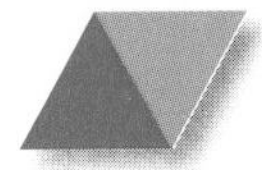 perimeter = 4 cm 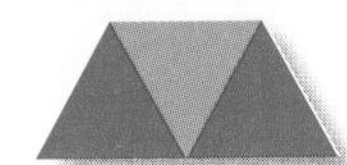 perimeter = 5 cm	Try solving a simpler problem when you can create a simpler case that is easier to solve.
Make a Graph	Mary was in a jump rope contest. How did her number of jumps change over the five days of the contest? 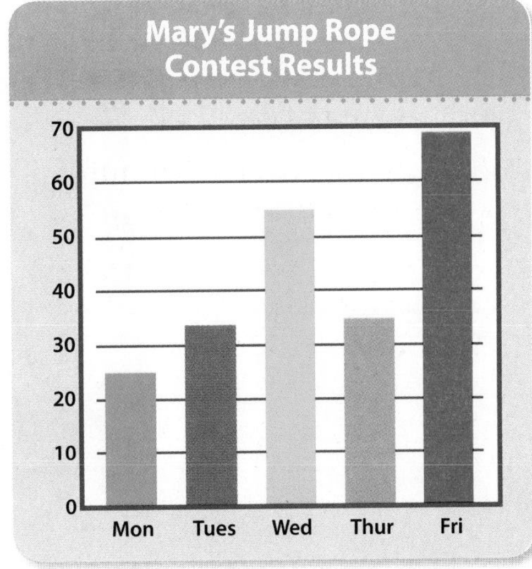	Make a graph when: • data for an event are given, • the question can be answered by reading the graph.

Writing to Explain

Here is a good math explanation.

Writing to Explain What happens to the area of the rectangle if the lengths of its sides are doubled?

■ = $\frac{1}{4}$ of the whole rectangle

The area of the new rectangle is 4 times the area of the original rectangle.

Tips for Writing Good Math Explanations....

A good explanation should be:

- correct
- simple
- complete
- easy to understand

Math explanations can use:

- words
- pictures
- numbers
- symbols

This is another good math explanation.

Writing to Explain Use blocks to show 13×24. Draw a picture of what you did with the blocks.

First we made a row of 24 using 2 tens and 4 ones. Then we made more rows until we had 13 rows. Then we said 13 rows of 2 tens is 13 x 2 tens = 26 tens or 260. Then we said 13 rows of 4 ones is 13 x 4 = 52. Then we added the parts 260 + 52 = 312 So, 13 x 24 = 312.

Problem-Solving Recording Sheet

Name Jane

Teaching Tool
1

Problem-Solving Recording Sheet

Problem:
On June 14, 1777, the Continental Congress approved the design of a national flag. The 1777 flag had 13 stars, one for each colony. Today's flag has 50 stars, one for each state. How many stars were added to the flag since 1777?

Find?

Number of stars added to the flag

Know?

Original flag
13 stars

Today's flag
50 stars

Strategies?

Show the Problem
- ☑ Draw a Picture
- ☐ Make an Organized List
- ☐ Make a Table
- ☐ Make a Graph
- ☐ Act It Out/Use Objects

- ☐ Look for a Pattern
- ☐ Try, Check, Revise
- ☑ Write an Equation
- ☐ Use Reasoning
- ☐ Work Backwards
- ☐ Solve a Simpler Problem

Show the Problem?

50	
13	?

Solution?

I am comparing the two quantities.
I could add up from 13 to 50. I can also subtract 13 from 50. I'll subract.

$$\begin{array}{r} 50 \\ -\ 13 \\ \hline 37 \end{array}$$

Answer?

There were 37 stars added to the flag from 1777 to today.

Check? Reasonable?

37 + 13 = 50 so I subtracted correctly.

50 − 13 is about 50 − 10 = 40
40 is close to 37. 37 is reasonable.

Here's a way to organize my problem-solving work

Name Benton

Teaching Tool 1

Problem-Solving Recording Sheet

Problem:

Suppose your teacher told you to open your math book to the facing pages whose pages numbers add to 85. To which two pages would you open your book?

Find?

Two facing page numbers

Know?

Two pages.
Facing each other.
Sum is 85.

Strategies?

Show the Problem
- ☑ Draw a Picture
- ☐ Make an Organized List
- ☐ Make a Table
- ☐ Make a Graph
- ☐ Act It Out/Use Objects

- ☐ Look for a Pattern
- ☑ Try, Check, Revise
- ☑ Write an Equation
- ☐ Use Reasoning
- ☐ Work Backwards
- ☐ Solve a Simpler Problem

Show the Problem?

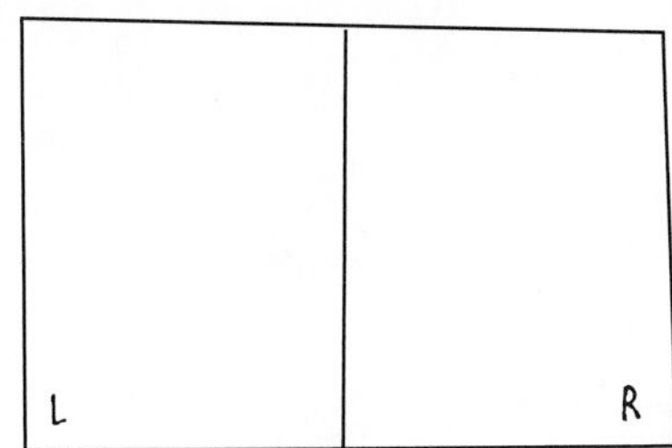

L + R = 85
L is 1 less than R

Solution?

I'll try some numbers in the middle.
40 + 41 = 81, too low
How about 46 and 47?
46 + 47 = 93, too high
Ok, now try 42 and 43.
42 + 43 = 85.

Answer?

The page numbers are 42 and 43.

Check? Reasonable?

I added correctly.
42 + 43 is about 40 + 40 = 80
80 is close to 85.
42 and 43 is reasonable.

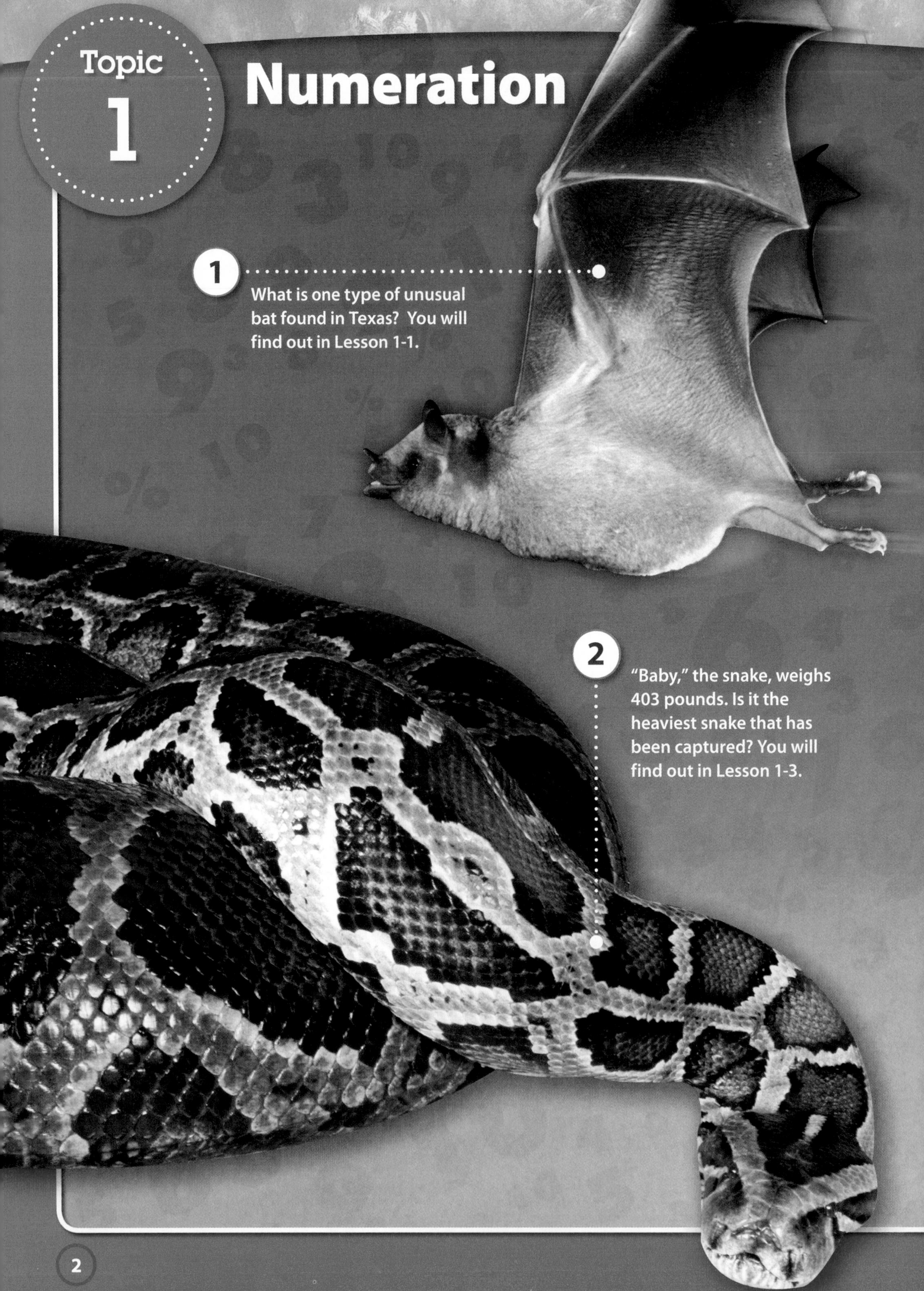
Topic
1
Numeration
1
What is one type of unusual bat found in Texas? You will find out in Lesson 1-1.
2
"Baby," the snake, weighs 403 pounds. Is it the heaviest snake that has been captured? You will find out in Lesson 1-3.

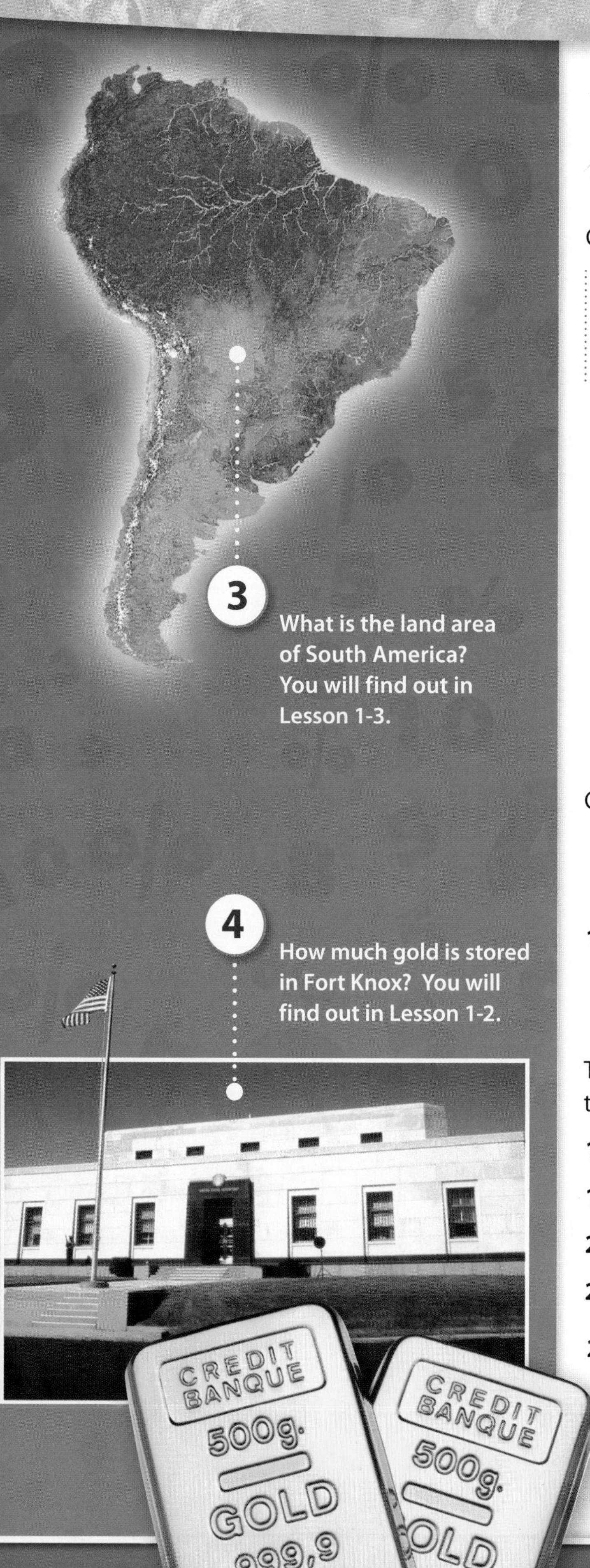

3
What is the land area of South America? You will find out in Lesson 1-3.
4
How much gold is stored in Fort Knox? You will find out in Lesson 1-2.
CREDIT BANQUE
500g.
GOLD
999,9

Review What You Know!

Vocabulary

Choose the best term from the box.

• digits	• period
• compare	• number line
• even	• odd

1. A group of three digits in a number separated by a comma is a ? .
2. A ? is a line that shows numbers in order using a scale.
3. The number 8 is an ? number.
4. The number 5 is an ? number.

Comparing Numbers

Compare each set of numbers using >, <, or =.

5. 13 ◯ 10 **6.** 7 ◯ 7 **7.** 28 ◯ 29

8. 14 ◯ 5 **9.** 43 ◯ 34 **10.** 0 ◯ 1

11. 52 ◯ 52 **12.** 13 ◯ 65 **13.** 22 ◯ 33

Place Value

Tell if the underlined digit is in the ones, tens, or hundreds place.

14. 34$\underline{6}$ **15.** $\underline{1}$7 **16.** 9$\underline{2}$1

17. $\underline{1}$06 **18.** 3$\underline{3}$ **19.** $\underline{4}$7

20. $\underline{2}$17 **21.** $\underline{3}$20 **22.** 81$\underline{0}$

23. 1,00$\underline{6}$ **24.** $\underline{9}$99 **25.** 1,4$\underline{0}$5

26. Writing to Explain How does using commas to separate periods help you read large numbers?

Lesson

1-1

TEKS 4.1A: Use place value to read, write, compare, and order whole numbers through 999,999,999.

Thousands

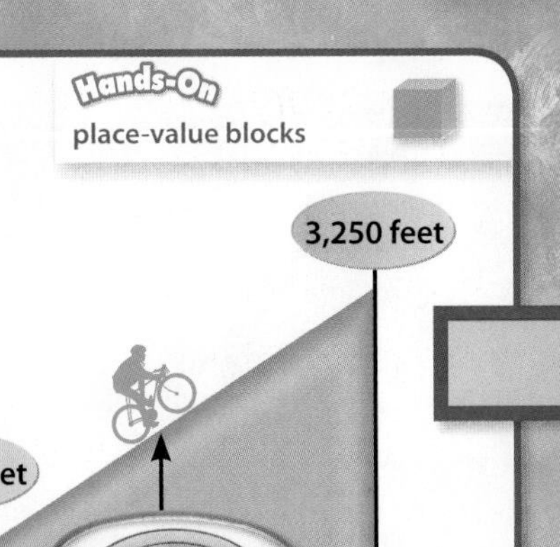

What are some ways to represent numbers in the thousands?

An altimeter measures height above sea level. Jill's altimeter shows she is 3,241 feet above sea level. There are different ways to represent 3,241.

Another Example **How do you read and write numbers in the thousands?**

Another bicycle racer's altimeter shows he is 5,260 feet above sea level. Write 5,260 in standard form, expanded form, and word form.

When writing a number in standard form, write only the digits: 5,260.

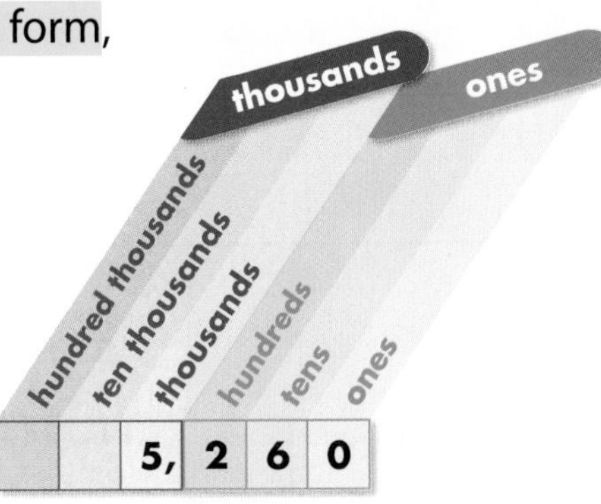

Each group of 3 digits starting from the right forms a period.

A number in expanded form is written as the sum of the value of the digits: 5,000 + 200 + 60 + 0.

Use periods in the place-value chart to write 5,260 in word form: five thousand, two hundred sixty.

Explain It

1. Explain why the value of 5 in 5,264 is 5,000.
2. Is the expanded form for 5,260 the same as for 5,206?

You can represent numbers using place-value blocks.

3,000 + 200 + 40 + 1

You can represent numbers on a number line.

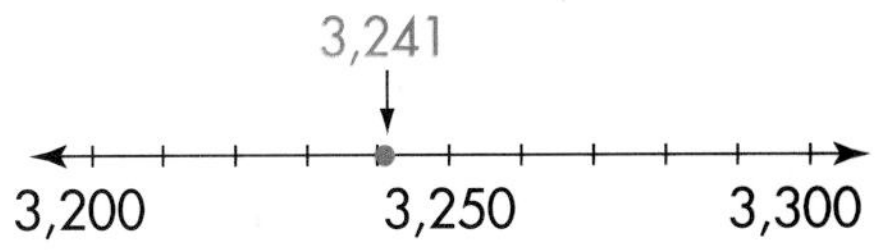

Guided Practice*

Do you know HOW?

In **1** through **4**, write the word form, and tell the value of the red digit in each number.

1. 15,324 **2.** 135,467

3. 921,382 **4.** 275,206

In **5** and **6**, write the expanded form.

5. 42,158 **6.** 63,308

Do you UNDERSTAND?

7. If Jill climbed 100 feet more, what would her altimeter read?

8. What is the value of the 2 in 3,261? the 3? the 1?

9. Write one hundred one thousand, eleven in standard form.

Independent Practice

Leveled Practice In **10** through **13**, write each number in standard form.

10.

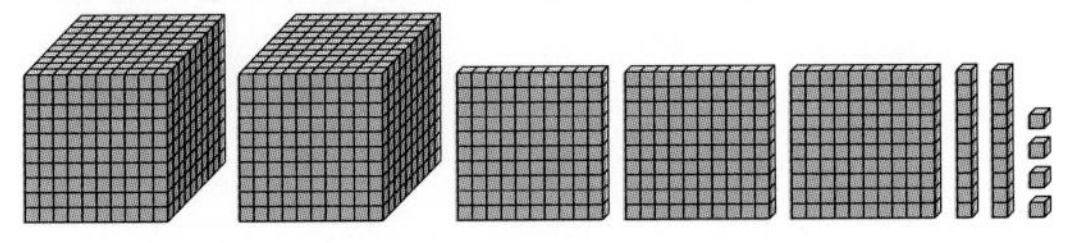

11.

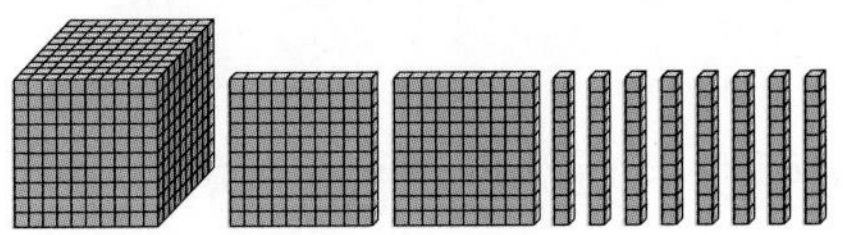

12.

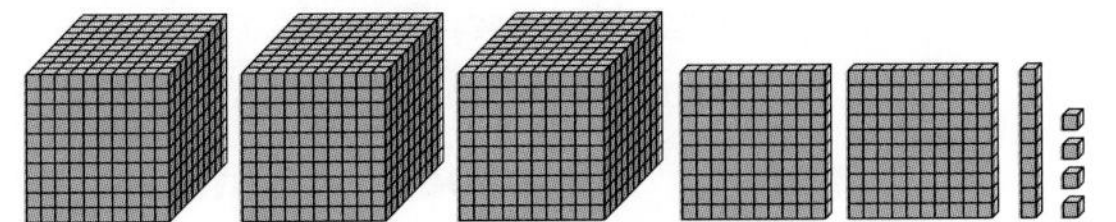

13.

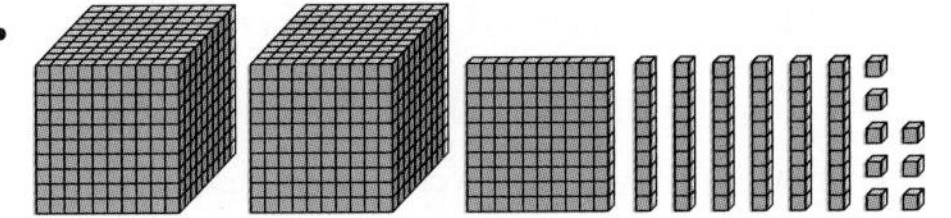

DIGITAL Animated Glossary, eTools, **www.pearsonsuccessnet.com**

For another example, see Set A on page 26.

Independent Practice

In **14** and **15**, write each number in standard form.

14. Eighty-three thousand, nine hundred two

15. Three hundred twenty-one thousand, two hundred nine

In **16** and **17**, write each number in expanded form.

16. Four hundred ninety-seven thousand, three hundred thirty-two

17. Twenty-one thousand, eight hundred seven

In **18** and **19**, write each number in word form.

18. 300,000 + 8,000 + 20 + 9

19. 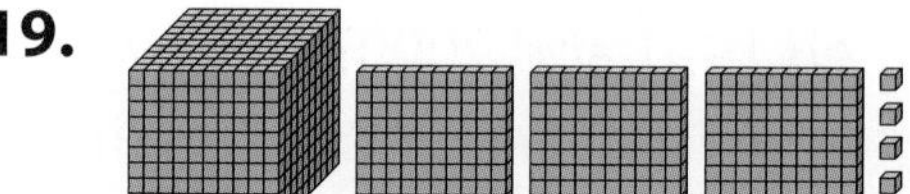

TAKS Problem Solving

20. Reasoning The pedometer below counts the number of steps you walk. It can show 5 digits. What is the greatest number it can show?

21. A town library has 124,763 books and 3,142 DVDs. This year, they bought 1,000 books and 2,000 DVDs. How many books does the library have now?

A 5,142 books

B 23,142 books

C 125,763 books

D 134,763 books

22. Number Sense Which digit is in the same place in all three numbers below? Name the place-value position.

574,632   24,376   204,581

23. Reasoning What is the greatest 4-digit number you can write? What is the least 4-digit number?

24. Greater Long-Nosed bats can be found in a cave at Big Bend National Park in Texas. In the table to the right, what was the number of bats in 1996? Use place-value blocks to represent the number. Then, write the number in expanded form.

Data

Greater Long-Nosed Bats in Big Bend National Park, Texas

Year	Number of Bats
1967	10,650
1993	2,859
1996	13,650

Mixed Problem Solving

The Texas Parks and Wildlife is helping with the recovery of Kemp's Ridley Sea Turtles.

1. How many more Kemp's Ridley Sea Turtles were there in 1947 than in 1968?

2. Did the population of Kemp's Ridley Sea Turtles increase or decrease between 1991 and 2000? What was the amount of increase or decrease?

3. Were there more or fewer sea turtles in 1968 than in 1991? How many more or fewer sea turtles were there?

Data

Kemp's Ridley Sea Turtles

Year	Female Kemp's Ridley Sea Turtles Found Nesting
1947	40,000
1968	5,000
1991	200
2000	6,000

Use the table for Exercises **4–6**.

4. Which is taller: the Pecos Sunflower or the Hinckley's Oak?

5. Which is shorter: the Terlingua Creek Cat's-eye or the Texas Poppy-Mallow?

6. Order the Texas Snowbell, the Hinckley's Oak, and the Pecos Sunflower from tallest to shortest.

Data

Heights of Plants in Texas

Plant	Height
Texas Snowbell	16 feet
Pecos Sunflower	5 feet
Terlingua Creek Cat's-eye	2 feet
Texas Poppy-Mallow	2.5 feet
Hinckley's Oak	4 feet

7. **Strategy Focus** Solve the problem by using the strategy Make a Table.

   Mr. Thomas was planting 5 rows of sunflowers. He planted 10 flowers in the first row, 8 flowers in the second row, and 6 flowers in the third row. If he continues this pattern, how many sunflowers will be in the fifth row?

Lesson

1-2

TEKS 4.1A: Use place value to read, write, compare, and order whole numbers through 999,999,999.

Millions

What are some ways to represent numbers in the millions?

From 2001 through 2005, 356,039,763 fans attended professional baseball games. Write the expanded form and word form for 356,039,763. Use a place-value chart to help.

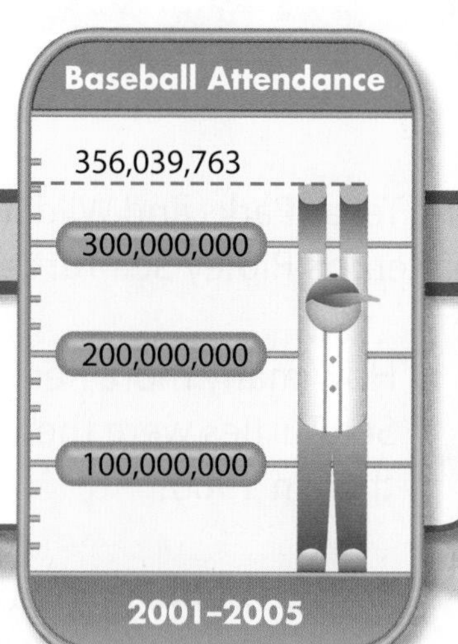

Guided Practice*

Do you know HOW?

In **1** and **2**, write the number in word form. Then, tell the value of the red digit in each number.

1. 75,600,295 **2.** 249,104,330

In **3** through **6**, write the number in expanded form.

3. 6,173,253 **4.** 75,001,432

5. 16,107,320 **6.** 430,290,100

Do you UNDERSTAND?

7. What is the value of 5 in 356,039,763?

8. What is the value of 9 in 356,039,763?

9. Between 1996 and 2000, 335,365,504 fans attended games. Which digit is in the millions place in 335,365,504?

Independent Practice

In **10** through **12**, write each number in standard form.

10. 300,000,000 + 40,000,000 + 7,000,000 + 300,000 + 10,000 + 6,000 + 20 + 9

11. 900,000,000 + 20,000,000 + 6,000,000 + 20,000 + 4,000 + 10

12. 80,000,000 + 1,000,000 + 600,000 + 20,000 + 900 + 40 + 8

In **13** through **16**, write the number in word form. Then, tell the value of the red digit in each number.

13. 7,915,878 **14.** 23,341,552 **15.** 214,278,216 **16.** 334,290,652

*For another example, see Set A on page 26.

Use a place-value chart to show 356,039,763.

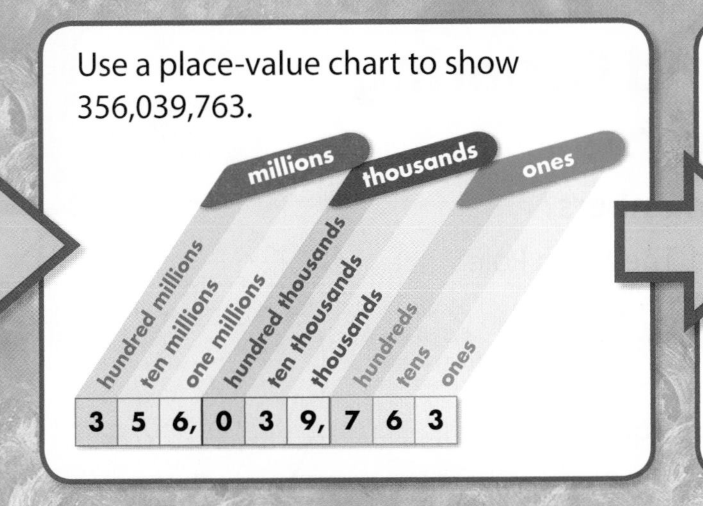

The 3 is in the hundred millions place. Its value is 300,000,000.

Expanded Form: 300,000,000 + 50,000,000 + 6,000,000 + 30,000 + 9,000 + 700 + 60 + 3

Word Form: Three hundred fifty-six million, thirty-nine thousand, seven hundred sixty-three

In **17** through **20**, write the number in expanded form. Then, tell the value of the red digit in each number.

17. 7,330,968 **18.** 30,290,447 **19.** 133,958,840 **20.** 309,603,114

TAKS Problem Solving

21. Writing to Explain Which number will take less time to write in expanded form, 800,000,000 or 267,423?

22. Write the expanded form of 123,456,789 and 987,654,321. Which digit has the same value in both numbers?

23. In 2005, seventy-four million, nine hundred fifteen thousand, two hundred sixty-eight fans attended baseball games. Which choice shows this number in standard form?

A 74,015,268 **C** 74,905,268

B 74,900,268 **D** 74,915,268

24. Write the standard form of a 9-digit number with a 5 in the millions place and a 9 in the tens place.

a Write a number that is ten million more than the number you chose.

b Write a number that is one million less than the number you chose.

25. Number Sense Fort Knox holds 147,300,000 ounces of gold. Write the number that is one million more.

147,300,000 ounces of gold in Fort Knox.

Lesson
1-3

TEKS 4.1A: Use place value to read, write, compare, and order whole numbers through 999,999,999.

Comparing and Ordering Whole Numbers

How do you compare numbers?

Earth is not perfectly round. The North Pole is 6,356 kilometers from Earth's center. The equator is 6,378 kilometers from the center. Which is closer to the Earth's center: the North Pole or the equator?

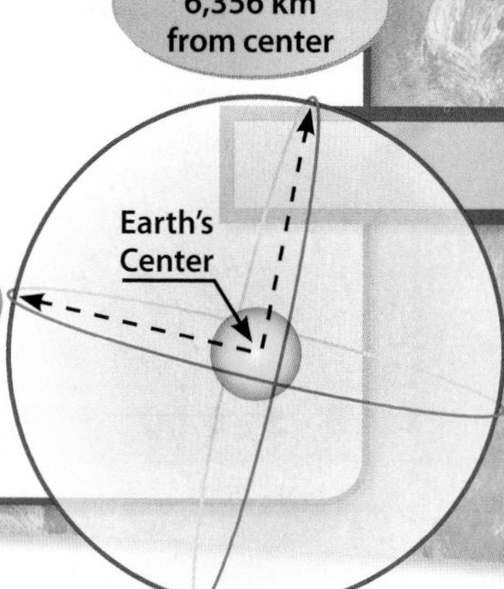

Another Example How do you order numbers?

The areas of 3 continents on Earth are shown in the table at the right. Which shows the areas in order from **least** to **greatest**?

A 9,450,000; 4,010,000; 6,890,000

B 4,010,000; 9,450,000; 6,890,000

C 6,890,000; 9,450,000; 4,010,000

D 4,010,000; 6,890,000; 9,450,000

Data

Continent	Areas (in square miles)
Europe	4,010,000
North America	9,450,000
South America	6,890,000

Step 1 Plot the numbers on a number line.

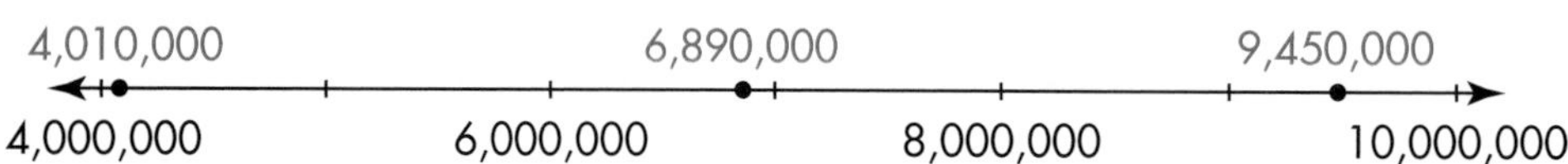

Step 2 Order the numbers. On a number line, numbers to the right are greater.

Reading from left to right, 4,010,000; 6,890,000; 9,450,000.

The correct choice is **D**.

Explain It

1. Describe how you would order the continents' areas using place value.
2. **Reasonableness** How can you rule out choices A and C as the correct answer?

Step 1

Use place value to compare numbers.

Write the numbers, lining up places. Begin at the left and compare.

6,356
6,378

The thousands digit is the same in both numbers.

Step 2

Look at the next digit.

6,356
6,378

The hundreds digit also is the same in both numbers.

Step 3

The first place where the digits are different is the tens place. Compare.

6,356
6,378

5 tens < 7 tens, so 6,356 < 6,378

The symbol > means is greater than, and the symbol < means is less than.

The North Pole is closer to Earth's center than the equator.

Guided Practice*

Do you know HOW?

In **1** through **4**, copy and complete by writing > or < for each ◯.

1. 2,643 ◯ 2,801 **2.** 6,519 ◯ 6,582

3. 2,643 ◯ 731 **4.** 6,703 ◯ 6,699

In **5** and **6**, order the numbers from least to greatest.

5. 7,502 6,793 6,723

6. 80,371 15,048 80,137

Do you UNDERSTAND?

7. Writing to Explain Why would you look at the hundreds place to order these numbers?

32,463 32,482 32,947

8. Compare the area of Europe and South America. Which is greater?

Independent Practice

In **9** through **18**, copy and complete by writing > or < for each ◯.

9. 221,495 ◯ 210,388

10. 52,744 ◯ 56,704

11. 138,752 ◯ 133,122

12. 4,937 ◯ 4,939

13. 22,873 ◯ 22,774

14. 1,912,706 ◯ 1,913,898

15. 412,632 ◯ 412,362

16. 999,999,999 ◯ 9,990,999

For another example, see Set B on page 26.

Independent Practice

Leveled Practice In **17** through **20**, copy and complete the number lines. Then use the number lines to order the numbers from greatest to least.

17. 27,505 26,905 26,950

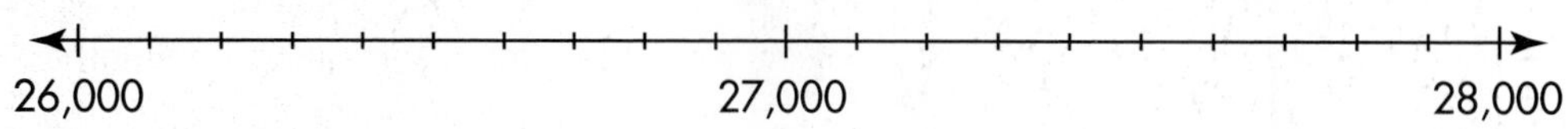

18. 3,422,100 3,422,700 3,422,000

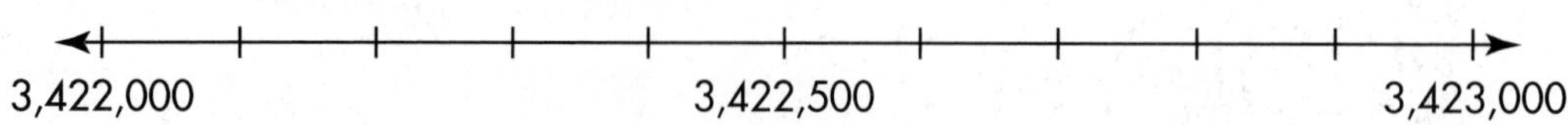

19. 7,502 7,622 7,523 7,852

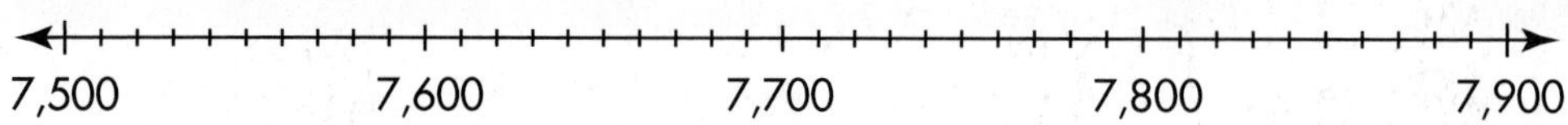

20. 3,030 3,033 3,003

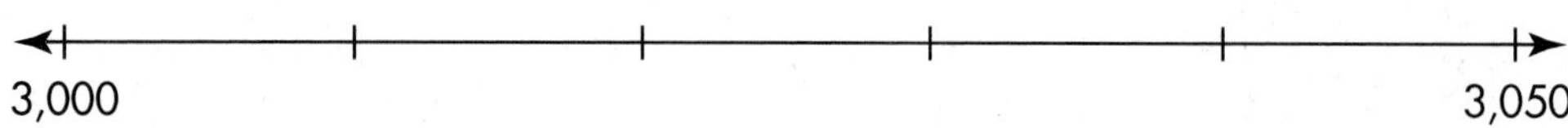

In **21** through **28**, write the numbers in order from least to greatest.

21. 57,535 576,945 506,495

22. 18,764 18,761 13,490

23. 25,988 25,978 25,998

24. 87,837 37,838 878,393

25. 43,783 434,282 64,382

26. 723,433 72,324 72,432

27. 58,028 85,843 77,893

28. 274,849,551 283,940,039 23,485,903

TAKS Problem Solving

29. **Estimation** Aaron added 57 and 20 and said the answer is greater than 100. Is Aaron correct?

30. **Number Sense** Write three numbers that are greater than 780,000 but less than 781,000.

31. **Reasoning** Could you use only the millions period to order 462,409,524 463,409,524 and 463,562,391?

32. Describe how to compare 7,463 74,633 and 74,366 from least to greatest.

33. The heaviest snake living in captivity is a Burmese Python named "Baby." An average Anaconda snake weighs 330 pounds. Which snake weighs more?

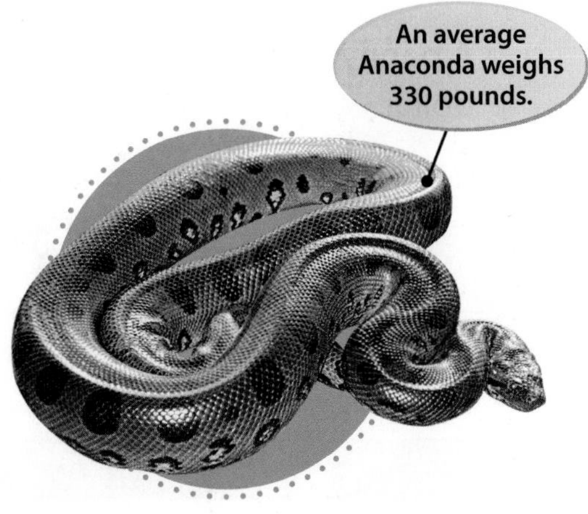
An average Anaconda weighs 330 pounds.

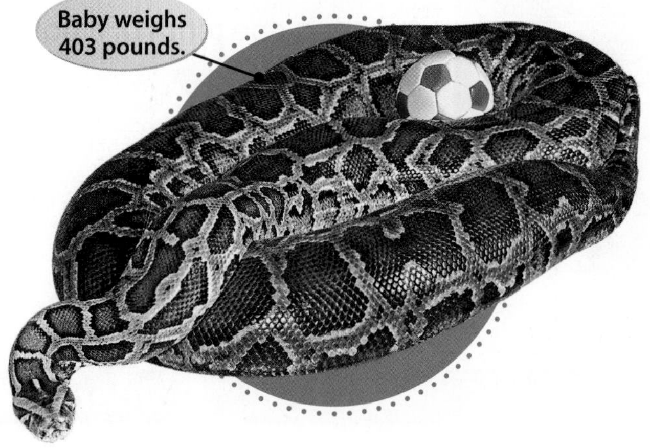
Baby weighs 403 pounds.

34. Which list of numbers is in order from least to greatest?

A 1,534 1,576 1,563

B 18,732 18,723 18,765

C 234,564 234,568 234,323

D 383,847 383,848 383,849

35. Asia and Africa are the two largest continents on Earth. Which continent is larger?

Data

Continent	Land Area (square miles)
Africa	11,608,000
Asia	17,212,000

36. The chart below shows the number of game cards owned by the top collectors in one school. Which student had the most cards?

F Shani **H** Ariel

G Lin **J** Jorge

Data

Collector	Number of cards
Shani	3,424
Ariel	3,443
Lin	2,354
Jorge	2,932

37. The Atlantic Ocean has an area of 33,420,000 square miles. This area is between which numbers?

A 33,400,000 and 33,440,000

B 33,000,000 and 33,040,000

C 33,100,000 and 33,419,000

D 33,430,000 and 33,500,000

Lesson
1-4

TEKS 4.1B: Use place value to read, write, compare, and order decimals involving tenths and hundredths, including money, using concrete objects and pictorial models.

Using Money to Understand Decimals

How are decimals related to money?

A dime is one tenth of a dollar.

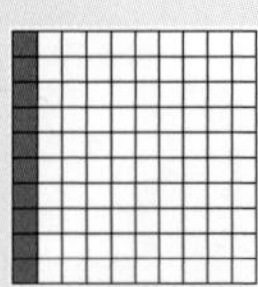

0.1

A penny is one hundredth of a dollar.

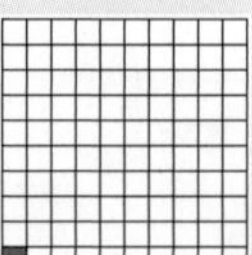

0.01

Guided Practice*

Do you know HOW?

In **1** and **2**, copy and complete.

1. \$9.75 = ☐ dollars + ☐ dimes + ☐ pennies

9.75 = ☐ ones + ☐ tenths + ☐ hundredths

2. \$3.62 = ☐ dollars + ☐ pennies

3.62 = ☐ ones + ☐ hundredths

Do you UNDERSTAND?

3. Writing to Explain How many hundredths are in one tenth? Explain using pennies and a dime.

4. How many pennies are equal to 6 dimes?

5. Gina's allowance is \$2.50. How much is this in dollars and dimes?

Remember, the number of dimes is the same as the number of tenths.

Independent Practice

In **6** through **9**, copy and complete.

6. \$5.83 = ☐ dollars + ☐ pennies

5.83 = ☐ ones + ☐ hundredths

7. \$7.14 = ☐ dollars + ☐ pennies

7.14 = ☐ ones + ☐ hundredths

8. \$2.19 = ☐ dollars + ☐ dime + ☐ pennies

2.19 = ☐ ones + ☐ tenth + ☐ hundredths

9. \$3.24 = ☐ dollars + ☐ dimes + ☐ pennies

3.24 = ☐ ones + ☐ tenths + ☐ hundredths

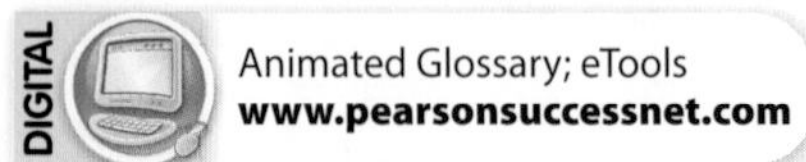

*For another example, see Set C on page 26.

One Way

You can use a place-value chart to show the decimal value of money.

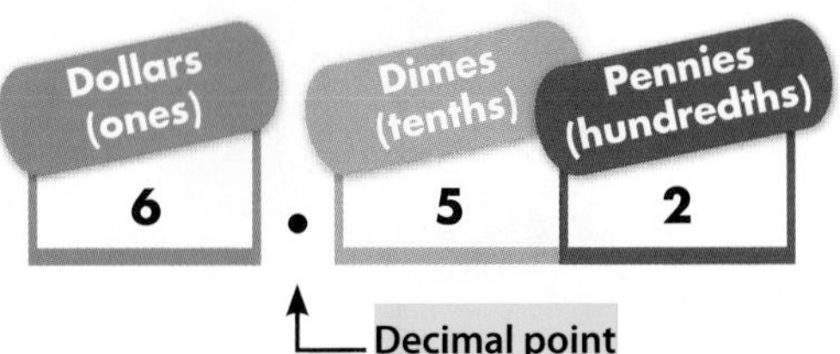

Read: six dollars *and* fifty-two cents.

Another Way

You can show $6.52 several ways.

$6.52 = 6 dollars + 5 dimes + 2 pennies
= 6 ones + 5 tenths + 2 hundredths

$6.52 = 6 dollars + 52 pennies
= 6 ones + 52 hundredths

In **10** through **13**, write the amount with a dollar sign and decimal point.

10. 6 dollars + 9 dimes + 3 pennies

11. 5 dollars + 8 pennies

12. 7 dollars + 3 dimes + 4 pennies

13. 4 dollars + 7 dimes

TAKS Problem Solving

14. Make a place-value chart to show the value of 5 dollars, 1 dime, and 3 pennies.

15. Writing to Explain Why do you only need to look at the number of dollars to know that $5.12 is greater than $4.82?

16. Pablo saves $1.20 each week. How much has he saved, in dollars and dimes, after one week? two weeks? three weeks?

17. Number Sense Which is more?

a 4 dimes and 6 pennies or 6 dimes and 4 pennies?

b 5 dimes or 45 pennies?

In **18** and **19**, use the information at the right.

18. How could you use only dollars, dimes, and pennies to buy the bubble blower?

19. How could you use only dollars, dimes, and pennies to buy the snow globe?

20. Which is equal to 6 dollars, 3 dimes, and 4 pennies?

A $3.46 **B** $3.64 **C** $6.34 **D** $6.43

Lesson

1-5

TEKS 4.1B: Use place value to read, write, compare, and order decimals involving tenths and hundredths, including money, using concrete objects and pictorial models.

Decimal Place Value

What are some ways to represent decimals?

A squirrel can weigh 1.64 pounds. There are different ways to represent 1.64.

Guided Practice*

Do you know HOW?

For **1** and **2**, write the expanded form for each number.

1. 3.91 **2.** 6.87

In **3** and **4**, draw and shade a grid for each number. Then, write the word form for each number.

3. 1.06 **4.** 2.36

Do you UNDERSTAND?

5. In Exercise 1, what digit is in the tenths place? in the hundredths place?

6. At the end of a basketball game, there are 3.29 seconds left on the clock. How would the referee say this number?

When you read a number or write a number in word form, replace the decimal point with the word and.

Independent Practice

In **7** through **9**, write the decimal for each shaded part.

7. 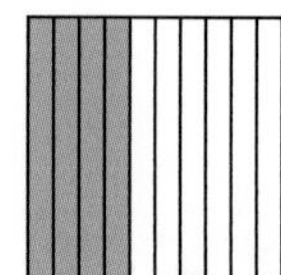

8. 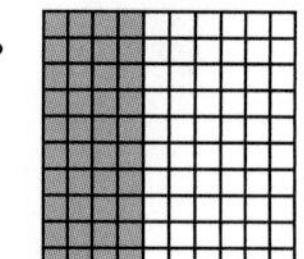

9. 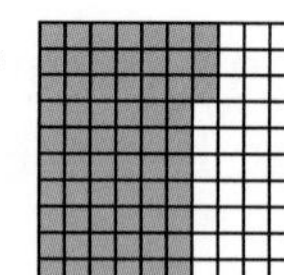

In **10** through **12**, write the number in standard form.

10. four and thirty-six hundredths **11.** 5 + 0.2 + 0.08 **12.** 2 + 0.01

*For another example, see Set D on page 27.

One Way

Use a decimal model.

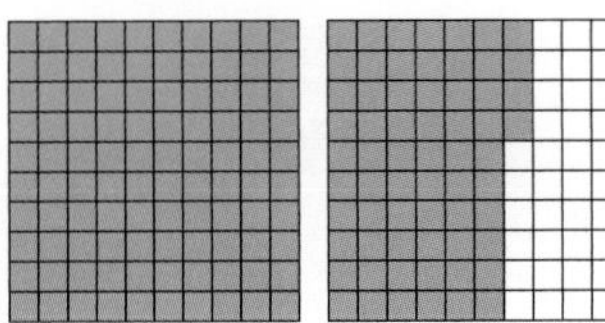

Expanded form: 1 + 0.6 + 0.04
Standard form: 1.64
Word form: one and sixty-four hundredths

Another Way

Use a place-value model.

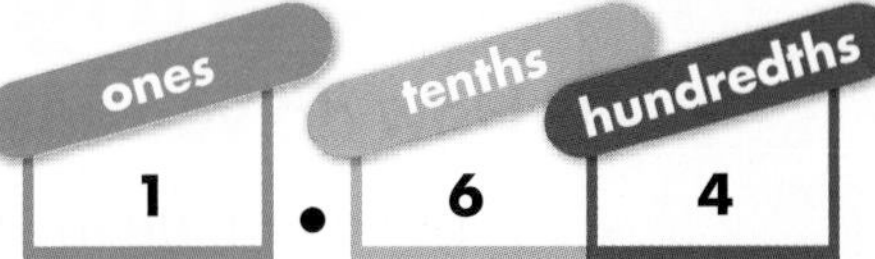

Expanded form: 1 + 0.6 + 0.04
Standard form: 1.64
Word form: one and sixty-four hundredths

In **13** through **17**, write the number in word form and give the value of the red digit for each number.

13. 2.47 **14.** 23.79 **15.** 1.85 **16.** 14.12 **17.** 9.05

In **18** through **22**, write each number in expanded form.

18. 3.19 **19.** 13.62 **20.** 0.78 **21.** 8.07 **22.** 17.2

TAKS Problem Solving

23. Reasoning Write a number that has a 4 in the tens place and a 6 in the hundredths place.

24. Mr. Cooper has 6 gallons of gas in his car. His car can hold 15 gallons in its gas tank. Will Mr. Cooper need more or less than 10 gallons to fill his tank?

25. Tisha wrote this amount: Five dollars and nine cents.

a What is the decimal word form for this amount?

b What is the decimal number?

26. Number Sense Write three numbers between 4.1 and 4.2.

Use hundredths grids or money to help.

27. Writing to Explain Use the decimal model below to explain why 0.08 is less than 0.1.

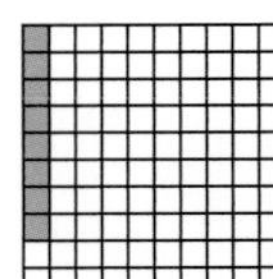

28. What is the value of the 5 in 43.51?

A five hundredths

B five tenths

C fifty-one hundredths

D five

TEKS 4.1B Use place value to read, write, compare, and order decimals involving tenths and hundredths, including money, using concrete objects and pictorial models.

Comparing and Ordering Decimals

Hands-On
Place-value blocks

How do you compare decimals?

A penny made in 1982 weighs about 0.11 ounces. A penny made in 2006 weighs about 0.09 ounces. Which penny weighs more, a 1982 penny or a 2006 penny?

Another Example How do you order decimals?

Patrick has a 1982 penny, a 2006 penny, and a dime in his pocket. Order the weights from least to greatest.

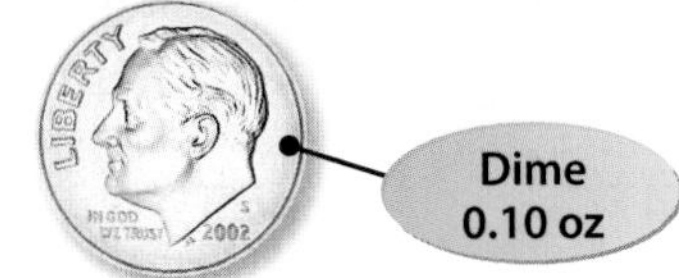

Use place-value blocks.

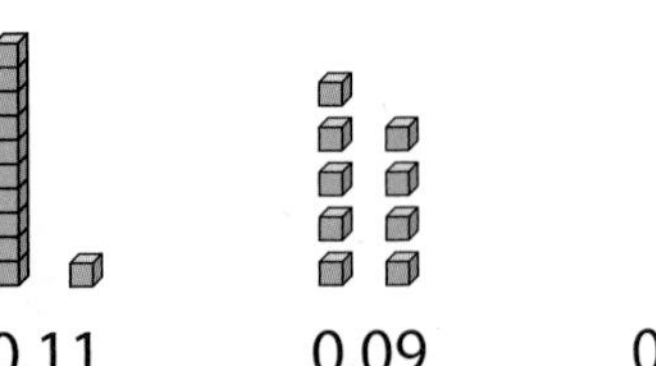

0.11	0.09	0.10
1982 penny	2006 penny	dime

Use hundredths grids.

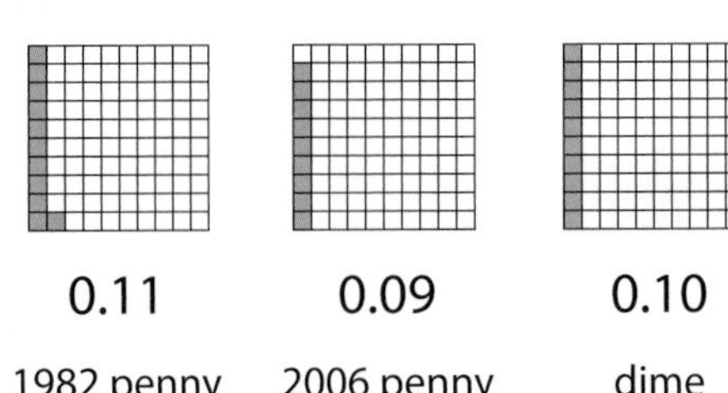

0.11	0.09	0.10
1982 penny	2006 penny	dime

The least number is 0.09. The greatest number is 0.11.
The order from least to greatest is 0.09, 0.10, 0.11.

Use place value.

First compare the digits in the tenths place.

0.11
0.09
0.10

The least number is 0.09. It has a 0 in the tenths place.

Then compare the digits in hundredths place.

0.10
0.11

1 > 0, so 0.11 is the greatest decimal.

The order from least to greatest is 0.09, 0.10, 0.11.

Explain It

1. Order the numbers above from greatest to least.

2. Which place did you use to compare 0.10 and 0.11?

Use place-value blocks.

11 hundredths > 9 hundredths

0.11 > 0.09

Use hundredths grids.

11 hundredths > 9 hundredths

0.11 > 0.09

Use place value.

Start at the left. Look for the first place where the digits are different.

0.11 0.09

1 tenth > 0 tenths

0.11 > 0.09

A penny made in 1982 weighs more than a penny made in 2006.

Guided Practice*

Do you know HOW?

In **1** through **4**, write >, <, or = for each ◯. Use place-value blocks or grids to help.

1. 0.7 ◯ 0.57 **2.** 0.23 ◯ 0.32

3. $1.01 ◯ $0.98 **4.** 0.2 ◯ 0.20

In **5** and **6**, order the numbers from least to greatest. Use place-value blocks or grids to help.

5. 0.7 0.6 0.5 **6.** 1.21 1.01 1.2

Do you UNDERSTAND?

7. **Number Sense** Which is greater, 2.02 or 0.22? Explain.

8. Maria told Patrick that her quarter weighs less than what a nickel weighs because 0.2 has less digits than 0.18. How can Patrick show Maria that 0.2 is greater than 0.18?

Independent Practice

For **9** through **16**, compare. Write >, <, or = for each ◯. Use place-value blocks or grids to help.

9. 0.01 ◯ 0.1 **10.** $7.31 ◯ $7.29 **11.** 6.56 ◯ 5.98 **12.** 1.1 ◯ 1.10

13. 3.22 ◯ 4.44 **14.** 9.01 ◯ 9.1 **15.** 2.01 ◯ 1.7 **16.** 0.01 ◯ 1.02

For **17** through **19**, order the numbers from least to greatest. Use place-value blocks or grids to help.

17. 1.2, 1.3, 1.1 **18.** 0.56, 4.56, 0.65 **19.** 0.21, 0.12, 0.22

*For another example, see Set E on page 27.

20. **Number Sense** A bag of 500 nickels weighs 5.5 pounds. A bag of 200 half dollars weighs 5 pounds. Which bag weighs more?

21. **Writing to Explain** Evan said the numbers 7.37, 7.36, 2.59, and 2.95 were in order from greatest to least. Is he correct?

22. **Number Sense** Tell which coin is worth more.

   a 1 quarter or 1 half dollar

   b 1 dime or 1 penny

   c 1 dollar or 1 penny

23. Which number is **NOT** greater than 0.64?

   A 6.4

   B 4.6

   C 0.46

   D 0.66

For **24** and **25**, use the clocks at the right.

24. Which clock shows the earliest time?

25. Order the clock times from latest to earliest.

26. Which numbers are **NOT** in order from the least to the greatest?

   F 0.3, 0.7, 0.9

   G 0.04, 0.09, 0.12

   H 0.15, 0.19, 0.23

   J 0.24, 0.09, 0.18

27. Ms. Alvarez has $0.83 in her change purse. She has 7 coins. She has the same number of pennies as quarters. What coins does she have?

28. Which number has a 3 in the ten-thousands place?

   A 23,604 **C** 593,100

   B 32,671 **D** 694,392

29. Which number is between 6.7 and 7.3?

   F 6.07 **H** 6.83

   G 6.26 **J** 7.4

30. Fishing lures are sold by weight. A yellow minnow lure weighs 0.63 ounce and a green minnow lure weighs 0.5 ounce. Which lure weighs more?

31. Tom has one $10 bill, one $5 bill, 4 dollars, 3 quarters, and 2 dimes. Janet has three $5 bills, three $1 bills, and 8 quarters. Who has more money?

Algebra Connections

Number Patterns

Number patterns can help you predict the next number or numbers that follow.

Example: 10, 20, 30, 40, ▒

Think *How is each number in the number pattern related?*

Compare 10 and 20.

10 + <u>10</u> = 20

Now, compare 20 and 30.

20 + <u>10</u> = 30

The pattern that best describes the list of numbers is: <u>add 10</u>.

The missing number in the number pattern is represented by a shaded box. Use the number pattern to find the missing number.

40 + <u>10</u> = 50

The missing number is 50.

Fill in each shaded box with the number that best completes the number pattern. Then, tell how you completed the pattern.

1. 2, 4, 6, 8, ▒

2. 5, 10, 15, 20, ▒

3. 5, 8, 11, 14, ▒

4. 1, 3, 5, ▒, 9

5. 5, 15, ▒, 35, 45

6. 30, 23, ▒, 9, 2

7. 28, ▒, 18, 13, 8

8. 32, 36, ▒, 44, 48, ▒

9. 47, 56, ▒, 74, ▒, 92

10. 98, 91, ▒, 77, ▒

11. 75, 59, 43, ▒, ▒

12. 3, 5, 4, 6, 5, 7, 6, ▒

13. What are the missing numbers in the number pattern? Describe the number pattern.

48, ▒, ▒, 33, 28, 23

14. Complete the table. Describe the pattern.

A	B	C
4	6	10
5	8	13
6		16
	11	19
15		30
20	14	

15. **Write a Problem** Write a real-world problem using one of the number patterns in Exercises 1 to 12.

Lesson

1-7

TEKS 4.14B: Solve problems that incorporate understanding the problem, making a plan, carrying out the plan, and evaluating the solution for reasonableness. Also, TEKS 4.1A

Problem Solving

Make an Organized List

Arthur is tiling a bathroom wall. He has 520 wall tiles. He wants to arrange them in patterns of hundreds and tens.

Using only hundreds and tens blocks, how many ways can he make 520?

520 tiles

Guided Practice*

Do you know HOW?

Solve. Make an organized list to help you.

1. It costs Celia 50¢ admission to enter the aquarium. How many different ways can Celia pay the admission using only quarters, dimes, and nickels?

Do you UNDERSTAND?

2. What were the titles for the columns of your list in problem 1?

3. **Write a Problem** Write a problem that you can solve using an organized list.

Independent Practice

Solve.

4. Using only hundreds blocks and tens blocks list the ways to show 340.

5. Simon asked Margaret to guess a number. He gave these hints.
   - The number has 3 digits.
   - The digit in the 100s place is less than 2.
   - The digit in the 10s place is greater than 8.
   - The number is even.

   What are the possible numbers?

6. Make a list showing the ways you can make a dollar using only quarters, dimes, and nickels using no more than one nickel and no more than 9 dimes.

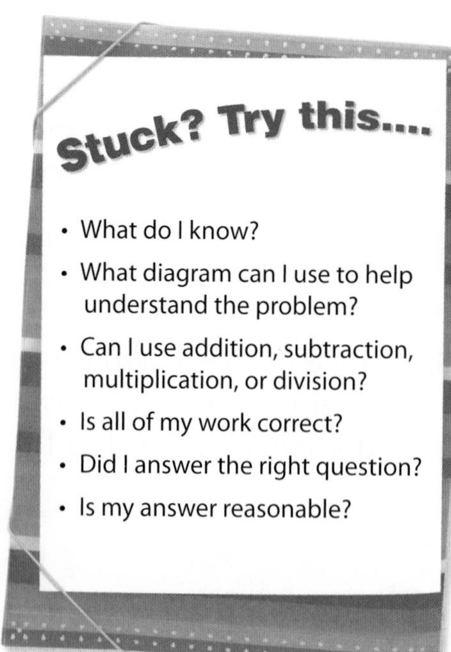
Stuck? Try this....
• What do I know?
• What diagram can I use to help understand the problem?
• Can I use addition, subtraction, multiplication, or division?
• Is all of my work correct?
• Did I answer the right question?
• Is my answer reasonable?

*For another example, see Set F on page 27.

Read & Understand

What do I know? I can use only hundreds blocks and tens blocks.

What am I asked to find? All of the combinations that show a total of 520

Plan

Record the combinations using an organized list.

Hundreds	5	4	3	2	1	0
Tens	2	12	22	32	42	52

There are 6 ways to make 520.

The answer is reasonable because the combinations have 5 or fewer hundreds blocks.

7. Lou's sandwiches are made with either wheat or white bread and have only one type of cheese—Swiss, Cheddar, American, or Mozzarella. How many different kinds of sandwiches can Lou make?

8. A magazine has a total of 24 articles and ads. There are 9 ads. How many articles are there?

24 articles and ads

9	?

9. Janie is making a bracelet. She has 1 red bead, 1 blue bead, and 1 white bead. How many possible ways can Janie arrange the beads?

10. Reasoning What two numbers have a sum of 12 and a difference of 4?

11. Alan has a cat, a goldfish, and a dog. He feeds them in a different order each day. How many different ways can he feed his pets?

12. Heather is writing a 3-digit number. She uses the digits 1, 5, and 9. What are the possible numbers she can write?

13. At the driving range, James wants to buy 200 golf balls. The golf balls are sold in buckets of 100, 50, and 10 golf balls. How many different ways can James buy 200 golf balls?

TAKS Test Prep

1. Which of the following is another way to write the numeral 10,220? (1-1)

   A One thousand, two hundred twenty

   B Ten thousand, two hundred two

   C Ten thousand, two hundred twenty

   D Ten thousand, twenty-two

2. Texas has about seventeen million, one hundred thousand acres of forested land. Which of the following is another way to write this number? (1-2)

   F 17,100

   G 17,000,100

   H 17,010,000

   J 17,100,000

3. Which of the following has a 9 in the hundredths place? (1-5)

   A 28.79

   B 65.91

   C 79.88

   D 926.7

4. What is the missing number? (1-4)

   \$5.47 = 5 dollars + ▢ dimes + 7 pennies
   5.47 = 5 ones + ▢ tenths + 7 hundredths

   F 4

   G 5

   H 7

   J 9

5. Which digit is in the ten millions place in 361,427,548? (1-2)

   A 1

   B 2

   C 4

   D 6

6. The table shows the areas of four states. Which of the four states has the least area? (1-3)

Data

State	Area (square miles)
Montana	147,042
Oklahoma	69,898
Oregon	98,381
Texas	268,581

   F Montana

   G Oklahoma

   H Oregon

   J Texas

7. What decimal is shown in the grid below? (1-5)

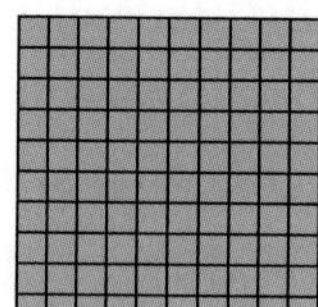
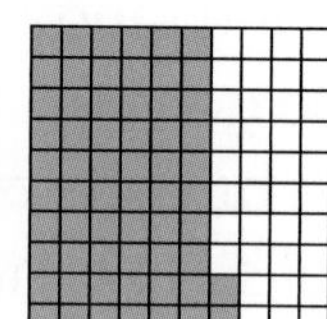

   A 6.12

   B 2.61

   C 1.62

   D 1.26

8. Which number is less than 4,329,349? (1-3)

F 4,359,219

G 4,329,391

H 4,329,319

J 4,359,291

9. Which statement is true? (1-6)

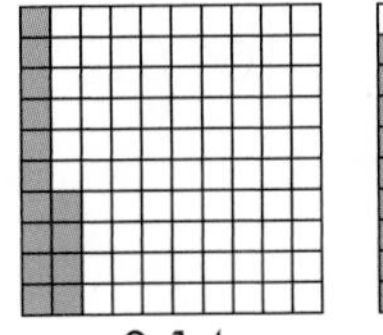
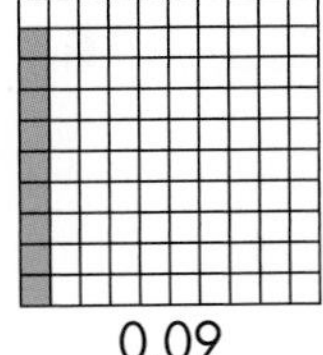

A 0.14 > 0.09

B 0.14 < 0.09

C 0.09 = 0.14

D 0.09 > 0.14

10. Which of the following is equal to 20 + 7 + 0.9 + 0.03? (1-5)

F 20.79

G 20.93

H 27.39

J 27.93

11. Which shows the gymnastic scores in order from the least to the greatest? (1-6)

A 9.72, 9.8, 9.78, 9.87

B 9.78, 9.72, 9.87, 9.8

C 9.78, 9.8, 9.72, 9.87

D 9.72, 9.78, 9.8, 9.87

12. The place value chart shows how many feet above sea level, Mt. McKinley, the highest point in the United States, is. Which of the following is another way to write the number in a place value chart? (1-1)

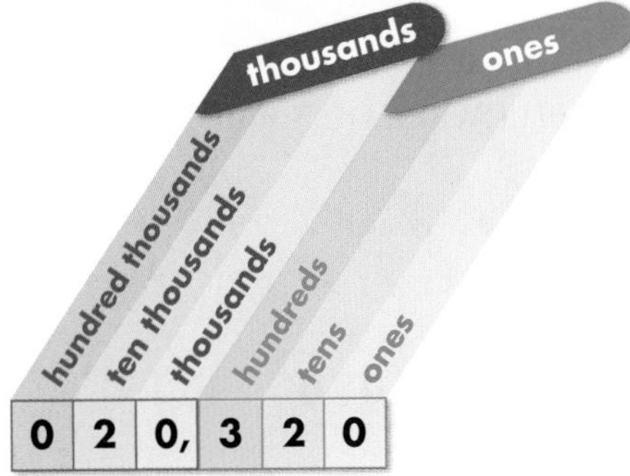

F 20,000 + 300 + 20

G 20,000 + 3,000 + 200

H 2,000 + 300 + 20

J 2,000 + 30 + 2

13. What number is best represented by point P on the number line? (1-1)

A 378

B 382

C 388

D 392

14. **Griddable Response** Estella is making a flag. She can choose three colors from red, white, blue, and yellow. How many different color combinations does Estella have to choose from? (1-7)

Reteaching

Set A, pages 4–6, 8–9

Use a place-value chart to write the expanded form and word form of 26,500.

Expanded form: 20,000 + 6,000 + 500

Word form: twenty-six thousand, five hundred

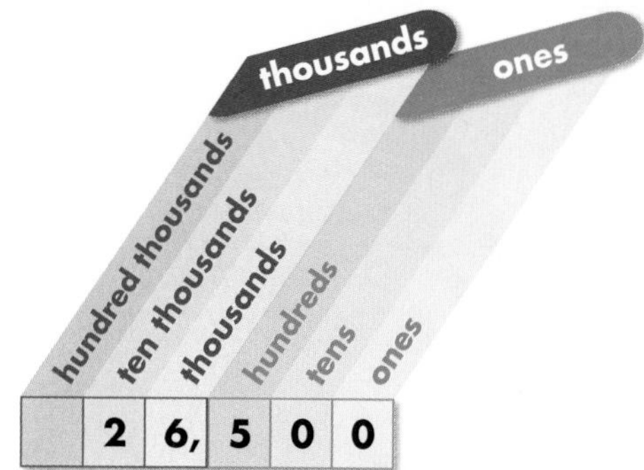

Remember that periods can help you read large numbers.

Use place-value charts to write each number in expanded form and word form.

1. 7,549
2. 27,961
3. 321,209
4. 3,454
5. 6,792,365
6. 15,164,612

Set B, pages 10–13

Write > or < for each ◯.

45,423 ◯ 44,897

Use place value to compare. Start comparing from the left. Look for the first digit that is different.

45,423 44,897 $5 > 4$

So, 45,423 > 44,897.

Remember that a number line can be used to compare numbers.

Write > or < for each ◯.

1. 11,961 ◯ 12,961
2. 735,291,000 ◯ 735,291,001

Order the numbers from greatest to least.

3. 22,981 14, 762 21, 046

Set C, pages 14–15

Write 4 dollars, 8 dimes, and 2 pennies with a dollar sign and a decimal point.

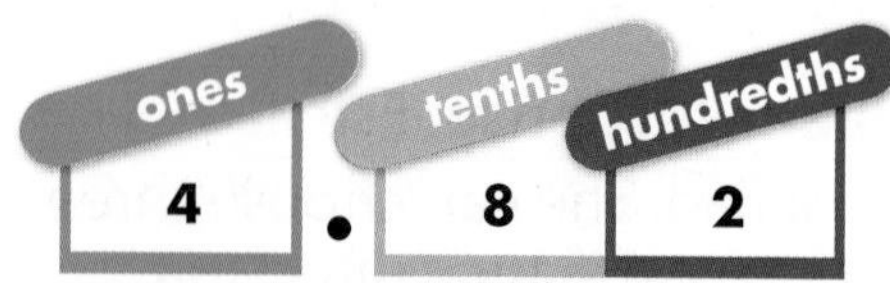

Read: four dollars and eighty-two cents

Write: $4.82

Remember that a dime is one tenth of a dollar, and a penny is one hundredth of a dollar.

Write each amount with a dollar sign and a decimal point.

1. 3 dimes + 4 pennies
2. 1 dollar + 5 dimes + 6 pennies
3. 9 dollars + 6 dimes
4. 4 dollars + 9 pennies

Set D, pages 16–17

Write the decimal shown in expanded, standard, and word form.

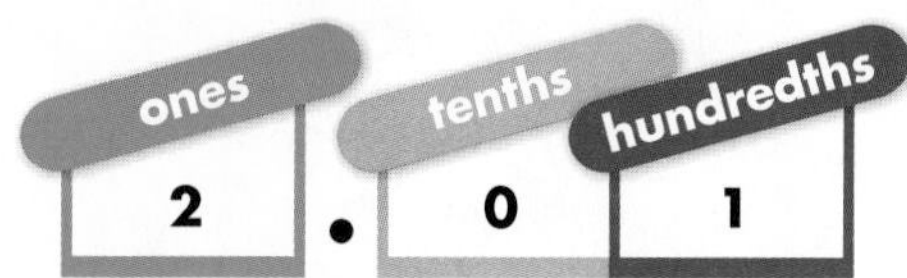

Expanded form: 2 + 0.01

Standard form: 2.01

Word form: Two and one hundredth

Remember to use the word and for the decimal point when you write a decimal in word form.

Write the following in word and expanded form.

1. 12.13
2. 1.09
3. 11.1
4. 88.08

Set E, pages 18–20

Order 0.2, 0.7, and 0.1 from least to greatest using place-value blocks.

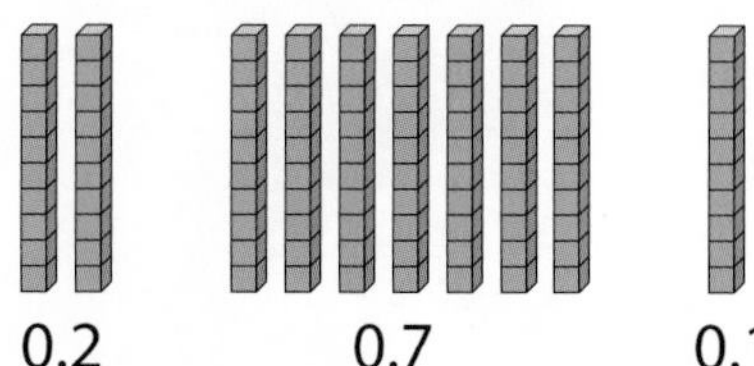

0.2 0.7 0.1

The least number is 0.1. The greatest number is 0.7. The order from least to greatest is 0.1, 0.2, 0.7.

Remember to check if you are ordering numbers from least to greatest or greatest to least.

Use place-value blocks to order the numbers from least to greatest.

1. 0.6, 0,3, 0.7
2. 0.9, 0.1, 0.5
3. 0.6, 0.4, 0.2
4. 0.8, 0.4, 0.9

Set F, pages 22–23

Using only hundreds and tens blocks, how many ways can you make 440?

What do I know? I can use only hundreds blocks and tens blocks

What am I asked to find? All of the combinations that make a total of 440.

Record the combinations using an organized list.

Hundreds	Tens
4	4
3	14
2	24
1	34

Remember the way you organize a list can help you find all the possibilities in a problem.

Solve. Make an organized list to help you.

1. Troy collects plastic banks. He has three different plastic banks: a pig, a cow, and a frog. How many ways can he arrange his banks on a shelf?

Topic 2

Addition and Subtraction Number Sense

1

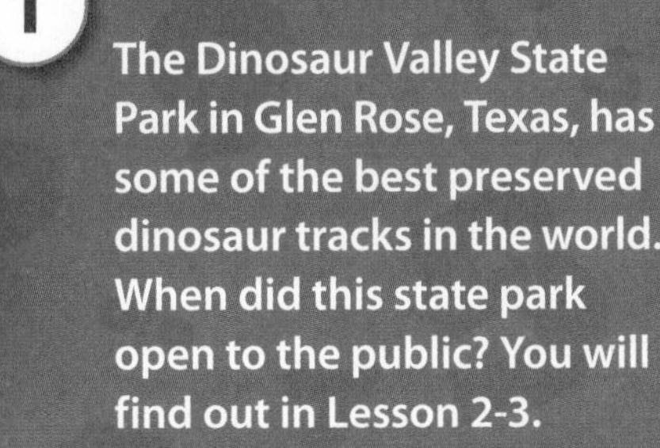

The Dinosaur Valley State Park in Glen Rose, Texas, has some of the best preserved dinosaur tracks in the world. When did this state park open to the public? You will find out in Lesson 2-3.

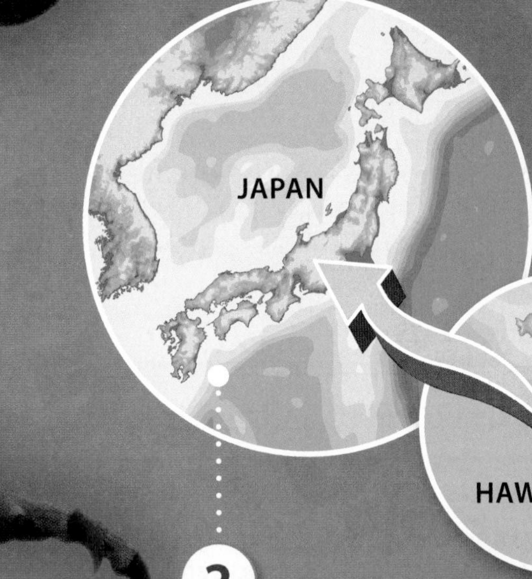

2

Did you know that Hawaii is moving closer to Japan every year? Find out how much closer in Lesson 2-4.

3 How many more bones are there in a child's body than an adult's body? You will find out in Lesson 2-1.

4 The lunar rover set the surface speed record on the moon. Find out the rover's estimated speed in Lesson 2-6.

Review What You Know!

Vocabulary

Choose the best term from the box.

- rounding
- sum
- difference
- mental math
- tens
- regroup

1. In order to subtract 141 from 530, you need to ?.

2. ? tells about how many or about how much.

3. When you subtract two numbers, the answer is the ?.

4. When you add numbers together, you find the ?.

Addition Facts

Find each sum.

5. 4 + 6 **6.** 7 + 5 **7.** 9 + 8

8. 14 + 5 **9.** 3 + 7 **10.** 37 + 7

11. 9 + 6 **12.** 6 + 5 **13.** 15 + 7

14. 3 + 8 **15.** 14 + 6 **16.** 25 + 5

Subtraction Facts

Find each difference.

17. 27 − 3 **18.** 6 − 4 **19.** 15 − 8

20. 11 − 8 **21.** 6 − 2 **22.** 17 − 8

23. 16 − 4 **24.** 20 − 5 **25.** 11 − 6

26. 14 − 6 **27.** 15 − 10 **28.** 13 − 7

29. **Writing to Explain** Why does 843 round to 840 rather than to 850?

Lesson

2-1

TEKS 4.3A: Use addition and subtraction to solve problems involving whole numbers.

Using Mental Math to Add and Subtract

How can you use mental math to add and subtract?

Properties can sometimes help you add using mental math. How many years have Ms. Walston and Mr. Randall been teaching? What is the total number of years all of the teachers in the chart have been teaching?

Data

Teacher	Years Teaching
Ms. Walston	12
Mr. Roy	5
Mr. Randall	30

Other Examples

Add using mental math.

Find 135 + 48.

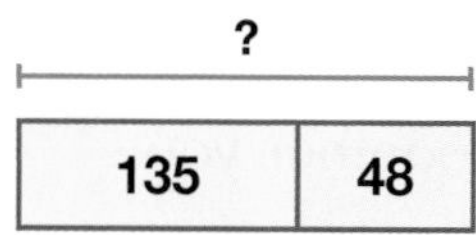

Use breaking apart to find a ten.

Adding 5 to 135 is easy. Break apart 48.

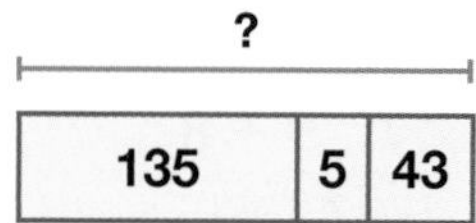

135 + 5 = 140
140 + 43 = 183
So, 135 + 48 = 183.

Use compensation.

135 + 48
135 + 50 = 185

I added 2 too many, so I will subtract 2.

185 − 2 = 183
So, 135 + 48 = 183.

Subtract using mental math.

Find 400 − 165.

Use counting on.

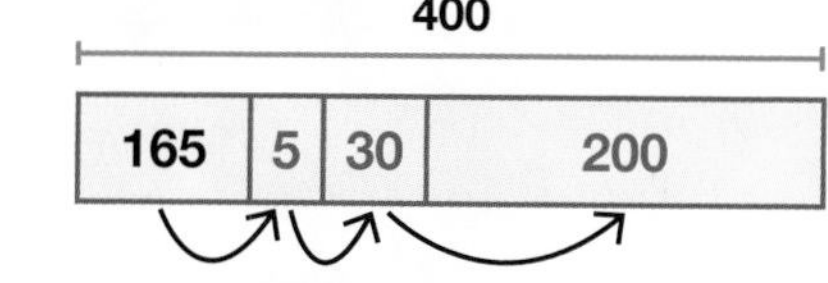

165 + 5 = 170
170 + 30 = 200
200 + 200 = 400

5 + 30 + 200 = 235
So, 400 − 165 = 235.

Use compensation.

Find 260 − 17.

It is easy to subtract 20.

260 − 20 = 240

Think I subtracted 3 too many, so I will add 3.

240 + 3 = 243
So, 260 − 17 = 243.

Commutative Property of Addition

You can add two numbers in any order.

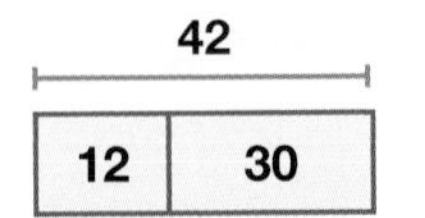

$12 + 30 = 30 + 12$

Ms. Walston and Mr. Randall have been teaching a combined total of 42 years.

Associative Property of Addition

You can change the grouping of addends.

47		
12	30	5

$(12 + 30) + 5 = 12 + (30 + 5)$

The total number of years the three teachers have been teaching is 47 years.

Identity Property of Addition

Adding zero does not change the number.

$12 + 0 = 12$

Guided Practice*

Do you know HOW?

In **1** through **6**, use mental math to add or subtract.

1. 86 + 25

2. 497 + 0

3. 566 − 359

4. 169 − 48

5. 239 + 509

6. (40 + 5) + 8

Do you UNDERSTAND?

7. How could you use compensation to find 391 – 26?

8. **Writing to Explain** Explain how you used mental math to find the answer to Exercise 4.

Independent Practice

Leveled Practice In **9** through **18**, use mental math to complete the calculation.

9. 400 − 227

400			
227	3	70	100

10. 500 − 89

500		
89	11	400

11. 906 − 289

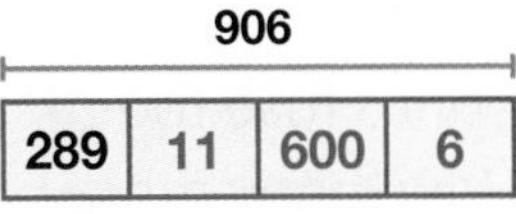

12. 7,000 + 2,130

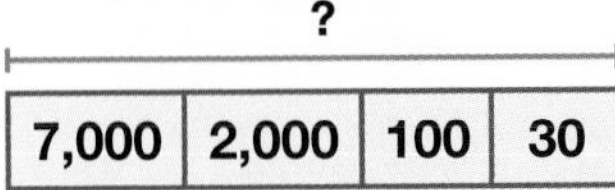

13. 583 + 317

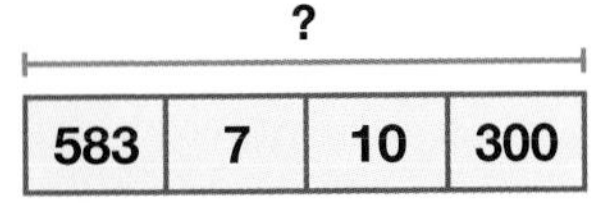

14. 125 + 28

?		
125	5	23

15. 1,700 − 315

16. 2,000 + 4,996

17. 438 − 129

18. 0 + 284

DIGITAL Animated Glossary www.pearsonsuccessnet.com

*For another example, see Set A on page 60.

TAKS Problem Solving

For **19** through **21**, use the table to the right.

19. Which state has the greatest land area in square miles?

20. Which two states shown in the table have the smallest difference in land area?

21. Which two states shown in the table have the greatest difference in land area?

Data

State	Total Square Miles
Alaska	571,951
Texas	261,797
California	155,959
Montana	145,552
New Mexico	121,356

22. Colin had 148 CDs in his collection. He traded 32 of them for 23 that he really wanted. How many CDs does Colin now have in his collection? Use mental math.

A 106 CDs

B 108 CDs

C 116 CDs

D 139 CDs

23. Ms. Gomez's class collected pencils for the community school supplies drive. Ethan's group brought in 143 pencils and Marcelina's group added 78 more. How many pencils did the groups contribute altogether?

F 184 pencils **H** 221 pencils

G 204 pencils **J** 245 pencils

24. **Number Sense** Is 881 – 262 more or less than 500? Explain how you can tell using mental math.

25. **Writing to Explain** How can you use mental math to subtract 158 – 29?

26. An adult human body has a total of 206 bones. There are 300 bones in a child's body because some of a child's bones fuse together as a child grows. How many more bones are in a child's body than in an adult's body?

300

206	4	90

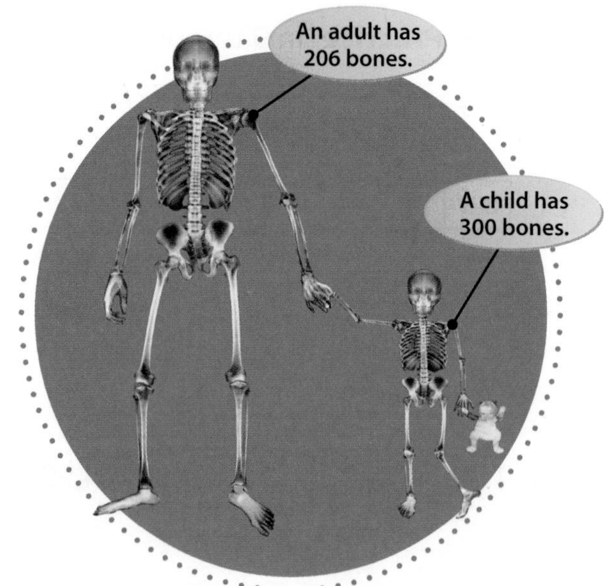
An adult has 206 bones.
A child has 300 bones.

27. **Number Sense** Write two numbers that have a 6 in the ones place and an 8 in the hundreds place.

Algebra Connections

Solving Number Sentences with Addition and Subtraction

A number sentence uses the equal sign (=) to show two expressions have the same value.

Fill in the box in each number sentence with the number that makes the number sentence true. Check your answers.

Example: 8 + ☐ = 35

Think *What number plus 8 equals 35?*

When solving an addition number sentence, use subtraction to identify the missing number.

What is 35 minus 8?

Subtract 8 from 35.
35 − 8 = 27

Now, add 8 and 27.
8 + 27 = 35

Copy and complete each number sentence.

1. 7 + ☐ = 31
2. ☐ + 6 = 21
3. 26 − ☐ = 25
4. 56 − ☐ = 38
5. ☐ − 47 = 12
6. 66 + ☐ = 85
7. ☐ − 98 = 1
8. 103 − ☐ = 72
9. 10 + ☐ = 13
10. ☐ − 8 = 12
11. 1 + ☐ = 7
12. 744 − ☐ = 327

For **13** through **16**, copy and complete the number sentence below each problem. Use it to help explain your answer.

13. Write a Problem Cheryl made 8 free-throw shots. She shot a total of 10 free-throw shots. How many free-throw shots did she miss?

8 + ☐ = 10

14. George delivered 118 newspapers in two days. He delivered 57 newspapers the first day. How many newspapers did George deliver the second day?

57 + ☐ = 118

15. 7 rabbits less than a certain number of rabbits is 13 rabbits. What is the value of the variable?

☐ − 7 = 13

16. The cost of an apple is 39¢. Robert had 25¢ in his pocket. How much more money did Robert need to purchase the apple?

25 + ☐ = 39

Lesson

2-2

TEKS 4.5A Round whole numbers to the nearest ten, hundred, or thousand to approximate reasonable results in problem situations.

Rounding Whole Numbers and Decimals

How can you round numbers?

Rounding replaces one number with another number that tells about how many or how much. A tortoise lived to be 176 years old. What is 176 rounded to the nearest ten?

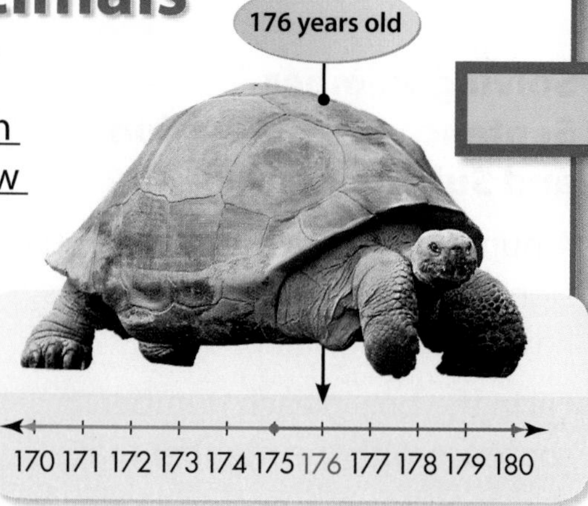

Other Examples

Round 2,364 to the nearest hundred.

hundreds place

2,364

The digit to the right of the hundreds place is 6.

Since 6 > 5, round 3 hundreds to 4 hundreds.

So, 2,364 rounds to 2,400.

Round 7.4 to the nearest whole number.

tenths place

7.4

The digit to the right of the ones place is 4.

Since 4 < 5, round to 7 ones.

So, 7.4 rounds to 7.

Guided Practice*

Do you know HOW?

In **1** through **8**, round each number to the place of the underlined digit.

1. 1.2

2. 85,639

3. 91.24

4. 4,542

5. 656

6. 7,893

7. 2,395

8. 187

Do you UNDERSTAND?

9. Writing to Explain When rounding to the nearest whole number, explain why 2.33 rounds to 2 and not to 3.

10. Number Sense Is it more precise to round 2,364 to the nearest or to the nearest hundred?

11. The oldest living tree is a Bristlecone pine that is about 4,760 years old. Round 4,760 to the nearest hundred.

For another example, see Set B on page 60.

One Way

You can use a number line to round 176 to the nearest ten.

Locate 176.

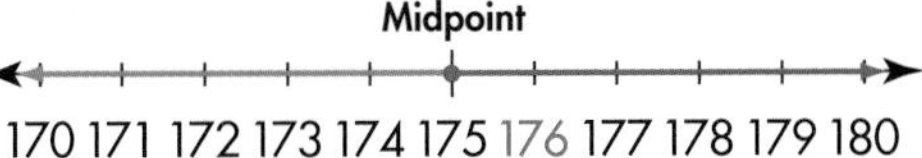

Compare 176 to the midpoint, 175.

176 is to the right of the midpoint, so round to 180.

Another Way

Round 176 to the nearest ten using place value.

Find the rounding place and look at the digit to the right. If it is 5 or more, add 1 to the rounding digit. If it is less than 5, leave the rounding digit alone.

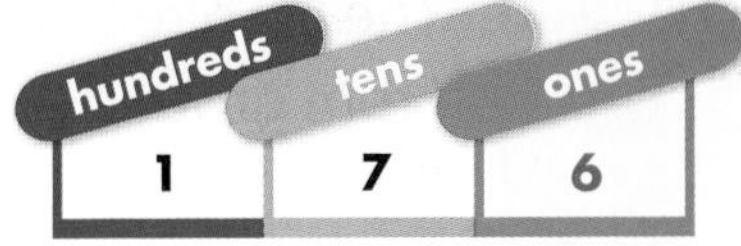

Since 6 > 5, round to 180.

Independent Practice

For **12** through **21**, round to the place of the underlined digit.

12. 8,493,695 **13.** 39,230 **14.** 77,292 **15.** 57,846 **16.** 4,028

17. 3,096 **18.** 87,312 **19.** 101,276 **20.** 524,188 **21.** 1,048,576

For **22** through **31**, round each decimal to the nearest whole number.

22. 0.4 **23.** 31.95 **24.** 2.59 **25.** 70.7 **26.** 1.63

27. 1.92 **28.** 2.84 **29.** 13.7 **30.** 3.42 **31.** 9.49

TAKS Problem Solving

32. Reasoning To what place do you think the number 93,734,000 is rounded? Explain.

33. Write a number that when rounded to the nearest thousand and to the nearest hundred will have the same result.

34. Writing to Explain The elevation of Fort Worth, Texas, is 612 feet. Round this number to the nearest hundred and to the nearest ten.

35. Reasoning Write four numbers that round to 9 when rounded to the nearest whole number.

36. Number Sense Write four numbers that round to 700 when rounded to the nearest hundred.

600 700 800

37. What is 57,681 rounded to the nearest thousand?

A 60,000 **C** 58,000

B 57,000 **D** 50,000

Lesson
2-3

TEKS 4.5A: Round whole numbers to the nearest ten, hundred, or thousand to approximate reasonable results in problem situations.

Estimating Sums and Differences of Whole Numbers

How can you estimate sums and differences of whole numbers?

The Empire State Building was completed in 1931. From ground to tip, it measures 1,250 feet. At the top of the building is a lightning rod which measures 204 feet. Estimate the total height of the structure.

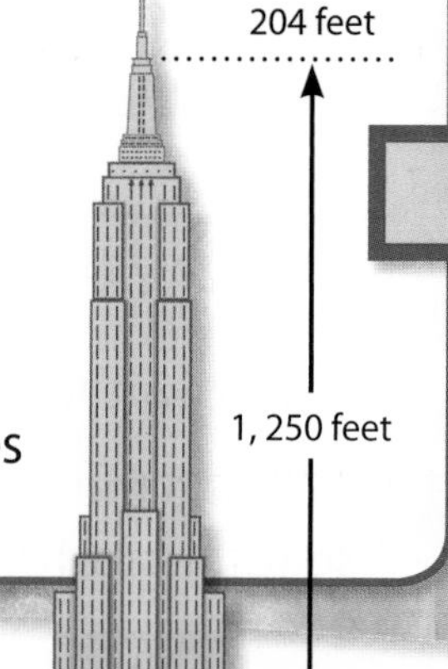

Guided Practice*

Do you know HOW?

In **1** through **6**, estimate each sum or difference.

1. 563 → ▢00
+ 375 → + ▢00

2. 288 → ▢▢0
− 171 → − ▢▢0

3. 645 + 253

4. 262 − 132

5. 952 − 402

6. 398 + 121

Do you UNDERSTAND?

7. Writing to Explain In the first example above, why can't you round both numbers to the nearest thousand?

8. The Statue of Liberty was completed in 1886. About how many years later was the Empire State Building completed than the Statue of Liberty?

Independent Practice

In 9 through 16, estimate by rounding to the nearest ten.

9. 542 + 27

10. 281 − 172

11. 5,323 − 2,611

12. 738 + 741

13. 6,324 + 3,842

14. 895 − 305

15. 755 − 344

16. 586 + 278

In 17 through 24, estimate by rounding to the nearest hundred.

17. 368 + 137

18. 918 + 391

19. 5,317 + 1,734

20. 778 + 95

21. 423 + 196

22. 891 + 223

23. 1,724 − 731

24. 551 − 249

*For another example, see Set C on page 61.

Estimate the total height of the structure.

Round each number to the nearest hundred.

1,250	→	1,300
+ 204	→	+ 200
		1,500

The total height is about 1,500 feet.

The answer is reasonable because the total height is greater than the height of the Empire State Building.

The Washington Monument was completed in 1884. About how many years after was the Empire State Building completed?

1931	→	1930	Round each number to the nearest ten. Show rounding to subtract.
− 1884	→	− 1880	
		50	

The Empire State Building was completed about 50 years later.

TAKS Problem Solving

25. The time line below shows the years that the Dinosaur Valley State Park and the Meridian State Park opened to the public. Use the time line to estimate the difference in years between the time they opened.

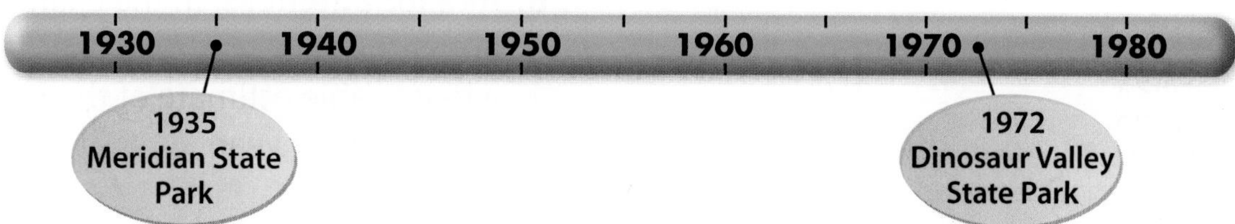

26. This year, 35,658 people ran in a marathon. Last year, 8,683 fewer people ran. About how many people ran last year?

27. During swimming practice, Juan swam 15 laps and Ted swam 9 laps. How many more laps did Juan swim than Ted?

28. The table below shows the number of students per grade. Estimate the total number of students in Grades 3, 4, and 5. About how many students are in Grades 4 and 5?

Data

Grade	Number of Students
3	145
4	152
5	144
6	149

29. Alex sold 86 tickets to a school talent show on Thursday and 153 tickets on Friday. About how many tickets to the talent show did Alex sell altogether?

A About 100

B About 200

C About 300

D About 400

Lesson

2-4

TEKS 4.5: Estimate to determine reasonable results.

Estimating Sums and Differences of Decimals

How do you estimate when you add and subtract decimals?

In Beijing, China, it rained 5.82 inches in the first half of the year. In the second half of the year, it rained 18.63 inches. Estimate the rainfall for the whole year.

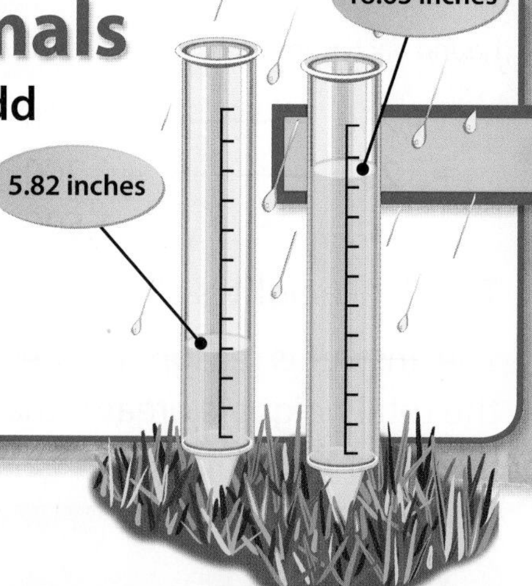

Guided Practice*

Do you know HOW?

In **1** through **4**, estimate each sum or difference.

1. 0.72 + 0.56

2. 18.54 − 1.99

3. $\begin{array}{r} 13.94 \\ +\ 4.72 \\ \hline \end{array}$

4. $\begin{array}{r} 47.31 \\ -\ 11.25 \\ \hline \end{array}$

Do you UNDERSTAND?

5. Explain why 1.4 and 0.75 both round to 1.

6. Reasonableness In the example above, explain why 2.5 inches is not a reasonable estimate of the rainfall for the whole year.

Independent Practice

In **7** through **22**, round to the nearest whole number to estimate each sum or difference.

You can write rounded numbers in vertical format before adding or subtracting.

7. 9.6 + 3.27

8. 9.51 + 8.61

9. 7.11 + 0.15

10. 1.45 + 6.85

11. 18.85 − 6.8

12. 4.31 − 1.28

13. 31.12 − 4.86

14. 0.66 − 0.34

15. $\begin{array}{r} 82.43 \\ -\ 3.90 \\ \hline \end{array}$

16. $\begin{array}{r} 5.78 \\ -\ 3.86 \\ \hline \end{array}$

17. $\begin{array}{r} 63.93 \\ +\ 3.31 \\ \hline \end{array}$

18. $\begin{array}{r} 3.73 \\ +\ 0.81 \\ \hline \end{array}$

19. $\begin{array}{r} 2.1 \\ +\ 7.5 \\ \hline \end{array}$

20. $\begin{array}{r} 3.45 \\ -\ 2.44 \\ \hline \end{array}$

21. $\begin{array}{r} 19.06 \\ +\ 1.99 \\ \hline \end{array}$

22. $\begin{array}{r} 4.84 \\ +\ 0.73 \\ \hline \end{array}$

*For another example, see Set D on page 61.

Estimate 5.82 + 18.63.

Round each decimal to the nearest whole number. Then add.

$$\begin{array}{r} 5.82 \\ +\ 18.63 \\ \hline \end{array} \longrightarrow \begin{array}{r} 6 \\ +\ 19 \\ \hline 25 \end{array}$$

About 25 inches of rain fell in Beijing.

In August, 6.7 inches of rain fell in Beijing. In September, it rained 2.3 inches. About how much more did it rain in August than in September?

$$\begin{array}{r} 6.7 \\ -\ 2.3 \\ \hline \end{array} \longrightarrow \begin{array}{r} 7 \\ -\ 2 \\ \hline 5 \end{array}$$

Round each decimal to the nearest whole number. Then subtract the rounded numbers.

It rained about 5 inches more in August.

TAKS Problem Solving

In **23** and **24**, use the table at the right.

Vegetable	Weight (pounds)
	2.0
	2.6
	1.2
	3.5

23. The table shows the weight of each type of vegetable Vanessa bought to make a large salad for her family picnic. About how much more did the cucumbers weigh than the lettuce?

24. About how much did all of the vegetables weigh altogether?

25. Hawaii is moving toward Japan at a rate of approximately 2.8 inches per year. About how much closer will Hawaii be to Japan in 3 years?

26. Kyle walked 13.43 miles last week, 15.33 miles the week before, and 14.82 miles this week. About how many miles has Kyle walked in the 3 weeks?

27. Neil is installing 38 square yards of carpet in his home. He uses 12.2 square yards in one room and 10.5 square yards in another room. About how much carpet does he have left?

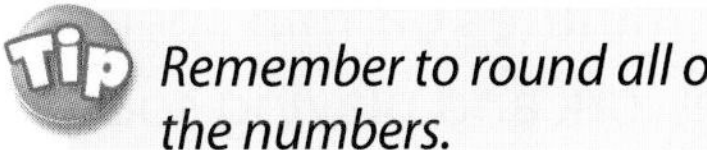

Tip *Remember to round all of the numbers.*

A about 13 square yards

B about 15 square yards

C about 17 square yards

D about 20 square yards

Lesson

2-5

TEKS 4.14A: Identify the mathematics in everyday situations.

Problem Solving

Missing or Extra Information

Kendra had $7. She bought a sandwich, a drink, and an apple at the cafeteria. She spent a total of $3 on the sandwich and the drink.

How much money did Kendra have left?

A drink and a sandwich cost $3.

Guided Practice*

Do you know HOW?

1. At the zoo, Julie saw 18 penguins. She saw 8 Adelie penguins. The rest of the penguins she saw were Rockhopper penguins. She learned that Rockhopper penguins grow to be about 5 to 8 pounds. How many Rockhopper penguins did Julie see?

Do you UNDERSTAND?

2. What information was not needed in Problem 1?
3. **Write a Problem** Write a problem that contains too much or too little information.

Independent Practice

Decide if each problem has extra information or not enough information. Tell any information that is not needed or that is missing. Solve if you have enough information.

4. Carmin spent 30 minutes completing his homework after school. Then he played soccer. What information do you need to find how many minutes Carmin spent completing his homework and playing soccer altogether?
5. June only has quarters and pennies in her coin collection. She has 85 coins in all. What would you need to know to find out how many quarters June has in her collection?

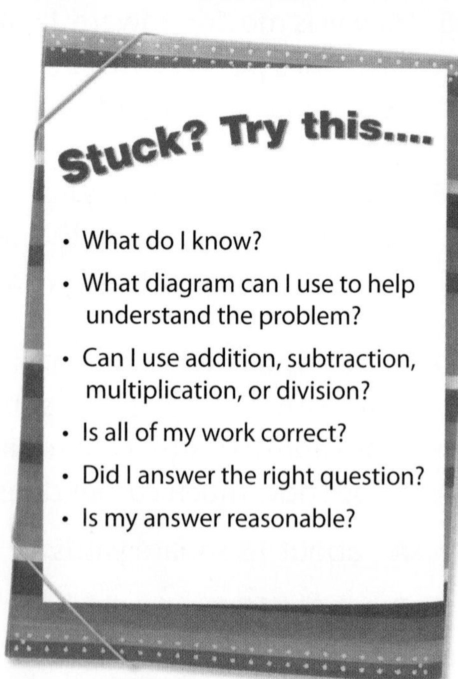
Stuck? Try this....
• What do I know?
• What diagram can I use to help understand the problem?
• Can I use addition, subtraction, multiplication, or division?
• Is all of my work correct?
• Did I answer the right question?
• Is my answer reasonable?

*For another example, see Set E on page 61.

Read & Understand

What do I know? Kendra had $7. She bought a sandwich, a drink, and an apple. The sandwich and the drink was $3.

What am I asked to find? The amount of money Kendra had left

Plan

Draw a diagram to show what you know and want to find.

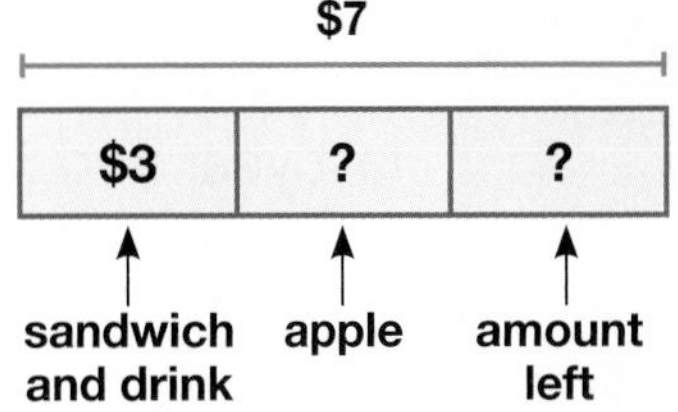

Think Is there missing information needed to solve the problem?

Is there any extra information not needed to solve the problem?

6. Kayla ate two tacos and an apple for lunch. The tacos had 260 calories. How many calories did Kayla eat for lunch?

7. There are 35 sopranos in the school choir. The 40 remaining choir members are altos. How many students are in the school choir?

8. There are 328 places for activity photographs in the yearbook. The yearbook club has decided to make most of the photographs black and white. How many color photographs will be in the yearbook?

9. A notebook costs $2.68 and a pen costs $1.79. Does Jasmine have enough money to buy a notebook and two pens?

10. The tallest steel roller coaster is in Jackson, New Jersey. It is 456 feet tall. The tallest wooden roller coaster is in Cincinnati, Ohio. The roller coaster is 7,032 feet long. How much taller is the steel roller coaster than the wooden roller coaster? Choose the letter that contains the information that is needed to solve the problem.

    A The tallest steel roller coaster travels at 128 miles per hour.

    B The tallest steel roller coaster is 3,118 feet long.

    C The tallest wooden roller coaster travels at 78.3 miles per hour.

    D The tallest wooden roller coaster is 218 feet tall.

11. Mrs. Song bought school supplies for her two children, Jason and Kevin. Jason is two years older than Kevin and is in the fourth grade. She spent $38 for Kevin's supplies and $46 for Jason's supplies. If she paid with a $100 bill, how much change did she get back?

$100 for school supplies

$38	$46	?

Lesson

2-6

TEKS 4.3A: Use addition and subtraction to solve problems involving whole numbers.

Adding Whole Numbers

How do you add whole numbers?

If an artificial coral reef grew 257 inches last year and 567 inches this year, how much did it grow in all?

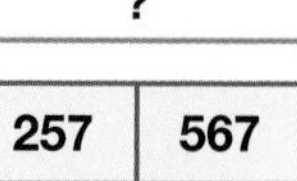

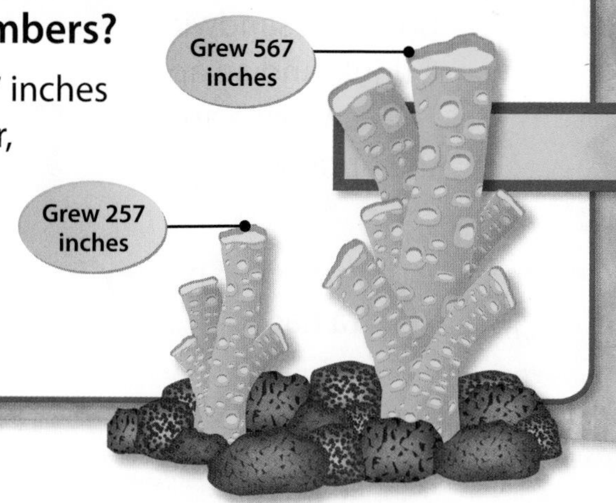

Estimate: 300 + 600 = 900

Another Example How do you add more than two numbers?

Find the sum.

9,348 + 102 + 5,802 + 1,933

A 17,185 **C** 16,175

B 17,175 **D** 15,175

Estimate: 9,000 + 100 + 6,000 + 2,000 = 17,100

Step 1

Add the ones. Regroup if necessary.

$$\begin{array}{r} {\scriptstyle 1} \\ 9,348 \\ 102 \\ 5,802 \\ +\ 1,933 \\ \hline 5 \end{array}$$

Step 2

Add the tens. Regroup if necessary.

$$\begin{array}{r} {\scriptstyle 1} \\ 9,348 \\ 102 \\ 5,802 \\ +\ 1,933 \\ \hline 85 \end{array}$$

Step 3

Add the hundreds, regroup, and then add the thousands.

$$\begin{array}{r} {\scriptstyle 2\ \ 1} \\ 9,348 \\ 102 \\ 5,802 \\ +\ 1,933 \\ \hline 17,185 \end{array}$$

The correct answer is **A**.

Explain It

1. How are the ones regrouped in the example above?

2. **Reasonableness** In Step 3 above, how can you tell that the answer is reasonable?

Step 1

Add 257 + 567.

Add the ones. Regroup if necessary.

```
   1
  257
+ 567
    4
```

Step 2

Add the tens. Regroup if necessary.

```
  11
  257
+ 567
   24
```

Step 3

Add the hundreds. Regroup if necessary.

```
  11
  257
+ 567
  824
```

The reef grew 824 inches in all.

Other Examples

Adding larger numbers

Add 36,424 + 24,842.

Estimate:

36,000 + 25,000 = 61,000

```
    1 1
   36,424
 + 24,842
   61,266
```

The sum is reasonable because it is close to the estimate of 61,000.

Adding more than two numbers

Add 130,283 + 263,823 + 396,538.

Estimate:

100,000 + 264,000 + 397,000 = 791,000

```
   111 1 1
   130,283
   263,823
 + 396,538
   790,644
```

The sum is reasonable because it is close to the estimate of 791,000.

Guided Practice*

Do you know HOW?

In **1** through **6**, find each sum.

1. 821 + 4,543

2. 14,926 + 3,832

3. 1,321 + 2,246

4. 24,593 + 16,861

5.
```
   3,258
 + 1,761
```

6.
```
   16,018
 +    135
```

Do you UNDERSTAND?

7. When adding 36,424 and 24,842 above, why is there no regrouping in the final step?

8. Volunteer teams identified 73 fish species, 30 corals, and 71 other invertebrates on the reef. How many species of fish, coral, and invertebrates were found in all?

*For another example, see Set F on page 62.

Independent Practice

In **9** through **24**, find each sum.

9. 78 + 421

10. 617 + 14,312

11. 873 + 4,893

12. 38,911 + 45,681

13. 327 + 886

14. 295 + 805

15. 3,751 + 4,736

16. 623 + 2,815

17. 4,231 + 76,118

18. 265 + 8,496

19. 9,634 + 2,958

20. 4,673 + 262

21. 7,845 + 509 + 3,746

22. 526 + 276 +1,086

23. 2,868 + 865

24. 15,891 + 527 + 1,086

TAKS Problem Solving

25. In 1972, the Apollo 16 lunar rover set the current lunar speed record at 11 miles per hour. In order to break free from Earth's orbit, Apollo missions had to go 24,989 miles per hour faster than the record speed of the lunar rover. How fast did the Apollo rockets travel?

26. There were 10,453 items checked out of the public library one week. The next week 12,975 items were checked out. A week later, 9,634 items were checked out. How many items were checked out in three weeks?

27. Sandy read 235 pages of a book. She had 192 more pages to read before she was done. How many pages are there in the book?

?

235	192

28. Cheryl and Jason collect baseball cards. Cheryl has 315 cards, and Jason has 186 cards. How many cards do they have altogether?

?

315	186

29. Number Sense The sum of 86, 68, and 38 is 192. What do you also know about the sum of 68, 38, and 86?

30. Estimation Maria added 45,273 and 35,687. Will her answer be greater or less than 80,000?

31. The population of New City is 23,945. Eastdale has a population of 12,774. What is the total population of the two communities?

A 35,719 **B** 36,619 **C** 36,719 **D** 37,619

Mixed Problem Solving

For Problems **1-3**, use the table below.

Some Facts About the Natural Regions of Texas	
Central Plains	Elevation ranges from 2,500 to 4,000 feet above sea level.
Coastal Plains	Home to Padre Island, which is about 110 miles long and up to 3 miles wide
Great Plains	Includes Palo Duro Canyon, which is 120 miles long, up to 20 miles wide, and more than 120 feet deep
Mountain and Basins	Contains the highest point in Texas, Guadalupe Peak, which reaches 8,749 feet above sea level

1. Estimate the difference of elevation between the highest and lowest point in the Central Plains Region.

2. Which is longer, Padre Island or Palo Duro Canyon? How much longer?

3. Fort Davis is the town with the highest elevation in Texas. It has an elevation of 5,050 feet. Guadalupe Peak, with an elevation of 8,749 feet, is the highest point in Texas. Estimate how much higher Guadalupe Peak is than Fort Davis.

4. Texas was governed by Spain from 1519 to 1685 and from 1690 to 1821. Estimate the total number of years that Texas was governed by Spain.

5. Texas was governed by Mexico from 1821 to 1836 and by France from 1685 to 1690. How much longer was Texas governed by Mexico than by France?

6. It is about 200 miles from Corpus Christi to Galveston, 200 miles from Galveston to Tyler, and about 85 miles from Tyler to Dallas. Following this route, about how far is it from Corpus Christi to Dallas?

? total miles

200	200	85

7. Strategy Focus Solve the problem by using the strategy, Draw a Picture.

Sam is in the middle of a line of dancers. His friend, Sara, is the third dancer to the right of Sam. If there are 21 dancers in the line, how many are to the right of Sara?

Lesson

2-7

TEKS 4.3A: Use addition and subtraction to solve problems involving whole numbers.

Subtracting Whole Numbers

How do you subtract numbers?

Brenda has a total of 221 songs in her computer. Her sister, Susan, has a total of 186 songs in her computer. How many more songs does Brenda have in her computer than Susan?

Choose an Operation Subtract to find how many more songs.

Guided Practice*

Do you know HOW?

In **1** through **4**, subtract.

1. 527 − 338

2. 716 − 254

3. 139 − 86

4. 1,268 − 429

Do you UNDERSTAND?

5. In the example at the top, why was the 0 in the hundreds place not written in the answer?

6. Brenda would like to have 275 songs on her computer by next year. How many more songs does she need to download?

Independent Practice

In **7** through **26**, subtract.

7. 336 − 259

8. 693 − 150

9. 881 − 79

10. 479 − 88

11. 1,931 − 509

12. 1,673 − 849

13. 2,173 − 108

14. 8,617 − 3,909

15. 552 − 228

16. 3,711 − 1,683

17. 217 − 166

18. 562 − 199

19. 7,475 − 5,130

20. 5,831 − 1,156

21. 9,385 − 720

22. 1,111 − 589

23. 8,476 − 2,185

24. 6,251 − 964

25. 7,374 − 1,246

26. 8,327 − 3,796

DIGITAL Animated Glossary **www.pearsonsuccessnet.com**

*For another example, see Set G on page 62.

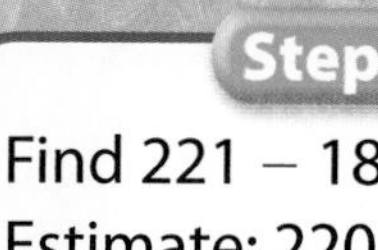

Step 1

Find 221 − 186.
Estimate: 220 − 190 = 30
Subtract the ones.

Regroup if necessary.

```
   1 11
  2 2̸ 1̸
− 1 8 6
      5
```

Step 2

Subtract the tens.
Subtract the hundreds.

Regroup if necessary.

```
  1 11 11
  2̸ 2̸ 1̸
− 1 8 6
    3 5
```

Step 3

Operations that undo each other are inverse operations. Addition and subtraction have an inverse relationship.

```
  1 1
  1 8 6
+   3 5
  2 2 1
```

Add to check your answer.

The answer checks.

TAKS Problem Solving

27. A crayon company makes 17,491 green crayons and 15,063 red crayons. How many more green crayons are made than red crayons?

A 3,463 **C** 10,456

B 2,428 **D** 32,554

28. Angela hiked a trail that climbed 526 feet. Raul hiked a trail that climbed 319 feet. How many more feet did Angela climb than Raul?

	526 feet	
Angela		
Raul	**319 feet**	**?**

29. Jermaine and Linda collected aluminum cans for one month. Look at the chart below to see how many aluminum cans each student collected.

a Who collected more cans?

b Find the difference between the number of cans collected.

Data

Jermaine	1,353 cans
Linda	1,328 cans

30. Mount Kilimanjaro is a mountain in Africa. A group of mountain climbers begin their descent from the peak. On Monday, the mountain climbers descended 3,499 feet. On Tuesday, they descended another 5,262 feet. How many feet have the mountain climbers descended?

Mount Kilimanjaro
is 19,341 feet high.

31. Mike's team scored 63 points in the first half of a basketball game. His team won the game by a score of 124 to103. How many points did his team score in the second half?

Lesson

2-8

TEKS 4.3A: Use addition and subtraction to solve problems involving whole numbers.

Subtracting Across Zeros

How do you subtract across zeros?

An airplane flight to Chicago has seats for 300 passengers. The airline sold 278 tickets for the flight. How many seats are still available for the flight?

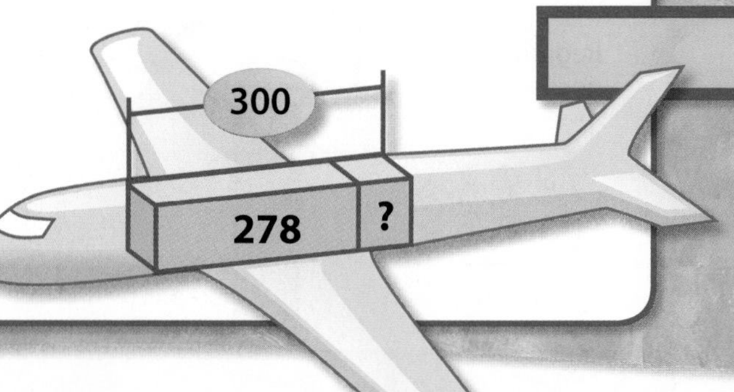

Guided Practice*

Do you know HOW?

In **1** through **6**, subtract.

1. 600 − 177

2. 1,086 − 728

3. 810 − 638

4. 3,304 − 1,137

5. 1,001 − 868

6. 4,000 − 1,698

Do you UNDERSTAND?

7. How would you check if the answer in the example above is correct?

8. One passenger flew from New York to Phoenix. The flight was 2,145 miles. Another passenger flew from Boston to Seattle. The flight was 2,496 miles. How many more miles was the flight to Seattle?

Independent Practice

In **9** through **28**, subtract.

9. 902 − 883

10. 502 − 380

11. 3,000 − 673

12. 5,604 − 1,717

13. 1,830 − 722

14. 7,006 − 3,529

15. 1,902 − 903

16. 6,008 − 4,879

17. 450 − 313

18. 5,025 − 178

19. 406 − 381

20. 1,001 − 35

21. 6,090 − 5,130

22. 2,700 − 1,699

23. 10,807 − 4,373

24. 504 − 319

25. 3,000 − 1,047

26. 5,001 − 368

27. 700 − 520

28. 900 − 406

For another example, see Set H on page 62.

One Way

Find 300 – 278.

Estimate: 300 – 280 = 20

Regroup hundreds to tens and tens to ones.

$$\begin{array}{r} \overset{2}{\cancel{3}}\,\overset{\overset{9}{\cancel{10}}}{\cancel{0}}\,\overset{10}{\cancel{0}} \\ -\ 2\ 7\ 8 \\ \hline 2\ 2 \end{array}$$

3 hundreds = 2 hundreds + 9 tens + 10 ones

There are 22 seats available for the flight.

Another Way

Find 300 – 278.

Estimate: 300 – 280 = 20

Think of 300 as 30 tens and 0 ones.

$$\begin{array}{r} \overset{29}{\cancel{30}}\,\overset{10}{\cancel{0}} \\ -\ 2\,7\,8 \\ \hline 2\,2 \end{array}$$

30 tens + 0 ones = 29 tens + 10 ones

There are 22 seats available for the flight.

TAKS Problem Solving

29. Shawn scored 10,830 points playing a video game. Miguel scored 9,645 points. How many more points did Shawn score than Miguel?

30. Writing to Explain Will the difference between 4,041 and 3,876 be greater or less than 1,000? Explain your answer.

31. Use the chart on the right. Music City sells CDs. Which of the following tells how many more Hip Hop CDs were sold than Latin CDs in April?

A 887 **C** 7,090

B 897 **D** 13,293

Data

CDs Sold in April

Music style	CDs sold in April
Rock	4,008
Hip Hop	7,090
Country	5,063
Latin	6,203

32. William drove from Atlanta, Georgia, to Portland, Oregon. The round trip was 5,601 miles. He traveled 2,603 miles to get to Portland, Oregon, but he decided to take a different route back. How many miles did he travel to get back to Atlanta?

33. On Thursday, 10,296 people attended a college basketball home game. The following week, 12,000 people attended an away game. How many more people attended the away game than the home game?

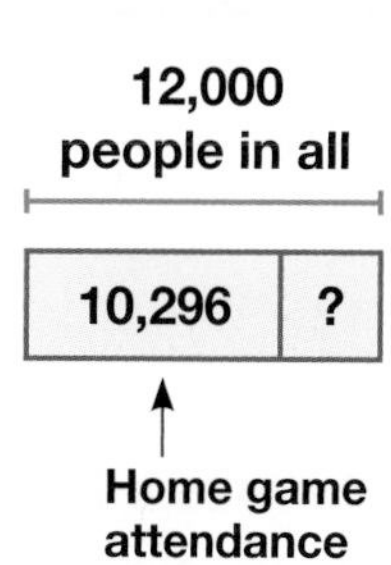

34. In a dart game, Casey scored 42 points, and Maggie scored 28 points. Jesse scored fewer points than Casey and more points than Maggie. Which is a possible score for Jesse?

F 50 points **H** 34 points

G 46 points **J** 26 points

Lesson

2-9

TEKS 4.3B: Add and subtract decimals to the hundredths place using concrete objects and pictorial models.

Modeling Addition and Subtraction of Decimals

Hands-On
grid paper
place-value blocks

How do you model adding decimals?

Use the table at the right to find the total monthly cost of using the dishwasher and the DVD player.

Data

Device	Cost/month
DVD player	$0.40
Microwave oven	$3.57
Ceiling light	$0.89
Dishwasher	$0.85

Another Example How do you model subtracting decimals?

Find the difference between the cost per month to run the microwave oven and the dishwasher.

One Way

Use place-value blocks to find $3.57– $0.85.
Subtract 5 hundredths.

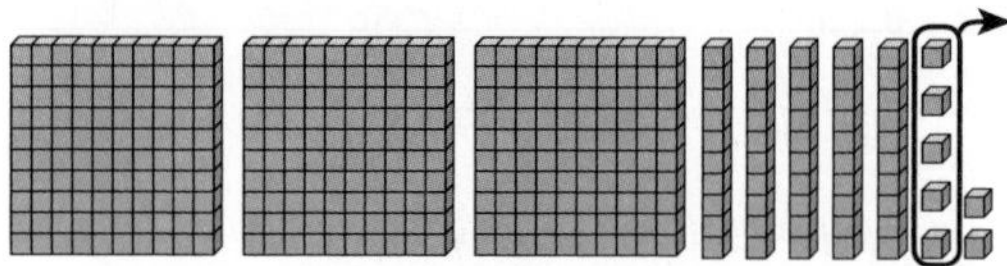

Regroup one whole as 10 tenths.
Subtract 8 tenths.

$3.57 – $0.85 = $2.72

Another Way

Use hundredths grids to find $3.57 – $0.85.

Shade three grids and 57 squares to show 3.57.

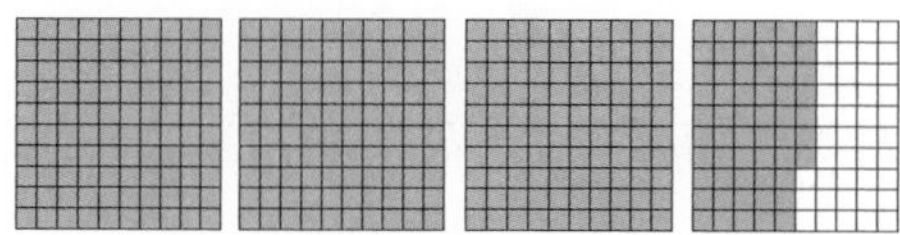

Cross out 8 columns and 5 squares of the shaded grids to show 0.85 being subtracted from 3.57

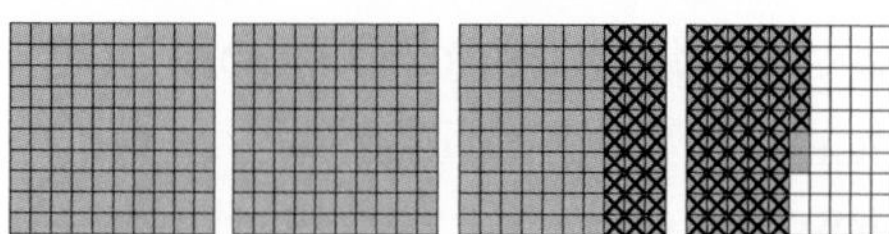

Count the squares that are shaded but not crossed out to find the difference.

$3.57 – $0.85 = $2.72

Explain It

1. **Reasonableness** How could you use the grids to check your answer above?

One Way

Use place-value blocks to add $0.85 + $0.40.

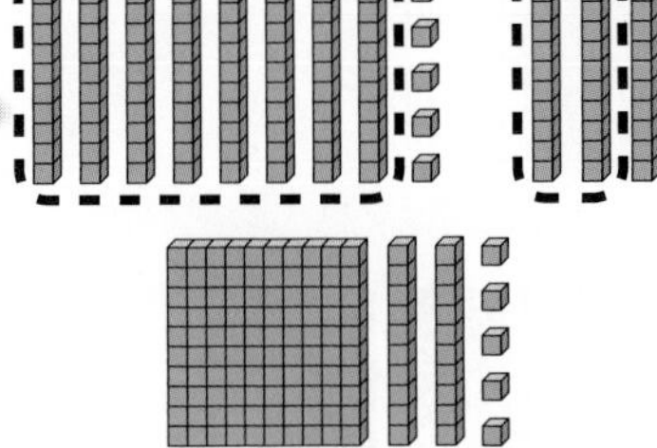

Add the hundredths. Add the tenths. Regroup the tenths as one whole.

$0.85 + $0.40 = $1.25

Another Way

Use hundredths grids to add $0.85 + $0.40.

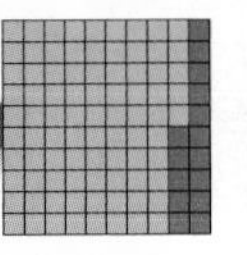
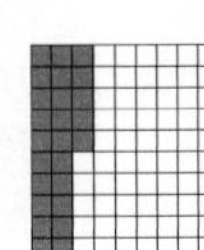

Shade 85 squares to show $0.85. Use a different color and shade 40 more squares to show $0.40. Count all of the shaded squares to find the sum.

$0.85 + $0.40 = $1.25

The monthly cost of using the dishwasher and DVD player is $1.25.

Guided Practice*

Do you know HOW?

In **1** through **6**, use place-value blocks or hundredths grids to add or subtract.

1. 1.22 + 0.34

2. 0.63 + 0.41

3. 2.73 − 0.94

4. 1.38 − 0.73

5. 0.47 − 0.21

6. 2.02 + 0.8

Do you UNDERSTAND?

7. If you were to shade 40 squares first, and then shade 85 more, would the answer be the same as shading 85 squares and then 40 more?

8. Show the difference between the monthly cost of using the DVD player and the dishwasher.

Independent Practice

In **9** through **18**, add or subtract. Use place-value blocks or hundredths grids to help.

9. 0.54 − 0.31

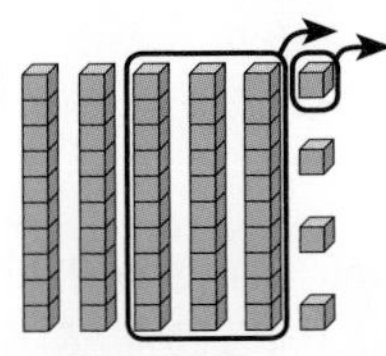

10. 0.37 + 0.47

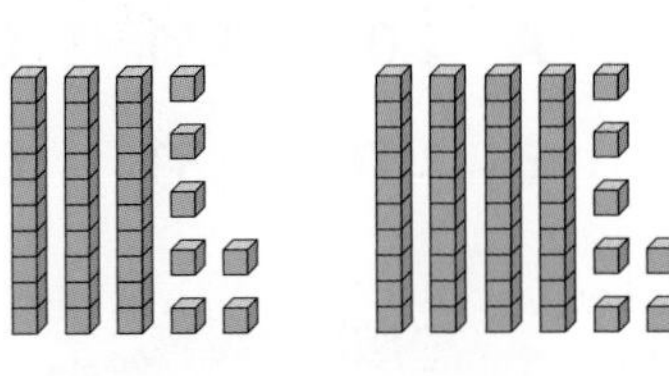

11. 1.2 + 0.56

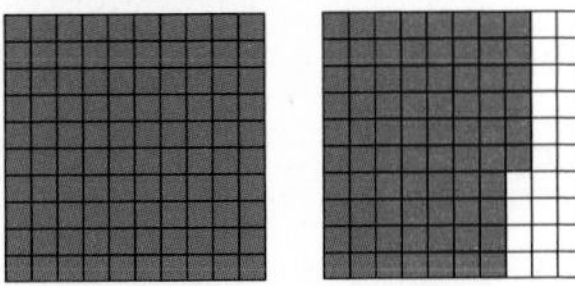

12. 1.33 − 0.35

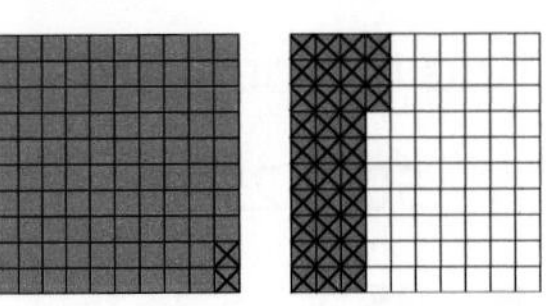

13. 3.0 − 1.47

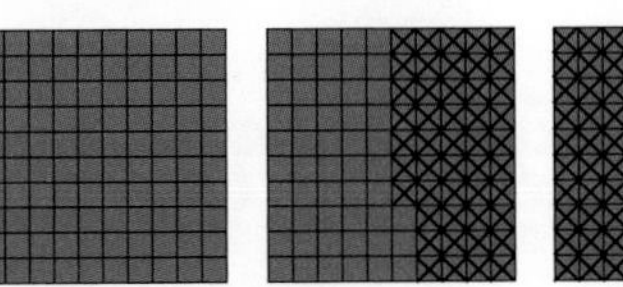

14. 1.11 + 0.89

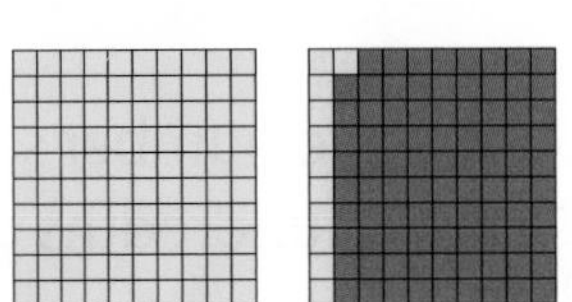

*For another example, see Set I on page 63.

Independent Practice

15. 2.23 − 1.8

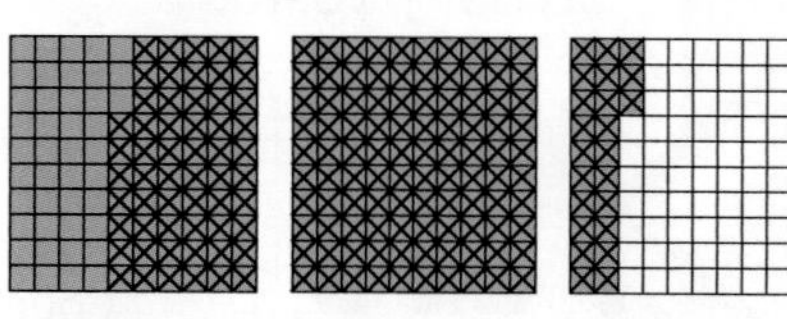

16. 0.4 − 0. 21

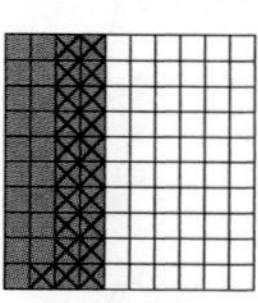

17. 0.58 + 2.4

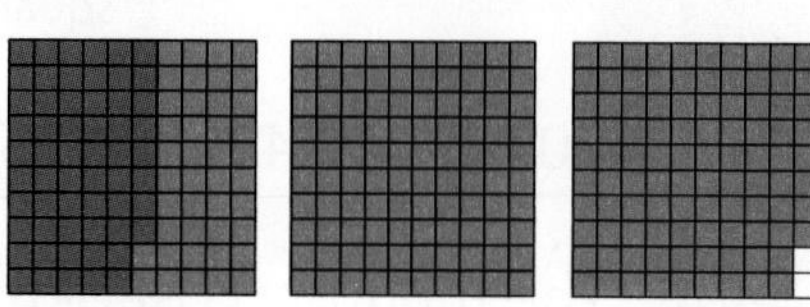

18. 1.31 − 0.55

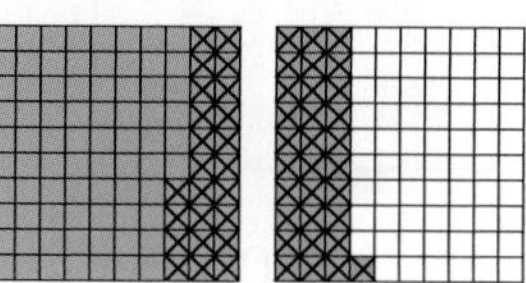

TAKS Problem Solving

19. Writing to Explain How is adding 4.56 + 2.31 similar to adding $2.31 + $4.56?

20. Number Sense Do you think the difference of 1.4 − 0.95 is less than one or greater than one? Explain.

21. Number Sense Is the sum of 0.46 + 0.25 less than or greater than one? Explain.

22. Estimation Estimate to decide if the sum of 314 + 175 is more or less than 600.

23. Which choice represents the problem below?

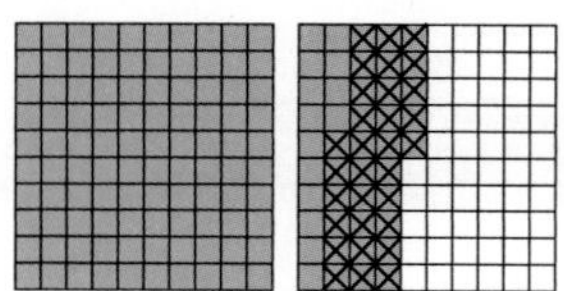

A 2.00 + 0.31 **C** 1.76 − 1.45

B 1.76 − 0.31 **D** 1.45− 0.31

24. Geometry What kind of angle is made when two lines are perpendicular?

F acute angle **H** obtuse angle

G right angle **J** vertex

25. Think About the Process Which expression can be used to find the perimeter of the pool shown to the right?

A 50 + 25 **C** 50 + 50 + 25 + 25

B 25 + 25 + 25 + 25 **D** 50 + 50 + 50 + 50

length = 50 meters

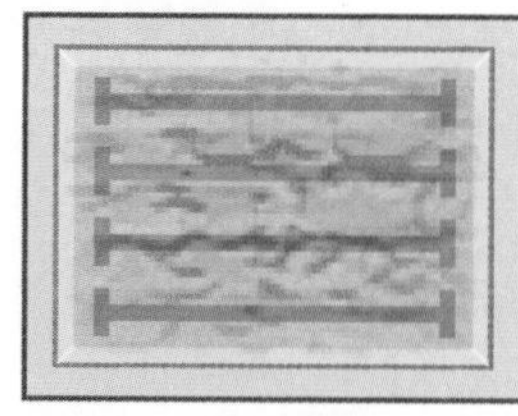

width = 25 meters

26. Write the number sentence that is shown by the hundredths grids to the right.

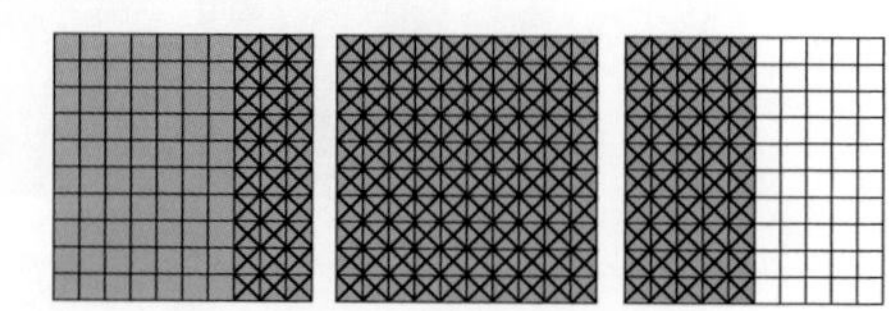

Reasonableness of Sums

Estimate 2,968 + 983 + 5,442. Use a calculator to find the sum. Then, explain whether or not the sum you found is reasonable.

Step 1 Estimate 2,968 + 983 + 5,442.

3,000 + 1,000 + 5,000 = 9,000

Step 2 Use a calculator to add.

Press: 2,968  983  5,442 ENTER =

Display:

9393

Step 3 Explain whether or not the sum is reasonable.

Since 9,393 is close to the estimate of 9,000, the sum is reasonable.

Practice

Estimate each sum. Find the sum on a calculator. Remember to check whether or not the sum is reasonable.

1. 956 + 1,495

2. 1,872 + 3,216

3. 4,857 + 5,679 + 3,298

4. 8,542 + 875 + 6,425

5. 1,978 + 7,435 + 2,986

6. 9,650 + 2,348 + 5,822

7. 2,726 + 1,247 + 3,476

8. 3,214 + 7,981 + 2,148 + 6,542

9. 872 + 2,729 + 221

10. 6,742+ 7,231

11. 8,792 + 3,864 + 298

12. 8,898 + 6,281

13. 1,372 + 6,261 + 204

14. 7,671 + 3,341

15. 3,634 + 8,916 + 192

16. 3,456 + 7,654 + 211

17. 101 + 3,561 + 41

18. 99 + 3,795 + 4,319

Lesson
2-10

TEKS 4.14C: Select or develop an appropriate problem-solving plan or strategy, including drawing a picture, looking for a pattern, systematic guessing and checking, acting it out, making a table, working a simpler problem, or working backwards to solve a problem.

Problem Solving

Draw a Picture and Write an Equation

The mass of a human brain is how much greater than the mass of a chimpanzee brain?

Average Masses of Brains

House cat	30 grams
Chimpanzee	420 grams
Human	1,350 grams
Dolphin	1,500 grams

The human brain has a mass of 1,350 grams.

Guided Practice*

Do you know HOW?

Solve. Draw a picture to help you.

1. In one week, Sandy earned $36 from her babysitting job. She got $15 more for doing her chores. How much money did Sandy earn?

? in all

$36	$15

Do you UNDERSTAND?

2. How can you show that 930 grams is a reasonable answer for the question asked above?

3. **Write a Problem** Write a problem using the table at the top.

Independent Practice

Solve. Draw a picture to help you.

4. Four cities are on the same road that runs east to west. Fleming is west of Bridgewater, but east of Clinton. Union is between Fleming and Bridgewater. It is 21 miles from Fleming to Union. It is 55 miles from Clinton to Union. How far is it from Clinton to Fleming?

5. Scott and his friends walk to school together. Scott leaves his home at 7:00 A.M. He meets Johnny and Zach at the end of the block. Next, they meet Paul, Tim, and Pete. Dan and Torey join them one block before the school. How many friends walk to school altogether?

Stuck? Try this....

- What do I know?
- What diagram can I use to help understand the problem?
- Can I use addition, subtraction, multiplication, or division?
- Is all of my work correct?
- Did I answer the right question?
- Is my answer reasonable?

*For another example, see Set J on page 63.

Read & Understand

What do I know? The average mass of a chimpanzee brain is 420 grams. The average mass of a human brain is 1,350 grams.

What am I asked to find? The difference between the masses

Plan and Solve

Draw a picture.

1,350 grams	
420 grams	?

Write an equation. Use subtraction to solve.

1,350 − 420 = ▢

The human brain has a mass that is 930 grams more than the chimpanzee brain.

6. The American Kennel Club recognizes 17 breeds of herding dogs and 26 breeds of terriers. Draw a picture that could help find the total number of herding dogs and terriers.

7. Using the information in Exercise 6, write an equation to find how many more breeds of terriers than herding dogs there are.

For **8** through **10**, use the table to the right.

8. There are about 200 more animals in the Minnesota Zoo than in the Phoenix Zoo. About how many species of animals are in the Minnesota Zoo?

9. About how many more species are in the Indianapolis Zoo than the Phoenix Zoo?

10. How can you find the number of species of animals at the San Francisco Zoo?

Data

Name of Zoo	Approximate Number of Animals
Phoenix	200
Minnesota	
San Francisco	▢
Indianapolis	360
Total Animals	1,210

11. A parking lot had a total of 243 cars in one day. By 6:00 A.M., there were 67 cars in the lot. In the next hour, 13 more cars joined these. How many more cars would come to the lot by the end of the day?

243 cars in all

67	13	?

12. A shoe store sold 162 pairs of shoes. The goal was to sell 345 pairs. How many pairs of shoes did they **NOT** sell?

345 pairs of shoes

162	?

Independent Practice

For **13** and **14**, use the table at right.

13. What equation can you write to help find the cost of the shoes and socks together?

14. What equation can you write to help find the difference between the cost of the shirt and the shorts?

Data

Cost of Gym Clothes	
Shirt	$12
Shorts	$19
Shoes	$42
Socks	$2
Hat	$15

15. Byron spent $7.75 on popcorn and a drink at the movie theater. The popcorn was $4.25. How much was the cost of the drink?

$7.75 in all

$4.25	?

16. Each school day, Mikaela sold the same number of tickets to the school play. On Monday she sold 4 tickets. How many tickets did she sell all together in 5 days?

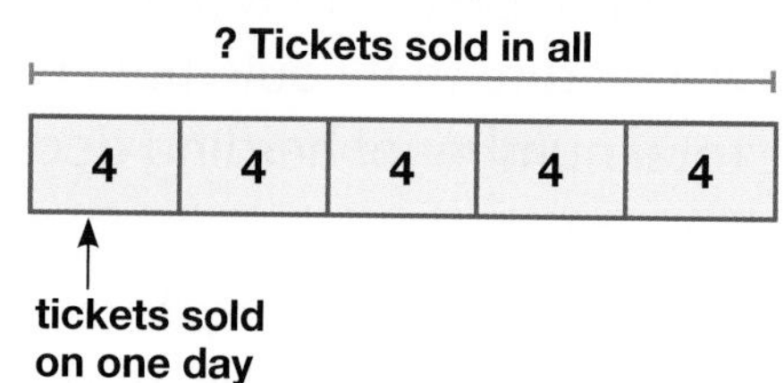

17. Writing to Explain Ken makes 2 nametags in the time it takes Mary to make 5 nametags. When Mary has made 15 nametags, how many has Ken made?

18. Mr. Lee had 62 pencils at the beginning of the school year. At the end of the school year he had 8 pencils left. How many pencils were given out during the year?

62 pencils in all

8	?

Think About the Process

19. Carlene bought a book for $13.58. She paid with a $10 bill and a $5 bill. Which expression would find the amount of change Carlene would receive?

A $15 − $13.58 **C** $10 + $5

B $15 − $1.42 **D** $13.58 + $1.42

20. Terrence rode 15 rides before lunch at the county fair. He rode 13 rides after lunch. Each ride requires 3 tickets. Which expression represents the number of rides he rode during the day?

F 15 − 13 **H** 15 − 3

G 15 + 13 **J** 13 − 3

Going Digital

Subtracting Decimals

Use eTools Place-Value Blocks to subtract 0.82 − 0.57.

Step 1 Go to the Place-Value Blocks eTool. Select a two-part workspace.

Step 2 Using the arrow tool, select a flat place-value block, and click in the top workspace to display one flat.

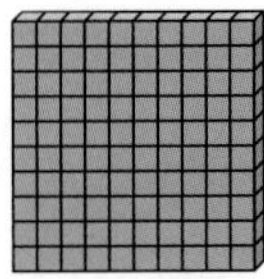

One

In the Select Unit Block drop-down menu, select Flat to let this block represent one.

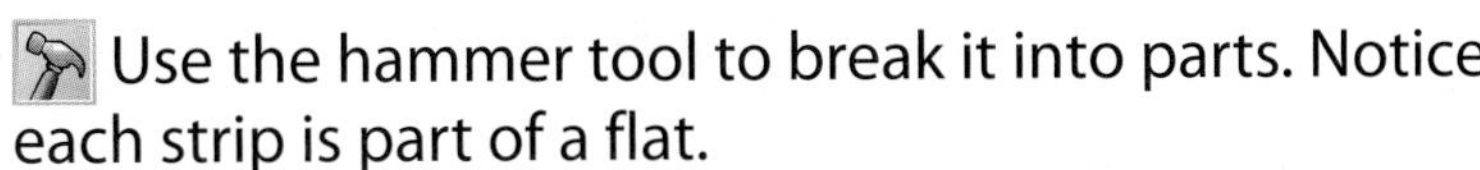

Use the hammer tool to break it into parts. Notice each strip is part of a flat.

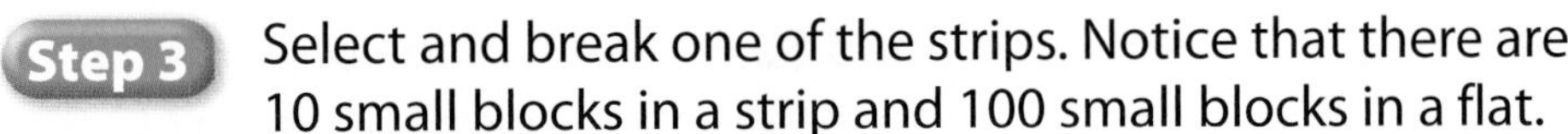

Step 3 Select and break one of the strips. Notice that there are 10 small blocks in a strip and 100 small blocks in a flat.

Step 4 Show 0.82 with the place-value blocks. Use the erase tool to erase any blocks you don't need.

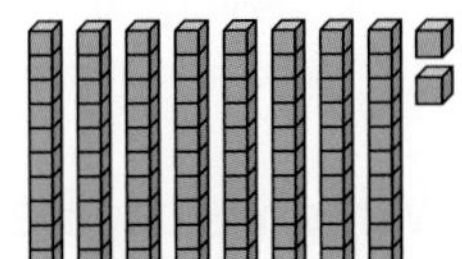

Step 5 Use the hammer tool to break one tenth strip into 10 hundredths. Use the erase tool to take away the 7 hundredths and then the 5 tenths in 0.57. Move them to the lower workspace. Look at the blocks that are left to find the difference, 0.82 − 0.57 = 0.25.

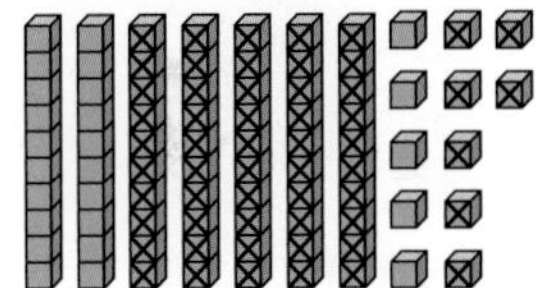

Practice

Solve.

1. 0.64 − 0.14	**2.** 0.27 − 0.13	**3.** 0.89 − 0.72	**4.** 0.93 − 0.27
5. 0.86 − 0.71	**6.** 0.38 − 0.19	**7.** 0.11 − 0.08	**8.** 0.35 − 0.21
9. 0.56 − 0.19	**10.** 0.74 − 0.49	**11.** 0.71 − 0.58	**12.** 0.85 − 0.38

TAKS Test Prep

1. Joe got 34,867 points playing a video game, and Carlos got 29,978 points. How many more points did Joe get than Carlos? (2-7)

   A 14,889

   B 4,999

   C 4,989

   D 4,889

2. The table shows tickets sold to the school play.

Tickets Sold	
Thursday	320
Friday	282
Saturday	375

   Which is the best estimate of the total tickets sold? (2-3)

   F 1,100

   G 1,000

   H 900

   J 800

3. David bought a 3-ring binder for $4.49, a package of pencils for $1.19, and two packages of paper. What information is needed to find the total amount David spent before tax? (2-5)

   A The cost of a package of paper

   B The cost of a package of erasers

   C The color of the binder

   D How much money David gave the clerk

4. The U. S. Constitution contains 4,543 words, including the signatures. What is this number rounded to the nearest hundred? (2-2)

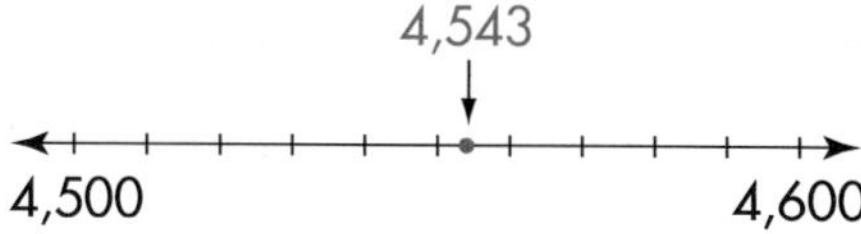

   F 4,600

   G 4,540

   H 4,500

   J 4,000

5. Larry spent $1.89 on a bottle of paint and $0.45 on a sponge brush. What was the total amount he spent? (2-9)

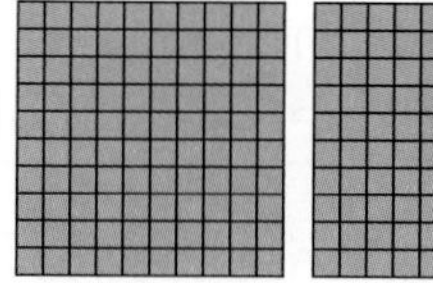
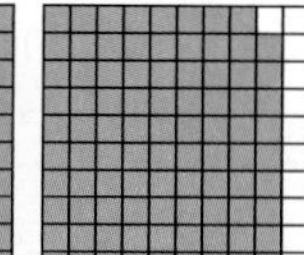
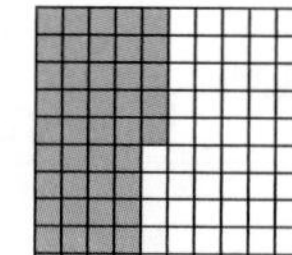

   A $2.34

   B $1.34

   C $1.32

   D $1.24

6. Garrett drove 239 miles on Saturday and 149 miles on Sunday. To find 239 + 149, Garrett made a multiple of ten, as shown below. What is the missing number? (2-1)

   $239 + 149 = 240 + \square = 388$

   F 129

   G 130

   H 147

   J 148

7. A musical group made 8,000 copies of a CD. So far, they have sold 6,280 copies. How many copies are left? (2-8)

A 2,720

B 2,280

C 1,820

D 1,720

8. In April, 5,326 books were checked out of the library. In May, 3,294 books were checked out. How many books were checked out in all? (2-6)

F 8,620

G 8,610

H 8,520

J 8,510

9. Lee's turtle's shell is 14.42 centimeters long. Ty's turtle's shell is 12.14 centimeters long. Which is the best estimate of the difference? (2-4)

A 1 centimeter

B 2 centimeters

C 4 centimeters

D 6 centimeters

10. The distance across the widest part of a quarter is 24.26 millimeters. What is 24.26 rounded to the nearest tenth? (2-2)

F 24

G 24.2

H 24.3

J 25

11. The last total solar eclipse seen in Dallas was in 1623. The next one will not be seen until 2024. Which number sentence shows the best way to estimate the number of years between the eclipses? (2-3)

A $2020 - 1630 = 390$

B $2030 - 1620 = 410$

C $2020 - 1620 = 400$

D $2020 - 1600 = 420$

12. Daria's book has 323 pages. She has read 141 pages. Which diagram models how to find the number of pages she has left to read? (2-10)

F Total: ?

323	141

G Total: 323

141	?

H Total: 141

323	?

J Total: 323

141	141	?

13. **Griddable Response** What number makes the number sentence true? (2-1)

$28 + 79 = \square + 28$

Reteaching

Set A, pages 30–32

Add 155 + 83. Use mental math.

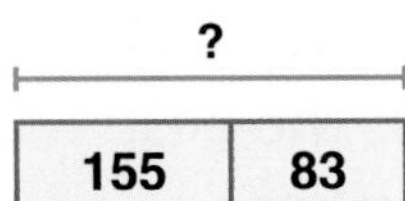

Look for a ten and use the breaking apart method. Adding 5 to 155 is easy.

Break apart 83.

?

155	5	78

155 + 5 = 160

160 + 78 = 238

So, 155 + 83 = 238.

Remember that when you use compensation, you must adjust the sum or difference.

1. 53 + 88 **2.** 372 + 226

3. 734 − 223 **4.** 147 − 56

5. 5,342 + 1,826 **6.** 283 − 169

7. 6,000 + 0 **8.** 854 + 353

9. 1,854 + 362 **10.** 3,874 + 121

11. 363 + 784 **12.** 841 + 1,024

13. 676 − 521 **14.** 1,089 − 961

15. 899 − 275 **16.** 1,444 − 1,225

17. 2,401 − 1,025 **18.** 2,499 + 2,601

Set B, pages 34–35

Use a number line to round 452 to the nearest ten.

Draw a number line from 450 to 460.

Locate 452.

Compare 452 to the midpoint, which is 455.

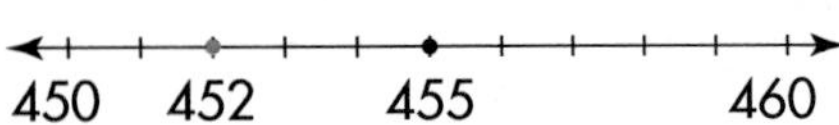

452 is to the left of midpoint, so round to 450.

Remember that you can us the midpoint to help you round.

Round each number to the place of the underlined digit.

1. $\underline{3}$.2 **2.** 4$\underline{6}$,928

3. 1$\underline{8}$.73 **4.** 5$\underline{2}$.09

5. 3$\underline{7}$2 **6.** $\underline{8}$,739

7. $\underline{4}$.6 **8.** $\underline{7}$5.6

9. 1$\underline{0}$.87 **10.** $\underline{1}$5.66

11. $\underline{2}$.15 **12.** $\underline{7}$.49

13. $\underline{8}$.92 **14.** $\underline{1}$6.34

15. 2$\underline{2}$.55 **16.** 9$\underline{9}$.3

17. 1,$\underline{2}$76 **18.** $\underline{8}$,572

Set C, pages 36–37

Estimate
$$\begin{array}{r} 1{,}579 \\ +\ 1{,}248 \\ \hline \end{array}$$

Round each number to the nearest hundred.

1,579 rounds to 1,600

1,248 rounds to 1,200

Add
$$\begin{array}{r} 1{,}600 \\ +\ 1{,}200 \\ \hline 2{,}800 \end{array}$$

Remember you can round numbers to the nearest hundred or thousand when estimating sums and differences.

1. 473 + 465
2. 8,352 − 3,421
3. 586 − 483
4. 4,094 + 246
5. 1,440 − 933
6. 748 − 392
7. 981 + 193
8. 725 + 635

Set D, pages 38–39

Estimate 23.64 + 7.36.

Round each decimal to the nearest whole number. Then add.

23.64 rounds to 24

7.36 rounds to 7

24 + 7 = 31

Remember to compare the digit in the tenths place to 5 when you round to the nearest whole number.

1. 0.57 + 0.98
2. 16.42 − 2.42
3. 19.35 + 8.74
4. 12.3 − 9.7
5. $\begin{array}{r} 14.04 \\ +\ \ 9.33 \\ \hline \end{array}$
6. $\begin{array}{r} 7.48 \\ -\ 3.92 \\ \hline \end{array}$

Set E, pages 40–41

The standard weight of a penny is 2.50 grams, a standard nickel is 5.0 grams, and a standard half dollar is 11.34 grams. Estimate how much greater the weight of a half dollar is than a nickel.

Use subtraction to solve.

11.34 rounds to 11.
11.0 − 5.0 = 6.0

The half dollar is about 6.0 grams heavier than a nickel.

What was the extra information?

Remember some problems have information you do not need.

1. Todd read 35 pages of his book on Saturday. He read for 10 minutes on Sunday. How many pages did Todd read over the weekend?
2. Molly bought 150 sheets of paper. She put 50 sheets in her math folder, 25 sheets in her science folder, 25 sheets in her social studies folder, and 40 sheets in her reading folder. How many sheets did Molly have left?

Set F, pages 42–44

Add 359 + 723.

Estimate: 400 + 700 = 1,100

Add the ones. Regroup if necessary.

```
   1
  359
+ 723
    2
```

Add the tens. Regroup if necessary.

```
   1
  359
+ 723
   82
```

Add the hundreds.

```
   1
  359
+ 723
1,082
```

The answer is reasonable.

Remember to regroup if necessary when adding whole numbers.

1. 215 + 8,823
2. 14,296 + 444
3. 2,417 + 3,573
4. 572 + 941
5. 32,834 + 17,384
6. 14,382 + 9,243
7. 10,294 + 26,326
8. 14,896 + 8,274

Set G, pages 46–47

Find 831 − 796.

Estimate: 830 − 800 = 30

Subtract the ones. Regroup if necessary.

```
   2 11
  8 3 1
− 7 9 6
      5
```

Subtract the tens. Subtract the hundreds. Regroup if necessary.

```
  7 12 11
  8  3  1
− 7  9  6
     3  5
```

Add to check your answer.

```
  1 1
  7 9 6
+   3 5
  8 3 1
```

The answer is reasonable.

Remember you may need to regroup before you subtract.

1. 415 − 323
2. 673 − 294
3. 186 − 77
4. 4,978 − 2,766
5. 18,823 − 4,634
6. 728 − 419
7. 1,296 − 377
8. 866 − 477

Set H, pages 48–49

Find 400 − 378.

Estimate: 400 − 380 = 20

Regroup 4 hundreds to tens and ones.

```
     9
  3 10 10
  4  0  0
− 3  7  8
     2  2
```

4 hundreds = 3 hundreds + 9 tens + 10 ones

The answer is reasonable.

Remember to use the inverse operation to check your answer.

1. 700 − 255
2. 1,054 − 438
3. 320 − 111
4. 4,508 − 2,613
5. 18,005 − 6,291
6. 601 − 482

Set I, pages 50–52

Use place-value blocks to find 0.49 − 0.27.

Show 0.49 using blocks.

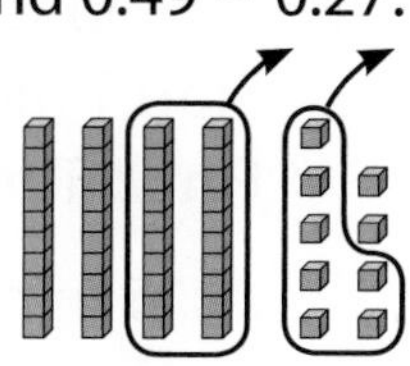

Subtract 7 hundredths and 2 tenths.

Count the remaining blocks. 0.49 − 0.27 = 0.22

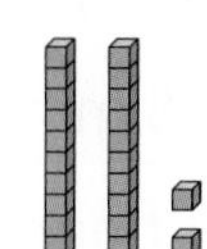

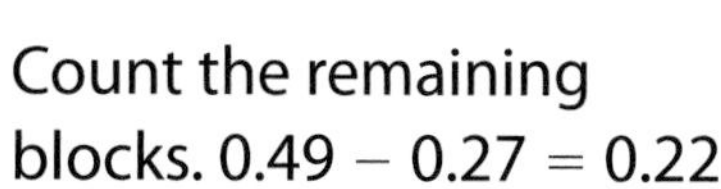

Use place-value blocks to find 0.12 + 0.24.

Show 0.12 using blocks. Add 4 hundredths and 2 tenths.

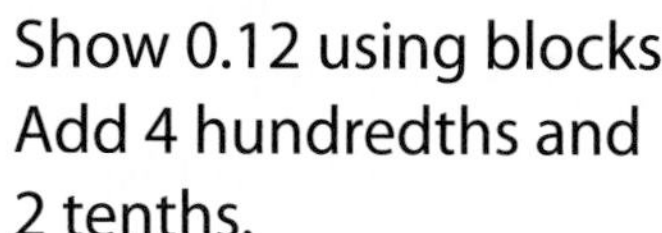

Count the total.

0.12 + 0.24 = 0.36

Remember when you add and subtract decimals, start with the least place value. Regroup if needed.

Use place-value blocks to solve.

1. 0.2 + 0.89

2. 0.67 − 0.31

3. 0.34 + 0.34

4. 0.81 − 0.78

5. 0.28 + 0.64

6. 0.7 − 0.52

7. 0.16 − 0.08

8. 0.62 + 0.12

9. 0.74 − 0.54

10. 0.28 − 0.25

11. 0.35 + 0.72

12. 0.95 − 0.83

Set J, pages 54–56

Cathy spent $8 on lunch. She bought a sandwich, a fruit cup, and a milk at the snack bar. She spent a total of $6 on the sandwich and milk. How much did the fruit cup cost?

What do I know? Cathy had $8. Cathy bought a sandwich, a milk, and a fruit cup.Cathy spent $6 on the sandwich and the milk.

What am I asked to find? The amount of money Cathy spent on the fruit cup

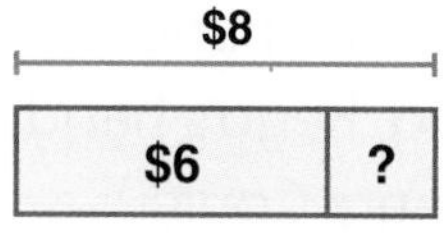

$8 – $6 = $2

Cathy spent $2 on the fruit cup.

Remember some problems have information you do not need.

Draw a picture and write an equation to solve.

1. Doug saw 5 Agile wallabies and 9 Rock wallabies at the zoo. How many wallabies did Doug see?

2. Luz had collected a total of 393 tokens from the games at Funland. To win a large stuffed animal, 500 tokens were needed. How many more tokens does Luz need to win the large stuffed animal?

Topics 1–2

Spiral Review

Number and Operations

1. Find 85 − 37.

A 33
B 41
C 48
D 50

2. Which digit is in the hundred thousands place in the number 372,993?

F 2
G 3
H 7
J 9

3. Which is equal to 8 dollars, 2 quarters, 2 dimes, and 3 pennies?

A $8.27
B $8.37
C $8.63
D $8.73

4. What is the value of the underlined digit?

<u>7</u>08,523

F 700
G 7,000
H 700,000
J 7,000,000

5. Nadia sold 341 tickets for the school play on the first night. On the second night she sold 187 more tickets. Estimate how many tickets Nadia sold?

6. If the sum of 56, 73, and 87 is 216, what do you know about the sum of 73, 87, and 56?

7. **Writing to Explain** Is one thousand, one hundred the same as eleven hundred?

Geometry and Measurement

8. How long did Leesa bake the pie?
Start Time: 3:10 P.M.
Finish Time: 3:55 P.M.

A 15 minutes
B 30 minutes
C 45 minutes
D 1 hour

9. The average temperature in July is 75.8°F. On July 25th, the high temperature reached 101.5°F. Estimate how much above average the temperature was that day.

F 24 degrees above average
G 26 degrees above average
H 28 degrees above average
J 30 degrees above average

10. How many lines of symmetry does the figure below have?

A 0
B 2
C 4
D 6

11. Ian's backyard is 10 yards long. How many feet long is the backyard?

12. **Writing to Explain** June's hand is 8 small paper clips long. Rego's hand is 3 large paper clips long. Could their hands be the same size?

Topics 1–2
Spiral Review

Probability and Statistics

13. The first year there were 48 squirrels and 30 rabbits in the park. The second year there were 58 squirrels and 25 rabbits. The third year there were 68 squirrels and 20 rabbits. Based on this data, predict how many squirrels and rabbits there will be in the park the following year.

F 93 squirrels and 15 rabbits

G 83 squirrels and 48 rabbits

H 83 squirrels and 25 rabbits

J 78 squirrels and 15 rabbits

14. What is the probability of drawing a red tile without looking?

A $\frac{1}{2}$ **B** $\frac{1}{5}$ **C** $\frac{2}{5}$ **D** $\frac{3}{5}$

15. What point on this coordinate grid is named by the ordered pair (3,2)?

F *Q*

G *R*

H *S*

J *T*

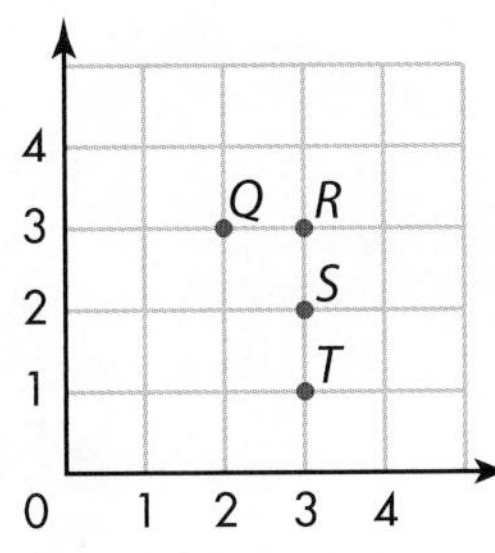

16. **Writing to Explain** In a game for 3 players, each player chooses a color and scores a point when the spinner lands on that color. What would the spinner look like that would make this game fair?

Algebraic Thinking

17. Which addition property explains why (6 + 8) +3 = (3 + 8) + 6?

A Commutative Property of Addition

B Associative Property of Addition

C Zero Property of Addition

D Identity Property of Addition

18. What is the missing number in 18 + ▢ = 36?

F 6

G 18

H 20

J 28

19. John had 32 CDs in his collection. He gave a certain number away to a friend. Now, John has 26 CDs in his collection. What number sentence gives the number of CDs John gave away?

A 32 − 6 = 26

B 32 − 26 = 6

C 50 − 44 = 6

D 32 + 26 = 58

20. Karen read 78 pages of a book. She has 82 more pages to read until she finishes. How many pages does the book have?

21. **Writing to Explain** How could you use the Identity Property of Addition to find 176 + 0?

Topic 3

Multiplication Meanings and Facts

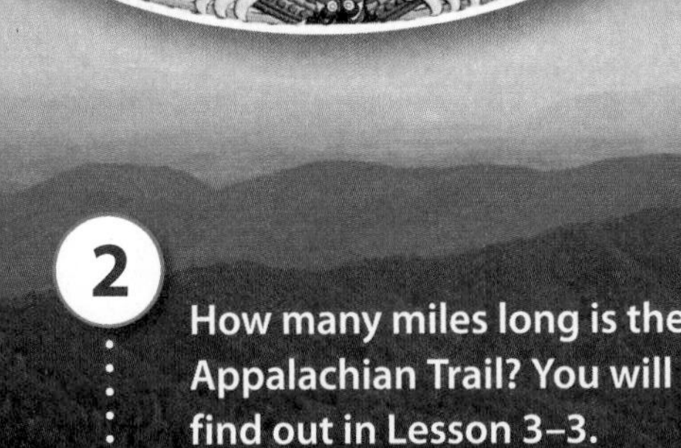

1 How many years were in one full cycle of the Aztec calendar? You will find out in Lesson 3-5.

2 How many miles long is the Appalachian Trail? You will find out in Lesson 3-3.

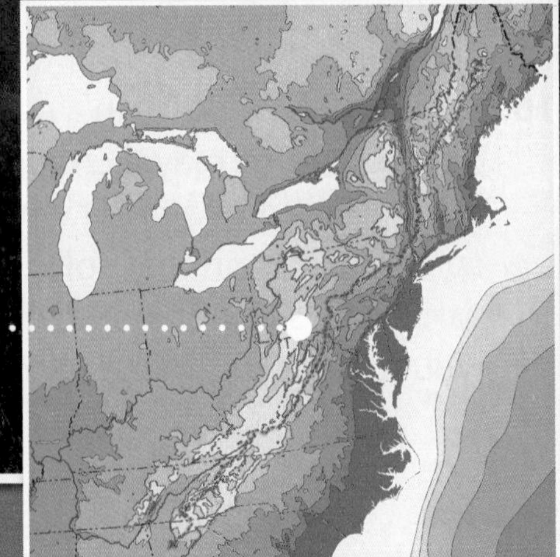

3

How much do tickets cost at the Texas Motor Speedway? You will find out in Lesson 3-7.

Review What You Know!

Vocabulary

Choose the best term from the box.

- breaking apart
- factor
- product
- multiples

1. In the number sentence $8 \times 3 = 24$, 8 is a ? .
2. In the number sentence $2 \times 6 = 12$, 12 is the ? .
3. $26 + 4 = (20 + 6) + 4$ is an example of using the ? strategy.
4. To find ? of the number 3, multiply numbers by 3.

Skip Counting

Find the term that comes next in the pattern.

5. 2, 4, 6, 8, ▢
6. 20, 25, 30, 35, ▢
7. 6, 9, 12, 15, ▢
8. 8, 16, 24, 32, ▢
9. 7, 14, 21, 28, ▢
10. 11, 22, 33, 44, ▢

Arrays

Copy each array and circle equal groups of 3.

11. ▢ ▢ ▢ ▢
▢ ▢ ▢ ▢
▢ ▢ ▢ ▢

12. ▢ ▢ ▢
▢ ▢ ▢

13. **Writing to Explain** Henry is thinking of a whole number. He multiplies the number by 5, but the result is less than 5. What number is Henry thinking about? Explain.

Lesson
3-1

TEKS 4.4A: Model factors and products using arrays and area models.

Meanings of Multiplication

How can multiplication be used when equal groups are combined?

How many ducks are there in 4 rows of 3? To find the total, multiply the number of equal groups by the number in each group. Objects arranged in equal rows form an array.

Another Example How can multiplication be used when you only know the number in one group?

Rudi and Eva collect plastic frogs. Rudi collected 5 frogs. Eva collected 3 times as many frogs. How many frogs did Eva collect?

A 3 frogs

B 5 frogs

C 10 frogs

D 15 frogs

Rudi's frogs

Eva's frogs

Eva collected 3 times as many frogs as Rudi.

Multiply by 3:

$3 \times 5 = 15$

Eva collected 15 frogs. The correct choice is **D**.

Explain It

1. Write an addition sentence that shows how many frogs Eva collected.
2. Draw an array of 16 frogs. Then, write a multiplication sentence describing the array.

One Way

There are 4 rows. Each row has 3 rubber ducks.

Repeated Addition: $3 + 3 + 3 + 3 = 12$
adding 4 rows of 3

Multiplication: $4 \times 3 = 12$
factors product

The product is the answer to a multiplication problem. Factors are the numbers multiplied together to find the product.

Another Way

The same rubber ducks can be arranged in another way.

Each group has 4 rubber ducks.

Repeated Addition: $4 + 4 + 4 = 12$

Multiplication: $3 \times 4 = 12$

There are 12 rubber ducks in all.

Guided Practice*

Do you know HOW?

In **1** and **2**, write an addition sentence and a multiplication sentence for each picture below.

1.

2.

Do you UNDERSTAND?

3. Beth saw 2 groups of 4 moths. Draw a picture to show 2 groups of 4. Then draw an array to show 2×4.

4. How could you use repeated addition to find the total number of objects in 3 groups of 2?

5. Martha has 5 rubber ducks. Jim has twice as many rubber ducks. How many rubber ducks does Jim have?

Independent Practice

Leveled Practice In **6** through **8**, write an addition sentence and a multiplication sentence for each picture.

6. 

7. 

8. 

In **9** through **11**, write a multiplication sentence for each addition sentence.

9. $3 + 3 + 3 + 3 = 12$

10. $5 + 5 + 5 + 5 + 5 = 25$

11. $8 + 8 + 8 = 24$

*For another example, see Set A on page 88.

12. Which number is three hundred three million, thirty-three thousand, three in standard form?

    A 300,333,003

    B 330,303,003

    C 300,303,033

    D 303,033,003

13. **Reasoning** Frank wrote 3×6 to describe the total number of paper clips shown. Alexa wrote 6×3. Who is correct? Explain.

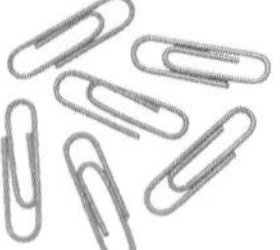
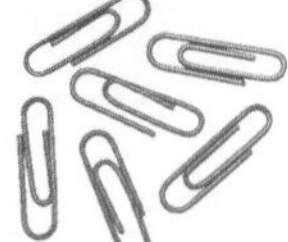
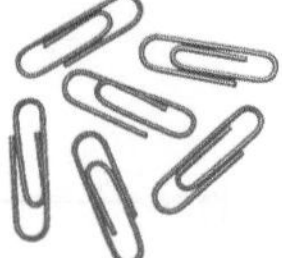

14. Jacob, Hannah, and their grandmother visited the petting zoo. One scoop of animal food cost two dollars. How much did their grandmother pay to buy a scoop for each child?

15. **Writing to Explain** Without multiplying, how do you know that a 4×4 array will have more items than a 3×3 array?

16. Taylor helped his father with the grocery shopping. He bought three bags of cheese sticks. Each bag contained 8 cheese sticks. How many cheese sticks were there in all?

    F 3 cheese sticks

    G 16 cheese sticks

    H 24 cheese sticks

    J 30 cheese sticks

17. Sam is setting the table for a family dinner. He needs to put two forks at each place setting. Ten people will come for dinner. Write a multiplication sentence to show how many forks Sam needs.

18. **Think About the Process** Harry arranged the marbles in the pattern shown to the right. Which number sentence best represents Harry's arrangement of marbles?

    A 3 groups of 9 marbles

    B 4 groups of 5 marbles

    C 2 groups of 13 marbles

    D 4 groups of 7 marbles

19. Lisa has 2 rings. Tina has 4 times as many rings. How many rings does Tina have?

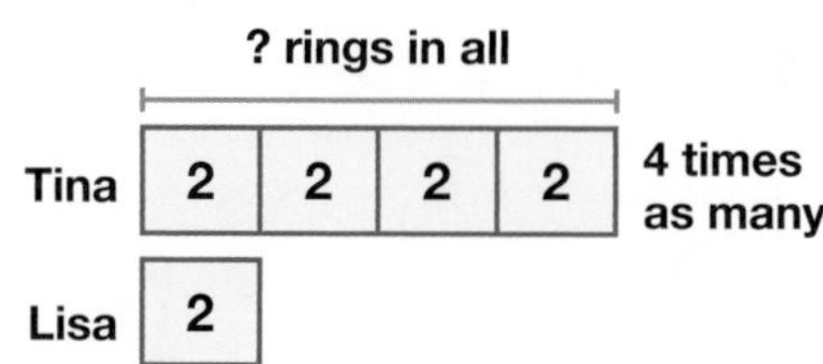

Mixed Problem Solving

Texas has several state animals in addition to the armadillo. They are listed in the table below.

Data

Texas State Animal	Facts
Animal: Nine-Banded Armadillo	Has 4 claws on each front foot, and 5 claws on each back foot
Mammal: Mexican Free-Tailed Bat	The largest colony can eat about 250 tons of insects per night
Mammal: Longhorn	Can have horn spans over 80 inches long
Dog: Blue Lacy	Adopted in 2005, is characterized by the unusual blue coat and blue nose
Bird: Mockingbird	Can sing up to 200 songs
Reptile: Texas Horned Lizard	Characterized by 2 long central head spines
Insect: Monarch Butterfly	Adopted in 1995, proposed by a group of Texas students

1. How many tons of insects can a bat colony eat in 4 days?

? tons in all

250	250	250	250

2. How many years after the Monarch Butterfly was adopted did Texas recognize the Blue Lacy as the official state dog?

2005

1995	?

3. How many claws does an armadillo have in all?

4. The Guadalupe Bass is the state fish of Texas. What is the range in the number of eggs that a female may lay?

5. If a female lays, on average, 5,000 eggs each year, how many eggs might she lay in her lifetime?

Data

Texas Guadalupe Bass	
Number of eggs	from 400 to 9,000

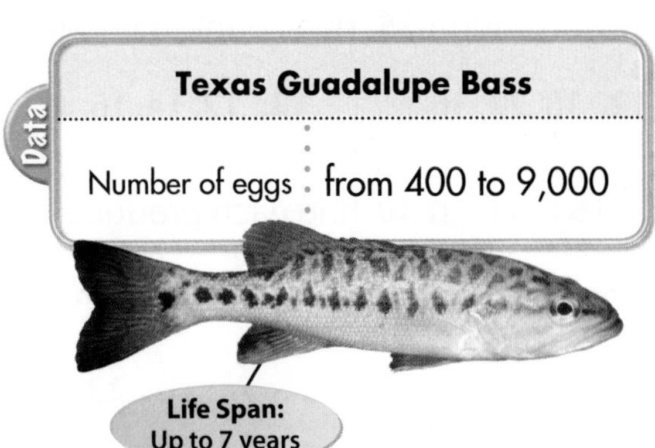

Lesson

3-2

TEKS 4.6A: Use patterns and relationships to develop strategies to remember basic multiplication and division facts.

Patterns for Facts

What are the patterns for multiples of 2, 5, and 9?

A multiple is the product of any two whole numbers.

○ multiples of 2

□ multiples of 5

△ multiples of 9

1	(2)	3	(4)	[5]	(6)	7	(8)	△9	[(10)]
11	(12)	13	(14)	[15]	(16)	17	△(18)	19	[(20)]
21	(22)	23	(24)	[25]	(26)	△27	(28)	29	[(30)]
31	(32)	33	(34)	[35]	△(36)	37	(38)	39	[(40)]

Guided Practice*

Do you know HOW?

In **1** through **4**, skip count to find the number that comes next.

1. 2, 4, 6, 8, ▢ **2.** 20, 22, 24, ▢

3. 20, 25, 30, ▢ **4.** 36, 45, 54, ▢

In **5** through **8**, find the product.

5. 9×1 **6.** 2×8

7. 5×4 **8.** 9×2

Do you UNDERSTAND?

9. In the chart above, what pattern do you see for the numbers that have both red circles and green squares?

10. How do you know that 63 is not a multiple of 2? Explain using the pattern for multiples of 2.

11. Felix is sorting socks. He has 11 pairs of socks. How many socks does he have in all?

Independent Practice

In **12** through **15**, skip count to find the number that comes next.

12. 18, 27, 36, ▢ **13.** 12, 14, 16, ▢ **14.** 5, 10, 15, ▢ **15.** 88, 90, 92, ▢

In **16** through **30**, find each product.

16. 2×6 **17.** 5×3 **18.** 9×2 **19.** 5×8 **20.** 9×1

21. 2×7 **22.** 5×7 **23.** 9×3 **24.** 9×6 **25.** 2×8

26. 2×3 **27.** 5×9 **28.** 5×6 **29.** 4×7 **30.** 5×4

*For another example, see Set B on page 88.

To find multiples of 2, skip count by 2s.

2, 4, 6, 8,
10, 12, 14, 16...

All multiples of 2 are even numbers.

To find multiples of 5, skip count by 5s.

5, 10, 15, 20,
25, 30, 35, 40...

All multiples of 5 have a 0 or 5 in the ones place.

To find multiples of 9, skip count by 9s.

9, 18, 27, 36,
45, 54, 63, 72...

The digits of multiples of 9 add to 9 or a multiple of 9.

For 99, for example, $9 + 9 = 18$, and 18 is a multiple of 9.

TAKS Problem Solving

31. How many arms do 9 starfish have

a if each starfish has 6 arms?

b if each starfish has 7 arms?

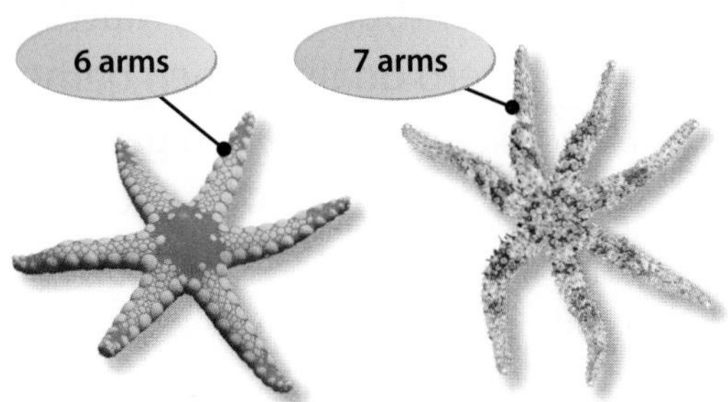

32. In wheelchair basketball, players use sports chairs that have 2 large wheels and 3 small wheels. If there are 5 players, how many

a large wheels do the sports chairs have?

b small wheels do the sports chairs have?

c wheels do the sports chairs have in all?

33. Jody is working on her model train. She adds 9 pieces of track. Each piece of track is attached with 4 screws. How many screws does she need in all?

A 18 screws **C** 54 screws

B 36 screws **D** 72 screws

34. **Geometry** Each pentagon shown below has 5 sides. How many sides are there in all? Skip count by 5s to find the answer. Then, write the multiplication sentence.

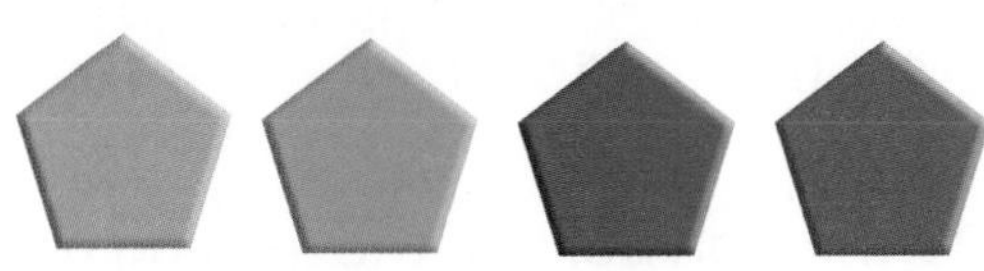

35. Use the digits 3, 4, and 6 to make as many 3-digit numbers as you can. Put the numbers in order from least to greatest.

36. Which is equal to 7 dollars, 8 dimes, and 7 pennies?

F \$8.87 **H** \$7.87

G \$8.78 **J** \$7.78

Lesson
3-3

TEKS 4.4C: Recall and apply multiplication facts through 12 × 12.

Multiplication Properties

How can properties help you multiply?

Multiplication properties can help you remember basic facts.

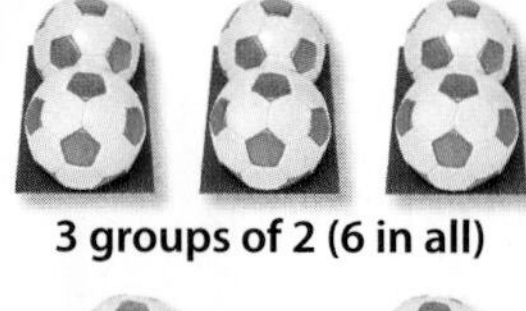

3 groups of 2 (6 in all)

Commutative Property of Multiplication
Two numbers can be multiplied in any order and the product will be the same.

2 groups of 3 (6 in all)

$3 \times 2 = 2 \times 3$

Guided Practice*

Do you know HOW?

In **1** through **4**, find the product.

1. 0×5 **2.** 1×6

3. 1×0 **4.** 1×9

In **5** and **6**, copy and complete.

5. $4 \times 7 = 7 \times \square$

6. $6 \times 10 = \square \times 6$

Do you UNDERSTAND?

7. When you multiply any number by one, what is the product?

8. In a soccer tournament, Matt's team scored zero goals in each game. They played a total of 6 games. Write a multiplication sentence to show how many goals they scored in all.

Independent Practice

In **9** through **18**, find the product.

9. 1×5 **10.** 5×0 **11.** 3×9 **12.** 0×8 **13.** 0×3

14. 4×0 **15.** 9×4 **16.** 2×7 **17.** 5×6 **18.** 1×1

In **19** through **26**, find the missing number.

19. $4 \times 5 = \square \times 4$ **20.** $9 \times 12 = 12 \times \square$ **21.** $0 \times 5 = \square \times 0$ **22.** $9 \times 8 = \square \times 9$

23. $8 \times 11 = \square \times 8$ **24.** $1 \times 9 = \square \times 1$ **25.** $6 \times 4 = \square \times 6$ **26.** $7 \times 5 = \square \times 7$

DIGITAL
Animated Glossary
www.pearsonsuccessnet.com

*For another example, see Set C on page 88.

Zero Property of Multiplication
The product of any number and zero is zero.

2 groups of 0

$2 \times 0 = 0$

Identity Property of Multiplication
The product of any number and one is that number.

1 group of 7

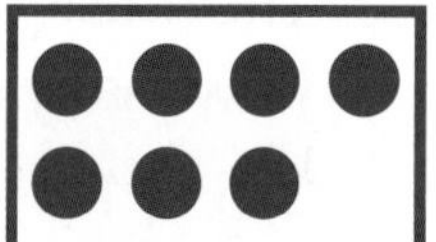

$1 \times 7 = 7$

TAKS Problem Solving

For **27** and **28**, use the table at the right.

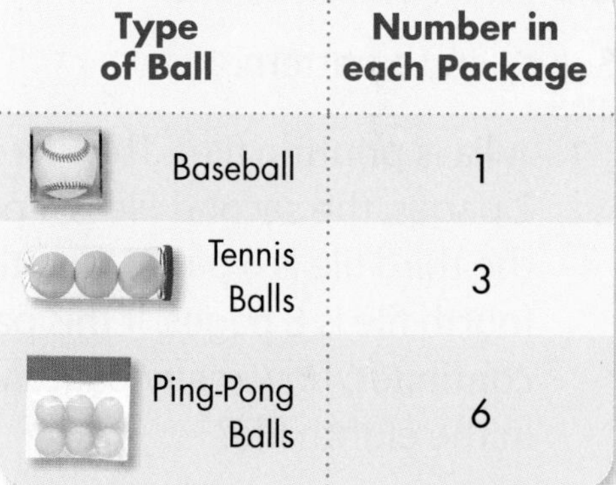

Type of Ball	Number in each Package
Baseball	1
Tennis Balls	3
Ping-Pong Balls	6

27. Annie has 6 packages of tennis balls. How many packages of yellow ping-pong balls would Annie need to have so that she has an equal number of ping-pong balls and tennis balls?

28. If Annie and her three friends each bought 1 package of baseballs, how many baseballs do they have in all?

29. Writing to Explain How do you know that $23 \times 15 = 15 \times 23$ without finding the products?

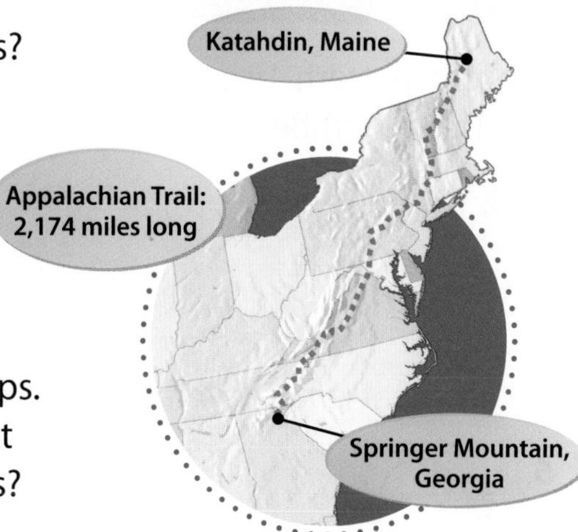

30. The Appalachian Trail is 2,174 miles long. If Andy hiked the entire trail one time, how many miles did he hike?

31. Mrs. Grayson has 27 students in her class. She wants to rearrange the desks in equal groups. If the desks are in 9 groups of 3 desks now, what is another way that she could arrange the desks?

Tip: Use a multiplication property.

A 3 groups of 9 desks

B 2 groups of 13 desks

C 5 groups of 6 desks

D 4 groups of 7 desks

Lesson

3-4

TEKS 4.14C: Select or develop an appropriate problem-solving plan or strategy, including drawing a picture, looking for a pattern, systematic guessing and checking, acting it out, making a table, working a simpler problem, or working backwards to solve a problem.

Problem Solving

Look for a Pattern

Ella is learning how to play a waltz on the piano. Her teacher gives her a beginner's exercise for her left hand.

The music shows 4 measures. If this pattern continues, how many notes will she play in 8 measures?

3, 6, 9, 12, ▢, ▢, ▢, ▢

Guided Practice*

Do you know HOW?

Solve. Find a pattern.

1. Julia is printing files. The first file is 2 pages, the second file is 4 pages, the third file is 6 pages, and the fourth file is 8 pages. If this pattern continues, how many pages will be in the eighth file?

Do you UNDERSTAND?

2. What multiplication facts can you use to help find the answer to Problem 1? Why?

3. **Write a Problem** Write a problem that uses a pattern for multiples of 5. Then answer your question.

Independent Practice

Look for a pattern. Use the pattern to find the missing numbers.

4. 5, 10, 15, 20, ▢, ▢, ▢, ▢

5. 9, 18, 27, ▢, ▢, ▢, ▢

Look for a pattern, Draw the next two shapes.

6. 

7. 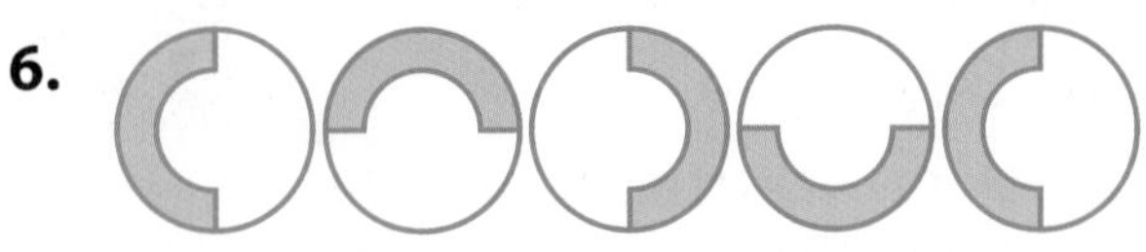

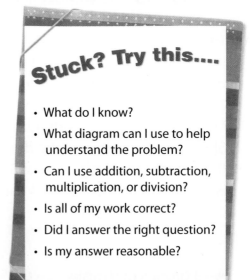

Stuck? Try this....

- What do I know?
- What diagram can I use to help understand the problem?
- Can I use addition, subtraction, multiplication, or division?
- Is all of my work correct?
- Did I answer the right question?
- Is my answer reasonable?

*For another example, see Set D on page 88.

Read and Understand

What do I know? The pattern for the first 4 measures is: 3, 6, 9, and 12.

What am I asked to find? The number of notes she will play in 8 measures.

Plan and Solve

Find a pattern. Skip count by 3s.

3, 6, 9, 12,...

What are the next four numbers?

3, 6, 9, 12, 15, 18, 21, 24

Ella plays 24 notes in 8 measures.

Look Back and Check

Is the answer reasonable?

There are 12 notes in 4 measures.

The number of notes in 8 measures is double the number in 4 measures.

The answer is reasonable.

Look for a pattern. Copy and complete each number sentence.

8. 30 + 5 = 35
300 + 5 = 305
3,000 + 5 = ▢
30,000 + 5 = ▢

9. 50 + 5 = 55
505 + 50 = 555
5,005 + 550 = ▢
50,505 + 5,050 = ▢

10. 60 + 8 = 68
608 + 60 = 668
6,008 + 660 = ▢
60,008 + 6,660 = ▢

11. Kaylee delivers invitations to everyone on her floor of her apartment building. There are 10 apartments on her floor. The numbers of the first four apartments are 2, 4, 6, and 8. If the pattern continues, what are the rest of the apartment numbers?

12. Look for a pattern in the table below to find the missing numbers.

300	320	340	▢	380
400	▢	440	460	▢
500	520	▢	560	580

13. Kerry has a newspaper route. The first four houses she delivers to are numbered 322, 326, 330, and 334. If this pattern continues, what will be the next four numbers?

14. Marvin is looking for a radio station on the AM dial. He tries these three stations: 1040, 1080, and 1120. If this pattern continues, what will be the next three numbers?

15. Jonas saves coins in his piggy bank. He drops in these groups of coins: 1 penny, 2 nickels, 3 dimes, 4 quarters, 5 pennies, 6 nickels, 7 dimes, and 8 quarters. If this pattern continues, what are the next four groups of coins?

16. **Writing to Explain** Suppose there are 18 bowls arranged in this pattern: big bowl, little bowl, big bowl, little bowl, and so on. Is the last bowl a big bowl or a little bowl? Explain.

Lesson

3-5

TEKS 4.4C: Recall and apply multiplication facts through 12 × 12.

3 and 4 as Factors

How can you break apart facts?

Darnel is replacing the wheels on 8 skateboards. Each skateboard has 4 wheels. How many wheels does he need in all?

Use the Distributive Property to break apart facts to find the product.

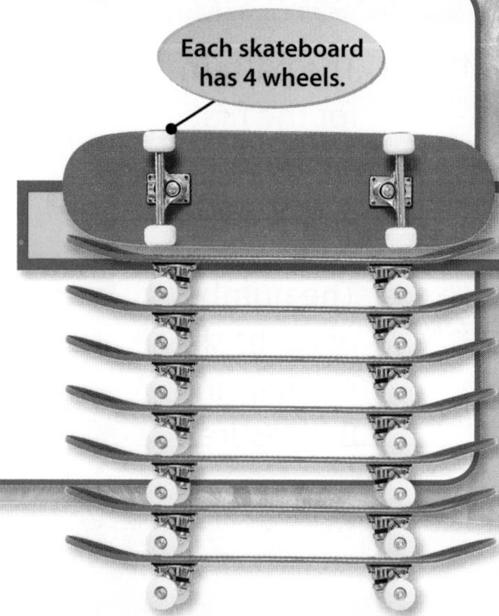
Each skateboard has 4 wheels.

Guided Practice*

Do you know HOW?

In **1** through **4**, use breaking apart to find each product.

1. $3 \times 4 = (1 \times 4) + (\ \square \times 4) = \square$

2. $4 \times 7 = (2 \times 7) + (\ \square \times 7) = \square$

3. 3×9

4. 4×6

Do you UNDERSTAND?

5. In Exercise 4, find 4 × 6 by breaking apart the 6.

6. On Friday, Darnel received a box of skateboard wheels from the factory. The box contained 12 sets of 4 wheels. How many wheels were there in all?

Independent Practice

Leveled Practice In **7** through **20**, use breaking apart to find each product.

7. $9 \times 5 = (5 \times 5) + (\ \square \times 5) = \square$

8. $8 \times 3 = (4 \times 3) + (4 \times \square\ ) = \square$

9. $3 \times 13 = (3 \times \square\ ) + (3 \times 3) = \square$

10. $12 \times 4 = (\ \square \times 4) + (2 \times 4) = \square$

11. 6×3

12. 0×4

13. 6×4

14. 8×4

15. 5×4

16. 3 × 5

17. 3 × 6

18. 4 × 7

19. 4 × 9

20. 3 × 7

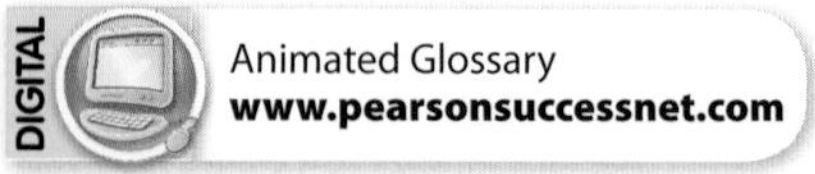
DIGITAL
Animated Glossary
www.pearsonsuccessnet.com

*For another example, see Set E on page 89.

One Way

Find 8×4. Break apart 4 into $2 + 2$.

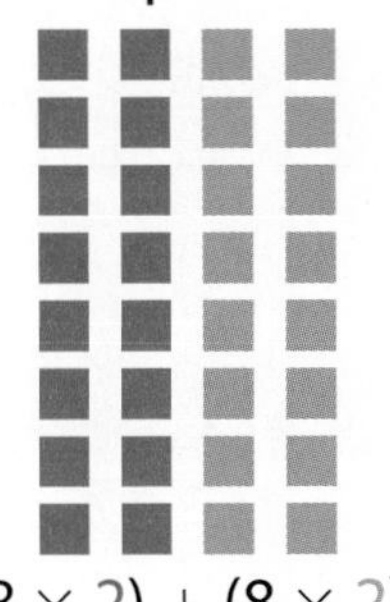

$(8 \times 2) + (8 \times 2)$

$16 + 16 = 32$

Darnel needs 32 wheels in all.

Another Way

Find 8×4. Break apart 8 into $3 + 5$.

$3 \times 4 = 12$

$5 \times 4 = 20$

$12 + 20 = 32$

So, $8 \times 4 = 32$.

TAKS Problem Solving

For **21** and **22**, use the table at the right.

21. In the Aztec calendar, each year has a number from 1 to 13. It also has one of 4 signs, as shown in the table. It takes 4×13 years to go through one complete cycle of years. How many years are in one cycle?

22. The year 2006 is the year 7-Rabbit in the Aztec calendar. What is the year 2010 in the Aztec calendar?

Aztec Year Names (first 16 years)

2-House	3-Rabbit	4-Reed	5-Flint
6-House	7-Rabbit	8-Reed	9-Flint
10-House	11-Rabbit	12-Reed	13-Flint
1-House	2-Rabbit	3-Reed	4-Flint

23. Writing to Explain Vicki scored 6 two-point baskets and 6 one-point free throws. Li scored 6 three-point baskets. Explain how you know each girl scored the same total.

24. In his last basketball game, Andrew scored 15 points. Which of the following is NOT a way he could have scored his points?

A 5 three-point shots

B 3 three-point shots in the first half and 2 three-point shots in the second half

C 3 two-point shots and 2 one-point free throws

D 5 two-point shots and 5 one-point free throws

Lesson

3-6

TEKS 4.4C: Recall and apply multiplication facts through 12 × 12.

6, 7, and 8 as Factors

Are there different ways to break apart a fact?

Mrs. White's class drew a map of their town. The map is 6 blocks by 6 blocks. How many square blocks are on the map?

Other Examples

Find 7×8.
Break the first factor, 7, into $5 + 2$.

$7 \times 8 = (5 \times 8) + (2 \times 8)$

$40 + 16 = 56$

Find 8×8.
Break the first factor, 8, into $5 + 3$.

$8 \times 8 = (5 \times 8) + (3 \times 8)$

$40 + 24 = 64$

Guided Practice*

Do you know HOW?

In **1** through **4**, use breaking apart to find each product.

1. $6 \times 8 = (6 \times 4) + (6 \times \square) = \square$

2. $7 \times 3 = (7 \times 1) + (\square \times 2) = \square$

3. 7×9

4. 8×8

Do you UNDERSTAND?

5. **Writing to Explain** In the example at the top, how can $3 \times 5 = 15$ help you find 6×5?

6. Two streets are added to one side of the map, so it now covers an area of 8 blocks by 6 blocks. How many square blocks is the map now?

Independent Practice

Leveled Practice In **7** through **18**, use breaking apart to find each product.

7. $9 \times 5 = (9 \times 1) + (9 \times \square) = \square$

8. $3 \times 5 = (2 \times \square) + (1 \times 5) = \square$

*For another example, see Set F on page 89.

What You Show

Find 6×6.

You can break apart the first factor or the second factor.

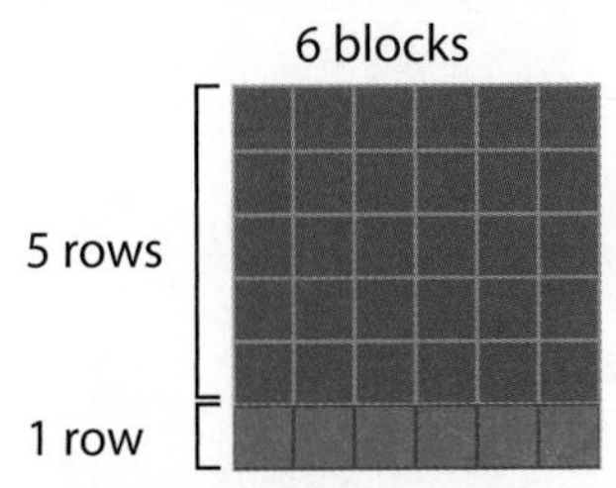

6 rows of 6 is the same as 5 rows of 6 and 1 row of 6.

What You Write

Break apart 6 into 5 + 1.

$6 \times 6 = (5 \times 6) + (1 \times 6)$

$30 + 6 = 36$

So, $6 \times 6 = 36$.

There are 36 square blocks on the map.

9. 6×6 **10.** 7×6 **11.** 8×7 **12.** 4×6 **13.** 3×7

14. 9×3 **15.** 8×9 **16.** 4×8 **17.** 6×3 **18.** 7×7

TAKS Problem Solving

19. Tara said she multiplied 6×6 to help her find the product of 7×6. Draw a picture and explain what she means.

20. Betsy's school needs $2000 to send the band to the state finals. So far, they have raised $465 in a fundraiser. How much more money do they need?

21. Joe, Vicki, and Tom took a hiking vacation. They traveled the distances shown in the table below. Who walked the farthest?

A Joe
B Tom
C Vicki
D They all walked the same distance.

Data

Hiker	Distance walked
Joe	9 miles each day for 8 days.
Vicki	8 miles each day for 4 days and 4 miles each day for 8 days.
Tom	7 miles each day for 5 days then 5 miles each day for 7 days.

22. For the chessboard shown below, write a multiplication sentence to find the total number of

a red pieces.
b squares with pieces.
c squares on the board.

Lesson
3-7

TEKS 4.4C: Recall and apply multiplication facts through 12 × 12.

10, 11, and 12 as Factors

What are the patterns for multiples of 10, 11, and 12?

How many plants are in 3 dozen containers if there is one plant in each container?

Patterns can help you when multiplying by 10, 11, or 12.

Guided Practice*

Do you know HOW?

In **1** through **4**, use patterns to find each product.

1. 10×3

2. 11×4

3. 11×7

4. 10×5

Do you UNDERSTAND?

5. Writing to Explain How can you use 7×10 to help you find 7×12?

6. A flower shop ordered one gross of flower pots. A gross is 12 dozen. Use breaking apart to find out how many flower pots they ordered.

Independent Practice

Leveled Practice In **9** through **26**, use breaking apart and patterns to find each product.

7. $12 \times 6 = (10 \times 6) + (\square \times 6) = \square$

8. $12 \times 8 = (10 \times 8) + (2 \times \square) = \square$

9. $9 \times 11 = (9 \times \square) + (9 \times 1) = \square$

10. $11 \times 11 = (11 \times 10) + (\square \times 1) = \square$

11. 11×6

12. 12×2

13. 10×6

14. 4×11

15. 4×10

16. 12×4

17. 11×8

18. 10×8

19. 10×3

20. 7×12

21. 11×10

22. 10×10

23. 11×2

24. 12×5

25. 10×1

26. 12×10

*For another example, see Set G on page 89.

Multiples of 10

$10 \times 1 = 10$
$10 \times 2 = 20$
$10 \times 3 = 30$
$10 \times 4 = 40$
$10 \times 5 = 50$
⋮

Place a zero to the right of the number to create a new ones digit.

Multiples of 11

$11 \times 1 = 11$
$11 \times 2 = 22$
$11 \times 3 = 33$
$11 \times 4 = 44$
$11 \times 5 = 55$
⋮

Multiply the factor that is not 11 by 10. Then add the factor to the product.

$11 \times 6 = (10 \times 6) + 6$

Multiples of 12

$12 \times 1 = 12$
$12 \times 2 = 24$
$12 \times 3 = 36$
$12 \times 4 = 48$
$12 \times 5 = 60$
⋮

Break apart 12.

$12 = 10 + 2$

$12 \times 3 = (10 \times 3) + (2 \times 3)$

There are 36 plants in 3 dozen containers.

TAKS Problem Solving

27. A pet store has 55 guppies. On Friday, Saturday, and Sunday, the store sold 11 guppies each day. How many guppies are left?

28. Reasonableness Jillian said that the product of 11×12 is 1,212. Is this reasonable? Why or why not?

29. Roger has 3 dimes and 6 pennies. He wrote a multiplication sentence to show the total value. His first factor was 12.

a What was the other factor?

b What is the product?

30. Think About the Process Mrs. Sanchez is installing new tile on her bathroom floor. If a 7×12 array of tiles fits perfectly, which expression shows how many tiles to use?

A $7 + 7 + 7 + 7 + 7 + 7 + 7$

B $(7 \times 10) - (7 \times 2)$

C $(7 \times 10) + (7 \times 2)$

D $(4 \times 10) + (3 \times 2)$

31. The Texas Motor Speedway in Fort Worth, Texas opened in 1996. If tickets for the O'Reilly 300, a race at the Speedway, are $24 each, how can you use multiples of 12 to find the cost of three tickets?

32. Steve, John, and Damon drove to a car race together. They each paid $34 for the day, including a $24 ticket and their portion of the parking fee. How much was the total parking fee?

F $10 **H** $40

G $30 **J** $60

Lesson

3-8

TEKS 4.14C: Select or develop an appropriate problem-solving plan or strategy, including drawing a picture, looking for a pattern, systematic guessing and checking, acting it out, making a table, working a simpler problem, or working backwards to solve a problem.

Problem Solving

Draw a Picture and Write an Equation

A stegosaurus was 5 times as long as a velociraptor. If a velociraptor was 6 feet long, how long was a stegosaurus?

Stegosaurus: ? feet long

Velociraptor: 6 feet long

Guided Practice*

Do you know HOW?

Solve. Write an equation to help you.

1. Manuel has a collection of coins, all of which are nickels and quarters. He has 8 nickels and three times as many quarters.

a How many quarters does he have?

b How many coins does Manuel have in all?

Do you UNDERSTAND?

2. How did the picture in the example above help you to write an equation?

3. **Write a Problem** The length of an iguanodon is 28 feet. A velociraptor is 6 feet long. Use this information to write a problem you can solve by writing an equation. Then solve.

Independent Practice

Solve.

4. For the science fair, James decided to make a model of sauroposeidon, the tallest dinosaur ever discovered. He made his model 3 feet tall. The actual dinosaur was 20 times the height of James' model. How tall was sauroposeidon?

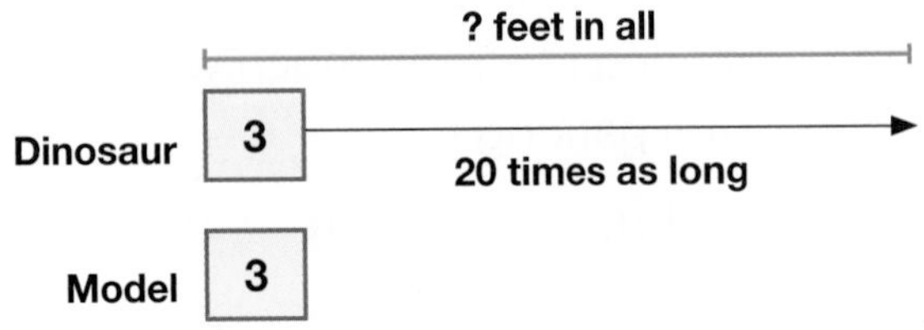

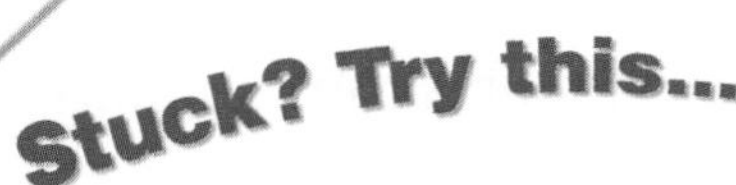

- What do I know?
- What diagram can I use to help understand the problem?
- Can I use addition, subtraction, multiplication, or division?
- Is all of my work correct?
- Did I answer the right question?
- Is my answer reasonable?

*For another example, see Set H on page 89.

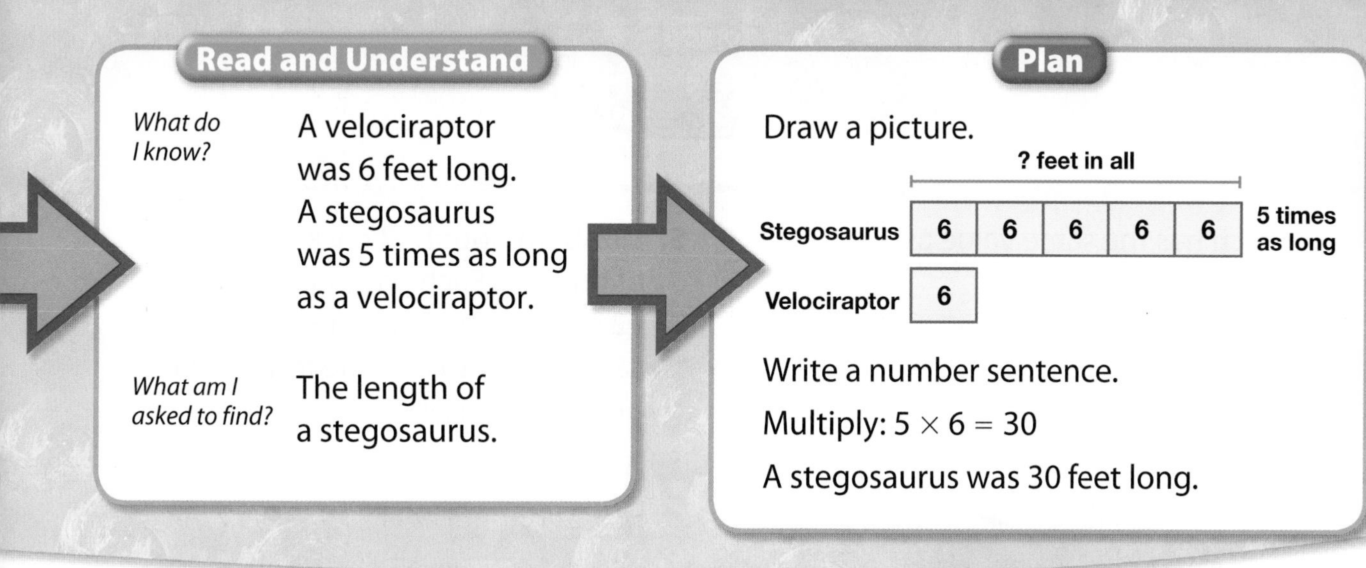

Read and Understand
What do I know?
A velociraptor was 6 feet long. A stegosaurus was 5 times as long as a velociraptor.
What am I asked to find?
The length of a stegosaurus.
Plan
Draw a picture.
? feet in all
Stegosaurus
6
6
6
6
6
5 times as long
Velociraptor
6
Write a number sentence.
Multiply: 5 × 6 = 30
A stegosaurus was 30 feet long.

5. Carmen's recipe calls for three times as many carrots as peas. If Carmen uses 2 cups of peas, how many cups of carrots will she use?

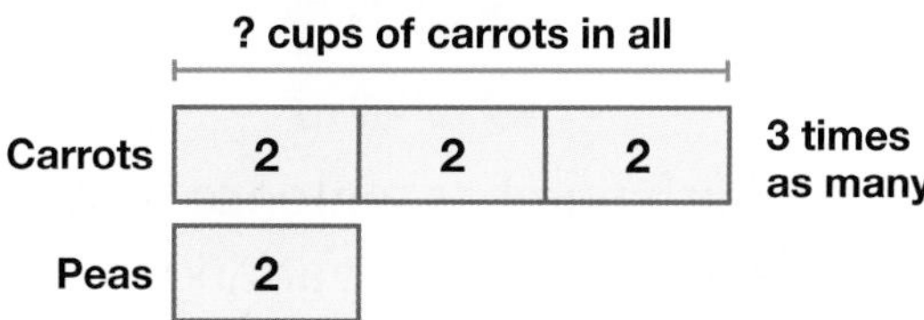

6. Rae's recipe calls for twice as many tomatoes as peppers. She uses 2 cups of peppers. How many cups of tomatoes and peppers will she use in all?

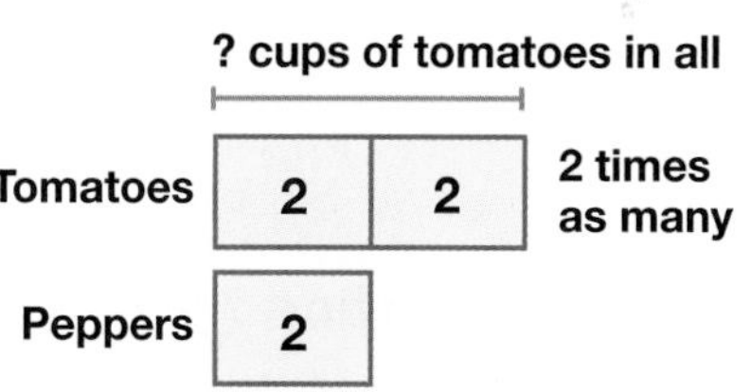

7. Marley, Jon, and Bart swim a relay race. Jon swims two more laps than Marley. Bart swims twice as many laps as Marley. If Marley swims 3 laps, how many laps do they swim altogether?

8. Jack's dog has a rectangular pen. The length is two feet longer than the width. The width is 6 feet. Write an equation to find the perimeter. What is the perimeter of the pen?

9. When Matilda was born, she was 20 inches tall. Matilda's mother is 3 times as tall as Matilda was at birth. Use the model below to find Matilda's mother height.

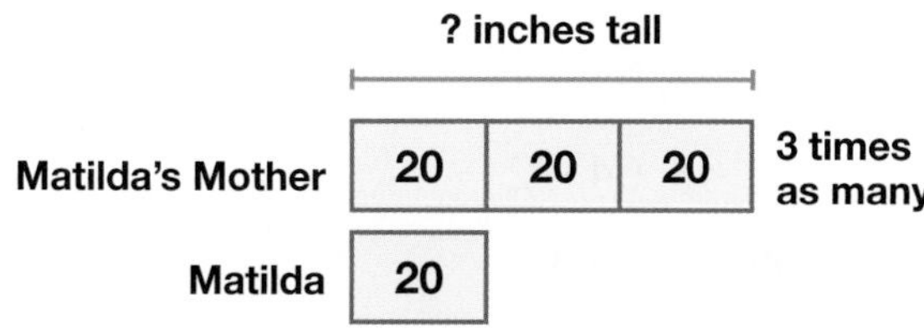

10. **Think About the Process** Four relay team members run an equal part of an 8-mile race. Which equation shows how far each member runs?

A $2 + 2 = 4$

B $4 \times 2 = 8$

C $4 + 4 + 4 + 4 = 16$

D $2 \times 2 = 4$

1. Which has the same value as 3×5? (3-1)

   A $5 + 3$

   B $5 + 5 + 5$

   C $5 + 5 + 5 + 3$

   D $3 + 3 + 3 + 3$

2. Grant made 4 Texas state flags for the school play. Each Texas flag had 1 white star. How many white stars did Grant need? (3-3)

   F 5

   G 4

   H 1

   J 0

3. Which is a way to find 7×8? (3-6)

   A $(7 \times 5) + (7 \times 2)$

   B $(4 \times 8) + (3 \times 8)$

   C $(7 \times 5) + (8 \times 1)$

   D $(5 \times 8) + (2 \times 7)$

4. Each flower has 5 petals.

   If Stephanie counted the petals in groups of 5, which list shows numbers she could have named? (3-2)

   F 12, 15, 18, 30

   G 15, 20, 34, 40

   H 15, 20, 25, 30

   J 10, 12, 14, 16

5. Elizabeth bought 3 packages of buttons. Each package had 12 buttons. Which number sentence can be used to find the total number of buttons Elizabeth bought? (3-7)

   A $12 - 3 = \square$

   B $3 + 12 = \square$

   C $3 \times \square = 12$

   D $3 \times 12 = \square$

6. Derrik arranged some balls on a table as shown.

   Which number sentence best represents Derrik's arrangement? (3-1)

   F $3 \times 4 = 12$

   G $3 \times 5 = 15$

   H $3 + 4 = 7$

   J $12 - 4 = 8$

7. Tad applies numbers on the back of football jerseys. Below are the first five numbers he applied. If the pattern continues, what are the next three numbers he will apply? (3-4)

   9, 18, 27, 36, 45, $\square$, $\square$, $\square$

   A 54, 63, 72

   B 54, 63, 71

   C 63, 64, 72

   D 63, 72, 81

8. Trevor's display case has 6 shelves. Each shelf displays 8 golf balls. Which number sentence shows how many golf balls are displayed in the case? (3-8)

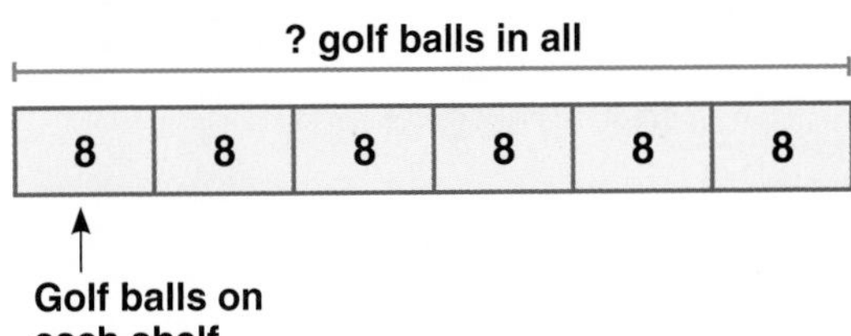

F $6 + 8 = 14$

G $6 - 3 = 3$

H $6 \times 8 = 48$

J $8 \times 8 = 64$

9. Sue collected 5 rocks. Angie collected 4 times as many rocks as Sue. Which of these shows the total number of rocks Angie collected? (3-1)

A The sum of 5 and 4

B The difference between 20 and 4

C The quotient of 20 and 4

D The product of 5 and 4

10. The Mendez family replaced tile on their kitchen counter. A 9×4 array of tiles fit the area. How many tiles did they use? (3-5)

F 13

G 27

H 34

J 36

11. Which number makes the number sentence true? (3-3)

$6 \times 2 = \square \times 6$

A 0

B 1

C 2

D 6

12. Which is a way to find 4×8? (3-5)

F $(4 \times 8) + (4 \times 8)$

G $(2 \times 5) + (2 \times 3)$

H $(2 \times 4) + (2 \times 4)$

J $(2 \times 8) + (2 \times 8)$

13. Before touring Kickapoo Cavern State Park, the 4th graders were put into 6 groups of 12 students. Which is a way to find 6×12? (3-7)

A $(3 \times 10) + (3 \times 2)$

B $(3 \times 6) + (3 \times 6)$

C $(6 \times 10) + (6 \times 2)$

D $(6 \times 12) + (6 \times 12)$

14. It takes Dave 7 minutes to paint one section of a fence. How many minutes would it take him to paint 3 sections? (3-6)

F 18

G 21

H 24

J 28

15. **Griddable Response** Gina made an invitation for each of her 10 friends. She used 11 stickers on each invitation. How many stickers in all did Gina use? (3-7)

Reteaching

Set A, pages 68–70

Write an addition sentence and a multiplication sentence.

$5 + 5 + 5 = 15$

$3 \times 5 = 15$

Remember you can multiply when adding the same number over and over.

1. 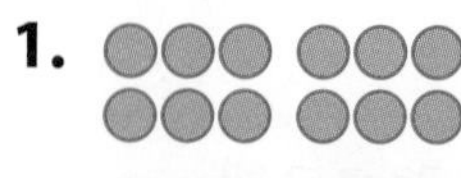

2. 

Set B, pages 72–73

Find 2×10.

When you multiply a number by 2, the product is always even.

$2 \times 10 = 20$

Remember you can solve some multiplication problems by using patterns of multiples.

1. 6×5 **2.** 9×8

3. 9×6 **4.** 2×3

5. 2×7 **6.** 5×7

Set C, pages 74–75

Find 9×10.

When you multiply any number by 0, the product is 0.

$9 \times 0 = 0$

Remember you can change the order of the factors when you multiply.

1. 10×0 **2.** 8×4

3. 4×8 **4.** 1×12

Set D, pages 76–77

Look for a pattern. Tell the missing numbers.

1, 5, 9, 13, ▢, ▢

Find the pattern.

$1 + 4 = 5$
$5 + 4 = 9$
$9 + 4 = 13$

Finish the pattern.

$13 + 4 = 17$
$17 + 4 = 21$

The missing numbers are 17 and 21.

Remember that in some patterns you do not add the same number each time.

1. 2, 10, 18, 26, ▢, ▢, ▢

2. 1, 2, 4, 7, 11, 16, 22, ▢, ▢, ▢

3. 3, 6, 9, 12, ▢, ▢, ▢

4. 5, 11, 17, 23, ▢, ▢, ▢

5. 14, 21, 28, 35, ▢, ▢, ▢

Reteaching

Set E, pages 78–79

Find 3×9 using breaking apart.

3 groups of 9 = 3 groups of 5 + 3 groups of 4.

$$3 \times 9 = (3 \times 5) + (3 \times 4)$$
$$15 + 12$$
$$27$$

Remember you can use breaking apart to remember multiplication facts.

1. 3×8 **2.** 4×9

3. 4×2 **4.** 3×10

Set F, pages 80–81

What are two ways to break apart 8×7?

Break apart the first factor.

$$8 \times 7 = (4 \times 7) + (4 \times 7)$$
$$28 + 28$$
$$56$$

Break apart the second factor.

$$8 \times 7 = (8 \times 5) + (8 \times 2)$$
$$40 + 16$$
$$56$$

Remember you can break apart either factor to find a multiplication fact.

1. 12×6 **2.** 8×8

3. 9×8 **4.** 6×9

Set G, pages 82–83

Find 7×12 using breaking apart.

7 groups of 12 = 7 groups of 10 + 7 groups of 2.

$$7 \times 12 = (7 \times 10) + (7 \times 2)$$
$$70 + 14$$
$$84$$

Remember you can use patterns or breaking apart to multiply.

1. 12×12 **2.** 9×9

3. 11×7 **4.** 10×6

Set H, pages 84–85

Marisol has 8 pennies in her collection. She has four times as many quarters as pennies. How many coins are in Marisol's collection?

? quarters in all

quarters	**8**	**8**	**8**	**8**	**4 times as many**
pennies	**8**				

$4 \times 8 = 32$ quarters

$32 + 8 = 40$ coins in all

Add 8 pennies to 32 quarters to find how many coins are in Marisol's collection.

Remember you can draw a picture to help you write an equation.

Draw a picture and write an equation to solve.

1. The length of Mel's basement is 10 times the length of a broom. The length of a broom is 3 feet. What is the length of the basement?

Topic 4

Division Meanings and Facts

1

When did people start riding carousels in the United States? You will find out in Lesson 4-4.

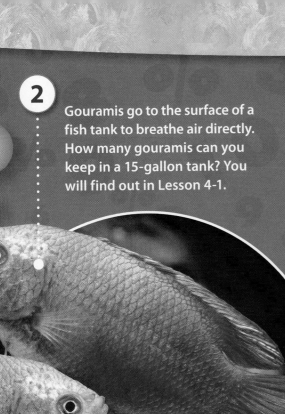

2

Gouramis go to the surface of a fish tank to breathe air directly. How many gouramis can you keep in a 15-gallon tank? You will find out in Lesson 4-1.

3

How many years will it take the U.S. Mint to release all of the 50 state quarters? You will find out in Lesson 4-2.

Review What You Know!

Vocabulary

Choose the best term from the box.

- divisor
- multiple
- factor
- quotient
- product

1. In the number sentence $9 \times 5 = 45$, 45 is the ?.
2. The number you divide by is the ?.
3. The answer in a division problem is the ?.

Multiplication Facts

Find each product.

4. 5×3	**5.** 7×2	**6.** 6×8
7. 8×0	**8.** 1×4	**9.** 2×8
10. 5×7	**11.** 3×6	**12.** 4×4
13. 4×5	**14.** 4×8	**15.** 2×6

Addition and Subtraction Facts

Write a subtraction fact for each addition fact.

16. $8 + 8 = 16$	**17.** $4 + 7 = 11$
18. $6 + 6 = 12$	**19.** $9 + 5 = 14$

20. Write a subtraction fact for the array below.

21. **Writing to Explain** Explain how you could subtract $146 - 51$ using mental math.

Lesson

4-1

TEKS 4.4B: Represent multiplication and division situations in picture, word, and number form.

Meanings of Division

When do you divide?

A museum wants to display a collection of 24 gems on four shelves, placing the same number of gems on each shelf. How many gems will be on each shelf?

Choose an Operation Think about sharing. Divide to find the number in each group.

24 gems on 4 shelves

Another Example How can you divide to find the number of groups?

Terri has 24 gems. She wants to display them on shelves. She decides to display 4 gems on each shelf. How many shelves does she need?

Choose an Operation Think about repeated subtraction. Divide to find the number of groups.

What You Show

To find the number of shelves, put 4 gems in each group. How many groups are there?

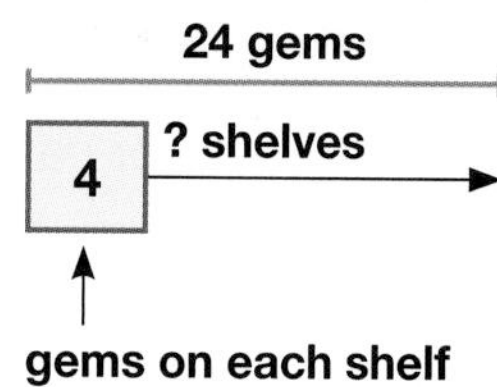

Terri needs 6 shelves.

What You Write

quotient

divisor → $4\overline{)24}$ ← dividend, with quotient 6

Explain It

1. How can repeated subtraction be used to find the number of shelves needed to hold 24 gems if each shelf holds 6 gems?
2. Explain what the quotient represents in each of the examples above.

What You Show

Think of sharing the gems equally among the 4 shelves. How many gems are on each shelf?

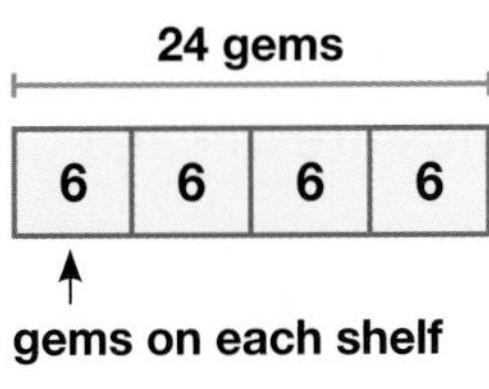

What You Write

divisor

$$24 \div 4 = 6$$

dividend quotient

Each shelf should have 6 gems.

Guided Practice*

Do you know HOW?

In **1** and **2**, draw pictures to help you divide.

1. You put 18 people into 3 rows. How many people are in each row?

2. Rocco is putting 14 drawings into 2 art binders. How many drawings are in each binder?

Do you UNDERSTAND?

3. Explain how you could use repeated addition to check the answer to the example above.

4. Sixteen players came to soccer practice. They formed four teams with the same number of players per team. How many players were on each team?

Independent Practice

Leveled Practice In **5** through **7**, copy and complete the diagrams to help you divide.

5. Kevin is arranging 12 chairs in 3 equal groups. How many chairs are in each group?

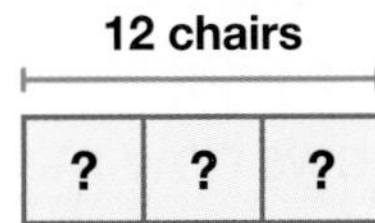

6. Meg has 36 beads. Each bracelet has 9 beads. How many bracelets does she have?

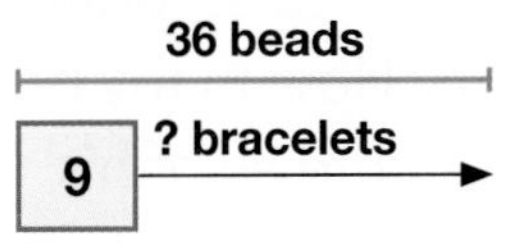

7. A farmer has 15 fruit trees. He plants 3 trees in each row. How many rows are there?

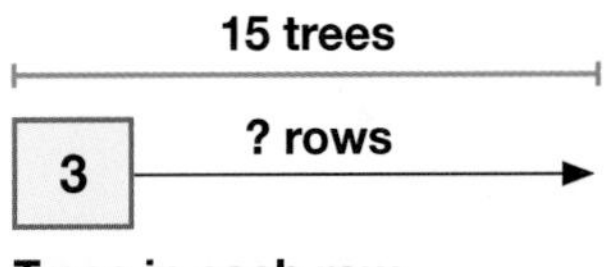

For another example, see Set A on page 108.

Independent Practice

In **8** through **11**, draw pictures to solve each problem.

8. Jeff puts 25 quarters into 5 equal groups. How many quarters are in each group?

9. Sally has 12 flower bulbs and divides them into 4 equal groups. How many flower bulbs are in each group?

10. Jena is making apple pies. She has 33 apples. She's putting 11 in each pie. How many pies will Jena make?

11. There are 30 stuffed bears in a gift shop arranged in 5 equal rows. How many bears are in each row?

TAKS Problem Solving

In **12** through **15**, use the table at the right.

12. How many students will be in each row for Mrs. Raymond's class photo?

13. How many more students will be in each row for Mr. Peterson's class than for Mr. Chen's class?

14. In which class will there be 7 students in each row?

15. If 3 students were absent from Miss Clifford's class on picture day, how many fewer students would be in each row?

Data

Class Picture Day

Each class must be arranged into three equal rows.

Name of Teacher	Number of Students
Mrs. Raymond	24
Mr. Chen	18
Miss Clifford	21
Mr. Peterson	27

16. Kissing gouramis do not get enough oxygen using their gills underwater, so they come to the surface to breathe. A fish store tells you that you need 3 gallons of water for each gouramis. How many gouramis can you keep in a 15-gallon tank?

17. Ray collects toy cars. He stores them in special boxes that fit 6 cars each. He had a total of 48 cars. Today he got 12 more cars. How many boxes will Ray need to store all of his cars now?

A 2 boxes

B 6 boxes

C 8 boxes

D 10 boxes

18. Think About the Process The drama club collects 242 bottles and 320 cans in a fundraiser. Each is worth a nickel. However, 48 cans were rejected. Which expression shows how many nickels they raised?

F $(242 + 320) - 48$

G $242 + 320 + 48$

H $(320 - 242) + 48$

J $(320 - 242) - 48$

Algebra Connections

Properties and Number Sentences

Remember multiplication properties can be used to help you solve multiplication problems:

- Commutative Property
  $3 \times 2 = 2 \times 3$
- Associative Property
  $(5 \times 2) \times 4 = 5 \times (2 \times 4)$
- Identity Property
  $9 \times 1 = 9$
- Zero Property
  $8 \times 0 = 0$

Example: $8 \times 5 = \square \times 8$

Think *The Commutative Property of Multiplication means you can multiply numbers in any order.*

Since $8 \times 5 = 5 \times 8$, the value of $\square$ must be 5.

Copy and complete. Check your answers.

1. $39 \times \square = 39$

2. $\square \times 12 = 12$

3. $(8 \times 5) \times 2 = \square \times (5 \times 2)$

4. $20 \times 4 = 4 \times \square$

5. $6 \times \square = 5 \times 6$

6. $0 = \square \times 9$

7. $\square \times 8 = 8 \times 9$

8. $1 \times \square = 24$

9. $\square \times 25 = 0$

10. $15 \times 3 = \square \times 15$

11. $16 \times \square = 16$

12. $\square \times 5 = 6 \times (4 \times 5)$

13. $12 \times 0 = \square$

14. $7 \times \square = 0$

15. $7 \times (1 \times \square) = (7 \times 1) \times 3$

For **16** through **18**, use the information in the table to find the answer.

16. Write two number sentences to represent the number of seats in 6 rows.

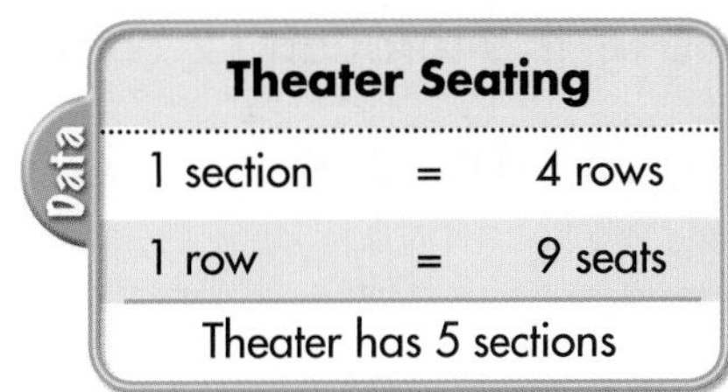

Theater Seating		
1 section	=	4 rows
1 row	=	9 seats
Theater has 5 sections		

17. No one is sitting in the last row of the theater that is otherwise filled. How many seats are being used?

18. How many rows of seats does the theater have?

Lesson
4-2

TEKS 4.6A: Use patterns and relationships to develop strategies to remember basic multiplication and division facts (such as the patterns in related multiplication and division number sentences (fact families) such as 9 x 9 = 81 and 81 ÷ 9 = 9).

Relating Multiplication and Division

Operations that undo each other are inverse operations. Multiplying by 3 and dividing by 3 are inverse operations.

Each trading card sheet has 3 rows with 2 pockets in each row. How many pockets are on each sheet?

Guided Practice*

Do you know HOW?

In **1** and **2**, copy and complete each fact family.

1. $8 \times \square = 32$
$32 \div \square = 4$
$32 \div \square = \square$
$\square \times \square = 32$

2. $6 \times 9 = \square$
$54 \div \square = 9$
$54 \div 9 = \square$
$9 \times \square = \square$

In **3** and **4**, write the fact family for each set of numbers.

3. 3, 6, 18

4. 5, 7, 35

Do you UNDERSTAND?

5. Why are there four number sentences in the example above?

6. Is $2 \times 6 = 12$ part of the fact family from the example above?

7. Why is $3 + 3 = 6$ **NOT** in the fact family of 2, 3, and 6?

8. If you know $7 \times 9 = 63$, what division facts do you know?

Independent Practice

Leveled Practice In **9** through **12**, copy and complete each fact family.

9. $5 \times \square = 35$
$35 \div 7 = \square$
$\square \times \square = 35$
$35 \div \square = \square$

10. $9 \times \square = 72$
$72 \div 8 = \square$
$\square \times \square = 72$
$72 \div \square = \square$

11. $3 \times \square = 18$
$18 \div 6 = \square$
$\square \times \square = 18$
$18 \div \square = \square$

12. $2 \times \square = 24$
$24 \div 12 = \square$
$\square \times \square = 24$
$24 \div \square = \square$

*For another example, see Set B on page 108.

A fact family shows all the related multiplication and division facts for a set of numbers. You can use fact families to help you remember division facts.

This is the fact family for 2, 3, and 6:

$2 \times 3 = 6$ $6 \div 2 = 3$

$3 \times 2 = 6$ $6 \div 3 = 2$

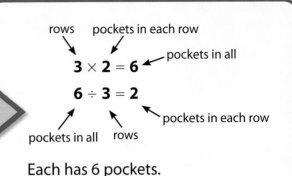

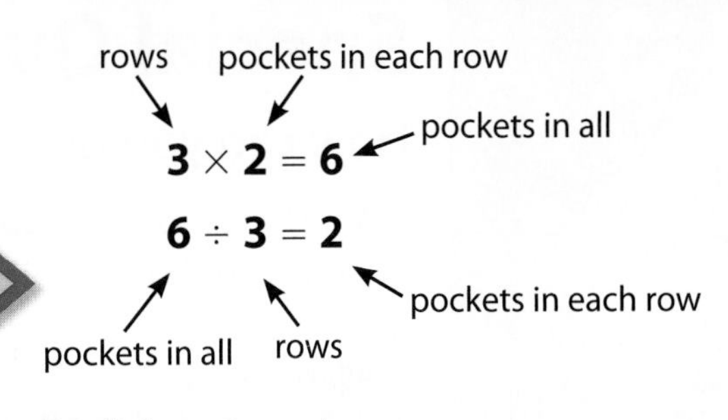

Each has 6 pockets.

In **13** through **20**, write a fact family for each set of numbers.

13. 7, 8, 56 **14.** 2, 8, 16 **15.** 6, 7, 42 **16.** 6, 6, 36

17. 3, 8, 24 **18.** 7, 10, 70 **19.** 6, 5, 30 **20.** 5, 8, 40

TAKS Problem Solving

21. How many years will it take to release all 50 quarters? Write a division fact you can use to find this quotient.

First quarters released	1999
Number of new quarters each year	5
Texas quarter released	2004

22. In the fact family for the numbers 5, 6, 30, which term can **NOT** be used to describe 5 or 6?

A factor **C** product

B divisor **D** quotient

23. Josh practiced his drums two hours before dinner and three hours after dinner. How many hours did he practice in all?

F 3 hours **H** 5 hours

G 4 hours **J** 6 hours

24. Write the fact family that has 9 as a factor and 45 as a product.

25. **Number Sense** Why does the fact family for 64 and 8 have only two number sentences?

Lesson

4-3

TEKS 4.6A: Use patterns and relationships to develop strategies to remember basic multiplication and division facts (such as the patterns in related multiplication and division number sentences (fact families) such as 9 × 9 = 81 and 81 ÷ 9 = 9).

Special Quotients

How can you divide with 1 and 0?

A sandwich is cut into 8 pieces. How many people can have 1 piece each? Find 8 ÷ 1.

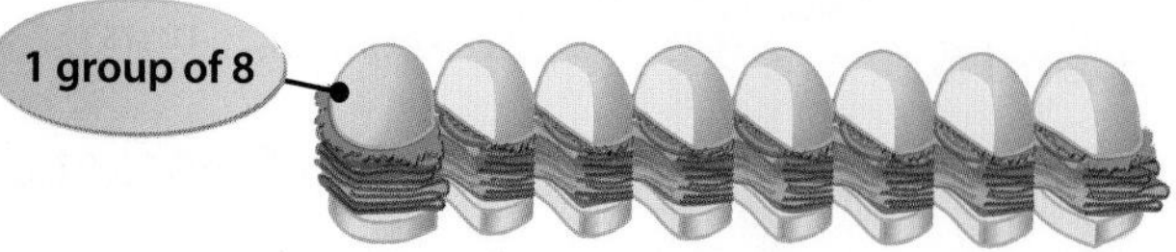

8 people can have 1 piece of sandwich

Dividing by 1

Think What number times 1 equals 8?

$1 \times 8 = 8$

So, $8 \div 1 = 8$.

Rule: Any number divided by 1 is itself.

Guided Practice*

Do you know HOW?

In **1** through **8**, use multiplication facts to help you divide.

1. 9 ÷ 9 **2.** 5 ÷ 1

3. 0 ÷ 4 **4.** 7 ÷ 1

5. $3\overline{)0}$ **6.** $1\overline{)1}$

7. $1\overline{)2}$ **8.** $6\overline{)6}$

Do you UNDERSTAND?

9. What multiplication sentence can help you find 0 ÷ 8?

10. What multiplication sentence can help you find 8 ÷ 8?

11. **Writing to Explain** If none of the bread is left, how many pieces can 4 people have?

Independent Practice

Use multiplication facts to help you divide.

12. $1\overline{)3}$ **13.** $8\overline{)0}$ **14.** $2\overline{)0}$ **15.** $4\overline{)4}$

Copy and complete by writing >, <, or = for each ◯.

16. 7 ÷ 7 ◯ 2 ÷ 2 **17.** 0 ÷ 5 ◯ 3 ÷ 1 **18.** 4 ÷ 1 ◯ 4 ÷ 4

19. 6 ÷ 6 ◯ 0 ÷ 4 **20.** 9 ÷ 1 ◯ 4 ÷ 1 **21.** 3 ÷ 3 ◯ 6 ÷ 1

22. 0 ÷ 3 ◯ 0 ÷ 8 **23.** 0 ÷ 5 ◯ 5 ÷ 5 **24.** 8 ÷ 1 ◯ 6 ÷ 1

25. 0 ÷ 9 ◯ 0 ÷ 7 **26.** 0 ÷ 1 ◯ 1 ÷ 1 **27.** 7 ÷ 1 ◯ 0 ÷ 6

For another example, see Set C on page 109.

1 as a Quotient

To find $8 \div 8$, think 8 times what number equals 8?

$8 \times 1 = 8$

So, $8 \div 8 = 1$.

Rule: Any number (except 0) divided by itself is 1.

Dividing 0 by a Number

To find $0 \div 8$, think 8 times what number equals 0?

$8 \times 0 = 0$

So, $0 \div 8 = 0$.

Rule: 0 divided by any number (except 0) is 0.

Dividing by 0

To find $8 \div 0$, think 0 times what number equals 8?

There is no such number.

Rule: You cannot divide by 0.

TAKS Problem Solving

28. Three friends decided to buy lunch. Anne spent $3.42, Saul spent $4.41, and Ryan spent $4.24. Write these numbers from least to greatest.

29. Tony's family is driving 70 miles to a fair. They have already traveled 30 miles. They are traveling at a speed of 40 miles per hour. How many more hours will it take them to complete the trip?

30. On a trip to the beach, the Torrez family brings 5 beach balls for their 5 children.

a If the beach balls are divided evenly, how many beach balls will each child get?

b If the children give the 5 balls to 1 parent, how many balls will the parent have?

31. **Algebra** If $\square \div \triangle = 0$, what do you know about $\square$?

A $\square$ cannot equal 0.

B $\square$ must equal 0.

C $\square$ must equal 1.

D $\square$ must equal $\triangle$.

32. **Write a Problem** Write a word problem in which 5 is divided by 5 and another problem in which 5 is divided by 1.

33. In one season, a baseball team will practice 3 times a week. If there are 36 practices, how many weeks will the team practice in the season?

34. **Number Sense** Write a fact family for 3, 3, and 9.

Lesson

4-4

TEKS 4.6A: Use patterns and relationships to develop strategies to remember basic multiplication and division facts (such as the patterns in related multiplication and division number sentences (fact families) such as $9 \times 9 = 81$ and $81 \div 9 = 9$).

Using Multiplication Facts to Find Division Facts

How does multiplication help you divide?

Matt wants to buy 28 super bouncy balls to give as prizes. How many packs does Matt need to buy?

Choose an Operation Divide to find the number of equal groups.

Guided Practice*

Do you know HOW?

In **1** through **6**, use multiplication facts to help you divide.

1. $27 \div 9$

2. $40 \div 5$

3. $24 \div 4$

4. $66 \div 6$

5. $9\overline{)63}$

6. $9\overline{)81}$

Do you UNDERSTAND?

7. What multiplication fact could you use to help you find $72 \div 9$?

8. Matt has 40 super bouncy balls to put in 10 bags. He puts the same number in each bag. What multiplication fact can you use to find the number of balls in each bag?

Independent Practice

Leveled Practice In **9** through **27**, use multiplication facts to help you find the quotient.

9. ☐ $\times 3 = 27$ $27 \div 3 =$ ☐

10. ☐ $\times 8 = 40$ $40 \div 8 =$ ☐

11. ☐ $\times 6 = 42$ $42 \div 6 =$ ☐

12. ☐ $\times 7 = 63$ $63 \div 7 =$ ☐

13. $7\overline{)49}$ **14.** $3\overline{)27}$ **15.** $6\overline{)48}$ **16.** $7\overline{)21}$ **17.** $4\overline{)16}$

18. $9\overline{)36}$ **19.** $5\overline{)15}$ **20.** $12\overline{)60}$ **21.** $6\overline{)36}$ **22.** $2\overline{)14}$

23. $3\overline{)24}$ **24.** $4\overline{)32}$ **25.** $2\overline{)18}$ **26.** $7\overline{)35}$ **27.** $7\overline{)56}$

*For another example, see Set D on page 109.

What You Think

How many groups of 7 are in 28?

Change this to a multiplication sentence:

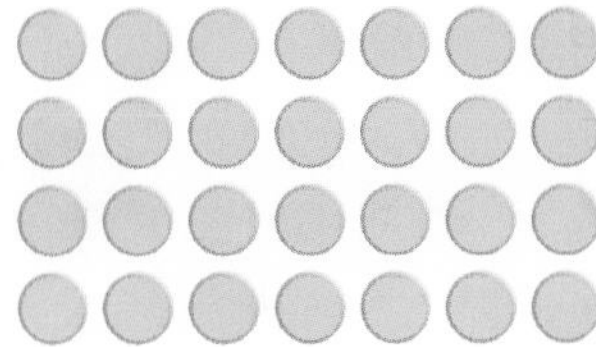

What number times 7 equals 28?

$\square \times 7 = 28$ $4 \times 7 = 28$

What You Write

There are two ways to write division facts.

$28 \div 7 = 4$

or

$7\overline{)28}$ with quotient 4

Matt needs to buy 4 packs of bouncy balls.

TAKS Problem Solving

For **28** and **29**, use the table at the right.

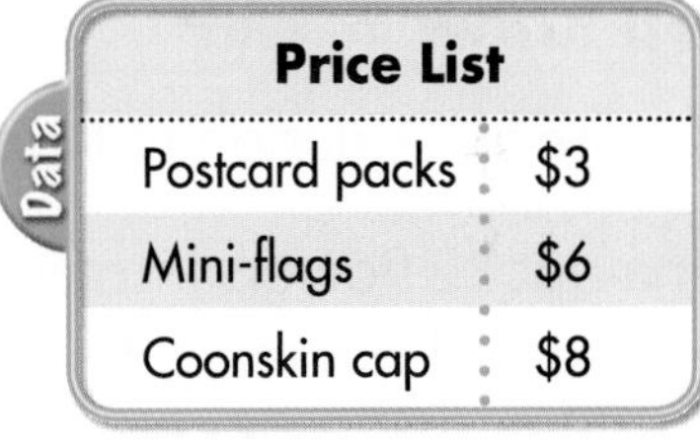

Price List	
Postcard packs	$3
Mini-flags	$6
Coonskin cap	$8

28. On a field trip to the Alamo, Shana spends $24 in the gift shop. Which item can Shana buy the most of? Explain.

29. How many mini-flags can Shana buy if she uses all of her money?

For **30**, use the diagram at the right.

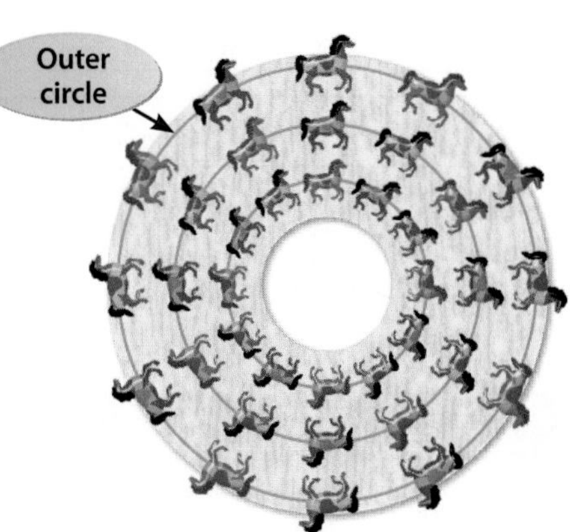

30. People started riding carousels in the United States in 1835. The carousel drawing, at the right, has a total of 36 horses with an equal number of horses on each circle. Write a division fact you can use to find the number of horses on the outer circle.

31. Carson plays a card word game. She gives the same number of cards to each of 4 players. If there are 20 cards in all, how many cards does each player get?

32. The total lunch bill for six people is $52. They add an $8 tip and split the bill evenly. How much is each person's equal share of the total bill?

A $6 **C** $10

B $8 **D** $12

Lesson
4-5

TEKS 4.14C: Select or develop an appropriate problem-solving plan or strategy, including drawing a picture, looking for a pattern, systematic guessing and checking, acting it out, making a table, working a simpler problem, or working backwards to solve a problem.

Problem Solving

Draw a Picture and Write an Equation

Ruben's scout troop is making 4 milk-jug birdfeeders. Each birdfeeder will use the same number of wooden dowels. If they have 24 dowels in all, how many dowels will be used for each feeder?

Guided Practice*

Do you know HOW?

Solve. Write an equation to help you.

1. Tina put 32 flowers into eight bouquets. How many flowers were in each bouquet if each had the same number of flowers?

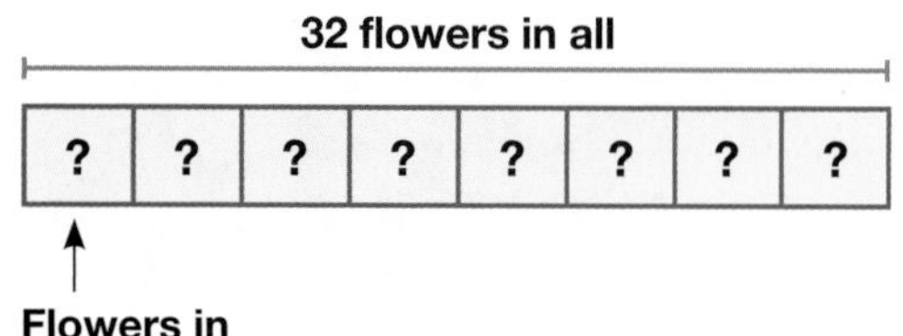

Do you UNDERSTAND?

2. How did the picture in Problem 1 help you to write an equation?

3. How many birdfeeders could Ruben make with 36 dowels?

4. **Write a Problem** Write a problem about sharing items that you can solve by drawing a picture. Then solve.

Independent Practice

Solve.

5. Kylie bought a bag of 30 beads to make bracelets. Each bracelet requires 5 beads. How many bracelets can Kylie make?

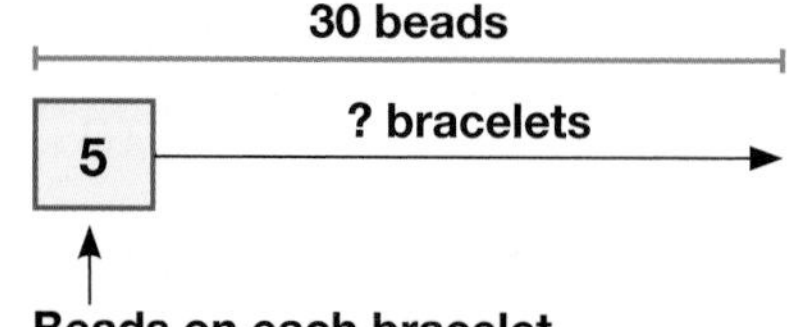

6. In Exercise 5, what equation can you write to answer the problem?

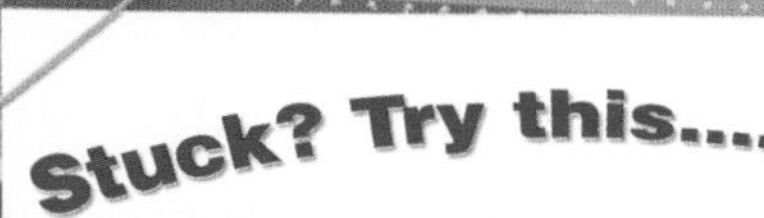

- What do I know?
- What diagram can I use to help understand the problem?
- Can I use addition, subtraction, multiplication, or division?
- Is all of my work correct?
- Did I answer the right question?
- Is my answer reasonable?

*For another example, see Set E on page 109.

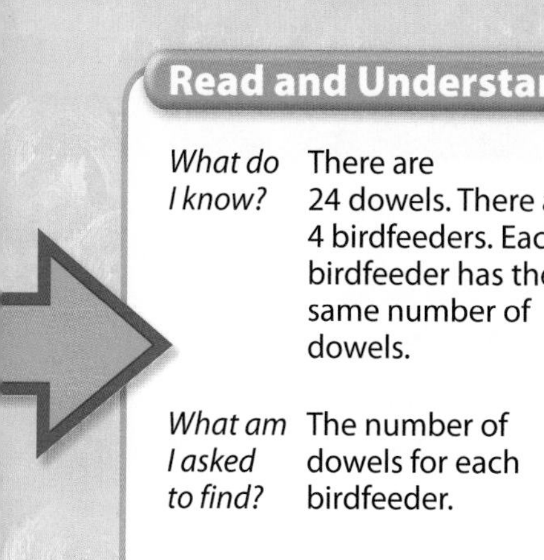

Read and Understand

What do I know? There are 24 dowels. There are 4 birdfeeders. Each birdfeeder has the same number of dowels.

What am I asked to find? The number of dowels for each birdfeeder.

Plan and Solve

Draw a picture.

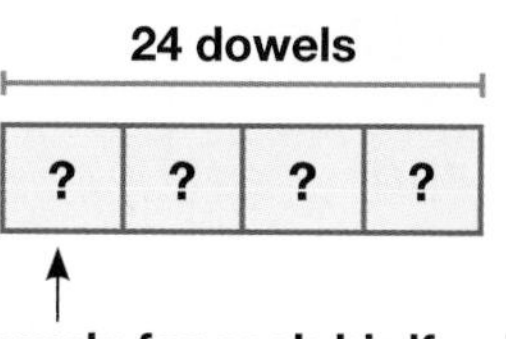

Write a number sentence.

Divide: $24 \div 4 = \square$

$24 \div 4 = 6$

There are 6 dowels for each birdfeeder.

Look Back and Check

Check the answer by multiplying.

Each birdfeeder has 6 dowels. There are 4 birdfeeders.

$4 \times 6 = 24$

The answer checks.

7. Sheena is packing 18 paperweights in boxes. She packs them in 6 boxes with the same number of paperweights in each box. How many paperweights are in each box?

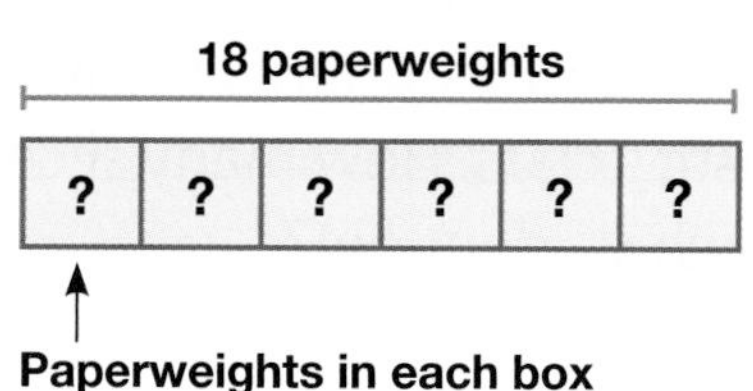

8. Jodi is bundling newspapers. She has 66 newspapers and puts 6 newspapers in each bundle. How many bundles does Jodi make?

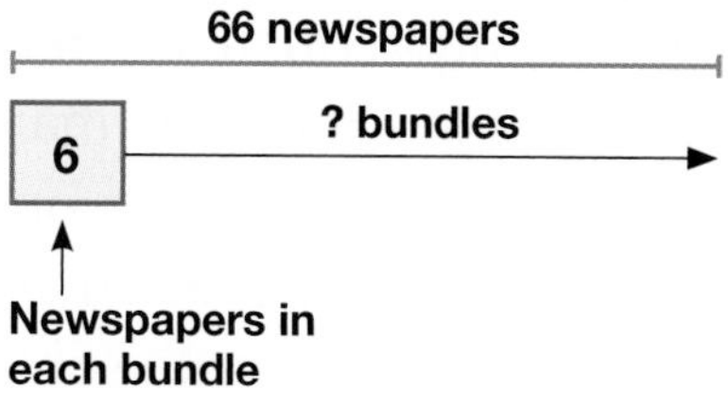

Use the bar graph at the right for **9** and **10**.

9. How much more money did Katie save in September than in October?

10. Katie used the money she saved in November and December to buy her mother a present. How much did she spend?

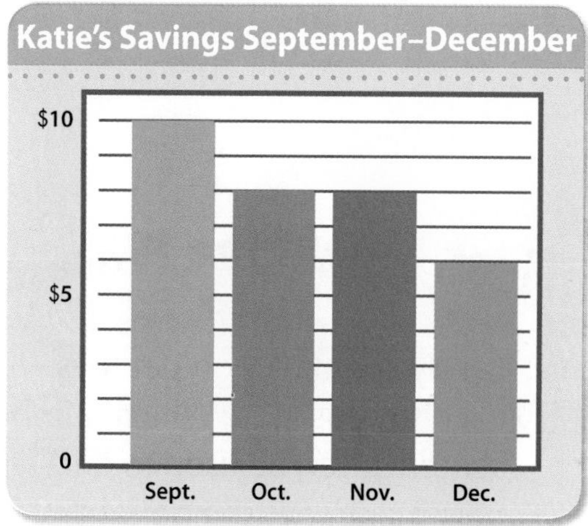

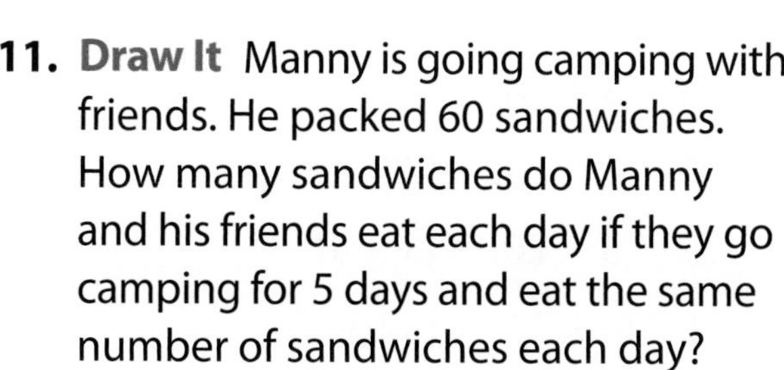

11. Draw It Manny is going camping with friends. He packed 60 sandwiches. How many sandwiches do Manny and his friends eat each day if they go camping for 5 days and eat the same number of sandwiches each day?

12. Draw It Jenna bought 36 pencils to give to her friends before the first day of school. If each friend received 6 pencils, how many friends did Jenna buy pencils for?

Independent Practice

Use the table at the right for **13** and **14**.

13. Everett bought a leash, collar, and bed at the sale. How much did Everett spend in all?

14. **Draw It** Everett has his dog groomed at the pet shop. The cost of grooming is three times the cost of a dog bowl. Find the cost of the grooming.

Dog Supplies Sale (Data)

Item	Price
Leash	\$8
Collar	\$6
Bowls	\$7
Medium Beds	\$15

15. Rena has 16 scarves. If 4 of her scarves are blue and one half of her scarves are red, how many are **NOT** red or blue?

16. Frank, Chuck, Bob and Dan arranged their exercise mats in a row. Bob's mat is next to only one other mat. Dan is on the third mat. Chuck is not next to Dan. Who is on which mat?

17. Emma is fencing a square garden with 52 feet of fencing. How many feet of fencing will Emma use on each side? Draw a bar diagram and write a number sentence to solve the problem.

18. Oliver has 75 apple slices that he distributes to 15 students in his gymnastics class. How many slices does each student get?

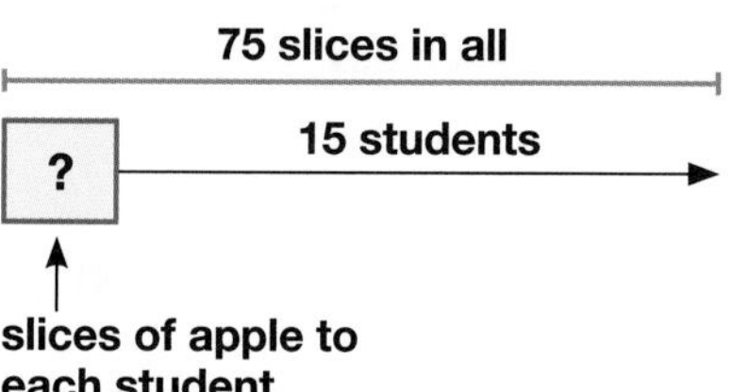

Think About the Process

19. Sandy spent \$36 on pet toys. Each toy cost \$12. Which number sentence can be used to find how many toys she bought?

A $12 + 24 = \square$

B $36 \div 12 = \square$

C $6 \times 6 = \square$

D $36 \div 6 = \square$

20. Three groups of 24 students each competed in the junior mathematics relay. What two simpler problems can you use to find the total number of students in the three groups?

F $(3 + 24) - (12 + 4)$

G $(3 \times 12) + (20 + 2)$

H $(3 \times 20) + (3 \times 4)$

J $(4 \times 12) + (32 + 4)$

Use Multiplication to Divide

Use eTools Counters

Use multiplication to find $28 \div 7$, $42 \div 7$, and $72 \div 8$

Step 1 Go to the Counters eTool. Select the array workspace. Drag the resize button in the upper right corner of the rectangle to make a row that is 7 counters long. Drag the button up to increase the number of rows until there are 28 counters in all. The total number of counters is shown in the odometer at the bottom of the page.

eTools Counters

Resize Button

Odometer

The array shows that $4 \times 7 = 28$, so $28 \div 7 = 4$.

Step 2 Increase the number of rows with 7 counters in each until there are 42 counters in all. The array shows that $6 \times 7 = 42$, so $42 \div 7 = 6$.

Step 3 Make an array with 8 counters in each row. Increase the number of rows until there are 72 counters in all. The array shows that $9 \times 8 = 72$, so $72 \div 8 = 9$.

Practice

Find the quotient by using multiplication.

1. $16 \div 2$ **2.** $24 \div 4$ **3.** $45 \div 5$ **4.** $49 \div 7$

5. $36 \div 6$ **6.** $63 \div 9$ **7.** $21 \div 3$ **8.** $35 \div 5$

9. $56 \div 7$ **10.** $32 \div 8$ **11.** $48 \div 6$ **12.** $20 \div 5$

13. $40 \div 8$ **14.** $30 \div 6$ **15.** $10 \div 2$ **16.** $72 \div 9$

17. $18 \div 9$ **18.** $27 \div 3$ **19.** $45 \div 9$ **20.** $24 \div 8$

21. $21 \div 7$ **22.** $54 \div 9$ **23.** $24 \div 12$ **24.** $33 \div 11$

TAKS Test Prep

1. Kent uses 8 nails to make each birdhouse. So far he has used 24 nails. Which number sentence can be used to find the number of birdhouses he has made so far? (4-4)

   A $24 + 8 = 32$

   B $24 - 8 = 16$

   C $24 \times 8 = 192$

   D $24 \div 8 = 3$

2. Tammy made 10 friendship rings to share equally among 5 of her friends. How can she find how many rings to give each friend? (4-1)

   F Divide the number of rings by 5

   G Add the number of rings 5 times

   H Subtract the number of rings from 5

   J Multiply the number of rings by 5

3. Sierra bought 30 shells for her 6 hermit crabs. Which number sentence is **NOT** in the same fact family as the others? (4-2)

   A $6 \times 5 = 30$

   B $5 \times 6 = 30$

   C $30 \div 5 = 6$

   D $5 \times 30 = 150$

4. In which number sentence does 7 make the number sentence true? (4-4)

   F $35 \div \square = 7$

   G $28 \div \square = 4$

   H $48 \div \square = 8$

   J $20 \div \square = 5$

5. Three friends have 27 water balloons to share equally. How many water balloons will each friend get? (4-1)

   27 water balloons

?	?	?

   Water balloons each friend gets

   A 9

   B 8

   C 7

   D 6

6. Which number sentence is in the same fact family as $63 \div 9 = \square$? (4-2)

   F $63 \times 9 = \square$

   G $\square \times 9 = 63$

   H $\square - 9 = 63$

   J $9 + \square = 63$

7. Which number makes the number sentence true? (4-4)

   $40 \div \square = 8$

   A 7

   B 6

   C 5

   D 4

8. Which number sentence is true? (4-3)

   F $4 \div 4 = 0$

   G $7 \div 1 = 1$

   H $2 \div 2 = 2$

   J $0 \div 8 = 0$

9. Which number makes both number sentences true? (4-4)

$4 \times \square = 32$

$32 \div 4 = \square$

A 9

B 8

C 7

D 6

10. Olivia has 48 daisies and 6 vases. Which number sentence shows how many daisies she can put in each vase if she puts the same number in each vase? (4-5)

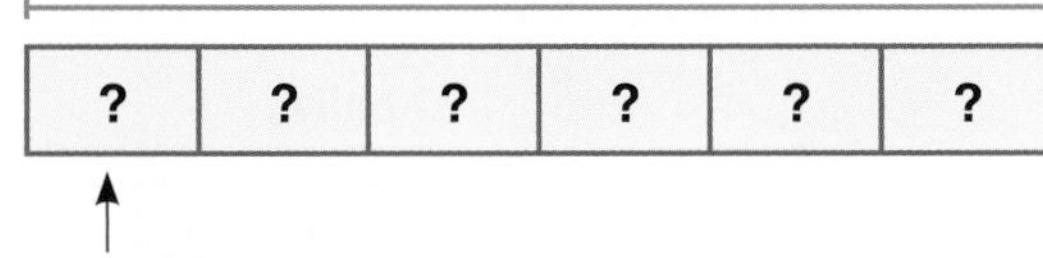

F $48 - 6 = 42$

G $48 + 6 = 54$

H $48 \div 6 = 8$

J $6 \times 48 = 288$

11. Which symbol makes the number sentence true? (4-3)

$0 \div 9 \bigcirc 6 \div 6$

A $\times$

B $=$

C $<$

D $>$

12. Mrs. Warren bought 3 packages of pencils for her students. Each package had 6 pencils. Which number sentence is in this fact family? (4-2)

F $2 \times 3 = 6$

G $6 - 3 = 3$

H $3 + 6 = 9$

J $18 \div 3 = 6$

13. Mason bought a package of 20 wheels. Each model car needs 4 wheels. How many cars can he make? (4-1)

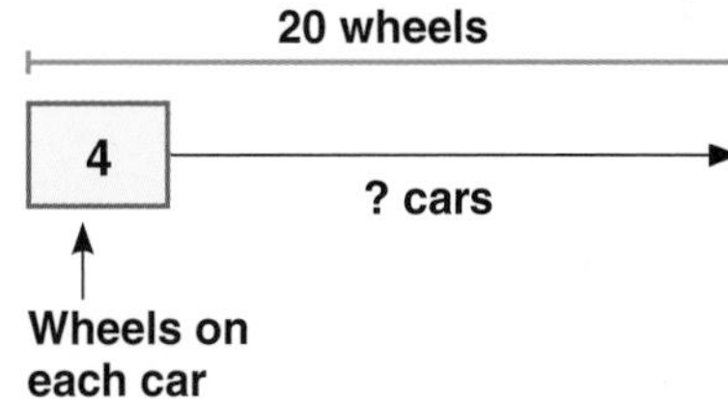

A 4

B 5

C 16

D 24

14. **Griddable Response** Mr. Nessels bought 14 apples to feed his horse. He wants to give the horse the same number of apples each day for 7 days. How many apples will the horse get each day? (4-4)

15. **Griddable Response** Five friends are sharing 5 chicken burritos equally. How many burritos will each person get? (4-3)

Reteaching

Set A, pages 92–94

Katherine is making 6 lunches. She has 30 carrot sticks. How many carrot sticks go in each lunch?

$30 \div 6 = 5$

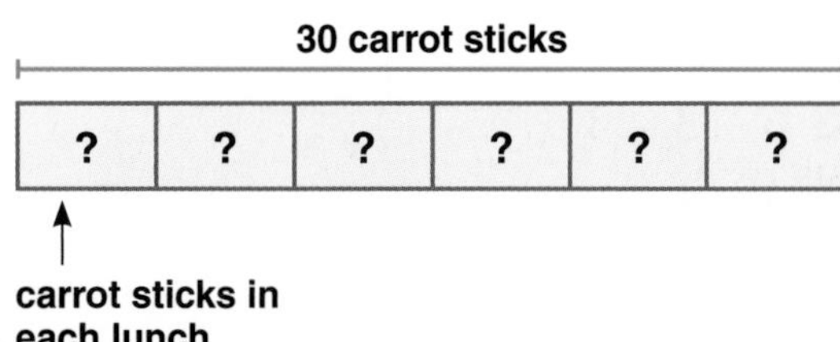

There are 5 carrot sticks in each lunch when 30 carrot sticks are shared equally in 6 lunches.

Remember you can think about sharing or repeated subtraction to divide.

Use the diagram to help you divide.

1. There are 15 chairs in 3 groups. How many chairs are in each group?

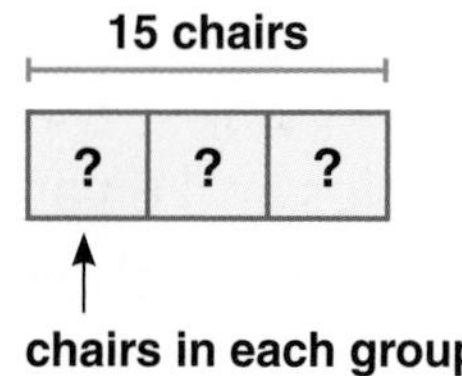

2. The soccer club has 32 balls for 8 teams to share equally. How many balls will each team get?

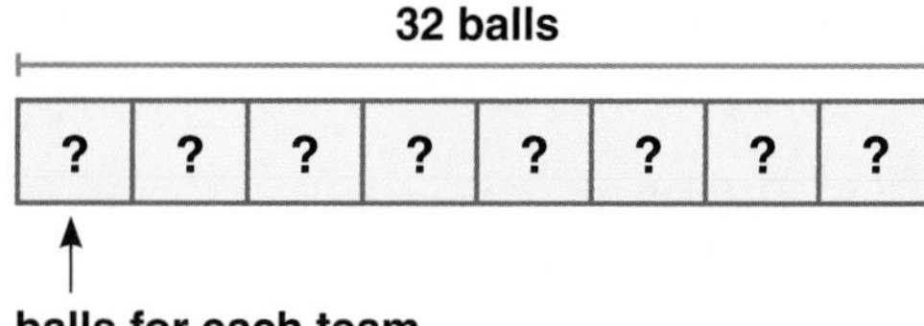

Set B, pages 96–97

Francine places 12 dolls on 3 shelves with the same number of dolls on each shelf.

shelves ↓ dolls on each shelf ↓

$3 \times \square = 12$ ← dolls in all

Use the fact family for 3, 4, and 12 to find how many dolls are on each shelf.

$3 \times 4 = 12$ $12 \div 3 = 4$

$4 \times 3 = 12$ $12 \div 4 = 3$

There are 4 dolls on each shelf.

Remember a fact family shows all of the related facts for a set of numbers.

Copy and complete each fact family.

1. $5 \times \square = 40$ $\square \div 5 = 8$

   $8 \times 5 = \square$ $\square \div 8 = \square$

2. $7 \times 9 = \square$ $\square \div 7 = 9$

   $9 \times \square = 63$ $63 \div \square = 7$

3. $3 \times \square = 21$ $\square \div 3 = 7$

   $7 \times 3 = \square$ $\square \div 7 = \square$

4. $6 \times 2 = \square$ $\square \div 6 = 2$

   $2 \times \square = 12$ $12 \div \square = 6$

Set C, pages 98–99

Find $6 \div 6$ and $6 \div 1$.

Any number divided by itself, except 0 is 1. So, $6 \div 6 = 1$.

Any number divided by 1 is that number. So, $6 \div 1 = 6$.

Remember zero divided by any number is zero, but you cannot divide by zero.

Compare. Use >, <, or = for each ◯.

1. $8\overline{)8}$ ◯ $3\overline{)3}$
2. $1\overline{)7}$ ◯ $6\overline{)0}$
3. $1\overline{)7}$ ◯ $1\overline{)4}$
4. $2\overline{)0}$ ◯ $9\overline{)0}$
5. $1\overline{)8}$ ◯ $5\overline{)1}$
6. $2\overline{)0}$ ◯ $2\overline{)1}$

Set D, pages 100–101

Find $24 \div 4$.

What number times 4 equals 24?

$\square \times 4 = 24$

$6 \times 4 = 24$

So, $24 \div 4 = 6$.

Remember use multiplication facts to help you divide.

1. $5\overline{)30}$
2. $2\overline{)18}$
3. $7\overline{)28}$
4. $9\overline{)81}$
5. $8\overline{)56}$
6. $8\overline{)48}$

Set E, pages 102–103

What do I know?	Mrs. Collins has 24 pairs of scissors. She puts the same number of each in 6 drawers. How many pairs of scissors are in each drawer?
What am I asked to find?	The number of scissors in each drawer.

Draw a picture.

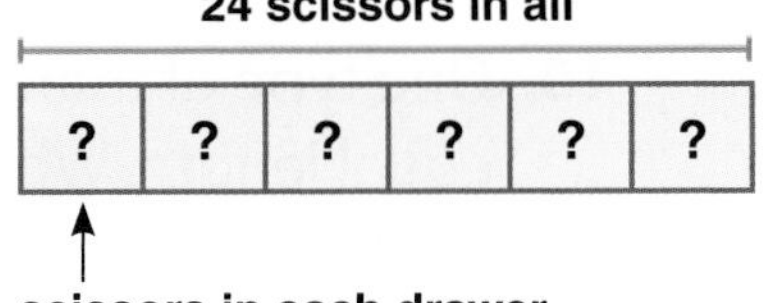

Divide to find the number of scissors in each drawer.

$24 \div 6 = \square$

$24 \div 6 = 4$

There are 4 pairs of scissors in each drawer.

Remember to draw a picture to help solve the problem.

Solve.

1. Winnie buys 20 bookmarks for herself and three of her friends. Each person received the same number of bookmarks. How many bookmarks did they each receive?

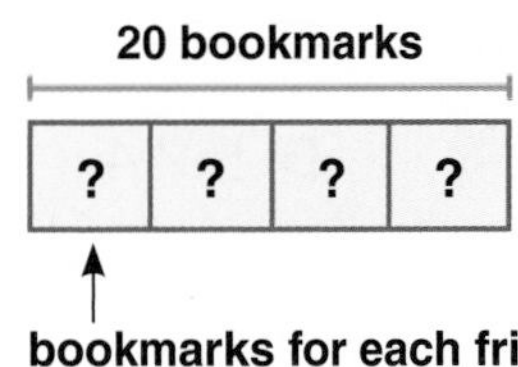

Spiral Review

Number and Operations

1. What number is equal to eight thousand, three hundred nine?

A 8,309
B 8,390
C 80,390
D 83,039

2.

City	Population
Folsom	154,907
Grove City	195,704
McHandy	159,407

Order the populations from least to greatest.

F Folsom, McHandy, Grove City
G McHandy, Grove City, Folsom
H Folsom, Grove City, McHandy
J Grove City, Folsom, McHandy

3. Round 17,856,000 to the nearest hundred thousand.

A 17,800,000
B 17,900,000
C 17,970,000
D 18,000,000

4. Todd read one book that had 177 pages and another book that had 187 pages. Estimate how many pages Todd read in all?

F 500 pages
G 400 pages
H 300 pages
J 200 pages

5. Which of the following is not in the fact family of 4, 5, 20?

A $4 \times 5 = 20$
B $4 \div 2 = 2$
C $20 \div 5 = 4$
D $5 \times 4 = 20$

Geometry and Measurement

6. Find the perimeter of the rectangle.

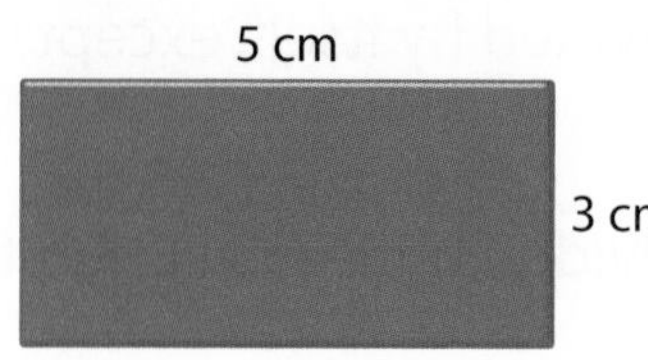

F 5 cm
G 10 cm
H 15 cm
J 16 cm

7. Name this figure.

A rectangular prism
B cylinder
C cube
D sphere

8. Which does not have a line of symmetry?

F  

H 

G  

J 

9. A football field is 100 yards long. How many feet long is the football field?

10. One type of triangle has 3 sides of equal length. What type of triangle is it?

11. **Writing to Explain** Explain why the length of a bus is measured in feet, but the height of a bus seat is measured in inches.

Spiral Review

Probability and Statistics

12. Predict the color you are most likely to pick from the bag without looking.

A blue

B yellow

C green

D orange

13. How likely is it you will pick a blue marble without looking from the bag of marbles shown in Question 12?

F impossible

G unlikely

H likely

J certain

The line plot below shows the number of points scored per game by a hockey team.

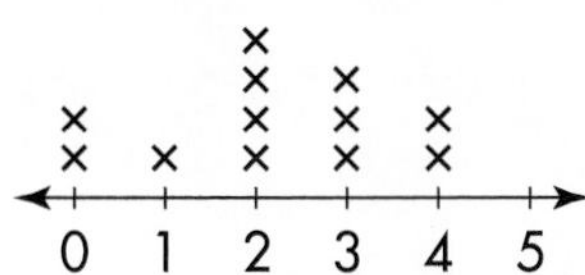

14. In how many games were no points scored?

15. What was the greatest number of points scored?

16. Writing to Explain What kind of graph would you choose to display data about the temperatures for a week?

Algebraic Thinking

17. Which number sentence is in the same fact family as $42 \div 6 = 7$?

A $6 \times 7 = 42$

B $40 + 2 = 42$

C $42 - 7 = 35$

D $6 + 7 = 13$

18. What is the missing number in the number pattern?

81, 72, ▢, 54, 45

F 18 **G** 36 **H** 42 **J** 63

19. John had 32 CDs in his collection. He gave a certain number away to a friend. Now, John has 26 CDs in his collection. What number of CDs did John give away?

A 4 **B** 6 **C** 7 **D** 8

20. Which number completes the last row of the table?

Data

Number of Automobiles	Number of Wheels
2	8
4	16
6	24
8	32
10	▢

21. Writing to Explain One pencil costs 9 cents. Three pencils cost 27 cents. How much would 7 pencils cost? Explain how you found your answer.

Topic 5

Multiplication Number Sense

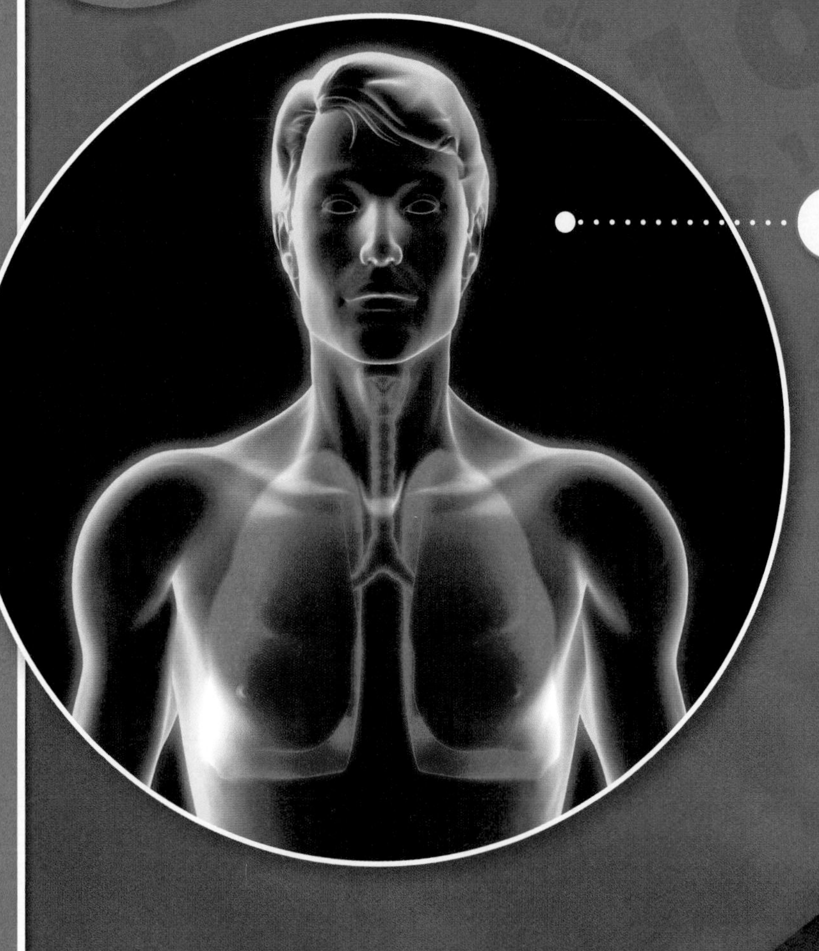

1

How many gallons of air does a student breathe each school day? You will find out in Lesson 5-1.

2

How much longer can a female Texas Brown tarantula live than a male Texas Brown tarantula? You will find out in Lesson 5-3.

3

How long was the longest blue whale? You will find out in Lesson 5-2.

Review What You Know!

Vocabulary

Choose the best term from the box.

- product
- factor
- array
- rounding

1. You multiply numbers to find a ? .
2. In the number sentence $8 \times 6 = 48$, 8 is a ? .
3. When you estimate to the nearest 10 or 100, you may use ? .

Multiplication Facts

Find each product.

4. 5×6
5. 7×3
6. 9×5
7. 6×8
8. 6×4
9. 12×3
10. 8×5
11. 9×9

Rounding

Round each number to the nearest ten.

12. 16
13. 82
14. 35
15. 52
16. 24
17. 96
18. 78
19. 472
20. 119

Round each number to the nearest hundred.

21. 868
22. 499
23. 625
24. 167
25. 772
26. 341
27. 1,372
28. 9,009
29. 919

30. **Writing to Explain** Explain how to round 743 to the hundreds place.

Lesson

5-1

TEKS 4.6B: Use patterns to multiply by 10 and 100. Also TEKS 4.4D: Use multiplication to solve problems.

Multiplying by Multiples of 10 and 100

What is the rule when you multiply by multiples of 10 and 100?

You can use basic multiplication facts to multiply by multiples of 10 and 100. Find 3 × 50.

? in all

Guided Practice*

Do you know HOW?

In **1** through **6**, use basic facts to help you multiply.

1. 7 × 10 **2.** 2 × 100

3. 3 × 20 **4.** 9 × 800

5. 6 × 10 **6.** 8 × 500

Do you UNDERSTAND?

7. How many zeros will be in the product for 5 × 200? Explain how you know.

8. Reasonableness Peter said the product of 4 × 500 is 2,000. Bob said it is 200. Who is correct?

Independent Practice

Leveled Practice In **9** through **32**, find each product.

9. 3 × 7 = ☐
3 × 70 = ☐
3 × 700 = ☐

10. 6 × 4 = ☐
6 × 40 = ☐
6 × 400 = ☐

11. 8 × 5 = ☐
8 × 50 = ☐
8 × 500 = ☐

12. 2 × 8 = ☐
2 × 80 = ☐
2 × 800 = ☐

13. 4 ×20 **14.** 7 × 40 **15.** 70 × 2 **16.** 8 × 60 **17.** 3 × 70

18. 5 × 500 **19.** 3 × 600 **20.** 9 × 700 **21.** 600 × 6 **22.** 100 × 9

23. 5 × 40 **24.** 200 × 6 **25.** 9 × 50 **26.** 900 × 4 **27.** 80 × 3

28. 8 × 70 **29.** 2 × 90 **30.** 300 × 4 **31.** 7 × 100 **32.** 800 × 5

*For another example, see Set A on page 126.

Find 3×50.

Think $3 \times 50 = 3 \times 5 \times 10$

Multiply:
$3 \times 5 = 15$

Write one zero after 15.

$3 \times 5\underline{0} = 15\underline{0}$

So, $3 \times 50 = 150$.

Find 3×500.

Think $3 \times 500 = 3 \times 5 \times 100$

Multiply:
$3 \times 5 = 15$

Write two zeros after 15.

$3 \times 5\underline{00} = 1{,}5\underline{00}$

So, $3 \times 500 = 1{,}500$.

When the product of a basic fact ends in zero, the answer will have an extra zero.

$6 \times 5 = 30$

$6 \times 50 = 300$

$6 \times 500 = 3{,}000$

TAKS Problem Solving

In **33** and **34**, use the table to the right.

Funland Ticket Prices

	Adult	Child
Plan A Waterpark	$30	$20
Plan B Amusement Park	$40	$30
Plan C Combined A + B	$60	$40

33. Tina visited Funland with her mom and a friend. They chose Plan C. How much did they save on the two children's tickets by buying combined tickets instead of buying separate tickets?

34. Aimee's scout troop has 8 girls and 4 adults. How much did the troop pay for tickets to the amusement park?

35. A fourth grader breathes about 50 gallons of air per hour. Shana, a fourth grader, arrives at school at 8:00 A.M. and leaves at 3:00 P.M. How many gallons of air does she breathe at school?

36. Number Sense Without calculating the answer, tell which has the greater product, 4×80 or 8×400. Explain how you know.

37. Last year, the fourth graders at Summit School collected 500 cans of food for the food drive. This year's fourth graders want to collect two times as many cans. How many cans do this year's fourth graders hope to collect?

A 250 cans
B 500 cans
C 1,000 cans
D 10,000 cans

38. Ted, Jason, and Angelina are trying to raise 200 dollars for a local shelter. Ted raised 30 dollars. Jason raised 90 dollars. How much money does Angelina need to raise in order to reach their goal?

Goal: $200

Amount raised: $30 | $90 | ?

Lesson
5-2

TEKS 4.4: Multiply and divide to solve meaningful problems involving whole numbers.

Using Mental Math to Multiply

What are some ways to multiply mentally?

Evan rode his bicycle for 18 miles each day for 3 days. How many miles did he ride his bicycle in all?

Find 3×18 mentally.

DAY 1 | DAY 2 | DAY 3

Guided Practice*

Do you know HOW?

In **1** and **2**, use the breaking apart method to find each product mentally.

1. 6×37 **2.** 51×3

In **3** and **4**, use compatible numbers to find each product mentally.

3. 33×4 **4.** 9×83

Do you UNDERSTAND?

5. Explain how to use mental math to multiply 56×4.

6. How could place-value blocks be used to model the breaking apart method in the example at the top?

You can draw place-value blocks to help you visualize the model.

Independent Practice

Leveled Practice In **7** through **20**, use mental math to find each product.

7. 4×36 Breaking apart: $(4 \times \square) + (4 \times \square) = \square$

8. 6×42 Breaking apart: $(6 \times \square) + (6 \times \square) = \square$

9. 5×17 Compatible numbers: $5 \times \square = 100$ $\square - 15 = \square$

10. 7×29 Compatible numbers: $7 \times \square = 210$ $\square - 7 = \square$

11. 7×28 **12.** 61×8 **13.** 14×5 **14.** 64×3 **15.** 2×58

16. 4×23 **17.** 3×27 **18.** 44×6 **19.** 5×35 **20.** 9×52

DIGITAL Animated Glossary **www.pearsonsuccessnet.com**

*For another example, see Set B on page 126.

One Way

Find 3×18.

Break apart 18 into 10 and 8.

Think of 3×18 as $(3 \times 10) + (3 \times 8)$.

$30 + 24$

Add to find the total.
$30 + 24 = 54$

So, $3 \times 18 = 54$.

Another Way

Compatible numbers are numbers that are easy to work with mentally. Substitute a number for 18 that is easy to multiply by 3.

3×18

↓

$3 \times 20 = 60$

Now adjust. Subtract 2 groups of 3.

$60 - 6 = 54$ So, $3 \times 18 = 54$.

Evan rode his bicycle 54 miles in all.

TAKS Problem Solving

For **21** and **22**, use the table to the right.

21. To raise money, the high school band members sold items shown in the table. Use mental math to find how much money the band raised in all.

Data

Item	Cost	Number Sold
Caps	$9	36
Mugs	$7	44
Pennants	$8	52

22. How much more do 10 caps cost than 10 pennants?

23. **Writing to Explain** Ashley and 3 friends took a bus to the Houston Space Center. The cost of the trip was 43 dollars per person. How much did the trip cost in all? Explain how you found the answer.

Total Cost

$43	$43	$43	$43

↑ Cost per person

24. 

Helen walked 5 miles every day for 37 days. Which choice shows how to find how many miles Helen walked?

A 35×5

B $(40 \times 5) + (3 \times 5)$

C $(5 \times 30) + (5 \times 7)$

D $(30 \times 5) - (3 \times 5)$

25. The height of one scuba diver is about 6 feet. The longest blue whale on record was about 18 scuba divers in length. Use breaking apart to estimate the length of the blue whale.

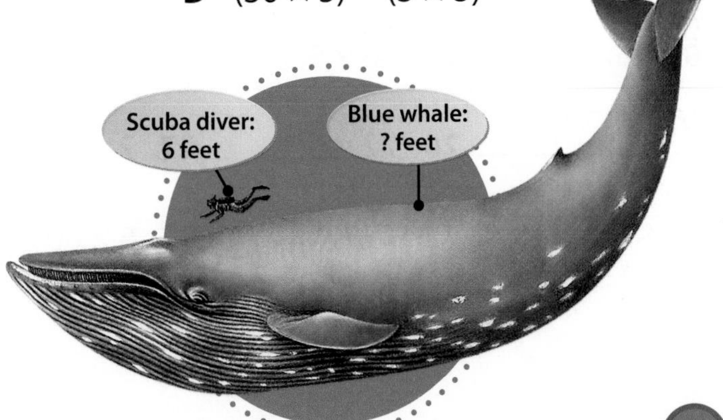

Lesson
5-3

TEKS 4.5B: Use strategies including rounding and compatible numbers to estimate solutions to multiplication and division problems.

Using Rounding to Estimate

How can you use rounding to estimate when you multiply?

Hoover School is holding a Read-a-thon. Any student who raises more than $500 earns a prize. Hector has pledges totaling $4 per page read. Alan has pledges totaling $3 per page read. Both want to know if they will earn a prize.

Hector reads 153 pages

Alan reads 115 pages

Guided Practice*

Do you know HOW?

In **1** through **8**, estimate each product.

1. 6 × 125 **2.** 39 × 5

3. 538 × 3 **4.** 7 × 314

5. 2 × 97 **6.** 4 × 261

7. 63 × 6 **8.** 9 × 48

Do you UNDERSTAND?

9. Is the estimate in Exercise 1 more or less than the actual answer? Explain how you know.

10. Alan collects pledges for 70 more pages. Estimate to see if he will now get a prize.

Independent Practice

Leveled Practice In **11** through **34**, estimate each product.

11. 7 × 34 is close to 7 × ▢ **12.** 6 × 291 is close to 6 × ▢

13. 41 × 9 is close to ▢ × 9 **14.** 814 × 3 is close to ▢ × 3

15. 117 × 4 **16.** 3 × 86 **17.** 9 × 476 **18.** 34 × 6 **19.** 7 × 77

20. 52 × 9 **21.** 46 × 5 **22.** 3 × 287 **23.** 6 × 131 **24.** 602 × 9

25. 354 × 2 **26.** 77 × 8 **27.** 2 × 863 **28.** 44 × 8 **29.** 303 × 5

30. 486 × 7 **31.** 719 × 5 **32.** 6 × 609 **33.** 249 × 4 **34.** 54 × 9

*For another example, see Set C on page 127.

Estimate 4×153 using rounding.

4×153

Round 153 to 150

$4 \times 150 = 600$

Two 150s is 300. Four 150s is 600.
So, 4×153 is about 600.

Hector raised more than 500 dollars.

He has earned a prize.

Estimate 3×115 using rounding.

3×115

Round 115 to 100.

$3 \times 100 = 300$

Alan has raised about 300 dollars.
This is not enough to earn a prize.

TAKS Problem Solving

35. Sam and his 2 brothers want to fly to San Antonio. One airline offers a round trip fare of $319. Another airline has a round trip fare of $389. About how much will Sam and his brothers save by buying the less expensive fare?

36. Male Texas Brown tarantulas can live about 15 years. Female Texas Brown tarantulas can live three times longer. How many years can a female Texas Brown tarantula live?

37. Reasonableness Ellie estimates that the product of 211 and 6 is 1,800. Is this estimate reasonable? Why or why not?

38. Number Sense Which has more pencils, 3 packs with 40 pencils or 40 packs with 3 pencils? Explain.

39. The students at Spring Elementary voted on a school mascot. The bar graph at the right shows the results of the vote.

Which mascot has about 4 times as many votes as the unicorn?

A Lion **C** Dragon

B Owl **D** Bear

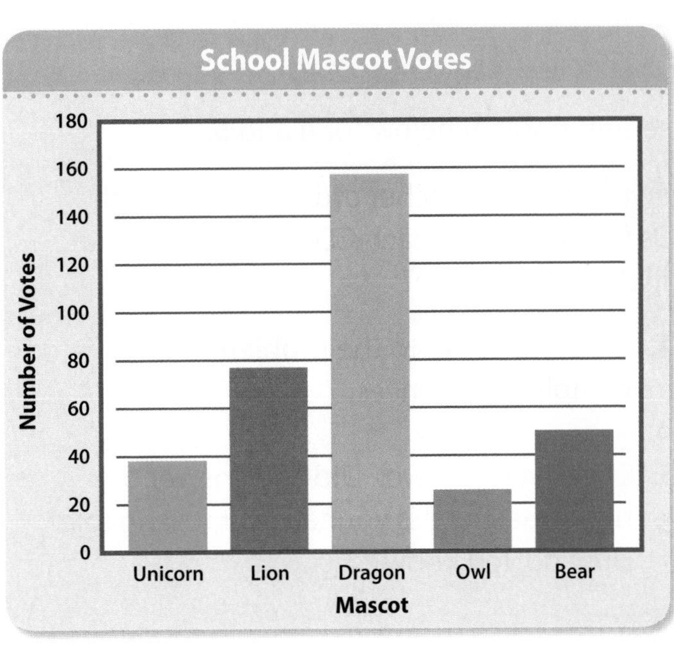

40. Which mascot had the least amount of votes?

Lesson

5-4

TEKS 4.16B: Justify why an answer is reasonable and explain the solution process. Also **TEKS 4.4D:** Use multiplication to solve problems (no more than two-digits times two digits without technology.)

Problem Solving

Reasonableness

Karen glued sequins onto her project. She used 7 rows with 28 sequins in each row. How many sequins did Karen glue in all?

After you solve a problem, check whether your answer is reasonable. Ask yourself: Did I answer the right question? Is the calculation reasonable?

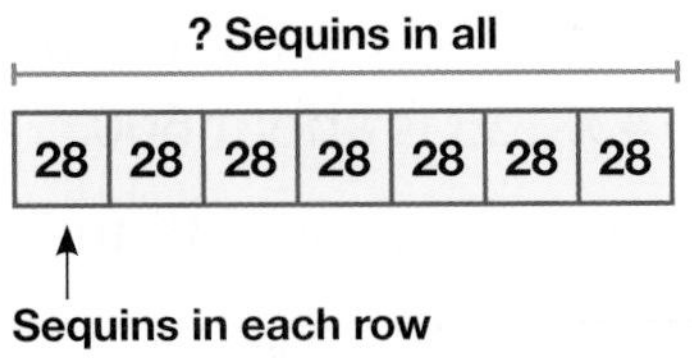

Guided Practice*

Do you know HOW?

Solve and make an estimate to show that your answer is reasonable.

1. A fish store has 8 empty tanks. After a delivery, they put 40 fish in each tank. How many fish were in the delivery?

? in all

40	40	40	40	40	40	40	40

Fish in each tank

Do you UNDERSTAND?

2. In Problem 1, if your estimate was about 40 more than your actual answer, what would you do?

3. **Write a Problem** Write a problem about fish that would have an answer near 80. Then solve and use an estimate to show that your answer is reasonable.

Independent Practice

Use the problem below for **4** and **5**.

Dawn's Spanish teacher ordered 20 Spanish CDs for her class. If each CD costs $9.00, what will the total cost be?

4. Give an answer to the problem using complete sentences.

5. Check your answer. Did you answer the right question? Is your answer reasonable? How do you know?

- What do I know?
- What diagram can I use to help understand the problem?
- Can I use addition, subtraction, multiplication, or division?
- Is all of my work correct?
- Did I answer the right question?
- Is my answer reasonable?

*For another example, see Set D on page 127.

Reasonable

There were 196 sequins in all.

Estimate: $7 \times 30 = 210$.

The answer is reasonable because 210 is close to 196.

The right question was answered and the calculation is reasonable.

Not reasonable

There were 140 sequins in all.

Estimate: $7 \times 20 = 140$.

The answer is not reasonable because 140 is not close to 196.

The right question was answered, but the calculation is not reasonable.

For **6** through **9**, use the problem below.

A plane increases its height at a rate of 400 feet per second.

6. How high will the plane be after 5 seconds?

7. What number sentence did you use to solve the problem?

8. Did you answer the right question?

9. Is your answer reasonable? How do you know?

For **10** through **12**, use the chart.

10. About how much money does an American family spend in 20 weeks to feed a child who is 11 years old?

11. In four weeks, how much more money does a family spend to feed a child who is 8 years old than a child who is 3 years old?

12. Is your answer for Problem 11 reasonable? How do you know?

Data

Money spent by an American Family to Feed a Child

Age of Child	Weekly Amount
3–5 years	$28
6–8 years	$37
9–11 years	$43

Independent Practice

For **13** through **16**, use the chart at the right.

1 [heart] = 10 stickers

13. How many stickers does Mr. Richardson have on rolls?

14. How many more stickers on sheets does Mr. Richardson have than stickers in boxes?

15. Is your calculation for Problem 14 reasonable? How do you know?

16. How many stickers does Mr. Richardson have in all?

17. The distance from Bethany's home to New York City is 180 miles. After Bethany drove 95 miles she said she had traveled over half the distance. Is Bethany correct?

180 miles to New York

95 miles	?

18. On her way from New York City, Bethany stopped for a break after driving 116 miles. How many miles does she have left to drive home?

180 miles to home

116 miles	?

Think About the Process

19. Which of the following uses the Distributive Property to solve the equation 4×9?

A $4 \times 9 = (3 \times 3) + (1 \times 6)$

B $4 \times 9 = (4 \times 9) + (4 \times 9)$

C $4 \times 9 = (2 \times 9) + (2 \times 9)$

D $4 \times 9 = (2 \times 3) + (2 \times 6)$

20. Louisa solved the equation $m - 16 = 54$ and got $m = 38$. Which statement best explains why Louisa's answer is **NOT** reasonable?

F Louisa subtracted incorrectly.

G Louisa forgot to regroup.

H Louisa should have added.

J Louisa forgot that 16 is less than 38.

Multiplying with Mental Math

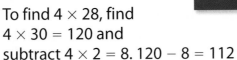

Use eTools Place-Value Blocks

Explain how to use compatible numbers to find 4×28.

Step 1 Go to the Place-Value Blocks eTool. Select the two-part workspace. 30 is the closest number to 28 that is easy to multiply. Click on the horizontal long block. Then click in the top workspace to show 4 rows with 3 longs in each row, or 4×30.

Step 2 Click on the hammer tool icon. Then click on the last long in each row to break each into ten ones. Use the arrow tool to select two ones from the first group, and move them to the bottom workspace. Do the same for the last two ones in each row.

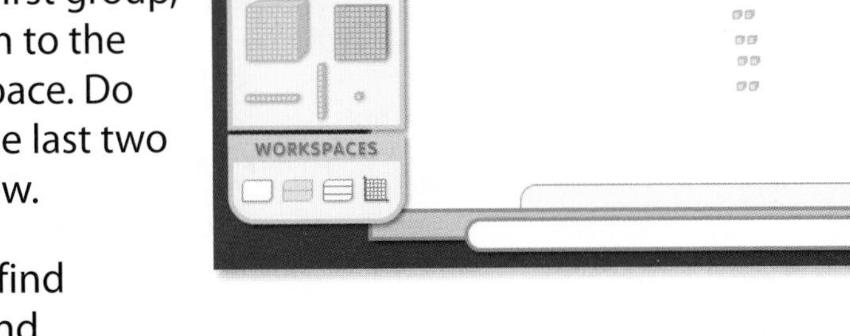

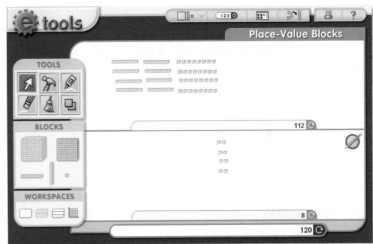

To find 4×28, find $4 \times 30 = 120$ and subtract $4 \times 2 = 8$. $120 - 8 = 112$

So, $4 \times 28 = 112$.

Practice

Use compatible numbers to find each product mentally.

1. 3×19 **2.** 4×18 **3.** 2×67 **4.** 6×29

5. 4×38 **6.** 3×47 **7.** 3×29 **8.** 4×49

9. 2×49 **10.** 3×58 **11.** 4×39 **12.** 2×39

13. 3×27 **14.** 3×28 **15.** 4×47 **16.** 2×48

17. 4×37 **18.** 4×48 **19.** 3×57 **20.** 3×68

21. 2×47 **22.** 3×38 **23.** 4×67 **24.** 4×58

TAKS Test Prep

1. Mrs. Ortiz can make 50 sopapillas out of one batch of dough. If she makes 4 batches of dough, how many sopapillas can she make? (5-1)

   A 8

   B 20

   C 200

   D 2,000

2. Mrs. Henderson bought 4 boxes of facial tissues. Each box has 174 tissues. Which number sentence shows the best way to use rounding to estimate the total number of tissues? (5-3)

   F $4 + 100 = 104$

   G $4 + 200 = 204$

   H $4 \times 100 = 400$

   J $4 \times 200 = 800$

3. Which shows one way to use breaking apart to find 7×32? (5-2)

   A $210 + 14 = 224$

   B $210 + 7 = 217$

   C $210 + 21 = 231$

   D $7 + 32 = 39$

4. A gallon of paint can cover about 400 square feet of wall space. How many square feet of wall space will 3 gallons cover? (5-1)

   F 12

   G 120

   H 1,200

   J 12,000

5. Each photo album can hold 300 photos. How many pictures are in 3 full albums? (5-1)

   A 90

   B 100

   C 900

   D 9,000

6. Which shows one way to use breaking apart to find 4×13? (5-2)

   F $(4 \times 10) + (4 \times 3)$

   G $(4 \times 10) \times (4 \times 3)$

   H $(4 \times 10) + (4 \times 13)$

   J $(2 \times 10) + (2 \times 3)$

7. A local restaurant ordered 8 boxes of toothpicks. Each box contained 800 toothpicks. How many toothpicks did the restaurant order? (5-1)

   A 64

   B 100

   C 640

   D 6,400

8. Ivan gets $22 a week for completing his chores. Which is the best estimate for the amount of money Ivan would have if he saved all his chore money for 6 weeks? (5-3)

   F $120

   G $180

   H $200

   J $1,200

9. The bike trail around Frontier Park is 8 miles long. This month, Ed rode around the trail 18 times. To find 18×8, Ed used compatible numbers and multiplied $20 \times 8 = 160$. What should Ed do next? (5-2)

A $160 - 8 = 152$

B $160 + 8 = 168$

C $160 + 16 = 176$

D $160 - 16 = 144$

10. Susanna's school has 5 grades with an average of 48 students in each grade. Which is a reasonable number of students in Susanna's school? (5-4)

F 205, because 5×48 is about $5 \times 40 = 200$.

G 240, because 5×48 is about $5 \times 50 = 250$.

H 285, because 5×48 is about $5 \times 60 = 300$.

J 315, because 5×48 is about $6 \times 50 = 300$.

11. One serving of soy milk contains 16 grams of sugar. If Mary drank 5 servings of soy milk in one day, how many grams of sugar would she get just from soy milk? Use mental math to solve. (5-2)

A 80

B 75

C 50

D 21

12. There are 52 weeks in a year. If Jean turned 9 today, which is the best estimate of the number of weeks Jean has been alive? (5-3)

F 300

G 350

H 400

J 450

13. Which pair of numbers best completes the number sentence? (5-1)

$\square \times 600 = \square$

A 5 and 30

B 5 and 300

C 5 and 3,000

D 5 and 30,000

14. Quinn finished 32 math facts in a 1 minute drill. At this rate, about how many math facts will he finish in a 3 minute drill? (5-3)

F 60

G 70

H 90

J 120

15. **Griddable Response** Lauren's punch recipe calls for four 64-ounce bottles of juice. Use mental math to find how many ounces of juice are in the punch. (5-2)

Reteaching

Set A, pages 114–115

Use basic multiplication facts to multiply by multiples of 10 and 100.

For a multiple of 10, multiply by the digit in the tens place. Then, write one zero in the product.

Find 4×60 → Multiply $4 \times 6 = 24$.

Write one zero after 24.

$4 \times 60 = 240$

So, $4 \times 60 = 240$.

For a multiple of 100, multiply by the digit in the hundreds place. Then, write two zeros in the product.

Find 4×600 → Multiply $4 \times 6 = 24$.

Write two zeros after 24.

$4 \times 600 = 2{,}400$

So, $4 \times 600 = 2{,}400$.

Remember when the product of a basic fact has a zero, the answer will have an extra zero.

Write the basic fact. Then find the product.

1. 8×60
2. 3×40
3. 6×50
4. 5×300
5. 700×4
6. 2×900
7. 300×7
8. 80×8
9. 100×4
10. 30×6
11. 20×9
12. 9×800
13. 5×70
14. 2×70
15. 300×3
16. 40×9
17. 7×70
18. 500×4

Set B, pages 116–117

One way to multiply mentally is to use compatible numbers.

Find 2×27.

Subtract 2 from 27 to make 25.

$2 \times 25 = 50$

Now adjust. Add 2 groups of 2.

$50 + 4 = 54$

So, $2 \times 27 = 54$.

Remember to check your answer for reasonableness.

Find each product.

1. 6×13
2. 3×46
3. 7×63
4. 9×24
5. 5×87
6. 6×14
7. 2×72
8. 28×6
9. 61×9
10. 49×4
11. 47×6
12. 81×8
13. 5×72
14. 76×4

Set C, pages 118–119

Estimate 9×83.

Round 83 to 80.

9×83
↓
9×80

$9 \times 80 = 720$

9×83 is about 720.

Remember when both rounded numbers are less than the factors they replace, their product will also be less than the product of the factors.

Estimate each product.

1. 8×76
2. 493×3
3. 96×5
4. 678×6
5. 707×4
6. 42×9
7. 148×3
8. 719×9
9. 5×299
10. 6×109
11. 4×253
12. 287×3

Set D, pages 120–122

Ty is making centerpieces for the tables at a banquet. There will be 12 tables with a centerpiece at each table. Each centerpiece needs 5 sheets of construction paper.

What do I know?	There are 12 tables at the banquet. Each centerpiece needs 5 sheets of construction paper.
What am I asked to find?	The number of sheets of construction paper that will be needed to make all the centerpieces.

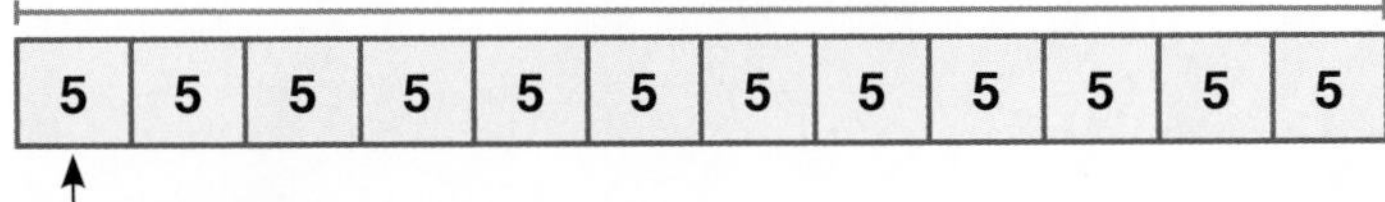

$12 \times 5 = 60$

Estimate to determine if the answer is reasonable.

12 rounds to 10.
$10 \times 5 = 50$

The answer is reasonable because 50 is close to 60.

Remember to check if your answer is reasonable

Solve.

1. Mitchell earns 8 dollars per hour delivering newspapers. How much will Mitchell earn if he works for 10 hours?

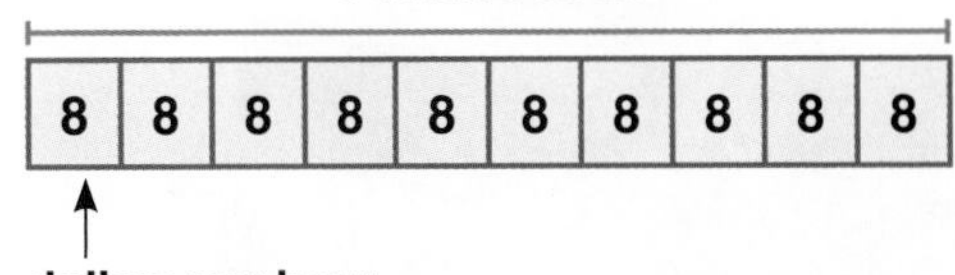

2. Joan needs envelopes. Each pack costs $4. How much will Joan pay for 9 packs of envelopes?

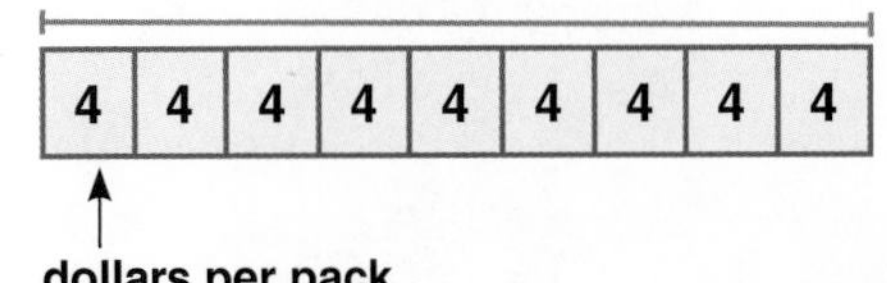

Topic 6 Multiplying by 1-Digit Numbers

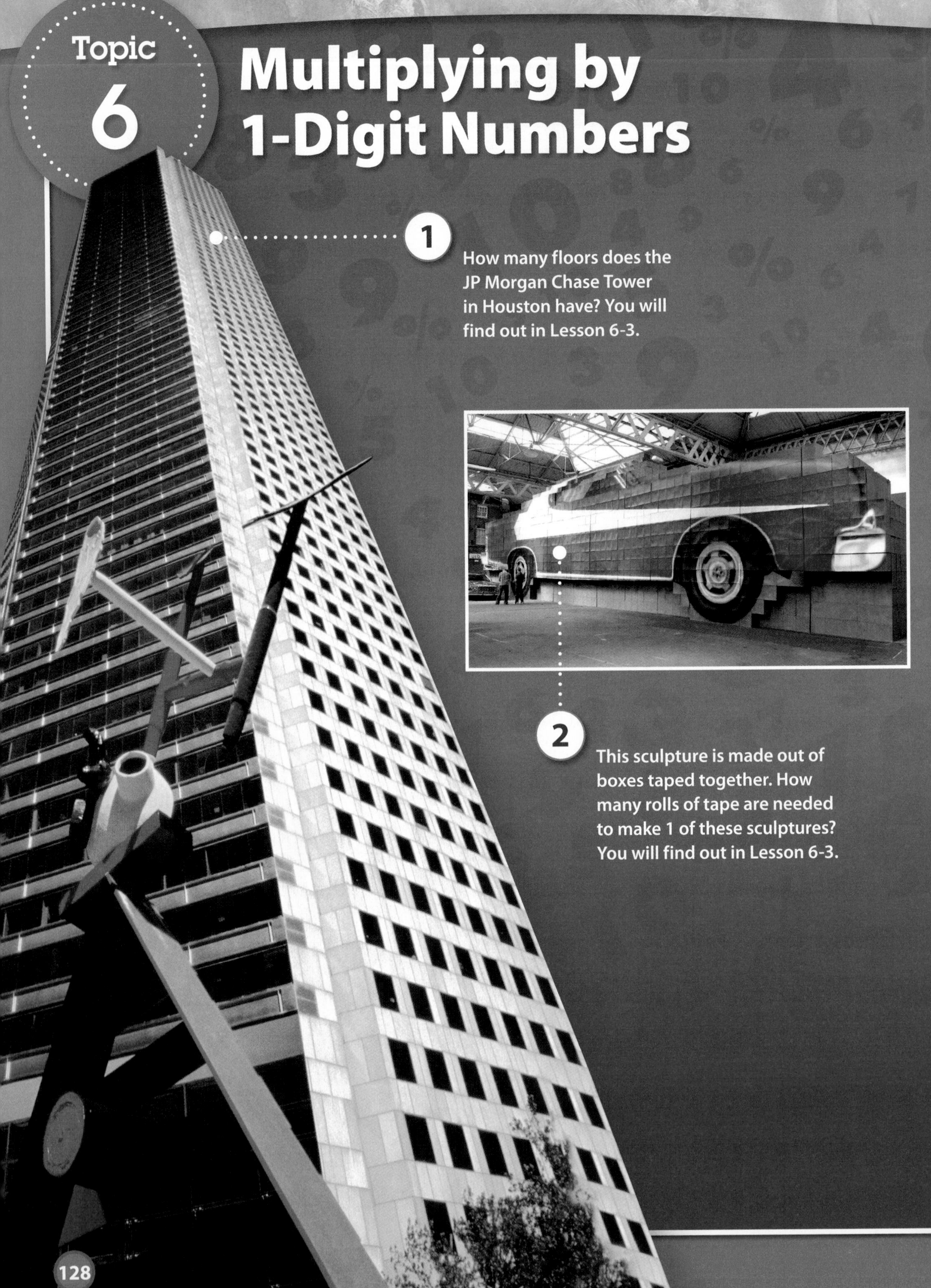

1 How many floors does the JP Morgan Chase Tower in Houston have? You will find out in Lesson 6-3.

2 This sculpture is made out of boxes taped together. How many rolls of tape are needed to make 1 of these sculptures? You will find out in Lesson 6-3.

3

How many passengers can fit in 7 cabins on the London Eye Ferris Wheel? You will find out in Lesson 6-1.

Review What You Know!

Vocabulary

Choose the best term from the box.

- array
- factor
- rounding
- product

1. In the number sentence $4 \times 7 = 28$, 4 is a _?_ and 28 is a _?_.
2. An arrangement of objects in rows and columns is called a(n) _?_.
3. When you estimate, you may use _?_.

Multiplication Facts

Find each product.

4. 8×6
5. 7×5
6. 9×8
7. 8×8
8. 6×9
9. 5×8
10. 4×6
11. 6×5
12. 8×7

Rounding

Round each number to the nearest hundred.

13. 436
14. 1,765
15. 652
16. 149
17. 351
18. 1,999

Arrays

19. Can you write a multiplication number sentence for the array below? Explain.

★ ★ ★ ★ ★ ★
★ ★ ★ ★ ★ ★

20. **Writing to Explain** Is an array for 3×4 the same or different than an array for 4×3? Explain.

6-1

TEKS 4.4A: Model factors and products using arrays and area models.

Breaking Apart Arrays

How can you use arrays to find products?

A display has 4 rows. Each row can hold 23 shampoo bottles. Each bottle is on sale for $6. How many shampoo bottles can the display hold?

Choose an Operation Multiply to find the total for an array.

Guided Practice*

Do you know HOW?

In **1** through **6**, use place-value blocks to build an array. Find the partial products and the product.

1. $3 \times 22 =$ ☐ **2.** $2 \times 17 =$ ☐

3. $5 \times 25 =$ ☐ **4.** $4 \times 21 =$ ☐

5. $2 \times 28 =$ ☐ **6.** $3 \times 14 =$ ☐

Do you UNDERSTAND?

7. In the example above, what are the two number sentences that give the partial products?

8. In the example at the top, what would you pay to buy one row of these shampoo bottles?

Independent Practice

Leveled Practice In **9** through **21**, use place-value blocks or draw a picture to show each array. Find the partial products and the product.

You can draw lines to show tens and Xs to show ones. This picture shows 2 × 28.

———— ———— XXXXXXXX
———— ———— XXXXXXXX

9. $3 \times 24 =$ ☐ Find the partial products: $3 \times 20 =$ ☐ $3 \times 4 =$ ☐
Add the partial products to find the product: $3 \times 24 =$ ☐

10. $2 \times 34 =$ ☐ **11.** $4 \times 26 =$ ☐ **12.** $5 \times 21 =$ ☐ **13.** $5 \times 17 =$ ☐

14. $7 \times 19 =$ ☐ **15.** $3 \times 27 =$ ☐ **16.** $6 \times 25 =$ ☐ **17.** $5 \times 22 =$ ☐

18. $3 \times 18 =$ ☐ **19.** $2 \times 26 =$ ☐ **20.** $4 \times 22 =$ ☐ **21.** $6 \times 16 =$ ☐

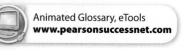

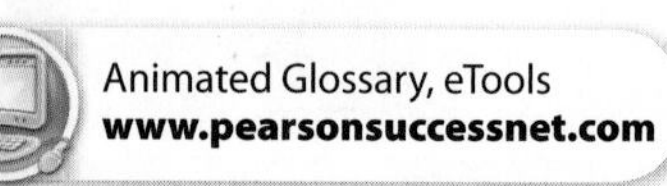

*For another example, see Set A on page 148.

Build an array for 4×23.
Break it into tens and ones. Find how many in each part.

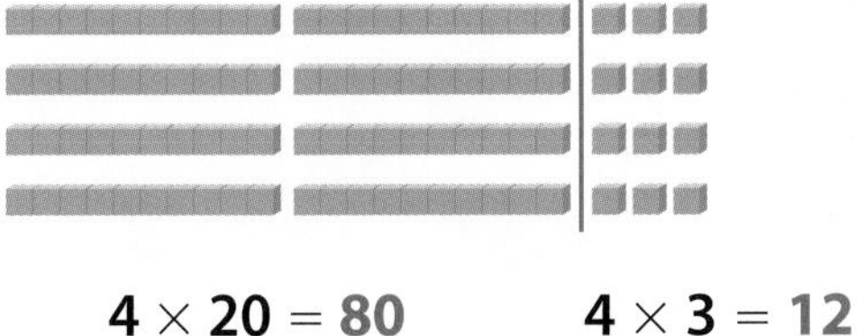

$4 \times 20 = 80$ $4 \times 3 = 12$

Add each part to get the product.

$4 \times 20 = 80$ $4 \times 3 = 12$

$80 + 12 = 92$

80 and **12** are called partial products because they are parts of the product.

The display can hold 92 bottles.

TAKS Problem Solving

22. Algebra Look for patterns in the table. Copy and complete.

x	■	3	4	5	■	9
y	20	60	?	100	140	■

23. Geometry How many 1-foot by 1-foot tiles does it take to cover a rectangular floor that measures 8 tiles on one side and 25 tiles on the other side?

Tip *Draw an array.*

24. Paul's gymnastic scores for his first three events are shown in the table below. He needs a total of 32 points to qualify for the state meet.

a What is the lowest score he can receive on the Horse routine to qualify for the state meet?

b The total time (in seconds) for his routine on the Bars was 12 times the points he earned. What was the total time for the Bars routine?

Data

Paul's Gymnastics Scores	
Vault	8
Bars	8
Floor	7
Horse	
Total	■

25. Each cabin on the London Eye Ferris Wheel can hold up to 25 passengers. How many passengers can 7 cabins hold?

A 150 passengers

B 175 passengers

C 200 passengers

D 225 passengers

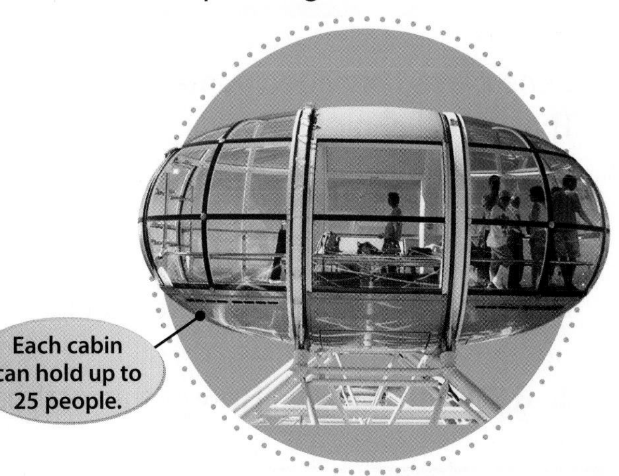
Each cabin can hold up to 25 people.

TEKS 4.4A: Model factors and products using arrays and area models.

Using an Expanded Algorithm

Hands-On
place-value blocks

How can you record multiplication?

A store ordered 2 boxes of video games. How many games did the store order?

Choose an Operation Multiply to join equal groups.

Another Example How do you record multiplication when the product has three digits?

Gene played his new video game 23 times each day for 5 days. How many times did he play his video game in 5 days?

A 18

B 28

C 115

D 145

Choose an Operation Since 5 equal groups of 23 are being joined, you will multiply. Find 5×23.

What You Write

$$\begin{array}{r} 23 \\ \times \quad 5 \\ \hline 15 \\ +\ 100 \\ \hline 115 \end{array}$$

Gene played his video game 115 times in 5 days. The correct choice is **C**.

Explain It

1. Explain how the partial products, 15 and 100, were found in the work above.

2. **Reasonableness** How can an estimate help you eliminate choices above?

What You Show

Build an array to show 2×16.

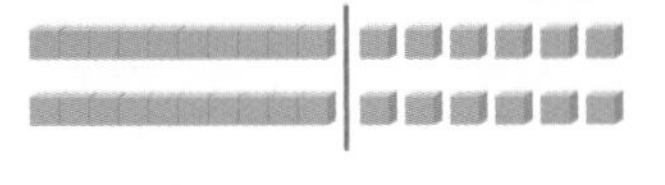

$2 \times 10 = 20$ $2 \times 6 = 12$

$20 + 12 = 32$

What You Write

Here is one way to record multiplication.

```
   16
 x  2
   12  ← Partial
 + 20  ← Products
   32
```

The store ordered 32 games.

Guided Practice*

Do you know HOW?

In **1** and **2**, use place-value blocks or draw pictures to build an array for each. Copy and complete the calculation.

1. $2 \times 34 =$ ▢

```
   34
 × 2
   ▢
 + ▢▢
   ▢▢
```

2. $3 \times 18 =$ ▢

```
   18
 × 3
   ▢▢
 + ▢▢
   ▢▢
```

Do you UNDERSTAND?

Use the array and the calculation shown for Problem 3.

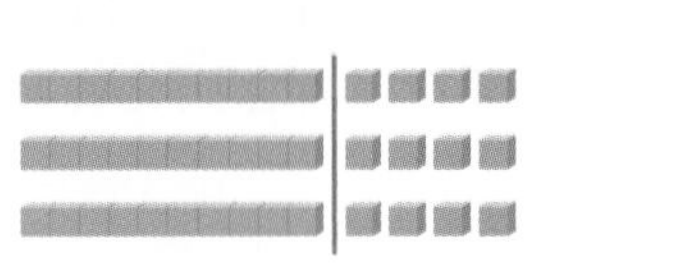

```
   14
 x  3
   12
 + 30
   42
```

3. What calculation was used to give the partial product 12? 30? What is the product of 3×14?

Independent Practice

Leveled Practice In **4** and **5**, use place-value blocks or draw pictures to build an array for each. Copy and complete the calculation.

4.

```
   27
 × 3
   ▢▢
 + ▢▢
   ▢▢
```

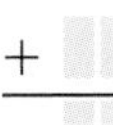

5.

```
   22
 × 4
   ▢
 + ▢▢
   ▢▢
```

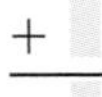

DIGITAL eTools www.pearsonsuccessnet.com

*For another example, see Set B on page 148.

Independent Practice

Leveled Practice In **6** through **15**, copy and complete the calculation. Draw a picture to help.

6. $\begin{array}{r} 26 \\ \times \ \ 5 \\ \hline \square\square \\ + \square\square\square \\ \hline \square\square\square \end{array}$

7. $\begin{array}{r} 18 \\ \times \ \ 3 \\ \hline \square\square \\ + \square\square \\ \hline \square\square \end{array}$

8. $\begin{array}{r} 24 \\ \times \ \ 2 \\ \hline \square \\ + \square\square \\ \hline \square\square \end{array}$

9. $\begin{array}{r} 21 \\ \times \ \ 4 \\ \hline \square \\ + \square\square \\ \hline \square\square \end{array}$

10. $\begin{array}{r} 24 \\ \times \ \ 3 \\ \hline \square\square \\ + \square\square \\ \hline \square\square \end{array}$

11. $\begin{array}{r} 22 \\ \times \ \ 8 \\ \hline \end{array}$

12. $\begin{array}{r} 17 \\ \times \ \ 3 \\ \hline \end{array}$

13. $\begin{array}{r} 24 \\ \times \ \ 8 \\ \hline \end{array}$

14. $\begin{array}{r} 16 \\ \times \ \ 5 \\ \hline \end{array}$

15. $\begin{array}{r} 23 \\ \times \ \ 7 \\ \hline \end{array}$

TAKS Problem Solving

16. Geometry The sides of each of the shapes below are the same whole-number length. Which figure has a perimeter of 64 units? How long is each side?

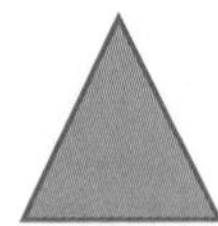

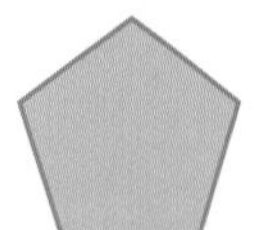

17. Algebra Copy and complete each number sentence.

a $\square \times 14 = A$ where A is greater than 100.

b $\square \times 24 = B$ where B is less than 100.

18. Large tables in the library have 8 chairs and small tables have 4 chairs. How many students can sit at 3 large tables and 5 small tables if each seat is filled?

A 20 students **C** 44 students

B 36 students **D** 52 students

19. Estimation Emma wants to put 3 smiley stickers on each of her note cards. Use estimation to decide if a roll of smileys has enough stickers for 42 note cards.

Type of Sticker	Number of Stickers per Roll
Star	50
Dog	75
Smiley	100
Flower	125

100 stickers

20. Writing to Explain Tim called 3×20 and 3×4 *simple calculations*. Explain what he meant.

Mixed Problem Solving

1. How many miles of track were laid in Texas from 1860 to 1900?

2. How many more people lived in Texas in 1900 than in 1860?

3. How much money would a railroad worker earn in 7 months?

? earnings in all

20	20	20	20	20	20	20

earnings per month

Data

Some Facts About Texas 1860–1900	
Miles of railroad track in 1860	400 miles
Miles of railroad track in 1900	8,000 miles
Population in 1860	400,000 people
Population in 1900	2,000,000 people
Railroad workers wages (26 days of work per month)	$20 per month and food

4. Railroad steam engines traveled at about 60 miles per hour and needed to stop every 30 minutes for water. As a result, many Texas towns are 30 miles apart. Look for patterns in the table below. Copy and complete the table.

Stop	1		5	?	9
Miles traveled	30	90		210	

5. A stamp collector collects stamps with Texas subjects. One page of the album can hold 15 stamps in each of 5 rows. What is the total number of stamps that can fit on one of these pages?

15 stamps

5 rows

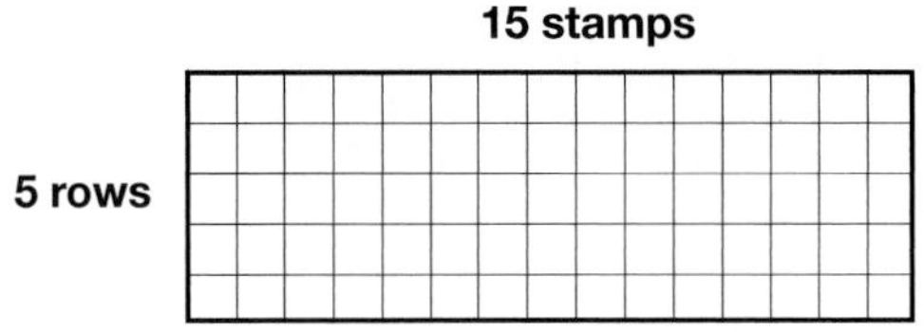

6. On a map of Texas, 1 inch represents 35 miles. How many miles would 5 inches represent on the map?

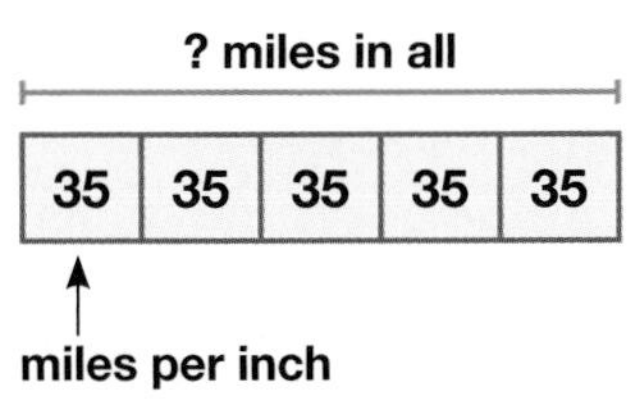

7. **Strategy Focus** Solve using the strategy Draw a Picture.

   A train boxcar has 8 wheels. How many more wheels are on 6 boxcars than on 6 bicycles?

Lesson

6-3

TEKS 4.4D: Use multiplication to solve problems (no more than two digits times two digits without technology).

Multiplying 2-Digit by 1-Digit Numbers

What is a common way to record multiplication?

How many T-shirts with the saying, *and your point is...* are in 3 boxes?

Choose an Operation Multiply to join equal groups.

Saying on T-shirt	Number of T-shirts per Box
Trust Me	30 T-shirts
and your point is...	26 T-shirts
I'm the princess that's why	24 T-shirts
Because I said so	12 T-shirts

Another Example **Does the common way to record multiplication work for larger products?**

Mrs. Stockton ordered 8 boxes of T-shirts with the saying, *I'm the princess that's why.* How many of the T-shirts did she order?

Choose an Operation Since you are joining 8 groups of 24, you will multiply. Find 8×24.

Step 1 Multiply the ones. Regroup if necessary.

$$\begin{array}{r} {}^{3} \\ 24 \\ \times \quad 8 \\ \hline 2 \end{array}$$

$8 \times 4 = 32$ ones
Regroup 32 ones as 3 tens 2 ones

Step 2 Multiply the tens. Add any extra tens.

$$\begin{array}{r} {}^{3} \\ 24 \\ \times \quad 8 \\ \hline 192 \end{array}$$

8×2 tens $= 16$ tens
16 tens $+$ 3 tens $= 19$ tens or 1 hundred 9 tens

Mrs. Stockton ordered 192 T-shirts.

Explain It

1. **Reasonableness** How can you use estimation to decide if 192 is a reasonable answer?
2. In the example above, is it 8×2 or 8×20? Explain.

Remember, one way to multiply is to find partial products.

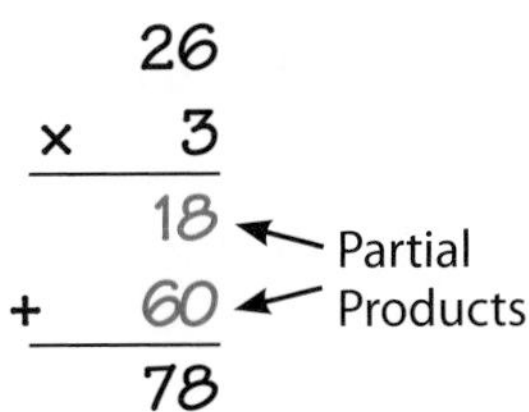

A shortcut for the partial products method is shown at the right.

Step 1

Multiply the ones. Regroup if necessary.

$$\begin{array}{r} {}^{1}\\ 26 \\ \times\ 3 \\ \hline 8 \end{array}$$

Step 2

Multiply the tens. Add any extra tens.

$$\begin{array}{r} {}^{1}\\ 26 \\ \times\ 3 \\ \hline 78 \end{array}$$

There are 78 T-shirts in 3 boxes.

Guided Practice*

Do you know HOW?

Find each product. Estimate to check reasonableness.

1. $\begin{array}{r} 15 \\ \times\ 5 \\ \hline \end{array}$

2. $\begin{array}{r} 28 \\ \times\ 3 \\ \hline \end{array}$

3. $\begin{array}{r} 34 \\ \times\ 7 \\ \hline \end{array}$

4. $\begin{array}{r} 43 \\ \times\ 4 \\ \hline \end{array}$

5. 5×70

6. 5×78

7. 3×24

8. 3×79

Do you UNDERSTAND?

9. Explain how you would estimate the answer in Exercise 3.

10. Carrie bought 8 boxes of T-shirts with the saying *Because I said so.* How many T-shirts did Carrie buy?

11. **Writing to Explain** Explain how the answer to Exercise 5 can be used to find the answer to Exercise 6.

Independent Practice

Find each product. Estimate to check reasonableness.

12. $\begin{array}{r} 12 \\ \times\ 6 \\ \hline \end{array}$

13. $\begin{array}{r} 18 \\ \times\ 7 \\ \hline \end{array}$

14. $\begin{array}{r} 72 \\ \times\ 5 \\ \hline \end{array}$

15. $\begin{array}{r} 49 \\ \times\ 8 \\ \hline \end{array}$

16. $\begin{array}{r} 31 \\ \times\ 4 \\ \hline \end{array}$

17. $\begin{array}{r} 52 \\ \times\ 6 \\ \hline \end{array}$

18. $\begin{array}{r} 79 \\ \times\ 7 \\ \hline \end{array}$

19. $\begin{array}{r} 87 \\ \times\ 7 \\ \hline \end{array}$

*For another example, see Set C on page 148.

Find each product. Estimate to check reasonableness.

20. 9×23	**21.** 6×51	**22.** 4×29	**23.** 8×42
24. 3×64	**25.** 5×56	**26.** 6×83	**27.** 4×47
28. 3×25	**29.** 2×43	**30.** 2×73	**31.** 9×26

TAKS Problem Solving

32. Use the diagram to the right. How many floors does the JP Morgan Chase Tower have if it has 5 times as many floors as a 15-story office building?

A 60 **B** 75 **C** 105 **D** 1,010

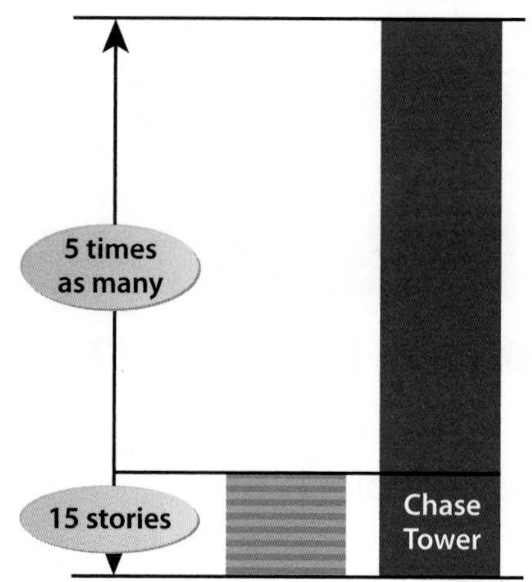

33. Estimation It takes 286 rolls of tape to make a car sculpture made of boxes. What is this number rounded to the nearest hundred?

F 200 **H** 300

G 280 **J** 380

34. Think About the Process Katie made 24 rag dolls. She gave away 8 of them as gifts. Which expression gives the number of rag dolls Katie had left?

A $24 + 8$

B 24×8

C $24 - 8$

D $24 \div 8$

35. A skateboard speed record of almost 63 miles per hour (about 92 feet per second) was set in 1998. At that speed about how many feet would the skateboarder travel in 6 seconds?

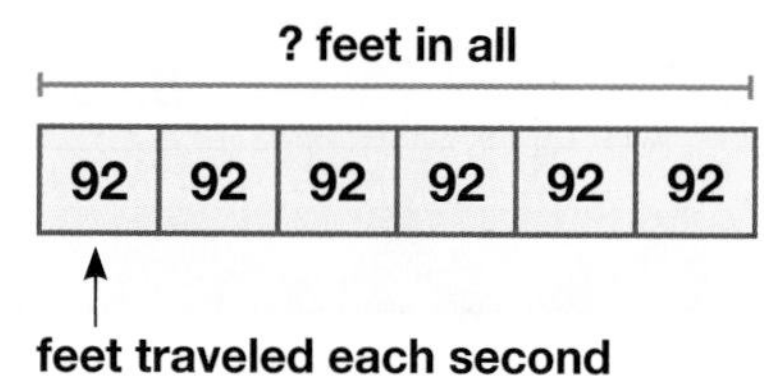

For **36** and **37**, use the table to the right.

36. What is the average length fingernails will grow in one year?

F 60 mm **H** 40 mm

G 50 mm **J** 5 mm

Data

Average Rate of Growth per Month	
Fingernails	5 mm
Hair	12 mm

37. How much longer will hair grow than fingernails in one year?

Algebra Connections

Multiplication and Number Sentences

Remember that a number sentence has two numbers or expressions connected by $<$, $>$, or $=$. Estimation or reasoning can help you tell if the left side or right side is greater.

Copy and complete. Write $<$, $>$, or $=$ in the circle. Check your answers.

Remember
$>$ *is greater than* $<$ *is less than* $=$ *is equal to*

Example: $7 \times 52 \bigcirc 7 \times 60$

Think *Is 7 groups of 52 more than 7 groups of 60?*

Since 52 is less than 60, the left side is less. Write "$<$".

$7 \times 52 \; (<) \; 7 \times 60$

1. $5 \times 71 \bigcirc 5 \times 70$ **2.** $8 \times 30 \bigcirc 8 \times 35$ **3.** $2 \times 90 \bigcirc 89 + 89$

4. $4 \times 56 \bigcirc 200$ **5.** $6 \times 37 \bigcirc 37 \times 6$ **6.** $190 \bigcirc 9 \times 25$

7. $3 \times 33 \bigcirc 100$ **8.** $80 \bigcirc 4 \times 19$ **9.** $10 \times 10 \bigcirc 9 \times 8$

10. $1 \times 67 \bigcirc 1 + 67$ **11.** $2 + 34 \bigcirc 2 \times 34$ **12.** $6 \times 18 \bigcirc 7 \times 20$

For **13** and **14**, copy and complete the number sentence below each problem. Use it to help explain your answer.

13. A red tray holds 7 rows of oranges with 8 oranges in each row. A blue tray holds 8 rows of oranges with 5 oranges in each row. Which tray holds more oranges?

____ × ____ ◯ ____ × ____

14. Look at the hats below. Mr. Fox bought 2 brown hats. Mrs. Lee bought 3 green hats. Who paid more for their hats?

____ × ____ ◯ ____ × ____

15. Write a Problem Write a real-world problem using one of the number sentences in Exercises 1 to 6.

Lesson

6-4

TEKS 4.4D: Use multiplication to solve problems (no more than two digits times two digits without technology).

Multiplying 3-Digit by 1-Digit Numbers

How do you multiply larger numbers?

Juan guessed that the large bottle had 3 times as many pennies as the small bottle. What was Juan's guess?

Choose an Operation Multiply to find "3 times as many."

Guided Practice*

Do you know HOW?

In **1** through **4**, find each product. Estimate to decide if the answer is reasonable.

1. 519×4

2. 337×2

3. 181×9

4. 6×268

Do you UNDERSTAND?

5. **Number Sense** In the example at the top, 3×6 tens is how many tens?

6. Sue guessed the large bottle had 8 times as many pennies as the small bottle. What was Sue's guess?

Independent Practice

Find each product. Estimate to check reasonableness.

7. 423×2

8. 506×4

9. 821×3

10. 159×5

11. 624×7

12. 124×6

13. 281×9

14. 114×7

15. 2×256

16. 3×300

17. 3×649

18. 5×410

19. 2×125

20. 3×310

21. 4×265

22. 5×412

*For another example, see Set D on page 149.

Step 1

Multiply the ones.
Regroup if needed.

$$\begin{array}{r} {}^{1} \\ 264 \\ \times \quad 3 \\ \hline 2 \end{array}$$

3×4 ones $= 12$ ones
or 1 ten 2 ones

Step 2

Multiply the tens.
Add any extra tens.
Regroup if needed.

$$\begin{array}{r} {}^{1\,1} \\ 264 \\ \times \quad 3 \\ \hline 92 \end{array}$$

$(3 \times 6$ tens$) + 1$ ten $= 19$ tens
or 1 hundred 9 tens

Step 3

Multiply the hundreds.
Add any extra hundreds.

$$\begin{array}{r} {}^{1\,1} \\ 264 \\ \times \quad 3 \\ \hline 792 \end{array}$$

$(3 \times 2$ hundreds$) + 1$ hundred
$= 7$ hundreds

Juan's guess was 792 pennies.

TAKS Problem Solving

In **23** through **25**, find the weight of the animal.

23. Horse

24. Rhino

25. Elephant

Bear:
Weighs
836 pounds

Horse:
Weighs 2 times as
much as the bear

Rhino:
Weighs 5 times as
much as the bear

Elephant:
Weighs 9 times as
much as the bear

26. Algebra What did Mr. Sims buy at the electronics sale if $(3 \times \$129) + \$180$ stands for the total price?

27. Number Sense Which costs more—2 laptop computers or 4 picture phones? Use number sense to decide.

Data

Electronics Sale	
Digital Camera	$295
Laptop Computer	$420
DVD Player	$129
Picture Phone	$180

28. Think About the Process Which tells how to find the total cost of a laptop computer and 5 digital cameras?

A $5 \times \$420 \times \$295$

B $(5 \times \$420) + \$295$

C $\$420 + \$295 + 5$

D $\$420 + (5 \times \$295)$

Lesson

6-5

TEKS 4.14B: Solve problems that incorporate understanding the problem, making a plan, carrying out the plan, and evaluating the solution for reasonableness. Also TEKS 4.14C

Problem Solving

Draw a Picture and Write an Equation

Pocket bikes are a lot smaller than cars but many can go 35 miles per hour. The length of the family car in the table to the right is 5 times the length of the pocket bike. How long is the family car?

	Pocket Bike Model 235	Family Car
Height (seat)	19 inches	?
Length	38 inches	?
Weight	39 pounds	3,164 lbs

Guided Practice*

Do you know HOW?

Solve.

1. Fran paid $8 a week for gasoline for her Superbike. How much did she pay for gasoline for 6 weeks?

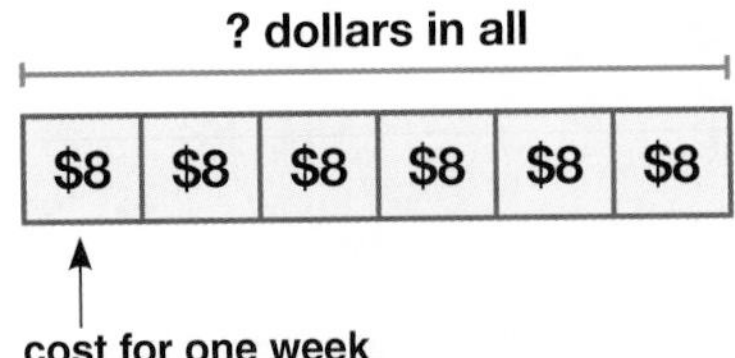

Do you UNDERSTAND?

2. What operation was needed to solve Problem 1? Tell why.

3. **Write a Problem** Write a problem that you can solve by
   - **a** adding.
   - **b** multiplying.

Independent Practice

Solve. Tell the operation or operations used.

4. Police officers walk about 1,632 miles per year. Mail carriers walk about 1,056 miles per year. About how many more miles does a police officer walk in a year than a mail carrier?

1,632 miles per year

1,056	?

$1{,}632 - 1{,}056 = ?$

5. On David's map, each half inch represents 13 miles. The airport is 2 inches from the state park. How many miles is this?

- What do I know?
- What diagram can I use to help understand the problem?
- Can I use addition, subtraction, multiplication, or division?
- Is all of my work correct?
- Did I answer the right question?
- Is my answer reasonable?

*For another example, see Set E on page 149.

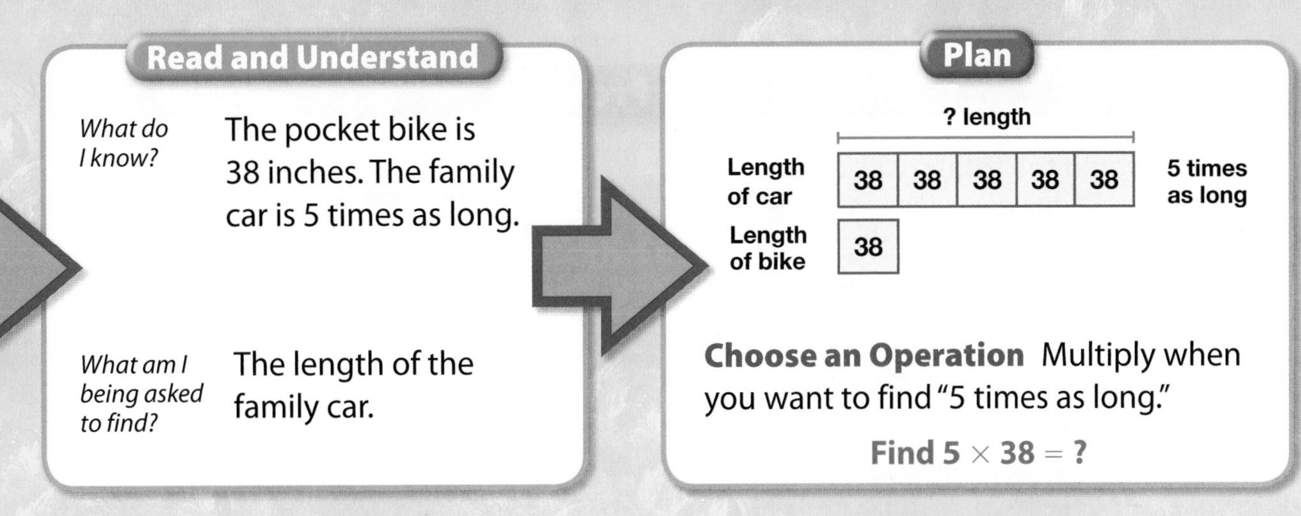

Read and Understand
What do I know?
The pocket bike is 38 inches. The family car is 5 times as long.
What am I being asked to find?
The length of the family car.
Plan
? length
Length of car
38
38
38
38
38
5 times as long
Length of bike
38
Choose an Operation Multiply when you want to find "5 times as long."
Find 5 × 38 = ?

6. In 1990, a high-school class in Indiana made a very large yo-yo. It weighed 6 times as much as a student who weighed 136 pounds. What was the weight of the yo-yo?

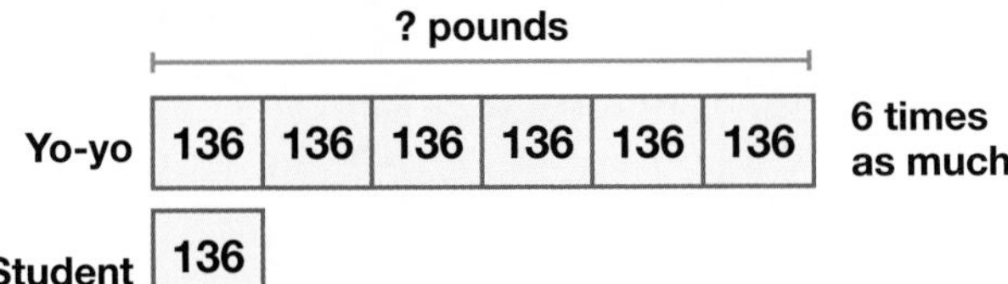

7. Yo-yos first appeared in the United States in 1866, but the name "yo-yo" was first used 50 years later. It is probably from a Filipino word for "come-come" or "to return." In what year did the toy get the "yo-yo" name?

8. What is the distance around (perimeter) the playground shown to the right?

9. If the length of this park at the right was increased by 10 feet, what is the new perimeter?

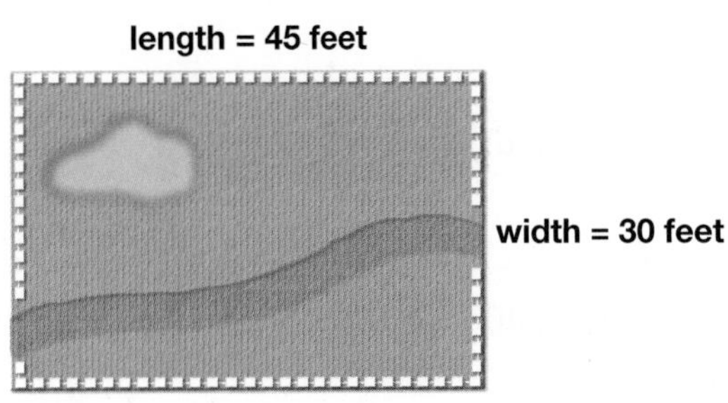

10. At a large dog show, there were 45 entries for each of the breeds in the chart at the right. What is the total number of dogs in this show?

11. A chihuahua weighs 6 pounds. A Great Pyrenees weighs 17 times as much. What is the weight of the Great Pyrenees dog?

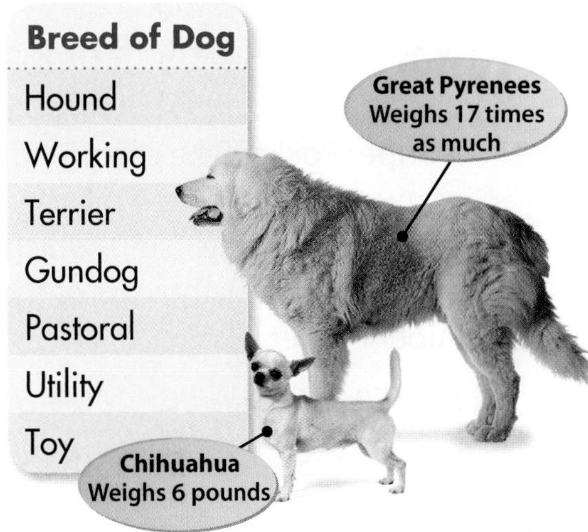

Breed of Dog
Hound
Working
Terrier
Gundog
Pastoral
Utility
Toy

Independent Practice

12. What would the total cost be for 3 round-trip tickets to Los Angeles?

The prices in the table are one way!

Destination	One-Way Price
Chicago	$296
New York	$239
Los Angeles	$349
Orlando	$189
Hawaii	$625

13. How much less does a one-way ticket to Orlando cost than a one-way ticket to Chicago?

$296

$189	?

14. Use the data to the right. How much more is a ton of dimes worth than a ton of pennies?

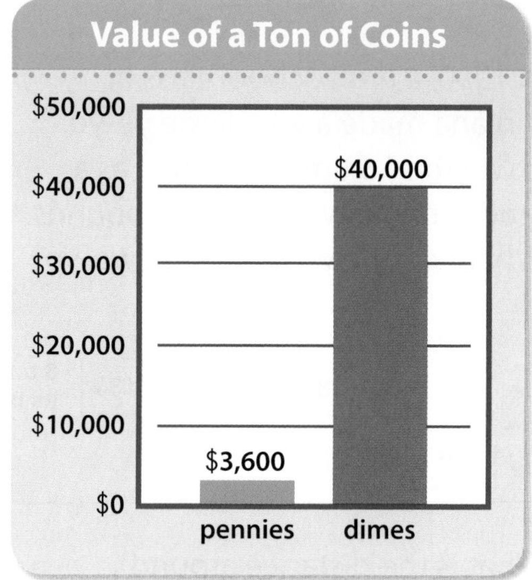

15. Four friends shared the cost of a boat ride. The total cost for the ride was $28. How much did each friend pay?

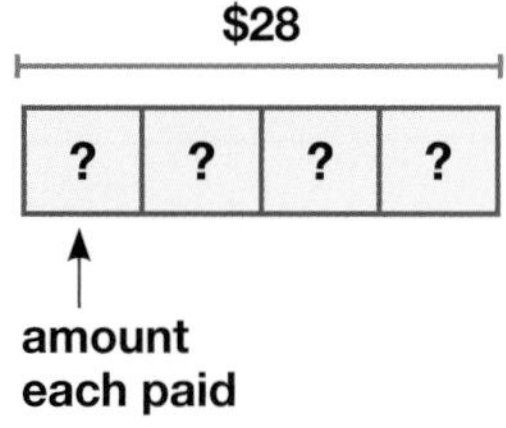

16. A food cart on an airplane has 6 slots. Each slot holds 2 food trays. How many trays are in 8 food carts?

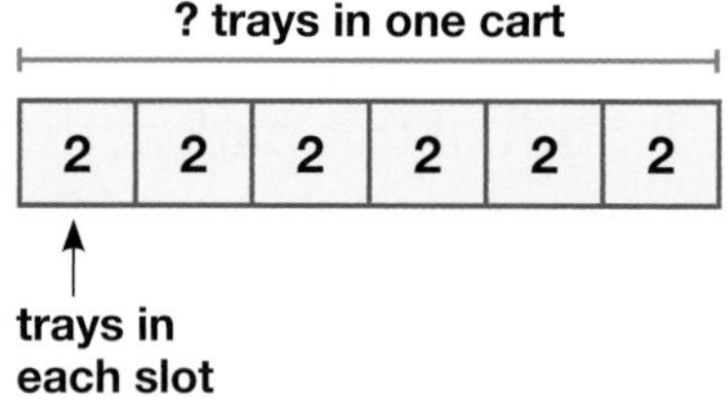

Think About the Process

17. A Super Pocket Bike costs 5 times as much as a 10-speed bicycle. If the bicycle costs $150, which expression gives the cost of the Super Pocket Bike?

A $150 - 5$ **C** $150 + 5$

B 150×5 **D** $150 \div 5$

18. Tickets for a movie cost $8 for an adult and $6 for a child. Wally is buying 2 adult tickets and 1 child ticket. Which expression can be used to find the total?

F $8 + 6 + 2 + 1$ **H** $8 + 6$

G $(2 \times 8) + (2 \times 6)$ **J** $(2 \times 8) + 6$

Operations on a Calculator

Jamie made 4 trips between Houston and Wichita Falls this summer. Each trip was 379 miles. How many miles were the 4 trips in all?

In September, Jamie traveled 379 miles from Wichita Falls to Houston, 244 miles from Houston to Dallas, and 137 miles from Dallas back to Wichita Falls. How many miles did Jamie travel in September?

Step 1 Draw a picture and choose an operation for the first question.

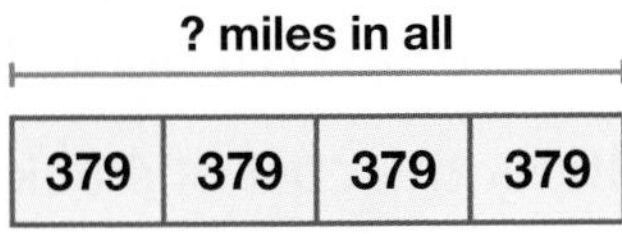

Multiply 4×379

Step 2 Press: 4 [×] 379 [ENTER =]

Display: 1516

Jamie's four trips were 1,516 miles in all.

Step 1 Draw a picture and choose an operation for the second question.

? miles in all

379	244	137

Add $379 + 244 + 137$

Step 2 Press: 379 [+] 244 [+] 137 [ENTER =]

Display: 760

Jamie traveled 760 miles in September.

Practice

For each problem, draw a picture, choose an operation, and solve.

1. How much farther did Jamie travel from Wichita Falls to Houston than from Houston to Dallas?

2. How many miles would Jamie travel if she went from Wichita Falls to Dallas and back to Wichita Falls?

TAKS Test Prep

1. Which product is shown by the following array? (6-1)

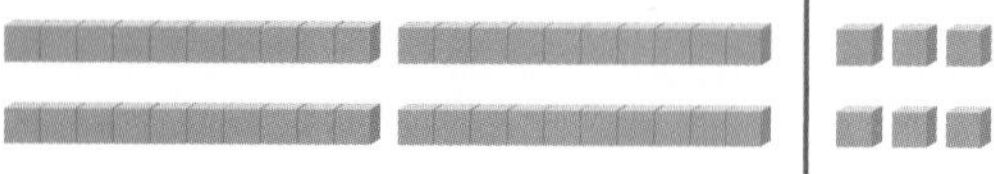

A $2 + 23$

B 2×20

C 2×23

D 2×40

2. Wally has 80 pennies. He put the pennies in stacks with the same number in each stack. Which arrangement is **NOT** possible, if Wally used all of the pennies? (6-3)

F 8 stacks of 10 pennies

G 16 stacks of 5 pennies

H 20 stacks of 4 pennies

J 6 stacks of 15 pennies

3. Ali ran for 19 minutes 7 days in a row. How many minutes did Ali run? (6-2)

A 26 minutes

B 70 minutes

C 106 minutes

D 133 minutes

4. Ray cut 6 pieces of rope. Each piece was between 67 and 84 inches long. Which could be the total length of the 6 pieces of rope? (6-3)

F 360 inches

G 390 inches

H 480 inches

J 540 inches

5. Jude used the table below to find the total price of tickets to a concert. How would Jude find the price of 8 tickets? (6-3)

Data

Tickets			
Number of tickets	3	4	6
Cost of tickets	\$51	\$68	\$102

A Add the total cost of the tickets

B Multiply the cost of 4 tickets by 2

C Subtract the cost of 6 tickets from the cost of 2 tickets

D Multiply the cost of 3 tickets by 3

6. The Lopez family plans to drive 500 miles. They have traveled 346 miles. How can they find how much farther they need to drive? (6-5)

500	
346	?

F Add 500 to 346

G Subtract 346 from 500

H Multiply 346 by 500

J Multiply 500 by 12

7. A school has 478 students. Each student was given 3 sheets of paper with information. Which of the following describes a reasonable number of sheets needed in all? (6-4)

A Between 120 and 150 sheets

B Between 1,000 and 1,100 sheets

C Between 1,200 and 1,500 sheets

D Between 1,600 and 2,000 sheets

8. Each movie theater has 278 seats. Which number sentence can be used to find the number of seats in 3 movie theaters? (6-5)

? Seats in all

278	278	278

F $3 \times 278 = \square$

G $278 + 278 = \square$

H $278 + 3 = \square$

J $278 - 3 = \square$

9. Use the picture below to find 2×24. (6-1)

A 12

B 28

C 40

D 48

10. A factory produced 275 cars in a week. At this rate, how many cars would the factory produce in 4 weeks? (6-4)

F 880 cars

G 1,000 cars

H 1,100 cars

J 8,300 cars

11. Nia has 5 piles with 48 paper clips in each. How many paper clips are there in all? (6-3)

A 340 paper clips

B 240 paper clips

C 140 paper clips

D 60 paper clips

12. The array shows 3×32. Which partial products are shown in the array? (6-1)

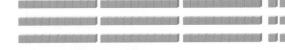

F 3 and 6

G 30 and 2

H 30 and 6

J 90 and 6

13. Part of the calculation for 3×26 is shown below. What partial product should replace $\square\square$? (6-2)

$$\begin{array}{r} 26 \\ \times \quad 3 \\ \hline \square\square \\ 60 \\ \hline 78 \end{array}$$

A 8

B 18

C 20

D 60

14. Blane earned 230 points playing a video game. Jane earned 7 times as many points as Blane. How many points did Jane earn? (6-4)

F 1,610 points

G 1,421 points

H 1,410 points

J 161 points

15. **Griddable Response** Each of 6 boxes weighs 67 ounces. What is the total weight of the boxes in ounces? (6-3)

Reteaching

Set A, pages 130–131

Build an array for 5 × 26. Break it into tens and ones. Find how many in each part.

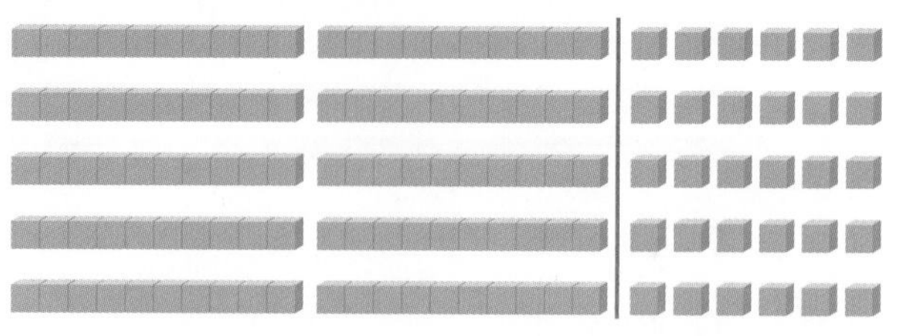

5 × 20 = 100 5 × 6 = 30

100 + 30 = 130

Remember partial products are parts of the product.

Use place-value blocks or draw a picture to show each array. Find the partial products and the product.

1. 4 × 27
2. 3 × 22
3. 5 × 16
4. 2 × 17
5. 3 × 29
6. 5 × 19

Set B, pages 132–134

Find 4 × 12.

Use blocks or draw a picture to build an array.

$$\begin{array}{r} 12 \\ \times\ 4 \\ \hline 8 \\ 40 \\ \hline 48 \end{array}$$

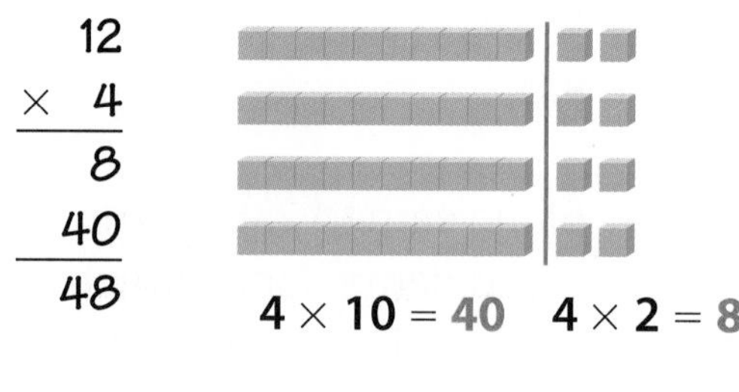

4 × 10 = 40 4 × 2 = 8

40 + 8 = 48

Remember to check that your picture accurately shows the numbers that are being multiplied.

1. $\begin{array}{r} 22 \\ \times\ 6 \\ \hline \end{array}$
2. $\begin{array}{r} 28 \\ \times\ 3 \\ \hline \end{array}$
3. $\begin{array}{r} 75 \\ \times\ 5 \\ \hline \end{array}$
4. $\begin{array}{r} 53 \\ \times\ 4 \\ \hline \end{array}$
5. $\begin{array}{r} 88 \\ \times\ 2 \\ \hline \end{array}$
6. $\begin{array}{r} 21 \\ \times\ 6 \\ \hline \end{array}$

Set C, pages 136–138

Find 5 × 13.

Step 1

Multiply the ones. Regroup if necessary.

$$\begin{array}{r} ^{1} \\ 13 \\ \times\ 5 \\ \hline 5 \end{array}$$

Step 2

Multiply the tens. Add any extra tens.

$$\begin{array}{r} ^{1} \\ 13 \\ \times\ 5 \\ \hline 65 \end{array}$$

5 × 13 = 65

Remember that you can use an array to help you multiply. Check your answer with an estimate.

1. $\begin{array}{r} 18 \\ \times\ 2 \\ \hline \end{array}$
2. $\begin{array}{r} 48 \\ \times\ 5 \\ \hline \end{array}$
3. $\begin{array}{r} 33 \\ \times\ 6 \\ \hline \end{array}$
4. $\begin{array}{r} 97 \\ \times\ 7 \\ \hline \end{array}$
5. $\begin{array}{r} 62 \\ \times\ 4 \\ \hline \end{array}$
6. $\begin{array}{r} 25 \\ \times\ 8 \\ \hline \end{array}$

Set D, pages 140–141

Find 768 × 6.

Step 1

Multiply the ones. Regroup if necessary.

$$\begin{array}{r} {}^{4}\\ 768 \\ \times \quad 6 \\ \hline 8 \end{array}$$

Step 2

Multiply the tens. Add any extra tens. Regroup if necessary.

$$\begin{array}{r} {}^{4\,4}\\ 768 \\ \times \quad 6 \\ \hline 08 \end{array}$$

Step 3

Multiply the hundreds. Add any extra hundreds.

$$\begin{array}{r} {}^{4\,4}\\ 768 \\ \times \quad 6 \\ \hline 4{,}608 \end{array}$$

Remember to check your answer with an estimate.

1. $\begin{array}{r} 239 \\ \times \quad 4 \\ \hline \end{array}$
2. $\begin{array}{r} 148 \\ \times \quad 5 \\ \hline \end{array}$
3. $\begin{array}{r} 233 \\ \times \quad 6 \\ \hline \end{array}$
4. $\begin{array}{r} 907 \\ \times \quad 7 \\ \hline \end{array}$
5. $\begin{array}{r} 261 \\ \times \quad 4 \\ \hline \end{array}$
6. $\begin{array}{r} 250 \\ \times \quad 8 \\ \hline \end{array}$

Set E, pages 142–144

An orchard has 3 times as many apple trees as cherry trees. If there are 52 cherry trees, how many apple trees are there?

What do I know? There are 52 cherry trees. There are 3 times as many apple trees.

What am I being asked to find? The number of apple trees

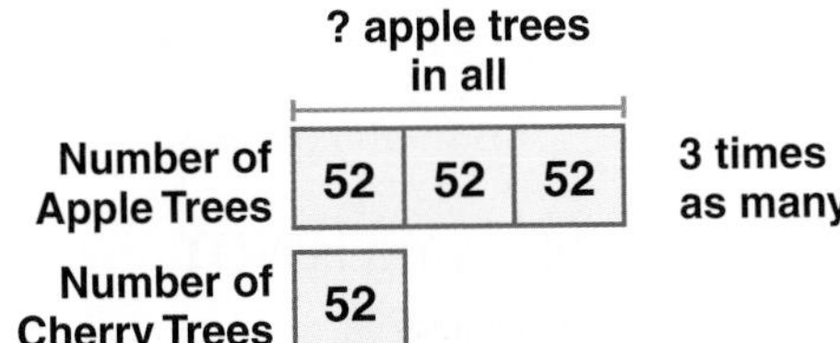

Choose an Operation Multiply when you want to find "times as many."

$3 \times 52 = 156$

There are 156 apple trees.

Remember to draw a picture to help you solve a problem.

1. There are 24 hours in one day. How many hours are in one week?

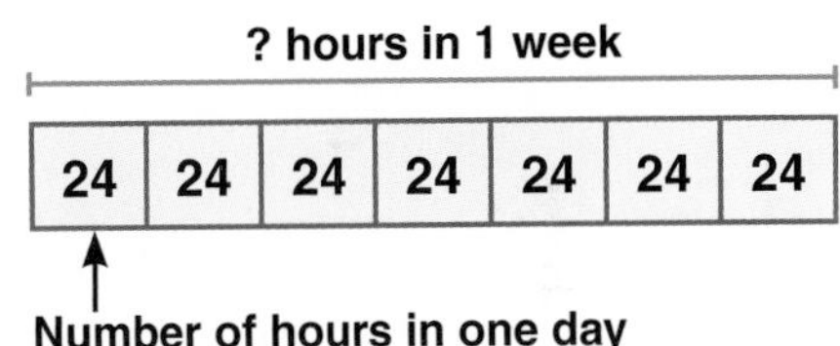

2. An office ordered 6 copy machines. Each machine weighed 108 pounds. Find the total weight of the order.

3. Celia has four weeks to save $58 for her vacation. In her first week, she saved $10, the second week, $21, and the third week, $17. How much more does she need to save?

Topics 1–6

Spiral Review

Number and Operations

1. What is three million, ninety-eight thousand, four hundred five written in standard form?

A 39,845

B 3,098,405

C 3,098,450

D 3,980,405

2. Estimate 6,742 – 2,938.

F 2,000

G 3,000

H 4,000

J 5,000

3. What is the quotient of 54 ÷ 9?

A 5

B 6

C 9

D 45

4. Write this number in standard form.

$8 \times 1{,}000 + 5 \times 100 + 6 \times 10$

5. Write these numbers in order from least to greatest.

75,175 75,715 75,571 75,751

6. Round 27,649 to the nearest thousand.

7. Carlos bought a camera for $28.75 and two rolls of film for $4.50 each. How much did Carlos spend in all?

8. **Writing to Explain** Explain how you can break numbers apart to find the product 8 × 12.

Geometry and Measurement

9. Which of these figures has a line of symmetry drawn through it?

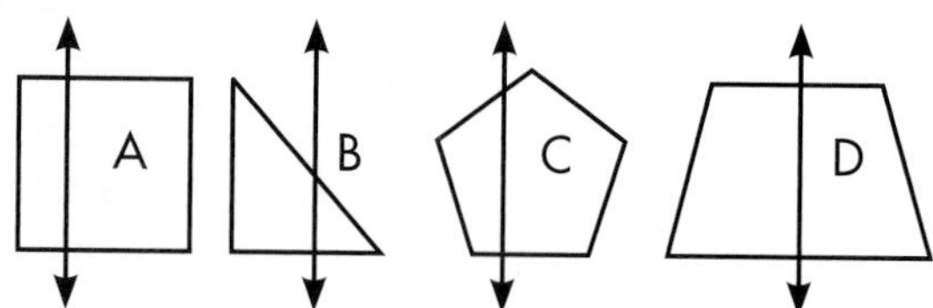

F Figure A

G Figure B

H Figure C

J Figure D

10. What time is shown on the clock?

A 2:35

B 6:10

C 7:10

D 7:35

11. Find the date 3 weeks after May 3.

12. A rectangle is 8 inches long and 5 inches wide. What is the perimeter of the rectangle?

F 3 inches

G 13 inches

H 26 inches

J 40 inches

13. Which of the following is **NOT** greater than 5 weeks?

A 1 month

B 4 weeks 10 days

C 40 days

D 2 months

14. **Writing to Explain** Explain two ways to find the elapsed time from 10:45 A.M. to 1:20 P.M.

Probability and Statistics

15. What point on this coordinate grid is named by the ordered pair (3, 4)?

F T

G V

H R

J S

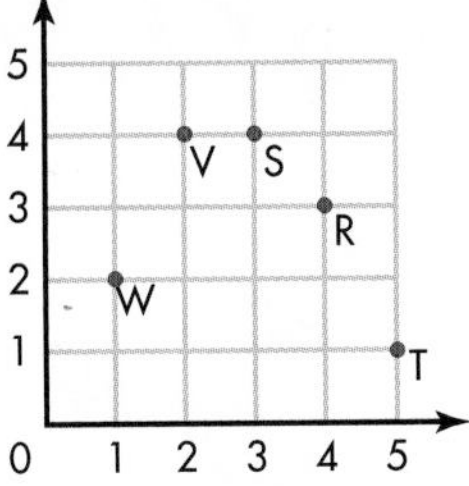

16. A bag has 3 red marbles, 2 blue marbles, 4 black marbles, and 3 green marbles. Without looking, if you pick only one marble, which color marble are you most likely to pick?

A Red

B Blue

C Black

D Green

Use the line graph for **17–19**.

Laptop Sales

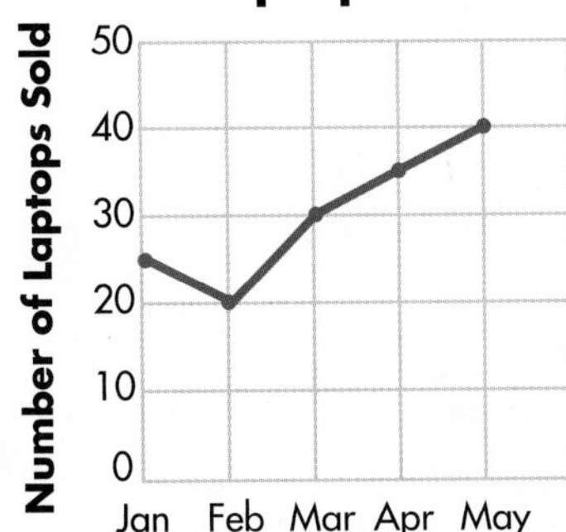

17. In which month were the most laptops sold? The least?

18. What was the total number of laptops sold from January through May?

19. **Writing to Explain** During which month did laptop sales increase the most? Explain how you used the graph to find your answer.

Algebraic Thinking

20. What number makes $47 - \square = 38$ true?

F 7

G 8

H 9

J 10

21. Which number completes the pattern?

9, 18, ☐, 36, 45

A 12

B 24

C 27

D 36

22. Which multiplication property explains why $3 \times 9 = 9 \times 3$?

F Commutative Property

G Distributive Property

H Identity Property

J Zero Property

23. The 24 desks in the classroom are arranged in *n* equal rows. Find how many desks are in each row if there are 6 rows.

24. **Writing to Explain** Complete the table. Then explain the pattern you used to find the distance traveled in 4 hours.

Time (h)	1	2	3	4
Distance (mi)	9	18	27	☐

Topic 7

Multiplying by 2-Digit Numbers

1 Ford Park Arena is the largest amphitheater in Texas. How many people sit in one of the upper sections? You will find out in Lesson 7–3.

2 The Pike's Peak Cog Railway is the highest cog railway in the world. How long does a train ride take to get to the top? You will find out in Lesson 7-4.

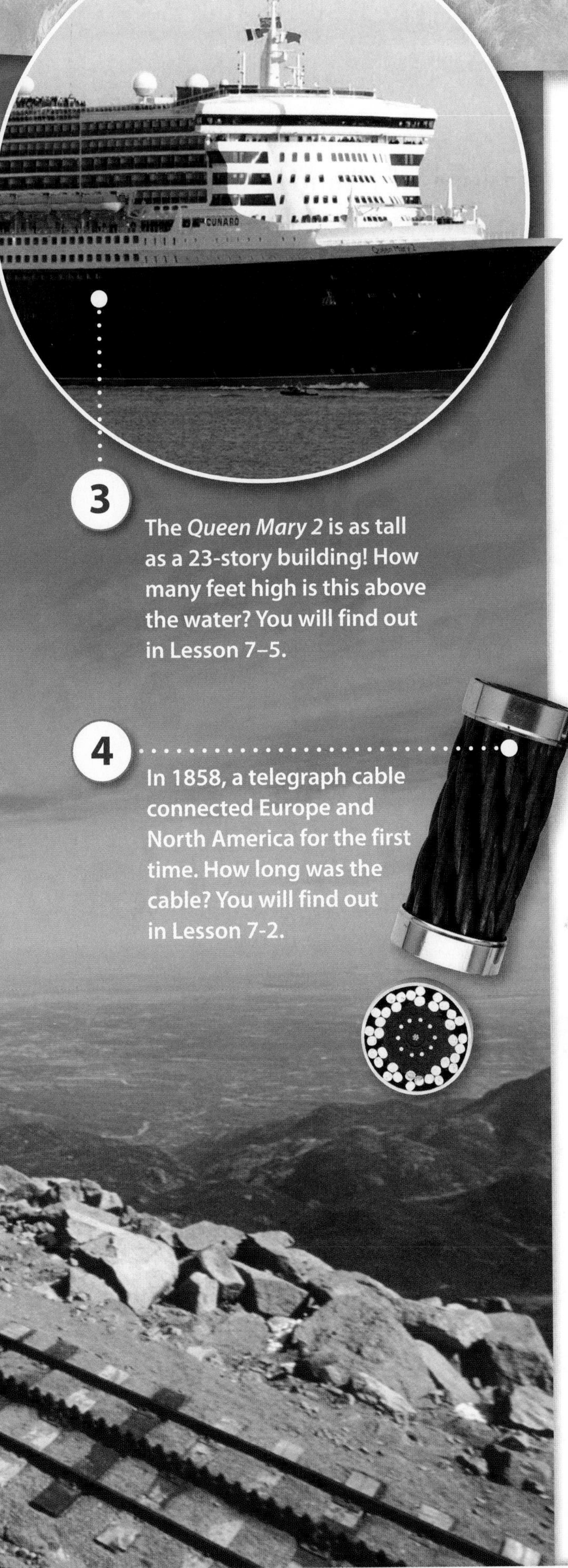

3 The *Queen Mary 2* is as tall as a 23-story building! How many feet high is this above the water? You will find out in Lesson 7–5.

4 In 1858, a telegraph cable connected Europe and North America for the first time. How long was the cable? You will find out in Lesson 7-2.

Review What You Know!

Vocabulary

Choose the best term from the box.

- rounding
- Commutative Property
- compatible
- Distributive Property

1. ? numbers are easy to compute mentally.
2. When you break apart factors in different ways but get the same product, you are using the ? of Multiplication.
3. You can use ? when you do not need an exact answer.

Estimating Products

Estimate each product.

4. 16×3
5. 52×7
6. 91×8
7. 24×8
8. 318×3
9. 624×5

Multiplying by 1-Digit Numbers

Find each product.

10. 53×9
11. 172×7
12. 512×6
13. 711×4
14. $2,152 \times 3$
15. $1,914 \times 5$

Partial Products

16. **Writing to Explain** Explain why the array shown below represents 3×21.

Lesson

7-1

TEKS 4.6B: Use patterns to multiply by 10 and 100. Also TEKS 4.4D: Use multiplication to solve problems.

Using Mental Math to Multiply 2-Digit Numbers

How can you multiply by multiples of 10 and 100?

How many adults under 65 visit the Sunny Day Amusement Park in 10 days? How many children visit the park in 100 days? How many adults 65 and over visit the park in 200 days?

Average Number of Visitors Each Day

Guided Practice*

Do you know HOW?

In **1** through **8**, use basic facts and patterns to find the product.

1. 30 × 100

2. 50 × 1,000

3. 25 × 10

4. 60× 200

5. 20 × 20

6. 40 × 100

7. 400 × 50

8. 80 × 500

Do you UNDERSTAND?

9. When you multiply 60 × 500, how many zeros are in the product?

10. In cold weather, fewer people go to Sunny Day Amusement Park. November has 30 days. If the park sells 300 tickets each day in November, how many would they sell for the whole month?

Independent Practice

For **11** through **34**, multiply using mental math.

11. 30 × 10

12. 100 × 60

13. 50 × 10

14. 80 × 40

15. 20 × 1,000

16. 70 × 900

17. 40 × 20

18. 500 × 30

19. 250 × 40

20. 20 × 40

21. 300 × 40

22. 60 × 90

23. 70 × 800

24. 30 × 80

25. 60 × 500

26. 700 × 30

27. 600 × 50

28. 30 × 900

29. 25 × 400

30. 30 × 600

31. 400 × 30

32. 800 × 30

33. 500 × 80

34. 600 × 90

*For another example, see Set A on page 172.

Adults under 65 in 10 Days

To multiply 400 × 10, use a pattern.

$4 \times 10 = 40$

$40 \times 10 = 400$

$400 \times 10 = 4{,}000$

4,000 adults under 65 visit the park in 10 days.

Children in 100 Days

The number of zeros in the product is the total number of zeros in both factors.

$800 \times 100 = 80{,}000$

2 zeros 2 zeros 4 zeros

80,000 children visit the park in 100 days.

Adults 65 and over in 200 Days

If the product of a basic fact ends in zero, include that zero in the count.

$5 \times 2 = 10$

$50 \times 200 = 10{,}000$

10,000 adults 65 and over visit the park in 200 days.

TAKS Problem Solving

For **35** and **36**, use the table at the right.

35. What is the total distance traveled in one triathlon?

36. Susan has completed 10 triathlons. How far did she bicycle in the races?

Data

Parts of an Olympic-Distance Triathlon	
Swimming	1,500 meters
Running	10,000 meters
Bicycling	40,000 meters

37. **Writing to Explain** Explain why the product of 50 and 800 has four zeros when 50 has one zero and 800 has two zeros.

38. Esther had 5 coins and two dollar bills to buy a snack at school. She paid $1.40 for her snack. She had exactly one dollar left. How did Esther pay for her snack?

39. For every 30 minutes of television air time, about 8 of the minutes are given to TV commercials. If 90 minutes of television is aired, how many minutes of commercials will be played?

A 8 minutes

B 24 minutes

C 38 minutes

D 128 minutes

40. If in one year a city recorded a total of 97 rainy days, how many of the days did it **NOT** rain?

365 days in one year

97	?

Lesson

7-2

TEKS 4.5B: Use strategies including rounding and compatible numbers to estimate solutions to multiplication and division problems.

Estimating Products

What are some ways to estimate?

In 1991, NASA launched the Upper Atmosphere Research Satellite (UARS). It orbits Earth about 105 times each week. There are 52 weeks in one year.

About how many orbits does it make in one year?

Orbits Earth about 105 times each week

Guided Practice*

Do you know HOW?

In **1** and **2**, use rounding to estimate each product.

1. 203×37

2. 177×14

In **3** and **4**, use compatible numbers to estimate each product.

3. 24×37

4. 15×27

Do you UNDERSTAND?

5. Writing to Explain In the example above, why are the estimates not the same?

6. About how many times does UARS orbit Earth in 3 weeks?

Independent Practice

For **7** through **30**, use rounding or compatible numbers to estimate each product.

You can round just one number or round both to make compatible numbers.

7. 32×83	**8.** 64×85	**9.** 31×46	**10.** 63×61
11. 42×703	**12.** 51×23	**13.** 27×41	**14.** 61×202
15. 62×20	**16.** 18×74	**17.** 12×89	**18.** 22×27
19. 79×43	**20.** 26×43	**21.** 346×18	**22.** 6×153
23. 602×43	**24.** 210×19	**25.** 79×79	**26.** 96×37
27. 840×49	**28.** 17×78	**29.** 35×45	**30.** 8×55

For another example, see Set B on page 172.

One Way

Use **rounding** to estimate the number of orbits in one year.

52×105

Round 105 to 100.

$52 \times 100 =$ **5,200**

UARS orbits Earth about 5,200 times each year.

Another Way

Use **compatible numbers** to estimate the number of orbits in one year.

Compatible numbers are easy to multiply.

52×105

Change 52 to 55.

Change 105 to 100.

$55 \times 100 =$ **5,500**

UARS orbits Earth about 5,500 times each year.

TAKS Problem Solving

31. A long-haul truck driver made 37 trips last year. If her average trip was 1,525 miles, about how far did she drive in all?

32. In one mission, an American astronaut spent more than 236 hours in space. About how many minutes did he spend in space?

There are 60 minutes in 1 hour.

33. Estimate to decide which has a greater product, 39×21 or 32×32. Explain.

34. The Mars Orbiter circles the planet Mars every 25 hours. About how many hours does it take to make 125 orbits?

35. Use the diagram below. In 1858, two ships connected a telegraph cable across the Atlantic Ocean for the first time. One ship laid out 1,016 miles of cable. The other ship laid out 1,010 miles of cable. Estimate the total distance of cable used.

36. Think About the Process About 57 baseballs are used in a professional baseball game. What is the best way to estimate how many baseballs are used in a season of 162 games?

A 6×100

B 60×160

C $60 \times 1{,}000$

D 200×200

1,010 miles

1,016 miles

Lesson **7-3**

TEKS 4.4A: Model factors and products using arrays and area models.

Arrays and an Expanded Algorithm

Hands-On: grid paper

How can you multiply using an array?

There are 13 bobble-head dogs in each row of the carnival booth. There are 24 equal rows. How many dogs are there?

Choose an Operation
Multiply to join equal groups.

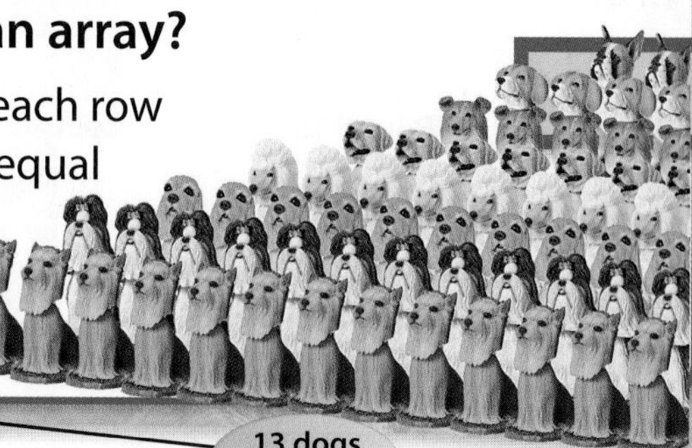

13 dogs per row

Another Example What is another way to show the partial products?

There are 37 rows with 26 seats set up at the ring at the dog show. How many seats are there?

Estimate $40 \times 25 = 1{,}000$

Step 1 Draw a table. Separate each factor into tens and ones. $(30 + 7) \times (20 + 6)$

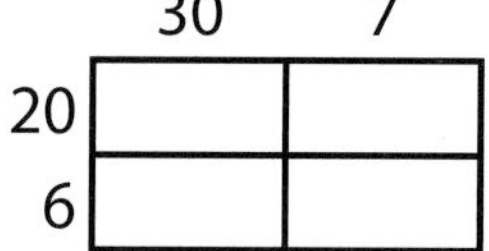

Step 2 Multiply to find the partial products.

	30	7
20	600	140
6	180	42

Step 3 Add the partial products to find the total.

$$\begin{array}{r} 42 \\ 180 \\ 140 \\ +\ 600 \\ \hline 962 \end{array}$$

$26 \times 37 = 962$
There are 962 seats at the dog show ring.

Explain It

1. How is breaking apart the problem 37×26 like solving four simpler problems?

2. **Reasonableness** Explain why the answer 962 is reasonable.

Step 1

Find 24 × 13.

Draw an array for 24 × 13.

Add each part of the array to find the product.

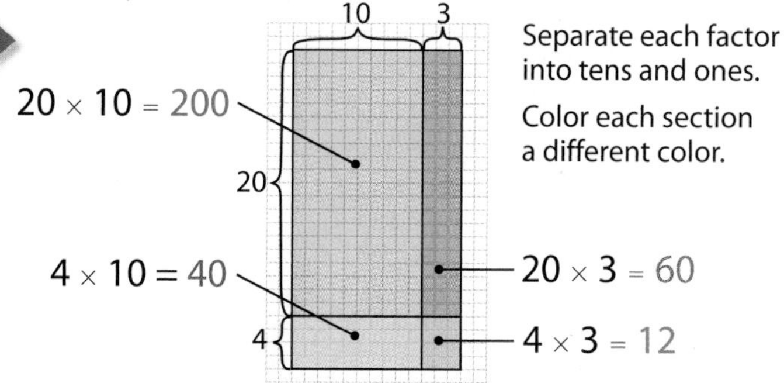

Step 2

Find the number of squares in each rectangle.

$$\begin{array}{r} 12 \\ 40 \\ 60 \\ +\ 200 \\ \hline 312 \end{array}$$

12, 40, 60, 200: partial products

In the booth there are 312 bobble-head dogs.

Guided Practice*

Do you know HOW?

In **1** and **2**, copy and complete the calculation by finding the partial products.

1. $\begin{array}{r} 13 \\ \times\ 17 \\ \hline \end{array}$

2. 24 × 16

	20	4
10		
6		

Do you UNDERSTAND?

3. In the example at the top, what four simpler multiplication problems were used to find 24 × 13?

4. At the dog show, the first 2 rows are reserved. How many people can sit in the remaining 35 rows?

Tip *There are 26 seats per row.*

Independent Practice

Leveled Practice Use grid paper to draw a rectangle. Then copy and complete the calculations.

Tip *You can solve the simpler problems in any order.*

5. 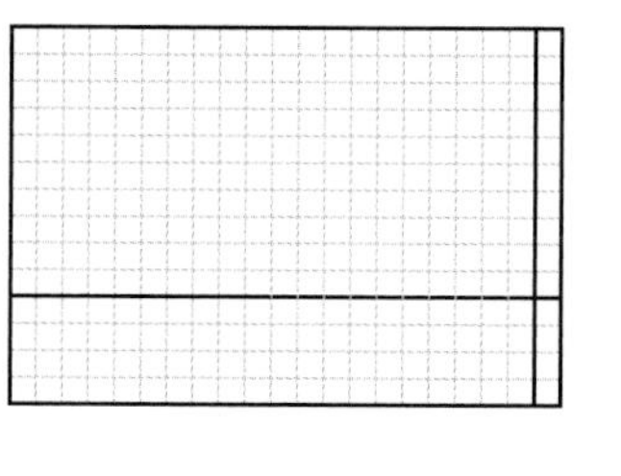

$\begin{array}{r} 21 \\ \times\ 14 \\ \hline \end{array}$

6. 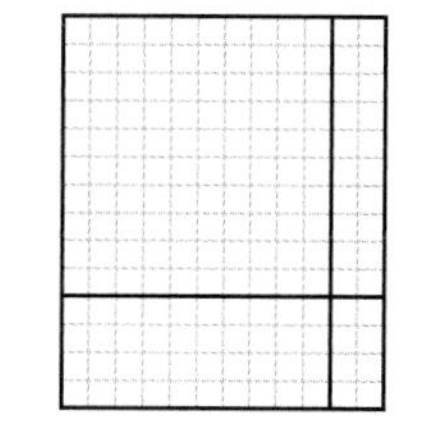

$\begin{array}{r} 12 \\ \times\ 14 \\ \hline \end{array}$

*For another example, see Set C on page 172.

Independent Practice

Leveled Practice For **7** and **8**, use grid paper to draw a rectangle. Then copy and complete the calculations.

7. 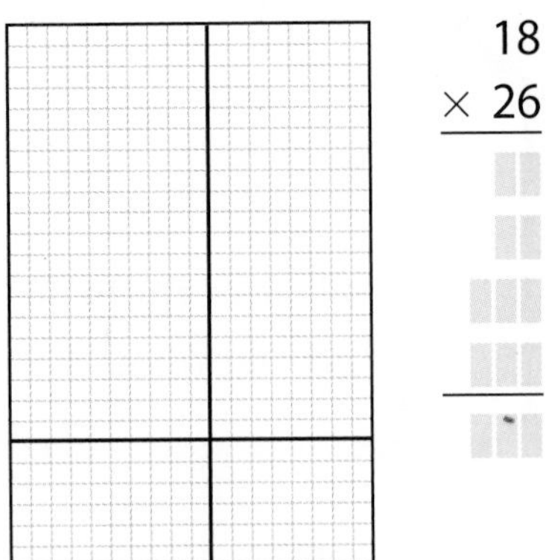

  18
× 26

8. 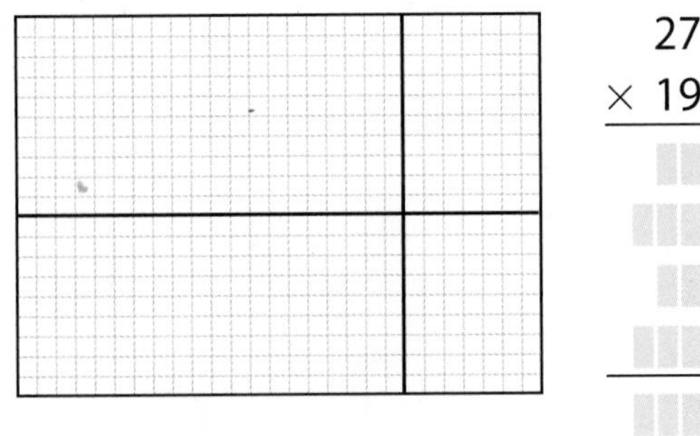

  27
× 19

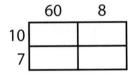

In **9** through **16**, copy and find the partial products. Then find the total.

9. 25 × 18

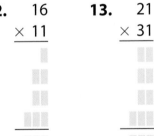

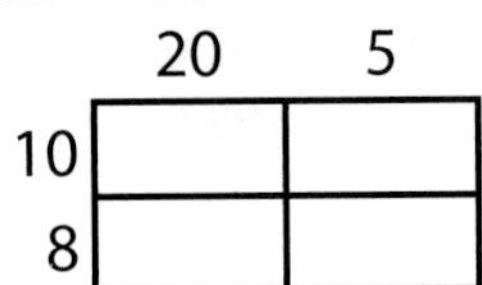

	20	5
10		
8		

10. 28 × 12

	20	8
10		
2		

11. 68 × 17

	60	8
10		
7		

12. 16 × 11

13. 21 × 31

14. 38 × 12

15. 29 × 17

16. 43 × 19

In **17** through **31**, find the products. Use partial products to help. Estimate to check for reasonableness.

17. 31 × 13

18. 21 × 33

19. 27 × 16

20. 59 × 41

21. 18 × 23

22. 28 × 29

23. 24 × 36

24. 43 × 39

25. 76 × 54

26. 88 × 22

27. 41 × 12

28. 38 × 27

29. 58 × 19

30. 29 × 15

31. 73 × 47

32. Writing to Explain Why is the product of 15×32 equal to the sum of 10×32 and 5×32?

33. The flagpole in front of City Hall in Luis' town is 35 feet tall. How many inches tall is the flagpole?

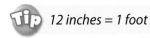

12 inches = 1 foot

34. The prices at Nolan's Novelties store are shown at the right. If 27 boxes of neon keychains and 35 boxes of glow-in-the-dark pens were purchased, what is the total cost?

Data

Item	Price per box
Neon Key chains	$15
Glow-in-the-dark pens	$10

35. Ford Park Arena is the largest amphitheater in Texas. The upper part of Section 108 has 17 rows with 16 seats in each row. How many seats are in this section?

36. Algebra Elijah has n customers in his lawn-mowing business. He mows each lawn once a week. Which expression shows how many lawns he mows in 12 weeks?

A $n + 12$ **C** $12 - n$

B $n \times 12$ **D** $12 \div n$

For **37** and **38**, use the diagram to the right.

37. Maggie is making a balloon game for the school fair. Kids will throw darts to try to pop the balloons. How many balloons are needed to set up the game?

38. Think About the Process Maggie knows that she will have to completely refill the balloon board about 15 times a day. Which expression shows how to find the number of balloons she will need?

F 15×13 **H** $15 \times (13 \times 14)$

G 15×14 **J** $15 \times (13 + 14)$

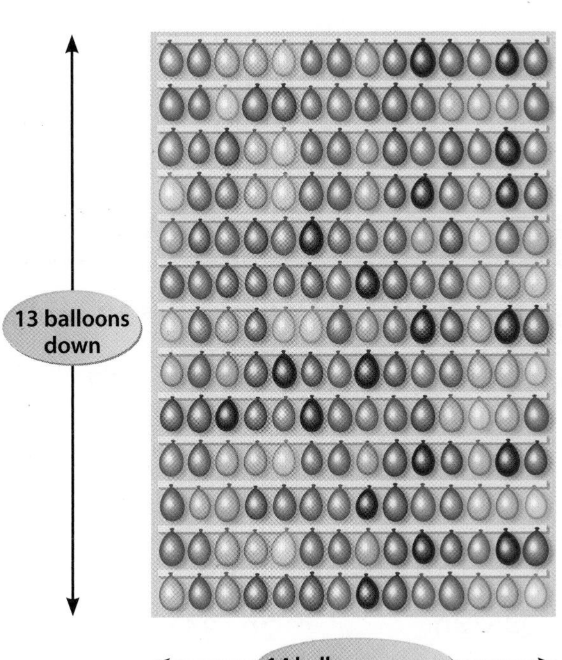

Lesson

7-4

TEKS 4.4D: Use multiplication to solve problems (no more than two digits times two digits without technology).

Multiplying 2-Digit Numbers by Multiples of Ten

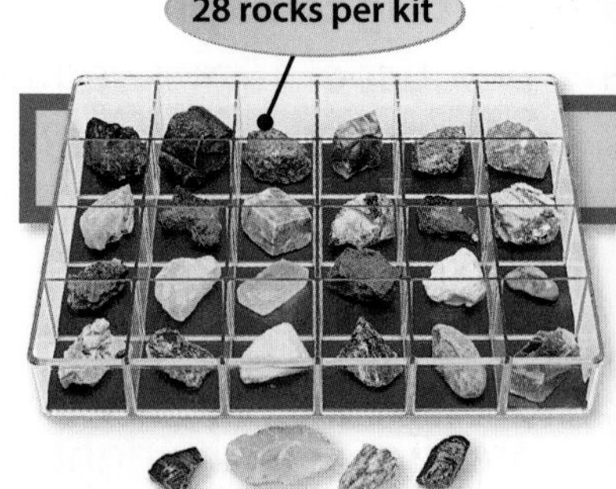

How can you find the product?

Mr. Jeffrey buys 20 rock identification kits for his science classes. If each kit has 28 rocks, how many rocks are there in all?

Choose an Operation

Multiply to find the number of rocks.

Guided Practice*

Do you know HOW?

In **1** through **6**, multiply to find each product.

1. $12 \times 20 = \square\square 0$

2. $21 \times 30 = \square\square 0$

3. 35 × 20

4. 63 × 20

5. 27 × 60

6. 66 × 40

Do you UNDERSTAND?

7. Writing to Explain Why is there a zero in the ones place when you multiply by 20 in the example above?

8. What simpler multiplication problem can you solve to find 38 × 70?

9. Each year, Mr. Jeffrey's school orders 100 rock kits. How many rocks are in all of the kits?

Independent Practice

Leveled Practice In **10** through **30**, multiply to find each product.

10. $12 \times 30 = \square\square 0$

11. $24 \times 10 = \square\square 0$

12. $33 \times 20 = \square\square 0$

13. $71 \times 30 = \square,\square\square 0$

14. $63 \times 40 = \square,\square\square 0$

15. 18 × 10,

16. 20 × 51

17. 32 × 30

18. 40 × 22

19. 24 × 40

20. 34 × 50

21. 40 × 73

22. 88 × 30

23. 75 × 40

24. 22 × 60

25. 13 × 50

26. 60 × 23

27. 32 × 20

28. 82 × 80

29. 62 × 60

30. 52 × 50

*For another example, see Set D on page 172.

One Way

Find 20 × 28.

Break 28 into tens and ones: 28 = 20 + 8.

Use a grid to find the partial products.

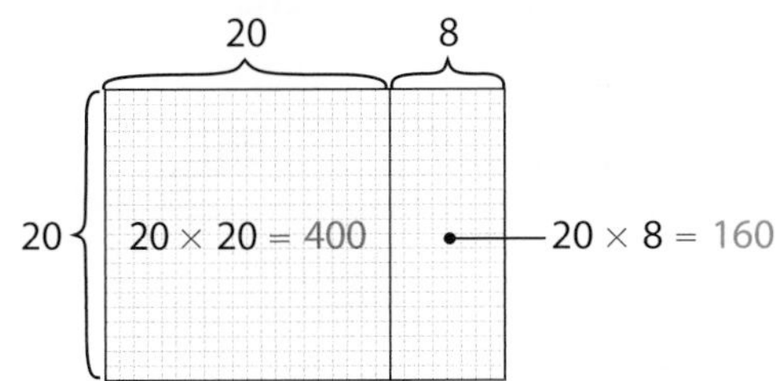

Add the partial products to find the total.

400 + 160 = 560

Another Way

Find 20 × 28.

Multiply 2 tens × 28.

$$\begin{array}{r} \scriptstyle 1 \\ 28 \\ \times\ 20 \\ \hline 560 \end{array}$$

Record a 0 in the ones place of the answer. This shows how many tens are in the answer.

There are 560 rocks in all.

TAKS Problem Solving

31. Number Sense Rex's class raised frogs from tadpoles. The class has 21 students, and each raised 6 tadpoles. All but 6 of the tadpoles grew to be frogs. Write a number sentence to show how many frogs the class has.

32. How many fossil kits with 12 samples each have the same number of fossils as 30 fossil kits with 8 samples each?

A 20 fossil kits
B 24 fossil kits
C 200 fossil kits
D 240 fossil kits

33. A ride on the Pike's Peak Cog Railway takes 75 minutes. If the train's average speed is 100 feet per minute how long is the Pike's Peak Cog Railway?

34. In the United States, students spend about 900 hours per year in school. How many hours would a student spend in 12 years of school?

35. A roller coaster runs rides 50 times an hour and reaches speeds of 70 miles per hour. If each ride takes 8 rows of 4 people, how many people ride each hour?

A 160 people
B 1,500 people
C 1,600 people
D 2,240 people

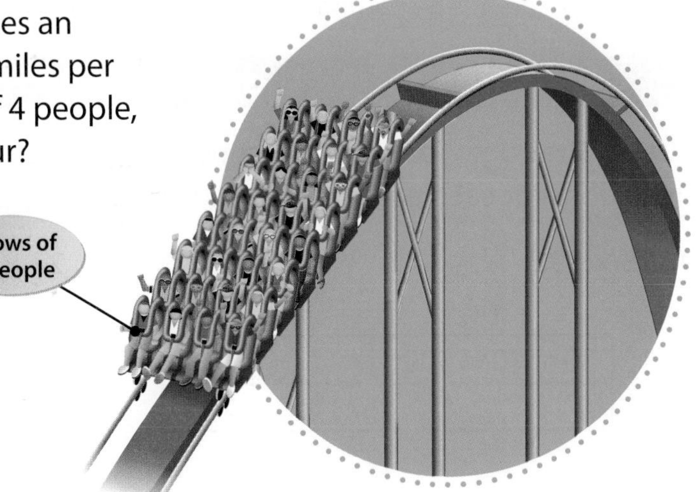

Lesson

7-5

TEKS 4.4D: Use multiplication to solve problems (no more than two digits times two digits without technology).

Multiplying 2-Digit by 2-Digit Numbers

What is a common way to record multiplication?

A ferry carried an average of 37 cars per trip on Saturday. If the ferry made 24 one-way trips, how many cars did it carry?

Choose an Operation Multiply to join equal groups.

37 cars per trip

Guided Practice*

Do you know HOW?

In **1** through **6**, draw a diagram and fill it in with partial products. Then find the product.

1. 41×23

2. 63×31

3. 12×27

4. 23×36

5. 42×18

6. 92×34

Do you UNDERSTAND?

7. In the example above, is 888 a reasonable answer for 37 × 24?

8. **Writing to Explain** The ferry made 36 one-way trips on Sunday and carried an average of 21 cars on each trip.

a How many cars were ferried on Sunday?

b On which day were more cars ferried, Saturday or Sunday? Explain.

Independent Practice

Leveled Practice For **9** and **10**, copy each diagram and show the calculations for each partial product. Then find the product.

9. 18 × 33

	30	3
10	30 × 10 = 300	
8		3 × 8 = 24

10. 22 × 46

	40	6
20		
2		

*For another example, see Set E on page 173.

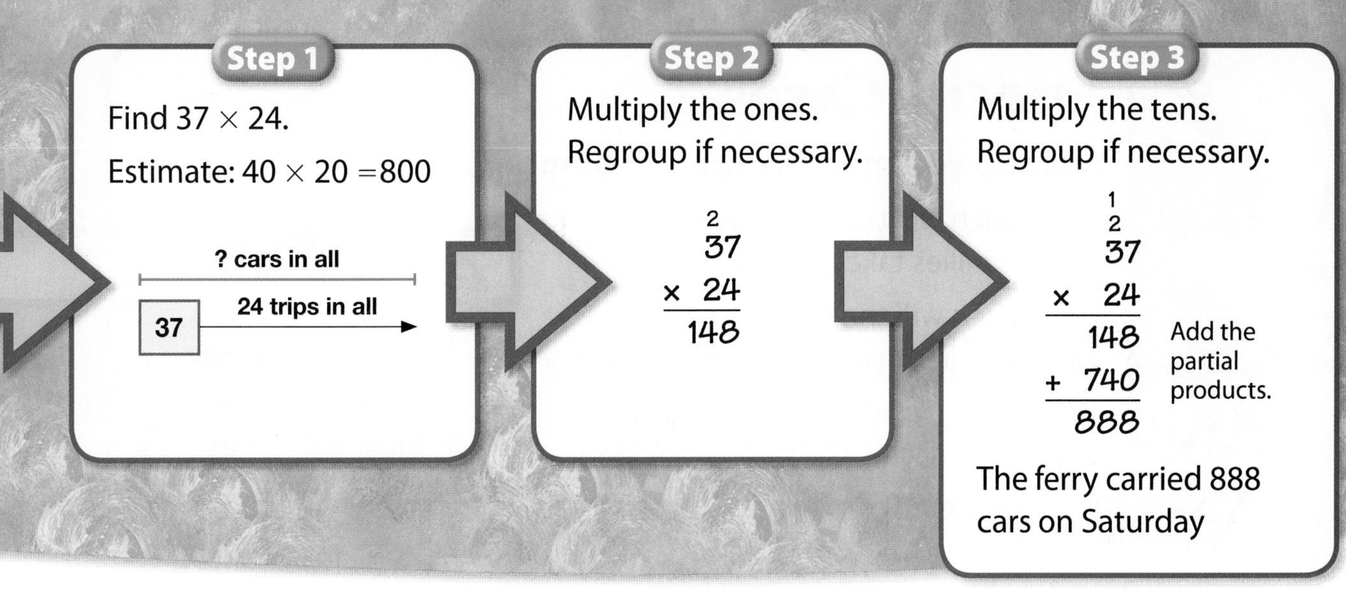

Step 1
Find 37 × 24.
Estimate: 40 × 20 =800
? cars in all
24 trips in all
37
Step 2
Multiply the ones.
Regroup if necessary.
2
37
× 24
148
Step 3
Multiply the tens.
Regroup if necessary.
1
2
37
× 24
148
+ 740
888
Add the partial products.
The ferry carried 888 cars on Saturday

In **11** through **20**, find the product.

11. 37×21 **12.** 54×37 **13.** 63×22 **14.** 34×41 **15.** 81×17

16. 56×31 **17.** 53×17 **18.** 81×46 **19.** 15×16 **20.** 17×21

TAKS Problem Solving

21. Algebra Evaluate the expression $7 \times (15 + m)$ when $m = 31$.

A 136 **C** 322

B 232 **D** 682

22. Reasonableness Sara estimated 32×45 by using 30×40. How could Sara make a more accurate estimate?

23. Use the diagram to the right. The *Queen Mary 2* is as high as a 21-story building. If a single story is 11 feet tall, how tall is the *Queen Mary 2?*

24. Mr. Morris bought sketch pads for 24 of his students. Each pad contained 50 sheets. How many sheets of paper were there altogether?

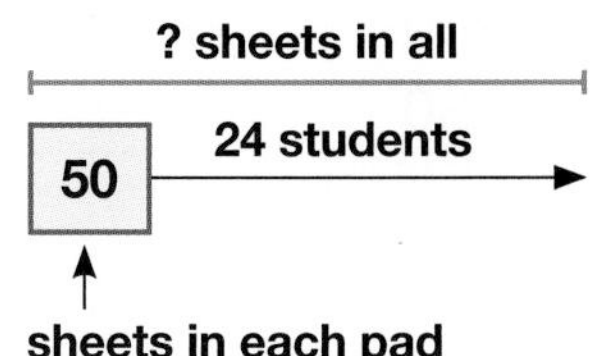

25. Geometry Jon's backyard is a rectangle that measures 32 feet by 44 feet. How many square feet will the garden be?

Tip *The area of a rectangle is length × width.*

Lesson

7-6

TEKS 4.4D: Use multiplication to solve problems.

Special Cases

How do you multiply greater numbers?

How much will the farm earn when 1,600 families take the one-hour tour?

How much will the farm earn when 2,000 families take the two-hour tour?

Choose an Operation Multiply the cost per family by the number of families.

Data

Barrington Farm Tours

Tours	Cost per Family
1-hour	$20
2-hour	$25

Guided Practice*

Do you know HOW?

In **1** through **6**, use mental math to find the product.

1. 100×25

2. 200×50

3. $3{,}000 \times 30$

4. $40{,}000 \times 50$

5. 30 × 600

6. 20 × 150

Do you UNDERSTAND?

7. Writing to Explain Why does the product of 25 × 2,000 have 4 zeros when 2,000 only has 3 zeros?

8. A school gets a special family-pass of $20 for each of its 134 families. How much will the school families be charged altogether?

Independent Practice

In **9** through **28**, use mental math to find the product.

9. 240×15

10. 440×20

11. $9{,}000 \times 60$

12. $1{,}000 \times 25$

13. 170×10

14. $1{,}500 \times 40$

15. $1{,}870 \times 20$

16. $20{,}000 \times 40$

17. 290×20

18. $4{,}200 \times 40$

19. $5{,}000 \times 70$

20. 660×40

21. $2{,}000 \times 25$

22. $1{,}200 \times 80$

23. $1{,}870 \times 30$

*For another example, see Set E on page 173.

Find $20 \times 1{,}600$.

Use mental math.

$16 \times 2 = 32$
$1{,}600 \times 20 = 32{,}000$

The farm earned 32,000 from the 1-hour tours.

Find $25 \times 2{,}000$.

Use mental math.

$25 \times 2 = 50$
$25 \times 2{,}000 = 50{,}000$

The farm earned \$50,000 from the 2-hour tours.

24. $2{,}500 \times 50$

25. 700×50

26. 600×25

27. $2{,}000 \times 15$

28. 800×30

TAKS Problem Solving

For **29** and **30**, use the table at the right.

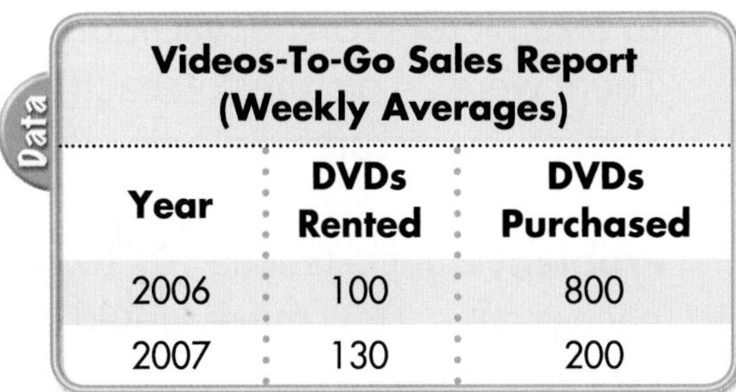

Videos-To-Go Sales Report (Weekly Averages)

Year	DVDs Rented	DVDs Purchased
2006	100	800
2007	130	200

29. In 2006, how many DVDs were rented in 52 weeks? How many DVDs were purchased in this same time?

30. In 2007, how many DVDs were rented? How many were purchased?

31. Think About the Process What are the partial products of 9×25?

A $(9 \times 20) + (9 \times 5)$

B $(9 \times 20) + (9 \times 25)$

C $(20 \times 20) + (5 \times 5)$

D $(3 \times 20) + (3 \times 5)$

32. A school buys 43 flat-screen computer monitors for \$270 each. What is the total amount of the purchase?

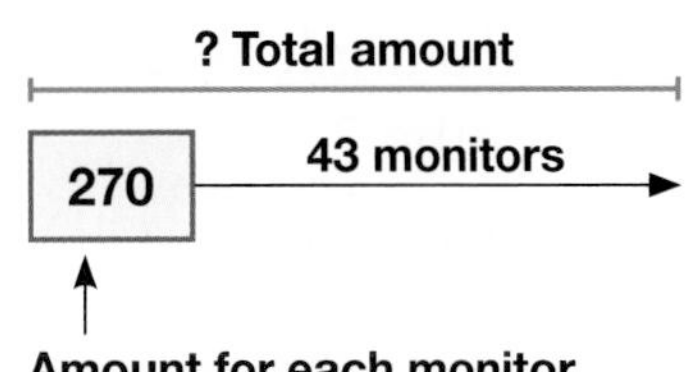

33. **Algebra** What is the value of the expression $\$752 + (\$20 \times t)$ if $t = 125$?

Lesson

7-7

TEKS 4.14C: Select or develop an appropriate problem-solving plan or strategy, including drawing a picture, looking for a pattern, systematic guessing and checking, acting it out, making a table, working a simpler problem, or working backwards to solve a problem.

Problem Solving

Two-Question Problems

Problem 1: Maya and Jose are preparing for a bike race. On Wednesday, they rode their bicycles 32 miles in the morning and 22 miles in the afternoon. How many miles did they ride in all?

Problem 2: Maya and Jose bicycled the same number of miles on Wednesday, Thursday, Friday, and Saturday. How far did they ride during the week?

Rode the same distance 4 days in a row

Guided Practice*

Do you know HOW?

Solve.

1. **Problem 1:** Julia used 3 rolls of film to take pictures on her vacation. There were 24 pictures on each roll. How many pictures did Julia take?

   Problem 2: It costs Julia 10¢ to print each picture. How much would it cost Julia to print every picture?

Do you UNDERSTAND?

2. Why do you need to know how many pictures Julia took to solve Problem 2?
3. **Write a Problem** Write a problem that uses the answer from Problem 1 below.
   Problem 1: Cal puts one vase on each of 5 tables. There are 6 flowers in each vase. How many flowers does Cal use?

Independent Practice

Solve. Use the answer from Problem 1 to solve Problem 2.

4. **Problem 1:** Martin buys a sandwich for $4, an apple for $1, and a drink for $2. How much did he pay altogether?

   ? Cost of Martin's lunch

$4	$1	$2

   Problem 2: How much change did Martin receive if he paid with a $20 bill?

   $20

Lunch	Change

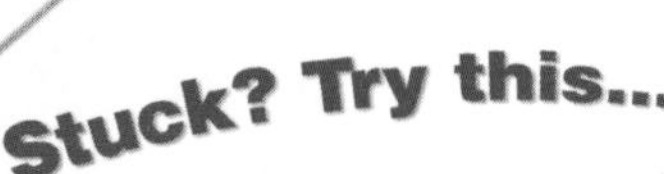

Stuck? Try this....

- What do I know?
- What diagram can I use to help understand the problem?
- Can I use addition, subtraction, multiplication, or division?
- Is all of my work correct?
- Did I answer the right question?
- Is my answer reasonable?

*For another example, see Set F on page 173.

Read & Understand

Sometimes you have to answer one problem to solve another problem.

32 miles + 22 miles = 54 miles

Maya and Jose bicycled 54 miles on Wednesday.

Plan

Use the answer from Problem 1 to solve Problem 2.

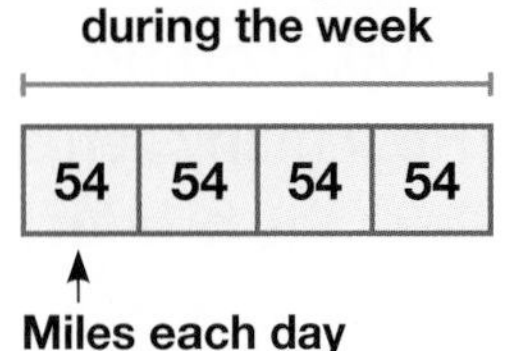

4×54 miles = 216 miles

Maya and Jose rode 216 miles during the week.

5. **Problem 1:** Sally and Byron mow their neighbors' lawns in the summer. Sally mows 5 lawns each week. Byron mows three times as many lawns as Sally. How many lawns does Byron mow each week?

Lawns mowed each week

Byron | 5 | 5 | 5 | 3 times as many

Sally | 5

Problem 2: Byron gets paid $20 for each lawn he mows. How much does Byron get paid each week?

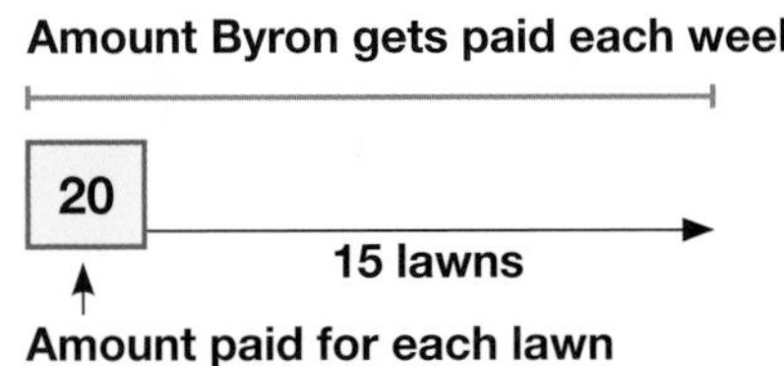

6. **Problem 1:** June's mom brought 3 bags of popcorn and 3 bottles of water to the park. How many bags of popcorn and bottles of water did June's mom take to the park?

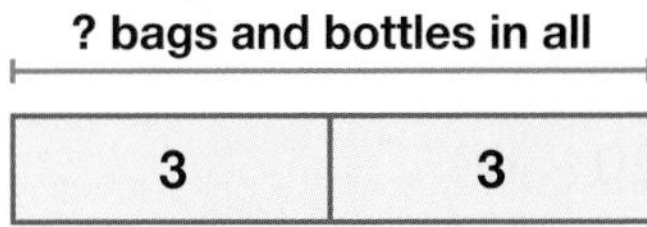

Problem 2: Each bag of popcorn that June's mom brought to the park contained 16 servings. How many servings of popcorn did June's mom bring to the park?

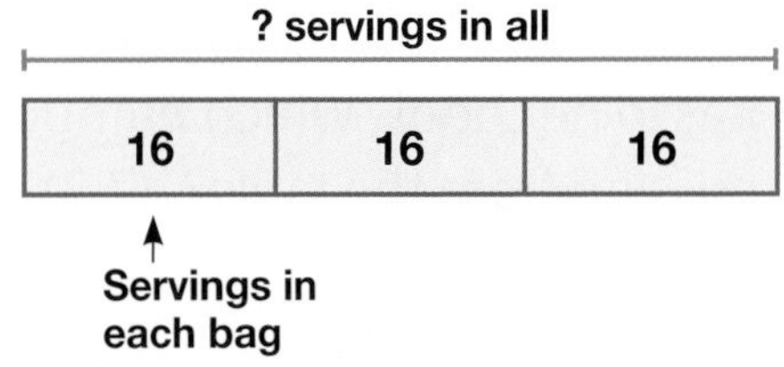

7. **Problem 1:** Sydney made wooden penguins to sell at a fair. She used 5 pompoms and 4 beads for each penguin. How many pompoms and beads are there all together on each wooden penguin?

Problem 2: Sydney made 21 wooden penguins. How many pompoms and beads did she use for the wooden penguins altogether?

8. **Problem 1:** Dave plans to retile his porch floor. He wants to buy 25 black tiles and 23 white tiles. How many tiles will he buy in all?

Problem 2: Each tile Dave plans to use is one square foot. Each tile costs 2 dollars. How much money will it cost to retile his porch floor?

TAKS Test Prep

1. To find 30×700, Scott first found $3 \times 7 = 21$. How many zeros should Scott include in the product? (7-1)

   A 1

   B 2

   C 3

   D 4

2. There are 27 schools participating in the regional band competition. Each school brought 38 band members. Which shows the best way to estimate how many band members are in the competition? (7-2)

   F 20×30

   G 20×40

   H 25×40

   J 30×30

3. Telly has 15 pages in her coin collector's book. Each page has 32 coins. Telly is using the table below to calculate how many coins she has in her book. Which number is missing from the table? (7-3)

	10	5
30	300	
2	20	10

   A 15

   B 150

   C 315

   D 480

4. Which partial products can be used to find 35×64? (7-5)

   F 140 and 210

   G 140 and 2,100

   H 120 and 2,100

   J 140 and 1,800

5. There are 16 ounces in a pound. Which is the best estimate of the number of ounces a 97 pound dog weighs? (7-2)

   A 160

   B 900

   C 1,600

   D 9,000

6. The bank ordered 24 cases of paper. Each case had 10 packs. How many packs of paper did the bank order? (7-4)

   F 240

   G 250

   H 2,400

   J 2,500

7. Mr. Taylor installed 10 dozen tiles on his kitchen floor. Each tile cost \$3. How much did Mr. Taylor spend, before tax? (7-7)

   A \$390

   B \$360

   C \$300

   D \$108

8. The school district bought 95 new microscopes. Each microscope cost \$52. How much did the district spend? (7-5)

F \$4,940

G \$4,930

H \$4,240

J \$655

9. Which pair best completes the number sentence? (7-1)

$\square \times 100 = \square$

A 300 and 3,000

B 30 and 30,000

C 30 and 3,000

D 30 and 300

10. Tom's goal is to learn 15 new words each day. At the end of day 40, how many new words will Tom have learned? (7-4)

F 55

G 400

H 450

J 600

11. An amusement park sold 500 adult admission tickets. Each adult ticket cost \$30. What is the total cost of the adult tickets? (7-6)

A \$800

B \$1,500

C \$8,000

D \$15,000

12. What is 15×29? (7-3)

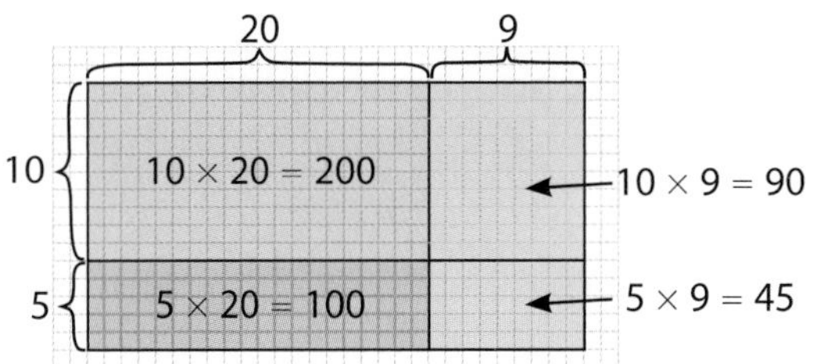

F 535

G 435

H 390

J 335

13. If 82 seats on a flight were sold for \$89 each, about how much money did the airline make? (7-2)

A \$7,200

B \$8,200

C \$9,200

D \$11,000

14. Which shows one way to use partial products to find 60×78? (7-4)

F $(30 \times 70) + (30 \times 8)$

G $(60 \times 70) + (60 \times 80)$

H $(60 \times 70) + (60 \times 78)$

J $(60 \times 70) + (60 \times 8)$

15. Griddable Response At the science fair, 42 cases are on display. Each case has 16 insects. How many insects are on display? (7-5)

Reteaching

Set A, pages 154–155

Use mental math to find 26 × 300.

You can think about the pattern.

26 × 3 = 78

26 × 30 = 780

26 × 300 = 7,800

Remember that when a product of a basic fact ends in zero, there is one more zero in the answer.

1. 4 × 10 **2.** 7 × 1,000

3. 80 × 600 **4.** 50 × 4,000

5. 3 × 900 **6.** 600 × 10

Set B, pages 156–157

Use multiplication to estimate 16 × 24.

Round 24 to 20.

Round 16 to 20.

20 × 20 = 400

Remember to check to see if your estimate is reasonable.

1. 41 × 54 **2.** 79 × 32

3. 64 × 86 **4.** 32 × 71

5. 26 × 626 **6.** 53 × 200

Set C, pages 158–161

Find 14 × 12. Draw a 14 × 12 array.

Separate each factor into tens and ones. Color each section a different color. Add each part to find the product.

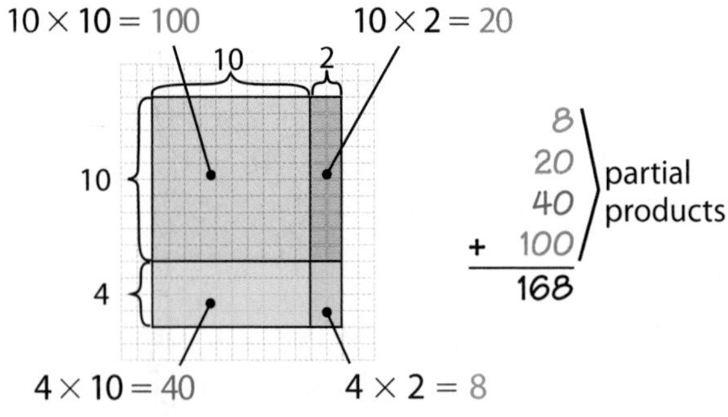

Remember you can solve the simpler problems in any order and the answer will remain the same.

Find the product. Use partial products to help.

1. 14 × 32 **2.** 64 × 12

3. 56 × 17 **4.** 72 × 15

5. 26 × 63 **6.** 47 × 27

Set D, pages 162–163

Find 16 × 30. Multiply 16 × 3 tens.

```
   1
  16
× 30
 480
```

The 0 in the ones places shows how many tens are in the answer.

Remember to record a 0 in the ones place of the answer.

1. 39 × 10 **2.** 56 × 30

3. 41 × 20 **4.** 60 × 13

Reteaching

Set E, pages 164–167

Find 19×14.

Multiply the ones.
Regroup if necessary.

$$\begin{array}{r} {}^{3}\\ 19 \\ \times\ 14 \\ \hline 76 \end{array}$$

Multiply the tens.
Regroup if necessary.

$$\begin{array}{r} 19 \\ \times\ 14 \\ \hline 76 \\ +\ 190 \\ \hline 266 \end{array}$$

Remember to regroup if necessary.

1. $\begin{array}{r} 53 \\ \times\ 36 \\ \hline \end{array}$

2. $\begin{array}{r} 23 \\ \times\ 18 \\ \hline \end{array}$

3. $\begin{array}{r} 73 \\ \times\ 33 \\ \hline \end{array}$

4. $\begin{array}{r} 31 \\ \times\ 74 \\ \hline \end{array}$

5. 56×64

6. 39×82

7. 700×40

8. 420×20

9. 250×30

10. $6{,}000 \times 15$

Set F, pages 168–169

When you solve two question problems, solve the first problem, and use that answer to help you solve the second problem.

Problem 1: It costs \$3 for a ticket to the pool, and \$7 for a ticket to the water park. How much does it cost for 4 people to go to each?

Cost of 4 pool tickets:
$\$3 \times 4 = \$12$

Cost of 4 water park tickets:
$\$7 \times 4 = \$28$.

Problem 2: How much more does it cost the group of 4 to go to the water park than to the pool?

$28 - 12 = 16$

It costs \$16 more.

Remember to use the information from Problem 1 to answer Problem 2.

Solve.

Problem 1: Rose visited 14 cities on her vacation. She bought 3 souvenirs in each city to send to her friends. How many souvenirs did Rose buy on her vacation?

Problem 2: It costs Rose \$2 to send each souvenir to her friends. How much did it cost Rose to send all of the souvenirs that she bought on vacation?

Topic 8

Division Number Sense

1

An ultralight plane tracks the trek of monarch butterflies from Canada, throughout the United States, and into Mexico. How many miles do the butterflies travel in Texas? You will find out in Lesson 8-4.

2

How many solar cells does it take to power a solar car? You will find out in Lesson 8-1.

3

How long does it take the International Space Station to orbit Earth one time? You will find out in Lesson 8-2.

Review What You Know!

Vocabulary

Choose the best term from the box.

- array
- compatible numbers
- factors
- partial product

1. An arrangement of objects in rows and columns is called a(n) ?.

2. When multiplying a two-digit number by a two-digit number, a ? is found by multiplying the first factor by the ones of the second factor.

3. Numbers that are easy to compute mentally are called ?.

Multiplying

Find each product.

4. 83×6 **5.** 71×3 **6.** 49×8

7. 87×7 **8.** 66×9 **9.** 52×4

Multiplying by 10 and 100

Find each product.

10. 62×10 **11.** 24×100 **12.** 65×100

13. 14×10 **14.** 35×100 **15.** 59×10

Arrays

16. Write a Problem Write a multiplication problem for the array at the right.

17. Writing to Explain Is an array for 4×3 the same or different from the array shown above? Explain.

Lesson

8-1

TEKS 4.4E: Use division to solve problems (no more than one-digit divisors and three-digit dividends without technology).

Mental Math

How can you use patterns to help you divide mentally?

Mr. Díaz ordered a supply of 320 pastels. He needs to divide them equally among four art classes. How many pastels does each class get?

Choose an Operation Division is used to make equal groups.

Guided Practice*

Do you know HOW?

In **1** and **2**, use patterns to find each quotient.

1. 28 ÷ 7 = ▢
280 ÷ 7 = ▢
2,800 ÷ 7 = ▢
28,000 ÷ 7 = ▢

2. 64 ÷ 8 = ▢
640 ÷ 8 = ▢
6,400 ÷ 8 = ▢
64,000 ÷ 8 = ▢

Do you UNDERSTAND?

3. How is dividing 320 by 4 like dividing 32 by 4?

4. José orders 240 binders and divides them equally among the 4 classes. How many binders will each class get? What basic fact did you use?

Independent Practice

Leveled Practice In **5** through **8**, use patterns to find each quotient.

5. 36 ÷ 9 = ▢
360 ÷ 9 = ▢
3,600 ÷ 9 = ▢
36,000 ÷ 9 = ▢

6. 10 ÷ 2 = ▢
100 ÷ 2 = ▢
1,000 ÷ 2 = ▢
10,000 ÷ 2 = ▢

7. 45 ÷ 5 = ▢
450 ÷ 5 = ▢
4,500 ÷ 5 = ▢
45,000 ÷ 5 = ▢

8. 24 ÷ 8 = ▢
240 ÷ 8 = ▢
2,400 ÷ 8 = ▢
24,000 ÷ 8 = ▢

For **9** through **23**, use mental math to divide.

9. 200 ÷ 5 **10.** 360 ÷ 4 **11.** 540 ÷ 9 **12.** 160 ÷ 4 **13.** 160 ÷ 2

14. 900 ÷ 3 **15.** 320 ÷ 8 **16.** 360 ÷ 6 **17.** 180 ÷ 3 **18.** 210 ÷ 7

19. 720 ÷ 8 **20.** 500 ÷ 5 **21.** 350 ÷ 7 **22.** 630 ÷ 9 **23.** 480 ÷ 6

*For another example, see Set A on page 192.

Find $320 \div 4$.

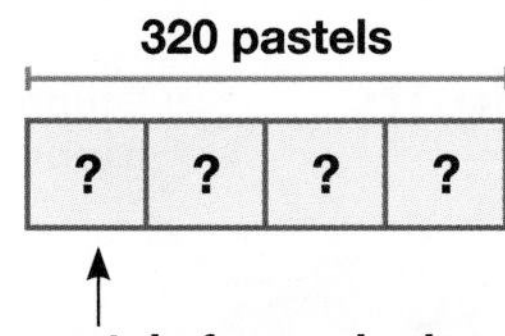

The basic fact is $32 \div 4 = 8$.

32 tens $\div 4 =$ 8 tens or 80.
$320 \div 4 = 80$

Each class will get 80 pastels.

Mr. Díaz wants to divide 400 erasers among 8 classes. How many erasers will each class get? Find $400 \div 8$.

The basic fact is $40 \div 8$.

40 tens $\div 8 =$ 5 tens or 50.
$400 \div 8 = 50$

Each class will get 50 erasers.

TAKS Problem Solving

24. Number Sense Selena used a basic fact to help solve $180 \div 6$. What basic fact did Selena use?

25. There are 52 weeks in 1 year. How many years are equivalent to 520 weeks?

26. At the North American Solar Challenge, teams use up to 1,000 solar cells to design and build solar cars for a race. If there are 810 solar cells in rows of 9, how many solar cells are in each row?

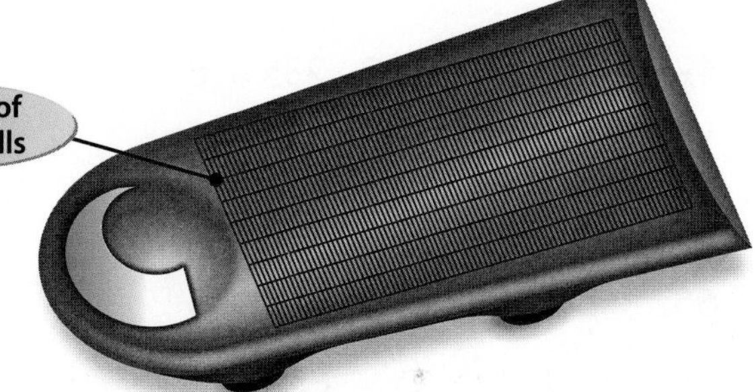

27. A bakery produced 37 loaves of bread an hour. How many loaves were produced in 4 hours?

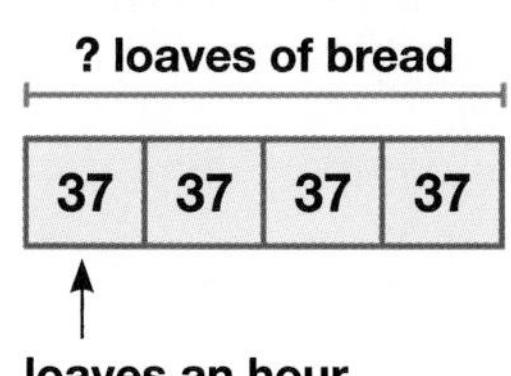

28. On Saturday afternoon, 350 people attended a play. The seating was arranged in 7 equal rows. How many people sat in each row? How do you know?

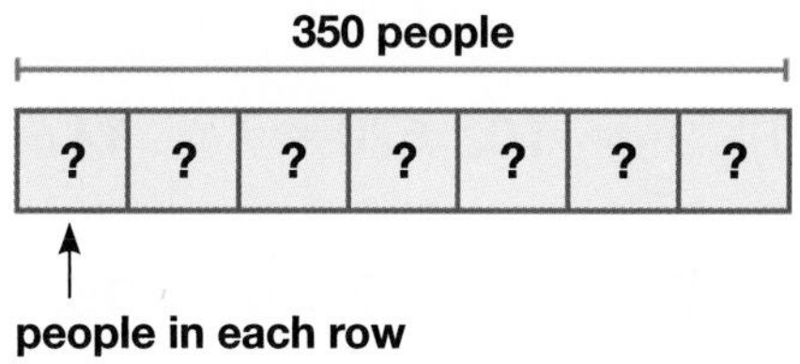

29. Each row of seats in a stadium has 32 chairs. If the first 3 rows are completely filled, how many people are in the first 3 rows?

A 9 people
B 10 people
C 96 people
D 256 people

30. Writing to Explain If you know that $20 \div 5 = 4$, how does that fact help you find $200 \div 5$?

Lesson
8-2

TEKS 4.5B: Use strategies including rounding and compatible numbers to estimate solutions to multiplication and division problems.

Estimating Quotients

When and how do you estimate quotients to solve problems?

Max wants to make 9 rubber-band balls. He bought a jar of 700 rubber bands. About how many rubber bands can he use for each ball?

700 rubber bands

Guided Practice*

Do you know HOW?

In **1** through **6**, estimate each quotient. Use rounding or compatible numbers.

1. 48 ÷ 5

2. 235 ÷ 8

3. 547 ÷ 6

4. 192 ÷ 5

5. 662 ÷ 8

6. 362 ÷ 3

Do you UNDERSTAND?

7. Writing to Explain In Exercise 4, to what number should you adjust 192? Why?

8. Reasonableness Max decides to use the 700 rubber bands to make 8 balls. Is it reasonable to say that each ball would contain about 90 rubber bands?

Independent Practice

Leveled Practice In **9** through **28**, estimate the quotient.

First round to the nearest ten. Then try multiples of ten that are near the rounded number.

9. 430 ÷ 9

10. 620 ÷ 7

11. 138 ÷ 5

12. 232 ÷ 6

13. 172 ÷ 3

14. 342 ÷ 8

15. 652 ÷ 6

16. 599 ÷ 9

17. 853 ÷ 6

18. 326 ÷ 4

19. 637 ÷ 6

20. 971 ÷ 2

21. 747 ÷ 8

22. 232 ÷ 9

23. 387 ÷ 4

24. 552 ÷ 7

25. 657 ÷ 4

26. 912 ÷ 4

27. 625 ÷ 3

28. 821 ÷ 3

*For another example, see Set B on page 192.

One Way

Use compatible numbers.

What number close to 700 is easily divided by 9?

Try multiples of ten near 700.

710 is not easily divided by 9.

720 is 72 tens and can be divided by 9.

$720 \div 9 = 80$

A good estimate is 80 rubber bands for each ball.

Another Way

Use multiplication.

9 times what number is about 700?

$9 \times 8 = 72$,
so $9 \times 80 = 720$.

$700 \div 9$ is about 80.

TAKS Problem Solving

Use the chart at the right for **29** and **30.**

29. Ada sold her mugs in 3 weeks. About how many did she sell each week?

30. Ben sold his mugs in 4 weeks. About how many did he sell each week?

31. Number Sense Jeff is asked to give two different estimates for $542 \div 8$. Name two numbers that are compatible with 8 that he could use to replace 542.

32. Writing to Explain Copy and complete by filling in the circle with > or <. Without dividing, explain how you know which quotient is greater.

$930 \div 4 \bigcirc 762 \div 4$

33. The International Space Station takes 644 minutes to orbit Earth 7 times. About how long does each orbit take?

A 80 minutes

B 90 minutes

C 95 minutes

D 100 minutes

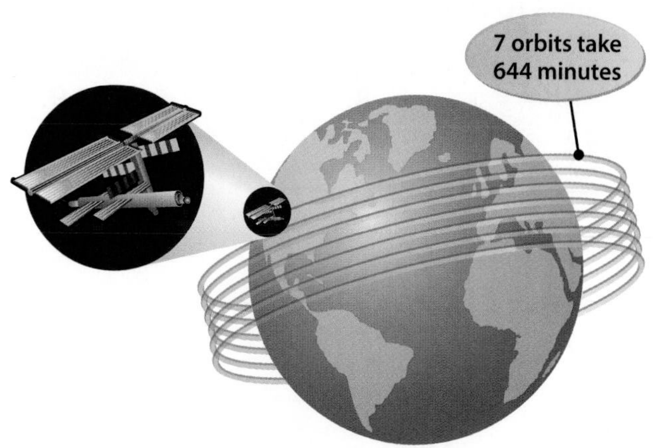

Lesson

8-3

TEKS 4.4E: Use division to solve problems (no more than one-digit divisors and three-digit dividends without technology).

Dividing with Remainders

Hands-On
counters

What happens when some are left?

Maria has 20 pepper plants to place in 3 rows. She has to plant the same number in each row. How many plants will go in each row? How many are left over?

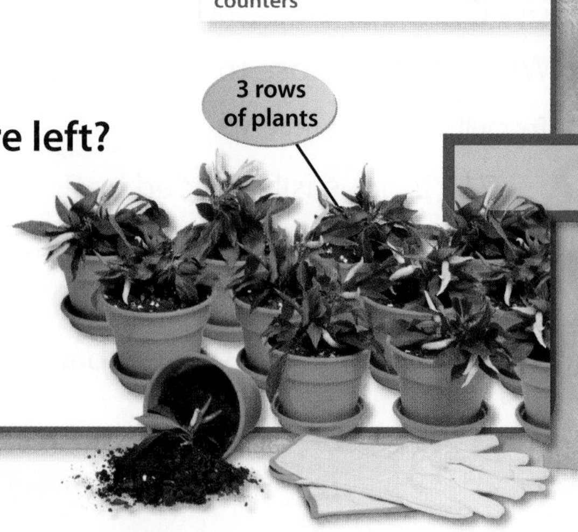

Guided Practice*

Do you know HOW?

In **1** through **4**, use counters or draw pictures. Tell how many items are in each group and how many are left over.

1. 26 pens
5 groups

2. 34 cars
7 boxes

3. 30 marbles
4 bags

4. 40 balls
6 bins

Do you UNDERSTAND?

5. Writing to Explain When you divide a number by 6, what remainders are possible?

6. Tia is planting her garden with 15 plants. She wants them planted in equal groups of 4. How many groups of 4 can she make? How many plants will she have left over?

Independent Practice

Leveled Practice In **7** through **14**, copy and then complete the calculations. Use counters or pictures to help.

The remainder should always be less than the divisor.

7. $8\overline{)35}$ R ▭, − ▭▭

8. $3\overline{)17}$ R ▭, − ▭▭

9. $9\overline{)51}$ R ▭, − ▭▭

10. $5\overline{)48}$ R ▭, − ▭▭

11. $6\overline{)47}$ R ▭, − ▭▭

12. $7\overline{)65}$ R ▭, − ▭▭

13. $9\overline{)77}$ R ▭, − ▭▭

14. $4\overline{)30}$ R ▭, − ▭▭

*For another example, see Set C on page 193.

Divide 20 counters among 3 rows.

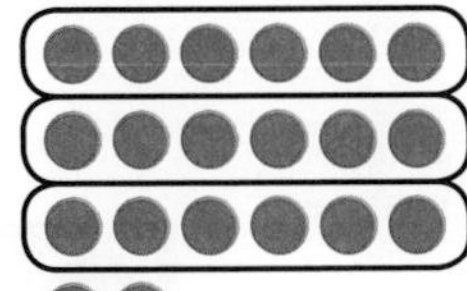

The part that is left after dividing is called the **remainder**.

There are 2 counters left over. This is not enough for another row, so the remainder is 2.

Check your answer.

$$\begin{array}{r} 6 \text{ R2} \\ 3\overline{)20} \\ -18 \\ \hline 2 \end{array}$$

Divide: 3 groups of 6 in 20

Multiply: $3 \times 6 = 18$

Subtract: $20 - 18 = 2$

Compare: $2 < 3$

$3 \times 6 = 18$, and $18 + 2 = 20$

Maria can plant 6 plants in each row. She will have 2 plants left over.

In **15** through **29**, divide. You may use counters or pictures to help.

15. $3\overline{)29}$	**16.** $7\overline{)41}$	**17.** $9\overline{)55}$	**18.** $8\overline{)62}$	**19.** $5\overline{)37}$
20. $7\overline{)45}$	**21.** $4\overline{)22}$	**22.** $6\overline{)28}$	**23.** $8\overline{)33}$	**24.** $8\overline{)75}$
25. $9\overline{)86}$	**26.** $6\overline{)34}$	**27.** $7\overline{)39}$	**28.** $5\overline{)23}$	**29.** $8\overline{)61}$

TAKS Problem Solving

30. **Algebra** If $69 \div 9 = n$ R6, what is the value of n?

31. How many pieces are left if 6 friends equally share 100 puzzle pieces?

32. Write a division sentence with a quotient of 7 and remainder of 3.

33. **Number Sense** When you divide by 3, can the remainder be 5?

34. **Reasonableness** Carl's teacher took 27 photos on their class trip. She wants to arrange them on the wall in 4 equal rows. Carl said if she does this, she will have 7 photos left over. Is this reasonable?

35. **Reasoning** Tanya is thinking of a number between 108 and 120. It is an odd number but the digit in the tens place is even. What is the number?

36. **Think About the Process** Jack helped Mrs. Sanchez pack 61 books in 7 boxes. Each box held 8 books. Which expression shows how to find how many books he had left?

A $61 - (7 + 8)$ **C** $61 + (7 \times 8)$

B $61 - (7 \times 8)$ **D** $61 + (7 + 8)$

37. At the school concert, there were 560 people seated in 8 rows. If there were no empty seats, how many people were in each row?

F 553 people **H** 70 people

G 480 people **J** 60 people

Lesson

8-4

TEKS 4.4B: Represent multiplication and division situations in picture, word, and number form.

Multiplication and Division Stories

When should you multiply or divide?

Multiply when you want to combine equal groups. Divide when you want to find the number of groups or the number in each group.

Each canoe holds four people, how many people can sit in 14 canoes?

Another Example How do you interpret a remainder?

Ben has 55 dollars to buy helium balloons for the end-of-summer camp party.

The balloons cost 9 dollars per bunch.

Sometimes you ignore the remainder.

How many bunches of balloons can Ben buy?

$$\begin{array}{r} 6 \text{ R1} \\ 9\overline{)55} \\ -54 \\ \hline 1 \end{array}$$

Ben can buy 6 bunches of balloons.

Sometimes the remainder is the answer.

How much money will Ben have left?

$$\begin{array}{r} 6 \text{ R1} \\ 9\overline{)55} \\ -54 \\ \hline 1 \end{array}$$

Ben will have 1 dollar left.

Explain It

1. Why is the remainder the answer to how much money Ben will have left?

2. How could you check that you divided 55 ÷ 9 correctly?

3. If Ben wanted to buy another bunch of balloons, how much more money does he need?

Find how many people can be seated in 14 canoes.

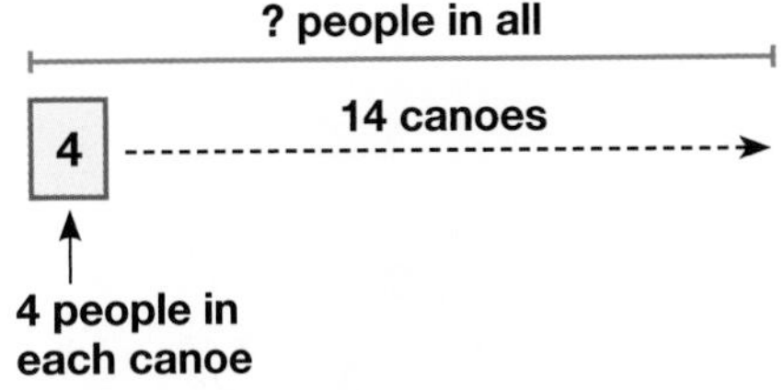

Multiply: $14 \times 4 = 56$

A total of 56 people can be seated in 14 canoes.

Find how many canoes will be needed for 36 people.

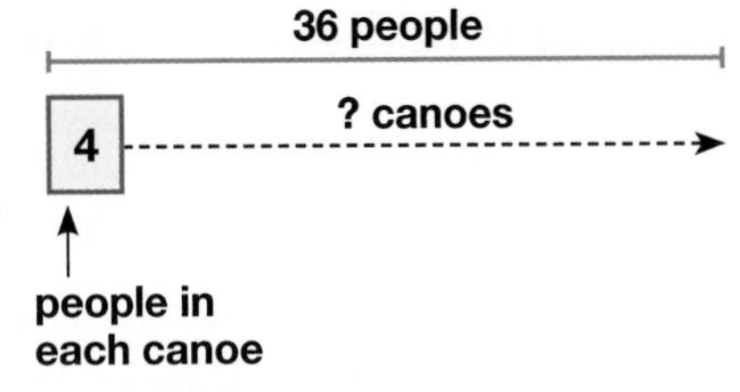

Divide: $36 \div 4 = 9$

A total of 9 canoes are needed for 36 people.

Guided Practice*

Do you know HOW?

Use the story below to solve **1** and **2**.

Ann is making costumes for a play. Each costume requires 3 yards of fabric.

1. How many yards of fabric are needed to make 12 costumes?

2. If Ann has 26 yards of fabric, how many costumes can she make?

Do you UNDERSTAND?

3. What does the remainder in Exercise 2 represent?

4. On a canoe trip, 12 paddles are shared among 5 canoes. How many canoes get an extra paddle?

5. Ben ordered 15 pizzas. Each pizza had 8 slices. How many slices of pizza were there in all?

Independent Practice

In **6** through **9**, write a multiplication or division story for each number fact. Then solve.

6. 22×7 **7.** $63 \div 9$ **8.** $34 \div 7$ **9.** 13×12

Solve **10** through **11**. If it is a multiplication story, explain how you knew to multiply. If it is a division story, explain how you know to divide.

10. There are 50 people signed up for a boat trip. Each boat holds 6 people. How many boats are needed?

11. Admission to a museum is 6 dollars a person. If 38 students are visiting the museum, how much will it cost in all?

*For another example, see Set D on page 193.

TAKS Problem Solving

Use the image at the right to answer **12**.

12. In 2005, an ultralight airplane tracked monarch butterflies migrating through Texas. The plane spent a total of 13 days in Texas. During this time, how many miles did the airplane travel?

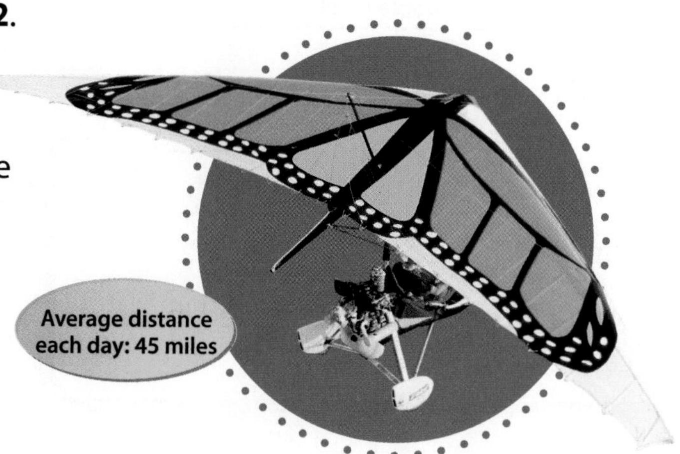

For **13** through **15**, use the table at the right.

13. Carl earns 23 tickets at the arcade. How many sticker packs can he get?

14. **Writing to Explain** Carlos has 39 tickets. If he gets as many glitter gels as possible, will he have enough tickets left over to get a sticker pack?

15. Tim wants to buy 4 toy airplanes. How many tickets does he need?

? tickets needed

22	22	22	22

tickets for each plane

Data

FunTime Arcade

Prize	Tickets Needed
Sticker packs	5
Glitter gel	8
Pencil case	14
Toy airplane	22

16. Joel has 5 packets of seeds. Each packet holds 12 seeds. He wants to divide the seeds evenly among 10 rows of his garden. How many seeds can he plant in each row?

F 4 seeds **H** 8 seeds

G 6 seeds **J** 10 seeds

17. Tina is making flag pins like the one shown below. How many of each color bead are needed to make 8 pins?

18. David is buying toys for a piñata. He wants to put 40 mini yo-yos in the piñata. Each bag has 8 yo-yos. If David spent 30 dollars on the yo-yos, how much did each bag cost?

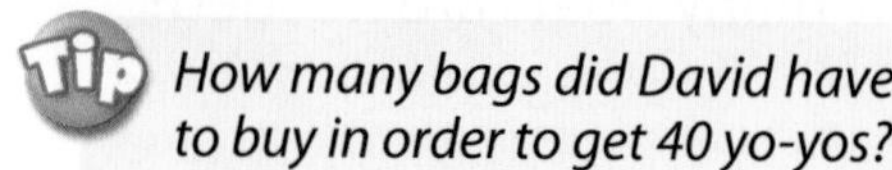

Tip
How many bags did David have
to buy in order to get 40 yo-yos?

A $4 **B** $5 **C** $6 **D** $7

Algebra Connections

Simplifying Number Expressions

In order to simplify a number expression you must follow the order of operations.

First, complete the operations inside the parentheses.

Then multiply and divide in order from left to right.

Then add and subtract in order from left to right.

Example: $(5 + 3) \times 4$

Start with the operation inside the parentheses. What is 5 + 3?

$5 + 3 = 8.$

Then, multiply 8 × 4.

$8 \times 4 = 32$

So, $(5 + 3) \times 4 = 32$

Simplify. Follow the order of operations.

1. $4 \times 8 - 6$

2. $12 + 8 \div 4$

3. $5 \times (8 - 2)$

4. $35 + (4 \times 6) - 7$

5. $7 \times 5 + 9$

6. $8 + 18 \div 3$

7. $6 + 4 + (12 \div 2)$

8. $(8 - 2) \div 3$

9. $(9 + 8) \times 2$

10. $10 + 4 \div (9 - 7)$

11. $(54 \div 9) + (6 \times 6)$

12. $(16 - 4) + (16 - 4)$

13. $(21 - 3) + 7$

14. $9 + 9 \div 3 \times 3$

15. $2 \div 2 + 2 - 1$

16. $3 \times 3 \div 3 + 6 - 3$

17. $5 + 4 \times 3 + 2 - 1$

18. $6 \div 3 \times 2 + 7 - 5$

For **19** through **24**, write the expression represented by each problem and then simplify the expression.

19. There are 2 teachers and 6 rows of 4 students in each classroom.

20. Three cartons of a dozen eggs each, with 4 eggs broken in each carton.

21. Two groups of 10 students are in a room. Four students leave the room.

22. Six rows of 5 small toys and 1 row of 7 large toys.

23. 4 baskets of 10 apples, with 2 bruised apples in each basket.

24. Five groups of 4 tulips, and 2 roses.

Lesson
8-5

TEKS 4.14: Apply Grade 4 mathematics to solve problems connected to everyday experiences and activities in and outside of school.

Problem Solving

Multiple-Step Problems

Paul and Libby sold some sock monkeys for a total of $72. Libby sold 5 monkeys from her collection. Paul sold 3 monkeys from his collection. If they sold each sock monkey for the same amount, how much did they sell each monkey for?

Paul sold
3 monkeys
Libby sold
5 monkeys

Guided Practice*

Do you know HOW?

Solve.

1. Adult admission to the town fair is $7. Child admission to the fair is $3. How much would it cost 2 adults and 4 children to enter the fair?

Do you UNDERSTAND?

2. What is the hidden question or questions?

3. **Write a Problem** Write a problem that contains a hidden question.

Independent Practice

Write the answer to the hidden question or questions. Then solve the problem. Write your answer in a complete sentence.

4. Charlie and Lola like to walk around the perimeter of their town park. The perimeter is 2 miles long. Last week Charlie walked around the perimeter 4 times and Lola walked around it 5 times. How many more miles did Lola walk than Charlie last week?

5. Abby buys 15 sunflower plants and 12 petunia plants to plant in her garden. She plans to plant 3 flowers in each row. How many rows of flowers will Abby plant?

6. What is the hidden question in Problem 5?

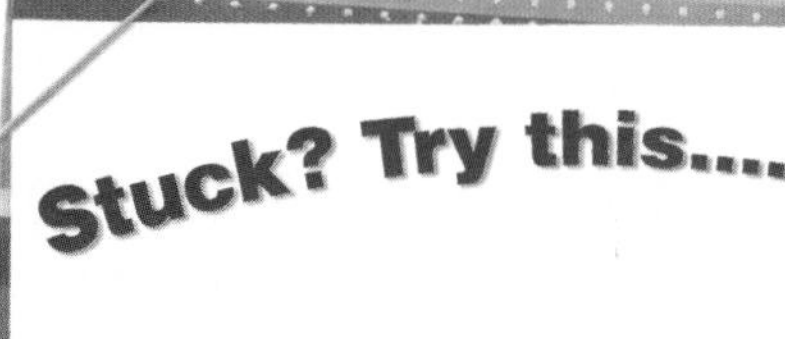
Stuck? Try this....

- What do I know?
- What diagram can I use to help understand the problem?
- Can I use addition, subtraction, multiplication, or division?
- Is all of my work correct?
- Did I answer the right question?
- Is my answer reasonable?

*For another example, see Set E on page 193.

Plan

Find the hidden question.
How many monkeys did Paul and Libby sell in all?

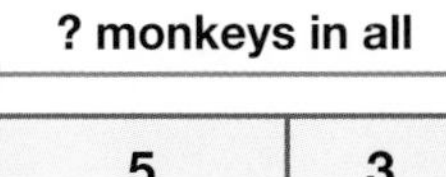

5 + 3 = 8 monkeys

They sold 8 sock monkeys.

Plan & Solve

Use the answer to the hidden question to solve the problem.

If they sold each sock monkey for the same amount, how much did they sell each sock monkey for?

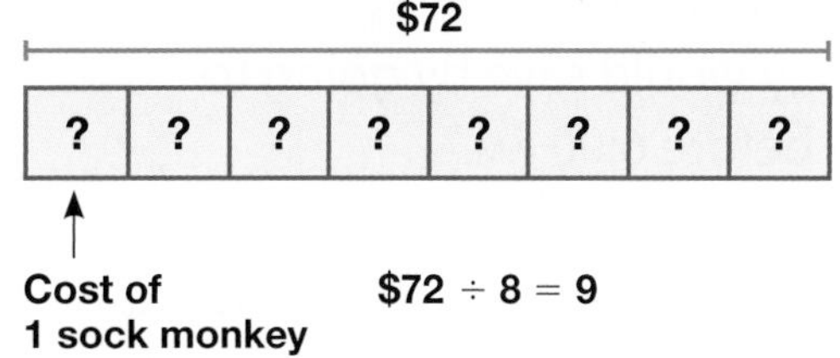

Cost of 1 sock monkey **$72 ÷ 8 = 9**

Paul and Libby sold each sock monkey for $9.

Use the data at the right for **7** through **9**.

Diner Delight

Item	Price
Hamburger	$4
Chicken Sandwich	$5
Baked Potato	$2
Salad	$3

7. Carlos's family bought 3 hamburgers and 2 salads from Diner Delight. They paid with a $20 bill. How much change did they receive?

8. Amber and her family bought 3 chicken sandwiches, 2 salads, and 1 baked potato. They spent $4 on drinks. How much did they spend in all?

9. Gene spent exactly $12 on lunch, including tax. He bought a chicken sandwich, a salad, and a baked potato. How much did Gene spend on tax?

For **10** through **12**, use the table to the right.

Al's Discount Music Store

Item	Price
3-pack blank CDs	$7
DVDs	$5
CDs	$10

10. Terrence and Jennifer went to Al's Discount Music Store. Terrence bought 4 CDs and two 3-packs of blank CDs. Jennifer bought 8 DVDs, 3 CDs, and one 3-pack of blank CDs. Together, how much did they spend?

11. Give an example of a hidden question in Problem 10.

12. In one hour, Al's Discount Music Store sold 22 DVDs, 36 CDs, and six 3-packs of blank CDs. How much was sold in one hour?

Independent Practice

Use the data at the right for **13** through **16**.

Samir and Maya are both under 12 years old. They are trying to find out how much they would save by going to a movie before 6:00 P.M.

Metro Movies Ticket Prices

	Children under 12	Adults under 65	65 and over
Before 6:00 P.M.	$4	$6	$3
Evening	$6	$7	$6

13. Look at Samir's work. What are the hidden questions Samir solved?

Samir's Work

$2 \times \$4 = \$8$

$2 \times \$6 = \$12$

$\$12 - \$8 = \$4$

14. Look at Maya's work. What is the hidden question Maya solved?

Maya's Work

$\$6 - \$4 = \$2$

15. What should Maya's next step be to find out how much money she and Samir would save?

16. What is the difference in the cost of 5 adult tickets for a movie before 6:00 P.M. and after 6:00 P.M.?

17. **Algebra** In $b \times c = 134$, b is a one-digit number and c is a two-digit number. What numbers could b and c represent?

18. A tractor-trailer is also known as an 18-wheeler, because it has 18 wheels. How many more wheels are on 2 tractor-trailers than on 5 cars?

Think About the Process

19. Justine's plant stand has 6 shelves. Each shelf holds 4 plants. Justine has already placed 16 plants on her stand. Which expression will answer the hidden question, "How many more plants can Justine's plant stand hold?"

A 4×16

B 6×16

C $24 - 16$

D $24 - 20$

20. Justine decided to buy more plants. She paid with two $20 bills. She received $12 in change. What must you first find before you can find the cost of each plant?

F The number of plants that she bought

G The amount Justine received in change

H The cost of each plant

J The amount Justine paid

Division Patterns

Use eTools Spreadsheet/Data/Grapher

Use a pattern to find 45,000 ÷ 9.

Step 1 Go to the Spreadsheet/Data/Grapher eTool. Use the arrow tool to select at least 3 rows and 4 columns. Set the number of decimal places at zero using the .00 pull-down menu. Enter 45, 450, 4500, and 45000 in one column. Enter 9 in each cell of the next column.

Step 2 In the first row of the third column enter =45/9. In the second row, enter =450/9. Continue entering formulas, where the first number is the number in the first column.

Step 3 Find a pattern and give the quotient.

45,000 ÷ 9 = 5,000.

Practice

Use patterns and the Spreadsheet/Data/Grapher eTool to find each quotient.

1. 30,000 ÷ 5

2. 56,000 ÷ 7

3. 64,000 ÷ 8

4. 1,200 ÷ 3

5. 14,000 ÷ 2

6. 25,000 ÷ 5

7. 40,000 ÷ 8

8. 8,000 ÷ 4

9. 24,000 ÷ 8

10. 36,000 ÷ 6

11. 49,000 ÷ 7

12. 32,000 ÷ 4

13. 10,000 ÷ 5

14. 2,400 ÷ 3

15. 81,000 ÷ 9

TAKS Test Prep

1. A stadium has 30,000 seats and 6 main gates. How many seats are served by each gate if each gate serves the same number of seats? (8-1)

   A 50

   B 500

   C 5,000

   D 50,000

2. What is the quotient? (8-3)

   $$\begin{array}{r} \square \text{ R } \square \\ 7\overline{)30} \\ -\ \square\square \\ \hline \square \end{array}$$

   F 3 R8

   G 4 R2

   H 4 R3

   J 5 R2

3. Which story could be solved with 64 ÷ 8? (8-4)

   A Tim used all but 8 of the 64 nails. How many nails were used?

   B Mrs. Pemberton bought 64 bags of hotdog buns for the picnic. Each bag had 8 buns. How many buns did she buy?

   C Alex made 64 placemats. If he makes 8 more, how many placemats will he have made?

   D Jeff has 64 ounces of juice. Each glass holds 8 ounces. How many glasses can he have?

4. Bracelets are on sale for 3 for $15. How much do 5 bracelets cost? (8-5)

   F $5

   G $20

   H $25

   J $30

5. There are 25 grapes for 4 girls. If each girl receives the same number of grapes, what is the most number of grapes each girl can receive? (8-4)

   A 7

   B 6

   C 5

   D 1

6. Which number sentence comes next in the pattern? (8-1)

   48 ÷ 6 = 8
   480 ÷ 6 = 80
   4,800 ÷ 6 = 800

   F 4,800 ÷ 6 = 8,000

   G 4,800 ÷ 60 = 800

   H 48,000 ÷ 6 = 8,000

   J 48,000 ÷ 60 = 800

7. The museum has 35 molecule models. They need to be packaged 4 to a box. After 8 boxes are filled, how many models will be left? (8-4)

   A 3

   B 2

   C 1

   D 0

8. Harold earned \$196 by mowing 5 lawns. Which number sentence shows the best way to estimate the amount he earned for each lawn? (8-2)

F $\$200 \div 5 = \$40$

G $\$150 \div 5 = \$30$

H $\$200 \div 10 = \$20$

J $5 \times \$200 = \$1{,}000$

9. Mandy bought 3 yards of material for \$3 a yard and 2 packages of buttons for \$2 a package. Which number sentence can be used to find the total amount Mandy spent on sewing supplies? (8-5)

A $9 + 4 = \square$

B $6 + 4 = \square$

C $9 \times 4 = \square$

D $6 + 6 = \square$

10. Eugenia bought 16 flowers. She used 3 flowers in each centerpiece. How many flowers were left over? (8-3)

F none

G 1 flower

H 2 flowers

J 6 flowers

11. Lee had 30 DVDs. He sold 12 for \$3 each. He used the money to buy 4 more DVDs. What needs to be answered to find how much Lee paid for each DVD he bought? (8-5)

A How many DVDs Lee did not sell

B Whether the DVDs were new

C Where Lee purchased the DVDs

D How much Lee earned on the 12 DVDs he sold

12. There are 49 students on a tour. Each guide can take 5 students. How many guides are needed? (8-4)

F 4

G 8

H 9

J 10

13. Holly uses 7 sheets of tissue paper to make one flower. If she bought a package with 500 sheets of tissue paper, about how many flowers will she be able to make? (8-2)

A 80

B 70

C 60

D 50

14. **Griddable Response** The soccer club has one package of 360 paper cups to use in the concession stands. If they split the cups evenly between the 4 concession stands, how many cups would each stand have? (8-1)

Reteaching

Set A, pages 176–177

A class shares 270 pens equally among 3 groups of students.

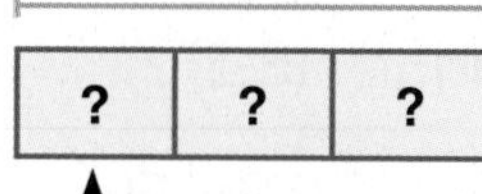

Find 270 ÷ 3.

The basic fact is 27 ÷ 3 = 9.
27 tens ÷ 3 = 9 tens or 90
So, 270 ÷ 3 = 90 pens.

Remember you can use patterns with zero to divide multiples of 10.

1. 250 ÷ 5
2. 81,000 ÷ 9
3. 3,200 ÷ 4
4. 42,000 ÷ 7
5. 1,000 ÷ 2
6. 240 ÷ 4
7. 450 ÷ 5
8. 72,000 ÷ 9
9. 3,600 ÷ 4
10. 49,000 ÷ 7
11. 2,000 ÷ 2
12. 280 ÷ 4

Set B, pages 178–179

Kenny read 130 pages in 7 days. Use estimation to find about how many pages Kenny read each day.

What number close to 130 is easily divided by 7?

Try multiples of ten near 130:

140 is 14 tens and can be divided by 7.

140 ÷ 7 = 20

So, 130 ÷ 7 is about 20.

Remember to try rounding the dividend to the nearest ten.

Estimate each quotient.

1. 718 ÷ 8
2. 156 ÷ 4
3. 482 ÷ 8
4. 117 ÷ 4
5. 843 ÷ 7
6. 321 ÷ 2
7. 428 ÷ 6
8. 811 ÷ 9
9. 561 ÷ 8
10. 723 ÷ 8
11. 632 ÷ 9
12. 362 ÷ 9
13. 402 ÷ 2
14. 122 ÷ 6
15. 251 ÷ 5
16. 362 ÷ 6

Topic 8

Reteaching

Set C, pages 180–181

Find $56 \div 9$.

$$\begin{array}{r} 6 \text{ R2} \\ 9\overline{)56} \\ -\ 54 \\ \hline 2 \end{array}$$

Divide: 6 groups of 9 in 56
Multiply: $6 \times 9 = 54$
Subtract: $56 - 54 = 2$
Compare $2 < 9$

Check: $9 \times 6 = 54$ and $54 + 2 = 56$

$56 \div 9 = 6$ R2

Remember that you can use pictures to help.

1. $3\overline{)22}$
2. $2\overline{)15}$
3. $5\overline{)43}$
4. $3\overline{)25}$
5. $3\overline{)28}$
6. $4\overline{)37}$
7. $4\overline{)35}$
8. $6\overline{)58}$

Set D, pages 182–184

Share 21 trading cards among 3 friends.

$$\begin{array}{r} 7 \\ 3\overline{)21} \\ -\ 21 \\ \hline 0 \end{array}$$

21 trading cards

?	?	?

Number of trading cards for each friend

Each friend will recieve 7 trading cards.

Remember to divide to find the number of equal groups.

Write a multiplication or division story for each number fact.

1. 32×5
2. $6\overline{)54}$
3. $6\overline{)36}$
4. 19×4
5. $3 \times \$10$
6. $7\overline{)49}$

Set E, pages 186–188

How can you use hidden questions to solve the problem?

Answer the hidden question first.

Joy bought 3 packages of balloons and 5 packages of party favors. There are 10 balloons and 8 favors in each package. How many more favors did Joy buy?

Hidden Questions: $3 \times 10 = 30$
$5 \times 8 = 40$

Solve the problem: $40 - 30 = 10$

Joy bought 10 more party favors than balloons.

Remember that you can use problem-solving strategies such as drawing a picture and work backward.

1. Adult admission to the dog show was \$8. Child admission to the dog show is \$5. How much would it cost 3 adults and 2 kids to enter the fair?

2. Juan bought 4 DVDs for \$10 each and 2 CDs for \$7 each. How much did Juan spend altogether?

Topics 1–8

Spiral Review

Number and Operations

1. What is the value of the 2 in 5,432,109?

   A 2,000 **C** 200,000

   B 20,000 **D** 2,000,000

2. The models are shaded to show 2 equivalent fractions. Which fraction is equal to $\frac{1}{3}$?

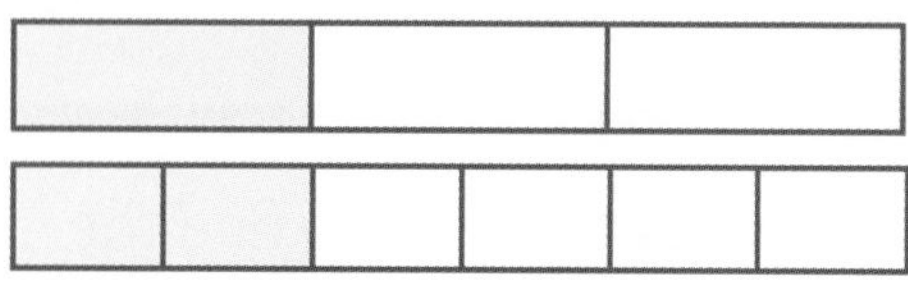

   F $\frac{2}{6}$ **G** $\frac{1}{4}$ **H** $\frac{2}{3}$ **J** $\frac{3}{1}$

3. What is 7,234 rounded to the nearest thousand?

   F 6,000 **H** 7,500

   G 7,000 **J** 8,000

4. Bill sold 25 tickets to the play on Thursday and 16 tickets on Friday. About how many tickets were sold in all?

   A About 40 **C** About 60

   B About 50 **D** About 75

5. An ad says, "Buy 3 notebooks, get 1 notebook free." If you purchase 15 notebooks in total, how many are free?

6. **Writing to Explain** How can you tell without dividing that 12 ÷ 3 will be greater than 12 ÷ 4?

Geometry and Measurement

7. Which space figure would you use to draw the plane figure shown in the box?

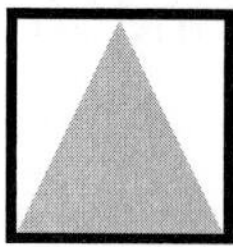

   A 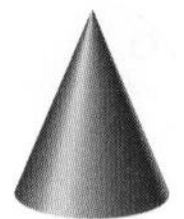 **C** 

   B 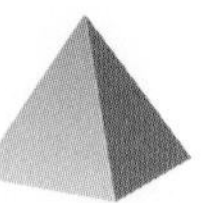 **D** 

8. Which figure represents a hexagon?

   F  **H** 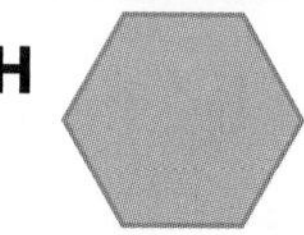

   G  **J** 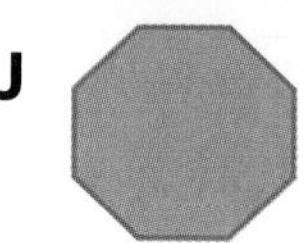

9. Which of the numbers below has one line of symmetry?

   A 9 **C** 7

   B 3 **D** 2

10. Which is not a metric unit used to measure length?

   F meter **H** centimeter

   G kilometer **J** liter

11. Jon began to exercise at 15 minutes before 7. Geraldine started to exercise at 45 minutes after 5. Who started to exercise first?

12. What is the date of the sixteenth day of the sixth month?

13. **Writing to Explain** Explain why it is impossible to measure a line or a ray.

Probability and Statistics

14. What is the probability that a bird will fly?

A Certain **C** Unlikely
B Likely **D** Impossible

15. On which color is the spinner most likely to land?

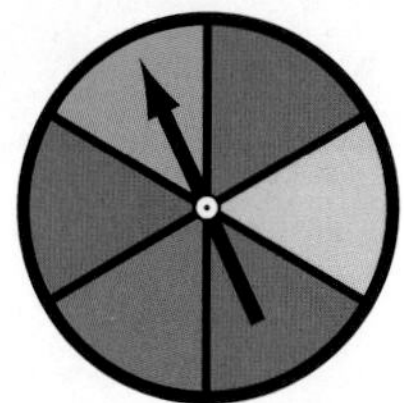

F Blue **H** Green
G Red **J** Yellow

This tally chart table shows the results of picking a marble from a bag, and then returning it to the bag 30 times.

Marbles picked from a bag

Outcome	Tally	Number
black	III	3
blue	~~IIII~~ I	6
red	~~IIII~~ IIII	9
green	~~IIII~~ ~~IIII~~ II	12

16. Predict the color of the marble most likely to be picked?

17. Predict the color of the next marble to be picked?

18. Writing to Explain A box is filled with 8 blue tiles and 2 white tiles. Why is it possible, but unlikely, to pick a white tile?

Algebra

19. Which number sentence completes the chart?

$7 \times 4 = 28$
$7 \times 40 = 280$
$7 \times 400 = 2{,}800$
$\square \times \square = \square$

A $4 \times 700 = 2{,}800$

B $7 \times 400 = 2{,}800$

C $7 \times 4{,}000 = 28{,}000$

D $7 \times 40{,}000 = 280{,}000$

20. If 18 divided by a number is 6, which number sentence could be used to find the number?

F $6 \times \square = 18$ **H** $18 \times 6 = \square$
G $18 - \square = 6$ **J** $18 + 6 = \square$

21. What is the missing number in the pattern?

9, 18, 27, ☐, 45, 54

A 30 **B** 32 **C** 34 **D** 36

22. What property of multiplication states that $a \times 1 = a$

F Identity **H** Associative
G Commutative **J** Distributive

23. Writing to Explain Blake is using the rule "add 3" to make a pattern. He started with 5 and wrote the numbers below. Which number should be removed?

5, 8, 11, 13, 14

Topic 9

Dividing by 1-Digit Divisors

1 Where was the world's largest American flag displayed? You will find out in Lesson 9-3.

2 Selenium is a mineral found in certain crystals. It is often used to conduct electricity. Some of the tallest selenite crystals are found in Chihuahua, Mexico. Find out how many times taller they are than a 4-foot-tall fourth grader in Lesson 9-2.

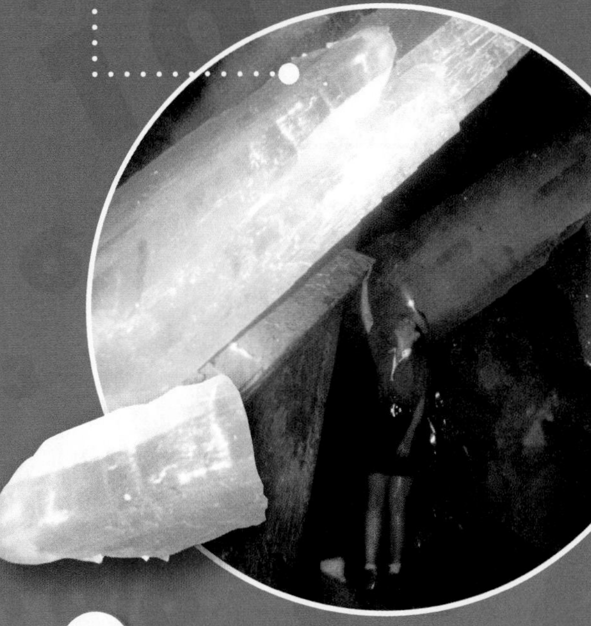

3 The Texas State Capitol is visited by over a million people per year. How many tours of the Capitol are run in one week? You will find out in Lesson 9-1.

Review What You Know!

Vocabulary

Choose the best term from the box.

- dividend
- divisor
- inverse operations
- quotient

1. In the number sentence 42 ÷ 6 = 7, 42 is the ?.

2. A ? is the answer to a division problem.

3. Operations that undo each other are ?.

Estimating Quotients

Estimate each quotient.

4. 88 ÷ 3 **5.** 249 ÷ 5 **6.** 634 ÷ 9

7. 448 ÷ 5 **8.** 101 ÷ 2 **9.** 372 ÷ 6

10. 241 ÷ 8 **11.** 472 ÷ 7 **12.** 352 ÷ 4

Dividing With Remainders

13. 3)20 **14.** 9)32 **15.** 7)60

16. 8)46 **17.** 6)59 **18.** 3)8

Multiplication and Division Stories

19. Each train coach can hold 40 people. How many people can ride in 3 coaches?

20. **Writing to Explain** A tennis pro buys 150 tennis balls in cans. Explain how there can be 3 balls in every can, but there cannot be 4 balls in every can.

Lesson
9-1

TEKS 4.4B: Represent multiplication and division situations in picture, word, and number form.

Connecting Models and Symbols

Hands-On
place-value blocks

How can place-value help you divide?

Mrs. Lynch displayed 57 student drawings on 3 walls in her art classroom. If she divided the drawings equally, how many drawings are on each wall?

Estimate: 60 ÷ 3 = 20

Another Example How do you model remainders?

Helen has 55 postcards. As an art project, she plans to glue 4 postcards onto sheets of colored paper.

How many pieces of paper can she fill?

Step 1 Divide the tens.

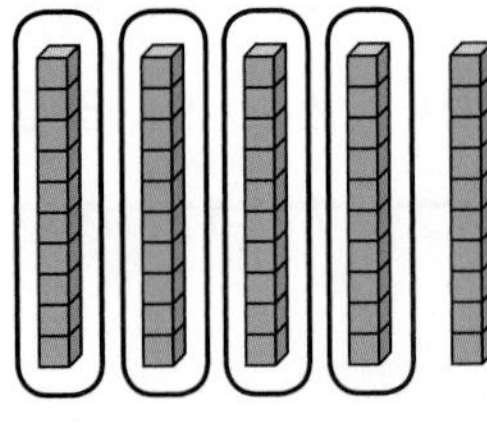

Division is used to find the number of equal groups.

```
  1
4)55
 -4
  1
```

There is 1 ten in each group and 1 ten left over.

Step 2 Regroup the 1 ten as 10 ones and divide.

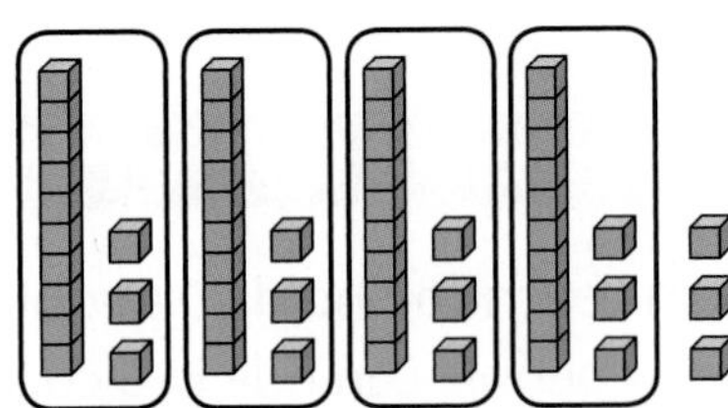

```
  13 R3
4)55
 -4
  15
 -12
   3
```

Trade the extra ten for ten ones.
The 1 ten and 5 ones make 15.
There are 3 ones in each group and 3 left over.

Helen will fill 13 pieces of colored paper.

Explain It

1. In the first step above, what does the 1 in the quotient represent?

2. **Reasonableness** How can you check that the answer is correct?

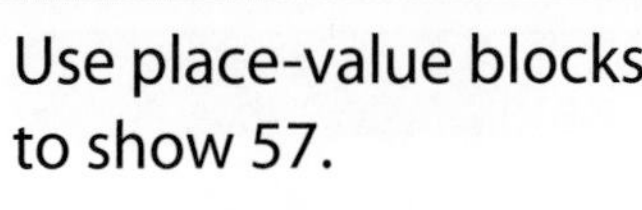

Use place-value blocks to show 57.

Divide the tens into three equal groups.

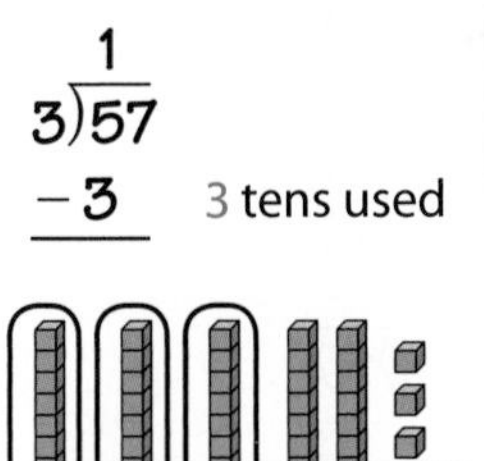

$$\begin{array}{r} 1 \\ 3\overline{)57} \\ -3 \\ \hline \end{array}$$ 3 tens used

Trade the extra tens for ones.

$$\begin{array}{r} 1 \\ 3\overline{)57} \\ -3 \\ \hline 27 \end{array}$$ 3 tens used, 27 ones left

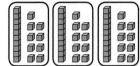

Divide the ones.

$$\begin{array}{r} 19 \\ 3\overline{)57} \\ -3 \\ \hline 27 \\ -27 \\ \hline 0 \end{array}$$ 27 ones used

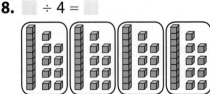

There are 19 drawings on each wall.

Guided Practice*

Do you know HOW?

In **1** through **4**, use place-value blocks or draw pictures. Tell how many are in each group and how many are left over.

1. 76 magazines
5 boxes

2. 56 marbles
3 bags

3. 82 muffins
7 boxes

4. 72 photos
3 albums

Do you UNDERSTAND?

5. Describe another way to show 57 using place-value blocks.

6. Mrs. Lynch displayed 48 paintings in 3 sets. If each set had the same number of paintings, how many were in each set?

Independent Practice

Leveled Practice In **7** through **10**, use the model to complete each division sentence.

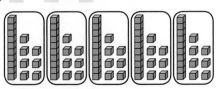

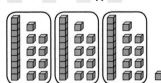

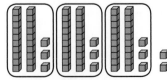

7. 71 ÷ ▢ = ▢ R2

8. ▢ ÷ 4 = ▢

9. ▢ ÷ ▢ = ▢

10. ▢ ÷ ▢ = ▢ R ▢

DIGITAL eTools www.pearsonsuccessnet.com

*For another example, see Set A on page 216.

Independent Practice

In **11** through **30**, use place-value blocks or draw pictures to solve.

11. $3\overline{)46}$	**12.** $8\overline{)96}$	**13.** $4\overline{)55}$	**14.** $2\overline{)51}$	**15.** $5\overline{)89}$
16. $6\overline{)76}$	**17.** $7\overline{)36}$	**18.** $3\overline{)72}$	**19.** $2\overline{)63}$	**20.** $4\overline{)92}$
21. $3\overline{)44}$	**22.** $4\overline{)67}$	**23.** $6\overline{)85}$	**24.** $3\overline{)56}$	**25.** $5\overline{)97}$
26. $2\overline{)39}$	**27.** $4\overline{)31}$	**28.** $5\overline{)87}$	**29.** $7\overline{)82}$	**30.** $5\overline{)22}$

TAKS Problem Solving

31. Maya used place-value blocks to divide 87. She made groups of 17 with 2 left over. Use place-value blocks or draw pictures to determine how many groups Maya made.

32. Writing to Explain Harold has 64 toy cars in 4 equal boxes. To find the number in each box, he divided 64 by 4. How many tens did he regroup as ones?

33. Think About the Process Jake walks dogs and delivers papers to earn money. This month, he earned $52 delivering papers and $43 walking dogs. Each month, he puts half of his money into the bank. Which shows how much Jake saved this month?

A $(52 + 43) + 2$ **C** $(52 + 43) \div 2$

B $(52 + 43) \times 2$ **D** $(52 + 43) - 2$

34. Number Sense Tina has 52 berries. She wants to have some each day for lunch. How many berries can she have each day if she wants to eat them all in 5 days?

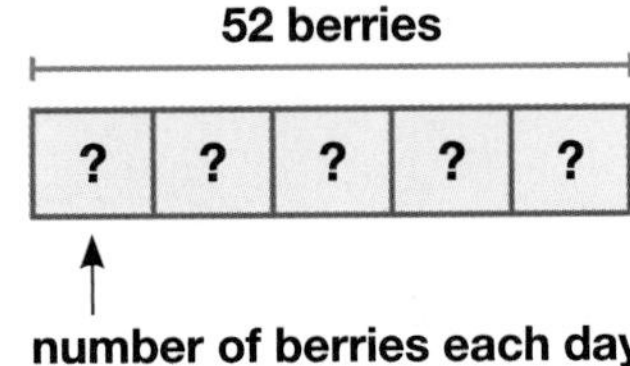

35. The 4 fourth-grade classes from Jameson Elementary School took a trip to the Texas State Capitol Building. Each class had 24 students. At the Capitol, the students were divided into 6 equal groups. How many students were in each group?

36. Every 4 weeks the Texas State Capitol runs about 244 tours. How many tours do they run in one week?

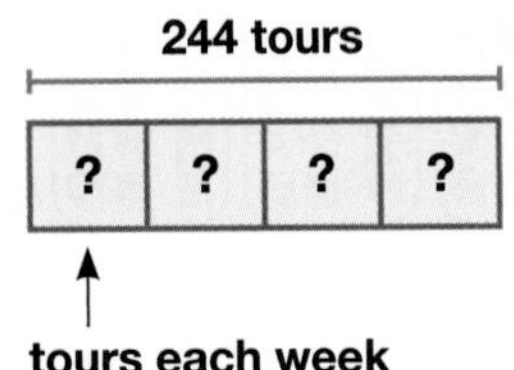

Mixed Problem Solving

Longhorn Cattle Herding in Texas

- The Chisholm Trail was a major route for herding Texas cattle. It was in use from 1867 to 1884.
- One cowboy was needed for every 250 head of cattle.
- Cowboys earned about $8 a month.
- The herd moved at a pace of about 12 miles per day for an average of 6 weeks.

1. For about how many years was the Chisholm Trail in use?

2. About how many miles would the herd travel in a week?

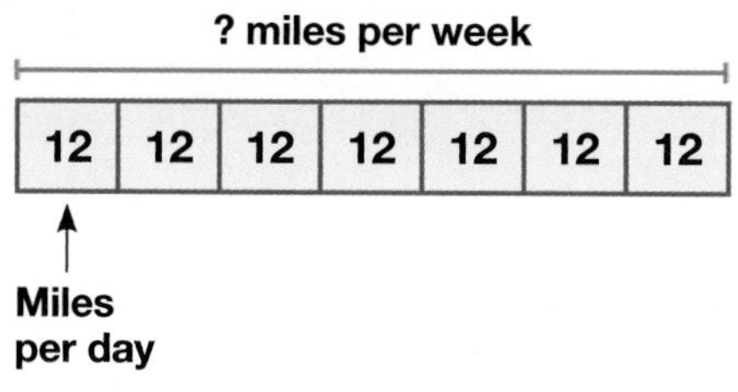

3. How many months would a cowboy have to work in order to earn $50?

4. Copy and complete the table below.

Cowboys	2	■	6	■	10
Cattle	500	1,000	■	2,000	■

5. Geometry A Texas rancher is building a pen for his sheep. The pen is 65 feet long and 22 feet wide. What is the area of the pen? How much fencing will be needed?

6. Estimation Cooks on a herding trip were paid $75 a month. About how much is this a week?

7. During the California Gold Rush, the demand for cattle was so great that a steer worth $14 in Texas was worth $95 in California. How much more would you spend for 5 cattle in California than in Texas at that time? Show how you found your answer.

8. Tanya has a poster with pictures of cowboy hats on it. The pictures are in 4 rows with 6 hats in each row. How many hats are shown in all?

Lesson
9-2

TEKS 4.4E: Use division to solve problems (no more than one-digit divisors and three-digit dividends without technology).

Dividing 2-Digit by 1-Digit Numbers

What is a common way to record division?

At the school food drive, Al needs to put the same number of soup cans into four boxes. How many soup cans will go in each box?

Choose an Operation Divide to find the number in each group.

Another Example How do you divide with a remainder?

Al collects 58 cans of vegetables. He puts the same number of cans in four boxes. How many cans of vegetables will go in each box? How many cans will be left over?

A 14 cans; 2 cans left over

B 15 cans; 2 cans left over

C 16 cans; 2 cans left over

D 18 cans; 2 cans left over

Step 1

Divide the tens.

Regroup the remaining ten as 10 ones.

```
  14
4)58
 -4
  1
```

Step 2

Divide the ones.

Subtract to find the remainder.

```
  14
4)58
 -4
  18
 -16
   2
```

Step 3

Check: $14 \times 4 = 56$ and $56 + 2 = 58$.

There will be 14 cans of vegetables in each box and 2 cans left over.

The correct choice is **A**.

Explain It

1. **Reasonableness** How can you use estimation to decide if 14 cans is reasonable?

2. Why is multiplication used to check division?

Step 1

Divide the tens.

$$\begin{array}{r} 1 \\ 4\overline{)76} \\ -4 \\ \hline 3 \end{array}$$

Think: There is 1 ten in each group and 3 tens left over.

Step 2

Divide the ones.

$$\begin{array}{r} 19 \\ 4\overline{)76} \\ -4 \\ \hline 36 \\ -36 \\ \hline 0 \end{array}$$

Think: Trade the 3 tens for 30 ones. 30 ones and 6 ones make 36 ones.

There will be 19 soup cans in each box.

Step 3

Check by multiplying.

$$\begin{array}{r} {}^{3} \\ 19 \\ \times\ 4 \\ \hline 76 \end{array}$$

The answer checks.

Guided Practice*

Do you know HOW?

In **1** and **2**, copy and complete each calculation.

1. $\begin{array}{r} 4\square \\ 2\overline{)94} \\ -\square \\ \hline \square 4 \\ -1\square \\ \hline 0 \end{array}$

2. $\begin{array}{r} \square 6\text{R}\square \\ 5\overline{)82} \\ -5 \\ \hline \square\square \\ -\square\square \\ \hline \square \end{array}$

Do you UNDERSTAND?

3. Explain how you would estimate the answer in Exercise 2.

4. Al collects 85 cans of fruit. He puts the same number of fruit cans in 4 boxes. Will he have any cans left over? If so, how many cans?

Independent Practice

Leveled Practice In **5** through **8**, copy and complete each calculation. Estimate to check reasonableness.

5. $\begin{array}{r} \square\square \\ 7\overline{)84} \\ -7 \\ \hline \square 4 \\ -\square\square \\ \hline 0 \end{array}$

6. $\begin{array}{r} \square 6 \\ 3\overline{)78} \\ -\square \\ \hline \square 8 \\ -1\square \\ \hline 0 \end{array}$

7. $\begin{array}{r} \square\square\text{R}\square \\ 4\overline{)93} \\ -8 \\ \hline \square\square \\ -1\square \\ \hline 1 \end{array}$

8. $\begin{array}{r} 1\square\text{R}\square \\ 6\overline{)80} \\ -\square \\ \hline \square\square \\ -\square\square \\ \hline \square \end{array}$

For **9** through **18**, find each quotient. Use multiplication to check.

9. $3\overline{)63}$ **10.** $7\overline{)88}$ **11.** $6\overline{)96}$ **12.** $4\overline{)52}$ **13.** $5\overline{)73}$

14. $5\overline{)93}$ **15.** $3\overline{)87}$ **16.** $4\overline{)72}$ **17.** $6\overline{)77}$ **18.** $2\overline{)37}$

For another example, see Set B on page 216.

Independent Practice

In **19** through **28**, find each quotient. Use multiplication to check.

19. $3\overline{)46}$ **20.** $7\overline{)65}$ **21.** $8\overline{)27}$ **22.** $9\overline{)86}$ **23.** $4\overline{)52}$

24. $8\overline{)59}$ **25.** $4\overline{)92}$ **26.** $3\overline{)74}$ **27.** $5\overline{)68}$ **28.** $2\overline{)89}$

TAKS Problem Solving

29. Some of the tallest selenite crystals in a cave in Chihuahua, Mexico, are 50 feet tall. About how many times taller are the tallest crystals than a 4-foot-tall fourth grader?

30. **Geometry** Zelda has a piece of fabric that is 74 inches long. She wants to divide it into 2 equal pieces. What is the length of each piece?

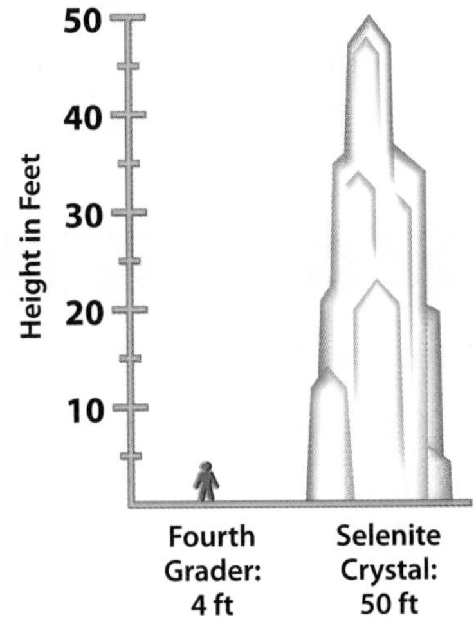

Use the recipe at the right for **31** and **32**.

31. How many ounces of Tasty Trail Mix are made following the recipe?

32. Maggie is making trail mix. She makes 4 batches of the recipe shown. Then she divides it into 3 equal sized bags. How many ounces are in each bag?

Data

Tasty Trail Mix	
granola	8 oz
nuts	5 oz
raisins	2 oz
cranberries	3 oz

33. **Writing to Explain** Why does $51 \div 4$ have two digits in the quotient, while $51 \div 6$ has only one digit in the quotient?

34. **Write a Problem** Write a problem that could be solved by dividing 78 by 5.

35. **Estimation** Paulo has 78 cattle on his ranch. He needs to divide them equally among 3 pastures. Which shows the best way to estimate the number of cattle in each pasture?

A $60 \div 3$ **C** $75 \div 3$

B $66 \div 3$ **D** $90 \div 3$

36. Every year the city of San Marcos holds a Cinco de Mayo festival. If 60 students perform in 5 groups, how many students are in each group?

F 10 students **H** 25 students

G 12 students **J** 55 students

Algebra Connections

Solving Equations

Remember that an equation is a number sentence which uses an equal sign to show that two expressions have the same value. You can use basic facts and mental math to help you find missing values in an equation.

Example:

$18 \div \square = 3$

Think *What number times 3 is 18?*

Since $6 \times 3 = 18$, the value of $\square$ must be 6.

Copy and complete. Check your answers.

1. $20 + \square = 34$ **2.** $64 \div \square = 8$ **3.** $5 \times \square = 45$ **4.** $54 - \square = 14$

5. $\square \times 6 = 42$ **6.** $36 \div \square = 4$ **7.** $\square + 15 = 31$ **8.** $\square - 8 = 6$

9. $26 - \square = 18$ **10.** $9 + \square = 20$ **11.** $12 \div \square = 6$ **12.** $4 \times \square = 28$

13. $72 \div \square = 8$ **14.** $\square \times 9 = 54$ **15.** $\square - 5 = 7$ **16.** $\square + 7 = 29$

17. $\square + 32 = 46$ **18.** $28 - \square = 9$ **19.** $\square \div 4 = 12$ **20.** $\square \times 3 = 30$

For **21** through **24**, copy and complete the equation using information from the problem. Then find the answer.

21. Jaina has \$4. She needs \$12 to buy a book. How much more money does Jaina need?

$4 + \square = 12$

22. Harrison's allowance is \$5 a week. How much money will he have if he saves his whole allowance for 4 weeks?

$\square \times 5 = \square$

23. There are 49 fourth graders. The gym teacher needs to divide them into groups of 7. How many groups can be made?

$49 \div \square = \square$

24. Write a Problem Write a problem in which 4 is subtracted from 28 to find a difference. Write the number sentence and then solve.

Lesson

9-3

TEKS 4.4E: Use division to solve problems (no more than one-digit divisors and three-digit dividends without technology).

Dividing 3-Digit by 1-Digit Numbers

How can you divide numbers in the hundreds?

A factory shipped 378 watches in 3 boxes. If the watches were equally divided, how many watches were there in each box?

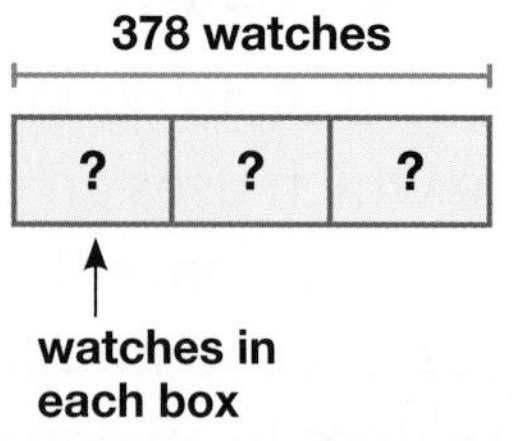

Choose an Operation Divide to find the size of equal groups.

Guided Practice*

Do you know HOW?

In **1** and **2**, copy and complete each calculation.

1. $2\overline{)658}$, quotient 3▯▯

2. $4\overline{)954}$, quotient ▯▯▯ R▯; first step − 8; final remainder 2

Do you UNDERSTAND?

3. When you divide the hundreds in the first step above, what does the 1 in the quotient represent?

4. Jenny paid $195 to take violin lessons for 3 months. How much did 1 month of lessons cost?

$195
? ? ?
Cost for 1 month

Independent Practice

Leveled Practice In **5** through **13**, divide. You may draw a picture to help you.

5. $5\overline{)595}$, quotient 1▯▯; partial result 4▯

6. $2\overline{)832}$, quotient ▯▯▯; partial results 3, ▯2

7. $3\overline{)866}$, quotient 2▯▯ R▯

8. $4\overline{)575}$, quotient ▯▯▯ R▯

9. $4\overline{)952}$ **10.** $3\overline{)761}$ **11.** $5\overline{)615}$ **12.** $2\overline{)871}$ **13.** $3\overline{)638}$

*For another example, see Set C on page 216.

Estimate:

$360 \div 3 = 120$

Divide the hundreds.

$$\begin{array}{r} 1 \\ 3\overline{)378} \\ -3 \\ \hline 7 \end{array}$$

Divide the tens.

$$\begin{array}{r} 12 \\ 3\overline{)378} \\ -3 \\ \hline 7 \\ -6 \\ \hline 1 \end{array}$$

Divide the ones.

$$\begin{array}{r} 126 \\ 3\overline{)378} \\ -3 \\ \hline 7 \\ -6 \\ \hline 18 \\ -18 \\ \hline 0 \end{array}$$

There are 126 watches in each box. The estimate is reasonable because 126 is close to 120.

TAKS Problem Solving

14. Geometry The largest United States flag ever created was displayed at the Hoover Dam. The flag measures 255 feet by 505 feet. How many feet wider is the flag than it is long?

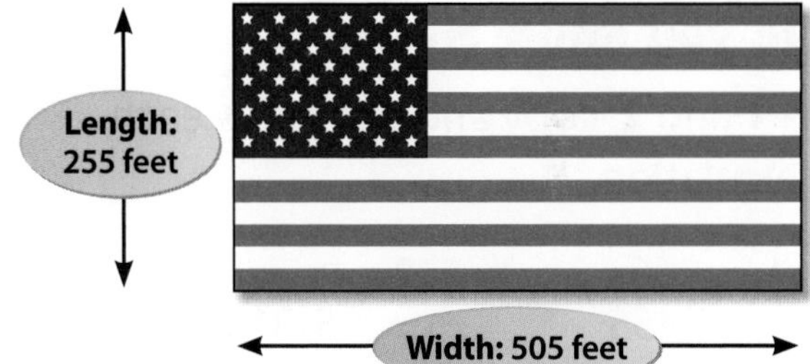

For **15** and **16**, use the table at the right.

15. There are 848 people getting on board the *Memphis Belle.* How many seats are needed for every person to sit?

16. Writing to Explain If 793 people are on the *Natchez Willie,* how many seats are needed for each person to sit?

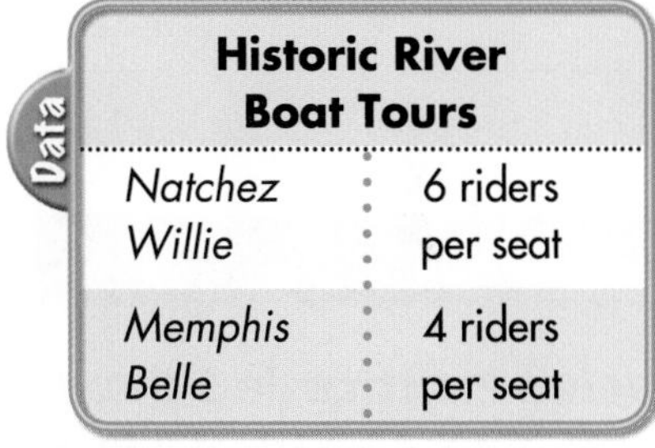

Data

Historic River Boat Tours	
Natchez Willie	6 riders per seat
Memphis Belle	4 riders per seat

17. Algebra If $698 \div 4 = 174$ R ▢, what is the value of ▢?

18. The Galveston-Port Bolivar Ferry takes cars across Galveston Bay. One day, the ferry transported a total of 685 cars over a 5-hour period. If the ferry took the same number of cars each hour, how many cars did it take each hour?

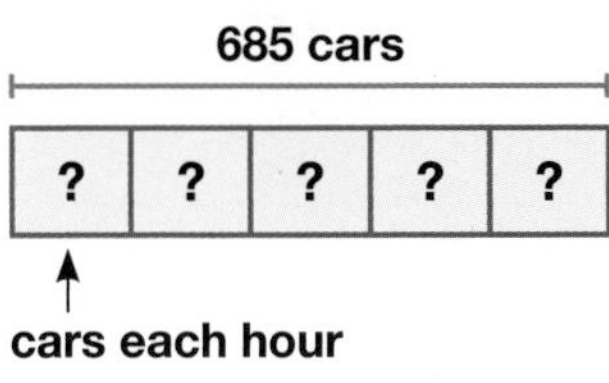

19. Theo bought a T-shirt for $21 and a pair of shorts for $16. He paid with two $20 bills. How much money did Theo get back?

A $1

B $2

C $3

D $4

Lesson

9-4

TEKS 4.4E: Use division to solve problems (no more than one-digit divisors and three digit dividends without technology).

Deciding Where to Start Dividing

What do you do when there aren't enough hundreds to divide?

Madison is making iguana key chains using pom-poms. She has 145 pink pom-poms. Are there enough pink pom-poms to make 36 key chains?

2 yellow pom-poms
4 pink pom-poms
7 blue pom-poms
31 green pom-poms
3 yards of plastic lace

4 pink pom-poms

Guided Practice*

Do you know HOW?

In **1** and **2**, copy and complete each calculation.

1.
$$\begin{array}{r} 6\square \\ 7\overline{)455} \\ -\square\square \\ \hline \square 5 \\ -\square\square \\ \hline \square \end{array}$$

2.
$$\begin{array}{r} \square\square \text{ R}\square \\ 5\overline{)319} \\ -3\square \\ \hline \square\square \\ -\square\square \\ \hline \square \end{array}$$

Do you UNDERSTAND?

3. Madison has 365 blue pom-poms. How many key chains can she make?

4. Explain how an estimated quotient can help you decide where to start.

Independent Practice

Leveled Practice In **5** through **13**, divide. You may draw a picture to help you.

5.
$$\begin{array}{r} \square\square \\ 6\overline{)444} \\ -\square\square \\ \hline \square\square \\ -\square\square \\ \hline \square \end{array}$$

6.
$$\begin{array}{r} 1\square\square \\ 3\overline{)588} \\ -\square \\ \hline \square 8 \\ -\square\square \\ \hline \square 8 \\ -\square\square \\ \hline \square \end{array}$$

7.
$$\begin{array}{r} 5\square \text{ R}\square \\ 8\overline{)417} \\ -\square\square \\ \hline \square\square \\ -\square\square \\ \hline \square \end{array}$$

8.
$$\begin{array}{r} \square\square\square \text{ R}\square \\ 2\overline{)935} \\ -8 \\ \hline \square\square \\ -\square\square \\ \hline \square\square \\ -\square\square \\ \hline \square \end{array}$$

9. $8\overline{)526}$ **10.** $5\overline{)690}$ **11.** $3\overline{)769}$ **12.** $4\overline{)923}$ **13.** $6\overline{)342}$

For another example, see Set D on page 217.

There are not enough hundreds to put one in each group.

Start by dividing the tens.

$$\begin{array}{r} 3 \\ 4\overline{)145} \\ -12 \\ \hline 25 \end{array}$$

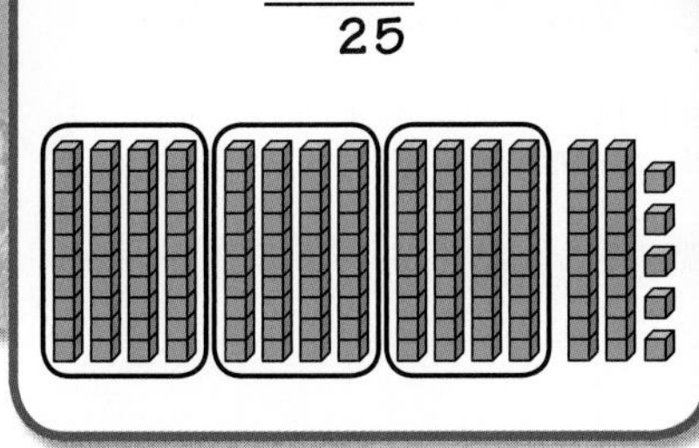

Divide the ones.

$$\begin{array}{r} 36 \text{ R1} \\ 4\overline{)145}\phantom{\text{ R1}} \\ -12\phantom{\text{ R1}} \\ \hline 25\phantom{\text{ R1}} \\ -\ 24\phantom{\text{ R1}} \\ \hline 1\phantom{\text{ R1}} \end{array}$$

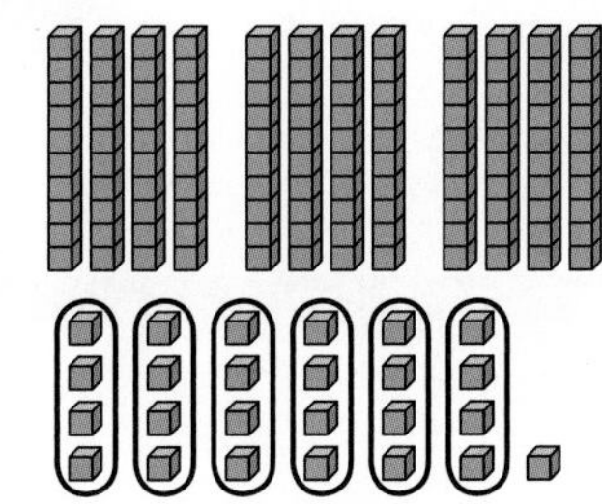

To check, multiply the quotient by the divisor and add the remainder.

$$\begin{array}{r} {\scriptstyle 2} \\ 36 \\ \times\ 4 \\ \hline 144 \end{array}$$

144 + 1 = 145

Madison has enough pink pom-poms to make 36 key chains.

In **14** through **23**, divide. Then check your answer.

14. $6\overline{)96}$ **15.** $5\overline{)295}$ **16.** $2\overline{)306}$ **17.** $9\overline{)517}$ **18.** $4\overline{)624}$

19. $7\overline{)430}$ **20.** $4\overline{)229}$ **21.** $5\overline{)655}$ **22.** $3\overline{)209}$ **23.** $6\overline{)438}$

TAKS Problem Solving

For **24** and **25**, use the bar graph at the right.

James is organizing his CDs. He plans to put them into stackable cubes that hold 8 CDs each.

24. How many cubes will James need for his entire collection?

25. If James decides to group his Rock and World Music CDs together, how many cubes would he need for them?

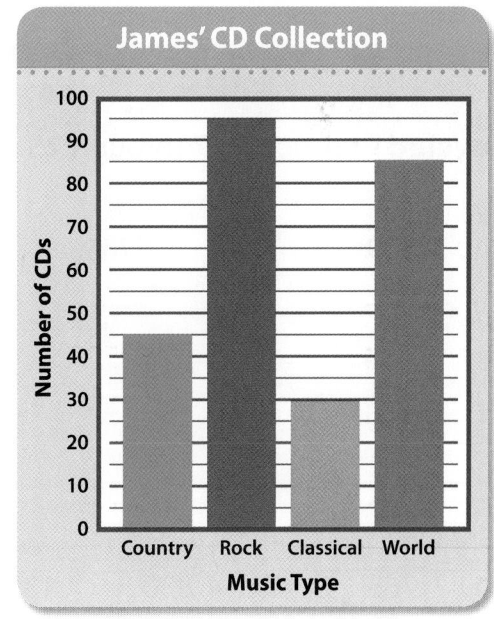

26. **Number Sense** How can you tell without dividing that 479 ÷ 6 will have a 2-digit quotient?

27. A family is going on a trip for 3 days. The total cost for the hotel is $336. They budgeted $100 a day for food. How much will each day of the trip cost?

A $33 **B** $112 **C** $145 **D** $212

Lesson
9-5

TEKS 4.4E: Use division to solve problems (no more than one-digit divisors and three-digit dividends without techonolgy).

Zeros in the Quotient

Do zeros matter?

Liam has 326 nails that he wants to store in 3 containers. He wants to put the same number in each container. How many nails will go in each container?

Estimate: $330 \div 3 = 110$

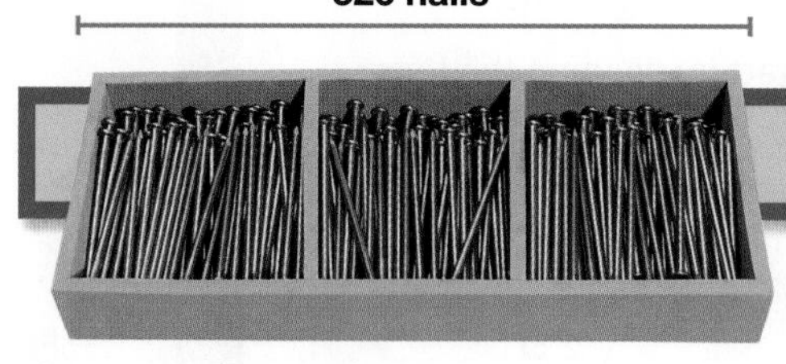

Guided Practice*

Do you know HOW?

In **1** through **4**, divide. Then check your answer.

1. $4\overline{)816}$ **2.** $2\overline{)608}$

3. $2\overline{)213}$ **4.** $3\overline{)619}$

Do you UNDERSTAND?

5. How can you check the answer in the problem above?

6. Liam sold some hammers at a market and made \$212. If he sold each hammer for \$2, how many hammers did he sell?

Independent Practice

Leveled Practice In **7** through **25**, divide. Then check your answer.

7. $3\overline{)309}$; − ▭; 0; − ▭; 9; − ▭; ▭

8. $7\overline{)749}$; − ▭; 4; − ▭; ▭▭; − ▭▭; ▭

9. $5\overline{)508}$ R ▭; − ▭; ▭; − ▭; 8; − ▭; ▭

10. $4\overline{)834}$ R ▭; − ▭; 3; − ▭; 34; − ▭▭; ▭

11. $7\overline{)763}$ **12.** $4\overline{)830}$ **13.** $2\overline{)818}$ **14.** $5\overline{)530}$ **15.** $8\overline{)823}$

16. $3\overline{)326}$ **17.** $6\overline{)658}$ **18.** $3\overline{)922}$ **19.** $8\overline{)482}$ **20.** $9\overline{)970}$

21. $9\overline{)927}$ **22.** $2\overline{)412}$ **23.** $5\overline{)525}$ **24.** $2\overline{)217}$ **25.** $7\overline{)717}$

*For another example, see Set E on page 217.

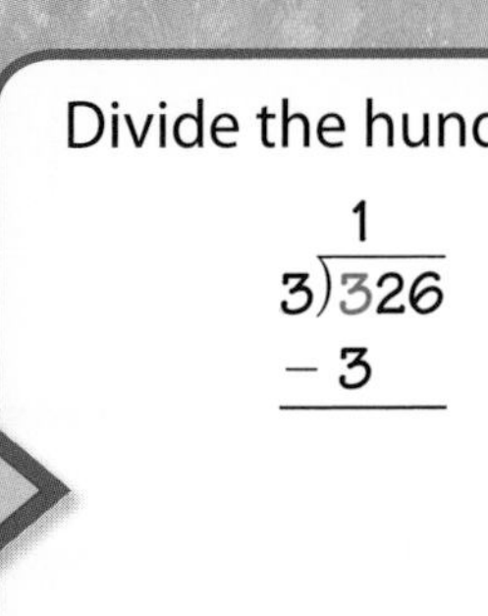
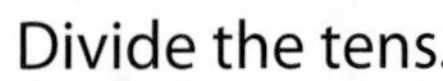

Divide the hundreds.

```
   1
3)326
 -3
```

Divide the tens.

```
   10
3)326
 -3
  2
 -0
  26
```

Since 3 > 2, there are not enough tens to put any in each group.

Place a zero in the quotient and bring down the 6.

Divide the ones.

```
  108 R2
3)326
 -3
  2
 -0
  26
 -24
   2
```

There will be 108 nails in each container with 2 left over.

TAKS Problem Solving

For **26** through **28**, use the information at right.

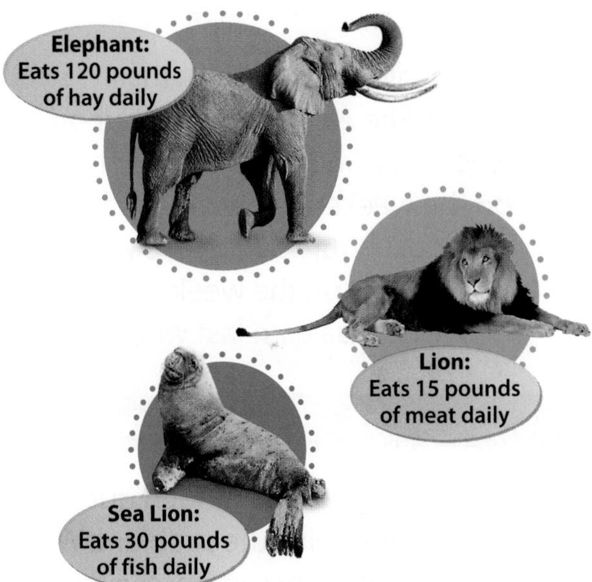

Elephant: Eats 120 pounds of hay daily
Lion: Eats 15 pounds of meat daily
Sea Lion: Eats 30 pounds of fish daily

26. Writing to Explain A zookeeper has 540 pounds of hay. Is this enough hay to feed one elephant for 5 days?

27. Another zookeeper has 324 pounds of meat. Is this enough to feed 3 lions for a full week? Explain.

28. Is 654 pounds of fish enough to feed 5 sea lions for 6 days? Explain.

29. Reasoning What digit belongs in the number sentence below?

8 ☐ 7 ÷ 4 = 206 R3

30. Claire divided 415 ÷ 2 and got a quotient of 27 R1. What mistake did Claire make?

A She divided the hundreds incorrectly.

B She forgot to record that there were not enough tens to divide.

C She regrouped the hundreds incorrectly.

D She wrote the wrong remainder.

31. The school band needs to raise money for 3 parades. They need $276 for each parade. The band plans to hold 4 fundraisers. If they raise an equal amount at each fundraiser, what is the least amount they can make at each fundraiser to reach their goal?

Lesson

9-6

TEKS 4.14: Apply Grade 4 mathematics to solve problems connected to everyday experiences and activities in and outside of school.

Problem Solving

Multiple-Step Problems

Justine and her father are going on a fishing trip. The prices for supplies, including tax, are shown in the table. Justine and her father have $25. They bought 2 box lunches, 2 bottles of water, 5 hooks, and 5 sinkers. How many pounds of bait can they buy?

Data

Captain Bob's Price List	
Bait	$3 per pound
Hooks	60¢ each
Sinkers	40¢ each
Bottled water	$1 each
Box lunch	$6 each

Guided Practice*

Do you know HOW?

Solve.

1. Elsa babysits for the Smyth family. She earns $10 per hour on weekdays. She earns $15 per hour on the weekend. Last week, she worked 3 hours during the week and 4 hours on the weekend. How much did Elsa earn last week?

Do you UNDERSTAND?

2. What is the hidden question or questions?

3. **Write a Problem** Write a problem that contains a hidden question.

Independent Practice

Write the answer to the hidden question or questions. Then solve the problem. Write your answer in a complete sentence.

4. Gabriella buys lunch for herself and her friend. She buys 2 sandwiches and 2 drinks. Each sandwich costs $4. Each drink costs $1.50. How much did Gabriella spend on lunch?

5. Jamie is buying bowls for a school ice cream social. She buys 5 packages of red bowls, 3 packages of orange bowls, 4 packages of green bowls, and 7 packages of white bowls. Each package contains 8 bowls. How many bowls did she buy in all?

- What do I know?
- What diagram can I use to help understand the problem?
- Can I use addition, subtraction, multiplication, or division?
- Is all of my work correct?
- Did I answer the right question?
- Is my answer reasonable?

*For another example, see Set E on page 217.

Read & Understand

What do I know? They bought:

2 lunches for \$6 each
2 bottles of water for \$1 each
5 hooks for 60¢ each
5 sinkers for 40¢ each

What am I asked to find? The number of pounds of bait they can buy with the money they have left.

Plan

Find the hidden question. How much money do Justine and her father have left?

The cost of lunches is	$2 \times \$6$	$= \$12$
The cost of water is	$2 \times \$1$	$= \$2$
The cost of hooks is	$5 \times 60¢$	$= \$3$
The cost of sinkers is	$5 \times 40¢$	$= \underline{\$2}$
	The total is	\$19

$\$25 - \$19 = \$6$ They have \$6 left.

Divide to find how many pounds of bait they can buy.

$6 \div 3 = 2$ They can buy 2 pounds of bait.

6. Kelly used 6 cups of apples, 4 cups of oranges, and 2 cups of grapes to make a fruit salad. She put an equal amount in each of 6 bowls. How many cups of fruit salad were in each bowl?

7. Muriel used the same recipe as Kelly to make her fruit salad. Muriel also added 1 cup of cherries and 1 cup of bananas. She put 2 cups of fruit salad into each bowl. How many bowls did Muriel need?

Use the data at the right for **8** through **11**.

8. The band needs to purchase 60 T-shirts. How much would it cost to purchase them from Shirt Shack?

9. How much would it cost the band to purchase 60 T-shirts from Just Jerseys?

10. How much more would it cost to buy 24 T-shirts at Just Jerseys than at Shirt Shack?

11. **Writing to Explain** Would it be less expensive to buy one shirt from Just Jerseys or Shirt Shack? Explain.

Data: **Shirt Shack**

Number of shirts	Price
10	\$90
20	\$180
50	\$450

Data: **Just Jerseys**

Number of shirts	Price
8	\$80
24	\$240
48	\$480

12. Each football practice is 45 minutes long. The team's next game is 6 practices away. How many minutes will they practice before the game?

A 135 minutes **C** 243 minutes

B 270 minutes **D** 2430 minutes

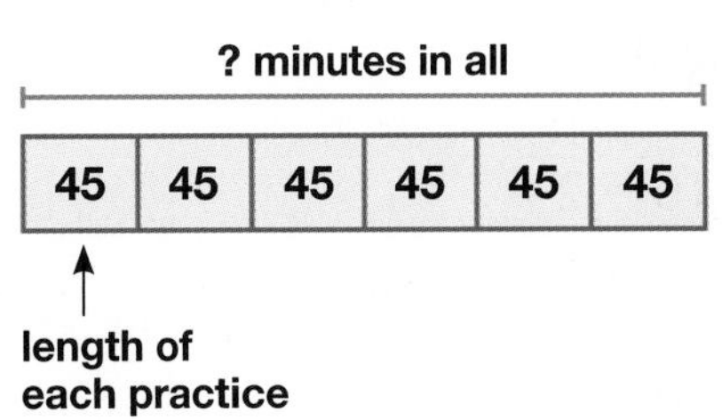

1. Nelly has 74 bricks to outline 5 different flower beds. How many bricks will she use for each flower bed if she uses the same number in each? (9-1)

A Each garden will use 10 bricks. There will be 4 left over.

B Each garden will use 13 bricks. There will be 9 left over.

C Each garden will use 14 bricks. There will be 0 left over.

D Each garden will use 14 bricks. There will be 4 left over.

2. Ty made 52 rolls. He put an equal amount in each of 4 baskets. How many rolls were in each basket? (9-2)

F 14

G 13

H 12

J 9

3. Tia has 15 metamorphic, 8 igneous, and 7 sedimentary rocks. She displays her rocks equally in 2 cases. Which shows how she found the number of rocks to put in each case? (9-6)

A 2×16

B $16 \div 2$

C 2×30

D $30 \div 2$

4. A riverboat offers 6 tours a day. Between 750 and 775 people take the tours. Which is a reasonable number of people who take each tour? (9-3)

F 200

H 150

G 125

J 120

5. Which number sentence does the diagram show? (9-1)

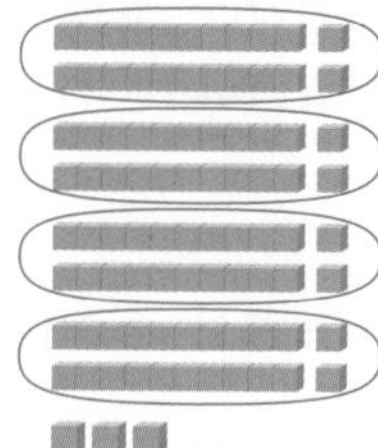

A $88 \div 22 = 4$ R3

B $88 \div 4 = 22$ R3

C $91 \div 4 = 22$

D $91 \div 4 = 22$ R3

6. Three friends shared 327 marbles equally. How many marbles did each friend get? (9-5)

F 981

G 190

H 109

J 19

7. Find $537 \div 5$. (9-5)

A 107 R2

B 107

C 101 R2

D 17 R2

8. To find 77 ÷ 3, Tim first divided the tens into 3 equal groups. What should Tim do next? (9-1)

$$\begin{array}{r} 2 \\ 3\overline{)77} \\ -6 \\ \hline 1 \end{array}$$

F Divide the ones.

G Trade the extra ten for 10 ones.

H Trade the two extra tens for ones.

J Nothing, he is finished.

9. Issac put 75 trading cards in a book. Each page of the book holds 6 cards. What is the fewest number of pages Issac could use? (9-2)

A 14

B 13

C 12

D 11

10. How many are left if 318 is divided into 4 equal groups? (9-3)

F 79

G 3

H 2

J 0

11. What can you tell about 427 ÷ 7 by only looking at the problem? (9-4)

A It will have a three-digit quotient.

B It will have a two-digit quotient.

C It will have a one-digit quotient.

D It will have a remainder.

12. Each costume requires 2 yards of material. How many costumes can Sara make out of 35 yards? How much material will she have left? (9-2)

F 17 costumes, 1 yard left

G 17 costumes, 0 yards left

H 16 costumes, 3 yards left

J 16 costumes, 1 yard left

13. Eatin' Good's menu is shown below.

Data

Lunch Specials			
Pizza	$4.25	Salad	$2.50
Breadsticks	$2.75	Fruit Cup	$1.25
Ravioli	$3.75	Tea	$0.75
Garlic Bread	$2.50	Apple Pie	$1.75

Jed spent $10.25 on lunch. He ordered a pizza, a salad, a tea, and 1 other item. What else did he order? (9-6)

A Breadsticks

B Garlic Bread

C Pudding

D Apple Pie

14. **Griddable Response** The cafeteria ordered 820 cartons of juice for the 4 days students are in school this week. How many cartons of juice did they allow for each day? (9-5)

15. **Griddable Response** Two boxes contain a total of 576 pencils. How many pencils are in each box? (9-3)

Reteaching

Set A, pages 198–200

Tom divides 54 pennies equally among 4 stacks. How many pennies are in each stack? How many are left over?

Use place-value blocks.

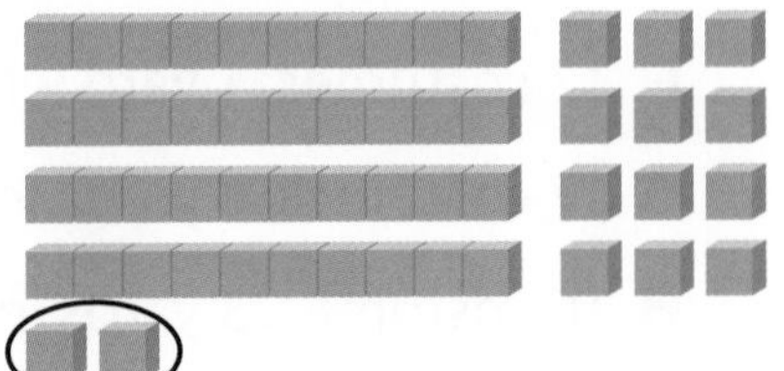

Each stack has 13 pennies. Two pennies are left over.

Remember to divide the tens and then the ones.

Divide. You may use place-value blocks or pictures to help.

1. 38 CDs 5 stacks

2. 42 nickels 3 stacks

3. 62 dimes 4 stacks

4. 77 nickels 6 stacks

Set B, pages 202–204

Find 67 ÷ 4.

$$\begin{array}{r} 1 \\ 4\overline{)67} \\ -4 \\ \hline 2 \end{array}$$

Divide. Multiply. Subtract.

$$\begin{array}{r} 16 \text{ R3} \\ 4\overline{)67} \\ -4\downarrow \\ \hline 27 \\ -24 \\ \hline 3 \end{array}$$

Bring down the 7. Divide. Multiply. Subtract.

Check:

$$\begin{array}{r} 16 \\ \times\ 4 \\ \hline 64 \end{array} \qquad \begin{array}{r} 64 \\ +\ 3 \\ \hline 67 \end{array}$$

The answer checks.

Remember that the remainder must be less than the divisor.

Divide. Check your answer.

1. 434 ÷ 7

2. 329 ÷ 2

3. 9 ÷ 5

4. 53 ÷ 2

5. 869 ÷ 7

6. 275 ÷ 3

7. 94 ÷ 4

8. 47 ÷ 3

Set C, pages 206–209

Find 915 ÷ 6.

Estimate: 900 ÷ 6 = 150

The estimate is more than 100, so you can start dividing the hundreds.

$$\begin{array}{r} 152 \text{ R3} \\ 6\overline{)915} \\ -6 \\ \hline 31 \\ -30 \\ \hline 15 \\ -12 \\ \hline 3 \end{array}$$

Divide the hundreds.

Divide the tens.

Divide the ones.

Include the remainder.

Remember that an estimate can tell you where to start dividing.

Tell whether you will start dividing the hundreds or the tens.

1. 524 ÷ 4

2. 601 ÷ 5

3. 398 ÷ 8

4. 265 ÷ 3

5. 710 ÷ 9

6. 429 ÷ 2

7. 820 ÷ 8

8. 372 ÷ 5

Set D, pages 210–211

Find 626 ÷ 6.

```
  104 R2
6)626     Divide the hundreds.
 - 6
   2      There are not enough tens to divide.
 - 0      Put a 0 in the quotient.
  26      Bring down the ones and divide.
 - 24
   2
```

Remember to write zeros in the quotient when needed.

1 815 ÷ 8

2. 218 ÷ 2

3. 417 ÷ 2

4. 428 ÷ 4

5. 423 ÷ 4

6. 619 ÷ 3

7. 386 ÷ 7

8. 642 ÷ 5

9. 521 ÷ 8

10. 793 ÷ 2

Set E, pages 212–213

Answer the hidden question first. Then solve the problem.

Brett and his family spent $50 for admission to the county fair. They bought 2 adult passes for $6 each, and 3 children passes for $3 each. How much more money did Brett's family spend on adult passes than children passes?

$6 × 2 = $12 → Price of adult passes

$3 × 3 = $9 → Price of children passes

Brett's family spent $12 on adult passes and $9 on children passes.

Use the hidden question to solve the problem.

How much more money did Brett's family spend on adult passes than children passes?

$12 – $9 = $3

Brett's family spent $3 more on adult passes.

Remember to find a hidden question to help you solve the problem.

1. Angelia works at a store at the mall. She earns a wage of $8 an hour, and earns $10 an hour if she works on weekends and holidays. Last week, she worked 24 hours during the week, and 16 hours during the weekend. How much did Angelique earn last week?

2. Brendan takes violin and guitar lessons. Each day, he practices 40 minutes on the violin and 25 minutes on the guitar. How many minutes does he practice his instruments in 5 days?

Topic 10 Fraction Concepts

1 The world's largest pumpkin pie was made in 2005. How much did the pie weigh? You will find out in Lesson 10-4.

2 Pandas eat up to 60 pounds of food a day. For what fraction of their time awake are pandas eating? You will find out in Lesson 10-5.

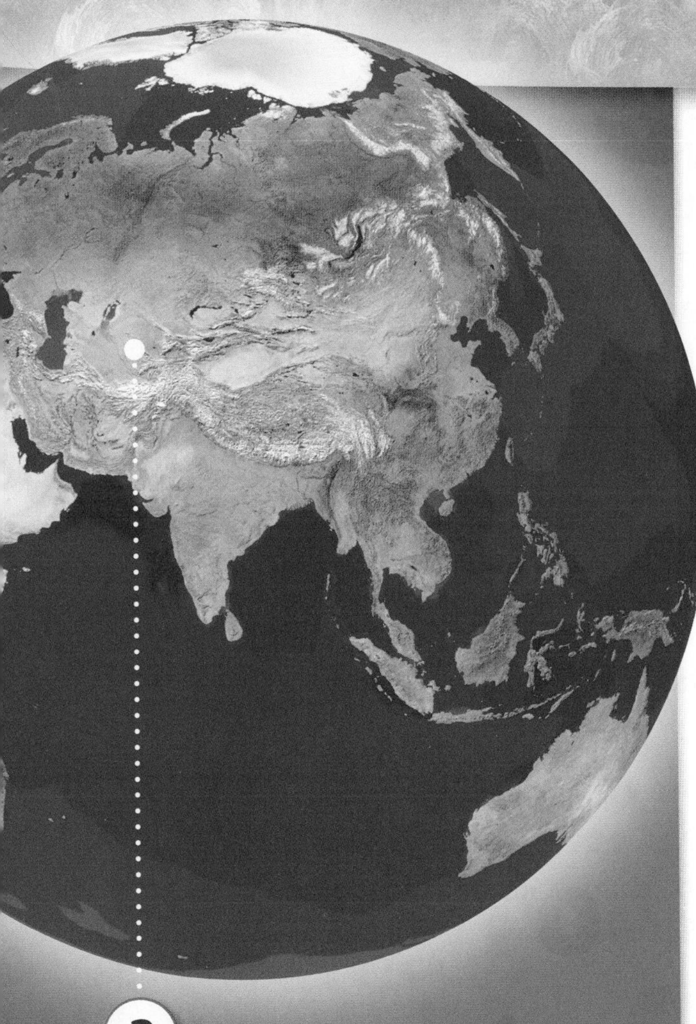

3 Asia is the largest continent, covering about $\frac{3}{10}$ of Earth's total land area. About what fraction of the people on Earth live in Asia? You will find out in Lesson 10-3.

4 The largest Texas flag can be seen at every home game for the University of Texas football team. What fraction of the flag is red? You will find out in Lesson 10-1.

Review What You Know!

Vocabulary

Choose the best term from the box.

- fraction
- denominator
- thirds
- numerator

1. Three equal parts of a shape are called __?__.
2. A __?__ can name a part of a whole.
3. The number below the fraction bar in a fraction is the __?__.

Division Facts

Divide.

4. $15 \div 3$
5. $48 \div 8$
6. $24 \div 6$
7. $72 \div 8$
8. $35 \div 7$
9. $12 \div 4$
10. $36 \div 6$
11. $14 \div 2$
12. $45 \div 9$
13. Amelia hiked 12 miles in 6 hours. How many miles did Amelia hike each hour?

Fraction Concepts

Name the number of equal parts in each figure.

14.

15. 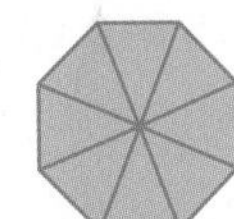

16. 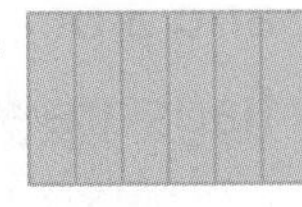

17.

18.

19. 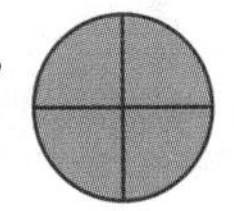

20. **Writing to Explain** Is $\frac{1}{4}$ of the figure below red? Explain why or why not.

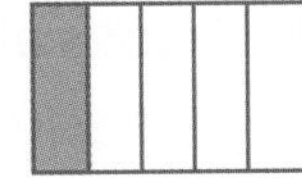

Lesson

10-1

TEKS 4.2: Describe and compare fractional parts of whole objects or sets of objects.

Regions and Sets

How can you name and show parts of a region and parts of a set?

A fraction is a symbol, such as $\frac{2}{3}$ or $\frac{5}{1}$, used to name a part of a whole, a part of a set, a location on a number line, or a division of whole numbers.

What fraction of the Nigerian flag is green?

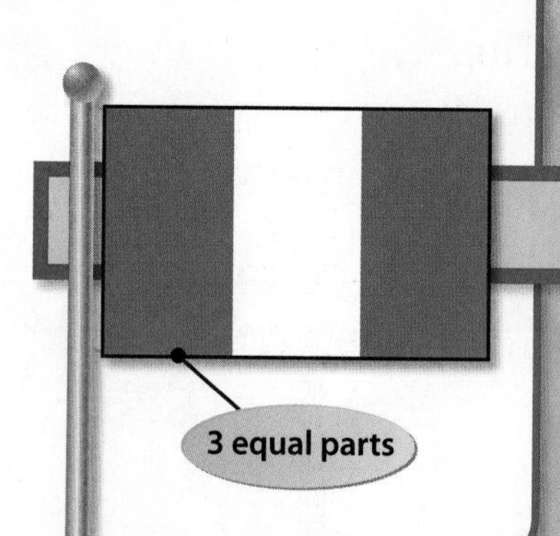

Another Example How can you draw parts of a region and parts of a set?

Draw Parts of a Region

Draw a flag that is $\frac{3}{5}$ green.

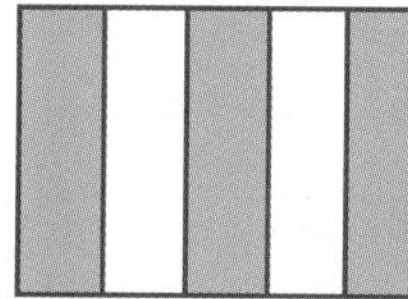

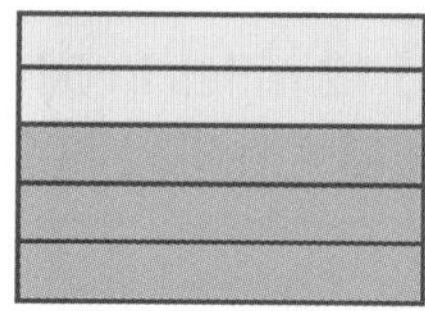

In both flags, there are 5 equal parts, and 3 of the parts are green. Both flags are $\frac{3}{5}$ green.

Draw Parts of a Set

Draw a set of shapes in which $\frac{4}{10}$ of the shapes are small triangles.

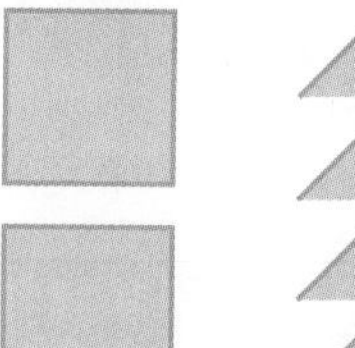

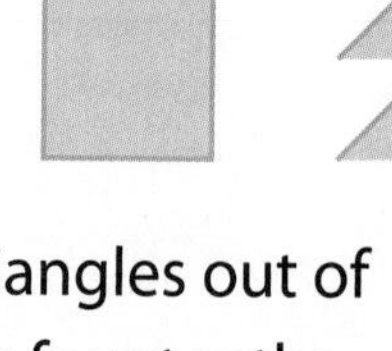

There are 4 small triangles out of 10 shapes. So, $\frac{4}{10}$, or four tenths, of the shapes are small triangles.

Explain It

1. Draw a flag that is $\frac{3}{6}$ green. How does this flag compare to a flag of the same size that is $\frac{3}{5}$ green?

2. What fraction of the set of shapes above is orange? What fraction of the shapes are squares? What is the same about these two fractions?

Parts of a region

The numerator tells how many equal parts are described. The denominator tells how many equal parts there are in all.

$\frac{2}{3}$ ← Numerator, Denominator

In the Nigerian flag, $\frac{2}{3}$ of the flag is green.

Parts of a set

These flags show the first 4 letters in the International Code of Signals:

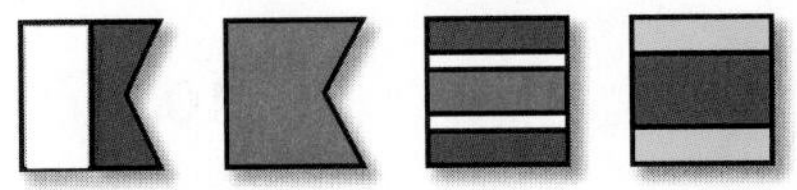

What fraction of these flags are rectangles? $\frac{2}{4}$ ← Number that are rectangles / Total number in set

In this set of 4 flags, $\frac{2}{4}$ are rectangles.

Guided Practice*

Do you know HOW?

In **1** and **2**, write a fraction to describe the part of each region or set that is green.

1. 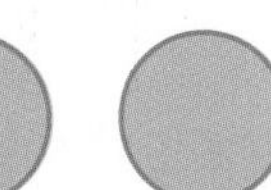 

2. 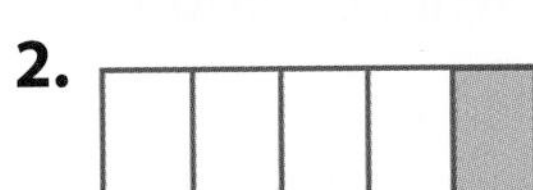

In **3** and **4**, draw a model for each fraction.

3. $\frac{4}{5}$ of a region **4.** $\frac{2}{9}$ of a set

Do you UNDERSTAND?

5. Writing to Explain What fraction of the signal flags at the top contain blue? What fraction of the flags contain yellow? Why do these fractions both have the same denominator?

6. What fraction of the squares below contain a red circle? What fraction of the circles are red?

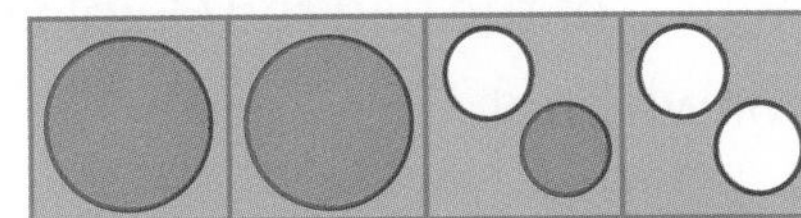

Independent Practice

In **7** and **8**, write a fraction to describe the part of each region or set that is green.

7. 

8.    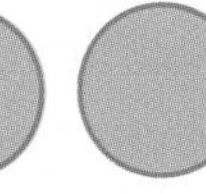 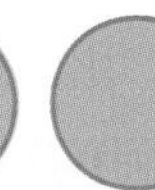   

DIGITAL Animated Glossary www.pearsonsuccessnet.com

*For another example, see Set A on page 240.

Independent Practice

In **9** and **10**, write a fraction to describe the part of each region or set that is blue.

9. 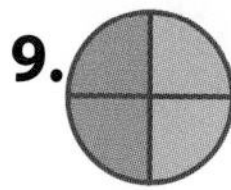

10.

In **11** through **18**, draw a model for each fraction.

11. $\frac{7}{10}$ of a region **12.** $\frac{2}{8}$ of a region **13.** $\frac{1}{6}$ of a region **14.** $\frac{3}{9}$ of a region

15. $\frac{1}{8}$ of a set **16.** $\frac{5}{6}$ of a set **17.** $\frac{3}{7}$ of a set **18.** $\frac{1}{10}$ of a set

TAKS Problem Solving

19. Maya tried a skateboard trick 12 times. She got it to work 3 times. What fraction describes the number of times the trick did **NOT** work?

20. Jane has a fish tank. Draw a model to show that $\frac{3}{10}$ of the fish are black and the rest of the fish are orange.

21. Students arranged 32 chairs in equal rows for a school concert. Describe two ways the students could have arranged the chairs.

22. When the numerator is the same as the denominator, what do you know about the fraction?

23. **Geometry** In the signal flag shown below, is $\frac{1}{3}$ of the flag red? Explain why or why not.

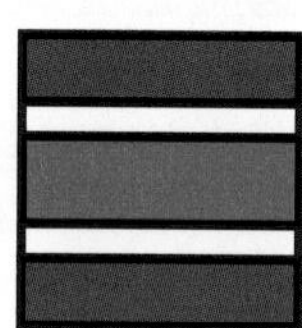

24. Alan's grandfather made 10 pancakes. Alan ate 3 pancakes. His sister ate 2 pancakes. What fraction of the pancakes did Alan eat?

A $\frac{3}{10}$ **C** $\frac{5}{10}$

B $\frac{2}{5}$ **D** $\frac{3}{5}$

Use the diagram at the right for **25**.

25. The largest Texas flag, like all official Texas flags, has 3 rectangles that each cover an equal area. Each rectangle is twice as long as it is wide. What fraction of the flag is red?

F $\frac{1}{3}$ **G** $\frac{1}{2}$ **H** $\frac{2}{3}$ **J** $\frac{3}{3}$

Mixed Problem Solving

Some poems are written in a patterned form.
Below are examples of two types of poems.

Pattern 1	Pattern 2
A-A-B-C-C-B	A-A-B-B-C-C
Example: Old Mother Hubbard (A) Went to the cupboard (A) To fetch her poor dog a bone; (B) But when she came there (C) The cupboard was bare, (C) And so the poor dog had none. (B)	Example: Little Boy Blue, come blow your horn, (A) The sheep's in the meadow, the cow's in the corn; (A) Where is the boy who looks after the sheep? (B) He's under a haycock, fast asleep. (B) Will you wake him? No, not I, (C) For if I do, he's sure to cry. (C)

1. If Pattern 2 has 6 lines, which line will also rhyme with the fifth line?

2. What pattern do you notice in Pattern 2?

3. Which of the patterns described above does this poem follow?

Jack and Jill
Went up the hill
To fetch a pail of water.
Jack fell down
And broke his crown
And Jill came tumbling after.

4. One type of poem is called a limerick. Below is an example of a limerick:

Hickory, dickory, dock,
The mouse ran up the clock.
The clock struck one,
And down he run,
Hickory, dickory, dock.

What is the rhyming pattern of the limerick?

5. If you knew the first three lines of a poem, would you be able to tell if it follows Pattern 1 or Pattern 2?

6. Is there a difference in the number of lines that rhyme in Pattern 1 than in Pattern 2?

7. A book contains poems with 15 poems that follow Pattern 2 and 10 poems that follow Pattern 1. How many sets of rhyming lines are there?

A 65 **C** 150

B 75 **D** 250

8. Another book has 18 poems that follow pattern 1. Each poem had 6 lines. How many lines are there in all?

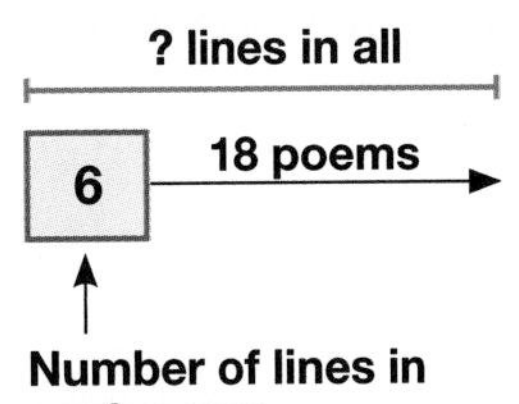

Lesson

10-2

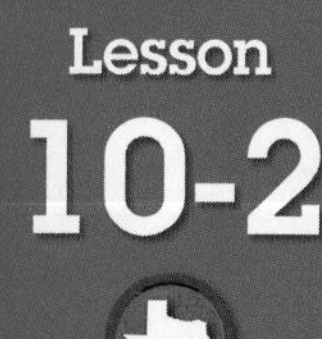

TEKS 4.2: Describe and compare fractional parts of whole objects or sets of objects.

Fractions and Division

How can you share items?

Tom, Joe, and Sam made clay pots using two rolls of clay. If they shared the clay equally, what fraction of the clay did each friend use?

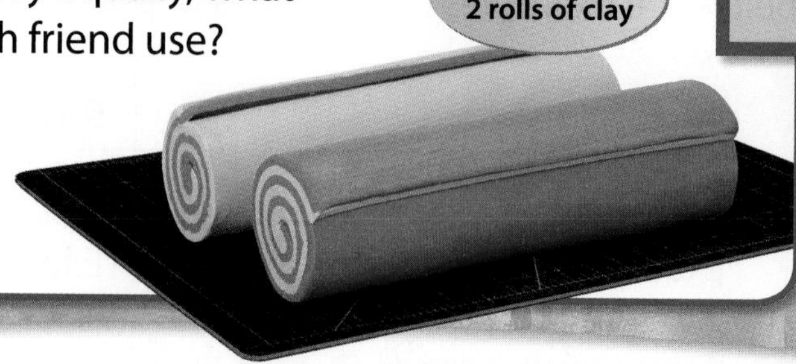
3 friends share
2 rolls of clay

Choose an Operation

Divide to find a fraction of the total.

Guided Practice*

Do you know HOW?

Tell what fraction each person gets.

1. Three people share 2 cans of paint.
2. Two students share 1 sheet of paper.
3. Four friends share 3 apples.
4. Five friends share 5 bagels.

Do you UNDERSTAND?

5. How do you write $3 \div 5$ as a fraction?
6. In Exercises 1 through 4, did you use the number of items as the denominator or as the numerator?
7. If 6 people equally shared 3 rolls of clay to make pots, how much clay did each person use?

Independent Practice

In **8** through **13**, tell what fraction each person gets when they share equally.

Tip *The number of items shared is the numerator and the number of people is the denominator.*

8. Four students share 3 breakfast bars.
9. Ten friends share 7 dollars.
10. Five women each run an equal part of a 3-mile relay.
11. Ten students share 1 hour to give their reports.
12. Six soccer players share 5 oranges.
13. Five friends pay for a 4 dollar gift.

*For another example, see Set B on page 240.

Step 1

Think about sharing 2 rolls of clay among 3 people. Divide each roll into 3 equal parts.

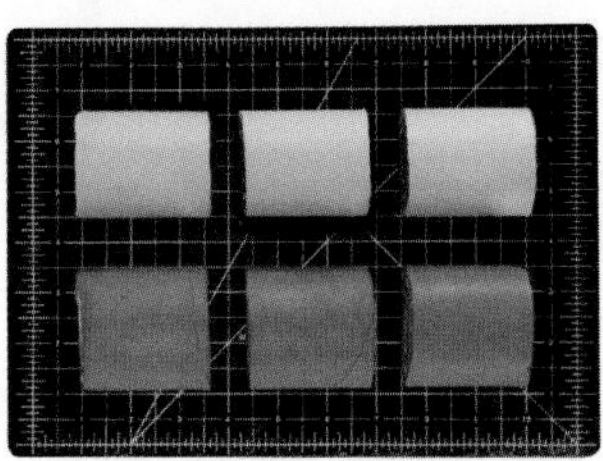

Each part is $1 \div 3$ or $\frac{1}{3}$.

Step 2

The parts were shared equally.

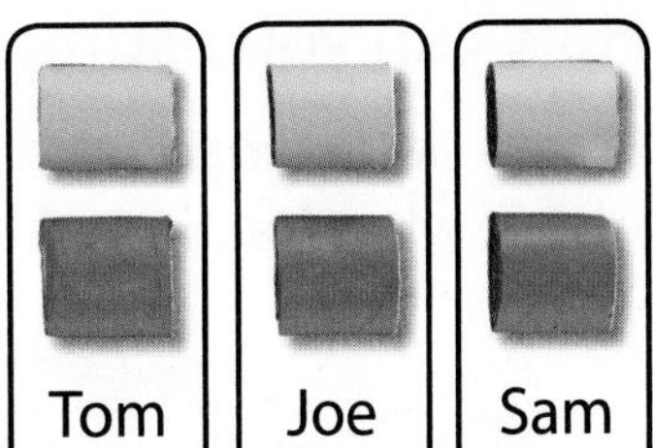

Each person used one part from each roll of clay for a total of 2 parts.

This is the same as $\frac{2}{3}$ of one roll of clay.

You can write division as a fraction. So, $2 \div 3 = \frac{2}{3}$.

TAKS Problem Solving

14. Eight friends divide 3 pizzas equally. How much pizza does each friend get?

15. Algebra Find the missing numbers in the following pattern:
1, 3, 9, ▢, 81, ▢

16. Reasoning A group of friends went to the movies. They shared 2 bags of popcorn equally. If each person got $\frac{2}{3}$ of a bag of popcorn, how many people were in the group?

17. When Sharon's reading group took turns reading aloud, every student had a chance to read. They finished a 12 page story. If each student read 3 pages, how many students are in the reading group?

18. There were 16 teams at a gymnastics meet. Each team had 12 members. How many gymnasts participated in the meet?

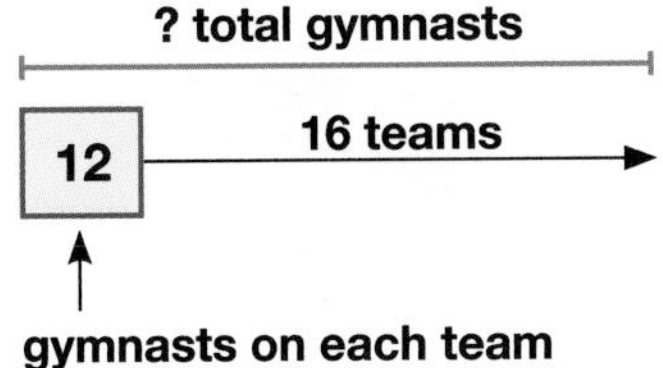

19. Twenty-one soccer players were put into 3 equal teams. How many players were on each team?

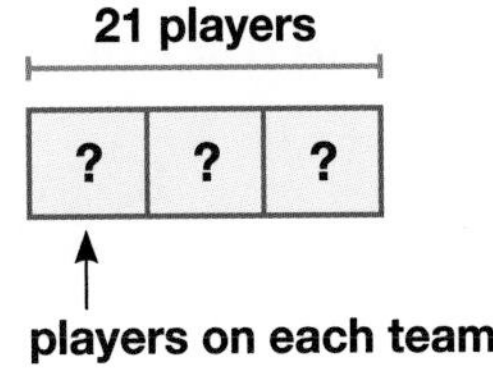

20. Think About the Process Four friends are baking bread. They equally share 3 sticks of butter. Which number sentence can be used to find the fraction of a stick of butter that each friend uses?

A $3 \div 12 =$ ▢ **C** $3 \div 4 =$ ▢

B $5 \div 12 =$ ▢ **D** $3 \div 5 =$ ▢

Lesson
10-3

TEKS 4.2: Describe and compare fractional parts of whole objects or sets of objects.

Estimating Fractional Amounts

How can you estimate parts?

Emma helped her mom begin to paint a mural downtown. About what fraction of the wall has been painted?

Guided Practice*

Do you know HOW?

For **1** through **3**, estimate the fractional part that is orange.

1.

2.

3.

Do you UNDERSTAND?

4. Writing to Explain How can you estimate whether a part of a region is about $\frac{1}{2}$ of the whole?

5. Which of the rectangles in Exercises 1 through 3 has the greatest fractional part that is orange?

6. About what fraction of the wall is **NOT** painted at all?

Independent Practice

In **7** through **9**, estimate the fractional part of each that is green.

7.

8.

9.

In **10** through **12**, estimate the fractional part of each that is flowers.

10.

11.

12.

*For another example, see Set C on page 240.

Step 1

Think about benchmark fractions.

A benchmark fraction is a simple fraction that is easy to visualize, such as $\frac{1}{4}$, $\frac{1}{3}$, $\frac{1}{2}$, $\frac{2}{3}$, and $\frac{3}{4}$.

You can use benchmark fractions to estimate fractional parts.

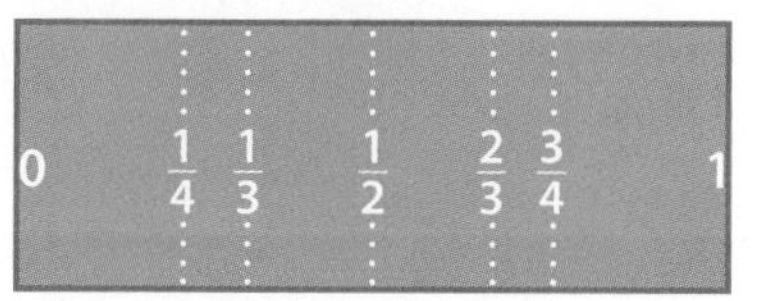

Step 2

Compare the benchmark fractions to the part of the wall that has been painted.

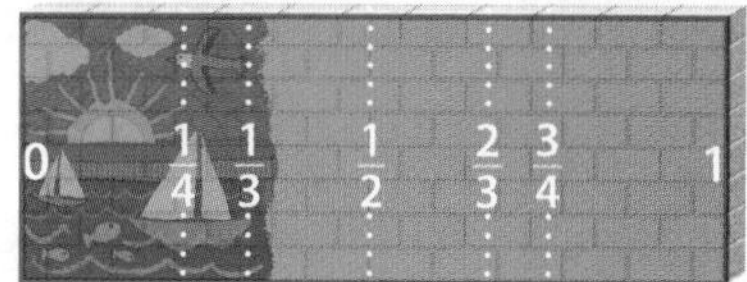

The painted part is more than $\frac{1}{4}$ but less than $\frac{1}{2}$. About $\frac{1}{3}$ of the wall is painted.

TAKS Problem Solving

13. Asia has more people than any other continent. About what fraction of the people on Earth live in Asia?

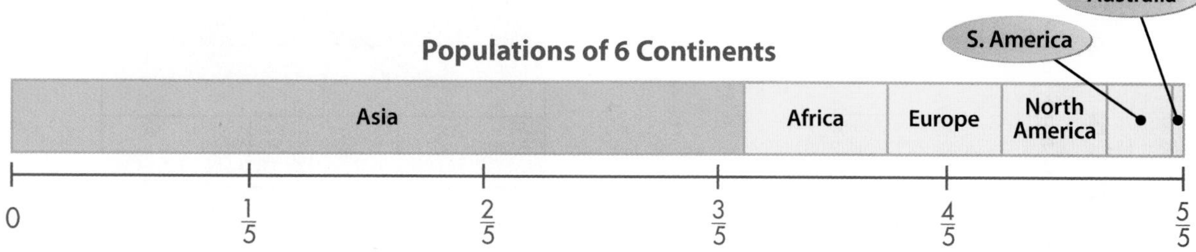

14. At the bowling alley, there are 32 bowling balls. Of these, 8 are blue, 5 are pink, 6 are red, and the rest are black. How many of the bowling balls are black?

15. Reasonableness If less than half of a garden is planted with corn, is it reasonable to estimate that $\frac{2}{3}$ of the garden is planted with corn? Explain.

16. Number Sense The numbers are missing from the graph below. Compare the bars to decide which farmer has about $\frac{1}{3}$ as many cows as Mr. Harris.

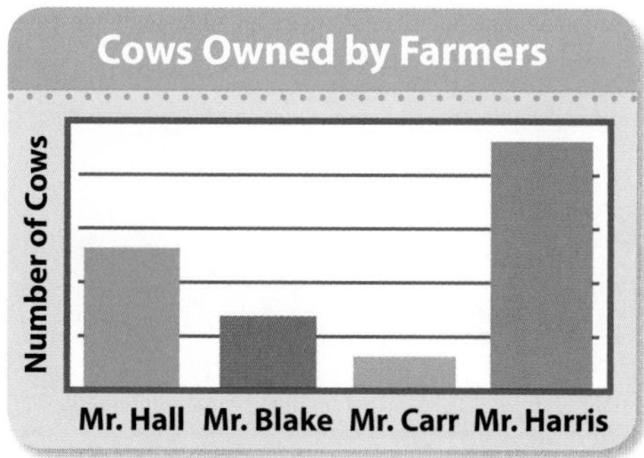

17. Geometry What is the perimeter of the figure shown below?

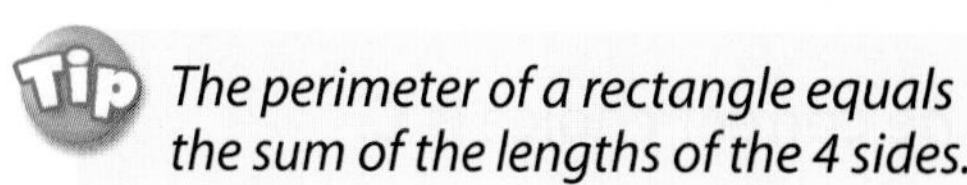

The perimeter of a rectangle equals the sum of the lengths of the 4 sides.

A 6 units

B 8 units

C 12 units

D 16 units

4

2

TEKS 4.2A: Use concrete objects and pictorial models to generate equivalent fractions.

Equivalent Fractions

Hands-On
fraction strips
counters

How can you find two fractions that name the same part of a whole?

Lee ate $\frac{4}{6}$ of a pizza. Write another fraction that is equivalent to $\frac{4}{6}$.

Equivalent fractions name the same part of a whole.

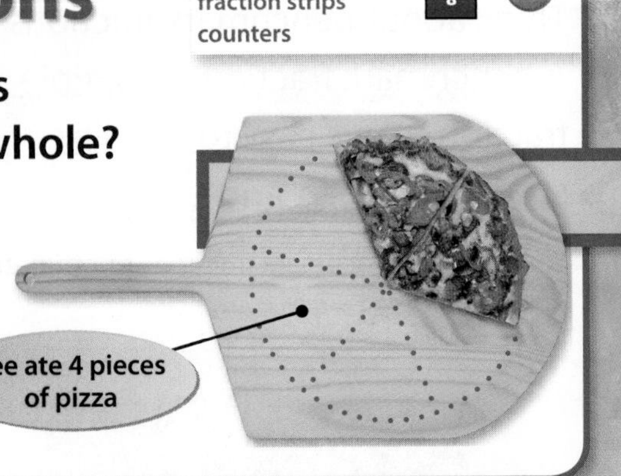

Another Example **How can you use fraction strips to find an equivalent fraction?**

Which fraction is equivalent to $\frac{3}{4}$?

A $\frac{1}{3}$

B $\frac{2}{4}$

C $\frac{6}{8}$

D $\frac{7}{8}$

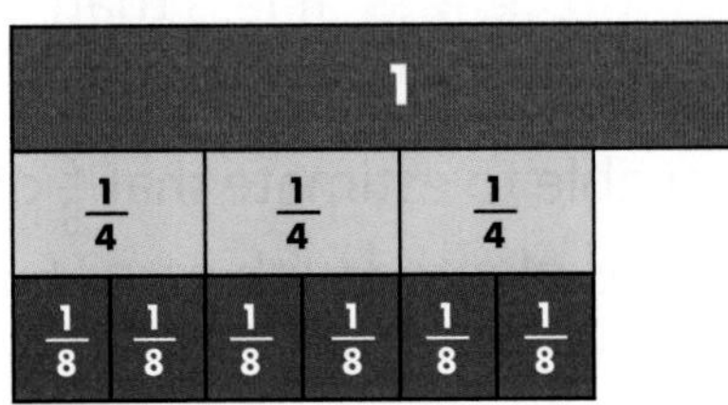

1
1/2 1/2
1/3 1/3 1/3
1/4 1/4 1/4 1/4
1/5 1/5 1/5 1/5 1/5
1/6 1/6 1/6 1/6 1/6 1/6
1/8 1/8 1/8 1/8 1/8 1/8 1/8 1/8
1/10 1/10 1/10 1/10 1/10 1/10 1/10 1/10 1/10 1/10
1/12 1/12 1/12 1/12 1/12 1/12 1/12 1/12 1/12 1/12 1/12 1/12

The regions covered by $\frac{3}{4}$ and $\frac{6}{8}$ are the same.

The correct choice is **C**.

Explain It

1. Using fraction strips, find another fraction that is equivalent to $\frac{3}{4}$.

2. Name a fraction that is equivalent to 1.

What You Show

Use counters to find equivalent fractions.

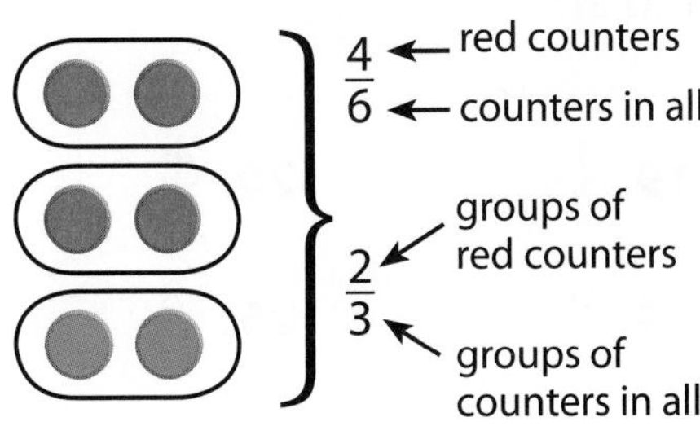

What You Write

$$\frac{4}{6} = \frac{2}{3}$$

So, $\frac{4}{6}$ and $\frac{2}{3}$ are equivalent fractions.

Guided Practice*

Do you know HOW?

In **1** through **6**, find an equivalent fraction. You can use counters or fraction strips to help.

1. $\frac{2}{5} = \frac{\square}{10}$

2. $\frac{9}{12} = \frac{3}{\square}$

3. $\frac{1}{4} = \frac{\square}{12}$

4. $\frac{2}{3} = \frac{8}{\square}$

5. $\frac{1}{3} = \frac{\square}{12}$

6. $\frac{5}{6} = \frac{\square}{12}$

Do you UNDERSTAND?

7. Suppose Lee's pizza had 12 equal slices instead of 6. How many slices are gone if he ate $\frac{1}{4}$ of the pizza? Explain.

8. Reasoning Josh, Lisa, and Vicki each ate $\frac{1}{2}$ of their own pizza. The pizzas were the same size, but Josh ate 1 slice, Lisa ate 3 slices, and Vicki ate 4 slices. How is this possible?

Independent Practice

Leveled Practice For **9** through **15**, use fraction strips to find equivalent fractions.

9. $\frac{4}{10} = \frac{2}{\square}$

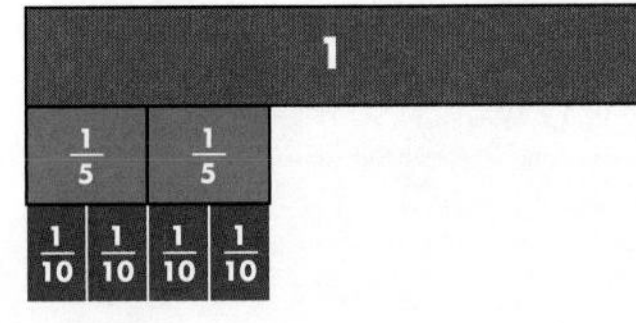

10. $\frac{8}{12} = \frac{\square}{6}$

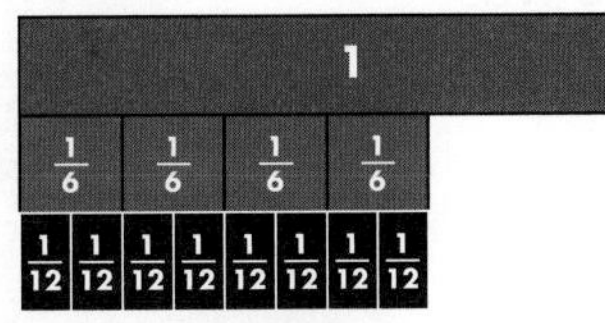

11. $\frac{4}{8} = \frac{2}{\square}$

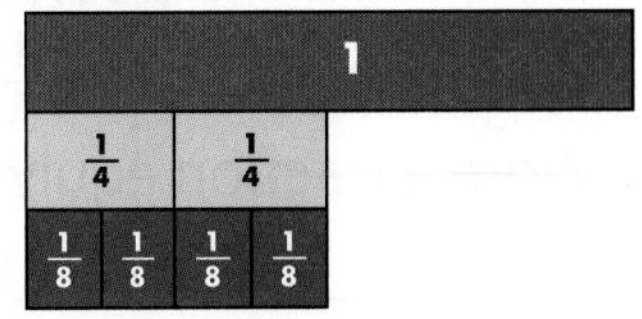

12. $\frac{10}{10} = \frac{1}{\square}$

13. $\frac{1}{2} = \frac{\square}{8}$

14. $\frac{2}{6} = \frac{1}{\square}$

15. $\frac{3}{5} = \frac{\square}{10}$

DIGITAL Animated Glossary, eTools **www.pearsonsuccessnet.com**

For another example, see Set D on page 241.

Independent Practice

In **16** through **25**, use counters or fraction strips to find an equivalent fraction for each.

16. $\frac{2}{3}$ **17.** $\frac{2}{10}$ **18.** $\frac{1}{3}$ **19.** $\frac{1}{6}$ **20.** $\frac{4}{5}$

21. $\frac{6}{8}$ **22.** $\frac{2}{8}$ **23.** $\frac{9}{12}$ **24.** $\frac{6}{6}$ **25.** $\frac{8}{12}$

TAKS Problem Solving

26. Draw fraction strips to show that $\frac{6}{8}$ and $\frac{9}{12}$ are equivalent.

27. Number Sense Write six facts that have a product of 12.

28. Using the model below, name three equivalent fractions for the region that is green.

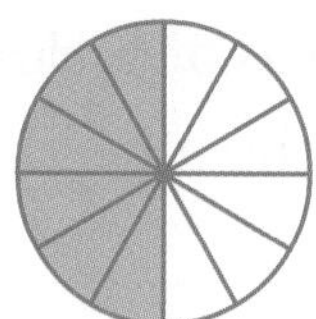

29. In a parking lot $\frac{5}{6}$ of the cars park for more than two hours. Which fraction is equivalent to $\frac{5}{6}$?

A $\frac{4}{12}$ **C** $\frac{6}{12}$

B $\frac{8}{12}$ **D** $\frac{10}{12}$

30. Susan used $\frac{1}{2}$ of a bucket of paint to paint a table. James used the same amount to paint another table. Which is **NOT** an amount James could have used?

F $\frac{2}{4}$ of a bucket **H** $\frac{5}{8}$ of a bucket

G $\frac{3}{6}$ of a bucket **J** $\frac{6}{12}$ of a bucket

31. In a school poetry contest, 15 out of 45 students who entered will win a small prize. Half of the remaining students receive a certificate. How many students win nothing?

32. The world's largest pumpkin pie weighed 2,020 pounds.The pie was $12\frac{1}{3}$ feet across and $\frac{1}{3}$ foot thick. Write a fraction equivalent to $\frac{1}{3}$.

$\frac{1}{3}$ foot thick

Algebra Connections

Divisibility

A number is divisible by another number when the quotient is a whole number and the remainder is 0.

Find which numbers in each list are divisible by the number shown.

1. 5
(5, 8, 10, 12, 15)

2. 8
(8, 14, 16, 19, 24)

3. 12
(12, 18, 25, 36, 48)

4. 14
(14, 27, 42, 56, 96)

5. 15
(15, 35, 45, 70, 90)

6. 16
(16, 32, 63, 80, 98)

7. 17
(17, 28, 34, 51, 69)

8. 22
(22, 33, 44, 55, 66)

9. 31
(31, 62, 83, 91, 124)

10. 4
(4, 8, 9, 12, 17)

11. 6
(6, 18, 21, 24, 35)

12. 7
(12, 14, 20, 28, 35)

13. 9
(18, 26, 36, 55, 63)

14. 18
(18, 35, 54, 72, 91)

Example:

Which of these numbers are divisible by 3?

(11, 14, 23, 42)

Use divisibility rules for 3s:

Is the sum of the digits of the number divisible by 3?

Try 14.

1 + **4** = **5**

5 is not divisible by 3, so 14 is not divisible by 3.

Now try 42.

4 + **2** = **6**

6 is divisible by 3, so 3 is a factor of 42.

Check: **42** ÷ **3** = **14**

15. Bonnie has 64 packets of pepper. She wants to store the same amount of packets in bags so that each bag has the same number of packets. What are three different ways Bonnie can do this?

16. How many pieces of cloth 7 yards long could you cut from a piece of cloth that is 42 yards long? Explain.

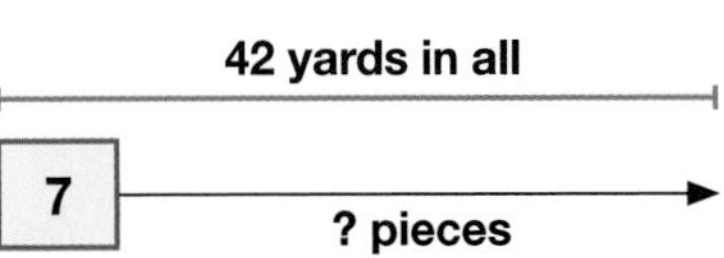

Lesson
10-5

TEKS 4.2A: Use concrete objects and pictorial models to generate equivalent fractions.

Finding Equivalent Fractions

Hands-On
fraction strips

How do you write a fraction in simplest form?

Stacy is using cubes, spheres, and a pyramid to make an abstract sculpture. What fraction of the shapes in her sculpture will be cubes? Write the fraction in simplest form.

4 cubes

Guided Practice*

Do you know HOW?

Write each fraction in simplest form. Use fractions strips to help you. If it is in simplest form, write simplest form.

1. $\frac{3}{9}$ **2.** $\frac{5}{12}$

3. $\frac{2}{10}$ **4.** $\frac{6}{12}$

5. $\frac{4}{5}$ **6.** $\frac{6}{8}$

Do you UNDERSTAND?

7. Writing to Explain Explain how you can tell $\frac{2}{6}$ is not in simplest form.

8. Stacy decided to not use 2 spheres, leaving a total of 10 shapes. Now what fraction of the shapes are cubes? Write this fraction in simplest form.

The number of cube shapes has not changed, so the numerator is still 4.

Independent Practice

In **9** through **28**, write each fraction in simplest form. Use fraction strips to help you. If it is in simplest form, write simplest form.

9. $\frac{3}{12}$ **10.** $\frac{5}{10}$ **11.** $\frac{4}{8}$ **12.** $\frac{8}{10}$ **13.** $\frac{4}{6}$

14. $\frac{2}{5}$ **15.** $\frac{2}{6}$ **16.** $\frac{3}{10}$ **17.** $\frac{8}{12}$ **18.** $\frac{5}{12}$

19. $\frac{1}{3}$ **20.** $\frac{2}{8}$ **21.** $\frac{9}{10}$ **22.** $\frac{6}{10}$ **23.** $\frac{4}{10}$

24. $\frac{5}{6}$ **25.** $\frac{6}{9}$ **26.** $\frac{10}{12}$ **27.** $\frac{2}{4}$ **28.** $\frac{2}{12}$

*For another example, see Set E on page 241.

Write $\frac{4}{12}$ in simplest form.

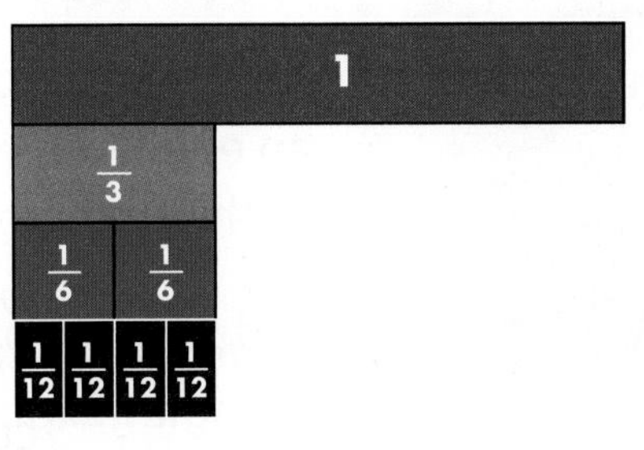

A common factor is a factor that two or more numbers have in common. Since 4 is a factor of 4 and a factor of 12, it is a common factor of 4 and 12.

A fraction is in simplest form if the numerator and denominator have no common factors other than 1.

In simplest form, $\frac{4}{12} = \frac{1}{3}$. So, $\frac{1}{3}$ of the shapes are cubes.

TAKS Problem Solving

Use the table at the right for **29** through **31**. Write your answers in simplest form.

Data

Band Member	Lessons (minutes)	Practice (minutes)
Will	90	60
Kaitlyn	60	210
Madison	45	105
Ryan	90	75
Kirk	75	240
Gina	60	45

29. What fraction of the band members practice for more than 120 minutes a week?

30. What fraction of the band members spend more time on lessons than on practice?

31. What is the total time spent each week on lessons? on practice? Which is greater?

32. Each day, pandas are awake for about 12 hours. They eat for about 10 hours. What fraction of their time awake are pandas eating?

33. Think About the Process Which of the following helps you find a fraction equal to $\frac{4}{8}$?

A Subtract 4 from 8.

B Divide 4 by 8.

C Compare fraction strips for fourths and eighths.

D Compare fraction strips for fourths and thirds.

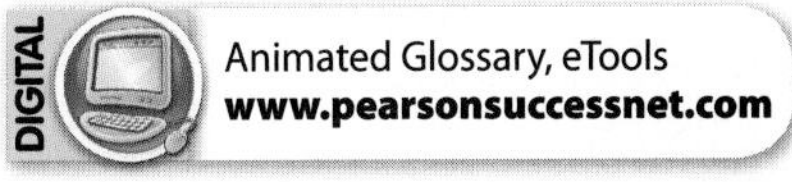

Lesson

10-6

TEKS 4.15A: Explain and record observations using objects, words, pictures, numbers, and technology.

Problem Solving

Writing to Explain

Jake found a piece of wood in the shape of an equilateral triangle. He cut off a section of the triangle as shown to the right.

Did Jake cut off $\frac{1}{3}$ of the triangle? Explain.

Another Example

Erin says that $\frac{1}{2}$ is always the same amount as $\frac{2}{4}$. Matthew says that $\frac{1}{2}$ and $\frac{2}{4}$ are equivalent fractions, but they could be different amounts. Which student is correct? Explain.

The circles are the same size.

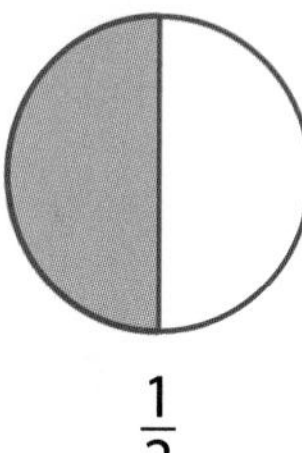

$\frac{1}{2}$

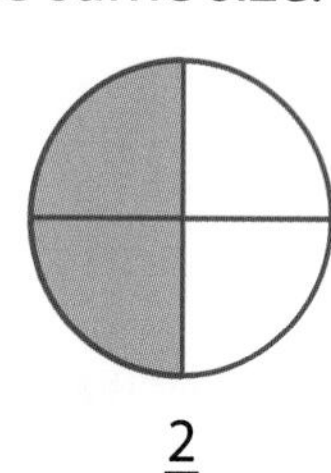

$\frac{2}{4}$

The amounts are the same.

The circles are not the same size.

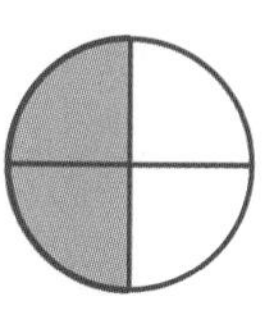

$\frac{2}{4}$

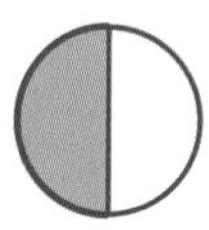

$\frac{1}{2}$

The amounts are different.

Matthew is correct. $\frac{1}{2}$ and $\frac{2}{4}$ are equivalent fractions but they could represent different amounts.

Explain It

1. When will amounts of $\frac{1}{2}$ and $\frac{2}{4}$ be equal?

2. When are the fractional amounts $\frac{3}{6}$ and $\frac{2}{4}$ not equal?

Read & Understand

What do I know? The triangle is an equilateral triangle. One piece is cut off.

What am I asked to find? Is the section that is cut off $\frac{1}{3}$ of the triangle?

Plan

Use words, pictures, numbers, or symbols to write a math explanation.

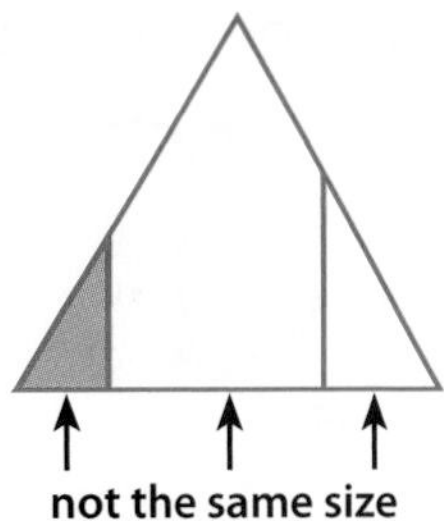

$\frac{1}{3}$ means that the whole has to be divided into 3 equal parts. The parts have to be the same size.

The shaded section is not $\frac{1}{3}$ of the triangle.

Guided Practice*

Do you know HOW?

1. A board is cut into 12 equal pieces. How many pieces together represent $\frac{3}{4}$ of the board? Explain how you arrived at your answer.

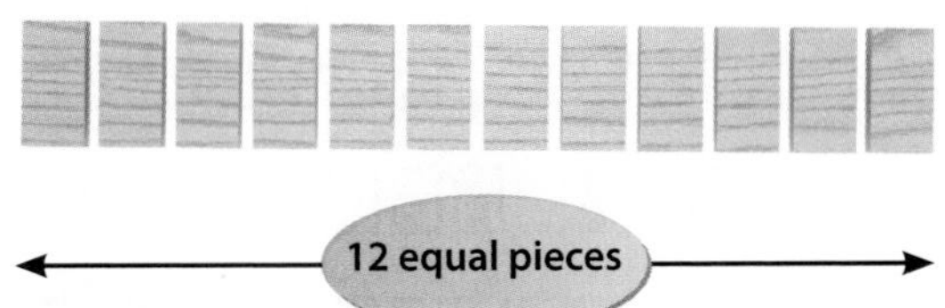

Do you UNDERSTAND?

2. Copy and draw the triangle above. Shade in $\frac{1}{3}$ of the triangle.

3. **Write a Problem** Write a problem that would use the figure below as part of its explanation.

Independent Practice

Write to explain.

4. Devon and Amanda knit the same size scarf. Devon's scarf is $\frac{3}{5}$ yellow. Amanda's scarf is $\frac{3}{4}$ yellow. How can you use a picture to show whose scarf is more yellow?

5. The school newspaper has a total of 18 articles and ads. There are 6 more articles than ads. How many articles and ads are there? Explain how you found your answer.

Stuck? Try this....

- What do I know?
- What diagram can I use to help understand the problem?
- Can I use addition, subtraction, multiplication, or division?
- Is all of my work correct?
- Did I answer the right question?
- Is my answer reasonable?

*For another example, see Set F on page 241.

Independent Practice

6. Look at the cell pattern below. Explain how the number of cells changes as the number of divisions changes.

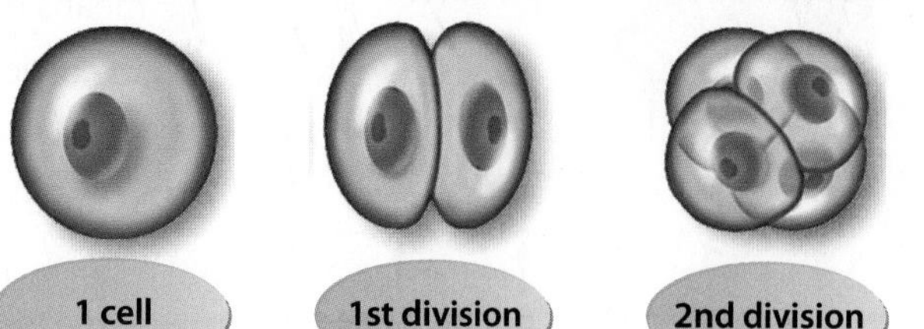

7. **Algebra** Look at the number sentences. What numbers replace ●, ▲, and ■? Explain your answer.

   ▲ + ■ = 18
   ● + ▲ = 20
   ■ + ■ = 14

8. **Geometry** Three streets intersect with one another. East Street runs horizontally, North Street runs vertically and Fourth Street runs diagonally and intersects both East Street and North Street. What geometric figure do the three streets form?

Use the data at the right for problems **9** and **10**.

9. How can you find the number of cards Linda has in her collection?

10. George has 100 rookie cards in his collection. How can you find the number of pictures in the pictograph that represent George's rookie cards?

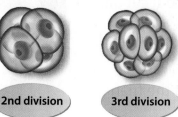

Baseball Card Collections

George	▣▣▣▣▣▣▣▣▣▣▣▣
Becky	▣▣▣▣▣▣▣▣▣▣▣▣
Trent	▣▣▣▣▣▣▣▣▣▣▣▣▣▣
Linda	▣▣▣▣▣▣▣▣▣▣▣▣

Each ▣ = 25 cards

Think About the Process

11. Janet gets $25 a week to buy lunch at school. She spends $4 each day and saves the rest. How much money will Janet save at the end of the 5 days?

   A $(4 \times 5) + 25$ **C** $(25 - 5) + 4$
   B $25 + (5 - 4)$ **D** $25 - (5 \times 4)$

12. During recess, Rachel played on the bars and swings. She spent 10 minutes on the bars and twice as long on the swings. How much time did she play on the equipment?

   F $10 - (2 + 10)$ **H** $(10 + 2) - 10$
   G $10 + (2 \times 10)$ **J** $(10 \div 2) + 10$

Equivalent Fractions

Use eTools Fractions

Find the numerator which makes the fractions equivalent. $\frac{3}{4} = \frac{\square}{8}$

Step 1 Go to the Fractions eTool. Select the equivalents workspace mode.

Select $\frac{1}{4}$ three times, to show $\frac{3}{4}$ in the first circle.

Step 2 Select the second circle by clicking on it. Select $\frac{1}{8}$ until the symbol changes from $>$ to $=$. Read the fractions at the bottom of the workspace. $\frac{3}{4} = \frac{6}{8}$

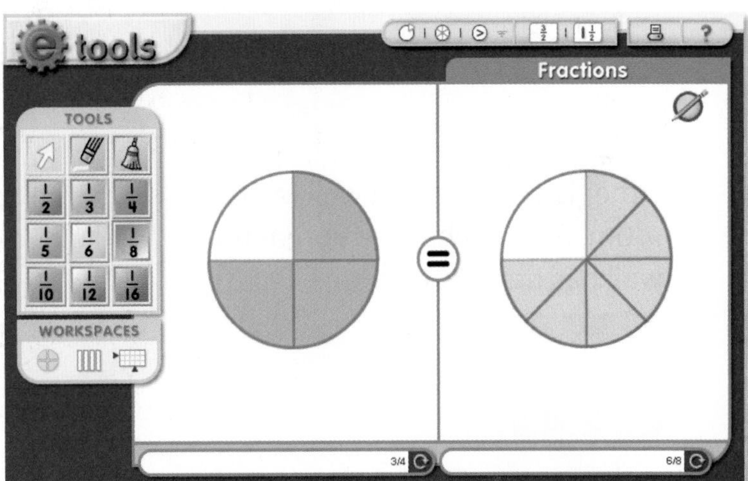

Step 3 Use the Broom tool to clear the workspace before doing another problem.

Practice

Use the Fractions eTool to find the numerator which makes the fractions equivalent.

1. $\frac{3}{4} = \frac{\square}{8}$
2. $\frac{2}{5} = \frac{\square}{10}$
3. $\frac{4}{6} = \frac{\square}{3}$
4. $\frac{6}{16} = \frac{\square}{8}$
5. $\frac{1}{2} = \frac{\square}{16}$
6. $\frac{1}{3} = \frac{\square}{12}$
7. $\frac{8}{10} = \frac{\square}{5}$
8. $\frac{3}{12} = \frac{\square}{4}$
9. $\frac{3}{4} = \frac{\square}{12}$
10. $\frac{5}{8} = \frac{\square}{16}$
11. $\frac{3}{4} = \frac{\square}{16}$
12. $\frac{4}{8} = \frac{\square}{2}$
13. $\frac{1}{2} = \frac{\square}{12}$
14. $\frac{1}{2} = \frac{\square}{10}$
15. $\frac{5}{6} = \frac{\square}{12}$
16. $\frac{4}{5} = \frac{\square}{15}$

1. Tonya bought the fruit shown below. What fraction of the fruit are apples? (10-1)

A $\frac{7}{10}$
B $\frac{3}{7}$
C $\frac{3}{10}$
D $\frac{3}{12}$

2. Elmer is painting one wall in his room. About what fraction of the wall has he painted blue? (10-3)

F $\frac{1}{2}$
G $\frac{1}{4}$
H $\frac{3}{4}$
J $\frac{2}{3}$

3. Which fraction is **NOT** equivalent to the shaded area of the rectangle? (10-4)

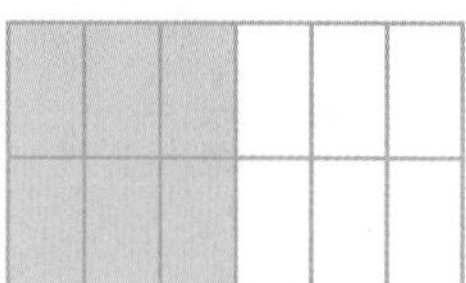

A $\frac{6}{12}$
B $\frac{1}{2}$
C $\frac{3}{6}$
D $\frac{2}{3}$

4. Eight students share 5 yards of ribbon equally. What fraction does each student get? (10-2)

F $\frac{8}{5}$ yard
G $\frac{8}{8}$ yard
H $\frac{5}{5}$ yard
J $\frac{5}{8}$ yard

5. Mallory had 12 grapes. She ate 8 of them. What fraction, in simplest form, of the grapes did she eat? (10-5)

A $\frac{3}{4}$
B $\frac{8}{12}$
C $\frac{2}{3}$
D $\frac{1}{3}$

6. Which model is shaded to show a fraction equivalent to $\frac{3}{9}$? (10-4)

F 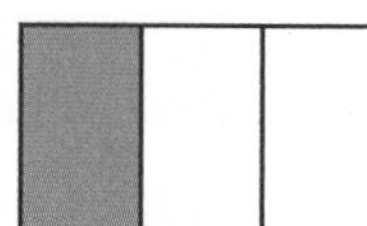

G 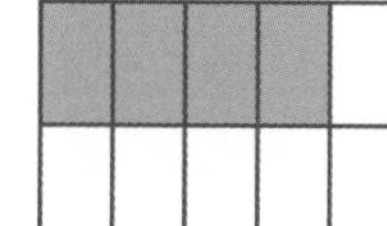

H 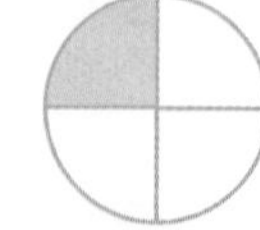

J 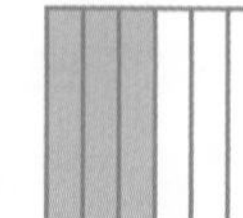

7. What fraction of Mr. William's garden contains carrots? (10-1)

A $\frac{1}{6}$

B $\frac{1}{5}$

C $\frac{2}{6}$

D $\frac{5}{6}$

8. Seven friends are sharing 3 bottles of juice. Which number sentence can be used to find the fraction of a bottle of juice that each friend gets? (10-2)

F $3 \times 7 = \square$

G $3 \div 4 = \square$

H $3 \div 7 = \square$

J $7 \div 3 = \square$

9. Which statement would **NOT** be used in an explanation of how the drawing shows that $\frac{2}{3} = \frac{4}{6}$? (10-6)

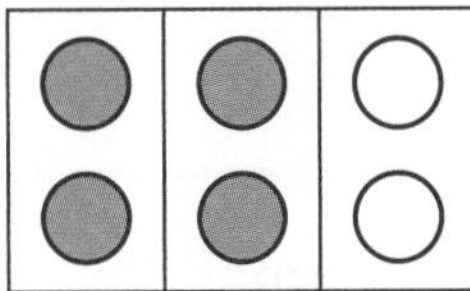

A 2 of the 3 rectangles are filled with shaded circles.

B 4 out of the 6 rectangles are shaded.

C Both $\frac{2}{3}$ and $\frac{4}{6}$ describe the part that is shaded.

D In the rectangles, 4 out of the 6 circles are shaded.

10. Jase completed 8 out of the 10 laps required to pass his swimming test. What fraction, in simplest form, of the laps did he complete? (10-5)

F $\frac{8}{10}$

G $\frac{4}{5}$

H $\frac{3}{4}$

J $\frac{2}{3}$

11. Mrs. Zenno made a vegetable pizza for dinner. About $\frac{1}{4}$ of the pizza is left. Which shows about $\frac{1}{4}$? (10-3)

A 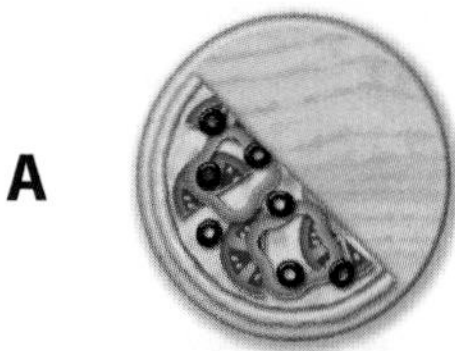

B 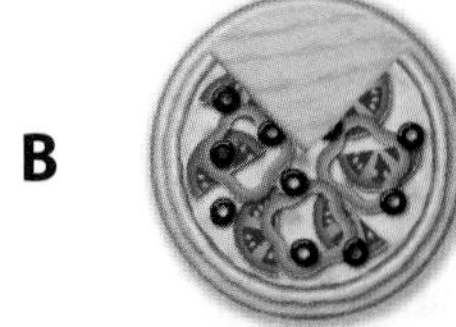

C 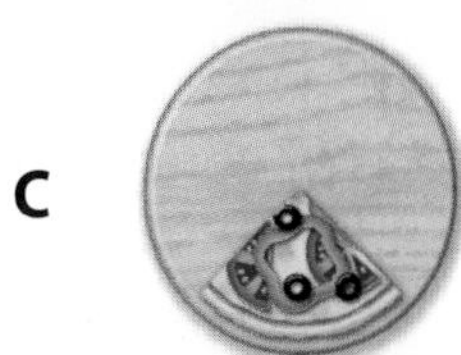

D 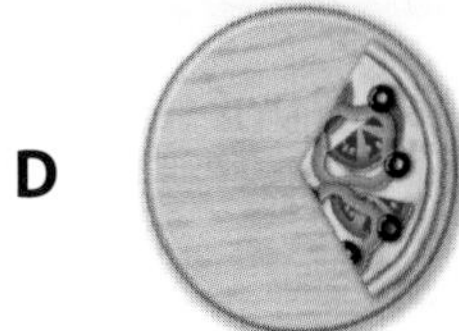

12. **Griddable Response** Steven bought a small bag of marbles at a yard sale. He found that $\frac{5}{12}$ of the marbles were red. What is the denominator of $\frac{5}{12}$? (10-1)

Set A, pages 220–222

You can write fractions to represent parts of a set. What part of the grapes are green?

$\frac{\text{numerator}}{\text{denominator}} = \frac{\text{green grapes}}{\text{parts in all}}$

$\frac{3}{5}$ of the grapes are green.

Remember the numerator tells how many equal parts are described, and the denominator tells how many equal parts in all.

Write a fraction for the part of each set that is red.

1. 2.

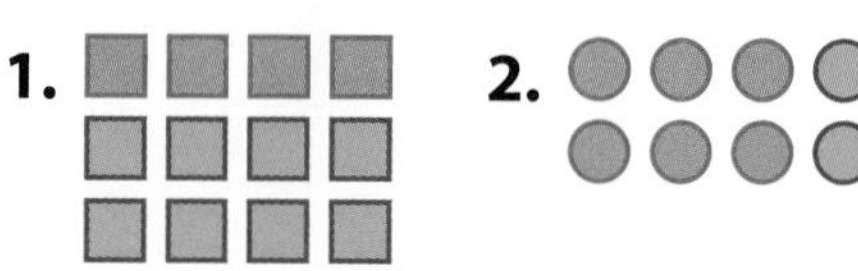

3. 4.

Set B, pages 224–225

Four friends cut up 3 pieces of construction paper. If they shared the paper equally, what fraction of the paper did each friend use?

  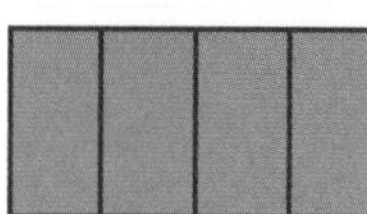

Each part is 1 ÷ 4, or $\frac{1}{4}$.

Each person used 3 parts. Each part is $\frac{1}{4}$, so each person used $\frac{3}{4}$ of a piece of construction paper.

Remember you can draw a model to show each fraction amount.

Tell what fraction each person gets.

1. Five students share 1 hour to give their reports.
2. Four people share two sandwiches.
3. Four friends share 3 cups of hot chocolate.

Set C, pages 226–227

Estimate the fractional part of the rectangle that is blue.

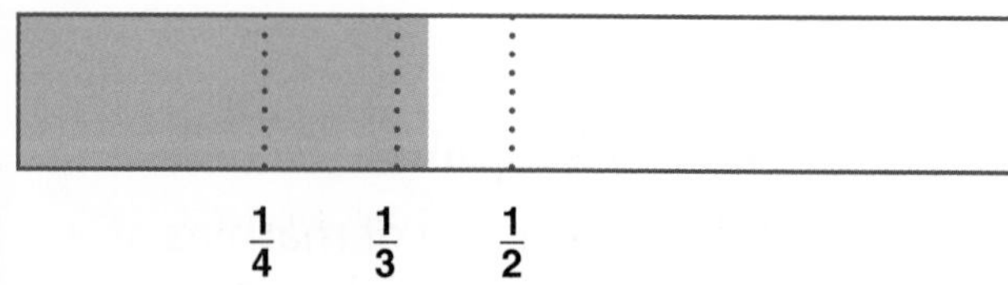

Compare the part that is blue. The blue part is more than $\frac{1}{3}$ but less than $\frac{1}{2}$ of the whole rectangle. About $\frac{1}{3}$ of the rectangle is blue.

Remember, the benchmark fractions are basic fractions, such as $\frac{1}{4}$, $\frac{1}{3}$, $\frac{1}{2}$, $\frac{2}{3}$, and $\frac{3}{4}$.

Estimate the fractional part of each that is green.

1. 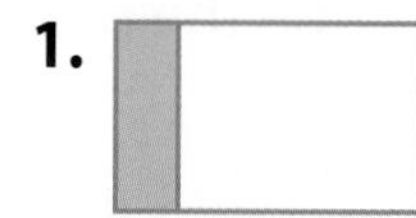

2. 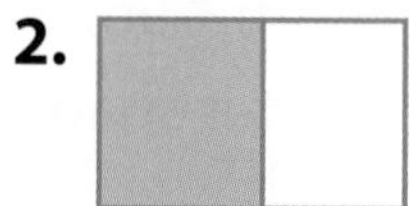

Reteaching

Set D, pages 228–230

Write an equivalent fraction for $\frac{1}{3}$.

Two of the sixths equal the same amount as one third. So, $\frac{1}{3} = \frac{2}{6}$.

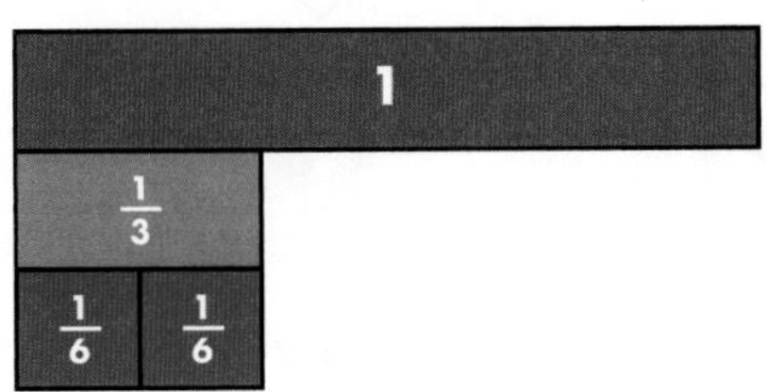

Remember when you compare fractions, they are equivalent if the shaded areas of the fraction strip are equal.

Use fraction strips to find an equivalent fraction.

1. $\frac{6}{10} = \frac{\square}{\square}$
2. $\frac{3}{4} = \frac{\square}{\square}$
3. $\frac{4}{12} = \frac{\square}{\square}$
4. $\frac{1}{5} = \frac{\square}{\square}$

Set E, pages 232–233

Write $\frac{4}{10}$ in simplest form.

The numerator, 4, and denominator, 10, have 2 as a common factor.

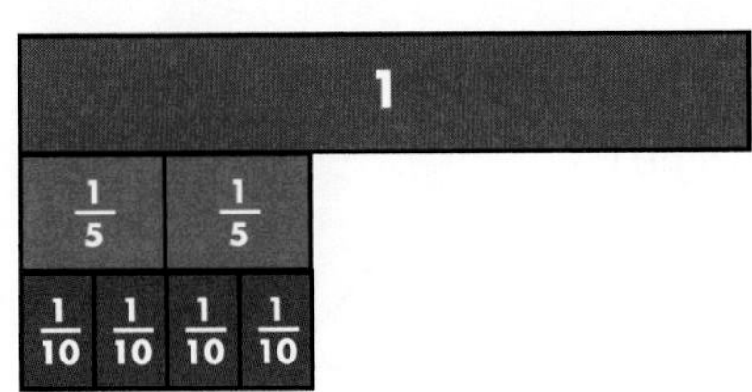

$\frac{4}{10} = \frac{2}{5}$

The only common factor for 2 and 5 is 1. So, $\frac{2}{5}$ is in simplest form.

Remember that a fraction is in simplest form if the numerator and the denominator have no common factor other than 1.

Use fraction strips to write each fraction in simplest form.

1. $\frac{3}{6}$
2. $\frac{2}{10}$
3. $\frac{6}{8}$
4. $\frac{10}{12}$
5. $\frac{9}{12}$
6. $\frac{4}{6}$

Set F, pages 234–236

Suppose a square is cut as shown. Is each section $\frac{1}{4}$ of the square?

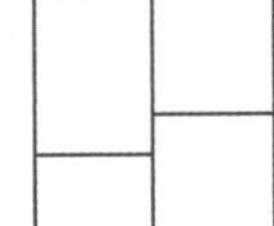

What do I know? The square is cut into 4 pieces.

What am I asked to find? Do all the cuts represent $\frac{1}{4}$ of the square?

If each part is $\frac{1}{4}$ then the whole is divided into 4 equal parts. The parts are not the same size. Each is not $\frac{1}{4}$ of the square.

Remember to explain your answer.

1. Peter says that $\frac{3}{4}$ of a pizza is always the same as $\frac{6}{8}$ of a pizza. Nadia says that while they are equivalent fractions, $\frac{3}{4}$ and $\frac{6}{8}$ of a pizza could represent different amounts. Who is correct?

Topics 1–10

Spiral Review

Number and Operations

1. What is 219 divided by 7?

   A 30 R3 C 31 R2

   B 31 D 39

2. Which model below shows $\frac{9}{16}$ shaded?

   F 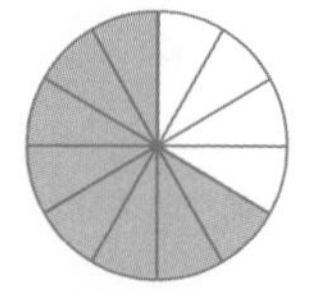 H 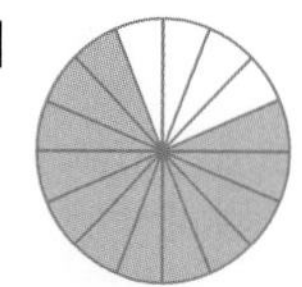

   G 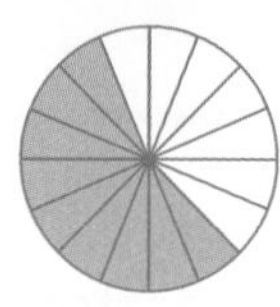 J 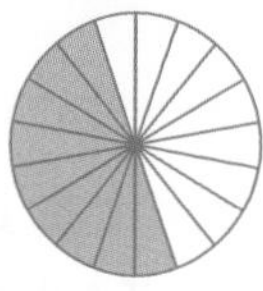

3. What is twenty seven million, thirty thousand, thirty-six written in standard form?

   A 27,030,036 C 27,000,036

   B 27,003,306 D 27,30,36

4. Which rectangle shows about $\frac{1}{4}$ shaded green?

   F  H 

   G 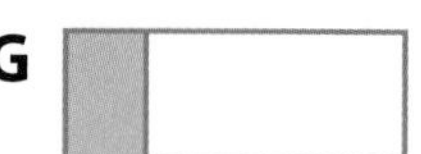 J 

5. What is the product of 18 and 14?

   A 212 C 252

   B 232 D 272

6. **Writing to Explain** Explain how you can break numbers apart to find the product of 7×13.

Geometry and Measurement

7. Which sign is a quadrilateral?

   F 

   H 

   G  J 

8. Which of the figures below is a solid figure?

   A  C 

   B 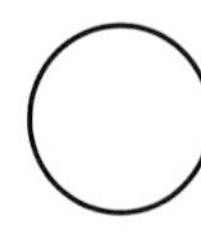 D 

9. Which of these figures is a right triangle?

   F  H 

   G J

10. What is the date three weeks after June 2nd?

11. Write the time shown in two different ways.

12. **Writing to Explain** Would a scale used to weigh a truck be the best tool to weigh a fourth-grader?

Probability and Statistics

13. Which describes the likelihood of landing on a 4?

A Certain

B Likely

C Unlikely

D Impossible

14. Rick tosses a number cube with the numbers 1 through 6. If Rick tosses an even number, what are the possible outcomes?

F 1, 2, 3 **H** 2, 3, 4

G 1, 3, 5 **J** 2, 4, 6

15. If these letter tiles are randomly selected, what letter is most likely to be selected?

A A **B** B **C** C **D** E

Use the picture below for **16** and **17**.

16. Without looking what color marble are you most likely to pull out?

17. **Writing to Explain** Explain why it is equally likely you will pull a green or yellow marble.

Algebraic Thinking

18. Which number is next in the pattern?

4, 8, 12, 16, 20, ▭

F 21 **H** 22

G 24 **J** 28

19. What number is next in the pattern?

6, 8, 11, 6, 8, 11, 6, ▭

A 8 **C** 10

B 9 **D** 11

20. Which is the equation for the sum of 5 and n is 20?

F $5 + 5 = n$

G $n + 20 = 5$

H $20 + n = 5$

J $5 + n = 20$

21. Which is part of the fact family for 6, 8, and 48?

A $6 + 8 = 14$

B $48 \div 8 = 6$

C $48 - 8 = 40$

D $48 \times 6 = 288$

22. What is the rule?

In	49	35	28	14
Out	7	5	4	2

23. **Writing to Explain** How can you use patterns to find $3{,}000 \div 6$ and $3{,}000 \div 60$?

Topic 11

Fractions and Decimals

1 The Roman Colosseum is one of the best examples of Roman architecture. The arena is what fractional part of the Colosseum? You will find out in Lesson 11-5.

2 How many gallons of milk does an average milk cow produce each day? You will find out in Lesson 11-1.

3 A hummingbird flaps its wings once every tenth of a second. What is this number as a decimal and as a fraction in simplest form? You will find out in Lesson 11-6.

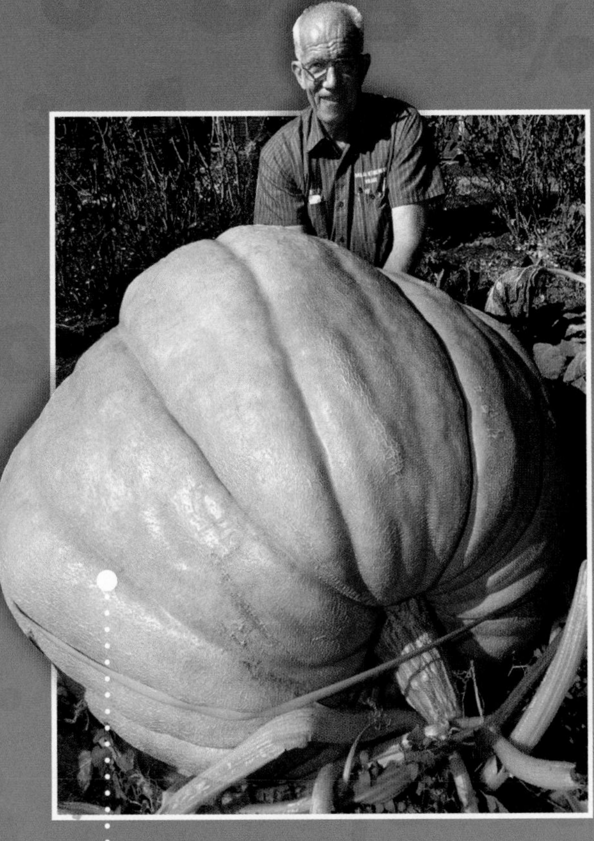

4 The largest pumpkin grown in the United States weighed 1,502 pounds. How much did the largest pumpkin grown in Texas weigh? You will find out in Lesson 11-2.

Review What You Know!

Vocabulary

Choose the best term from the box.

- common factor
- numerator
- denominator
- simplest form

1. The factor that two or more numbers have in common is called a(n) ___?___.
2. A ___?___ represents the total number of equal parts in all.
3. The number above the fraction bar in a fraction is known as the ___?___.

Parts of a Region or Set

4. What fraction of the set below is red?

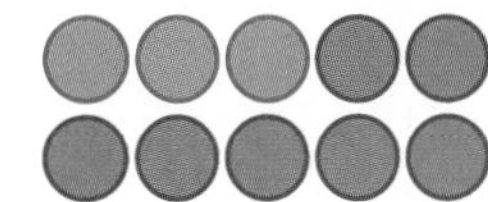

5. What fraction of the rectangle below is not green?

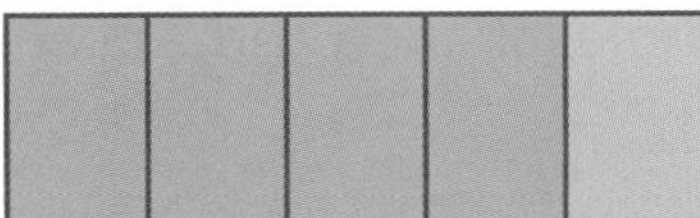

Fraction Concepts

Draw a model to show each fraction.

6. $\frac{4}{5}$
7. $\frac{1}{4}$
8. $\frac{2}{3}$
9. $\frac{1}{4}$
10. $\frac{6}{8}$
11. $\frac{3}{5}$
12. $\frac{6}{10}$
13. $\frac{11}{12}$
14. $\frac{5}{5}$
15. **Writing to Explain** Why are $\frac{3}{4}$ and $\frac{4}{8}$ not equivalent fractions?

Lesson

11-1

TEKS 4.2B: Model fraction quantities greater than one using concrete objects and pictorial models.

Improper Fractions and Mixed Numbers

Hands-On
fraction strips

$\frac{1}{8}$

How can you name an amount in two different ways?

How many times will Matt need to fill his $\frac{1}{4}$-cup container to make $2\frac{1}{4}$ cups of punch?

$2\frac{1}{4}$ is a mixed number. A mixed number has a whole number part and a fraction part.

Another Example How can you write an improper fraction as a mixed number or whole number?

Jack used $\frac{10}{3}$ cups of water to make lemonade. Write $\frac{10}{3}$ as a mixed number.

A $10\frac{1}{3}$ cups

B $3\frac{1}{3}$ cups

C $3\frac{1}{10}$ cups

D $\frac{3}{3}$ cups

Use a model. Show $\frac{10}{3}$ or 10 thirds.

There are 3 wholes shaded and $\frac{1}{3}$ of another whole shaded.

So, $\frac{10}{3} = 3\frac{1}{3}$.

Jack made $3\frac{1}{3}$ cups of lemonade.

The correct answer choice is **B**.

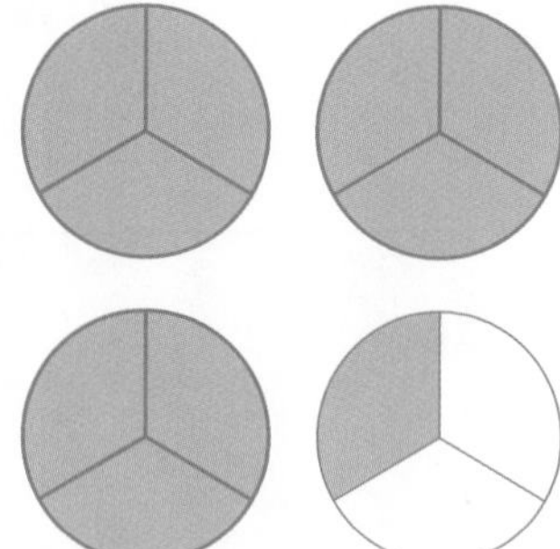

Explain It

1. Explain why $\frac{6}{3} = 2$. Draw a model to help you.

2. Jacquelyn made punch using $\frac{7}{2}$ cups of water. Write $\frac{7}{2}$ as a mixed number.

One Way

Use a model to write $2\frac{1}{4}$ as an improper fraction.

An improper fraction <u>has a numerator greater than or equal to its denominator</u>.

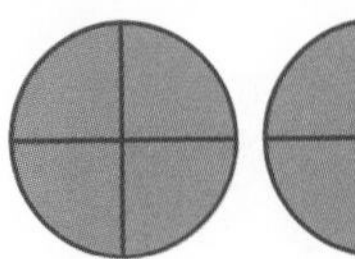
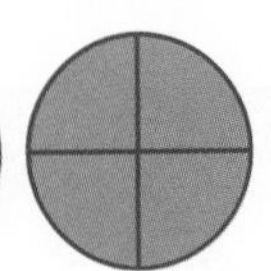
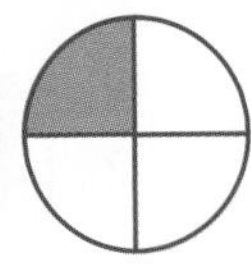

Count the shaded fourths.

There are 9 fourths or $\frac{9}{4}$ shaded. So, $2\frac{1}{4} = \frac{9}{4}$.

$\frac{9}{4}$ is an improper fraction.

Matt needs to fill the $\frac{1}{4}$-cup container 9 times.

Another Way

Use fraction strips.

1			
$\frac{1}{4}$	$\frac{1}{4}$	$\frac{1}{4}$	$\frac{1}{4}$
$\frac{1}{4}$	$\frac{1}{4}$	$\frac{1}{4}$	$\frac{1}{4}$
$\frac{1}{4}$			

So, $2\frac{1}{4} = \frac{9}{4}$.

Guided Practice*

Do you know HOW?

Write each mixed number as an improper fraction. Write each improper fraction as a mixed number or whole number. Use models to help you.

1. $1\frac{3}{8}$

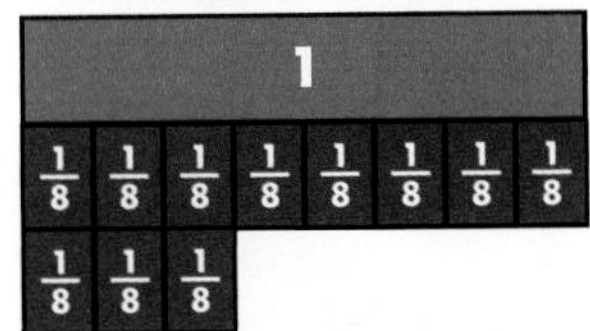

2. $\frac{4}{3}$

1		
$\frac{1}{3}$	$\frac{1}{3}$	$\frac{1}{3}$
$\frac{1}{3}$		

Do you UNDERSTAND?

3. How else could you model $2\frac{1}{4}$ using fraction strips?

4. If Matt filled a $3\frac{1}{4}$ cup container, how many $\frac{1}{4}$ cups would he need to use?

5. Nancy bought $7\frac{1}{2}$ gallons of milk for the school cafeteria. She bought only half-gallon containers. How many half-gallon containers did she buy?

Independent Practice

For **6** through **8**, write each mixed number or improper fraction using fraction strips.

6. $1\frac{3}{4}$

1			
$\frac{1}{4}$	$\frac{1}{4}$	$\frac{1}{4}$	$\frac{1}{4}$
$\frac{1}{4}$	$\frac{1}{4}$	$\frac{1}{4}$	

7. $\frac{7}{3}$

1		
$\frac{1}{3}$	$\frac{1}{3}$	$\frac{1}{3}$
$\frac{1}{3}$	$\frac{1}{3}$	$\frac{1}{3}$
$\frac{1}{3}$		

8. $3\frac{1}{5}$

1				
$\frac{1}{5}$	$\frac{1}{5}$	$\frac{1}{5}$	$\frac{1}{5}$	$\frac{1}{5}$
$\frac{1}{5}$	$\frac{1}{5}$	$\frac{1}{5}$	$\frac{1}{5}$	$\frac{1}{5}$
$\frac{1}{5}$	$\frac{1}{5}$	$\frac{1}{5}$	$\frac{1}{5}$	$\frac{1}{5}$
$\frac{1}{5}$				

*For another example, see Set A on page 266.

Independent Practice

For **9** through **11**, write each number as a mixed number or improper fraction.

9. $4\frac{2}{3}$

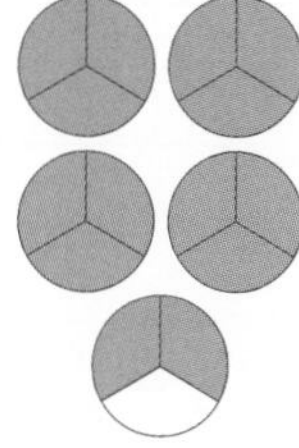

10. $\frac{10}{3}$

11. $1\frac{1}{2}$

TAKS Problem Solving

12. Jeremy used this recipe to make a smoothie. How many $\frac{1}{2}$ cups of ice does Jeremy need?

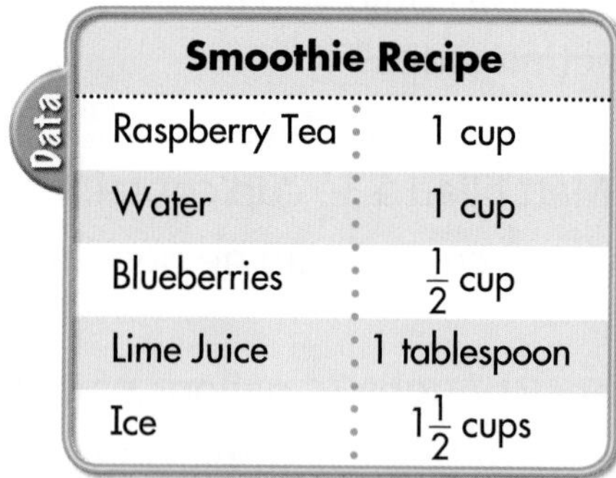

Smoothie Recipe	
Raspberry Tea	1 cup
Water	1 cup
Blueberries	$\frac{1}{2}$ cup
Lime Juice	1 tablespoon
Ice	$1\frac{1}{2}$ cups

13. Chris finished eating his lunch in 11 minutes. His brother took 3 times as long. How many minutes did it take his brother to finish his lunch?

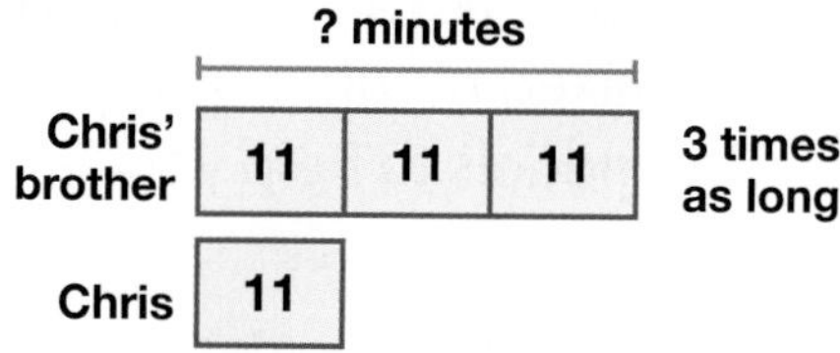

14. Sara bought a box of 6 granola bars. The total weight was $7\frac{1}{3}$ ounces. Write $7\frac{1}{3}$ as an improper fraction.

15. Kathy wrote the mixed number for $\frac{35}{5}$ as $\frac{7}{5}$. Is she correct? Why or why not?

16. Julia bought $3\frac{1}{4}$ yards of fabric. How many $\frac{1}{4}$ yards of fabric did Julia buy?

17. In one week Nate drank $\frac{17}{3}$ cups of milk. Write $\frac{17}{3}$ as a mixed number.

18. What fraction or mixed number does this model show?

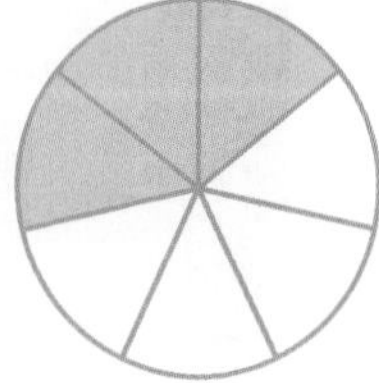

19. The average milk cow produces $4\frac{1}{2}$ gallons of milk a day. How much milk is this amount as an improper fraction?

A $\frac{11}{9}$ gallons

B $\frac{19}{9}$ gallons

C $\frac{9}{2}$ gallons

D $\frac{19}{2}$ gallon

Mixed Problem Solving

Artists frequently mix base colors together to create different hues of paint for use in paintings. They begin with three primary colors: blue, red, and yellow. The colors that are produced depend upon the fraction of paints that are combined.

Mr. McCrory is mixing paints together to create colors to use in some oil paintings.

Data

Paint 1	$\frac{1}{4}$ blue	$\frac{1}{6}$ red	$\frac{5}{6}$ yellow
Paint 2	$\frac{3}{4}$ red	$\frac{1}{3}$ yellow	$\frac{5}{8}$ blue
Color	Light Purple	Orange	Deep Green

1. Use fraction strips to compare the fractions of color paint that were used to make the shade of deep green and the shade of light purple. Write the fractions from *greatest* to *least*.

2. Use fraction strips to order all the fractions of paint used from *least* to *greatest*.

3. Jared painted on a canvas using fractional amounts of colored paint. The chart at the right shows the fractional amount of each color that was used. Order each fraction from *least* to *greatest*.

Data

Color of paint	Blue	Red	Yellow	White
Amount used	$\frac{2}{3}$	$\frac{6}{12}$	$\frac{8}{9}$	$\frac{4}{10}$

4. Elsie took a course on making stained glass at the community art center. She used $\frac{2}{6}$ of green colored glass, $\frac{1}{2}$ of yellow colored glass, and $\frac{1}{6}$ of red colored glass to make a sun catcher. Was more of her sun catcher made up of green or yellow colored glass? Draw a model to show your answer.

5. A flag is made up of fractional colors. $\frac{1}{2}$ of the flag is blue, and $\frac{1}{4}$ is white. The rest of the flag is made up of $\frac{2}{12}$ red and $\frac{1}{12}$ green. Order the fractions of color from *least* to *greatest*.

Lesson

11-2

TEKS4.2C: Compare and order fractions using concrete objects and pictorial models.

Using Models to Compare and Order Fractions

Hands-On fraction strips

How can you use fraction strips to compare and order fractions?

The table shows the amount of time three students spent practicing guitar each day. Who spent more time practicing—Jack or Lynn? Who spent less time practicing—Chase or Jack?

Data

Guitar Practice	
Jack	$\frac{3}{4}$ hour
Chase	$\frac{2}{3}$ hour
Lynn	$\frac{1}{4}$ hour

Another Example How can you use fraction strips to order fractions?

Use the table above. Which choice below shows the amount of time the students practiced in order from least to greatest?

A $\frac{3}{4}$ h, $\frac{2}{3}$ h, $\frac{1}{4}$ h

B $\frac{2}{3}$ h, $\frac{3}{4}$ h, $\frac{1}{4}$ h

C $\frac{1}{4}$ h, $\frac{3}{4}$ h, $\frac{2}{3}$ h

D $\frac{1}{4}$ h, $\frac{2}{3}$ h, $\frac{3}{4}$ h

You can use fraction strips to order the fractions.

$\frac{1}{4} < \frac{2}{3} < \frac{3}{4}$

So, the order of the practice times from least to greatest is $\frac{1}{4}$ h, $\frac{2}{3}$ h, $\frac{3}{4}$ h.

The correct choice is **D**.

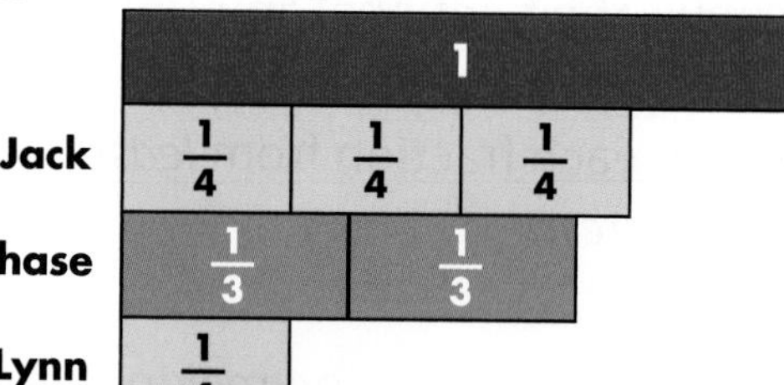

Explain It

1. Look at the fraction strips for $\frac{3}{4}$, $\frac{2}{3}$, and $\frac{1}{4}$. Which of the fractions are greater than $\frac{1}{2}$? Explain how you found your answer.

2. Look at the fraction strips for $\frac{1}{4}$, $\frac{5}{6}$, and $\frac{5}{12}$. Which of the fractions are less than $\frac{1}{2}$? Explain how you found your answer.

Who practiced more—Jack or Lynn? Compare $\frac{3}{4}$ and $\frac{1}{4}$.

You can use fraction strips to compare.

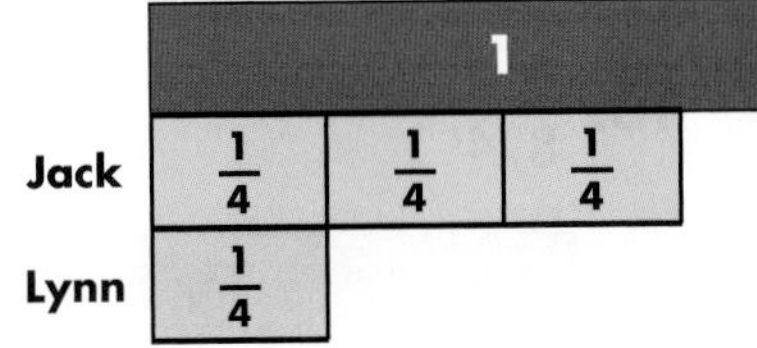

$\frac{3}{4} > \frac{1}{4}$

Jack spent more time practicing than Lynn.

Who practiced less—Chase or Jack? Compare $\frac{2}{3}$ and $\frac{3}{4}$.

You can use fraction strips to compare.

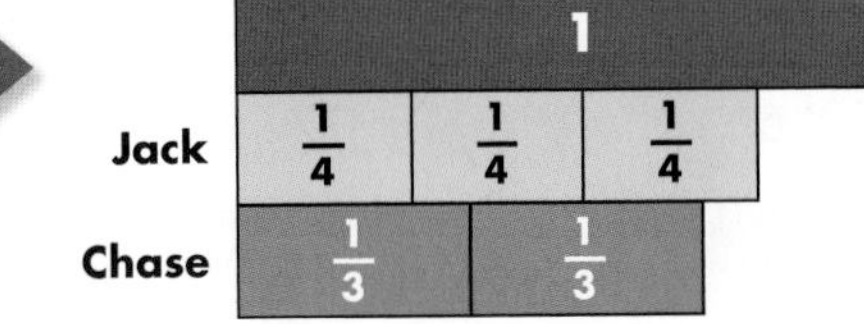

$\frac{2}{3} < \frac{3}{4}$

Chase spent less time practicing than Jack.

Guided Practice*

Do you know HOW?

Write >, <, or = for the ◯. Use fraction strips to help.

1. $\frac{1}{2}$ ◯ $\frac{3}{8}$

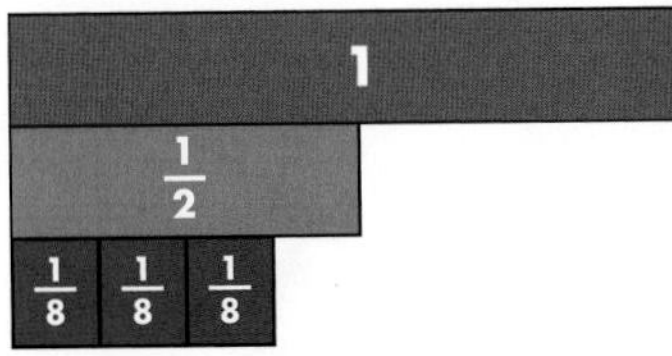

Order the numbers from least to greatest. Use fraction strips.

2. $\frac{1}{3}, \frac{1}{6}, \frac{3}{4}$

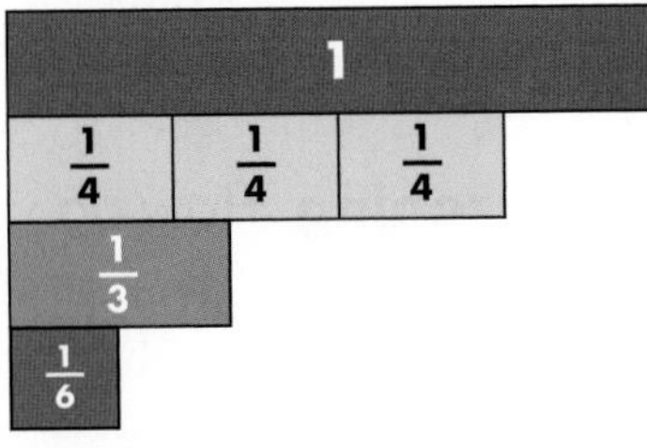

Do you UNDERSTAND?

3. Who practiced more—Chase or Lynn? Use fraction strips to compare.

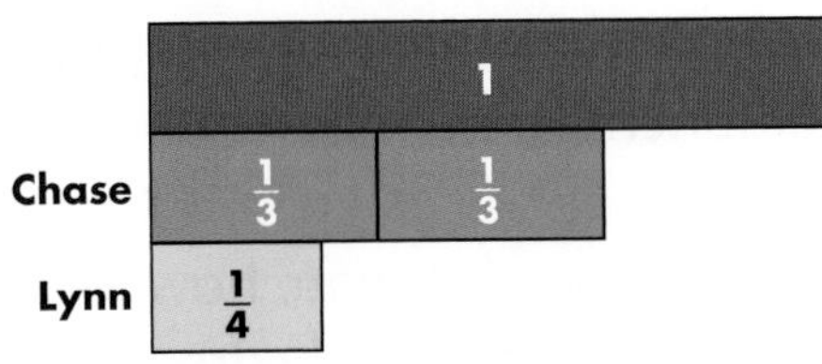

4. Three students practiced piano for $\frac{5}{8}$ hour, $\frac{1}{3}$ hour, and $\frac{7}{12}$ hour. Write these amounts of time in order from least to greatest.

Independent Practice

For **5** through **7**, write >,< or = for each ◯. Use fraction strips or drawings to help.

5. $\frac{5}{12}$ ◯ $\frac{1}{2}$

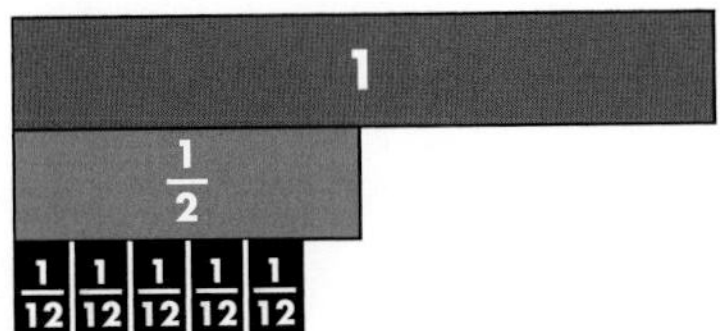

6. $\frac{3}{4}$ ◯ $\frac{7}{8}$

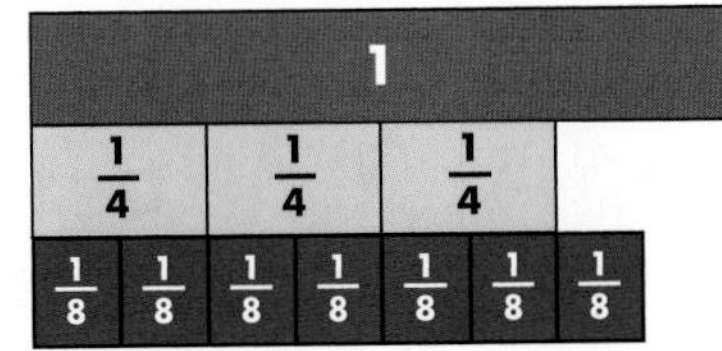

7. $\frac{7}{8}$ ◯ $\frac{3}{10}$

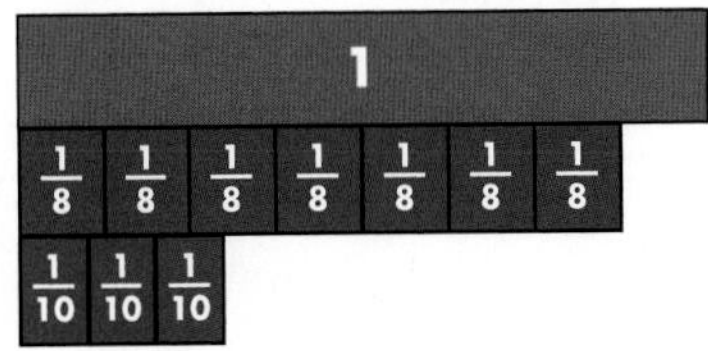

*For another example, see Set B on page 266.

Independent Practice

For **8** through **10**, order the numbers from least to greatest. Use fraction strips or drawings to help.

8. $\frac{1}{3}, \frac{3}{12}, \frac{3}{6}$

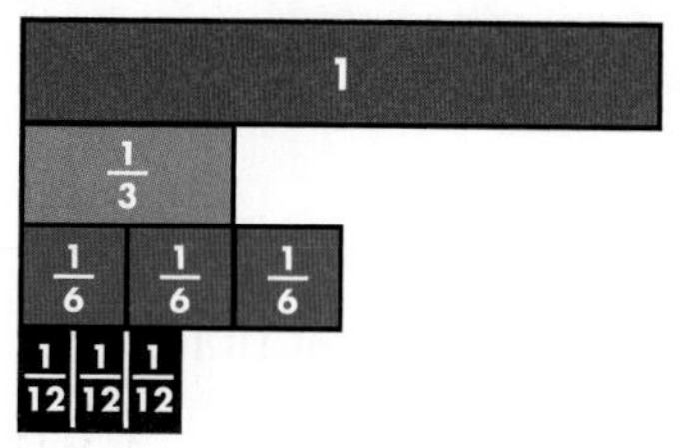

9. $\frac{3}{4}, \frac{3}{8}, \frac{1}{2}$

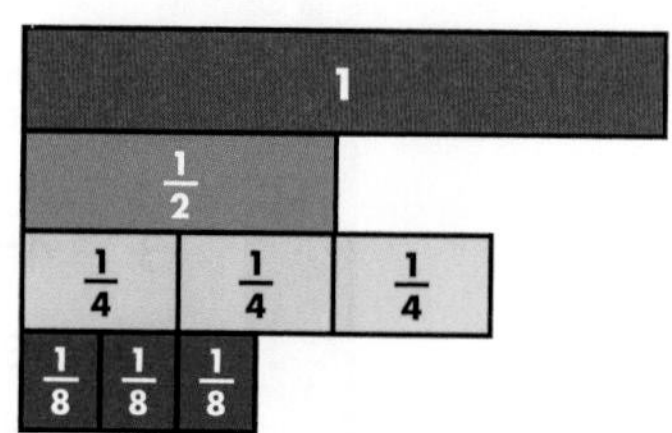

10. $\frac{5}{8}, \frac{3}{4}, \frac{1}{2}$

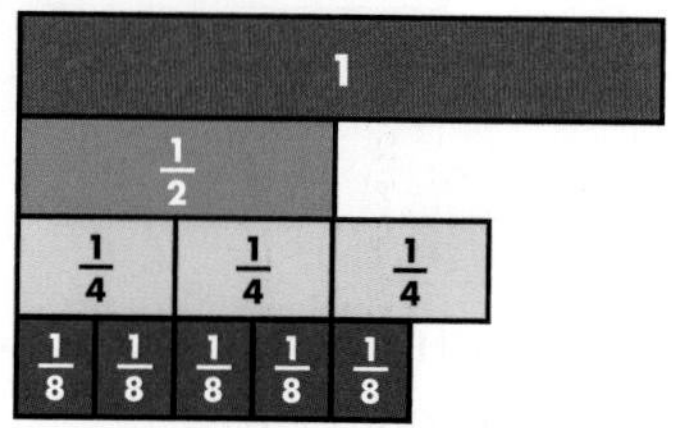

TAKS Problem Solving

For problems **11** and **12**, use the graph at right.

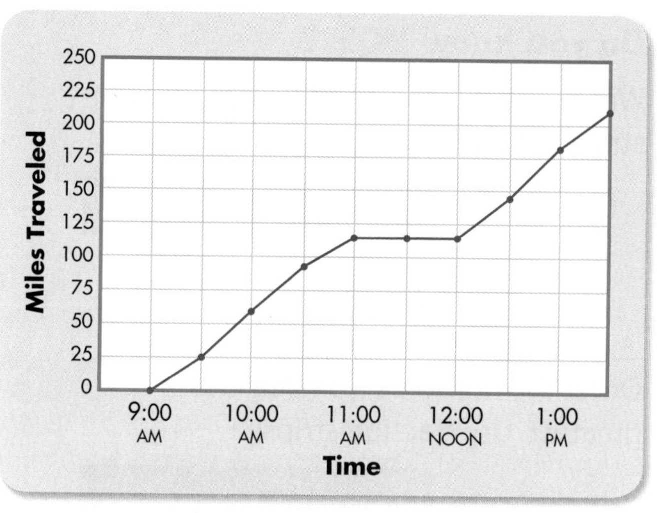

11. The line graph shows how many miles Michael's family drove on their vacation. Between which two times do you think the family stopped for lunch?

12. Estimation Estimate how many miles Michael's family drove from 12:00 NOON to 1:30 P.M..

13. Write three different improper fractions that are equal to 3.

14. Reasoning How do you know that $\frac{3}{8}$ is greater than $\frac{3}{10}$?

15. In 2006, the largest pumpkin grown in the United States weighed 1,502 pounds. The largest pumpkin ever grown in Texas weighed 845 pounds less than this. How much did the largest pumpkin grown in Texas weigh?

16. **Think About the Process** Linda bought 2 board games for $11.25 each and 1 art kit for $24.75. Which tells how to find the total cost?

A $11.25 × 2

B ($11.25 × 2) + $24.75

C ($24.75 × 2) + $11.25

D $24.75 × 2

Comparing Fractions

Use e tools Fractions
Model each fraction using the Fractions eTool and write >, <, or = for ◯.

$\frac{3}{5}$ ◯ $\frac{3}{4}$

Step 1 Go to the Fractions eTool. Select the equivalents workspace mode by using the pull-down menu at the top of the page. Select $\frac{1}{5}$ three times to show $\frac{3}{5}$ in the first circle.

Step 2 Select the second circle by clicking on it. Select $\frac{1}{4}$ three times to show $\frac{3}{4}$ in the second circle. Notice that less of the first circle is shaded than the second one. Also, see the symbol in the middle of the workspace. Both show that $\frac{3}{5} < \frac{3}{4}$.

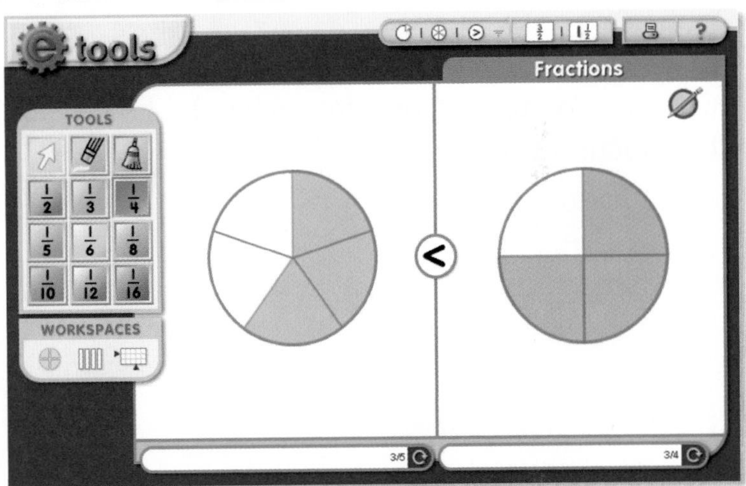

Step 3 Click on the Broom Tool icon to clear the workspace before starting another problem.

Practice

Model each fraction using the e tools Fractions and write >, <, or = for each ◯.

1. $\frac{2}{3}$ ◯ $\frac{2}{5}$
2. $\frac{5}{8}$ ◯ $\frac{5}{6}$
3. $\frac{7}{8}$ ◯ $\frac{7}{10}$
4. $\frac{2}{5}$ ◯ $\frac{2}{7}$
5. $\frac{5}{12}$ ◯ $\frac{7}{12}$
6. $\frac{1}{4}$ ◯ $\frac{3}{4}$
7. $\frac{4}{5}$ ◯ $\frac{3}{5}$
8. $\frac{3}{6}$ ◯ $\frac{3}{4}$
9. $\frac{5}{8}$ ◯ $\frac{1}{2}$
10. $\frac{5}{12}$ ◯ $\frac{1}{2}$
11. $\frac{7}{16}$ ◯ $\frac{1}{2}$
12. $\frac{1}{3}$ ◯ $\frac{3}{9}$
13. $\frac{8}{12}$ ◯ $\frac{2}{3}$
14. $\frac{5}{6}$ ◯ $\frac{9}{10}$
15. $\frac{1}{2}$ ◯ $\frac{9}{18}$
16. $\frac{5}{6}$ ◯ $\frac{1}{6}$

Lesson
11-3

TEKS4.2C: Compare and order fractions using concrete objects and pictorial models.

Comparing Fractions

fraction strips

How can you compare fractions?

Isabella's father is building a model dinosaur with spare pieces of wood that measure $\frac{1}{4}$ of an inch and $\frac{5}{8}$ of an inch. Which are longer, the $\frac{1}{4}$ inch pieces or the $\frac{5}{8}$ inch pieces?

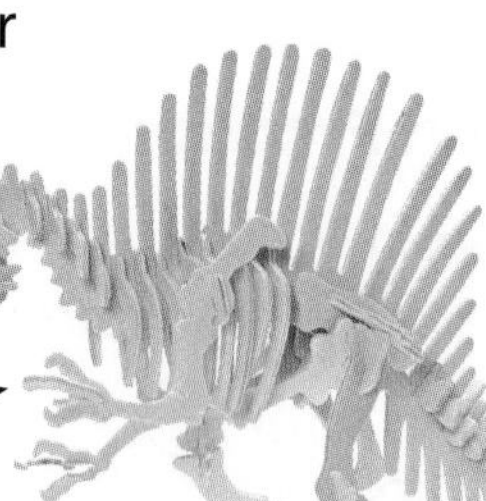

$\frac{1}{4}$ of an inch

Guided Practice*

Do you know HOW?

Compare. Write >, <, or = for each ◯. Use fraction strips or drawings to help.

1. $\frac{3}{4} \bigcirc \frac{6}{8}$
2. $\frac{1}{4} \bigcirc \frac{1}{10}$
3. $\frac{3}{5} \bigcirc \frac{7}{12}$
4. $\frac{1}{2} \bigcirc \frac{4}{5}$

Do you UNDERSTAND?

5. Mary says that $\frac{1}{8}$ is greater than $\frac{1}{4}$ because 8 is greater than 4. Is she right? Explain your answer.

6. Mr. Arnold used wood measuring $\frac{2}{5}$ foot, $\frac{1}{3}$ foot, and $\frac{3}{8}$ foot to build a birdhouse. Compare these lengths of wood.

Independent Practice

For **7** through **38**, compare, and then write >, <, or = for each ◯. Use fraction strips or benchmark fractions to help.

7. $\frac{5}{6} \bigcirc \frac{10}{12}$
8. $\frac{3}{10} \bigcirc \frac{7}{8}$
9. $\frac{5}{12} \bigcirc \frac{1}{2}$
10. $\frac{7}{8} \bigcirc \frac{3}{4}$
11. $\frac{1}{3} \bigcirc \frac{2}{8}$
12. $\frac{1}{4} \bigcirc \frac{2}{3}$
13. $\frac{7}{12} \bigcirc \frac{3}{4}$
14. $\frac{2}{3} \bigcirc \frac{2}{12}$
15. $\frac{3}{8} \bigcirc \frac{2}{3}$
16. $\frac{3}{4} \bigcirc \frac{1}{8}$
17. $\frac{2}{3} \bigcirc \frac{5}{12}$
18. $\frac{1}{2} \bigcirc \frac{3}{4}$
19. $\frac{7}{10} \bigcirc \frac{11}{12}$
20. $\frac{7}{12} \bigcirc \frac{4}{10}$
21. $\frac{5}{12} \bigcirc \frac{4}{5}$
22. $\frac{2}{6} \bigcirc \frac{3}{12}$
23. $\frac{8}{10} \bigcirc \frac{3}{4}$
24. $\frac{3}{8} \bigcirc \frac{11}{12}$
25. $\frac{2}{3} \bigcirc \frac{10}{12}$
26. $\frac{7}{8} \bigcirc \frac{1}{6}$

*For another example, see Set C on page 266.

Use benchmark fractions.

Compare $\frac{1}{4}$ and $\frac{5}{8}$.

You can use fraction strips to compare both fractions to $\frac{1}{2}$.

$\frac{1}{4} < \frac{1}{2}$,

$\frac{5}{8} > \frac{1}{2}$,

So, $\frac{1}{4} < \frac{5}{8}$

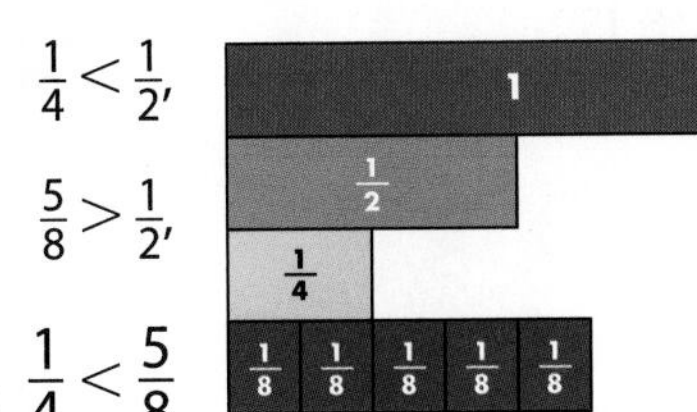

The $\frac{5}{8}$ inch pieces are longer.

Compare $\frac{1}{4}$ and $\frac{3}{4}$.

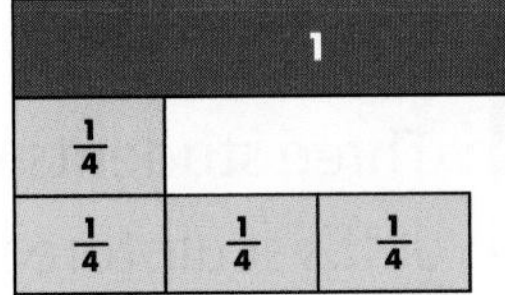

When the two fractions have the same denominators, you compare the numerators.

3 > **1**

So, $\frac{3}{4} > \frac{1}{4}$.

27. $\frac{3}{8} \bigcirc \frac{7}{8}$

28. $\frac{2}{4} \bigcirc \frac{4}{8}$

29. $\frac{6}{8} \bigcirc \frac{8}{12}$

30. $\frac{1}{3} \bigcirc \frac{4}{9}$

31. $\frac{6}{8} \bigcirc \frac{8}{10}$

32. $\frac{3}{5} \bigcirc \frac{3}{6}$

33. $\frac{2}{12} \bigcirc \frac{2}{10}$

34. $\frac{5}{6} \bigcirc \frac{4}{5}$

35. $\frac{4}{4} \bigcirc \frac{1}{1}$

36. $\frac{2}{4} \bigcirc \frac{8}{10}$

37. $\frac{7}{8} \bigcirc \frac{3}{5}$

38. $\frac{3}{9} \bigcirc \frac{1}{3}$

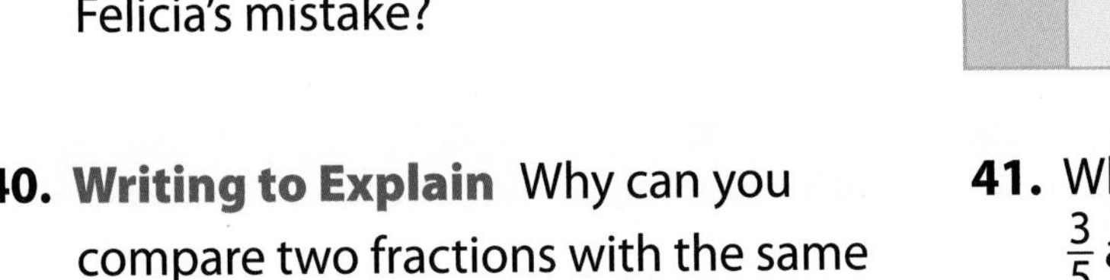

TAKS Problem Solving

39. Number Sense Felicia drew the picture at the right to show that $\frac{3}{8}$ is greater than $\frac{3}{4}$. What was Felicia's mistake?

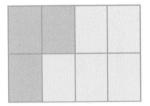

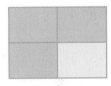

40. Writing to Explain Why can you compare two fractions with the same denominator by only comparing the numerators?

41. What can you conclude about $\frac{3}{5}$ and $\frac{12}{20}$ if you know that $\frac{3}{5} = \frac{6}{10}$ and that $\frac{6}{10} = \frac{12}{20}$?

42. Reasoning Which is longer, $\frac{1}{4}$ foot or $\frac{1}{4}$ yard? Explain.

43. If $34 \times 20 = 680$ then $34 \times 200 = \square$.

44. A melon was divided into 8 equal slices. Juan ate three slices. Tom and Stacy ate the remaining slices. What fraction of the melon did Tom and Stacy eat?

A $\frac{1}{4}$ **B** $\frac{2}{8}$ **C** $\frac{2}{3}$ **D** $\frac{5}{8}$

45. Neil is setting up for a dinner party. He has 6 tables each seating 5 guests and another table seating the left over 3 guests. How many people are coming to Neil's dinner party?

Lesson
11-4

TEKS 4.2C: Compare and order fractions using concrete objects and pictorial models.

Ordering Fractions

Hands-On
fraction strips

How can you order fractions?

Three students made sculptures for a school project. Jeff's sculpture is $\frac{9}{12}$ foot tall, Scott's sculpture is $\frac{1}{3}$ foot tall, and Kristen's sculpture is $\frac{3}{6}$ foot tall. List the heights of the sculptures in order from least to greatest.

$\frac{9}{12}$ foot tall

Guided Practice*

Do you know HOW?

For **1** through **6**, order the fractions from least to greatest. Use fraction strips or drawings to help.

1. $\frac{2}{3}, \frac{1}{2}, \frac{5}{12}$
2. $\frac{5}{6}, \frac{1}{3}, \frac{1}{6}$
3. $\frac{7}{8}, \frac{3}{8}, \frac{3}{4}$
4. $\frac{2}{3}, \frac{3}{12}, \frac{3}{4}$
5. $\frac{7}{8}, \frac{2}{3}, \frac{5}{6}$
6. $\frac{2}{3}, \frac{1}{4}, \frac{1}{6}$

Do you UNDERSTAND?

7. What denominator would you use to find equivalent fractions when comparing $\frac{2}{3}, \frac{2}{4}, \frac{2}{12}$?
8. Three other students made sculptures with these heights: $\frac{2}{3}$ foot, $\frac{5}{6}$ foot, and $\frac{2}{12}$ foot. Write these heights in order from least to greatest.

Independent Practice

For **9** through **20**, find equivalent fractions with a common denominator and order from least to greatest. Use drawings or fraction strips to help.

9. $\frac{1}{4}, \frac{1}{6}, \frac{1}{2}$
10. $\frac{2}{4}, \frac{2}{6}, \frac{2}{12}$
11. $\frac{2}{3}, \frac{5}{6}, \frac{7}{12}$
12. $\frac{5}{12}, \frac{2}{3}, \frac{1}{4}$
13. $\frac{3}{5}, \frac{4}{10}, \frac{1}{2}$
14. $\frac{1}{2}, \frac{3}{5}, \frac{2}{10}$
15. $\frac{5}{6}, \frac{3}{4}, \frac{8}{12}$
16. $\frac{8}{12}, \frac{1}{2}, \frac{3}{4}$
17. $\frac{6}{8}, \frac{1}{2}, \frac{3}{8}$
18. $\frac{2}{5}, \frac{3}{10}, \frac{3}{5}$
19. $\frac{10}{12}, \frac{1}{2}, \frac{3}{4}$
20. $\frac{2}{4}, \frac{3}{12}, \frac{2}{3}$

*For another example, see Set D on page 267.

Step 1

Find equivalent fractions with a common denominator.

$\frac{3}{6} = \frac{6}{12}$

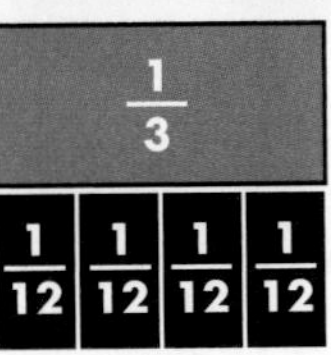

$\frac{1}{3} = \frac{4}{12}$

Step 2

Compare the numerators.

$\frac{4}{12} < \frac{6}{12} < \frac{9}{12}$ Order the fractions from least to greatest.

So, $\frac{1}{3} < \frac{3}{6} < \frac{9}{12}$.

The heights of the sculptures in order from least to greatest are $\frac{1}{3}$ foot, $\frac{3}{6}$ foot, $\frac{9}{12}$ foot.

TAKS Problem Solving

21. Writing to Explain Sandy's sculpture is taller than Jason's. Becca's sculpture is taller than Sandy's sculpture. If Sandy's sculpture is $\frac{2}{3}$ foot tall, how tall could Jason's and Becca's sculptures be?

22. Estimation The fraction $\frac{2}{3}$ is $\frac{1}{3}$ less than 1 whole. Without finding equivalent fractions, order the fractions $\frac{7}{8}$, $\frac{2}{3}$, and $\frac{5}{6}$ from least to greatest.

23. The table at the right shows the number of pages four students read. Which lists the number of pages in order from least to greatest?

A 25, 69, 96, 64 **C** 64, 25, 69, 96

B 25, 64, 69, 96 **D** 25, 64, 96, 69

Data

Students	Number of Pages
Francine	25
Ty	69
Greg	96
Vicki	64

24. Algebra Find the missing numbers in the pattern below.

▭, 36, 54, ▭, ▭, 108, ▭

25. Katie asked Kerry to name 3 fractions between 0 and 1. Kerry said $\frac{5}{12}$, $\frac{1}{4}$, and $\frac{2}{6}$. Order Kerry's fractions from least to greatest.

26. Geena had 6 pairs of earrings. Kiera had 3 times as many. How many pairs of earrings did Kiera have?

27. Each student in fourth grade had the same book to read. Charles read $\frac{2}{3}$ of the book, and Drew read $\frac{3}{5}$ of the book. Who read more?

Lesson

11-5

TEKS 4.2D: Relate decimals to fractions that name tenths and hundredths using concrete objects and pictorial models. Also TEKS 4.15A

Fractions to Decimals

How can you write a fraction as a decimal?

On Kelsey Street, six out of 10 homes have swing sets in their backyards. Write $\frac{6}{10}$ as a decimal.

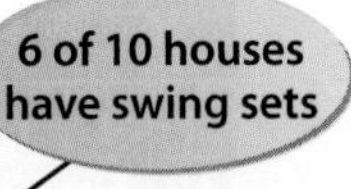

Other Examples

Use place-value blocks to model $\frac{4}{10}$ and $\frac{37}{100}$. Then write a decimal that shows the same amount.

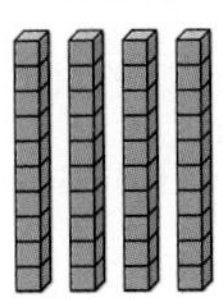

$\frac{4}{10} = 0.4$

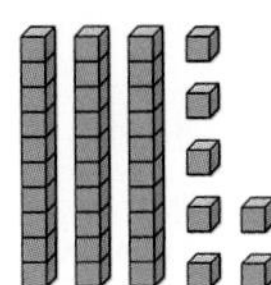

$\frac{37}{100} = 0.37$

Tip

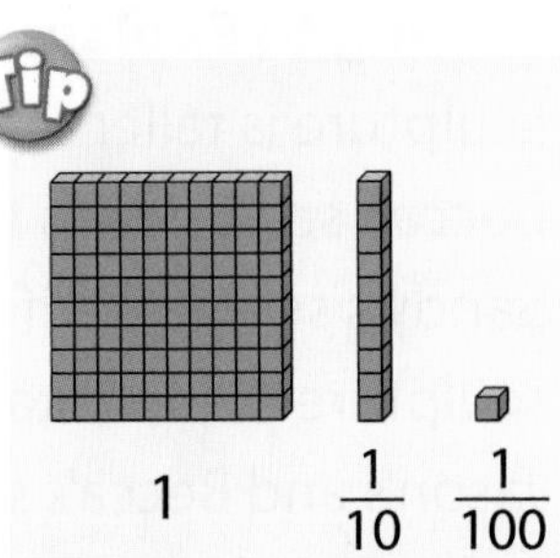

1 $\frac{1}{10}$ $\frac{1}{100}$

Guided Practice*

Do you know HOW?

For **1** and **2**, write a decimal for each model shown.

1. 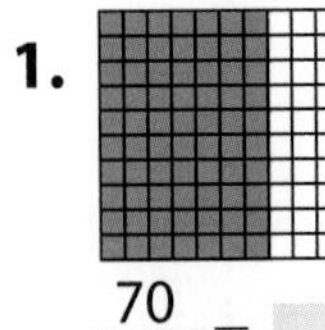

$\frac{70}{100} =$ ▢

2. 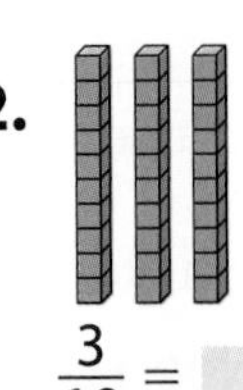

$\frac{3}{10} =$ ▢

Do you UNDERSTAND?

3. Are the word names for $\frac{30}{100}$ and 0.30 the same?

4. How could you use place-value blocks to model $\frac{7}{10}$? What decimal shows the same amount?

Independent Practice

For **5** through **8**, write a decimal and fraction for the part of the grid that is shaded.

5. 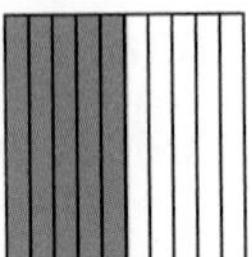

6. 

7. 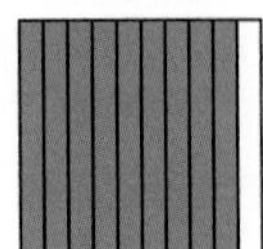

8. 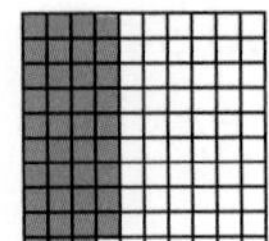

*For another example, see Set E on page 267.

Write $\frac{6}{10}$ as a decimal.

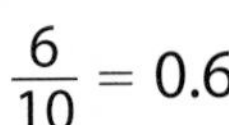

$\frac{6}{10}$ is six tenths, or 0.6.

$\frac{6}{10} = 0.6$

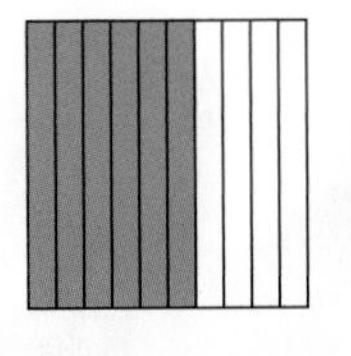

So, 0.6 of the houses have swing sets.

In Rolling Hills, 75 out of 100 houses are two-story homes. Write $\frac{75}{100}$ as a decimal.

$\frac{75}{100}$ is seventy-five hundredths, or 0.75.

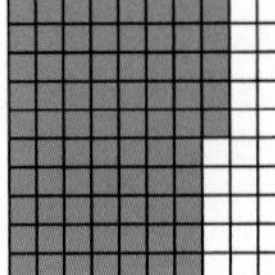

$\frac{75}{100} = 0.75$

So, 0.75 houses are two-story homes.

For **9** through **12**, write a fraction and a decimal for each model.

9. 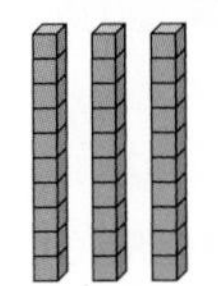

10. 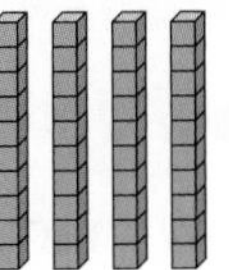

11. 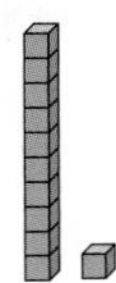

12. 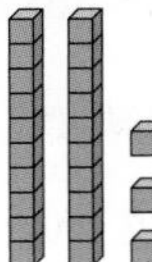

For **13** through **16**, write each fraction as a decimal.

13. $\frac{47}{100}$ **14.** $\frac{8}{10}$ **15.** $\frac{60}{100}$ **16.** $\frac{1}{10}$

17. Use place-value blocks to model $\frac{5}{10}$ and $\frac{67}{100}$. Then write a decimal that shows the same amount.

TAKS Problem Solving

18. Estimation About what fraction of the rectangle is shaded green?

19. Algebra Find the missing numbers in the pattern below.

▢, 21, 28, ▢, ▢, ▢, 56, ▢

20. The arena of the Colosseum in Rome was about $\frac{3}{20}$ of the entire Colosseum. Write this amount as a decimal.

Tip
$\frac{1}{20} = \frac{5}{100}$

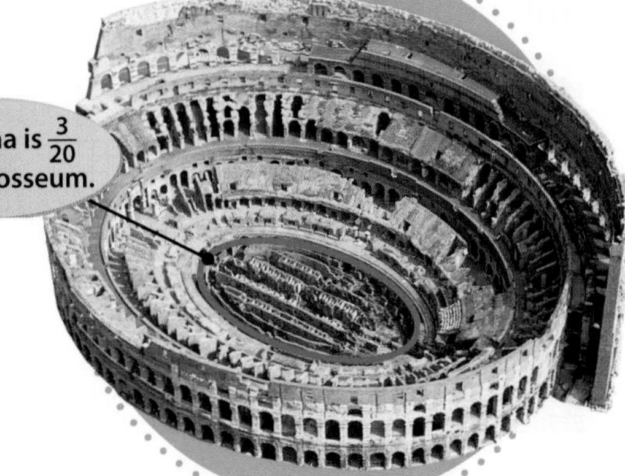

The arena is $\frac{3}{20}$ of the Colosseum.

21. Which choice below shows the fractions in order from least to greatest?

A $\frac{3}{10}, \frac{6}{10}, \frac{9}{10}$

B $\frac{3}{5}, \frac{2}{5}, \frac{4}{5}$

C $\frac{6}{8}, \frac{2}{8}, \frac{3}{8}$

D $\frac{5}{6}, \frac{4}{6}, \frac{2}{6}$

Lesson

11-6

TEKS 4.2D: Relate decimals to fractions that name tenths and hundredths using concrete objects and pictorial models.

Decimals to Fractions

How can you write a decimal as a fraction?

Hands-On
grid paper
place-value blocks

A hummingbird flaps its wings once every 0.1 second.

Write 0.1 as a fraction.

Guided Practice*

Do you know HOW?

For **1** through **4**, write a fraction for each model.

1. 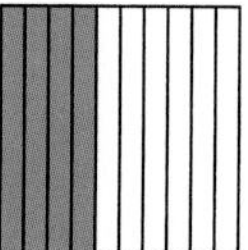

0.4 = $\frac{\square}{\square}$

2. 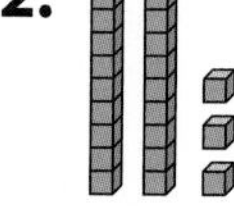

0.23 = $\frac{\square}{\square}$

3. 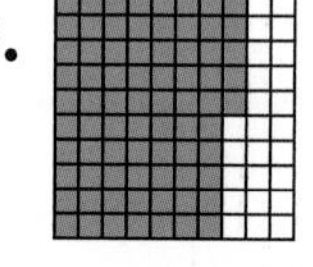

0.75 = $\frac{\square}{\square}$

4.

0.3 = $\frac{\square}{\square}$

Do you UNDERSTAND?

5. How many hundredths are shaded?

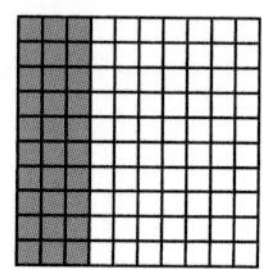

6. Write 1.0 as a fraction.

7. Some hummingbirds can flap their wings once every 0.02 seconds. Model 0.02 with place-value blocks and then write 0.02 as a fraction.

Independent Practice

For **8** through **15**, write a fraction and a decimal for each model.

8. 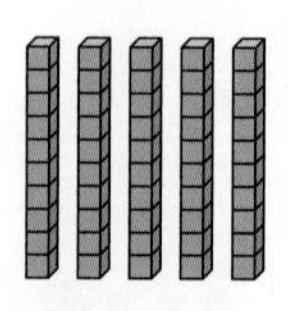

9. 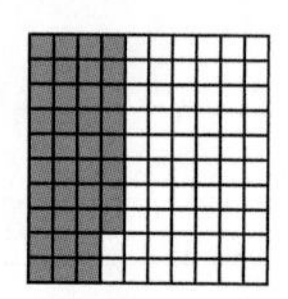

10. 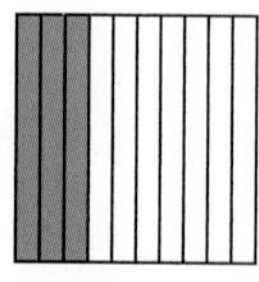

11. 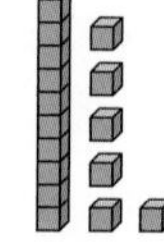 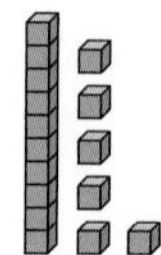

12. 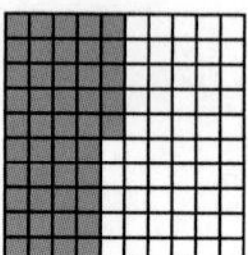

13. 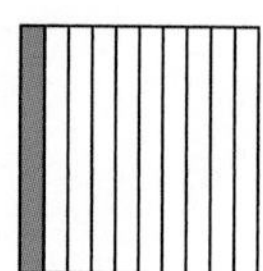

14. 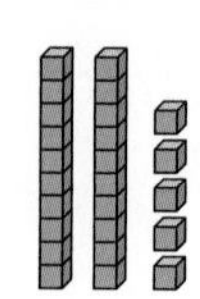

15. 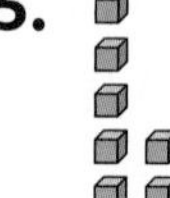

eTools
www.pearsonsuccessnet.com

*For another example, see Set E on page 267.

Model with place-value blocks and on a grid.

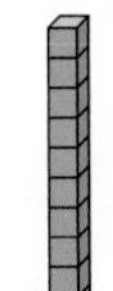

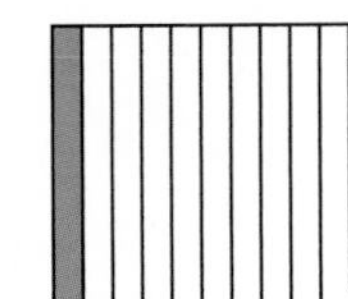

$0.1 = \frac{1}{10}$

0.1 is 1 tenth or $\frac{1}{10}$.

A hummingbird flaps its wings once every $\frac{1}{10}$ second.

Place-value blocks or drawings can model 0.05.

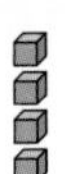

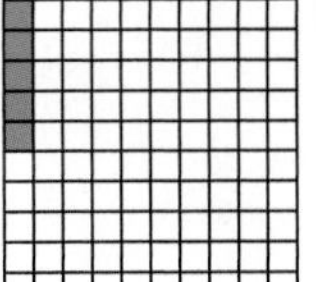

Write 0.05 as a fraction.

$0.05 = \frac{5}{100}$

In **16** through **25**, write each decimal as a fraction. Use place-value blocks or grids to help.

16. 0.2 **17.** 0.07 **18.** 0.55 **19.** 0.9 **20.** 0.88

21. 0.6 **22.** 0.18 **23.** 0.14 **24.** 0.09 **25.** 0.04

TAKS Problem Solving

26. Roberta used a hundredths grid to model a decimal. She shaded 72 squares. What decimal and fraction represent the part that is not shaded?

27. Geometry The figure below is a regular pentagon. Find its perimeter.

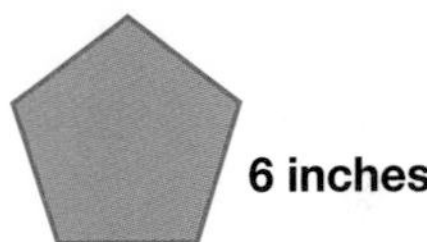

28. Reasoning Four friends, James, Victoria, Jaime, and Jill, are in line for tickets to the basketball game. Jaime is first. Victoria is behind Jill. Jill is not last. James is in front of Jill. How are the friends ordered?

29. There are 35 more chickens than twice the number of rabbits on the farm. There are 27 rabbits. How many chickens are on the farm?

30. Which model below shows 0.75?

A

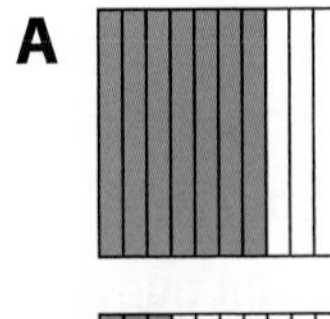

C

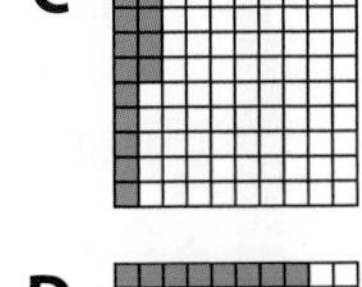

B **D**

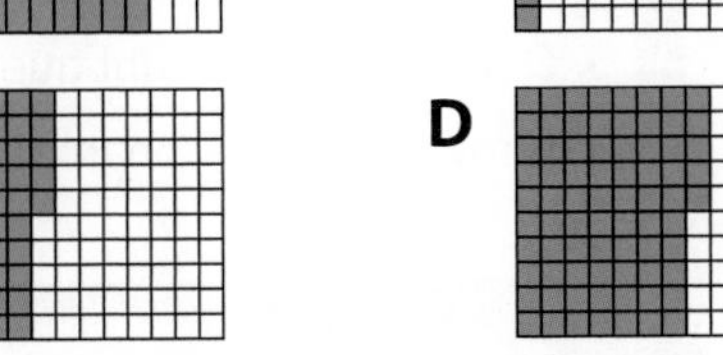

31. If three out of ten cars in the parking lot are red, what fraction of the cars are **NOT** red?

F $\frac{1}{10}$ **H** $\frac{4}{10}$

G $\frac{3}{10}$ **J** $\frac{7}{10}$

Lesson

11-7

TEKS 4.14C: Select or develop an appropriate problem-solving plan or strategy, including drawing a picture, looking for a pattern, systematic guessing and checking, acting it out, making a table, working a simpler problem, or working backwards to solve a problem.

Problem Solving

Use Objects and Make a Table

Hands-On
Cubes

Al has 12 containers of sand. One way to show $\frac{1}{2}$ is two groups of 6.

Using 12 or fewer cubes, how many other fractions can Al find that are equivalent to $\frac{1}{2}$?

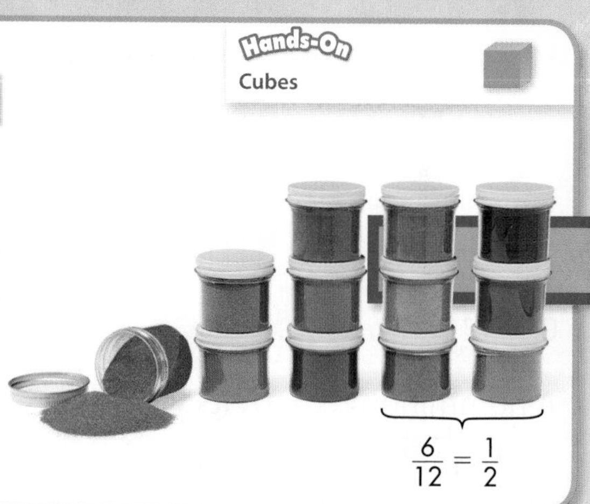

Guided Practice*

Do you know HOW?

Solve. Use object to help.

1. One way to show $\frac{1}{3}$ using cubes is three groups of 4 cubes each. Using 12 or fewer cubes, how many other fractions can you find that are equivalent to $\frac{1}{3}$? Make a table to help.

Do you UNDERSTAND?

2. How many cubes are in each group to show $\frac{3}{6}$?
3. How many cubes are in each group to show $\frac{2}{4}$?
4. **Write a Problem** Write a word problem that uses the table you created in Problem 1 as an answer.

Independent Practice

Solve. Use objects or make a table or list to help.

5. Marianne has 12 cubes. She uses all 12 cubes and separates them into 4 groups. Then she uses 8 cubes and separates them into 4 groups. What fraction is Marianne trying to make?
6. Using 12 or fewer cubes, how many fractions can you find that are equivalent to $\frac{1}{5}$?
7. At a car wash, Jim washed 8 cars per hour, and David washed 6 cars per hour. How many cars did Jim wash if David washed 24 cars?

Stuck? Try this....

- What do I know?
- What diagram can I use to help understand the problem?
- Can I use addition, subtraction, multiplication, or division?
- Is all of my work correct?
- Did I answer the right question?
- Is my answer reasonable?

*For another example, see Set F on page 267.

Al can use cubes to solve this problem.

Using two groups of 7 gives $\frac{7}{14} = \frac{1}{2}$.

This uses more than 12 cubes.

Using two groups of 5 gives $\frac{5}{10} = \frac{1}{2}$.

This works. Al only used 10 cubes.

Make a table to show the other fractions equivalent to $\frac{1}{2}$.

First group	*Second group*	*Fraction equivalent to* $\frac{1}{2}$
4	4	$\frac{4}{8}$
3	3	$\frac{3}{6}$
2	2	$\frac{2}{4}$

Count all of the different ways to make $\frac{1}{2}$.

There are 4 other fractions that are equivalent to $\frac{1}{2}$ using 12 cubes or less.

8. Charlie had 12 cubes. He showed $\frac{8}{12}$ is equivalent to $\frac{2}{3}$ by making three groups of 4 and drawing a circle around two of the groups. Using 12 or fewer cubes, what is another fraction that is equivalent to $\frac{2}{3}$?

9. At Tara's Video Outlet you can buy any 6 DVDs for 72 dollars. At Sam's DVD Palace you can buy any 4 DVDs for 52 dollars. In which store do DVDs cost less? How much less?

10. Tyrone runs 4 miles each week. Francis runs 4 times as many miles each week. How many miles does Francis run each week?

Miles each week

Francis	4	4	4	4	**4 times as many**
Tyrone	4				

11. **Writing to Explain** If you know a person runs a certain number of miles every week, then how would you find out how many miles that person runs in one year?

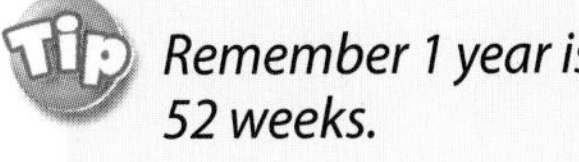

Tip *Remember 1 year is 52 weeks.*

12. Jane has 24 pennies. She separated the pennies equally into 4 cups with 6 pennies in each cup. Complete the table at the right to show how many ways Jane can separate the pennies.

Number of cups	*Number of pennies in each cup*	*Total number of pennies*
4		24
	12	24
3		24

13. A store sells school-supply packs that contain 6 pencils and 4 pens. A customer bought enough packs to get 36 pencils. How many pens did the customer get?

DIGITAL eTools
www.pearsonsuccessnet.com

TAKS Test Prep

1. What mixed number does this model show? (11-1)

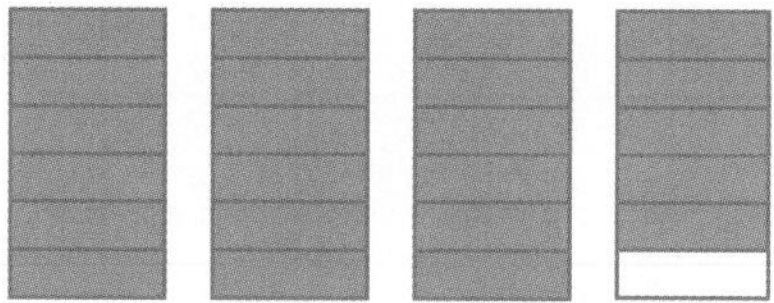

A $4\frac{5}{6}$

B $3\frac{5}{6}$

C $3\frac{4}{5}$

D $3\frac{1}{6}$

2. During the allotted time, Mark finished $\frac{2}{3}$ of the obstacle course. Jeremy finished $\frac{5}{8}$ of it. Use the models to find which comparison is true. (11-2)

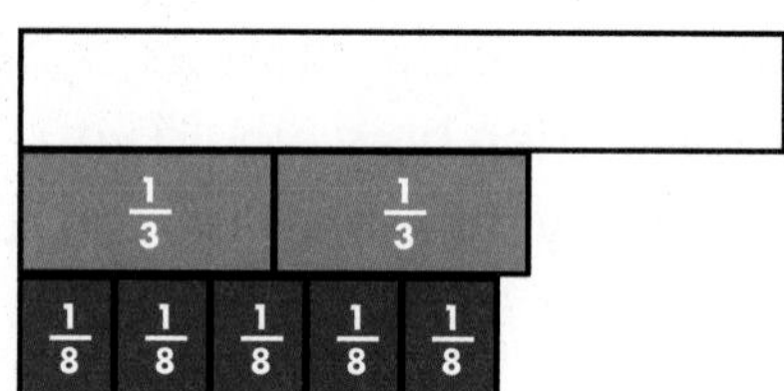

F $\frac{2}{3} > \frac{5}{8}$

G $\frac{1}{3} = \frac{3}{8}$

H $\frac{1}{3} > \frac{5}{8}$

J $\frac{5}{8} > \frac{2}{3}$

3. What is 1.47 written as a fraction or mixed number? (11-6)

A $\frac{1}{147}$

B $\frac{47}{100}$

C $1\frac{47}{100}$

D $1\frac{47}{10}$

4. The table shows the different types of berries Darcy picked at a berry farm. (11-4)

Type of Berry	Pound
Blackberry	$\frac{1}{2}$
Raspberry	$\frac{7}{8}$
Strawberry	$\frac{3}{4}$

$\frac{1}{8}$	$\frac{1}{8}$	$\frac{1}{8}$	$\frac{1}{8}$	$\frac{1}{8}$	$\frac{1}{8}$	$\frac{1}{8}$	$\frac{1}{8}$

Which type of berry did Darcy pick the most of?

F Blackberry

G Raspberry

H Strawberry

J Both raspberries and strawberries

5. Use 15 or fewer cubes. Which fraction completes the table? (11-7)

Cubes in Group 1	Cubes in Group 2	Cubes in Group 3	Fraction Equivalent to $\frac{1}{3}$
2	2	2	$\frac{2}{6}$
3	3	3	$\frac{3}{9}$
4	4	4	$\frac{4}{12}$
5	5	5	

A $\frac{10}{15}$

B $\frac{3}{5}$

C $\frac{5}{10}$

D $\frac{5}{15}$

Topic 11 TAKS Test Prep

6. Javier and Mark drew straws to see who would go down the waterslide first. Javier's straw was $\frac{5}{12}$ inch long and Mark's was $\frac{7}{12}$ inch long. Which symbol makes the comparison true? (11-3)

$\frac{5}{12} \bigcirc \frac{7}{12}$

F $\times$

G $=$

H $<$

J $>$

7. In the kennel, 7 out of the 10 dogs weigh less than 20 pounds. What is $\frac{7}{10}$ written as a decimal? (11-5)

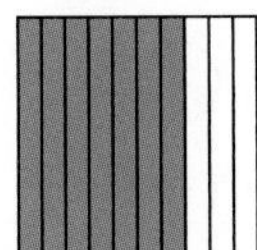

A 0.007

B 0.07

C 0.7

D 7.7

8. Yao drank $1\frac{1}{4}$ bottles of water. What is this number written as an improper fraction? (11-1)

$\frac{1}{4}$ $\frac{1}{4}$ $\frac{1}{4}$ $\frac{1}{4}$ 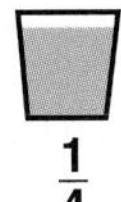 $\frac{1}{4}$

F $\frac{2}{4}$

G $\frac{5}{4}$

H $\frac{6}{4}$

J $\frac{8}{4}$

9. What fraction and decimal represent the part that is green? (11-6)

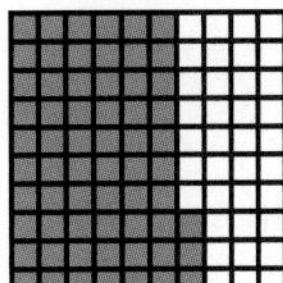

A $\frac{63}{100}$ and 0.63

B $\frac{63}{100}$ and 0.063

C $\frac{63}{100}$ and 6.3

D $\frac{63}{10}$ and 0.63

10. The student council ordered pizza for their meeting. Half of the members voted for cheese pizza, $\frac{1}{10}$ for pepperoni, and $\frac{2}{5}$ for vegetable.

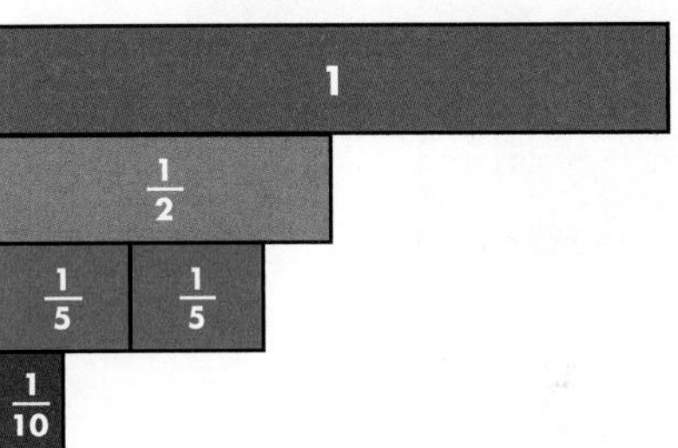

Which shows the fractions in order from the least to greatest? (11-4)

F $\frac{1}{2}, \frac{1}{10}, \frac{2}{5}$

G $\frac{2}{5}, \frac{1}{10}, \frac{1}{2}$

H $\frac{1}{10}, \frac{1}{2}, \frac{2}{5}$

J $\frac{1}{10}, \frac{2}{5}, \frac{1}{2}$

11. **Griddable Response** A puppy weighs $7\frac{1}{2}$ pounds. What number makes the statement true? (11-1)

$7\frac{1}{2} = \frac{\square}{2}$

Set A, pages 246–248

Write $\frac{7}{4}$ as a mixed number.

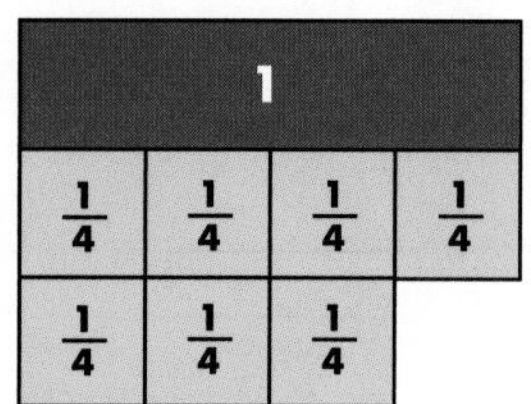

4 fourths in one whole

3 fourths

How many wholes can you make with 7 fourths?

So, $\frac{7}{4} = 1\frac{3}{4}$.

Remember you can use fraction strips to write a mixed number as an improper fraction.

Write each number as a mixed number or an improper fraction.

1. $2\frac{2}{5}$

2. $\frac{9}{4}$

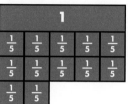

Set B, pages 250–252

Compare $\frac{4}{6}$ and $\frac{3}{4}$.

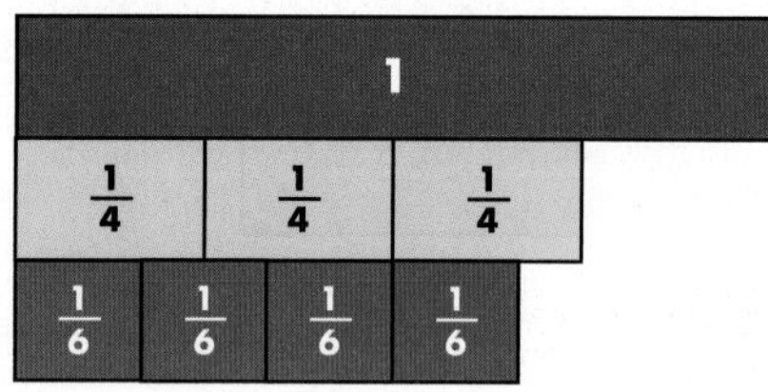

$\frac{4}{6}$ is less than $\frac{3}{4}$.

So, $\frac{4}{6} < \frac{3}{4}$.

Remember when you compare two fractions, a larger numerator does not always mean that the fraction is greater.

Write >, <, or = for each ◯.

1. $\frac{5}{6}$ ◯ $\frac{2}{3}$

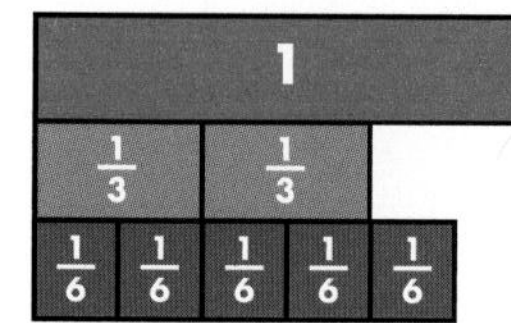

2. $\frac{1}{3}$ ◯ $\frac{3}{10}$

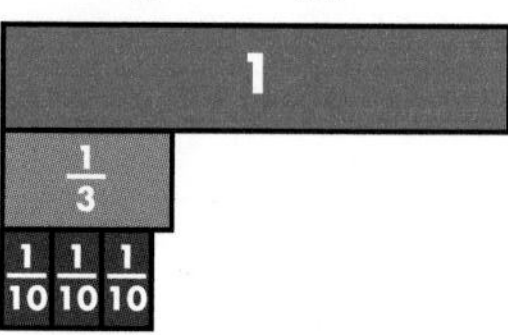

Set C, pages 254–255

Compare $\frac{1}{6}$ and $\frac{3}{6}$.

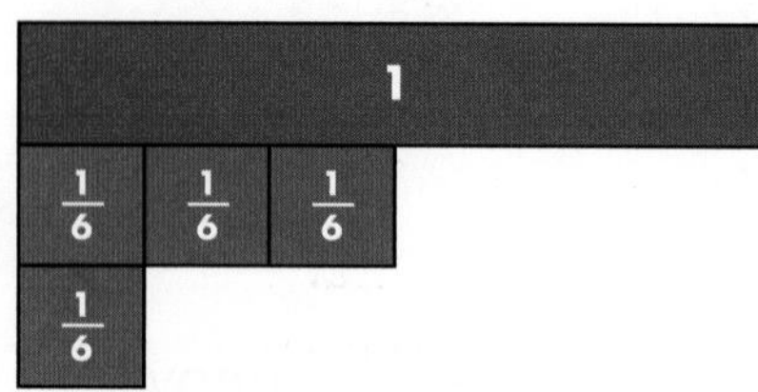

$1 < 3$

So, $\frac{1}{6} < \frac{3}{6}$.

Remember when comparing fractions with different denominators, you can use benchmark fractions such as $\frac{1}{4}$, $\frac{1}{3}$, $\frac{1}{2}$, $\frac{2}{3}$, and $\frac{3}{4}$.

Compare. Write >, <, or = for each ◯.

1. $\frac{5}{10}$ ◯ $\frac{1}{2}$

2. $\frac{3}{4}$ ◯ $\frac{5}{12}$

3. $\frac{3}{8}$ ◯ $\frac{1}{3}$

4. $\frac{4}{10}$ ◯ $\frac{3}{12}$

5. $\frac{7}{8}$ ◯ $\frac{5}{8}$

6. $\frac{1}{5}$ ◯ $\frac{2}{10}$

Reteaching

Set D, pages 256–257

Order $\frac{5}{6}, \frac{2}{3}, \frac{1}{2}$ from least to greatest.

Find equivalent fractions with a common denominator.

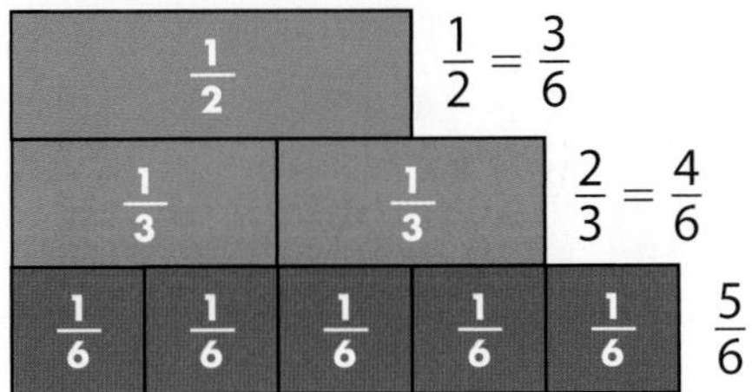

$\frac{1}{2} = \frac{3}{6}$

$\frac{2}{3} = \frac{4}{6}$

$\frac{5}{6}$

$\frac{3}{6} < \frac{4}{6} < \frac{5}{6}$

So, $\frac{1}{2}, \frac{2}{3}, \frac{5}{6}$.

Remember you can use fraction strips to find equivalent fractions with common denominators.

Order from least to greatest.

1. $\frac{1}{2}, \frac{2}{3}, \frac{5}{12}$
2. $\frac{7}{8}, \frac{3}{8}, \frac{3}{4}$
3. $\frac{1}{3}, \frac{1}{6}, \frac{3}{6}$
4. $\frac{2}{3}, \frac{5}{6}, \frac{11}{12}$
5. $\frac{6}{8}, \frac{5}{8}, \frac{1}{2}$
6. $\frac{2}{5}, \frac{3}{10}, \frac{6}{10}$

Set E, pages 258–261

Write $\frac{1}{100}$ as a decimal.

$\frac{1}{100}$

one hundredth

0.01

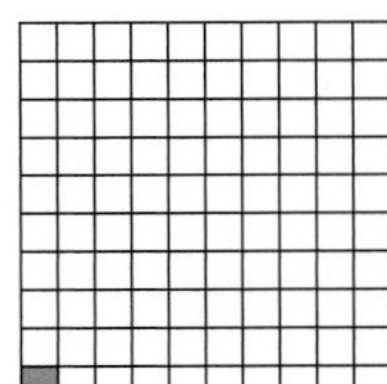

Remember read the decimal and write what you say when writing a decimal as a fraction.

Write each fraction as a decimal.

1. $\frac{8}{10}$
2. $\frac{94}{100}$
3. $\frac{4}{10}$
4. $\frac{50}{100}$

Set F, pages 262–263

You have 10 cubes. One way to show $\frac{1}{2}$ is two groups of 5. How many other fractions can you make with 10 or fewer cubes that are equivalent to $\frac{1}{2}$?

Make a table and count all the ways to make $\frac{1}{2}$.

Data

Group 1	Group 2	Fraction
4	4	$\frac{4}{8} = \frac{1}{2}$
3	3	$\frac{3}{6} = \frac{1}{2}$
2	2	$\frac{2}{4} = \frac{1}{2}$
1	1	$\frac{1}{2} = \frac{1}{2}$

Remember you can act it out, use objects, or make a table.

You have 16 cubes. One way to show $\frac{1}{4}$ is four groups of 4. Using 16 or fewer cubes, how many other fractions can you find that are equivalent to $\frac{1}{4}$?

Topic 12

Patterns and Expressions

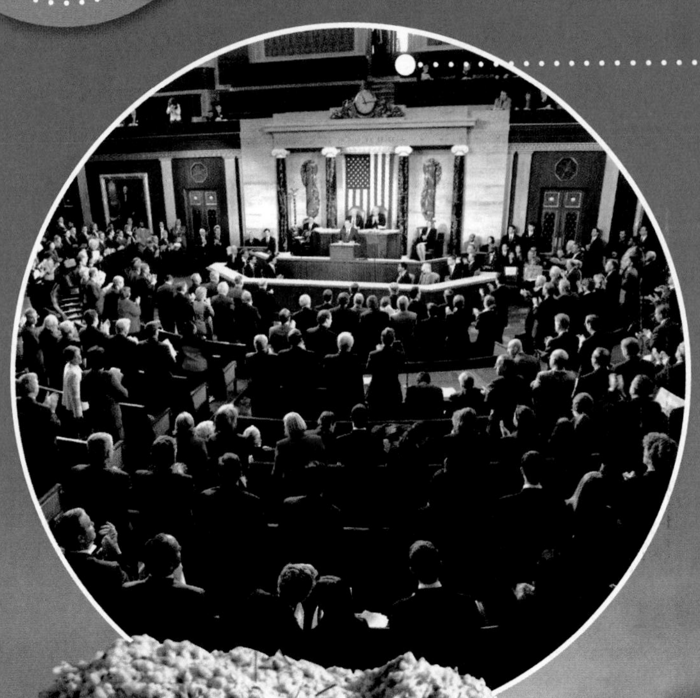

1 The United States Congress has 535 members that represent the country. How many members does Texas have in Congress? You will find out in Lesson 12–2.

2 How much cotton does Texas produce each year? You will find out in Lesson 12-3.

3

In a leap year, one day is added to February. What will be the fifth leap year after the year 2000? You'll find out in Lesson 12-1.

Review What You Know!

Vocabulary

Choose the best term from the box.

- expression
- ordered pair
- factors
- multiple

1. A ? is the product of a whole number and any other whole number.
2. A(n) ? may include numbers and at least one operation.
3. A(n) ? is a pair of numbers used to name a point on a coordinate grid.
4. ? are numbers multiplied together to find a product.

Patterns

For each set of numbers, find the missing number.

5. 2, ▢, 4, 5, 6
6. ▢, 10, 15, 20
7. 3, 6, 9, ▢
8. 4, 8, ▢, 16
9. 17, ▢, 35, 44
10. 1.5, 2, ▢, 3

Multiplication and Division

Solve.

11. 5×6
12. $120 \div 4$
13. 35×2
14. 9×8
15. $60 \div 3$
16. $33 \div 11$
17. In baseball, there are 6 outs in 1 full inning. Would you multiply or divide to find the number of outs in 2 innings?
18. **Writing to Explain** How would you describe the pattern for multiples of 2? multiples of 5?

Lesson

12-1

TEKS 4.7: Describe the relationship between two sets of related data such as ordered pairs in a table.

Variables and Expressions

How can you use expressions with variables?

A variable is a symbol that stands for a number.

A Tae Kwon Do class has 23 people. If n more people sign up, how many people will be taking the class?

n	$23 + n$
3	
5	
7	

Other Examples

An algebraic expression is a mathematical phrase that contains numbers or variables and at least one operation.

Word form	Expression
add 5	$n + 5$
multiply by 2	$2 \times n$

Guided Practice*

Do you know HOW?

In **1** through **3**, copy and complete the table.

	c	$c + 8$
1.	4	
2.	9	
3.	13	

Do you UNDERSTAND?

4. **Writing to Explain** Could you use the variable k instead of n to represent more students signing up for the Tae Kwon Do class?

5. If n is 12, how many people will be taking the Tae Kwon Do class?

Independent Practice

For **6** through **8**, copy and complete the table for each problem.

6.

d	$d + 30$
3	
7	
12	

7.

g	$5 \times g$
6	
9	
15	

8.

m	$m \div 10$
350	
240	
120	

DIGITAL Animated Glossary **www.pearsonsuccessnet.com**

*For another example, see Set A on page 280.

What You Show

Use the expression, $23 + n$, to find the missing numbers.

$23 + n$
↓
$23 + 3 = 26$

n	$23 + n$
3	$23 + 3$
5	$23 + 5$
7	$23 + 7$

What You Write

If 3 more people sign up, there will be 26 people in the class.

If 5 more people sign up, there will be 28 people in the class.

If 7 more people sign up, there will be 30 people in the class.

For **9** through **12**, fill in the missing numbers.

9.

z	152	128	112	88
$z \div 8$	19		14	11

10.

t	43	134	245	339
$t + 47$	90	181		386

11.

y	387	201	65	26
$y - 13$	374	188		

12.

x	5	7	10	20
$x \times 12$	60	84		

TAKS Problem Solving

13. The year 2020 will be the fifth leap year after the year 2000. Name the years between 2000 and 2020 that are leap years.

A leap year occurs every 4 years between 2000 and 2020.

14. Which expression represents how many seconds are in 5 minutes?

A $s + 5$

B $s \div 5$

C $s \times 5$

D $s - 5$

15. A Ferris wheel has 12 cars. The operator needs to keep 2, 4, or 6 cars empty. Make a table to show how many people can ride if each car holds 4 people.

16. Write an expression to represent the cost of parking a car for n hours in a lot that charges $7.00 per hour. Find the cost of parking the car for 3 hours.

17. Reasonableness Edgar used $10 \times d$ to represent the number of pennies in d dollars. Is this reasonable?

18. Reasoning How could you make $36.32 with exactly 4 bills and 4 coins?

Lesson

12-2

TEKS 4.7: Describe the relationship between two sets of related data such as ordered pairs in a table.

Addition and Subtraction Expressions

How can you find a rule and write an expression?

What is a rule for the table? How can you use a rule to write an expression and find the sale price when the regular price is $18?

Let *p* stand for the regular price.

Regular price (p)	$21	$20	$19	$18
Sale price	$16	$15	$14	

Guided Practice*

Do you know HOW?

For **1** and **2**, use the table below.

Total number of test questions (q)	20	30	40	50
Number of multiple-choice questions	10	20	30	

1. What is a rule for the table in words? in symbols?

2. How many multiple-choice questions would be on a 50-question test?

Do you UNDERSTAND?

3. **Writing to Explain** How could you use place-value blocks to find a rule in the table to the left?

4. Tony earns $7 and saves $2. When he earns $49, he saves $44. When he earns $10, he saves $5. Write an expression for the amount he saves.

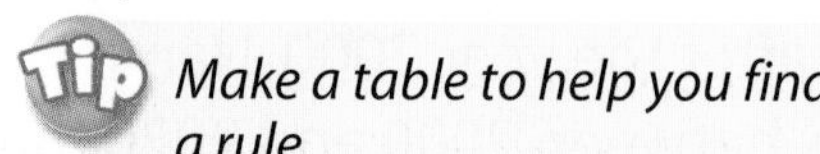

Tip *Make a table to help you find a rule.*

5. In the example at the top, what is the sale price when the regular price is $30?

Independent Practice

Leveled Practice For **6** through **11**, find a rule.

6.

n	3	4	5
n +	7	8	9

7.

b	31	42	55
b –	23	34	47

8.

q	0	2	8
q +	15	17	23

9.

p	3	4	5
p +	68	69	70

10.

x	18	21	26
x –	5	8	13

11.

r	112	96	62
r –	73	57	23

**For another example, see Set B on page 280.*

Subtract to find the sale price.

For a regular price of \$21:

$21 - 5 = 16$ 

For a regular price of \$20:

$20 - 5 = 15$ 

For a regular price of \$19:

$19 - 5 = 14$ 

A rule is subtract 5.
So, the expression is $p - 5$.

Use the expression $p - 5$ to find the missing value when $p = 18$.

Subtract 5 from the regular price, p.

Regular price (p)	\$21	\$20	\$19	\$18
Sale price	\$16	\$15	\$14	\$18 − 5

When the regular price is \$18, the sale price is \$13.

For **12** through **15**, copy and complete each table, and find a rule.

12.

n	15	18	20	27
n + ■	58	61	63	■

13.

u	212	199	190	188
u − ■	177	164	155	■

14.

c	31	54	60	64
c − ■	5	28	34	■

15.

a	589	485	400	362
a − ■	575	471	386	■

TAKS Problem Solving

For **16** and **17**, use the table at the right.

16. The United States Congress includes 2 senators from each state plus members of the House of Representatives. The number of representatives, r, is based on the state's population. Write a rule for the total number of members each state has in Congress.

Data

Number of Members in the United States Congress

State	House	Senate
Texas	32	2
Missouri	9	2
Hawaii	2	2
New York	29	2

17. How many members in Congress does each state in the table have?

18. Reasoning Don, Wanda, and Stu each play softball, basketball, or football. Each person plays only one sport. Wanda doesn't play football. Don doesn't play softball. Stu doesn't play basketball or softball. What sport does each person play?

19. Writing to Explain Chang has driven 1,372 miles. If the total mileage for his trip is 2,800 miles, how many miles does Chang have left to drive? Explain.

Lesson

12-3

TEKS 4.7: Describe the relationship between two sets of related data such as ordered pairs in a table.

Multiplication and Division Expressions

How can you find a rule and write an expression?

What is a rule for the table? How can Josie use a rule to write an expression and find the number of cards in 4 boxes? Let b equal the number of boxes.

Number of boxes (b)	1	2	3	4
Number of note cards	15	30	45	

Guided Practice*

Do you know HOW?

For **1** and **2**, use the table below.

Number of tickets (t)	2	4	6	8
Total Price	\$60	\$120	\$180	

1. What is a rule for the table in words? in symbols?

2. How much would 8 tickets cost?

Do you UNDERSTAND?

3. Writing to Explain How could you use place-value blocks to describe a rule in the table to the left?

4. How could you find the price of 1 ticket using the information from Exercises 1 and 2?

5. In the example above, how many note cards are in 13 boxes?

Independent Practice

Leveled Practice For **6** through **8**, find a rule.

6.

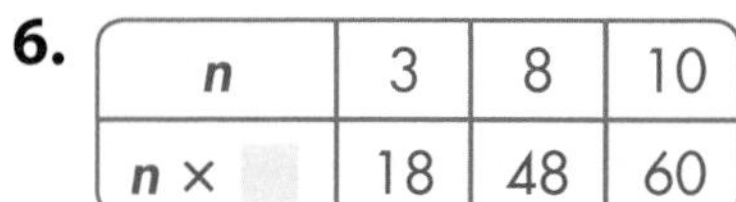

n	3	8	10
$n \times$ ▢	18	48	60

7.

p	2	4	8
$p \div$ ▢	1	2	4

8.

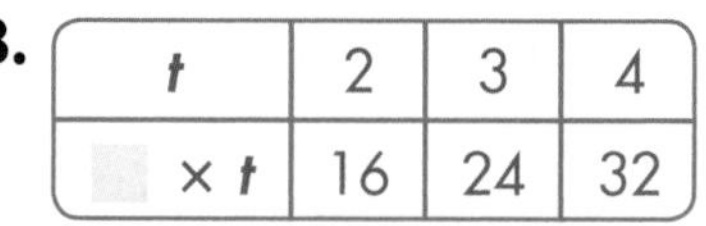

t	2	3	4
▢ $\times t$	16	24	32

For **9** through **12**, copy and complete each table, and find a rule.

9.

e	4	8	12	16
$e \div$ ▢	1	2	3	

10.

j	7	9	11	16
▢ $\times j$	98	126	154	

11.

w	5	7	8	10
▢ $\times w$	35	49	56	

12.

s	60	80	85	90
$s \div$ ▢	12	16	17	

*For another example, see Set C on page 281.

Multiply to find the number of cards.

For 1 box:
$1 \times 15 = 15$

For 2 boxes:
$2 \times 15 = 30$

For 3 boxes:
$3 \times 15 = 45$

A rule is multiply by 15. So, the expression is $b \times 15$.

Use the expression $b \times 15$ to find the missing value when $b = 4$.

$b \times 15 = 4 \times 15$

Number of boxes (b)	1	2	3	4
Number of note cards	15	30	45	4×15

There are 60 note cards in 4 boxes.

TAKS Problem Solving

For **13** and **14**, use the table at the right.

The Baker family is deciding which type of television to purchase for their family room.

Data

Type of Television	Cost
50-inch Plasma	$2800.00
34-inch Flat Screen	$900.00
26-inch LCD	$500.00

13. How much more does a 50-inch Plasma cost than a 34-inch Flat Screen?

14. How much less does a 26-inch LCD cost than a 50-inch Plasma?

15. There are 60 minutes in one hour and 7 days in one week. About how many minutes are in a week?

A About 1,500 minutes

B About 6,000 minutes

C About 10,000 minutes

D About 42,000 minutes

16. Jan spent $\frac{1}{4}$ hour doing chores, $\frac{2}{5}$ hour eating, and $\frac{1}{2}$ hour studying. Which activity did she spend the most time on?

F Doing chores

G Studying

H Eating

J Eating and studying

For **17**, use the table at the right.

17. Reasoning Texas produced about 4,000,000 bales of cotton in 2005. At harvest time, most of the cotton in the fields is compressed into bales. How many bales of cotton are in 7 tons?

Tons of Cotton	1	3	5	7
Bales of Cotton	4	12	20	■

Lesson
12-4

TEKS 4.14B Solve problems that incorporate understanding the problem, making a plan, carrying out the plan, and evaluating the solution for reasonableness.

Problem Solving

Use Objects and Reasoning

Cubes

Annette's shell collection has snail shells, yellow shells, and red shells. Use cubes to show the objects and solve the problem.

How many of each type of shell are in Annette's collection?

Annette's Collection

- 2 snail shells
- 3 times as many yellow shells as red shells
- 6 shells in all

2 snail shells

Guided Practice*

Do you know HOW?

Solve.

1. Patty made a picnic lunch for her friends. She made 6 sandwiches. Three of the sandwiches were turkey. There is 1 fewer chicken sandwich than roast beef. How many of each type of sandwich is there?

Do you UNDERSTAND?

2. **Reasonableness** Is your answer to Problem 1 reasonable? What number sentence can you write to check?

3. **Write a Problem** Write a problem that uses the following information:
   - 5 shirts in all
   - 2 blue shirts
   - 1 more yellow shirt than red shirts

Independent Practice

Solve. Use objects to help.

4. Margo takes juice boxes to the park. She brings apple, orange, and grape juice boxes. There are 9 juice boxes in all. There is 1 more apple juice box than grape. There are 2 grape juice boxes. How many of each type of juice box is there?

5. Jamie brings dried fruit, pretzels, and carrots to the clubhouse. There are 4 packages of dried fruit. There is 1 fewer package of pretzels than carrots. There are 7 packages of snacks in all. How many of each type of snack are there?

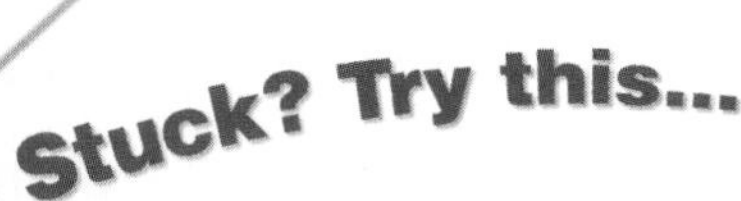

- What do I know?
- What diagram can I use to help understand the problem?
- Can I use addition, subtraction, multiplication, or division?
- Is all of my work correct?
- Did I answer the right question?
- Is my answer reasonable?

*For another example, see Set D on page 281.

Read and Understand

Use objects to show what you know. Use reasoning to make conclusions.

There are 6 shells in all.
There are 2 snail shells.

That leaves a total of 4 yellow shells and red shells.

There are 4 yellow shells and red shells.

There are 3 times as many yellow shells as red shells.

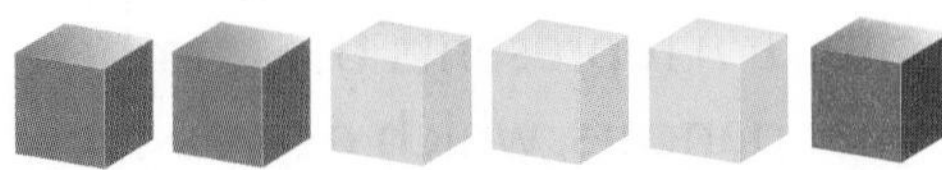

There has to be 2 snail shells, 3 yellow shells, and 1 red shell.

$2 + 3 + 1 = 6$

So, the answer is reasonable.

6. Mark is saving his allowance for a new bike. The bike he wants will cost him \$240. He can save \$30 each week. How many weeks will Mark need to save his allowance to be able to buy the bike?

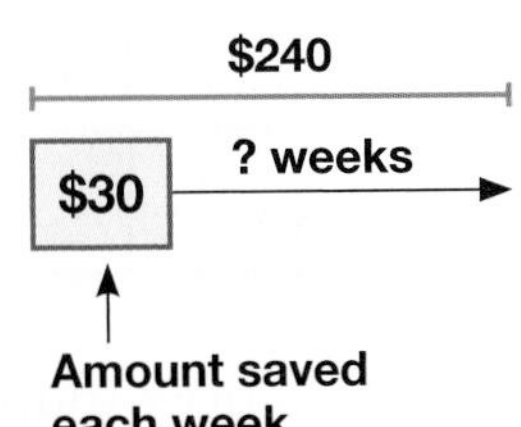

7. Leah's garden has 11 rows. There are 4 rows of tomatoes. There is 1 more row of cucumbers than tomatoes. The rest of the rows are peppers. How many rows of each type of vegetable are in Leah's garden?

8. There are 14 campers in Group 1. Six campers are boating, and $\frac{1}{2}$ as many campers are doing arts and crafts as boating. How many campers are in each activity?

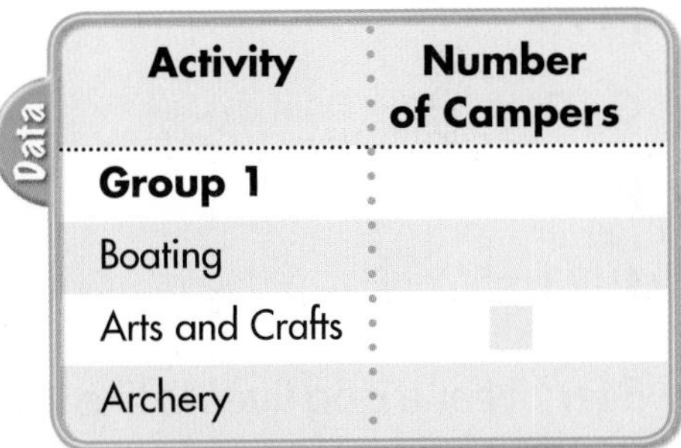

Activity	Number of Campers
Group 1	
Boating	
Arts and Crafts	
Archery	

9. There are 13 campers in Group 2. There are 4 campers playing tennis and one camper fishing. There are twice as many campers swimming as playing tennis. How many campers from Group 2 are in each activity?

Activity	Number of Campers
Group 2	
Swimming	
Tennis	
Fishing	

10. One more camper was added to Group 1 and each camper did a different activity. There are now 8 campers boating and $\frac{1}{2}$ as many campers doing archery than boating. How many campers from Group 1 are in each activity?

DIGITAL eTools **www.pearsonsuccessnet.com**

1. There are 24 dancers in Joy's recital. If *n* represents the number of jazz dancers, which expression represents the number of other types of dancers? (12-1)

A $24 + n$

B $24 - n$

C $24 \times n$

D $24 \div n$

2. Based on the pattern in the table, how many runs will Shanna's softball team have for the season if they score 6 runs in their game? (12-2)

Shanna's Softball Team

Runs Scored in Game	1	3	4	6
Total for Season	16	18	19	

F 20

G 21

H 22

J 23

3. Every year a dog lives is like 7 years a human lives. Which is a way to find the number of human years that are like 9 dog years? (12-3)

Dog Years	1	2	3	4
Human Years	7	14	21	28

A Subtract 7 from 9

B Add 7 and 9

C Divide 9 by 7

D Multiply 9 by 7

4. What is a rule for a table? (12-2)

Regular Price (p)	\$157	\$145	\$133	\$121
Price with the Coupon	\$145	\$133	\$121	\$109

F $p + 13$

G $p - 13$

H $p + 12$

J $p - 12$

5. Mr. Robinson used the table below to calculate how many adults need to help on the 4th grade trip to the observatory.

Number of Students (s)	8	16	24	32
Number of Adults	1	2	3	4

Which rule shows how many adults are needed for *s* students? (12-3)

A $s - 7$

B $8 \times s$

C $s \div 8$

D $8 + s$

6. Tennis balls are sold 3 to a canister. Vera and Tia bought 12 canisters all together. Tia bought twice as many canisters as Vera. How many canisters did Vera buy? (12-4)

F 12

G 8

H 4

J 3

7. Al participated in a reading contest. He read for the same amount of time each night for 2 weeks. The table shows the running total of how many minutes he read.

Number of Days	3	7	10	14
Total Minutes Read	60	140	200	280

Using the pattern in the table, how would the teacher be able to tell how many minutes Joey read each night? (12-3)

A Multiply Number of Days by Total Minutes Read

B Subtract the number in Total Minutes Read from Number of Days

C Divide the Total Minutes Read by the Number of Days

D Add all the numbers in Total Minutes Read and divide by 4

8. Which number completes the table? (12-1)

w	108	90	72	42
$w \div 6$	18	15		7

F 12

G 13

H 66

J 576

9. What is the rule for the table? (12-2)

d	7	11	17	21
	42	46	52	56

A $d + 35$

B $d + 4$

C $d + d + d + d + d + d$

D $d - 35$

10. Solar lights were installed along a city park's sidewalk. The table shows how many lights were installed.

Number of Yards of Sidewalk	*Number of Solar Lights*
400	80
600	120
750	150
900	

Using the pattern in the table, how can the number of solar lights installed in 900 yards of sidewalk be found? (12-3)

F Multiply 5 by 900

G Divide 900 by 5

H Add 900 to 5

J Subtract 900 from 5

11. **Griddable Response** Corrina already has \$138. After babysitting, she will have \$138 + x, where x equals the amount she earns babysitting. If x is \$25, how much money will she have after babysitting? (12-1)

Reteaching

Set A, pages 270–271

Each car on a ride holds 8 children. For c children, $c \div 8$ cars will be full on the ride. How many cars will be full if there are 16, 24, or 40 children?

Find the value of $c \div 8$ for each value of c.

c	$c \div 8$
16	2
24	3
40	5

If there are 16 children, 2 cars will be full.

If there are 24 children, 3 cars will be full.

If there are 40 children, 5 cars will be full.

Remember, to find unknown values you replace the variable with known values.

1.

e	16	25	36
$20 + e$			

2.

h	14	16	18
$h \times 4$			

3.

n	112	56	28
$n - 14$			

4.

f	96	36	144
$f \div 6$			

Set B, pages 272–273

Look at the table below. Start with the number in the first column. What rule tells you how to find the number in the second column?

Regular price (p)	Sale price
$43	$41
$45	$43
$46	$44
$47	

$43 - 2 = 41$

$45 - 2 = 43$

$46 - 2 = 44$

A rule is subtract 2, or $p - 2$.

Use the rule to find the missing number in the table.

$47 - 2 = 45$

Remember to ask "What is a rule?"

Copy and complete each table and find a rule.

1.

n	$\square - n$
3	12
5	10
8	7
12	

2.

x	$\square + x$
34	100
0	66
8	74
13	

3.

t	4	6	8	13
$t - \square$		4	6	11

4.

r	80	48	27	13
$r + \square$	88	56	35	

Reteaching

Set C, pages 274–275

Look at the table below. What rule tells you how to find each number in the second column?

Hours worked (*h*)	Wage
2	$10
4	$20
6	$30
8	▢

Think

$2 \times 5 = 10$

$4 \times 5 = 20$

$6 \times 5 = 30$

A rule is multiply by 5, or $h \times 5$.

Use the rule to find the missing number in the table.

$8 \times 5 = 40$

Remember, a rule must work with all of the numbers in the table.

1.

n	2	6	8	10
▢ × *n*	6	18	24	▢

2.

r	88	64	56	16
r ÷ ▢	11	8	▢	2

3.

e	800	700	600	500
e ÷ ▢	400	350	▢	250

4.

s	150	100	75	50
s ÷ ▢	30	20	▢	10

Set D, pages 276–277

Janet collects rocks. Her collection has black rocks, white rocks, and brown rocks. Use cubes to show the objects and solve the problem.

Janet's collection:

2 black rocks

2 times as many brown rocks as white rocks

14 objects in all

What do I know? The collection has black, white, and brown rocks. There are 2 times as many brown rocks as white rocks. There are 14 objects in all.

What am I asked to find? The number of black rocks, brown rocks, and white rocks in Janet's collection

There are 2 black rocks, 4 white rocks, and 8 brown rocks.

$2 + 4 + 8 = 14$, so the answer is reasonable.

Remember you can make a list, use objects, and use reasoning to solve a problem.

1. Six friends play on three different teams: Orioles, Cardinals, and Blue Jays. There are an equal number of players on each team. Two of the friends play on the Cardinals. The names of the remaining friends are Fedor, Lisa, John, and Ashton. Fedor is on the Orioles. John is on the same team as Lisa. Ashton is not on the Blue Jays. What team is Lisa on?

Topics 1–12

Spiral Review

Number and Operations

1. What is the value of the red digit? 106,712

A 70 **C** 700

B 100 **D** 712

2. Which number is **NOT** between 3,283 and 3,823?

F 3,278 **H** 3,592

G 3,287 **J** 3,822

3. Use fraction strips to find a fraction greater than $\frac{7}{10}$.

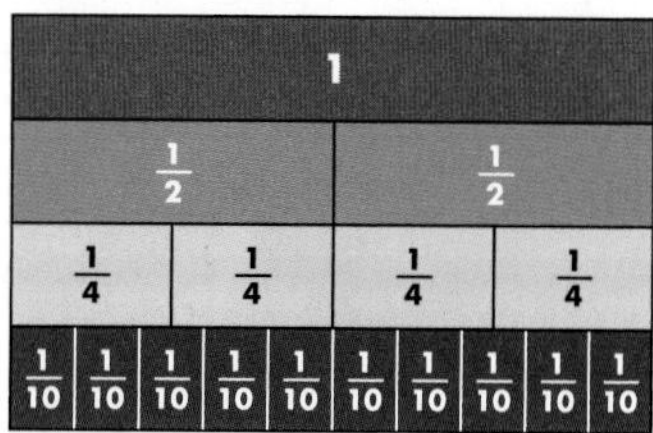

4. A pizza parlor offers a $10 discount after every 15 pizzas are ordered. Toni's family ordered 75 pizzas last year. What was the total value of discounts they saved last year? You can make a table to help solve the problem.

5. **Writing to Explain** Give the product of this array, and explain how you found it.

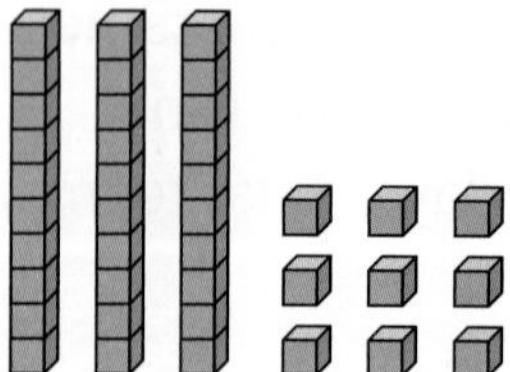

Geometry and Measurement

6. Which names the angle shown?

A acute angle

B right angle

C obtuse angle

D straight angle

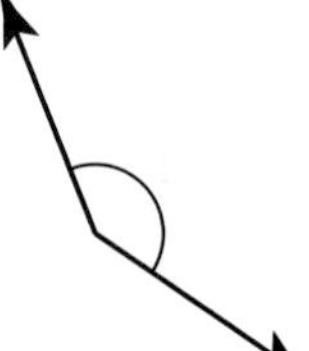

7. Which names a triangle with three angles that measure less than 90 degrees?

F acute triangle

G right triangle

H obtuse triangle

J equilateral triangle

8. Which solid does the figure represent?

A rectangular prism

B cone

C cylinder

D sphere

9. There are 2 cups in one pint and 2 pints in a quart. How many cups are in 1 quart?

10. If 1 mile is equal to 5,280 feet, how many feet are in 2 miles?

11. **Writing to Explain** Would you most likely measure a horse's weight using ounces or pounds?

Spiral Review

Probability and Statistics

12. What number is shown by ~~||||~~ |?

F 1 **G** 6 **H** 8 **J** 11

Use the graph below for Items **13** and **14**.

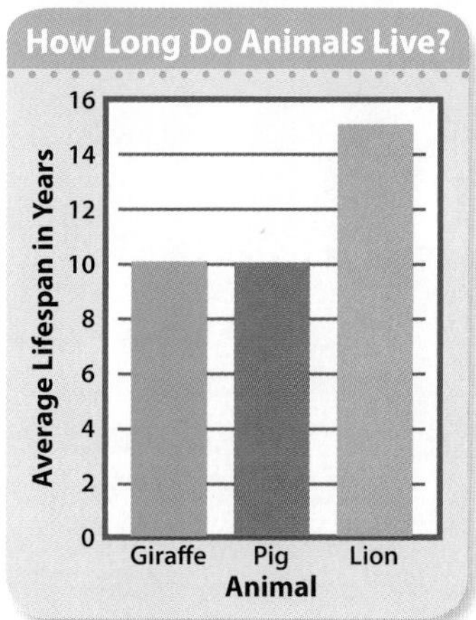

13. What are the numbers that show the units on a bar graph called?

A horizontal axis **C** scale

B bar graph **D** vertical axis

14. What is the average lifespan of a giraffe?

For **15** and **16**, use the spinner and number tiles below.

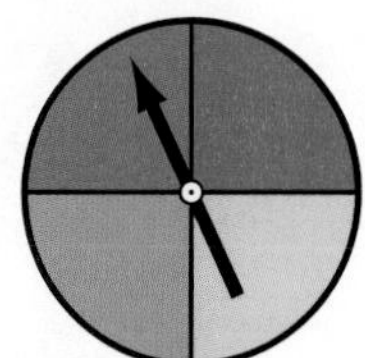

15. How many possible outcomes are there for the spinner?

16. Writing to Explain How do you find how many possible outcomes there are when you spin the spinner and pick one tile?

Algebraic Thinking

17. What is the missing number in the table below?

Pounds of Cheese	1	3	4	6
Price	$4	$12	$16	

18. Evaluate the expression $x - 18$ when $x = 30$.

F 12 **H** 36

G 24 **J** 48

19. What comes next in the pattern?

12, 16, 20, ▢

A 10 **C** 23

B 22 **D** 24

20. Write a multiplication sentence to represent the array shown below.

21. The table shows how many sheets of paper you get when you buy boxes of paper. Find the number of sheets you get when b is 7.

Boxes (b)	2	5	6	7
Sheets of Paper	200	500	600	

22. Writing to Explain An array has n rows and 60 columns. How do you find the total when $n = 4$?

Topic 13

Whole Numbers, Fractions, and Decimals on the Number Line

1

Located in College Station, Texas, the World Speedway is known as one of the world's fastest speedways. What are the lengths of two of its fastest tracks? You will find out in Lesson 13-2.

2

How many times per second do the world's fastest drummers hit their drums? You will find out in Lesson 13-3.

3

According to the Greek mathematician, Zeno, who lived in the fourth century B.C., this ball will never stop bouncing. You will find out why in Lesson 13-1.

Review What You Know!

Vocabulary

Choose the best term from the box.

- fraction
- decimal
- mixed number
- whole number

1. A ? names part of a whole.
2. A number that has a whole number and a fraction is a ?.
3. The ? equivalent of $\frac{1}{4}$ is 0.25.

Ordering Decimals

Order the numbers from least to greatest.

4. 0.4, 0.32, 0.25
5. 18.75, 18.7, 19.5
6. 2.4, 4.1, 1.5, 0.9
7. 3.5, 2.9, 4.6

Decimals and Fractions

Write each fraction as a decimal. Write each decimal as a fraction.

8. $\frac{2}{10}$
9. 0.4
10. $\frac{41}{100}$
11. $\frac{6}{100}$
12. 0.7
13. 0.75

Equivalent Fractions

Write each fraction in simplest form.

14. $\frac{2}{4}$

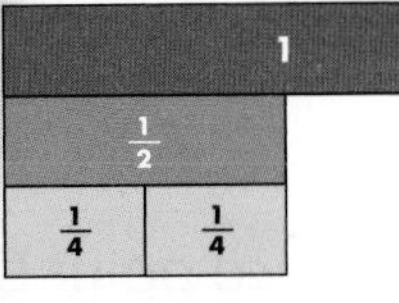

15. $\frac{4}{10}$

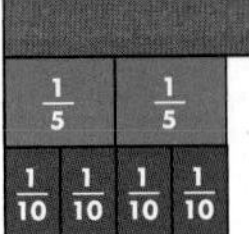

16. **Writing to Explain** How do you know that $\frac{3}{8}$ is in simplest form?

Lesson

13-1

TEKS 4.10: Locate and name points on a number line using whole numbers, fractions such as halves and fourths, and decimals such as tenths.

Locating Fractions and Decimals

How can you locate points on a number line?

In short-track speed skating, each lap is $\frac{1}{9}$ kilometer.
In long-track speed skating, each lap is 0.4 kilometer.
How can you use a number line to show these distances?

One lap = 0.4 km

One lap = $\frac{1}{9}$ km

Another Example How can you name points on a number line?

Naming fractions on a number line

What number is at point *P*?

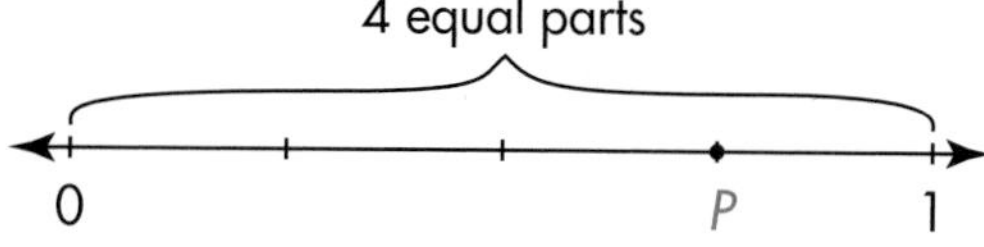

There are 4 equal parts between 0 and 1. There are 3 equal parts between 0 and point *P*. So, point *P* is at $\frac{3}{4}$.

Naming decimals on a number line

What number is at point *Q*?

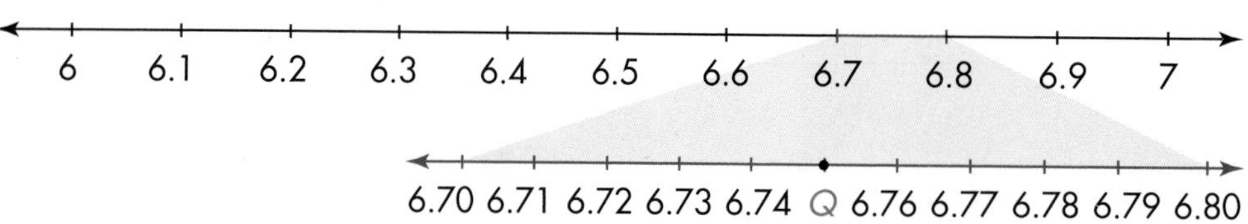

There are 5 equal parts between 6.70 and point *Q*. Each of these parts is 0.01, so point *Q* is at 6.75.

Explain It

1. Describe where you would place point *Q* on a number line that shows only tenths.

2. What number is at point *R*?

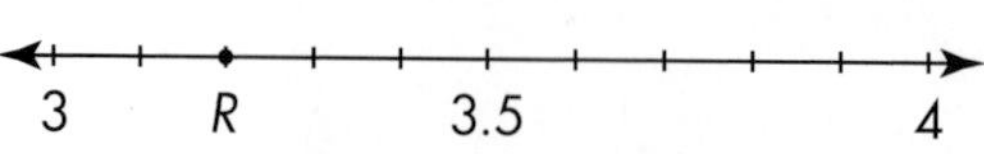

Locate $\frac{1}{9}$ on a number line.

Draw a number line, and label 0 and 1. Divide the distance from 0 to 1 into 9 equal parts.

Draw a point at $\frac{1}{9}$.

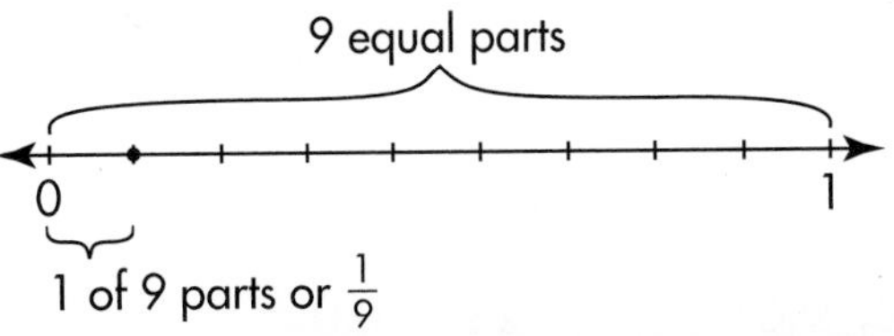

Locate 0.4 on a number line.

Draw a number line, and divide the distance from 0 to 1 into 10 equal parts to show tenths.

Draw a point at 0.4.

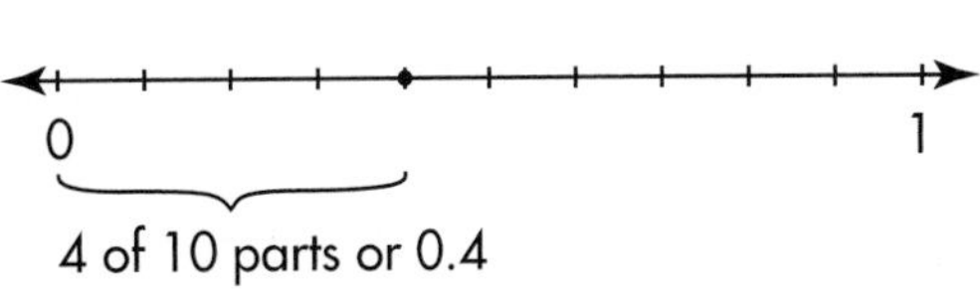

Guided Practice*

Do you know HOW?

For **1** and **2**, use the number line below to name the fraction.

1. *A*

2. *B*

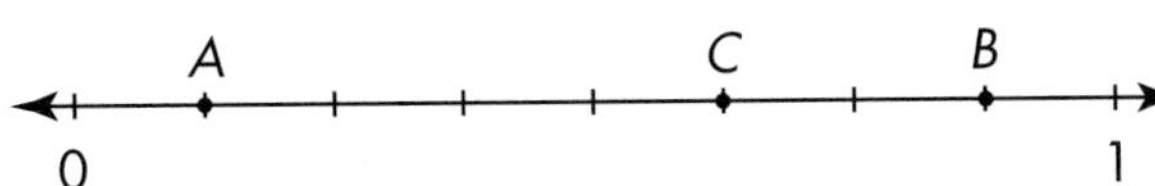

For **3** and **4**, name the point on the number line for each decimal.

3. 1.33

4. 1.39

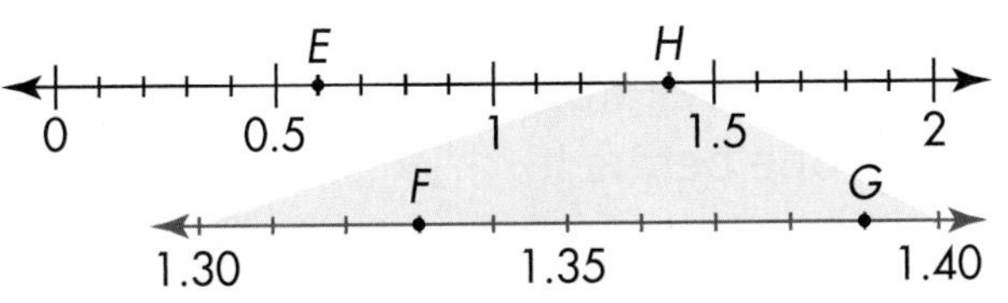

Do you UNDERSTAND?

5. Where would you locate 0.46 on the number line at the top?

6. In the number line for Exercises 1 and 2, what fraction is located at point *C*?

7. A 1,500-meter speed-skating race is $13\frac{1}{2}$ laps around a short track. Show $13\frac{1}{2}$ on a number line.

8. In the number line for Exercises 3 and 4, what point is at 0.6?

Independent Practice

For **9** through **13**, use the number line below to name the decimal.

9. *J*

10. *K*

11. *L*

12. *M*

13. *N*

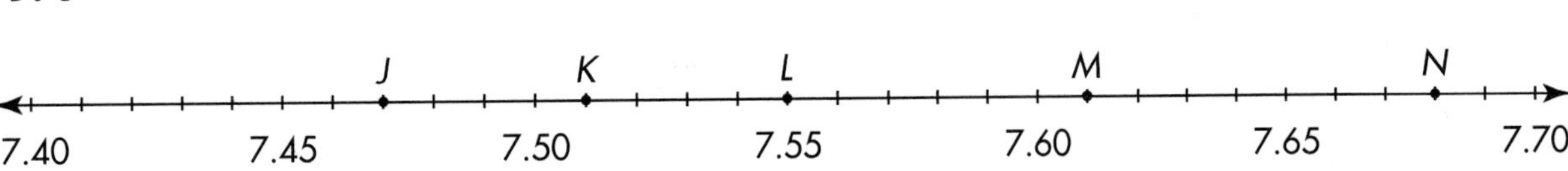

*For another example, see Set A on page 298.

Independent Practice

For **14** through **18**, name the fraction that should be written at each point.

14. *V* **15.** *Z* **16.** *X* **17.** *W* **18.** *Y*

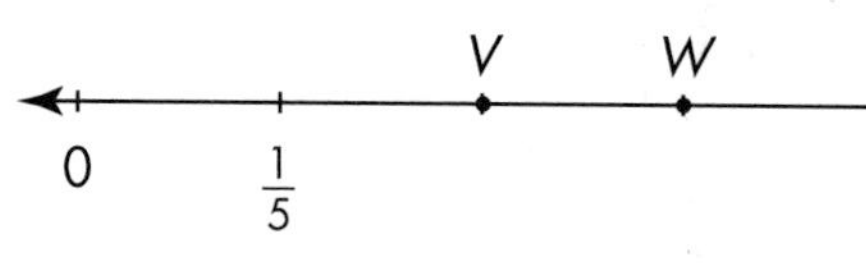
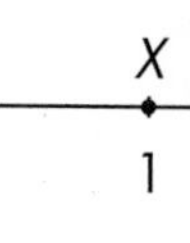
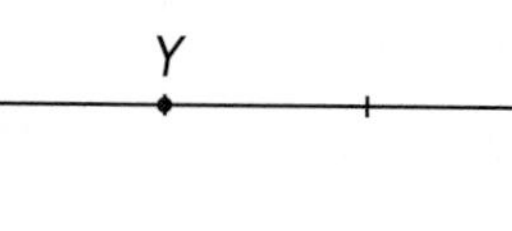
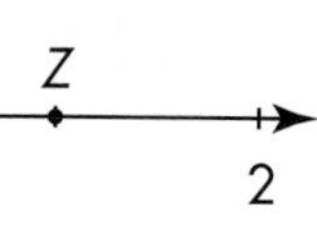

For **19** through **23**, name the point on the number line for each decimal.

19. 10.1 **20.** 10.28 **21.** 10.25 **22.** 9.6 **23.** 10.0

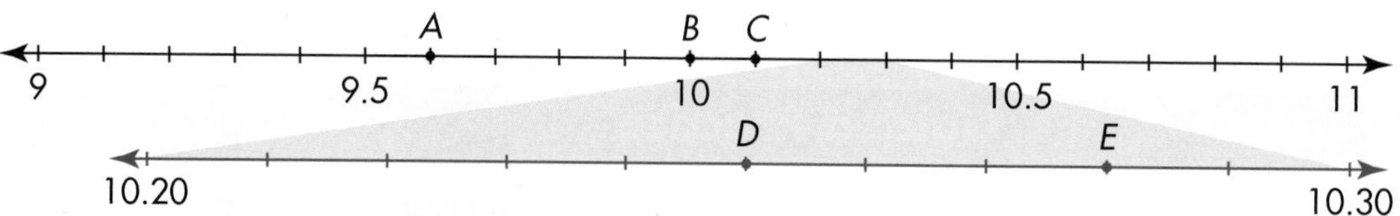

TAKS Problem Solving

24. Writing to Explain Which two points on the number line to the right represent the same point?

8 8.5 Z 9

8.70 X Y

25. Jack's distance in the shot-put throw was $8\frac{3}{4}$ meters. What is this distance as a decimal?

26. Write an expression that tells how to find the perimeter of a triangle with each side 2 inches long.

Use the diagram below for **27** and **28**.

According to the Greek mathematician Zeno, a ball will never stop bouncing because each bounce is half as high as the one before it.

27. Name the points at *D* and *E* for the next two bounces.

28. Writing to Explain Do you think it would be possible for the ball to reach zero by moving halfway closer at every step? Why or why not?

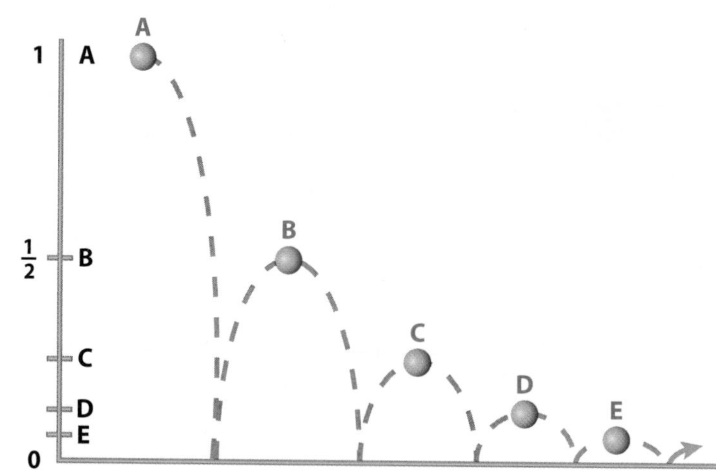

Algebra Connections

Repeating Shape Patterns

Look at the shapes below. Can you identify a pattern?

The pattern is 1 triangle, 2 circles, and 1 square.

Example: Name the 10th shape in the pattern at the left.

Think *Where does the pattern repeat itself?*

The pattern of 1 triangle, 2 circles, 1 square repeats after 4 shapes.

First group of shapes *Second group of shapes*

$4 + 4 + 2 = 10.$

Add two more

The 2nd shape in the pattern is a circle, so the 10th shape is also a circle.

In **1** through **10**, name the shape asked for in each pattern.

1. What is the 15th shape?

2. What is the 9th shape?

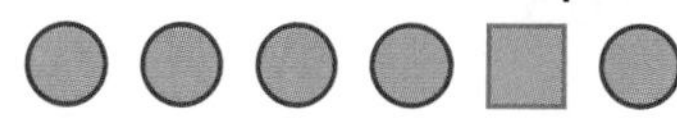

3. What is the 12th shape?

4. What is the 28th shape?

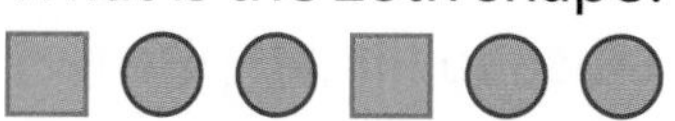

5. What is the 11th shape?

6. What is the 45th shape?

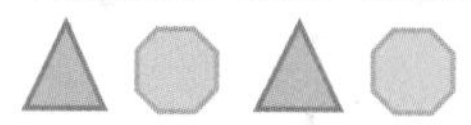

7. What is the 31st shape?

8. What is the 21st shape?

9. What is the 50th shape?

10. What is the 19th shape?

For **11** and **12**, use patterns.

11. Silvana used 8 red mugs, 7 purple mugs, and 6 green mugs in the display. Following the pattern, how many blue mugs come next?

12. Peter used 20 placemats in the display. The mats were blue, orange, and yellow. Arrange them in a pattern.

Lesson

13-2

TEKS 4.2C: Compare and order fractions using concrete objects and pictorial models.
TEKS 4.2D: Relate decimals to fractions that name tenths and hundredths using concrete objects and pictorial models.

Comparing and Ordering Fractions and Decimals

How can you use a number line to compare and order fractions and decimals?

Which container is larger, the glass bottle or the can? Order the size of the containers from least to greatest.

Juice Containers	
Glass bottle	$\frac{6}{10}$ liter
Plastic bottle	0.5 liter
Can	0.7 liter
Juice box	$\frac{2}{10}$ liter

Glass Bottle: $\frac{6}{10}$ liter

Guided Practice*

Do you know HOW?

In **1** through **4**, use a number line to compare. Write >, <, or = for each ◯.

1. $\frac{3}{10}$ ◯ $\frac{4}{10}$ **2.** $\frac{5}{10}$ ◯ $\frac{3}{10}$

3. 0.80 ◯ 0.8 **4.** 0.8 ◯ 0.5

In **5** and **6**, use a number line to order the numbers from least to greatest.

5. 0.3, 0.4, $\frac{2}{10}$ **6.** 0.8, $\frac{4}{10}$, 0.3

Do you UNDERSTAND?

7. What fraction is the same as 0.6?

8. Suppose you wanted to compare the containers using only fractions. What denominator would you use?

9. Writing to Explain A pitcher holds $\frac{4}{10}$ liter. Which juice containers could you use to fill the pitcher completely? Explain.

Independent Practice

Leveled Practice In **10** through **19**, use the number line to compare the fractions and decimals.

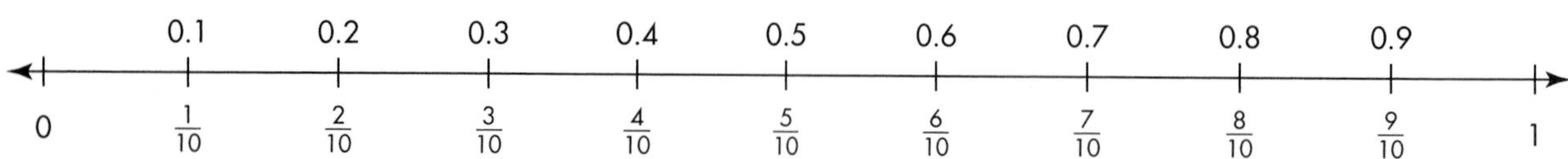

10. $\frac{4}{10}$ ◯ 0.4 **11.** $\frac{2}{10}$ ◯ 0.1 **12.** $\frac{3}{10}$ ◯ 0.2 **13.** $\frac{8}{10}$ ◯ 0.9 **14.** $\frac{3}{10}$ ◯ 0.3

15. $\frac{6}{10}$ ◯ 0.5 **16.** $\frac{6}{10}$ ◯ 0.6 **17.** $\frac{8}{10}$ ◯ 0.4 18. $\frac{5}{10}$ ◯ 0.5 **19.** $\frac{6}{10}$ ◯ 0.7

*For another example, see Set B on page 298.

Locate the numbers on a number line. Compare the numbers. Since 0.7 is to the right of 0.6, $0.7 > \frac{6}{10}$.

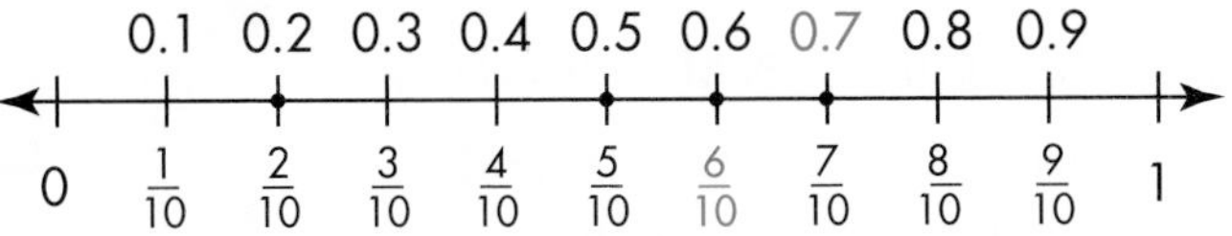

The can is larger than the glass bottle.

Put the numbers in order.

Numbers on a number line are in order from least on the left to greatest on the right.

$0.2 < 0.5 < 0.6 < 0.7$

$\frac{2}{10} < 0.5 < \frac{6}{10} < 0.7$

The order from least to greatest is $\frac{2}{10}$, 0.5, $\frac{6}{10}$, and 0.7.

In **20** through **27**, use a number line to order the numbers from least to greatest.

20. 0.5, 0.4, $\frac{1}{10}$ **21.** $\frac{4}{10}$, $\frac{3}{10}$, 0.5 **22.** 0.7, $\frac{4}{10}$, $\frac{1}{10}$ **23.** 0.6, $\frac{4}{10}$, 0.2

24. $\frac{3}{10}$, $\frac{5}{10}$, 0.1 **25.** 0.9, 0.4, $\frac{2}{10}$ **26.** 0.5, $\frac{3}{10}$, 0.8 **27.** $\frac{4}{10}$, 0.7, $\frac{2}{10}$

TAKS Problem Solving

28. Speed records have been set at the Texas World Speedway on two of its tracks. One track is 1.8 miles long. The other is $1\frac{1}{2}$ miles long. Which track is longer?

29. Jason got $\frac{8}{10}$ of the questions right on his first quiz and $\frac{7}{10}$ of the questions right on his second quiz. His third quiz score was 0.9. Order his scores from least to greatest.

30. Dan is taking two travel bags on a plane. Each bag weighs 36.5 pounds. If the total baggage limit is 70 pounds, how much weight must he remove?

31. Bella is making a quilt using 8 red squares, 3 blue squares, and 4 yellow squares. What fraction of the squares are blue?

Use the ruler at the right for **32** and **33**.

32. **Reasoning** Sam measures the length of a moth as $\frac{12}{16}$ inch. Bill says the same moth is $\frac{3}{4}$ inch. How can you use the ruler to show these are equivalent fractions?

33. Name four pairs of equivalent fractions using the ruler.

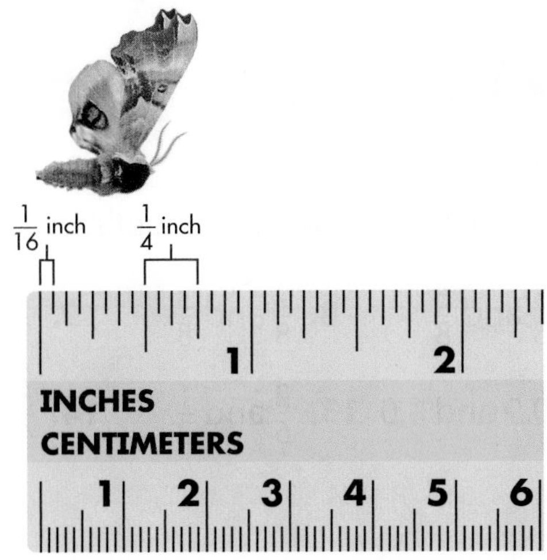

Lesson

13-3

TEKS 4.10: Locate and name points on a number line using whole number, fractions such as halves and fourths, and decimals such as tenths.

Numbers Between Numbers

How can you find a number between two numbers?

Tara is bolting together a metal sculpture. She needs to drill holes that are greater than $\frac{1}{4}$ inch across but less than $\frac{2}{4}$ inch across or the bolt will fall through the holes. Find three fractions between $\frac{1}{4}$ and $\frac{2}{4}$.

Other Examples

Find numbers between 0.2 and 0.3.

Divide the length between 0.2 and 0.3 into 10 equal parts to show hundredths.

Some numbers between 0.2 and 0.3 are 0.22, 0.25, and 0.28.

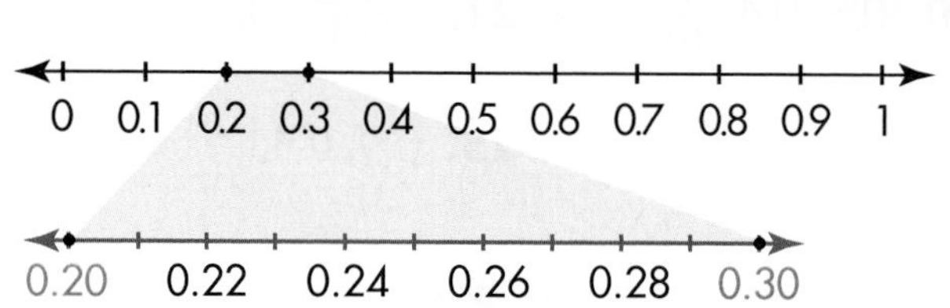

Guided Practice*

Do you know HOW?

In **1** through **4**, find a number that is between the two numbers given.

1. $\frac{5}{8}$ and $\frac{7}{8}$ **2.** $\frac{2}{4}$ and $\frac{3}{4}$

3. 1.0 and 1.1 **4.** 0.7 and 0.8

Do you UNDERSTAND?

5. How would you find more fractions between $\frac{1}{4}$ and $\frac{2}{4}$?

6. Name three sizes of holes that are between $\frac{1}{8}$ inch and $\frac{1}{4}$ inch.

Independent Practice

In **7** through **16**, find a number between each pair of numbers. Use a number line to help.

Use the given numbers as the endpoints on a number line.

7. $\frac{5}{8}$ and $\frac{6}{8}$ **8.** $\frac{2}{8}$ and $\frac{3}{8}$ **9.** $\frac{1}{5}$ and $\frac{2}{5}$ **10.** 1.4 and 1.5 **11.** 0.4 and 0.47

12. 0.9 and 1.0 **13.** $\frac{2}{6}$ and $\frac{1}{2}$ **14.** $\frac{3}{4}$ and $\frac{4}{4}$ **15.** 3.6 and 3.7 **16.** 14.4 and 14.5

*For another example, see Set C on page 299.

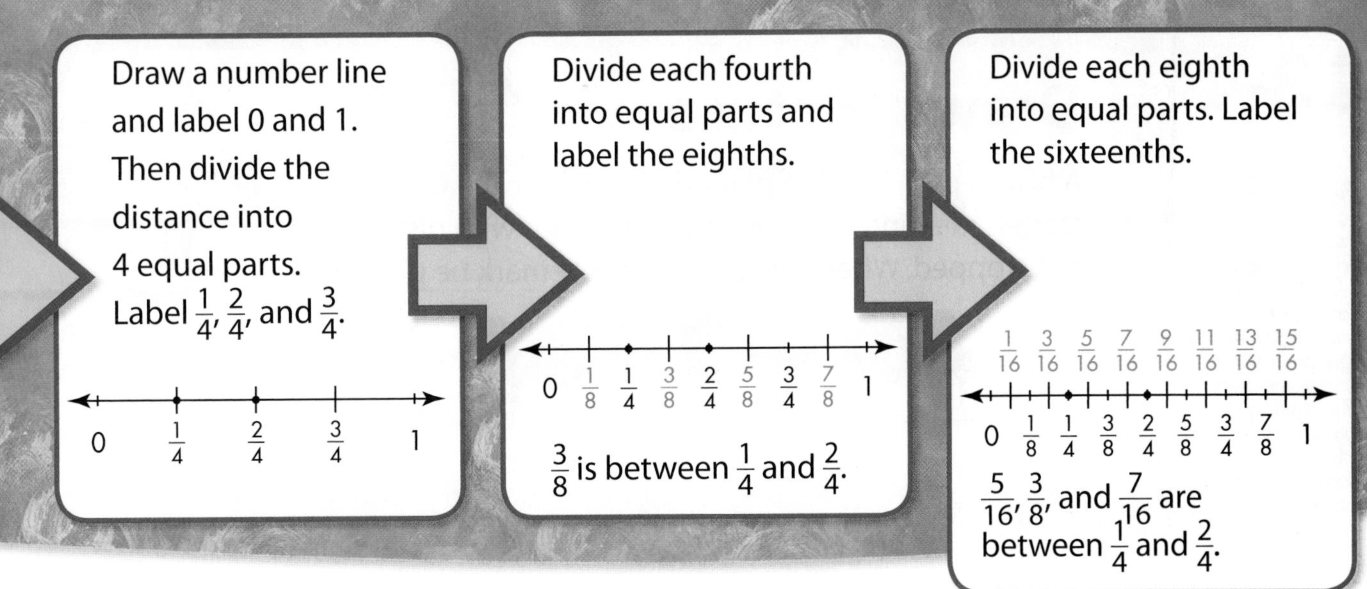

Draw a number line and label 0 and 1. Then divide the distance into 4 equal parts. Label $\frac{1}{4}$, $\frac{2}{4}$, and $\frac{3}{4}$.
0 $\frac{1}{4}$ $\frac{2}{4}$ $\frac{3}{4}$ 1
Divide each fourth into equal parts and label the eighths.
0 $\frac{1}{8}$ $\frac{1}{4}$ $\frac{3}{8}$ $\frac{2}{4}$ $\frac{5}{8}$ $\frac{3}{4}$ $\frac{7}{8}$ 1
$\frac{3}{8}$ is between $\frac{1}{4}$ and $\frac{2}{4}$.
Divide each eighth into equal parts. Label the sixteenths.
$\frac{1}{16}$ $\frac{3}{16}$ $\frac{5}{16}$ $\frac{7}{16}$ $\frac{9}{16}$ $\frac{11}{16}$ $\frac{13}{16}$ $\frac{15}{16}$
0 $\frac{1}{8}$ $\frac{1}{4}$ $\frac{3}{8}$ $\frac{2}{4}$ $\frac{5}{8}$ $\frac{3}{4}$ $\frac{7}{8}$ 1
$\frac{5}{16}$, $\frac{3}{8}$, and $\frac{7}{16}$ are between $\frac{1}{4}$ and $\frac{2}{4}$.

TAKS Problem Solving

For **17** and **18**, use the ruler at the right.

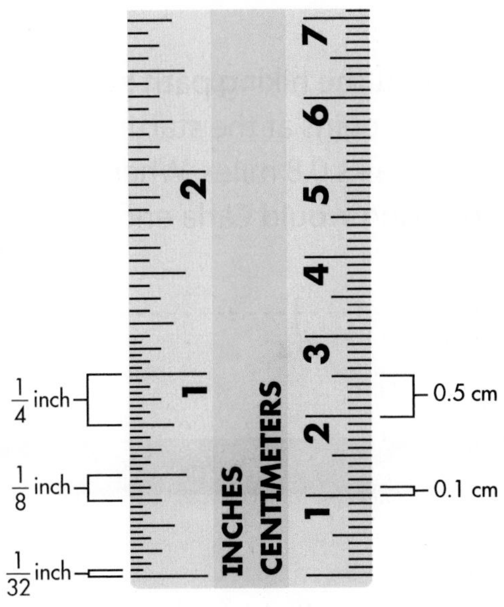

17. Felicia is drawing a tree house. She wants to make the ladder more than $\frac{1}{2}$ inch, but less than $\frac{5}{8}$ inch long. How many tick marks can she use on the ruler between $\frac{1}{2}$ inch and $\frac{5}{8}$ inch? What are the values for each tick mark?

18. Jeff uses the ruler to measure the height of the tree house in Felicia's diagram. The measurement falls exactly on a tick mark between 13 centimeters and 13.5 centimeters. What are the possible heights?

19. The world's fastest drummer hits the drum 20 times a second. So, it takes $\frac{1}{20}$ of a second for each drum beat. Between which two fractions would you find $\frac{1}{20}$ on a number line?

A $\frac{1}{4}$ and $\frac{1}{8}$

B $\frac{1}{8}$ and $\frac{1}{16}$

C $\frac{1}{16}$ and $\frac{1}{32}$

D $\frac{1}{32}$ and $\frac{1}{64}$

20. Katie has 15 quarters, 10 dimes, and 5 nickels.

a What fraction of the coins are quarters? What fraction are dimes? What fraction are nickels?

b How much money does Katie have in quarters? dimes? nickels?

Lesson
13-4

TEKS 4.14C Select or develop an appropriate problem-solving plan or strategy, including drawing a picture, looking for a pattern, systematic guessing and checking, acting it out, making a table, working a simpler problem, or working backwards to solve a problem.

Problem Solving

Draw a Picture

A hiking path is being planned for the local park. The planner started marking the drawing of the path with distances, but stopped. Where should the 1-mile mark be placed?

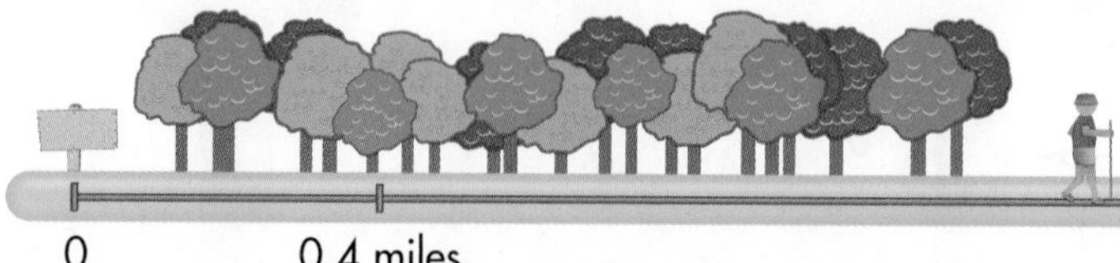

Guided Practice*

Do you know HOW?

Solve.

1. Look at the hiking path below. Carla begins at the starting point and walks 0.8 miles. Where on the drawing would Carla end her walk?

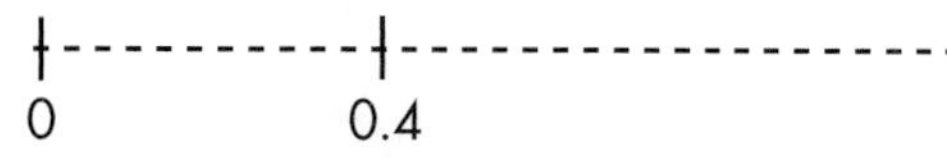

Do you UNDERSTAND?

2. How are the numbers 0.4 and 0.8 related? How can this help you to find where 0.8 is located on the drawing?

3. **Write a Problem** Write a problem that uses the drawing below to solve.

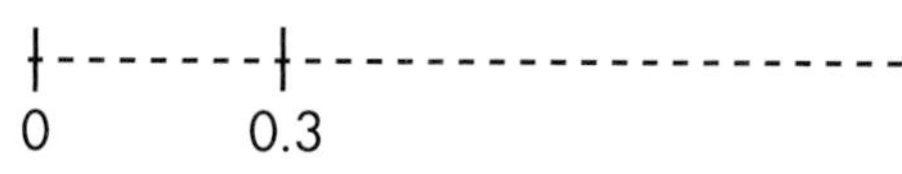

Independent Practice

Solve.

4. Look at the line below. How can you use the mark on the line to find where 1.0 should be located?

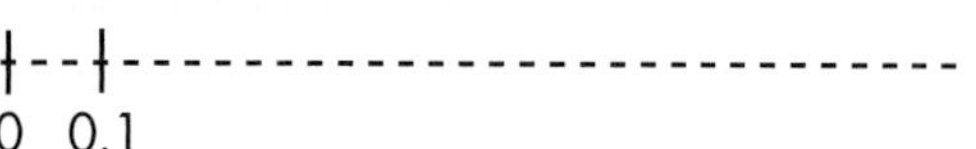

5. Copy the line segment from Problem 4. Find 1.0.

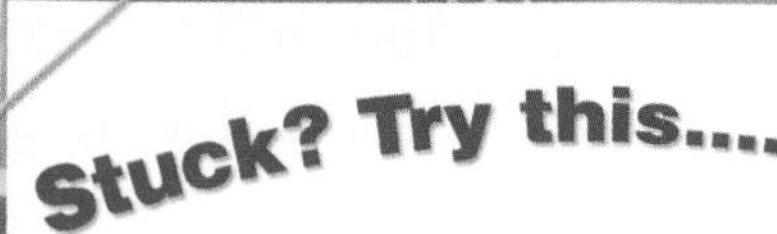

- What do I know?
- What diagram can I use to help understand the problem?
- Can I use addition, subtraction, multiplication, or division?
- Is all of my work correct?
- Did I answer the right question?
- Is my answer reasonable?

*For another example, see Set D on page 299.

Read & Understand

What do I know? The hiking path must be 1 mile long. The marker for 0.4 mile is located on the drawing.

What am I asked to find? Where the 1-mile mark should be located on the drawing.

Plan

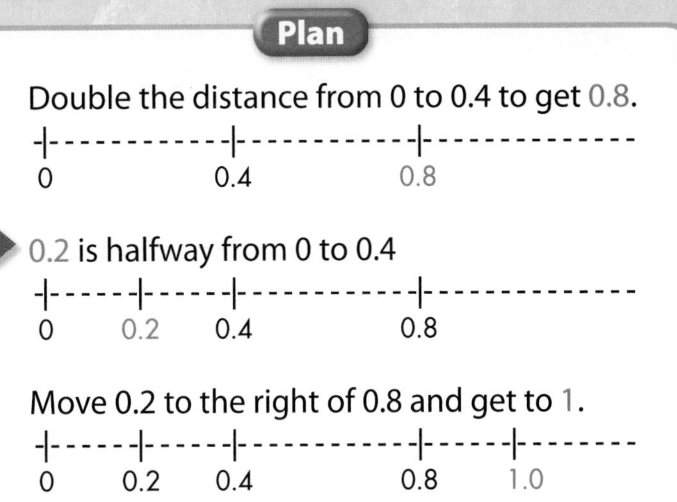

Double the distance from 0 to 0.4 to get 0.8.
0
0.4
0.8
0.2 is halfway from 0 to 0.4
0
0.2
0.4
0.8
Move 0.2 to the right of 0.8 and get to 1.
0
0.2
0.4
0.8
1.0

6. Allie needed to design a banner for field day. She wanted her banner to be 2 feet long. Allie marked 0.5 feet on her drawing. How can she use this distance to find 2 feet?

Allie's drawing: 0, 0.5

7. Dawn has 45 customers on her paper route. She delivers newspapers every day. How many newspapers does she deliver in five days?

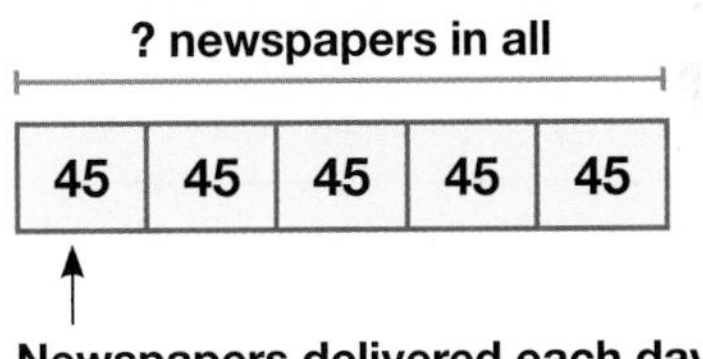

8. **Writing to Explain** Terrence has 8 comic books and 4 detective books. His sister says $\frac{2}{3}$ of his books are comic books. Terrence says $\frac{8}{12}$ of his books are comic books. Who is correct?

9. What would be a good estimate for *G* on the drawing below?

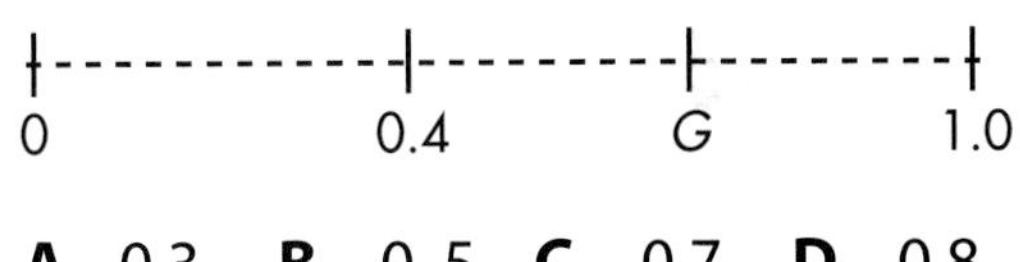

A 0.3 **B** 0.5 **C** 0.7 **D** 0.8

10. Shawn marked 0.8 feet on the chalkboard. How can Shawn use this distance to find 2 feet?

Shawn's drawing: 0, 0.8

11. **Algebra** John has twice as many brothers as Bob. If Bob has *b* brothers, how many brothers does John have?

12. Nick wrote a four-digit number. He used the digits 2, 4, 6, and 8. How many four-digit numbers could Nick have written?

13. Mary has 3 coin purses with 58 coins in each. How many coins does Mary have?

1. Which number is best represented by point *R* on the number line? (13-1)

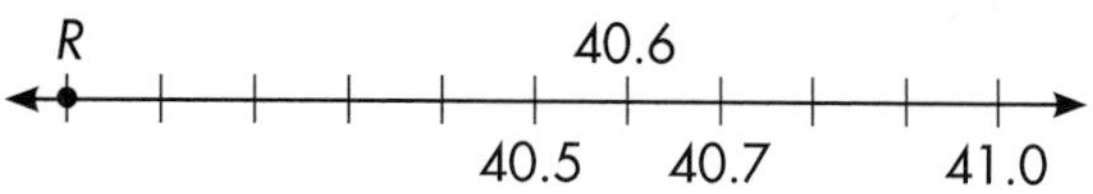

A 40.1

B 40.0

C 39.9

D 39.0

2. The black snake measured $\frac{4}{10}$ meter long. The green snake measured 0.7 meter long. Which symbol makes the comparison true? (13-2)

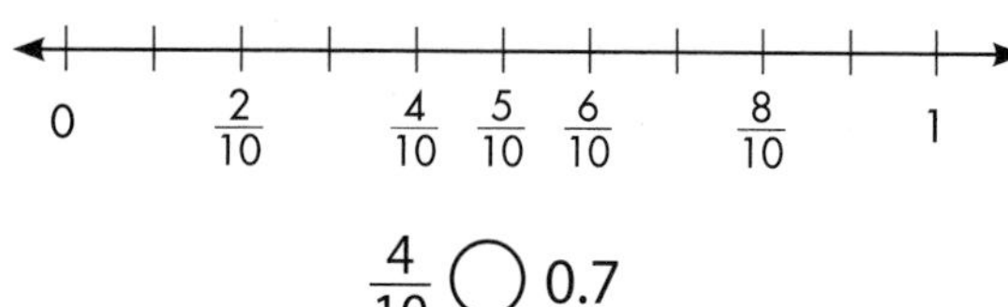

F ×

G =

H <

J >

3. Garrison is building a toy box. The $\frac{3}{8}$ inch wrench is too small and the $\frac{1}{2}$ inch wrench is too large. Which size wrench does he need? (13-3)

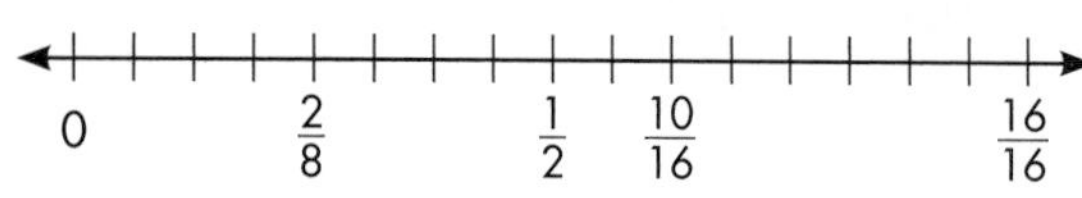

A $\frac{1}{4}$ inch

B $\frac{5}{16}$ inch

C $\frac{7}{16}$ inch

D $\frac{5}{8}$ inch

4. Whitney and her friends guessed the distance, in feet, around one of the nation's largest Sitka spruce trees. Whitney's guess was correct. Which point of $55\frac{9}{12}$ feet represents Whitney's guess? (13-1)

F Point *L*

G Point *M*

H Point *N*

J Point *O*

5. Which number is the greatest? (13-2)

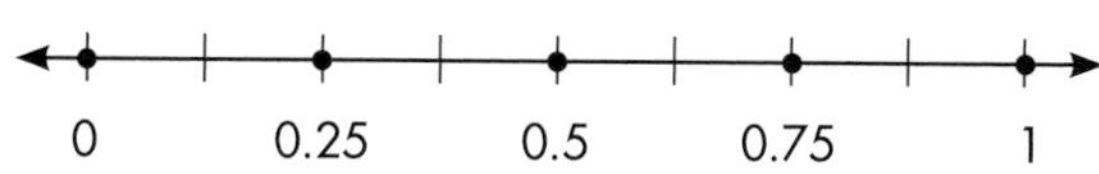

A $\frac{7}{8}$

B 0.75

C 0.25

D $\frac{1}{2}$

6. Write the fraction for point B. (13-1)

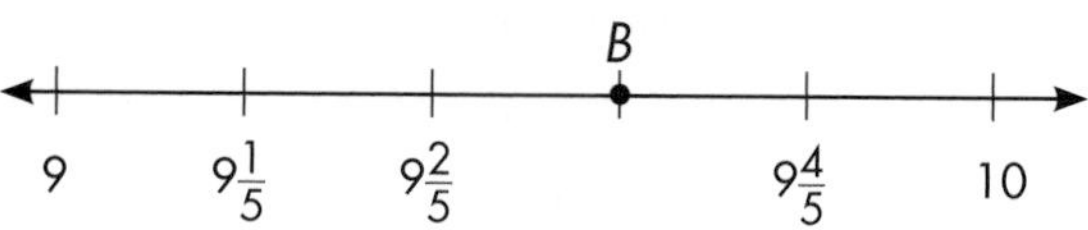

F $9\frac{1}{5}$

G $9\frac{3}{5}$

H $9\frac{4}{5}$

J 10

7. Four friends packed their own lunch for school on the same day. The table below shows the weight of each person's lunch.

	Weight in Kilograms
Loren	0.7
Larry	0.5
Penny	$\frac{9}{10}$
Ralph	$\frac{6}{10}$

Use the number line to find whose lunch weighs the least. (13-2)

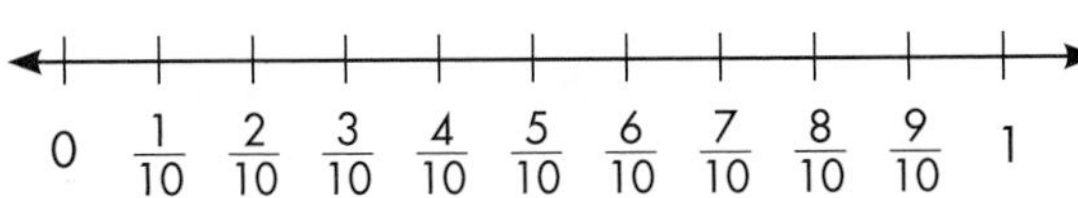

A Loren

B Larry

C Penny

D Ralph

8. Gwen sold 0.6 of her carnival tickets. Which point on the number line best represents 0.6? (13-1)

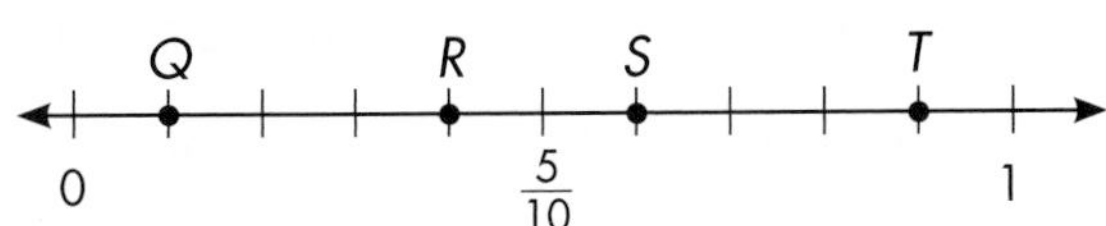

F Point *Q*

G Point *R*

H Point S

J Point *T*

9. Louise is creating a 1-foot long comic strip. If she has marked 0.5 on her paper, what should she do to find 1 foot? (13-4)

A Subtract 0.5

B Add 0.2

C Multiply 0.5

D Add 0.5

10. The Kitti's hog-nosed bat can weigh as little as 0.25 ounces. Between which two decimals would you place 0.25? (13-3)

F 0.2 and 0.3

G 0.2 and 0.24

H 0.2 and 0.25

J 0.02 and 0.03

11. Quinton's frog leaped $2\frac{3}{4}$ feet on its first leap. Which point on the number line represents $2\frac{3}{4}$? (13-1)

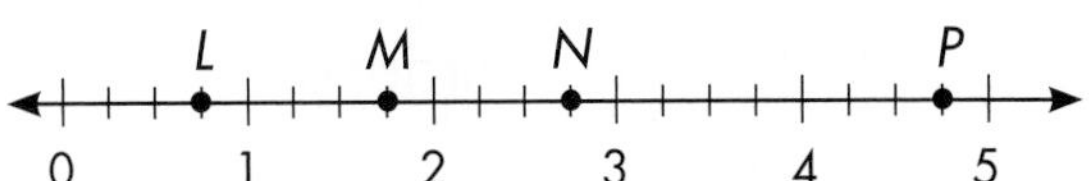

A L

B M

C N

D P

12. **Griddable Response** Angie drew a number line and labeled 0 and 1. To show $\frac{5}{12}$, how many parts should she divide the distance from 0 to 1? (13.4)

Reteaching

Set A, pages 286–288

Show $6\frac{1}{4}$ on a number line.

Divide the distance from 6 to 7 into 4 equal lengths.

Label the tick marks and draw a point at $6\frac{1}{4}$.

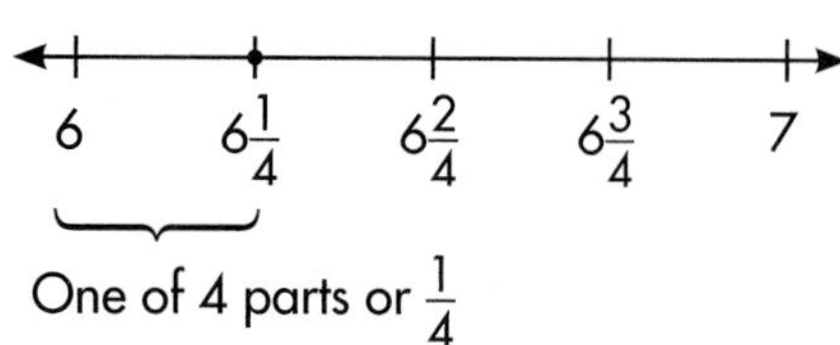

Show 7.7 on a number line.

Divide the distance from 7 to 8 into 10 equal lengths.

Label the tick marks, and draw a point at 7.7.

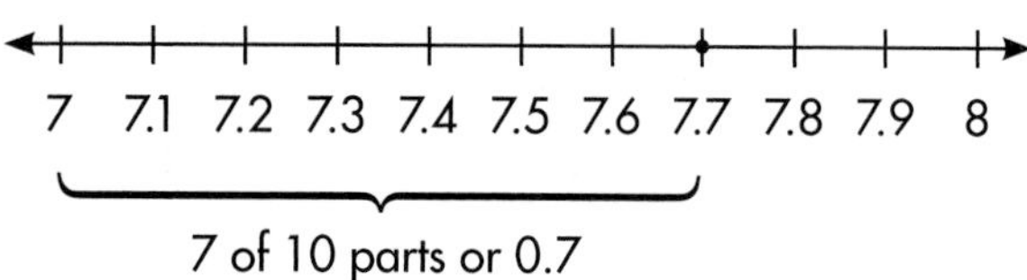

Remember that the distance between each tick mark is set evenly apart.

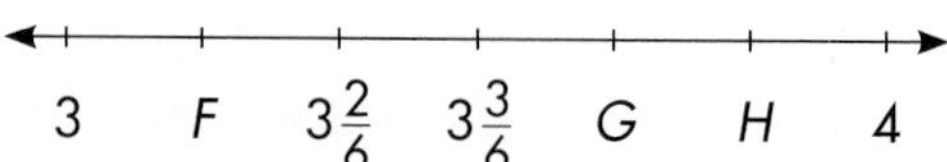

Name the fraction at each point.

1. *G* **2.** *F* **3.** *H*

J K L M N O

5.40 5.45 5.50 5.55 5.60 5.65 5.70

Name the decimal at each point.

4. *K* **5.** *M* **6.** *O*

Identify the correct point on the number line for each number.

7. 5.6 **8.** $5\frac{1}{2}$ **9.** 5.42

Set B, pages 290–291

Use a number line to order 0.4, $\frac{2}{10}$, 0.1 from least to greatest.

0.1 0.2 0.3 0.4 0.5 0.6 0.7 0.8 0.9 1.0

$\frac{1}{10}$ $\frac{2}{10}$ $\frac{3}{10}$ $\frac{4}{10}$ $\frac{5}{10}$ $\frac{6}{10}$ $\frac{7}{10}$ $\frac{8}{10}$ $\frac{9}{10}$ 1

$0.1 < 0.2 < 0.4$

↓ ↓ ↓

0.1 $\frac{2}{10}$ 0.4

The order from least to greatest is 0.1, $\frac{2}{10}$, 0.4.

Remember that numbers on a number line are in order from least on the left to greatest on the right.

Use a number line to order the numbers from least to greatest.

1. 0.5, $\frac{1}{10}$, 0.2 **2.** 0.7, $\frac{9}{10}$, 0.4

3. $\frac{1}{2}$, 0.3, $\frac{6}{10}$ **4.** $\frac{4}{10}$, 0.5, $\frac{2}{10}$

5. 0.8, 0.6, $\frac{5}{10}$ **6.** $\frac{4}{10}$, 0.2, 0.7

Set C, pages 292–293

Find a number between $\frac{1}{6}$ and $\frac{2}{6}$.

Draw a number line and label 0 and 1.
Then divide the distance into 6 equal parts. Label $\frac{1}{6}, \frac{2}{6}, \frac{3}{6}, \frac{4}{6}$, and $\frac{5}{6}$.

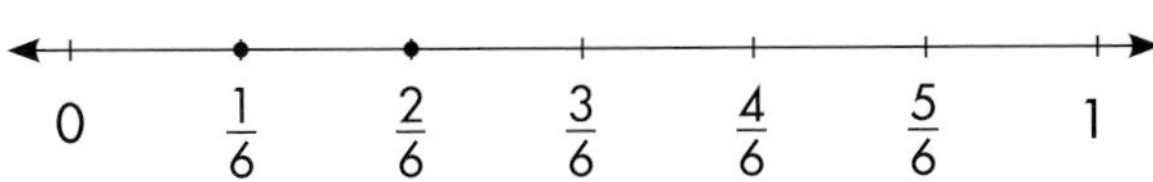

Divide each sixth into equal parts. Label the fractions of the new parts.

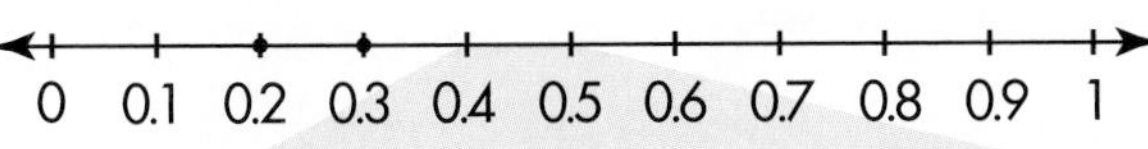

One possible answer is $\frac{3}{12}$.

Find a decimal between 0.4 and 0.5.

0 0.1 0.2 0.3 0.4 0.5 0.6 0.7 0.8 0.9 1

0.40 0.41 0.42 0.43 0.44 0.45 0.46 0.47 0.48 0.49 0.50

One possible answer is 0.44.

Remember that it is easy to compare fractions with the same denominator.

Find a number that is between the numbers given.

1. $\frac{1}{3}$ and $\frac{2}{3}$
2. 0.2 and 0.37
3. 0.42 and 0.5
4. $\frac{3}{5}$ and $\frac{4}{5}$
5. $\frac{2}{5}$ and $\frac{4}{5}$
6. 0.1 and 1.0
7. 0.6 and 0.7
8. 0.53 and 0.6
9. $\frac{1}{2}$ and $\frac{5}{6}$
10. $\frac{3}{6}$ and $\frac{10}{12}$

Set D, pages 294–295

A biking trail is being planned for a town. Where should the 2-mile marker be placed?

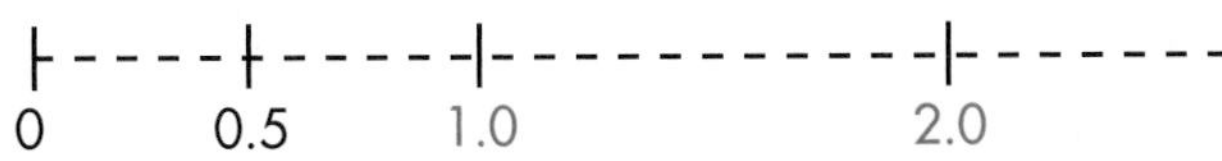

What do I know? The biking trail must be at least 2 miles long. The 0.5-mile mark is located on the drawing.

What am I asked to find? Where would the 2-mile mark be located on the drawing?

1.0 is double 0.5 and 1.0 is half of 2.0.

Measure the distance from 0 to 0.5. Double this distance. Mark 1.0. Now double this distance and mark 2.0.

Remember you can use a ruler to measure the distance between each mark.

1. Look at the walking path below. Will begins at the starting point and walks 0.6 miles. Where on the path would Will end his walk?

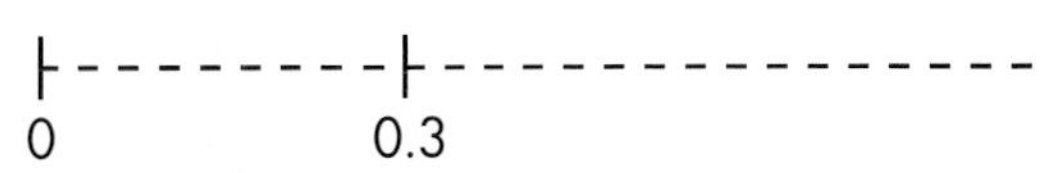

Topic 14 Lines, Angles, Shapes, and Solids

1 The Headquarters for the United States Department of Defense is named after the polygon it resembles. Which polygon does it look like? You will find out in Lesson 14-3.

2 The Great Pyramid of Giza was built so well by the ancient Egyptians that even current architects can't equal its exactness. What is the length of one of its sides? You will find out in Lesson 14-6.

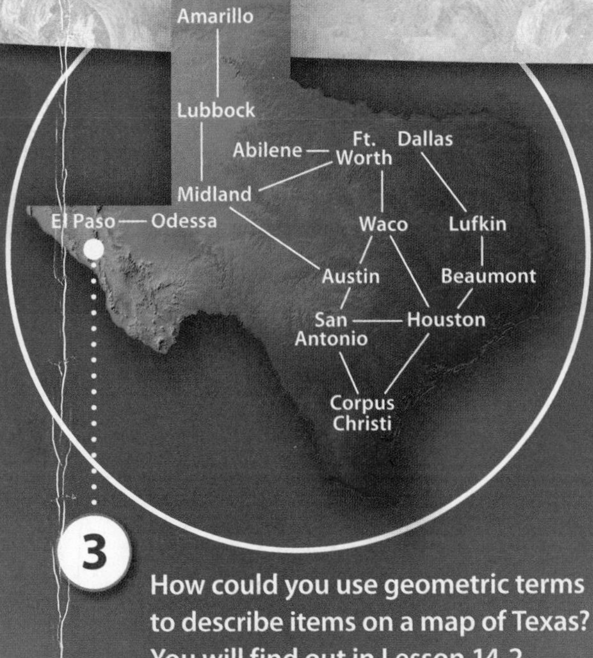

3 How could you use geometric terms to describe items on a map of Texas? You will find out in Lesson 14-2.

4 There are 3 muscles in your neck that are critical for breathing and singing. They are named after a type of triangle that has a similar shape. What kind of triangle is it? You will find out in Lesson 14-4.

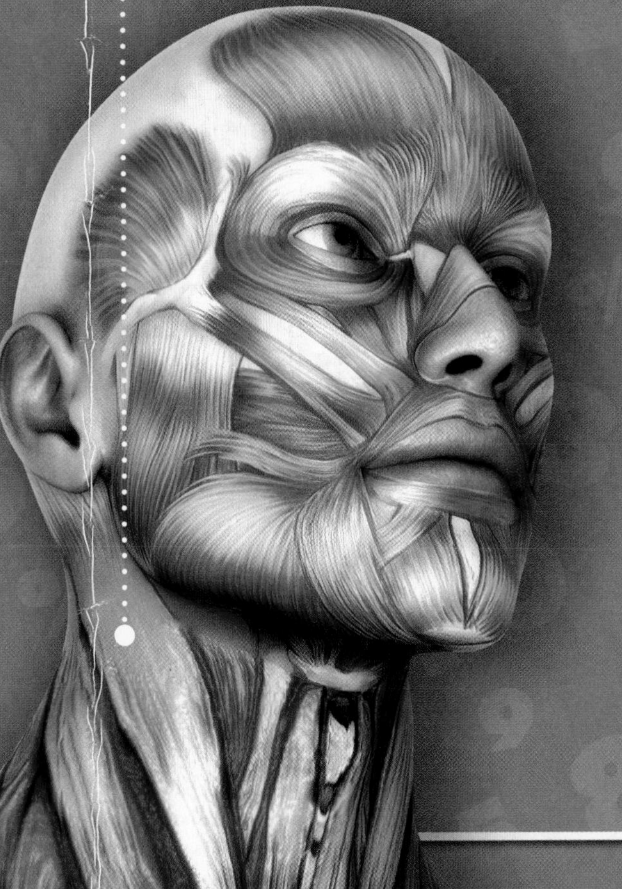

Review What You Know!

Vocabulary

Choose the best term from the box.

- height
- length
- perimeter
- width

1. Measuring the ? would tell you how wide a shape is.
2. To find the ? of an object you would have to add up the lengths of all of its sides.
3. Measuring the ? would tell you how long a shape is.

Solids

Name what each figure looks like.

4. 

5. 

6. 

7. 

Addition

Solve.

8. 35 + 39	**9.** 72 + 109	**10.** 44 + 12
11. 145 + 238	**12.** 642 + 8	**13.** 99 + 41
14. 984 + 984	**15.** 22 + 888	**16.** 72 + 391

17. **Writing to Explain** To find the sum of 438 + 385, how many times will you need to regroup? Explain.

Lesson
14-1

TEKS 4.8B: Identify and describe parallel and intersecting (including perpendicular) lines using concrete objects and pictorial models.
TEKS 4.8C: Use essential attributes to define two- and three-dimensional geometric figures.

Points, Lines, and Planes

What are some important geometric terms?

A point is an exact location in space.	• Z
A line is a straight path of points that goes on and on in two directions.	⟷
A plane is an endless flat surface.	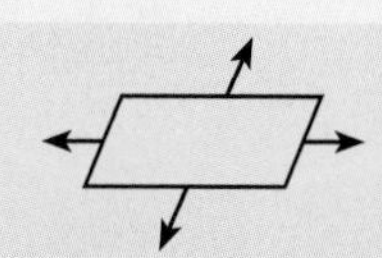

Guided Practice*

Do you know HOW?

For **1–4**, use the diagram at the right.

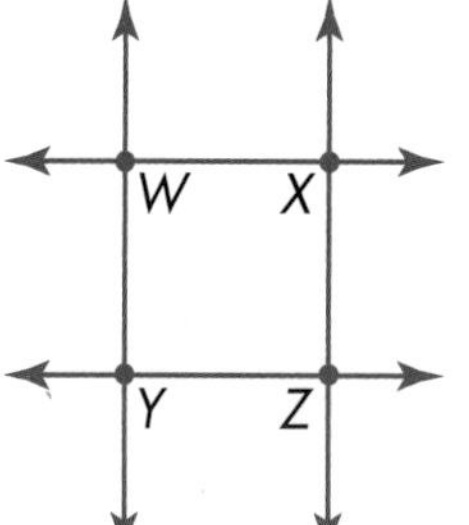

1. Name four points.
2. Name four lines.
3. Name two pairs of parallel lines.
4. Name two pairs of perpendicular lines.

Do you UNDERSTAND?

5. What geometric term could you use to describe the top and bottom sides of a chalkboard? Why?
6. Take two pens and make a plus symbol. Describe the type of lines the pens represent.
7. What geometric term could you use to describe the tip of your pencil?

Independent Practice

In **8** through **14**, use geometric terms to describe what is shown.

8.

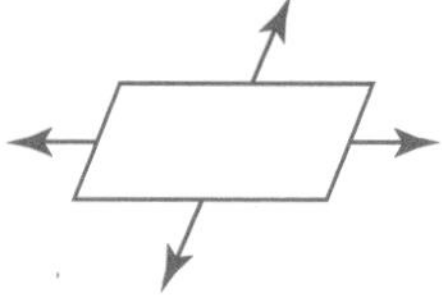

9.

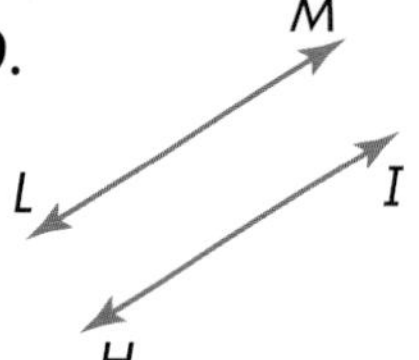

10.

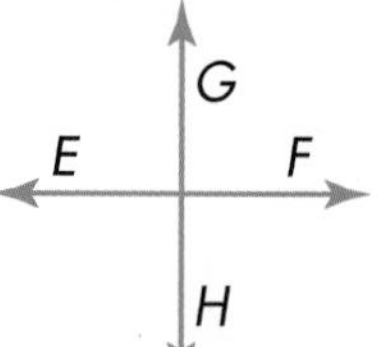

11.

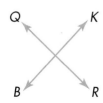

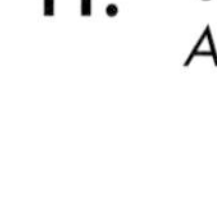

12.

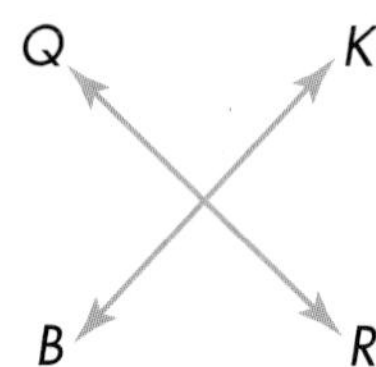

13.

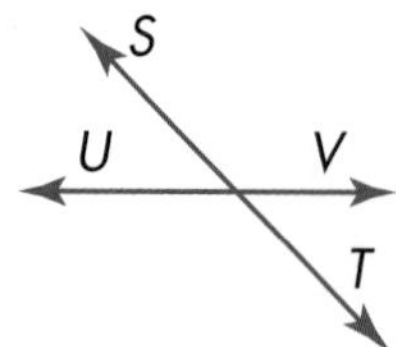

14.

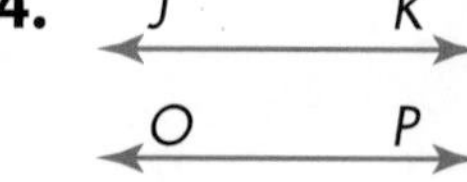

*For another example, see Set A on page 320.

Pairs of lines are given special names depending on their relationship. Use pencils to show pairs of lines.

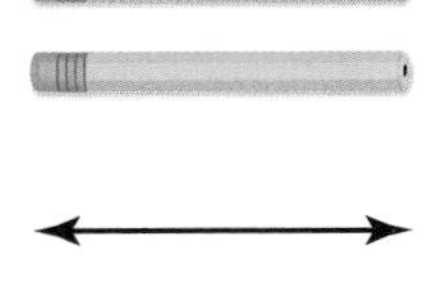

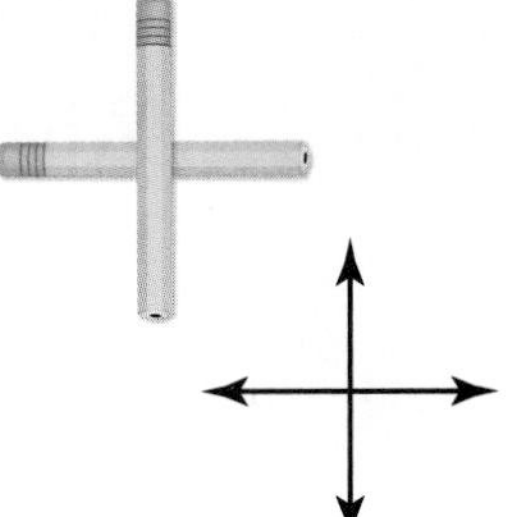

Parallel lines never intersect.

Intersecting lines pass through the same point.

Perpendicular lines are lines that form square corners.

For **15** through **17**, describe each image shown using a geometric term.

15. 

16. 

17. 

TAKS Problem Solving

18. Estimation Georgia purchased items to make dinner. She bought chicken for $5.29, salad items for $8.73, and rice for $1.99. Estimate how much Georgia spent in all.

19. I have 6 square faces and 8 vertices. What am I?

A Cube
B Square
C Pyramid
D Circle

For **20**, use the diagram at the right.

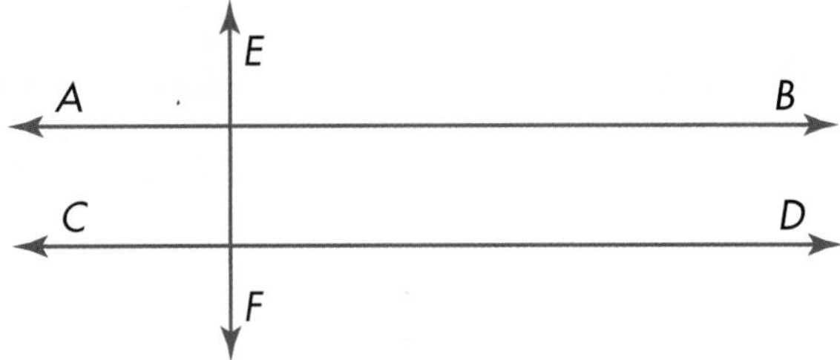

20. Reasoning Line *AB* is parallel to line *CD* and line *CD* is perpendicular to line *EF*. What can you conclude about *AB* and *EF*?

21. The Web site of a company that sells sports equipment averages 850 visitors a day. How many visitors would the web site average in 7 days?

22. Which geometric term below best describes the surface of a desk?

F Point
G Plane
H Line
J Parallel

23. Writing to Explain If all perpendicular lines are also intersecting lines, are all intersecting lines also perpendicular? Explain.

24. Cross your arms above your head. Describe the type of lines your arms represent.

Lesson

14-2

TEKS 4.8A: Identify and describe right, acute, and obtuse angles.
TEKS 4.8: Identify and describe attributes of geometric figures using formal geometric language.

Line Segments, Rays, and Angles

What geometric terms are used to describe parts of lines and types of angles?

A line segment is a part of a line with two endpoints.

A ray is a part of a line that has one endpoint and continues on forever in one direction.

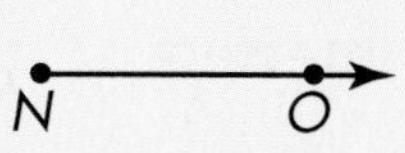

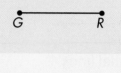

Guided Practice*

Do you know HOW?

In **1** through **4**, use geometric terms to describe what is shown.

1. P X

2. P Q R

3. B Y

4.

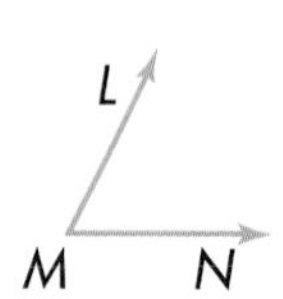

Do you UNDERSTAND?

5. What geometric term describes a line that has only one endpoint?

6. What geometric term describes a line that has two endpoints?

7. Which geometric term describes what two edges of a book make when a corner is formed?

Independent Practice

In **8** through **11**, use geometric terms to describe what is shown.

8.

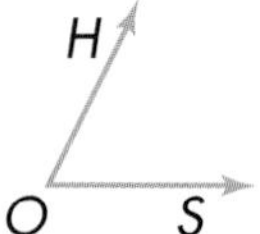

9.

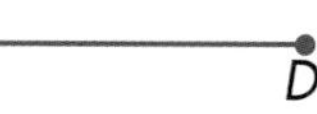

10.

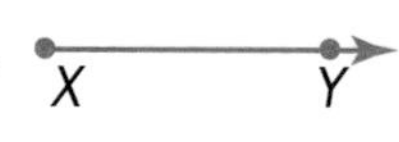

11.

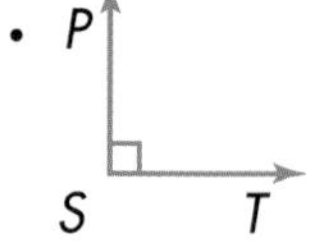

For **12** through **14**, use the figure shown to the right.

12. Name four line segments.

13. Name four rays.

14. Name 2 right angles.

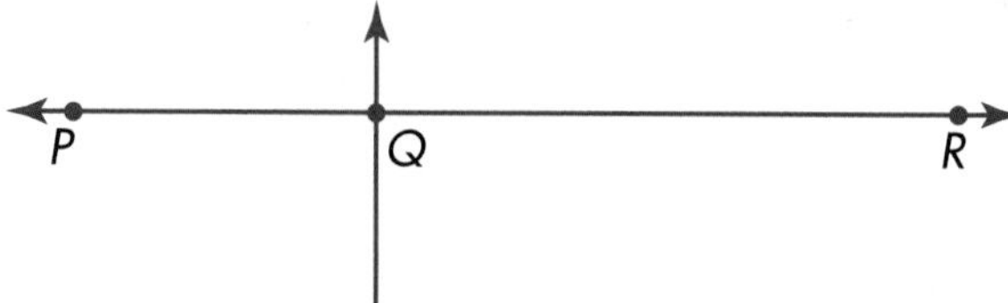

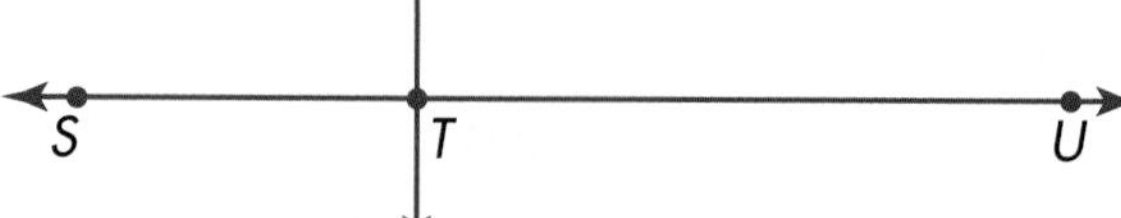

*For another example, see Set B on page 320.

An angle is a figure formed by two rays that have the same endpoint. Angles are given special names depending upon their size.

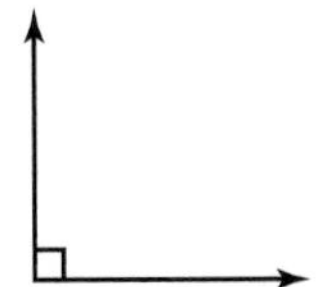

A right angle is a square corner.

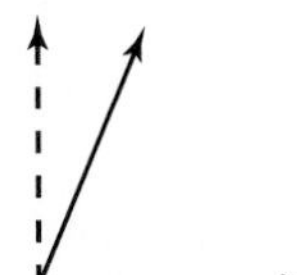

An acute angle is less than a right angle.

An obtuse angle is greater than a right angle.

A straight angle forms a straight line.

TAKS Problem Solving

15. **Writing to Explain** Is the figure shown below formed by two rays with a common endpoint? If so, is it an angle? Explain.

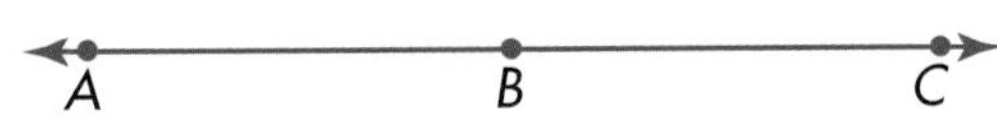

16. Which choice names the figure shown below?

G H

A Ray *GH**C** Line segment *GH*

B Line *GH**D** Angle *GH*

17. What three capital letters can be written by drawing two parallel line segments and then one line segment that is perpendicular to the line segments you already drew?

18. Lexi said that two lines can both intersect a line and form perpendicular lines. Draw a picture to explain what she means.

For **19** through **21**, use the map of Texas to the right.

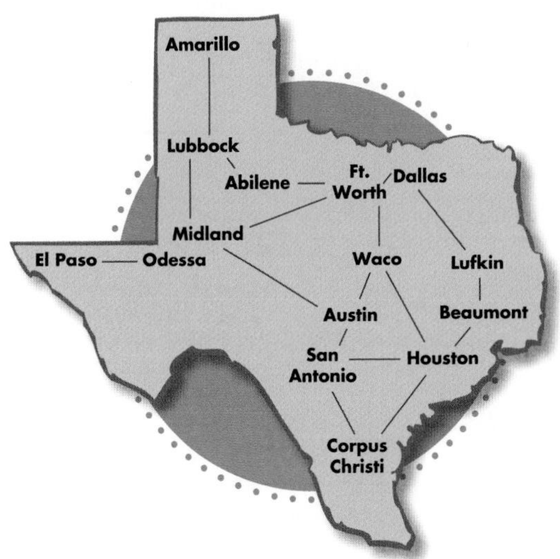

19. In geometric terms, how would you describe the route between 2 cities?

20. How would you describe the cities?

21. How would you describe the map of the state of Texas?

22. **Draw It** Randy used 96 sticks to build a model project. Bryan used 3 times as many. Draw a diagram showing how many sticks Bryan used.

Lesson
14-3

TEKS 4.8C: Use essential attributes to define two-and three-dimensional geometric figures.
TEKS 4.8: Indentify and describe attributes of geometric figures using formal geometric language.

Polygons

How do you identify polygons?

A polygon is a closed plane figure made up of line segments. Each line segment is a side. The point where the two sides meet is called a vertex.

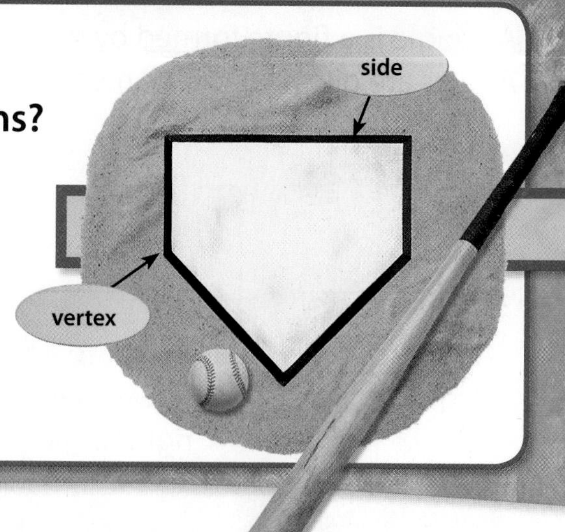

Guided Practice*

Do you know HOW?

Draw an example of each polygon. Write the number of sides and vertices it has.

1. pentagon
2. triangle
3. octagon
4. quadrilateral

Do you UNDERSTAND?

5. Is a circle a polygon? Why or why not?
6. **Writing to Explain** Does every hexagon have the same shape?

Independent Practice

In **7** through **18**, name each polygon, if possible. Write the number of sides and vertices it has.

7. 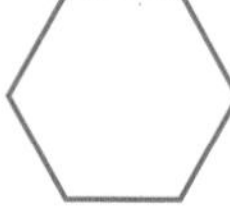
8. 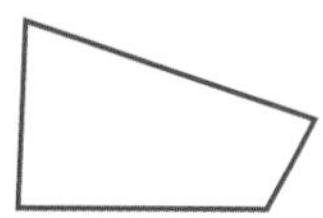
9. 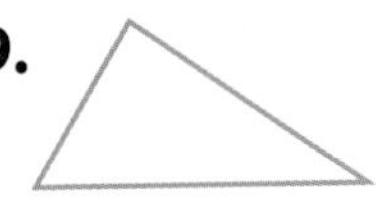
10. 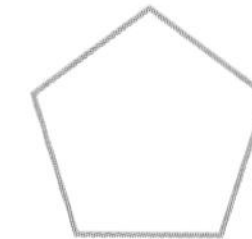
11. 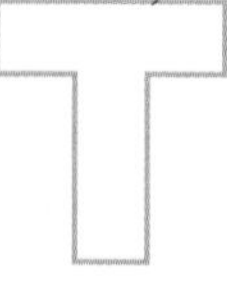
12. 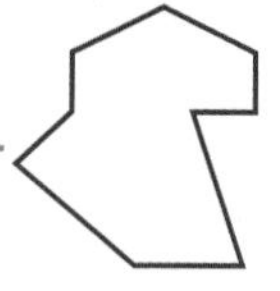
13. 
14. 
15. 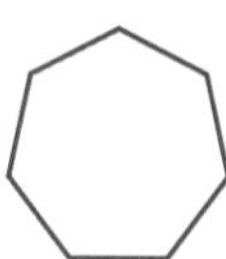
16. 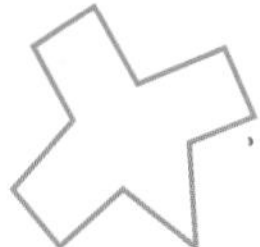
17. 
18. 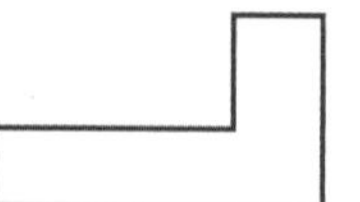

DIGITAL Animated Glossary www.pearsonsuccessnet.com

*For another example, see Set C on page 320.

Here are some examples of polygons.

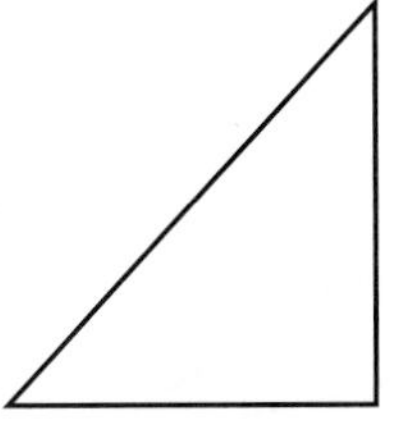

Triangle
3 sides

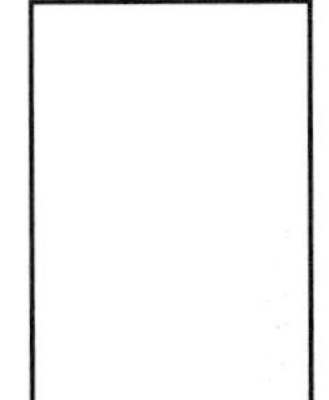

Quadrilateral
4 sides

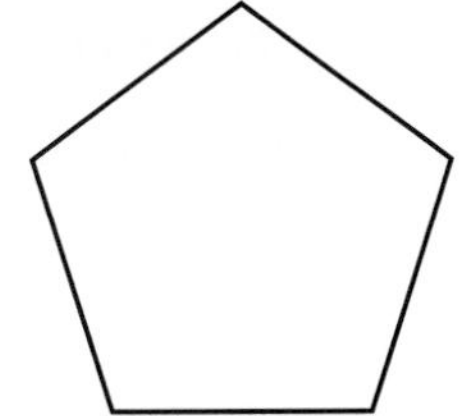

Pentagon
5 sides

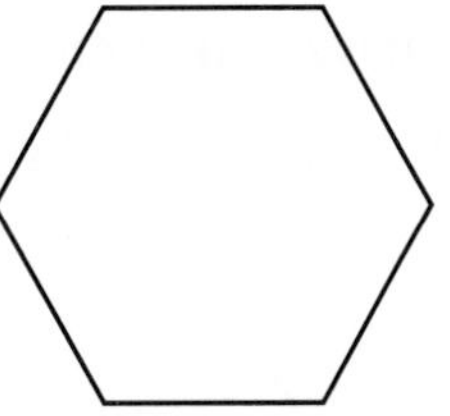

Hexagon
6 sides

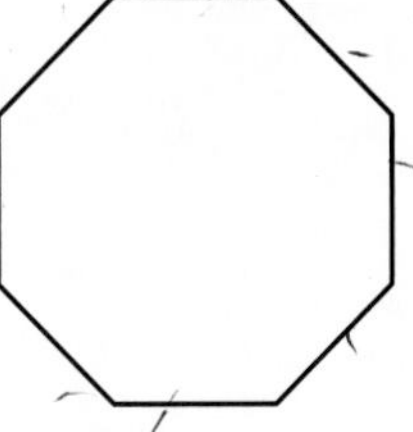

Octagon
8 sides

TAKS Problem Solving

19. The building to the right is named for the polygon it looks like. What is the name of the polygon?

A Quadrilateral **C** Hexagon

B Pentagon **D** Octagon

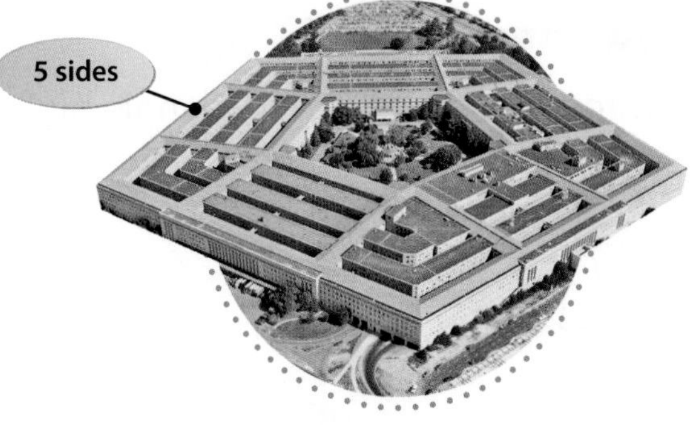

20. What rule could be used to sort these polygons?

Group A	[shapes]
Group B	[shapes]

21. Draw It Tim and Peter both are on a swimming team. In one week, Tim swam 244 laps and Peter swam 196 laps. Draw a bar diagram to show how many more laps Tim swam than Peter.

22. Carla gathered a total of 124 seashells. How many seashells would she have if she gathered 4 times that amount?

23. Tasha is hosting a party for 216 people. If 6 people can sit at each table, how many tables will Tasha need to set up?

24. Writing to Explain What do you notice about the number of sides and the number of vertices a polygon has? How many vertices would a 20-sided polygon have?

25. Which polygon does **NOT** have at least 4 sides?

F Octagon **H** Quadrilateral

G Hexagon **J** Triangle

Lesson

14-4

TEKS 4.8C: Use essential attributes to define two- and three-dimensional geometric figures.
TEKS 4.8A: Identify and describe right, acute, and obtuse angles.

Triangles

How can you classify triangles?

Triangles can be classified by their sides.

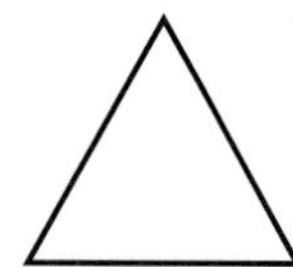

Equilateral Triangle
3 equal sides

Isosceles Triangle
2 equal sides

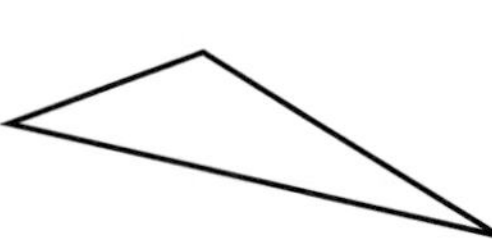

Scalene Triangle
0 equal sides

Guided Practice*

Do you know HOW?

In **1** through **4**, classify each triangle by its sides and then by its angles.

1. 

2. 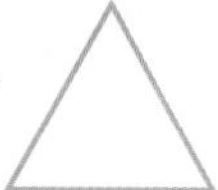

3. 

4. 

Do you UNDERSTAND?

5. Can a triangle have more than one obtuse angle? Explain.

6. Can you draw a right isosceles triangle? If so, draw an example.

7. Can a triangle have more than one right angle? If so, draw an example.

Independent Practice

In **8** through **16,** classify each triangle by its sides and then by its angles.

8. 

9. 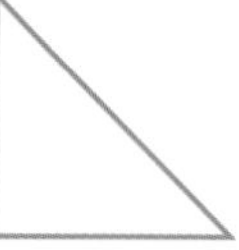

10. 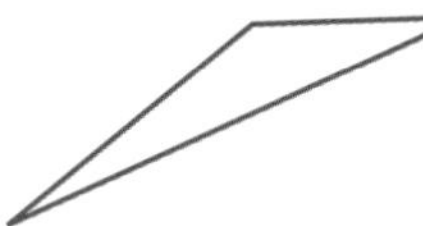

11. 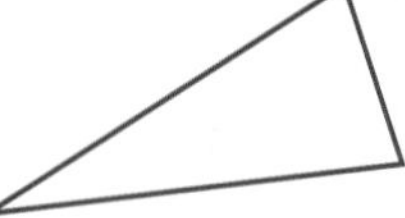

12. 

13. 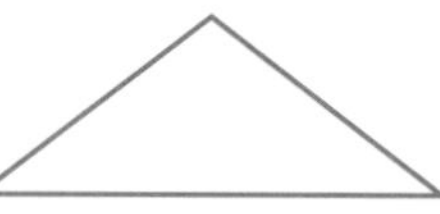

14. 

15. 

16. 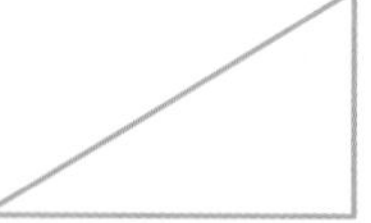

*For another example, see Set D on page 321.

Triangles also can be classified by their angles.

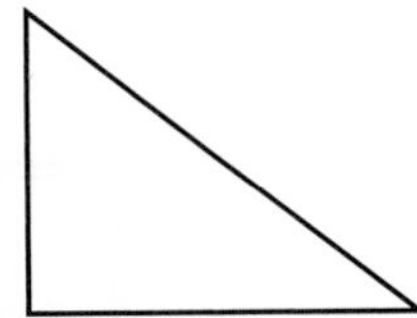

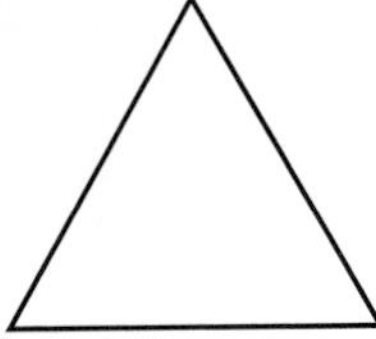

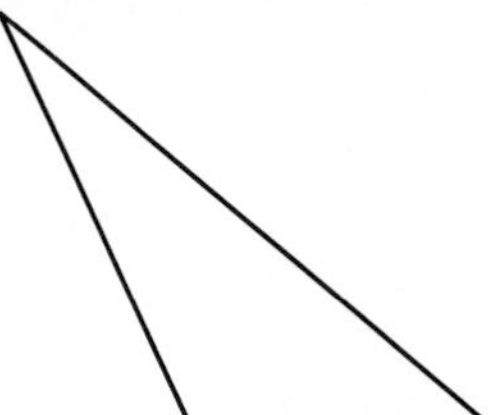

A right triangle has one right angle.

An acute triangle has three acute angles. All of its angles measure less than 90°.

An obtuse triangle has one obtuse angle. One angle has a measure greater than 90°.

In **17** through **19**, classify each triangle by its sides and then by its angles.

17.

18.

19.

TAKS Problem Solving

20. Reasoning Use the diagram below. If the backyard is an equilateral triangle, what do you know about the lengths of the other two sides?

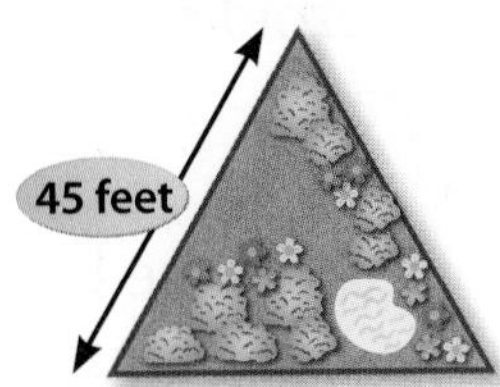

21. If Chris uses a third line to make a triangle, what kind of triangle will it be?

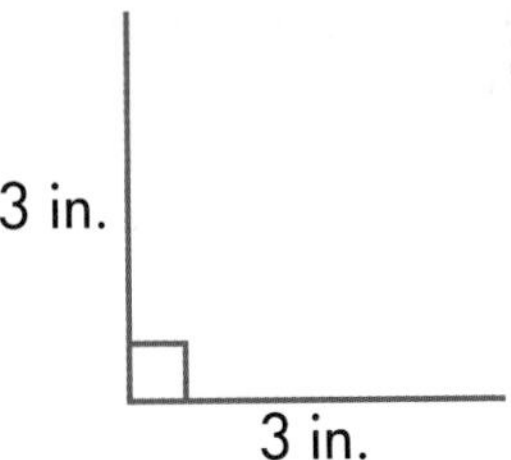

22. Writing to Explain Is an equilateral triangle always an isosceles triangle?

23. When you multiply any number by 1, what is the product?

Use the diagram at the right for **24**.

24. Which is the best name for this muscle group shown at the right?

A Right muscle group

B Scalene muscle group

C Isosceles muscle group

D Equilateral muscle group

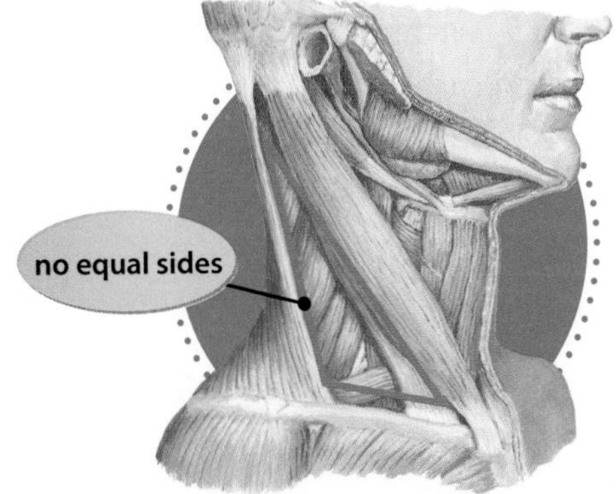

Lesson
14-5

TEKS 4.8C: Use essential attributes to define two- and three-dimensional geometric figures.
TEKS 4.8: Identify and describe attributes of geometric figures using formal geometric language.

Quadrilaterals

How can you classify quadrilaterals?

Quadrilaterals can be classified by their angles or pairs of sides.

Other Examples

A rhombus is a quadrilateral that has opposite sides that are parallel and all of its sides are the same length.

A trapezoid is a quadrilateral with only one pair of parallel sides.

Guided Practice*

Do you know HOW?

In **1** through **4**, write all the names you can use for each quadrilateral.

1. 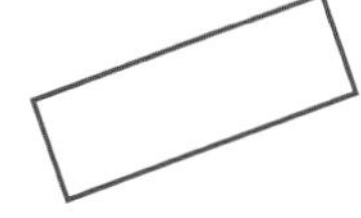

2. 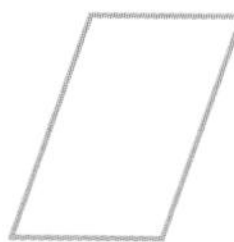

3. 

4.  

Do you UNDERSTAND?

5. What is true about all quadrilaterals?

6. Why is a trapezoid not a parallelogram?

7. What is the difference between a square and a rhombus?

Independent Practice

In **8** through **15**, write all the names you can use for each quadrilateral.

8. 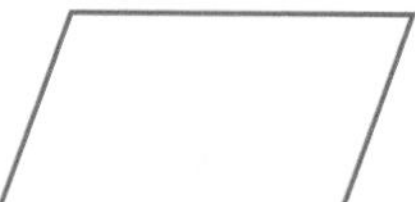

9. 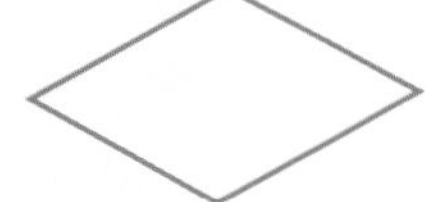

10. 

11. 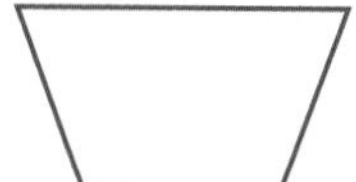

*For another example, see Set D on page 321.

A parallelogram has 2 pairs of parallel sides.

A rectangle has 4 right angles. It is also a parallelogram.

A square has 4 right angles and all sides are the same length. It is a parallelogram, rectangle, and rhombus.

12. 

13. 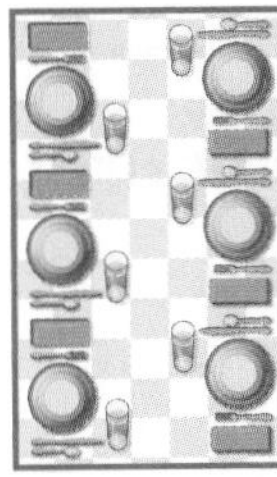

14. 

15. 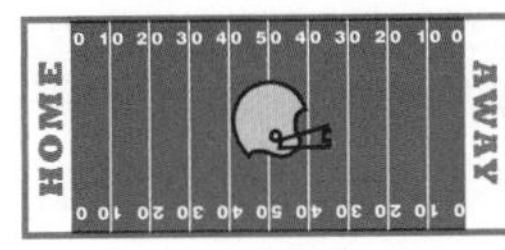

TAKS Problem Solving

16. A quadrilateral has two pairs of parallel sides and exactly 4 right angles. What quadrilateral is being described?

17. Reasoning Is it possible for a quadrilateral to be both a rhombus and a parallelogram?

18. Algebra What shape comes next in the pattern?

19. Writing to Explain All the sides of an equilateral triangle are congruent. Is an equilateral triangle also a rhombus? Explain.

20. Valley Ridge Elementary has 108 fourth-grade students and 4 fourth-grade teachers. If split equally, how many students should be in each class?

21. If a theater can hold 235 people for one showing of a movie and they show the movie 5 times a day, how many people could view the movie in one day?

22. In math class, Mr. Meyer drew a quadrilateral on the board. It had just one set of parallel sides and no right angles. What shape was it?

A Square
B Rhombus
C Rectangle
D Trapezoid

23. Jamie went to exercise at a swimming pool. The length of the pool was 25 yards. If she swam a total of 6 laps, how many yards did Jamie swim?

? yards

25	25	25	25	25	25

Length of pool

Lesson

14-6

TEKS 4.8C: Use essential attributes to define two- and three-dimensional geometric figures.
TEKS 4.8: Identify and describe attributes of geometric figures using formal geometric language.

Solids

How can you describe and classify solids?

A solid figure has three dimensions —length, width, and height.

Solids can have curved surfaces.

Sphere

Cylinder

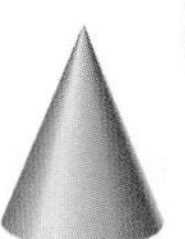

Cone

Another Example How can you build a solid figure?

A net is a pattern that can be used to make a solid.

This is a net for a cube. Each of the faces is connected to at least one other face.

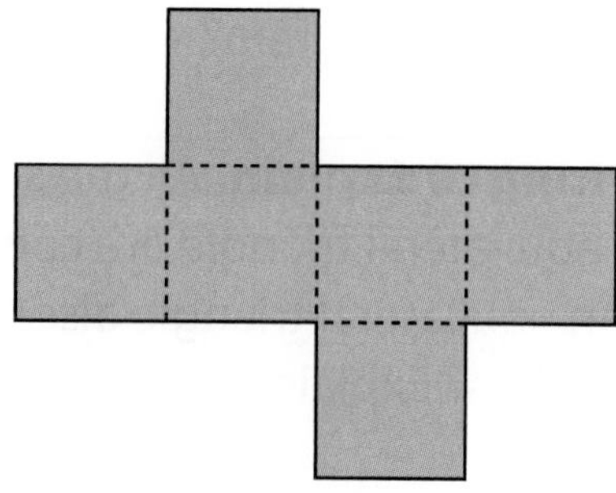

This is a net for a triangular prism.

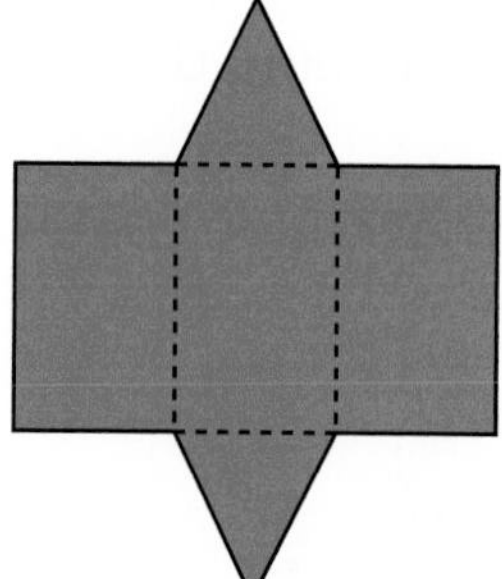

Explain It

1. Explain why the net for a cube has six squares.

2. Why does the net for a triangular prism have two triangles and three rectangles?

Some solids have all flat surfaces. They are named by referring to their faces.

face-flat surface of a solid

vertex-point where 3 or more edges meet. (plural: vertices)

edge-line segment where 2 faces meet.

rectangular prism
6 rectangular faces

cube
6 square faces

triangular prism
2 triangular faces
3 rectangular faces

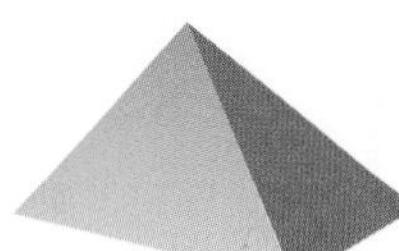

rectangular pyramid
1 rectangular face
4 triangular faces

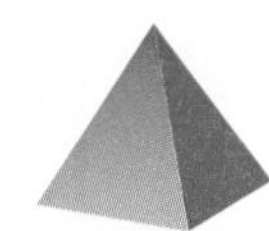

square pyramid
1 square face
4 triangular faces

Guided Practice*

Do you know HOW?

For **1** through **4**, identify each solid.

1. 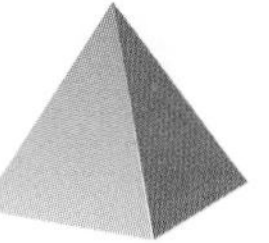

2. 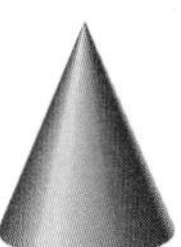

3. 

4. 

Do you UNDERSTAND?

5. Which solid figure has four triangular faces and one square face?

6. Why is a cube a special kind of rectangular prism?

7. Does a sphere have any edges or vertices? Explain.

Independent Practice

Leveled Practice For **8** through **10**, copy and complete the table.

	Solid Figure	Faces	Edges	Vertices	Shape(s) of Faces
8.	Rectangular prism				6 rectangles
9.	Cube	6			
10.	Rectangular pyramid		8		

For another example, see Set E on page 321.

Independent Practice

In **11** through **14**, trace each net and cut it out. Fold on the dashed line segments and tape together to make a solid. Name each solid figure.

11.

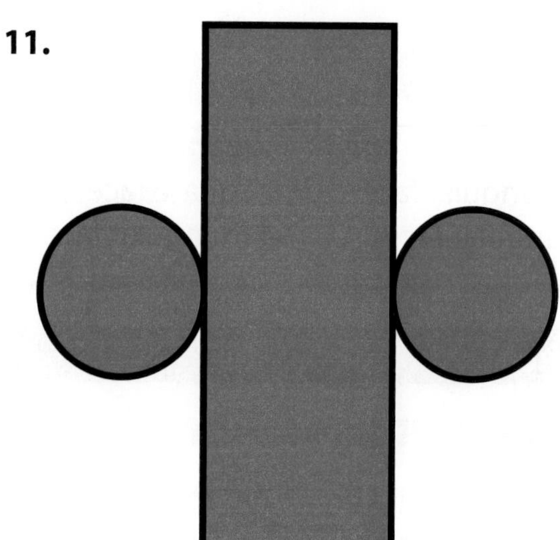

12.

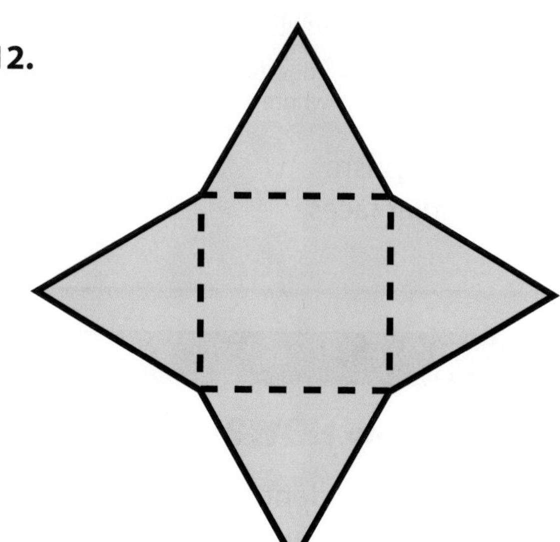

13.

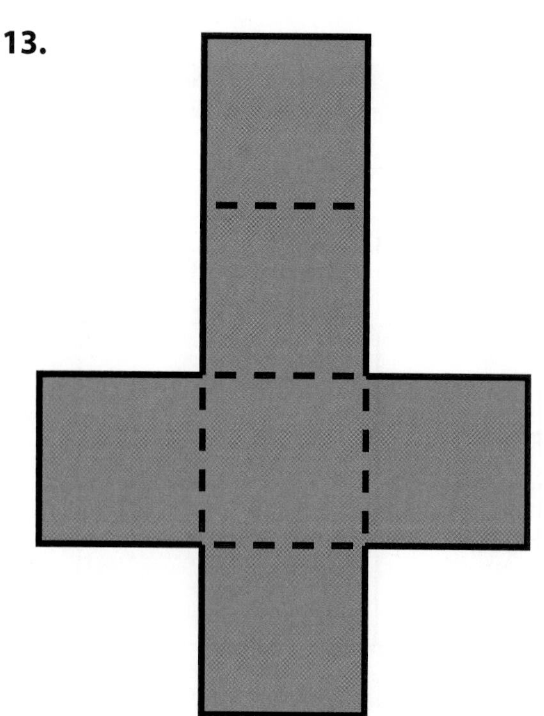

14.

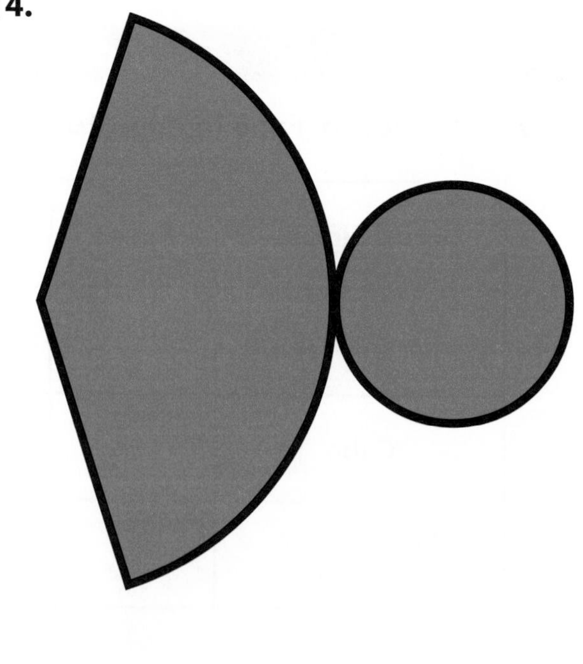

TAKS Problem Solving

For **15** through **18**, tell what solid figure best represents each object.

15. 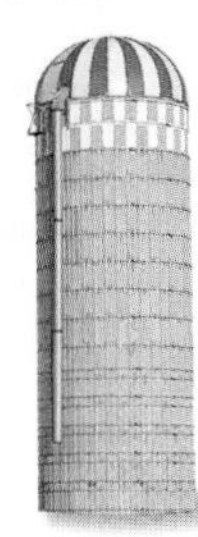

16. 

17. 

18. 

19. Todd's father offered to drive some members of the soccer team to a game. His car can fit 4 players. He drives 10 players from his home to the game. How many one-way trips must he make if he stays to watch the game?

Draw a picture to show each one-way trip.

20. **Writing to Explain** The length of the base of each side of the Great Pyramid of Giza is 756 feet long. If the Great Pyramid of Giza is a square pyramid, what is the distance around the base of the pyramid?

For **21** and **22**, use the rectangular pyramid shown at the right.

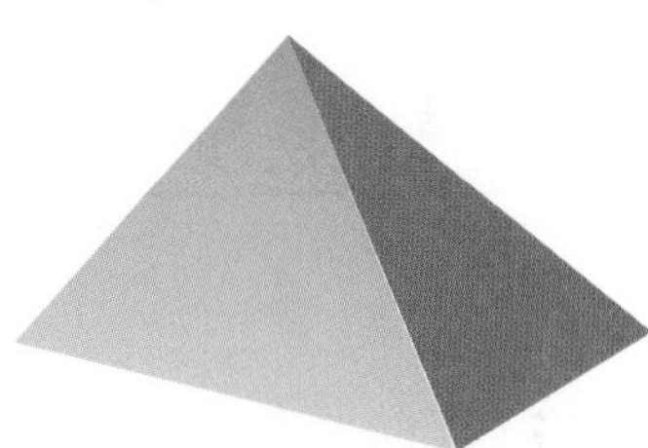

21. How many edges does the rectangular pyramid have?

22. How many vertices does the rectangular pyramid have?

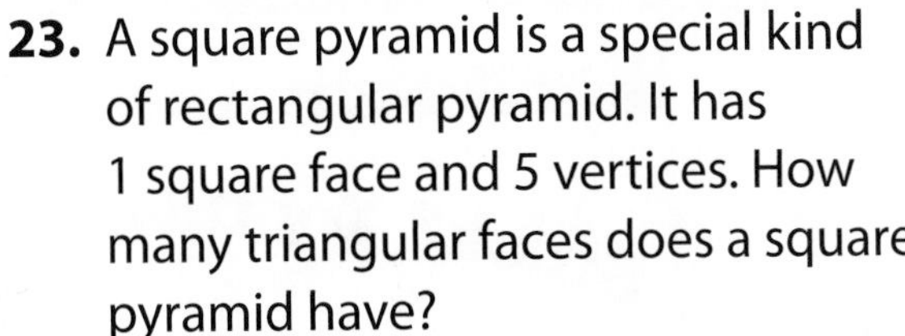

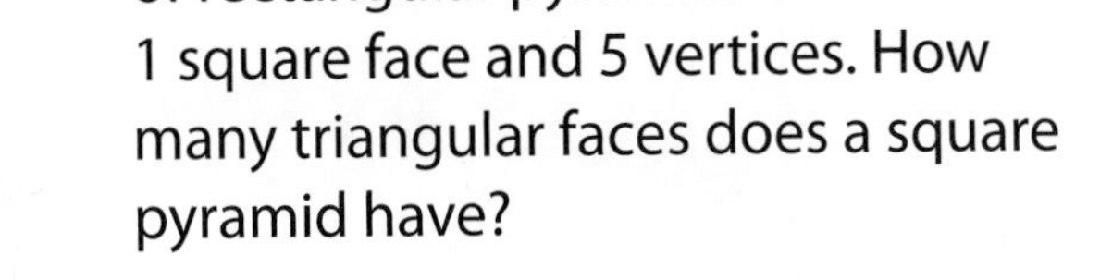

23. A square pyramid is a special kind of rectangular pyramid. It has 1 square face and 5 vertices. How many triangular faces does a square pyramid have?

24. Which number is **NOT** between 0.5 and $\frac{3}{4}$ on a number line?

A $\frac{5}{8}$

B 0.6

C $\frac{13}{16}$

D 0.7

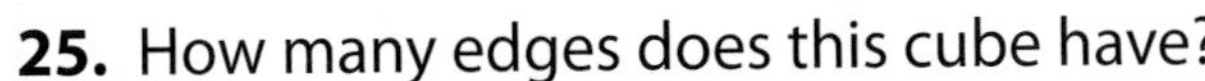

25. How many edges does this cube have?

F 6 edges

G 10 edges

H 8 edges

J 12 edges

26. In one soccer season, the Cougars scored six times as many goals as Jason made all season. Jason scored 12 goals. How many goals did the Cougars score throughout the season?

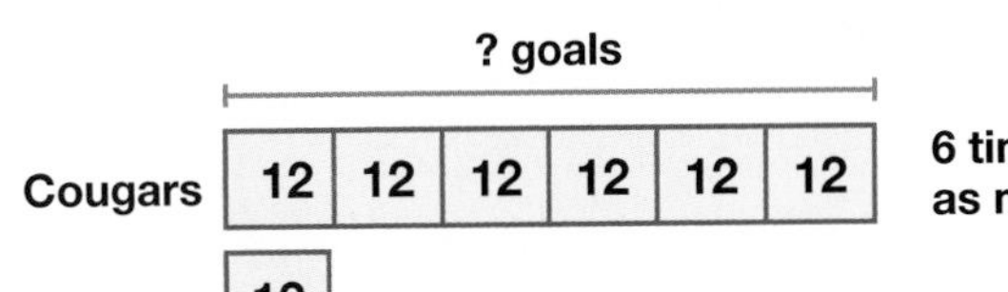

Lesson

14-7

TEKS 4.14C Select or develop an appropriate problem-solving plan or strategy, including drawing a picture, looking for a pattern, systematic guessing and checking, acting it out, making a table, working a simpler problem, or working backwards to solve a problem. Also **TEKS 4.16A**

Problem Solving

Make and Test Generalizations

What is true about all of these shapes?

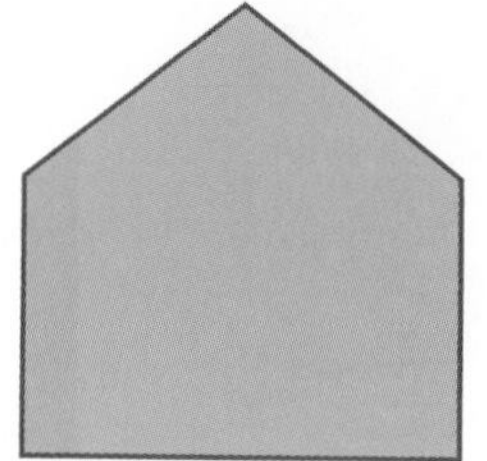

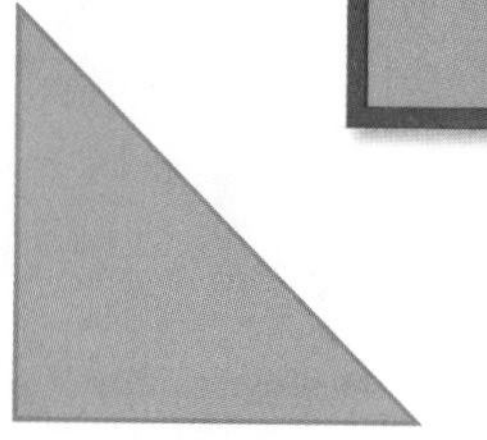

Guided Practice*

Do you know HOW?

1. Look at each group of three letters below. Give a generalization for each group of letters that does not apply to the other group of three letters.

EFT	COS

Do you UNDERSTAND?

2. Writing to Explain Is the generalization that every four sided polygon has at least one right angle correct? If not, draw a picture to show why not.

3. Write a Problem Select 3 items and make two correct generalizations about them.

Independent Practice

Solve.

4. Look at each group of numbers below. Compare the size of the factors to each product. What generalization can you make about factors and products for whole numbers?

$6 \times 8 = 48$ $46 \times 5 = 230$ $1 \times 243 = 243$

5. Write the factors for 8, 16, and 20. What generalization can you make about all multiples of 4?

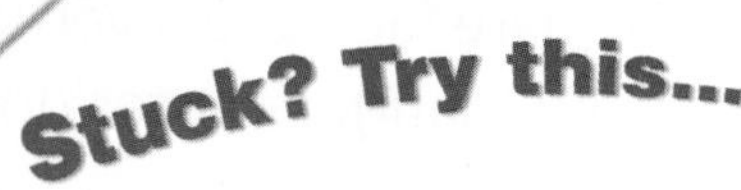

- What do I know?
- What diagram can I use to help understand the problem?
- Can I use addition, subtraction, multiplication, or division?
- Is all of my work correct?
- Did I answer the right question?
- Is my answer reasonable?

*For another example, see Set F on page 321.

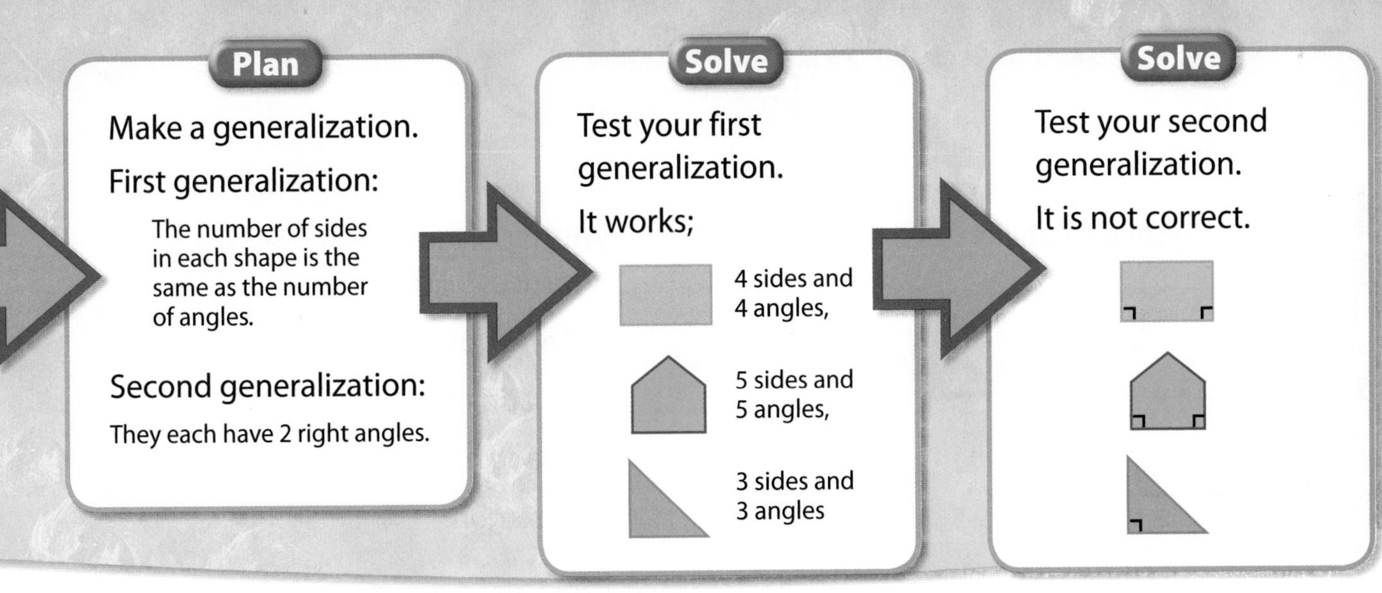

Plan
Make a generalization.
First generalization:
The number of sides in each shape is the same as the number of angles.
Second generalization:
They each have 2 right angles.
Solve
Test your first generalization.
It works;
4 sides and 4 angles,
5 sides and 5 angles,
3 sides and 3 angles
Solve
Test your second generalization.
It is not correct.

6. What generalization can you make about each of the polygons at the right?

A All sides of each polygon are the same length.

B All polygons have 5 sides.

C All polygons have 4 angles.

D All polygons have 3 angles.

7. The factors for 3 and 6 are shown in the table to the right. Jan concluded if you double a number, then you double the number of factors. Is Jan correct? Why or why not?

Number	3	6
Factors	1, 3	1, 2, 3, 6

8. How many faces does a rectangular pyramid have?

9. How many acute angles can an isosceles triangle have?

10. Look at the pattern below. Draw the shape that would come next.

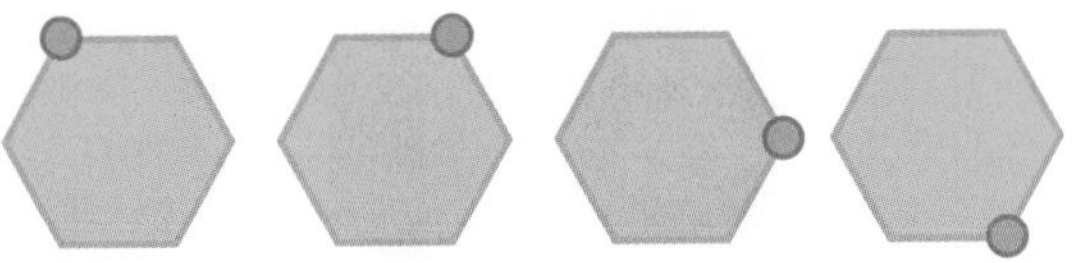

11. What generalization could be made about the triangles below?

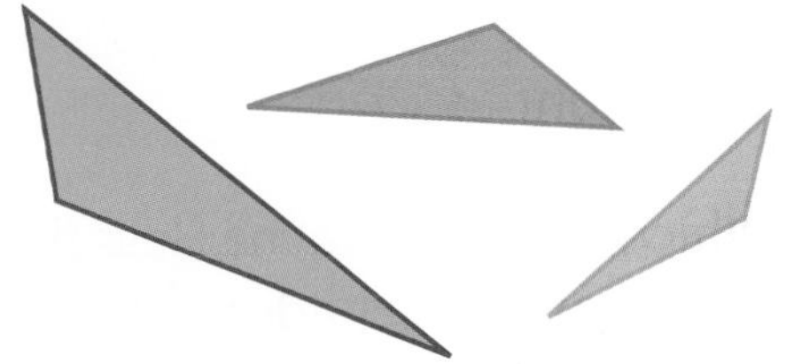

12. **Writing to Explain** Susan said that all squares are rectangles and therefore all rectangles are squares. Is Susan correct? Why or why not?

13. Michael lives on the 22nd floor of a 25 story building. If each floor is 12 feet in height, how many feet above ground level is Michael's apartment?

TAKS Test Prep

1. Which stick is parallel to stick S? (14-1)

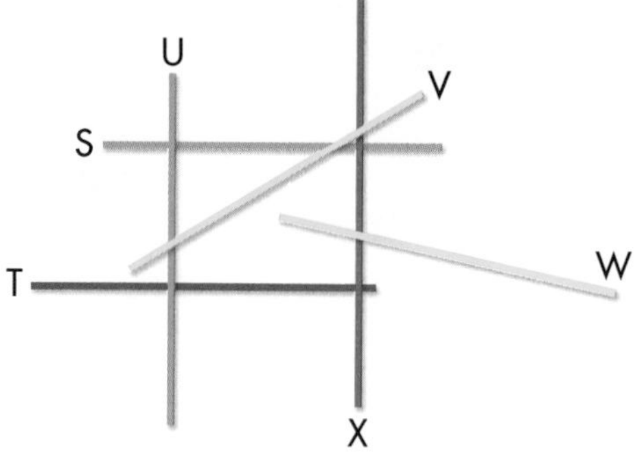

A Stick T

B Stick U

C Stick W

D Stick X

2. Which type of angle is angle A? (14-2)

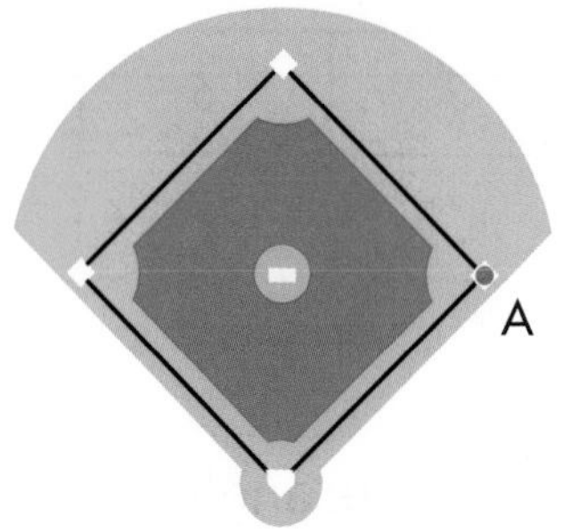

F Acute

G Obtuse

H Right

J Straight

3. Which quadrilateral has less than 2 pairs of parallel sides? (14-5)

A Square

B Parallelogram

C Trapezoid

D Rhombus

4. Which polygon has more than 5 vertices? (14-3)

F Pentagon

G Quadrilateral

H Triangle

J Hexagon

5. Laney used drinking straws in art to form a figure that had perpendicular sides. Which could be her figure? (14-1)

A 

B 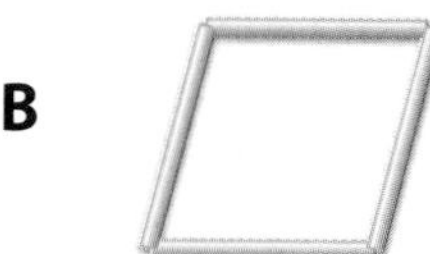

C 

D 

6. Which best describes a tissue box? (14-6)

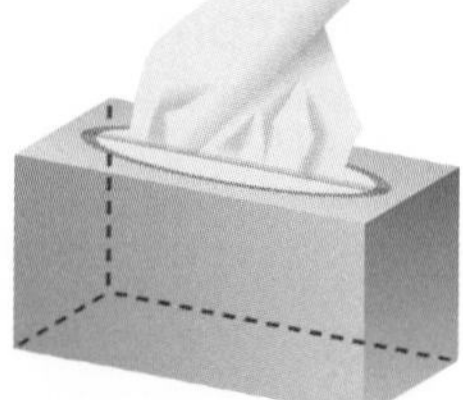

F 5 faces and 12 edges

G 6 faces and 8 edges

H 6 faces and 12 edges

J 12 faces and 6 edges

7. Which geometric term best describes the light that shines from a flashlight? (14-2)

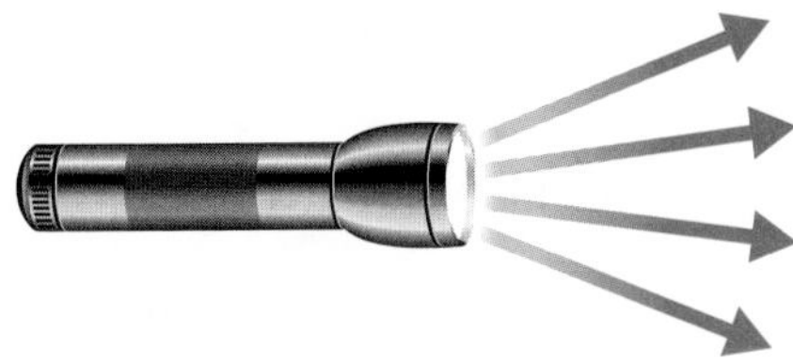

A Point

B Ray

C Line segment

D Plane

8. Which geometric terms best describe the triangle of the tepee below? (14-4)

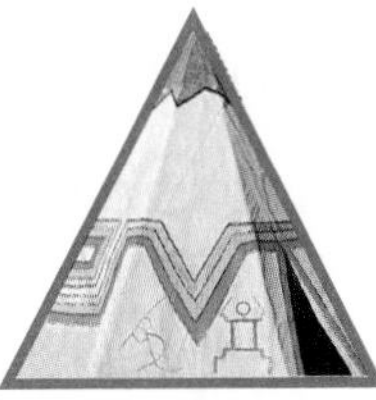

F Isosceles; acute

G Isosceles; right

H Equilateral; obtuse

J Scalene; acute

9. What solid figure can be made from the net shown at right? (14-6)

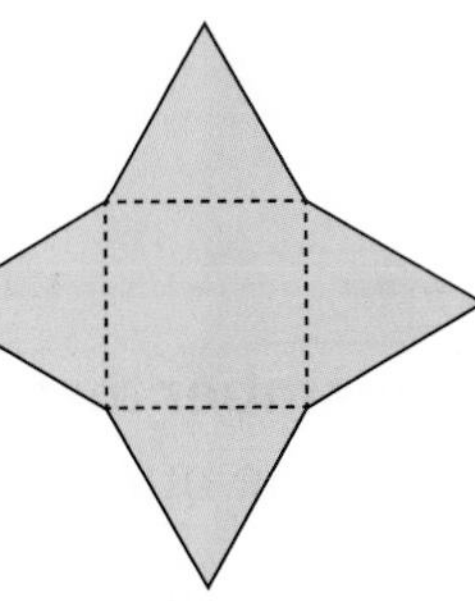

A Triangular pyramid

B Square pyramid

C Rectangular pyramid

D Rectangular prism

10. Which triangle has no congruent sides? (14-4)

F Isosceles

G Scalene

H Equilateral

J Straight

11. Which statement is true about the quadrilaterals shown below? (14-5)

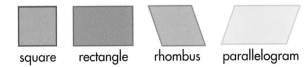

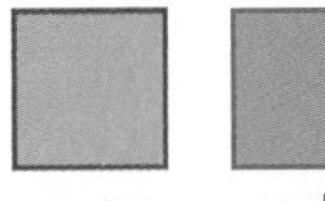

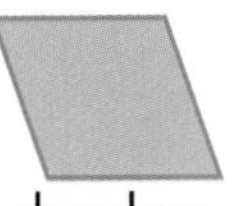

A They are all rhombuses.

B They are all squares.

C They are all rectangles.

D They are all parallelograms.

12. Thomas chose these shapes.

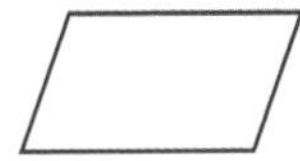
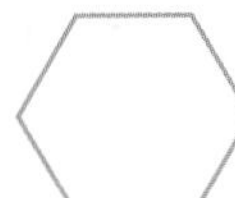
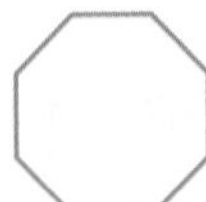

He said the following shapes did not belong with the ones he chose.

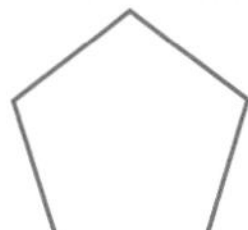
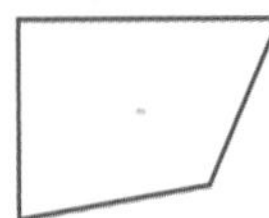

Which is the best description of the shapes Thomas chose? (14-7)

F Polygons with more than 4 sides

G Polygons with parallel sides

H Polygons with all sides congruent

J Polygons with a right angle

13. **Griddable Response** How many sides does an octagon have? (14-3)

Set A, pages 302–303

Pairs of lines are given special names.

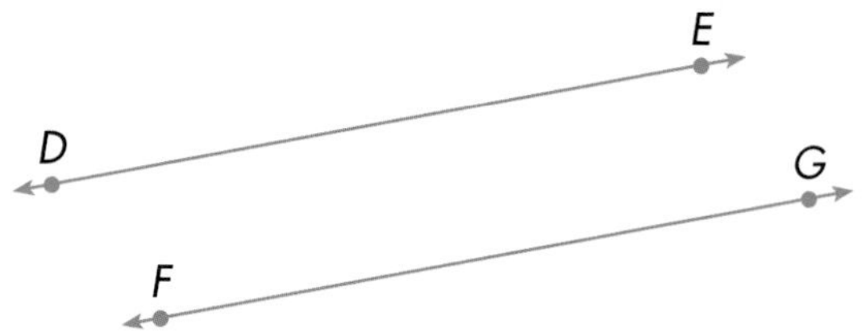

Line *DE* and line *FG* are parallel lines.

Remember that perpendicular lines intersect.

Match each term on the left with the correct image on the right.

1. ____ parallel lines **a**

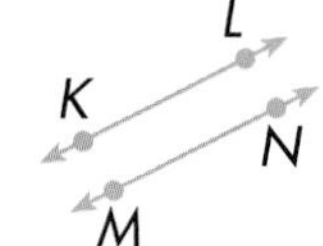

2. ____ point **b**

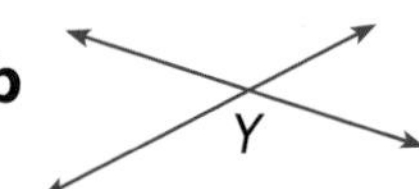

3. ____ intersecting lines **c** • *B*

Set B, pages 304–305

Geometric terms are used to describe figures.

A ray has one endpoint and continues on forever in one direction.

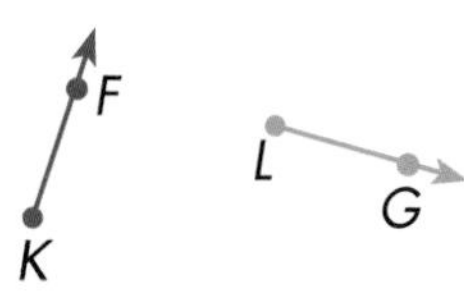

An angle is formed by two rays or line segments with a common endpoint.

S, *T*, *U*

Remember that a line segment does not continue beyond its endpoints.

Use geometric terms to describe what is shown.

1.

2.

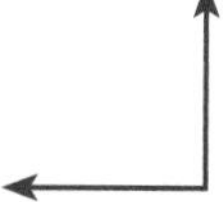

3.

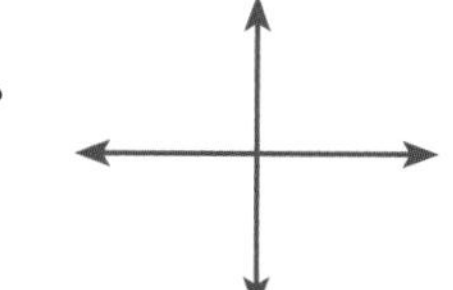

4.

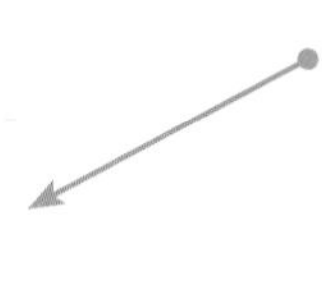

Set C, pages 306–307

A polygon is a closed figure made up of line segments called sides. Each side meets at a point called a vertex.

Count the number of sides and vertices to identify the polygon.

side

vertex

The polygon is a hexagon.

Remember that polygons have the same number of sides and vertices.

Write the number of sides and vertices of each polygon.

1. octagon **2.** square

3. triangle **4.** trapezoid

Set D, pages 308–311

Triangles can be classified by their sides and angles.

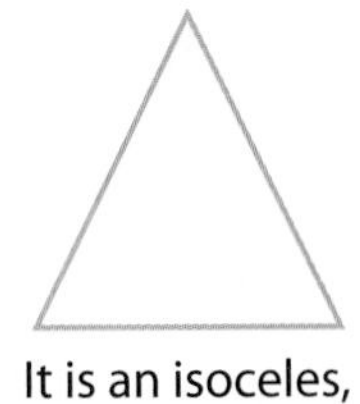

It is an isoceles, acute triangle.

Name the quadrilateral.

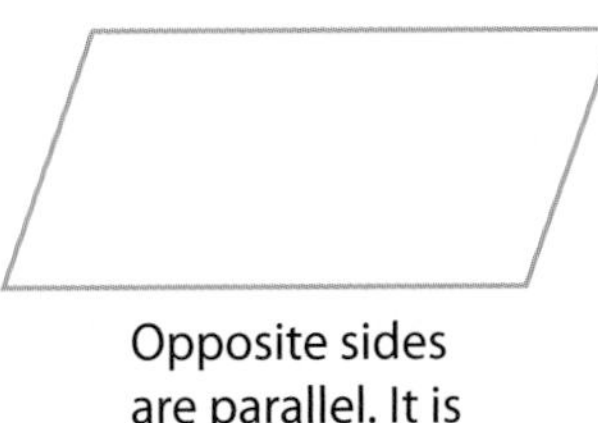

Opposite sides are parallel. It is a parallelogram.

Remember that a quadrilateral can be a rectangle, square, trapezoid, parallelogram, or rhombus.

Classify each shape by its sides and angles.

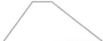

1. 
2.
3.
4. 

Set E, pages 312–315

Identify the solid figure. It has a square base. How many faces, edges, and vertices does this solid figure have?

It is a square pyramid. It has 5 faces, 8 edges, and 5 vertices.

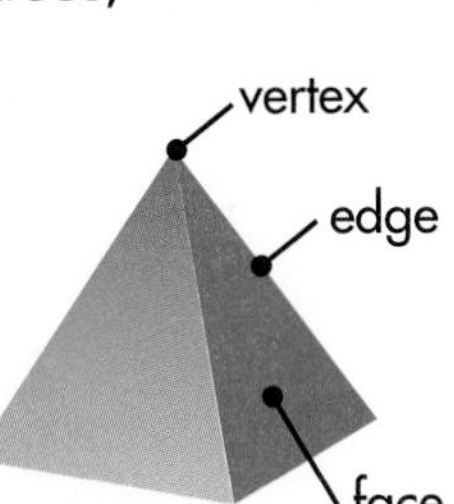

Remember that some solid figures have curved surfaces.

1. How many faces does a rectangular prism have?
2. How many edges does a cube have?
3. How many vertices does a cylinder have?

Set F, pages 316–317

What is true about all of these shapes?

 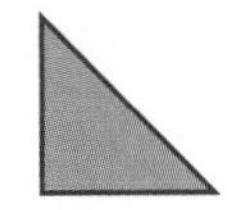 

The number of sides in each is the same as the number of angles. Test your generalization.

4 sides, 4 angles

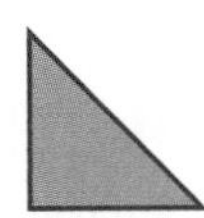

3 sides, 3 angles

4 sides, 4 angles

Remember to test your generalizations.

1. Look at each group of numbers below. Give a generalization for each group of numbers that does not apply to the other group of three numbers.

1 4 7   **3 6 9**

Topics 1–14

Spiral Review

Number and Operations

1. Which fraction does the letter A represent on the number line?

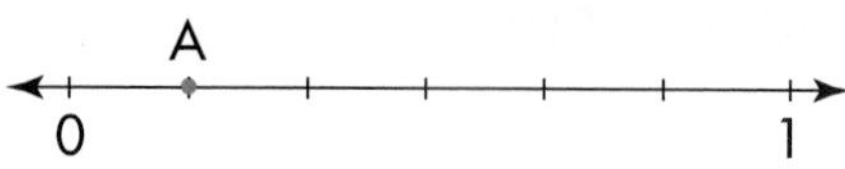

A $\frac{1}{6}$ **C** $\frac{3}{6}$

B $\frac{2}{6}$ **D** $\frac{4}{6}$

2. Which shows $\frac{5}{6}$ shaded?

F 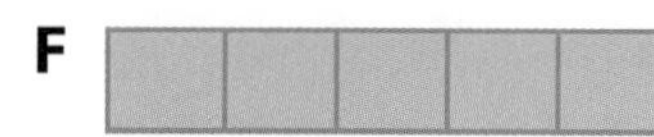

G

H

J

3. What is 4,392 rounded to the nearest thousand?

4. A freight train has 100 cars. Thirty-four of the cars are oil tanker cars. Write a fraction and a decimal to show what part of the train is made up of oil tanker cars.

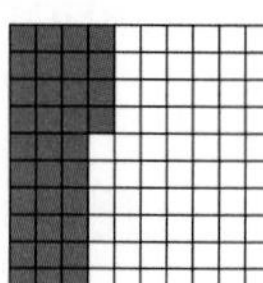

5. Write these numbers in order from least to greatest.

63,098 64,632 63,908 64,236

6. **Writing to Explain** Explain how to round 47,723 to the nearest thousand. Give the answer.

Geometry and Measurement

7. Which pair of lines never intersect?

A Parallel lines

B Intersecting lines

C Perpendicular lines

D All line pairs intersect

8. How many lines of symmetry does the figure to the right have?

F One

G Two

H Three

J Four

9. How many vertices does a square pyramid have?

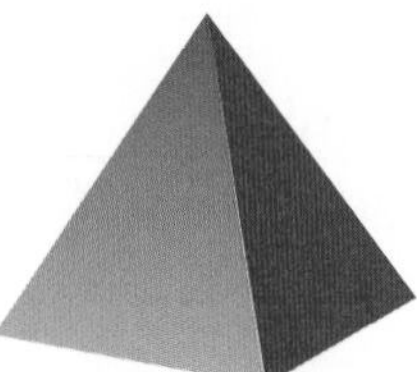

10. A square has a side that is 8 centimeters in length. What is the perimeter?

11. Describe how a square is different from a trapezoid.

12. In the morning, the temperature was 2°C. Four hours later it was 15°C. How many degrees did the temperature rise?

13. **Writing to Explain** Elyse made a sign that had 7 sides. How many angles did the sign have? Explain.

Probability and Statistics

14. Mia tosses a number cube that has the numbers 10, 20, 30, 45, 51, and 60 on its sides. What is the probability that Mia will toss an even number?

A $\frac{3}{4}$ **C** $\frac{4}{10}$

B $\frac{4}{6}$ **D** $\frac{5}{60}$

15. In 10 spins, which color will the spinner most likely point to the greatest number of times?

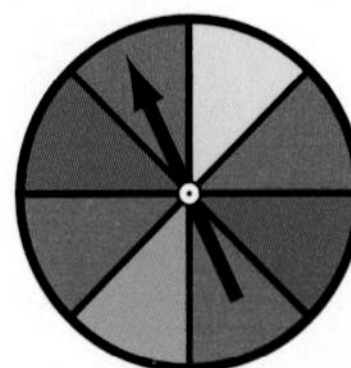

Use the bar graph for **16** through **18**.

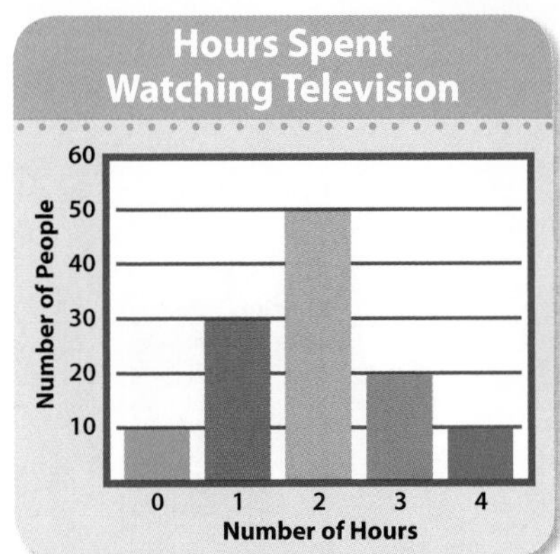

16. How many more people watch 3 hours of television than 4 hours of television?

17. How many more people watch 2 hours of television a day than watch no television at all?

18. **Writing to Explain** Explain how you know if more or less people watch 0 hours of television or 4 hours of television.

Algebraic Thinking

19. Which equation shows 649 decreased by 128?

F $649 - 128 = n$

G $649 + 128 = n$

H $128 + 649 = n$

J $128 - 649 = n$

20. Which number sentence is **NOT** true?

A $36 \div 4 = 9$

B $45 \div 9 = 5$

C $45 \div 9 = 6$

D $54 \div 6 = 9$

21. How do you evaluate the expression $(20 + 4) \div 6$?

22. How many cubes are needed to build the 7th figure if the pattern continues? Use cubes to help solve the problem.

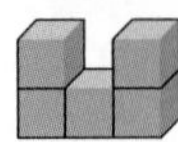

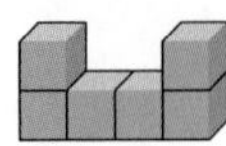

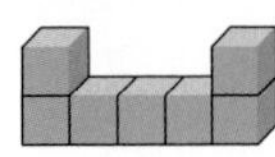

23. **Writing to Explain** Is the solution of $6 + d = 42$ greater than or less than 37?

Topic
15
Transformations, Symmetry, and Congruence
1
The Hall of Mirrors in Versailles, France, contains 357 mirrors. How long is the room? You will find out in Lesson 15-2.
2
How many lines of symmetry does the Alamo have? You will find out in Lesson 15-5.

3

In this M.C. Escher drawing, what are some of the ways these horses have been moved? You will find out in Lesson 15-1.

Review What You Know!

Vocabulary

Choose the best term from the box.

• line	• ray	• quadrilateral
• line segment	• rhombus	• triangle

1. A polygon with three sides is known as a ?.
2. A part of a line that has one endpoint is a ?.
3. A four-sided polygon in which opposite sides are parallel, and all sides are the same length is a ?.
4. A ? is a straight path of points that goes on forever in two directions.

Solid Figures

Name the solid figure for each object.

5. 
6. 
7. 

Shapes

Identify each shape.

8. 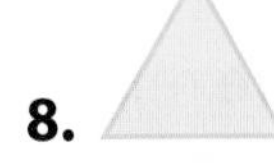
9. 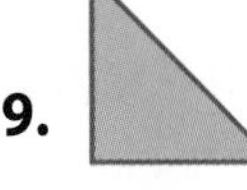
10. 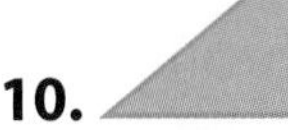
11. 
12. 
13. 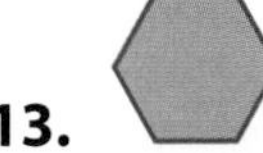
14. 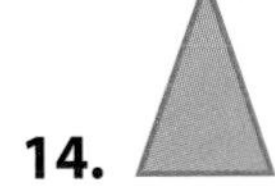
15. 
16. 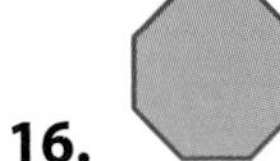
17. **Writing to Explain** Explain how the figures in Exercise 8–10 are alike and how they are different.

Lesson
15-1

TEKS 4.9A: Demonstrate translations, reflections, and rotations using concrete models.

Translations

What is one way to move a figure?

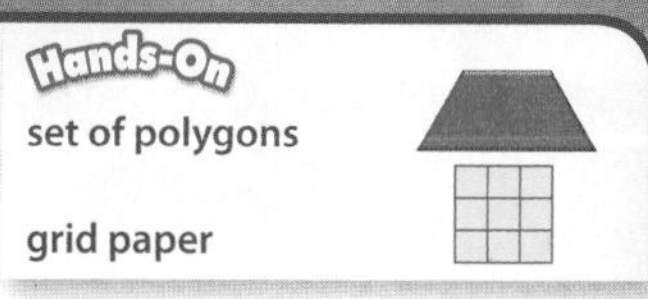

A translation moves a figure up, down, left, or right.

In this honeycomb, the hexagon is translated to the right.

Guided Practice*

Do you know HOW?

For **1** through **4**, tell if the figures are related by a translation.

1. 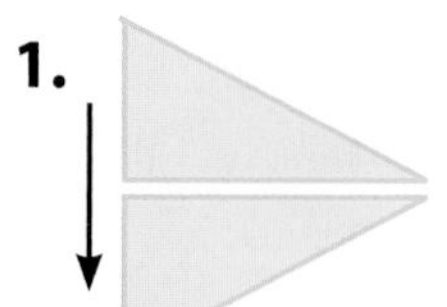

2. 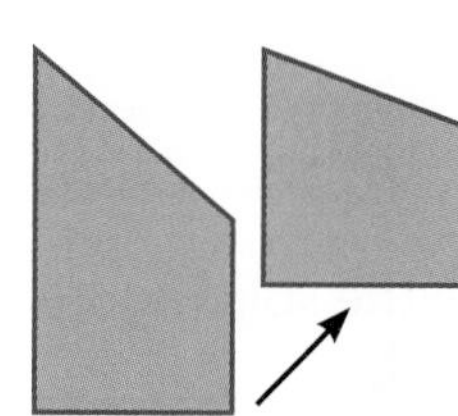

3. 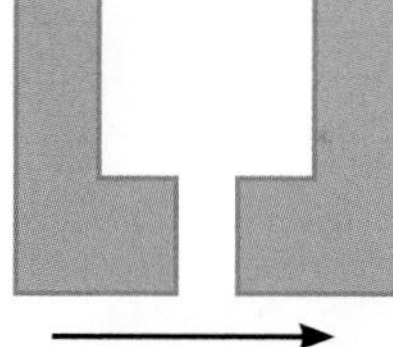

4. 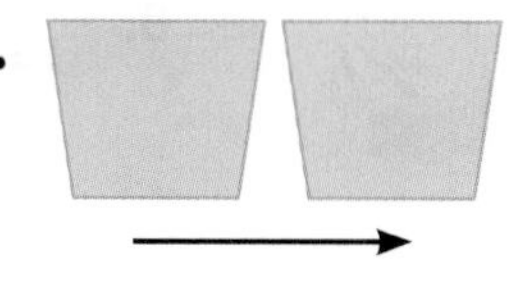

Do you UNDERSTAND?

5. Does a translation change a figure's shape or size?

6. Is moving a figure horizontally a translation?

7. Does moving a ruler across your desk affect its shape?

8. **Writing to Explain** Can a translation of a figure be done in many different directions?

Independent Practice

For **9** through **17**, tell if the figures are related by translation. You may use pattern blocks or grid paper to decide.

9. 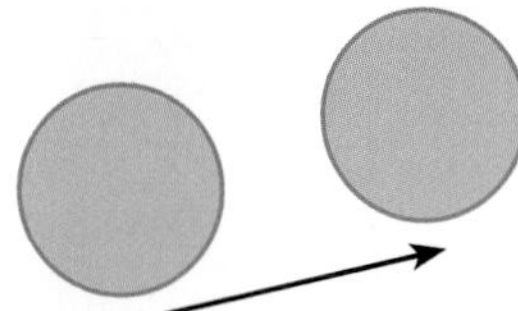

10. 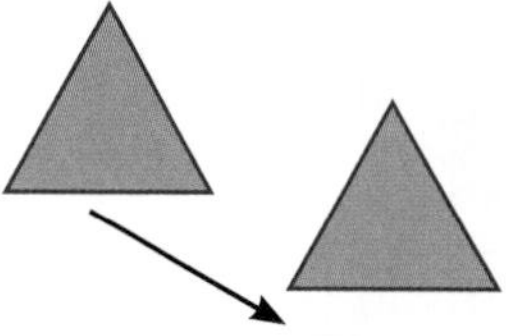

11. 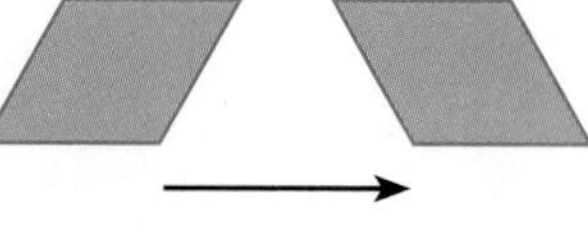

12. 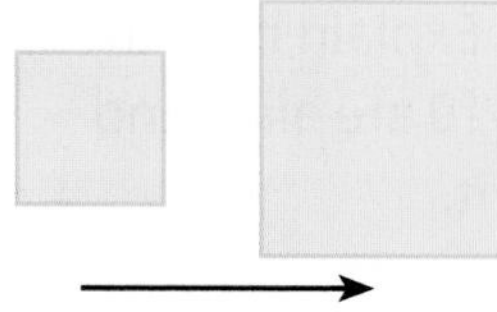

13. 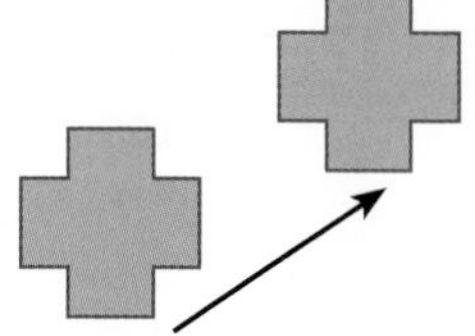

14. 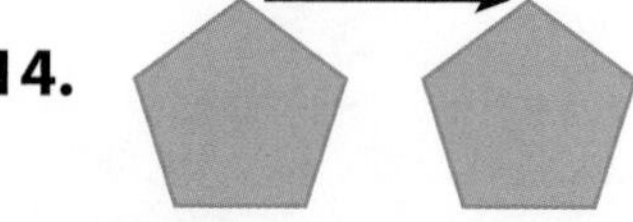

*For another example, see Set A on page 340.

When a figure is translated, the size and shape of the figure do not change.

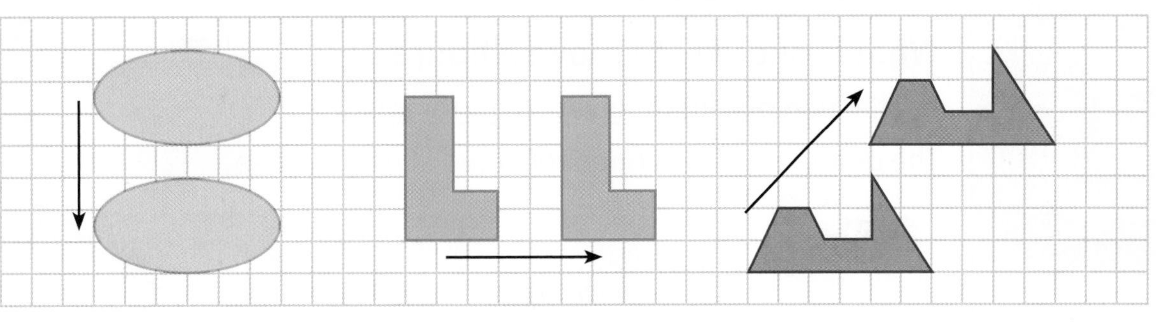

15. 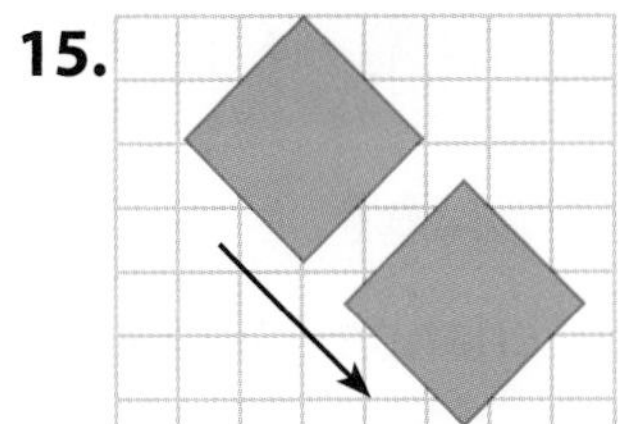

16. 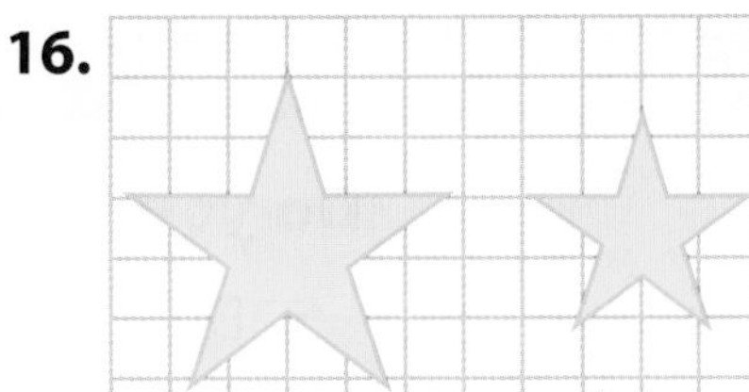

17. 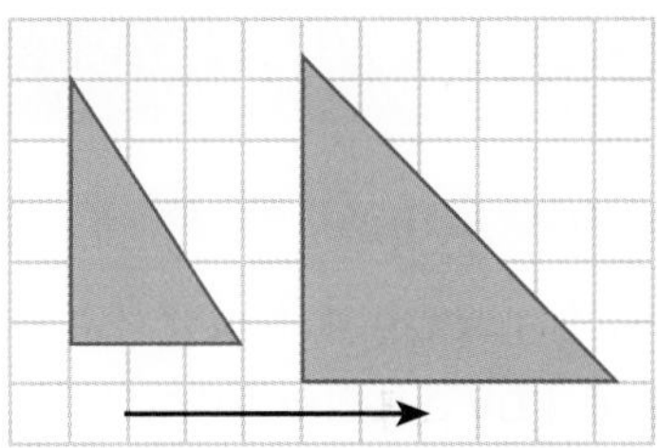

TAKS Problem Solving

For **18** and **19**, use the table at the right.

18. How many sticks would you need to make 10 kites?

19. How many kites could you make with 60 sticks?

Data

Number of Kites	Number of Sticks
1	2
2	4
3	6

20. A triangle has two congruent sides and a 140° angle. What type of triangle is it?

21. Which of the following best represents a translation?

A A bouncing ball **C** A snake slithering

B A leaf falling **D** A hockey puck sliding

22. In the M.C. Escher drawing at the right, which horse(s) are a translation of the horse labeled X?

F Horse A **H** Horses A and C

G Horse B **J** Horses A, B, and C

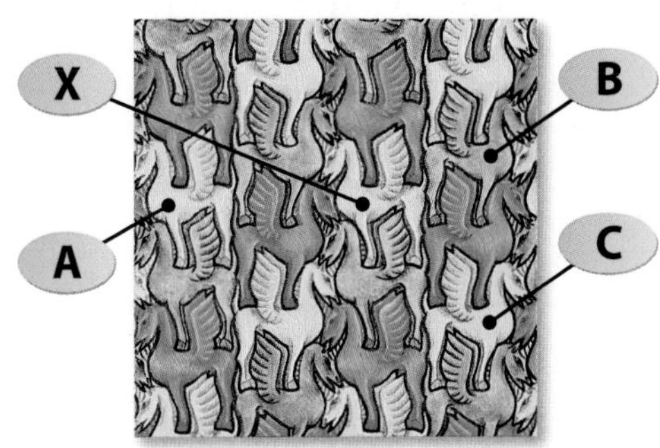

Symmetry Drawing 78 By M.C. Escher

23. On grid paper, draw a rectangle that moves to the right 3 units and then down 5 units. Is this a translation? Explain.

Lesson
15-2

TEKS 4.9A: Demonstrate translations, reflections, and rotations using concrete models.

Reflections

Hands-On
set of polygons
grid paper

What is one way to move a figure?

A reflection of a figure gives its mirror image.

The guitar below has been reflected across the line.

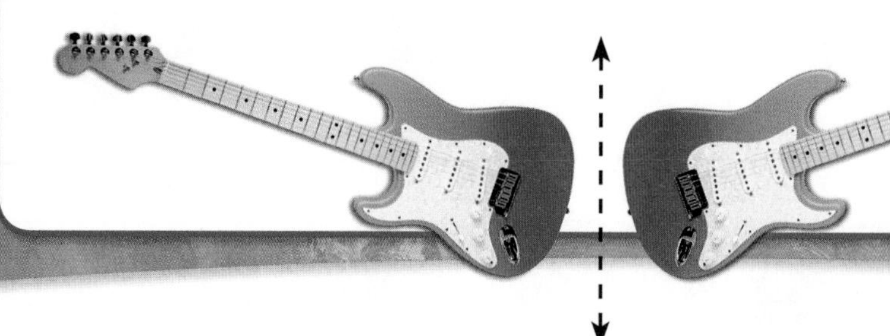

Guided Practice*

Do you know HOW?

For **1** through **4**, tell if the figures are related by a reflection.

1. 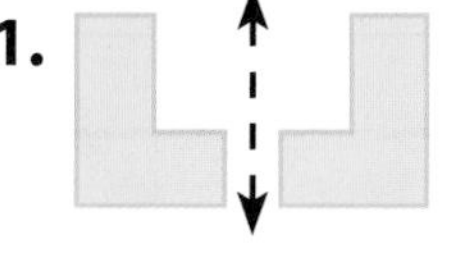

2. 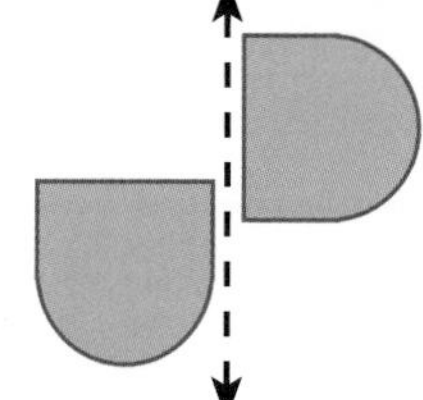

3. 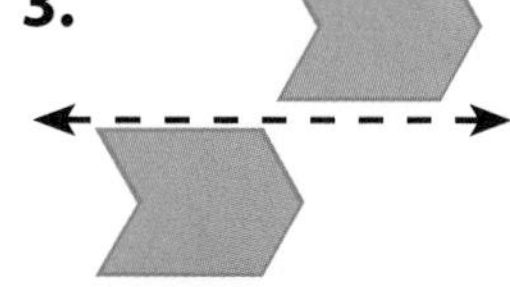

4. 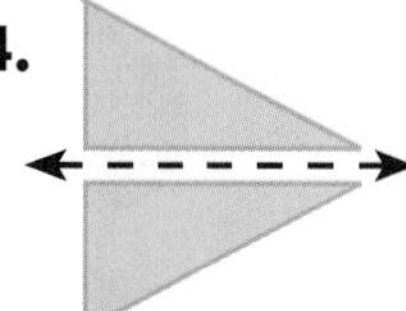

Do you UNDERSTAND?

5. Does a reflection change a figure's size or shape?

6. Writing to Explain Is the second triangle a reflection of the first triangle?

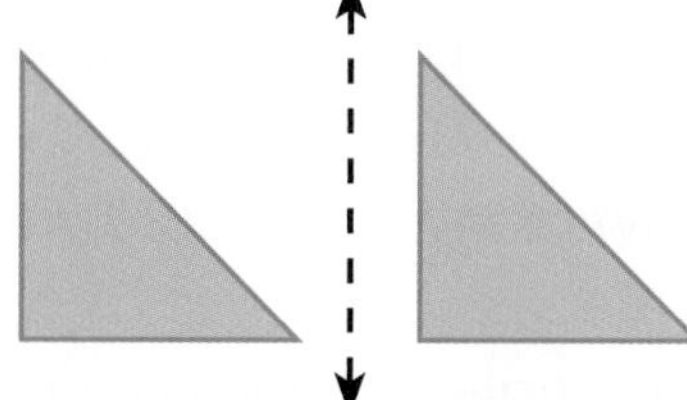

Independent Practice

For **7** through **12**, tell if the figures are related by reflection. You may use pattern blocks or grid paper to decide.

7. 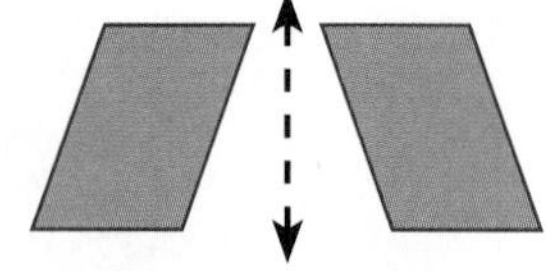

8. 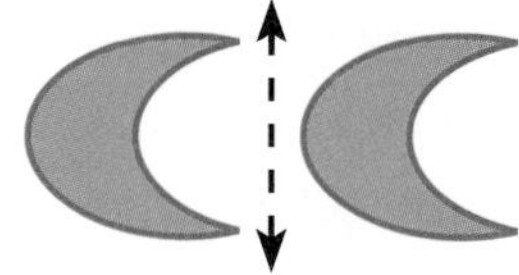

9. 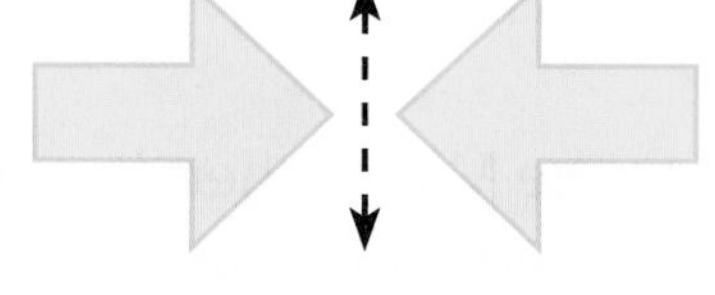

10. 

11. 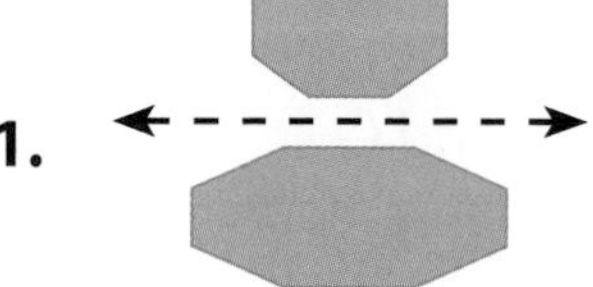

12. 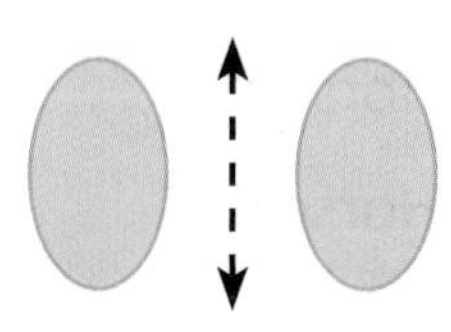

Animated Glossary, eTools
www.pearsonsuccessnet.com

*For another example, see Set B on page 340.

When a figure is reflected, the size and shape of the figure do not change.

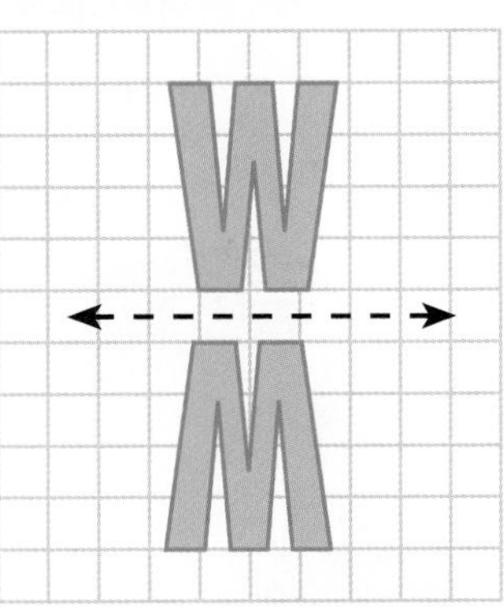

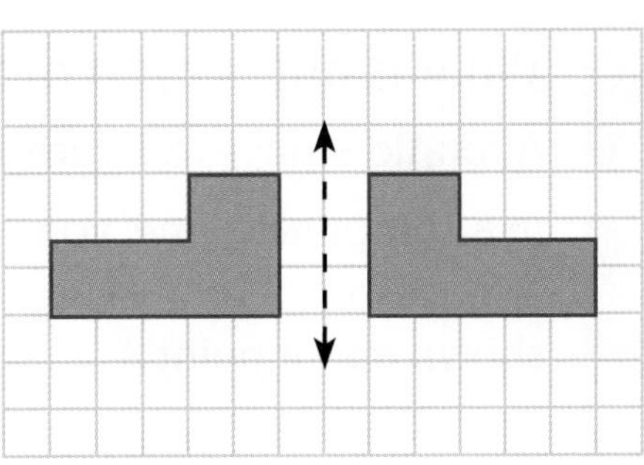

For **13** through **15**, draw the reflection of the given figure.

13.

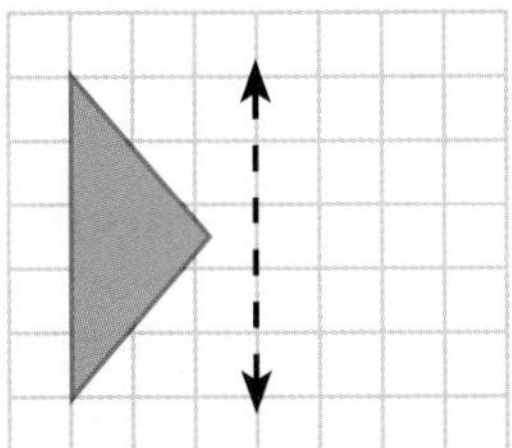

14.

15.

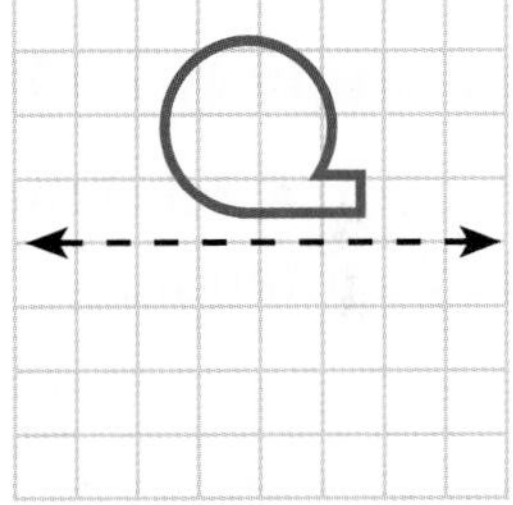

TAKS Problem Solving

16. In the drawing below explain why the figure on the right is not a reflection of the figure on the left.

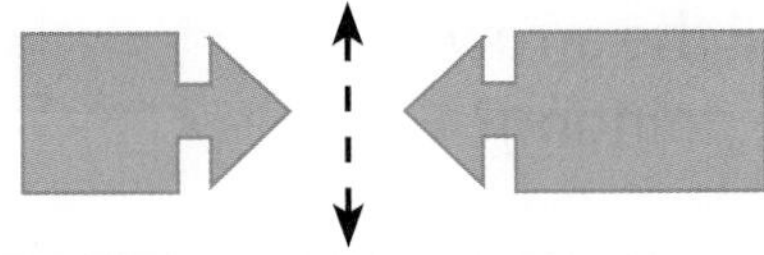

17. Draw an example of two figures that look the same when they are translated and when they are reflected.

18. Vanessa can run five miles in fifty minutes. If she keeps this pace, how many miles can she run in sixty minutes?

19. **Number Sense** How can you tell that you have made a mistake if you find that $540 \div 5 = 18$?

20. Which shows a pair of figures related by reflection?

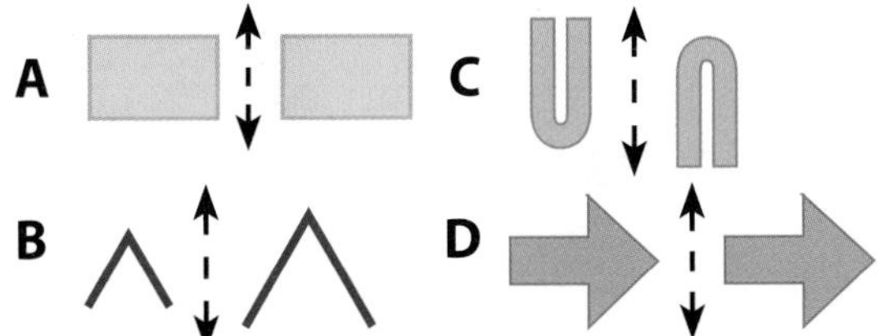

21. The Hall of Mirrors in the Palace of Versailles in France is 73 meters long. If you stand at one end and look at yourself in the mirror at the other end, how far away would your reflection appear to be?

? meters total

73	73

22. **Writing to Explain** How is a reflection different from a translation?

Lesson

15-3

TEKS 4.9A: Demonstrate translations, reflections, and rotations using concrete models.

Rotations

Hands-On
set of polygons
grid paper

What is one way to move a figure?

A rotation moves a figure around a point.

In a computer game, you rotate a spaceship. It rotates as shown about point A.

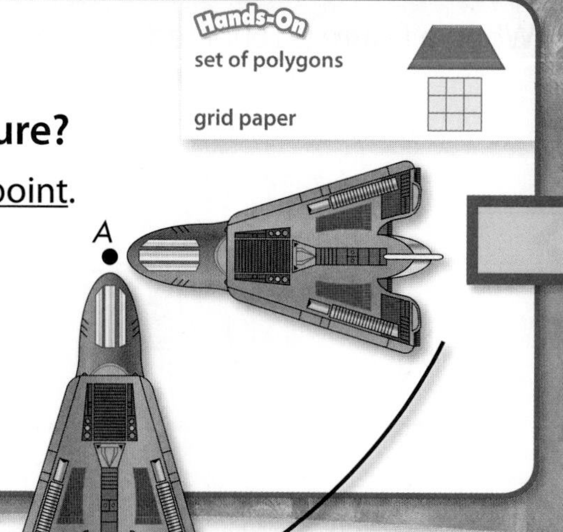

Guided Practice*

Do you know HOW?

For **1** through **4**, tell if the figures are related by a rotation.

1.

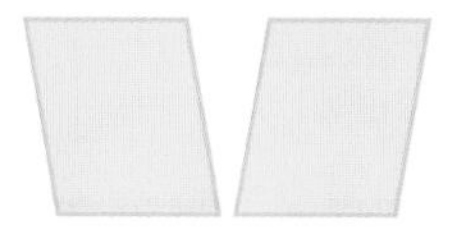

2.

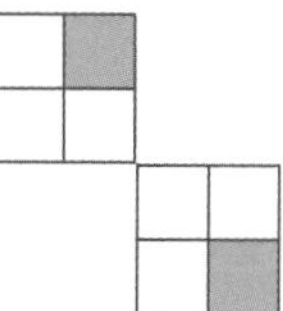

3.

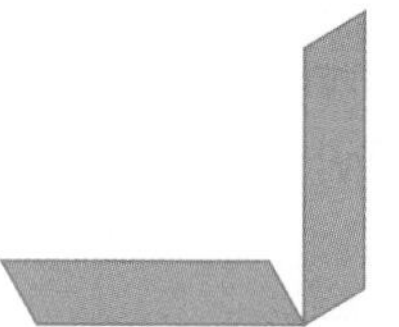

4.

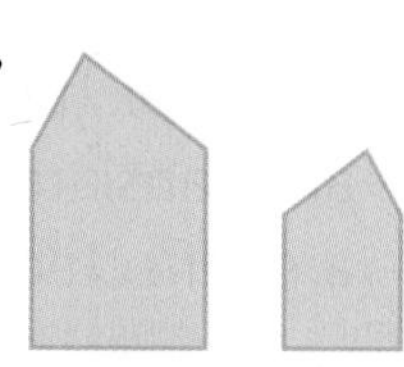

Do you UNDERSTAND?

5. Does a rotation change a figure's size or shape?

6. Can every figure be rotated so that it lands on top of itself?

7. If you rotate the arrow below 180 degrees about point x, in which direction will the arrow be pointing?

x

Independent Practice

For **8** through **13**, tell if the figures are related by rotation. You may use pattern blocks or grid paper to decide.

8.

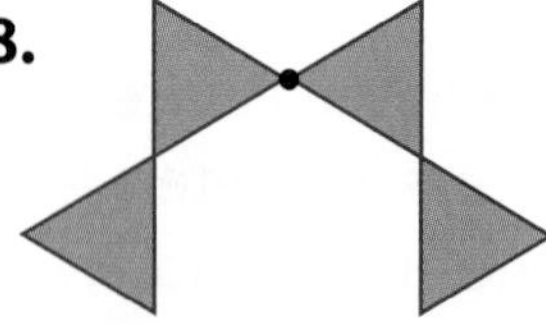

9.

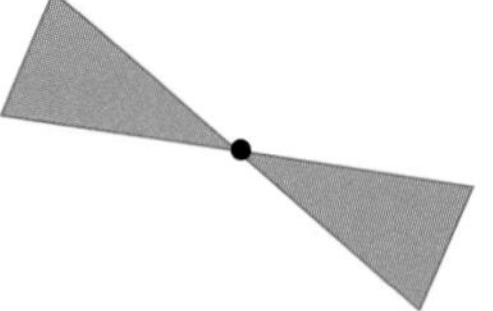

10.

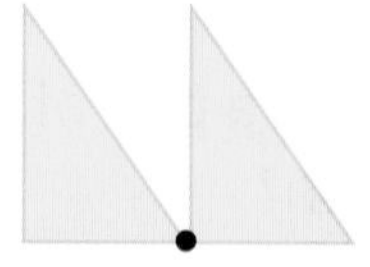

11.

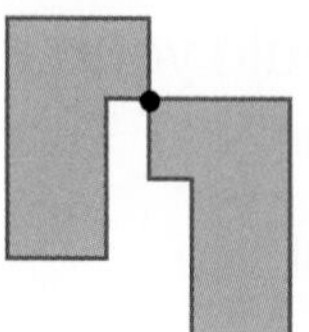

12.

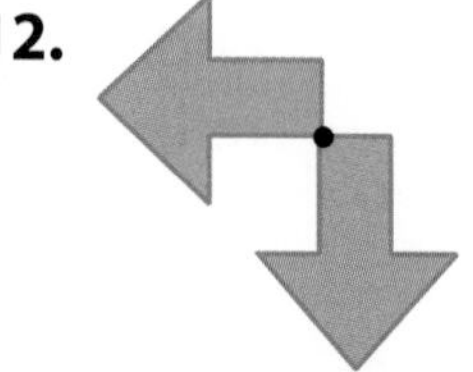

13.

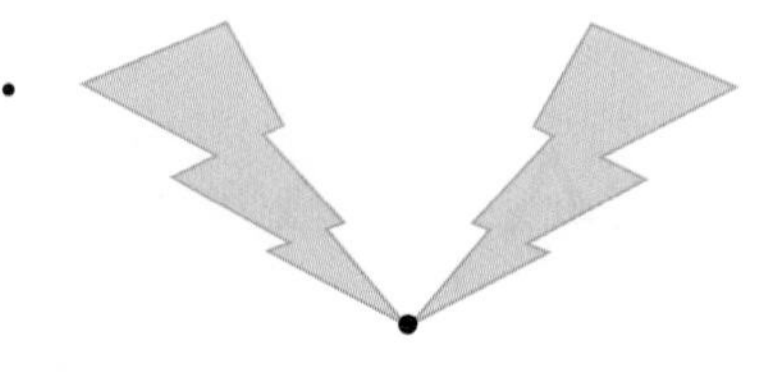

*For another example, see Set C on page 340.

When a figure is rotated, the size and shape of the figure do not change.

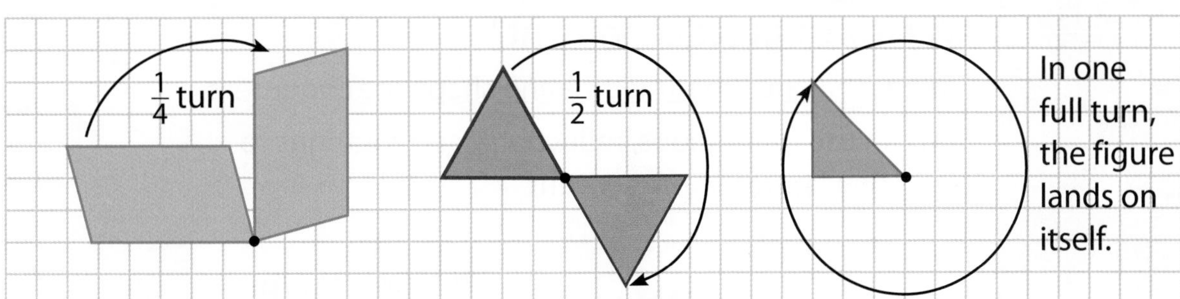

For **14** through **16**, copy each figure on grid paper. Then draw a rotation of the figure $\frac{1}{4}$ turn to the right.

14. 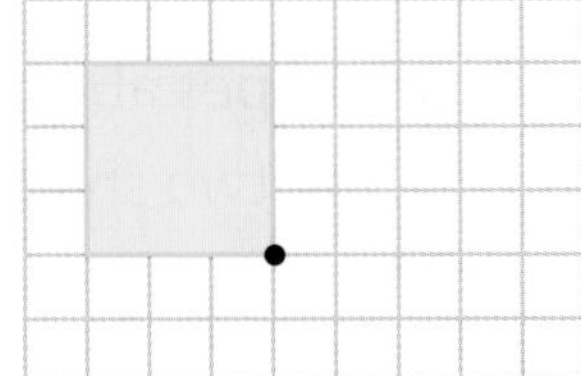

15. 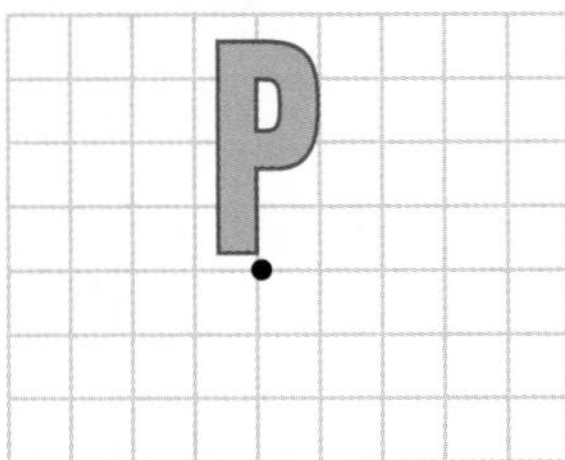

16. 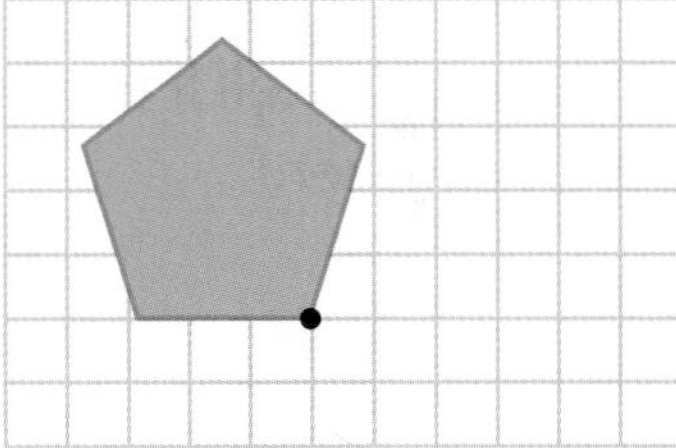

TAKS Problem Solving

17. The sum of the angles of a pentagon is 540°. If every angle of the pentagon is the same measure, what is the measure of each of its angles?

18. What figure is formed when a triangle has rotated $\frac{1}{4}$ turn?

A Circle **C** Rectangle

B Square **D** Triangle

19. The shape on the right shows a pattern of translations, reflections, and rotations. Describe each step.

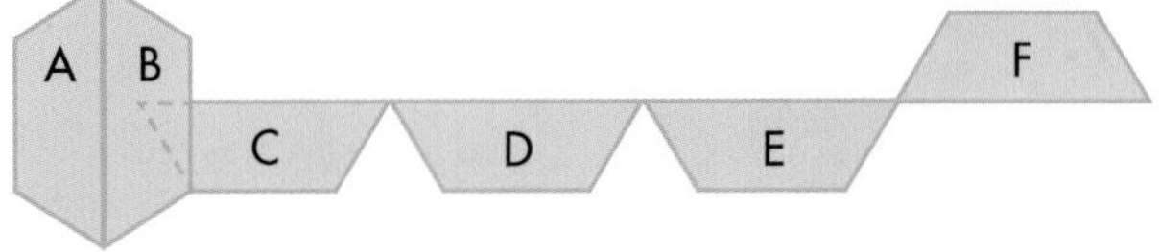

For **20** through **22**, use the table at the right.

20. How much does one Tetra cost?

21. Cal bought 2 guppies and 4 tiger barbs. How much did he pay?

22. How much would it cost to buy 1 of each fish?

Fish	Price
Guppies	5 for $1.50
Tetras	3 for $6.00
Tiger Barbs	4 for $4.00

Lesson

15-4

TEKS 4.9B: Use translations, reflections, and rotations to verify that two shapes are congruent.

Congruent Figures

Hands-On
grid paper

When are figures congruent?

Figures that are the same size and shape are congruent.

You can use translations, reflections, and rotations to test if two figures are congruent.

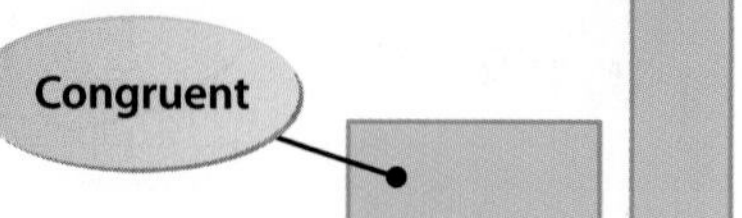

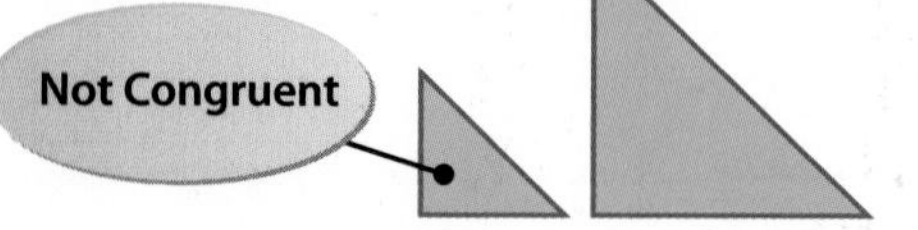

Guided Practice*

Do you know HOW?

For **1** through **4**, tell if the figures in each pair are congruent.

1. 

2. 

3. 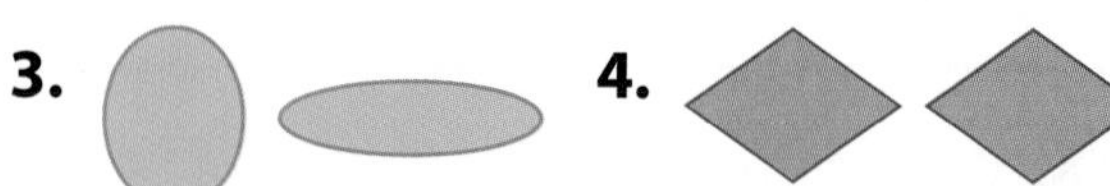

4.

Do you UNDERSTAND?

5. If one of the house shapes above is rotated $\frac{1}{4}$ turn, will the two shapes still be congruent?

6. **Writing to Explain** Can a circle and a square ever be congruent? Why or why not?

Independent Practice

For **7** through **15**, tell if the figures in each pair are congruent.

7. 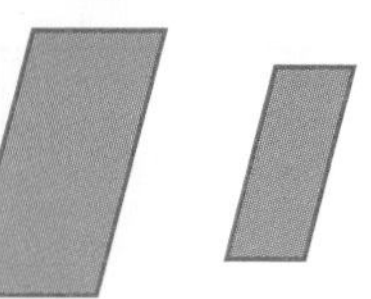

8. 

9. 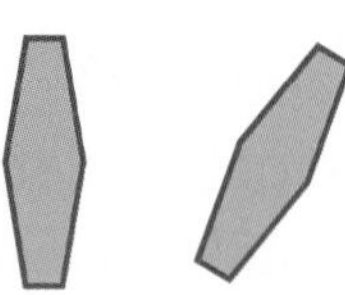

10. 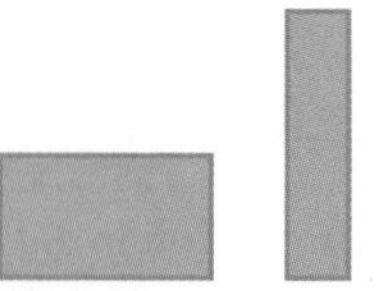

11. 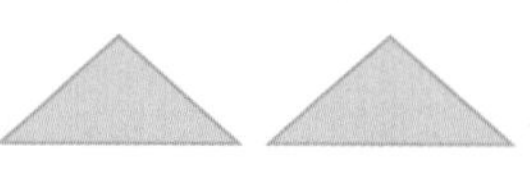

12. 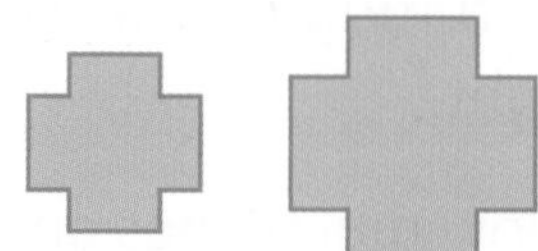

13. 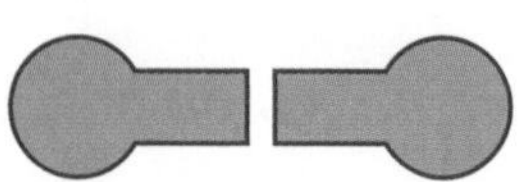

14. 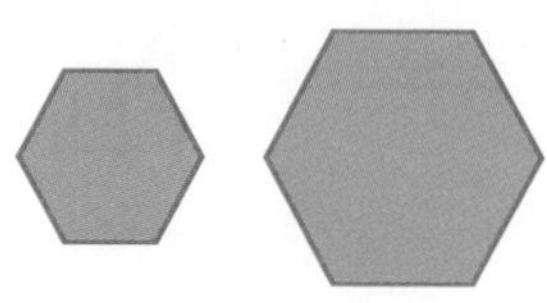

15. 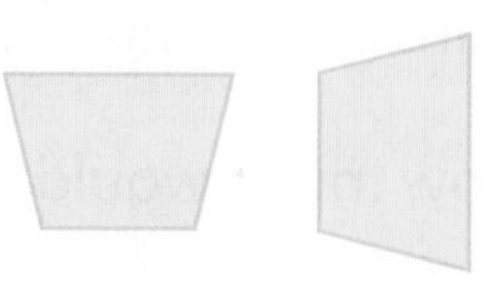

For another example, see Set D on page 341.

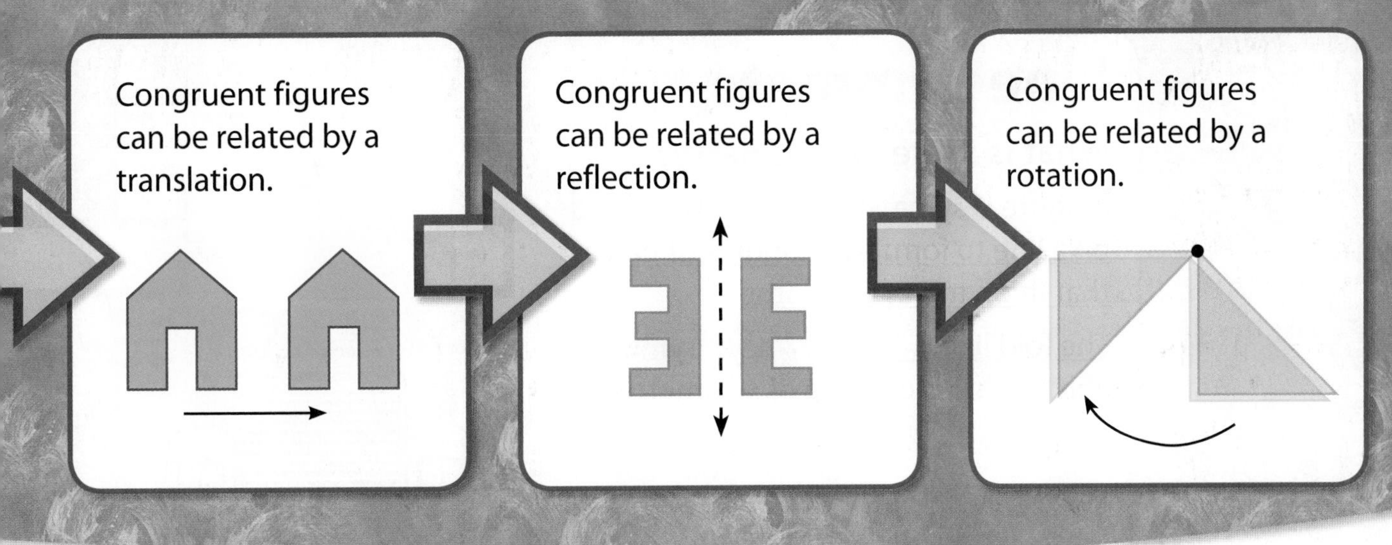
Congruent figures can be related by a translation.
Congruent figures can be related by a reflection.
Congruent figures can be related by a rotation.

TAKS Problem Solving

For **16** and **17**, describe everything that is the same and everything that is different about each pair of figures. Then tell if the figures are congruent.

16. 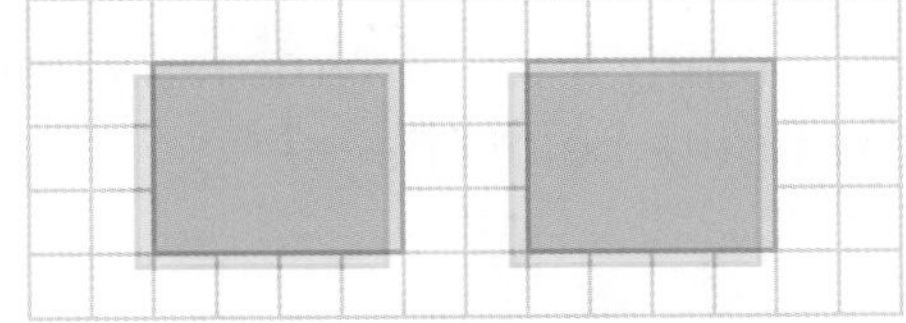

17. 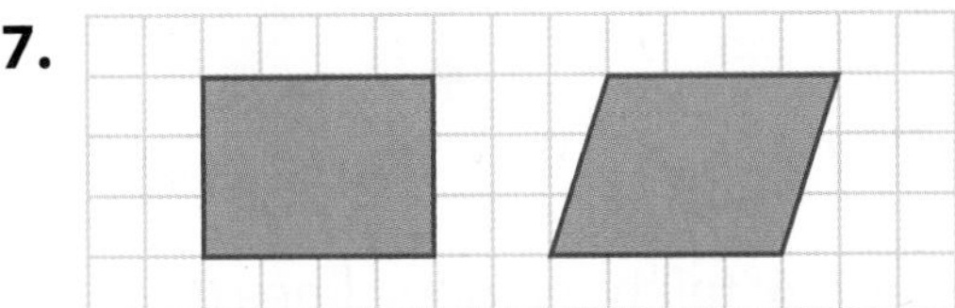

18. Draw one line segment to connect the opposite corners of a square. What polygons have you created? Are these polygons congruent?

19. On a bus ride, Jasmine counted 24 taxis and 12 buses. How many buses and taxis did she count in all?

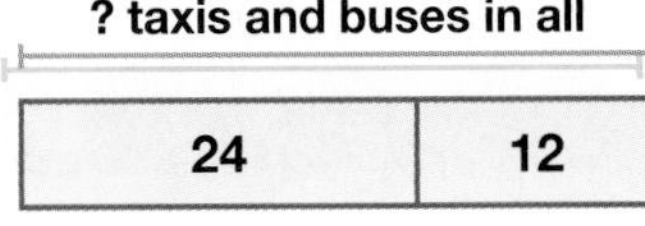
? taxis and buses in all
24
12

20. **Reasoning** Use the diagram below. Frida wrote a message on paper and held it up to a mirror. What does the message say?

THIS IS A REFLECTION.

21. Ozzie and Sam both travel 30 minutes to get to work each day. To get to work last week, Ozzie drove for three hours, and Sam drove for an hour and thirty minutes. How many more days did Ozzie work than Sam?

22. How many days are in 52 weeks?

A 59 days

B 364 days

C 365 days

D 366 days

DIGITAL
Animated Glossary
www.pearsonsuccessnet.com

Lesson
15-5

TEKS 4.9C: Use reflections to verify that a shape has symmetry.

Line Symmetry

Hands-On
grid paper

What is a line of symmetry?

A figure is symmetric if it can be folded on a line to form two congruent halves that fit on top of each other.

The fold line is called a line of symmetry. This truck has one line of symmetry.

Guided Practice*

Do you know HOW?

For **1** and **2**, tell if each line is a line of symmetry.

1. 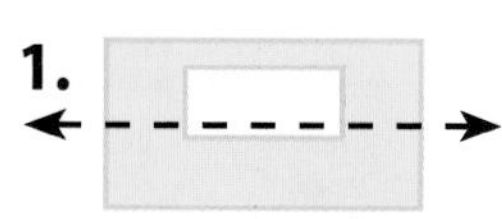

2. 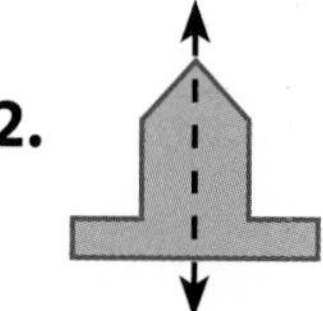

For **3** and **4**, tell how many lines of symmetry each figure has.

3.

4.

Do you UNDERSTAND?

5. Do some figures have no lines of symmetry?

6. How many lines of symmetry does the figure below have?

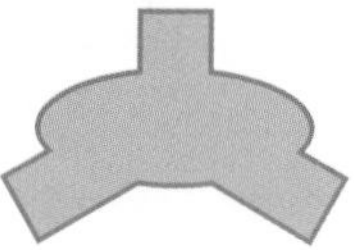

7. Writing to Explain How many lines of symmetry does a bicycle tire have?

Independent Practice

For **8** through **11**, tell if each line is a line of symmetry.

8. 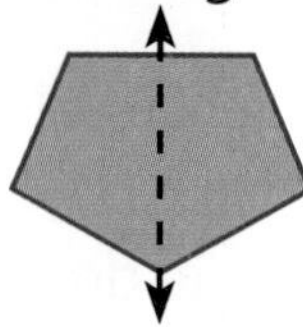

9. 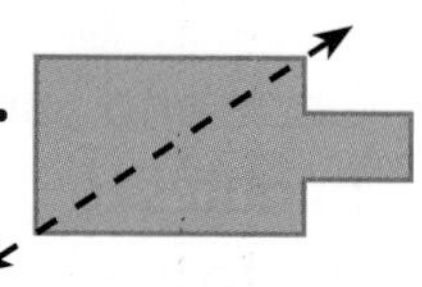

10. 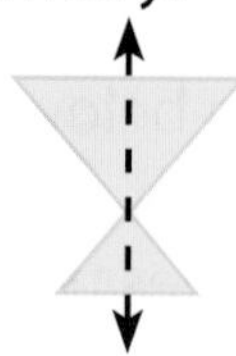

11. 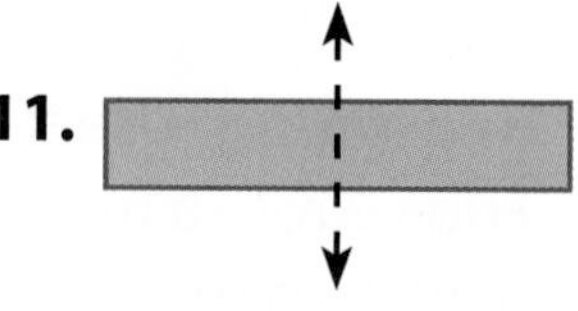

For **12** through **15**, tell how many lines of symmetry each figure has.

12. 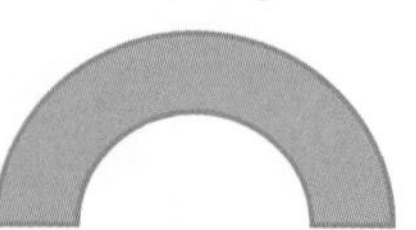

13. 

14. 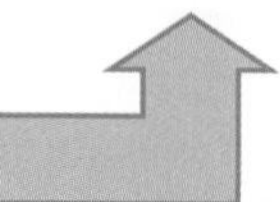

15. 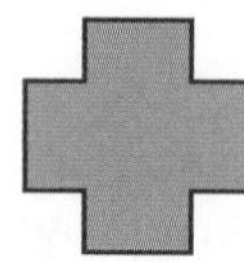

*For another example, see Set E on page 341 .

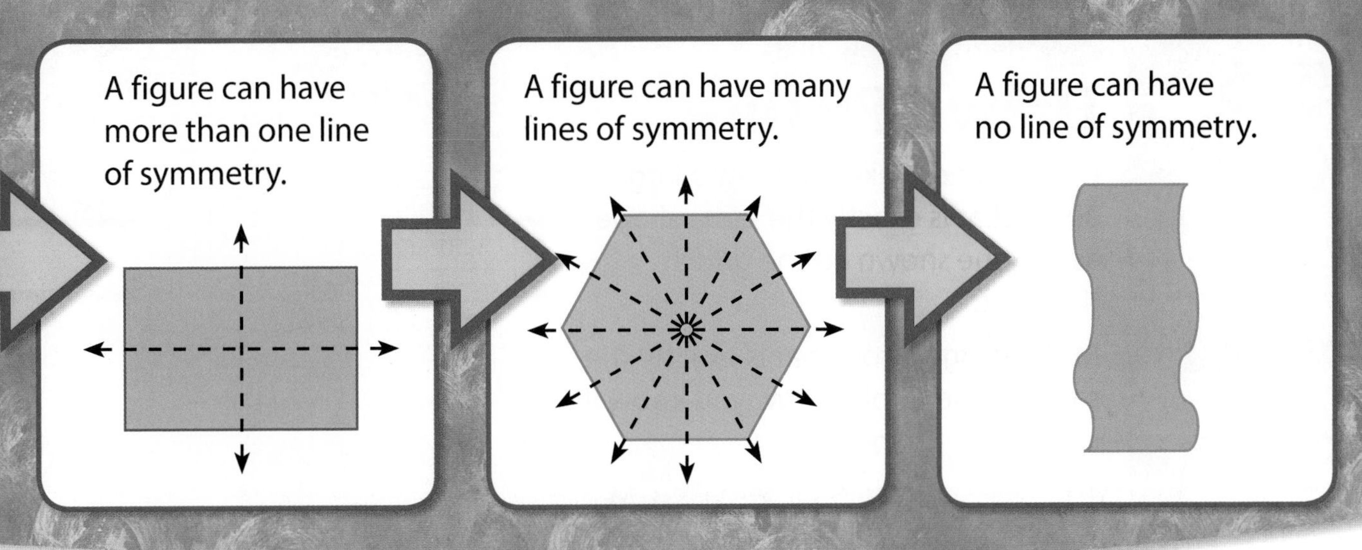
A figure can have more than one line of symmetry.
A figure can have many lines of symmetry.
A figure can have no line of symmetry.

For **16** through **23**, trace each figure and draw lines of symmetry if you can.

16. 

17. 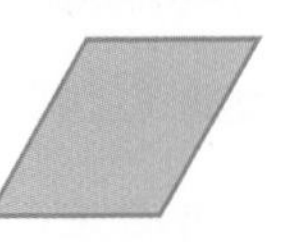

18. 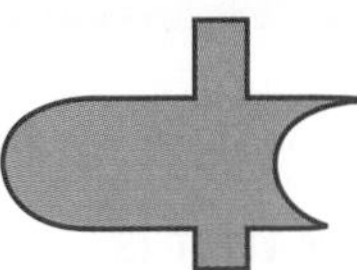

19. 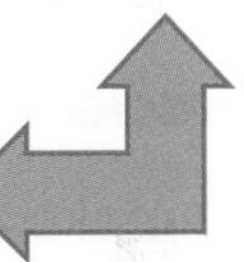

20. 

21. 

22. 

23. 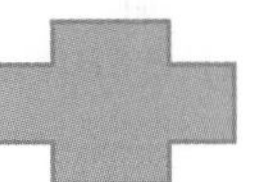

TAKS Problem Solving

24. How many lines of symmetry does a scalene triangle have?

25. How many lines of symmetry does an isosceles triangle have?

26. Reasoning Vanessa drew a figure and said that it had an infinite number of lines of symmetry. What figure did she draw?

27. Draw a quadrilateral that does not have a line of symmetry.

28. The Alamo is a key symbol of Texas independence. Use the picture at the right to describe where the line of symmetry is.

29. Write 5 capital letters that have at least one line of symmetry.

30. How many lines of symmetry does a square have?

A None

B 2 lines

C 4 lines

D 6 lines

DIGITAL
Animated Glossary, eTools
www.pearsonsuccessnet.com

Lesson
15-6

TEKS 4.14C Select or develop an appropriate problem-solving plan or strategy, including drawing a picture, looking for a pattern, systematic guessing and checking, acting it out, making a table, working a simpler problem, or working backwards to solve a problem.

Problem Solving

Draw a Picture

Hands-On
grid paper

Lisa has been asked to draw a large arrow that is exactly the same shape as the one shown on the grid at the right.

Make a large arrow that is exactly the same shape. Explain how you know it is the same shape.

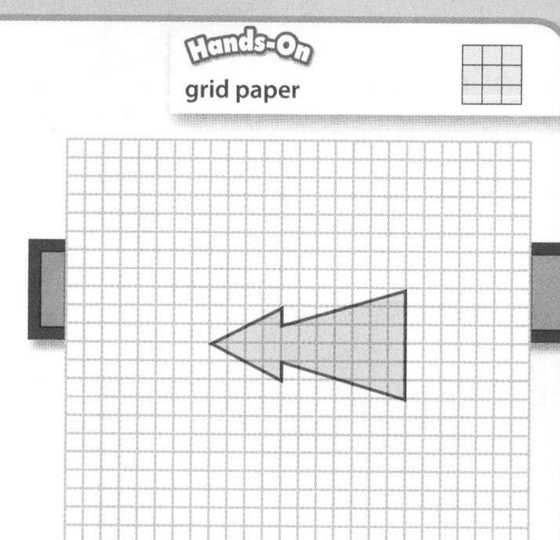

Guided Practice*

Do you know HOW?

For **1** and **2** make a large figure that is exactly the same shape. Explain how you know it is the same shape.

1. 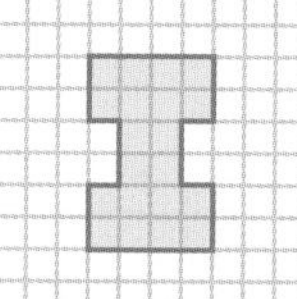

2. 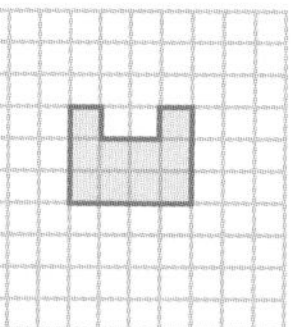

Do you UNDERSTAND?

3. Suppose that you drew the arrow above so that it was pointing vertically. Would the shape of the arrow change?

4. Draw a picture of a shape. Then triple each side.

Independent Practice

Solve.

Jackie and Kendall are part of their school's relay race team. Each member of the team has to run for a half mile of a 3-mile race.

5. Draw a picture to help you find how many members are on the relay team.

6. How many other members are on the relay team besides Jackie and Kendall?

7. Draw a large figure. Then draw a smaller figure that is exactly the same shape.

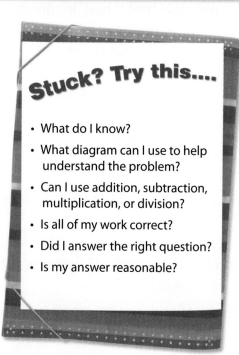

Stuck? Try this....

- What do I know?
- What diagram can I use to help understand the problem?
- Can I use addition, subtraction, multiplication, or division?
- Is all of my work correct?
- Did I answer the right question?
- Is my answer reasonable?

*For another example, see Set F on page 341.

Plan

What do I know? I know the length of each side of the arrow. The arrow is 11 units long from left to right.

What am I asked to find? To make an arrow that is exactly the same shape.

Solve

Double the length of each side.

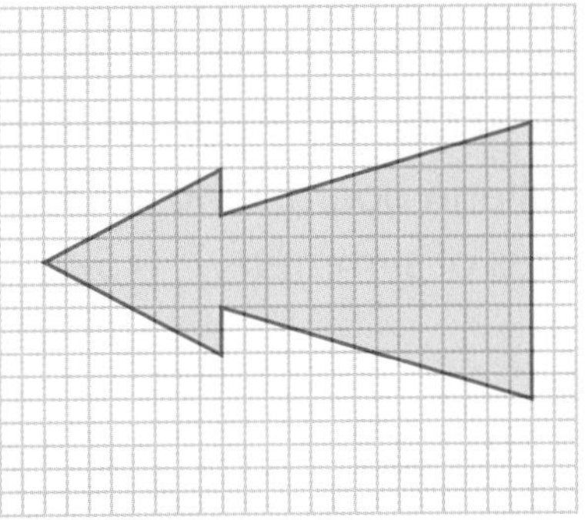

The shapes are the same because the lengths of each side were doubled.

8. Stephen is listening to a book on tape. The book has 17 chapters and each chapter is about 22 minutes long. How many minutes will it take to listen to the complete book?

9. Six people are taking part in a charity walk. Two people walked for 8 miles, three people walked for 6 miles, and one person walked for 10 miles. How many miles did they walk in all?

10. Which can be rotated less than one complete turn and look exactly the same?

A B

B V

C H

D R

11. Which of the following shapes has exactly four lines of symmetry?

F

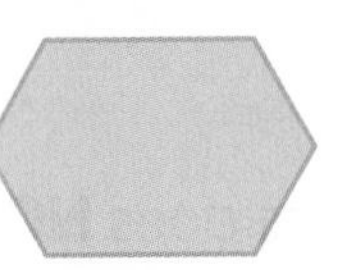

H

G

J

12. Writing to Explain Roxanne says for any figure you draw, if you translate it, reflect it, or rotate it, the result will still be congruent to the original figure. Is she correct?

13. Lawrence's father said that he would put 12 dollars into Lawrence's savings account for every 20 dollars Lawrence put into it. If after a year his father had put 96 dollars into Lawrence's account, how much did Lawrence put into his account?

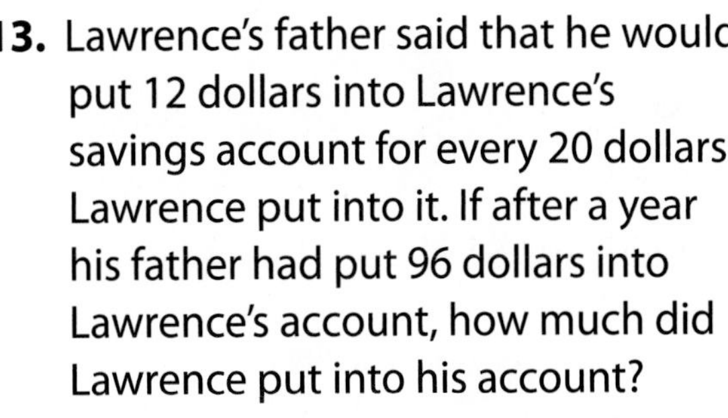

14. If you were to cut out a hexagon to make a sign similar to the shape at the right, how would you draw it to make it twice the size?

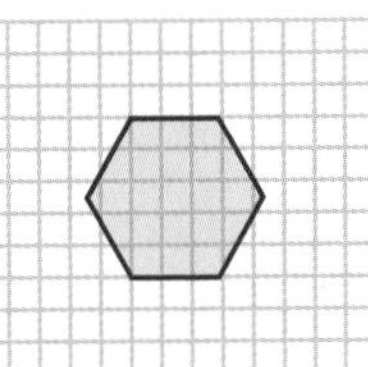

TAKS Test Prep

1. Four of Mrs. Li's students decorated a bulletin board. Whose shape has 4 lines of symmetry? (15-5)

Ralph

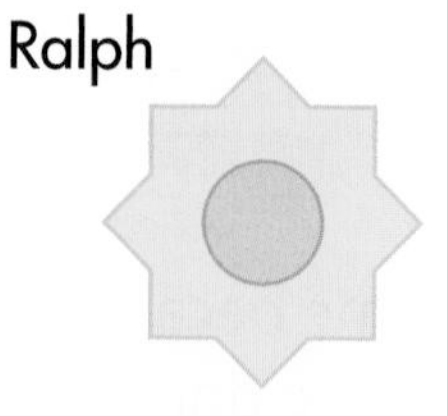

Liza

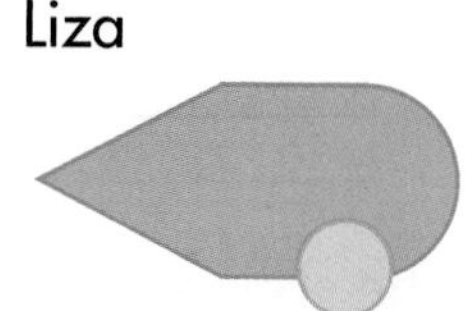

Patricia

Dan

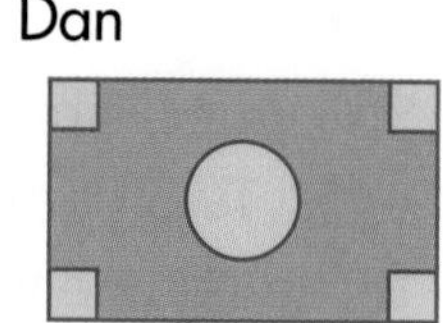

A Ralph

B Liza

C Patricia

D Dan

2. Which pair of shapes does **NOT** show a rotation? (15-3)

F 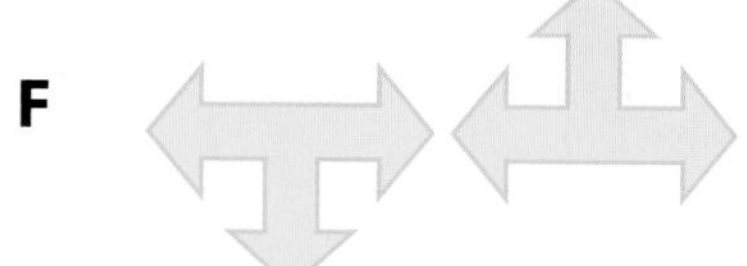

G  

H 

J 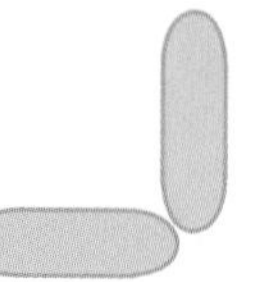

3. Which transformation can be used to show that the figures are congruent? (15-4)

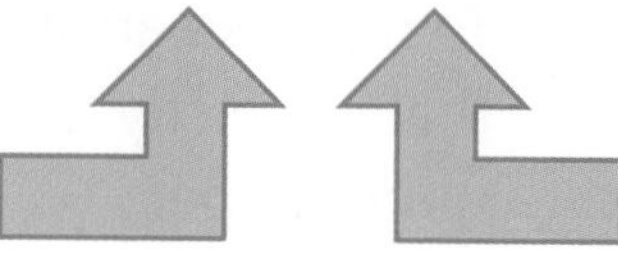

A Turn

B Translation

C Rotation

D Reflection

4. Corby made a pattern with geometric tiles. Which shows his pattern reflected over the line? (15-2)

F 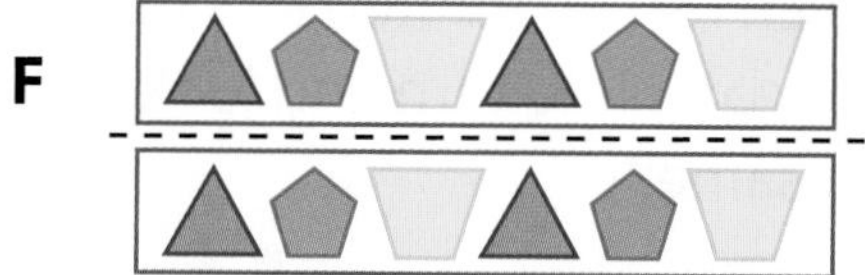

G 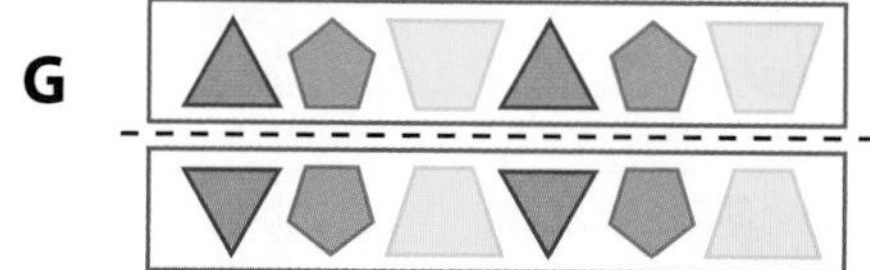

H 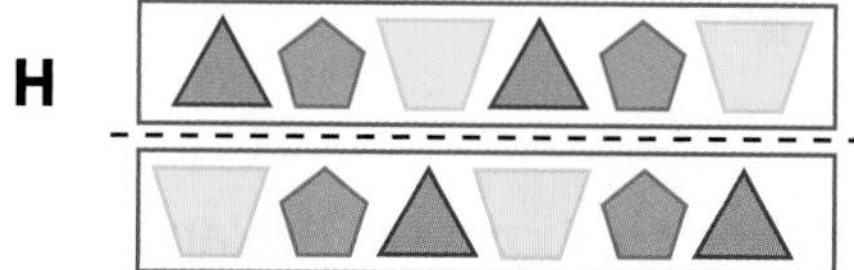

J 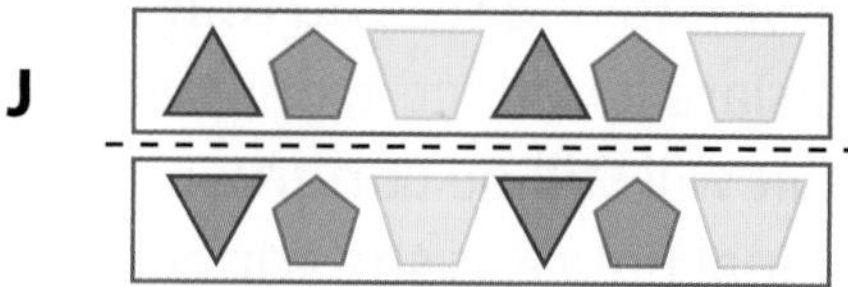

5. Which of the following represents a translation? (15-1)

A Turning over a pancake

B Seeing yourself in a mirror

C Moving a checker diagonally on a checker board

D A dog rolling over

6. Which letter of the alphabet is a reflection of the letter b? (15-2)

   F The letter d or the letter p

   G The letter d or the letter q

   H Only the letter p

   J Only the letter d

7. Which figures are related by translation? (15-1)

   A 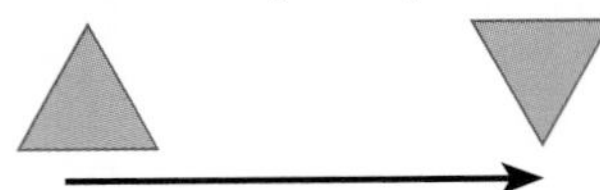

   B 

   C 

   D 

8. Cassidy made the shape to the right. Which shape below is the same shape? (15-6)

   F 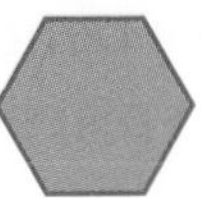

   G 

   H 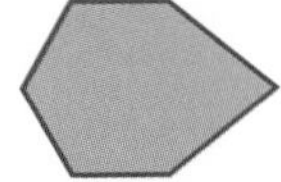

   J 

9. What is the new position of this shape after it makes a $\frac{1}{2}$ turn rotation? (15-3)

   A 

   B 

   C 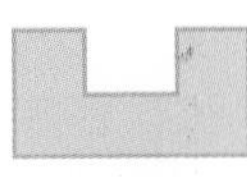

   D 

10. Which motion can be used to show the two figures are congruent? (15-4)

   F Turn

   G Rotation

   H Reflection

   J Translation

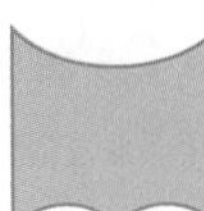

11. Which of the following represents a rotation? (15-3)

   A Riding a sled down a hill

   B A fan blade on a moving fan

   C The image of a tree in a lake

   D Jumping straight up

12. **Griddable Response** How many lines of symmetry does the logo on Gentry's t-shirt have? (15-5)

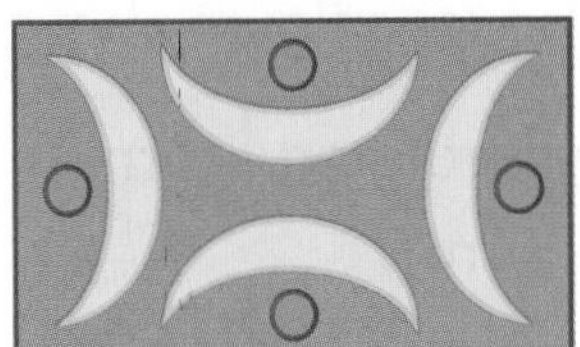

Reteaching

Set A, pages 326–327

Which triangle is a translation of Triangle *A*?

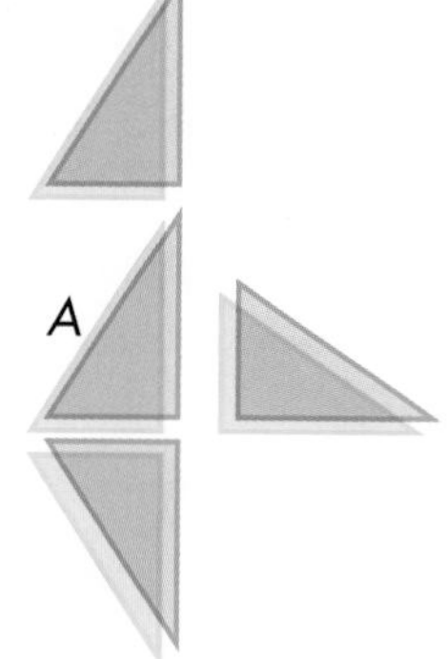

A translation moves a figure in a straight direction.

The triangle above Triangle *A* is a translation.

Remember that translated figures remain the same size and shape.

Are the figures related by translation?

1. 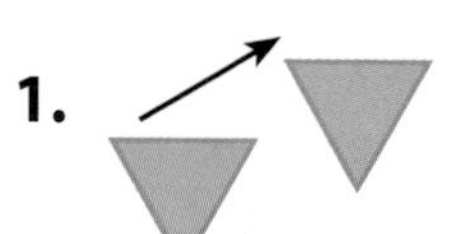
2. 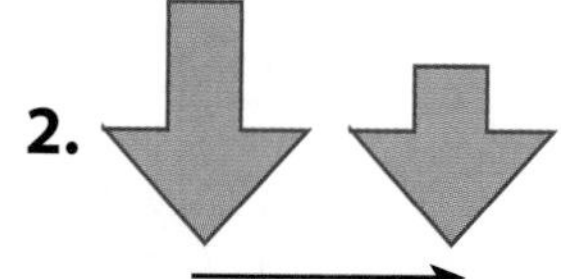
3. 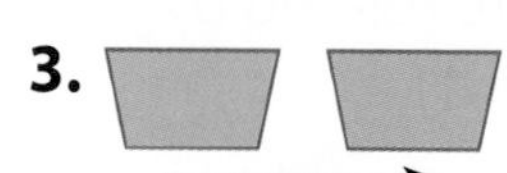
4. 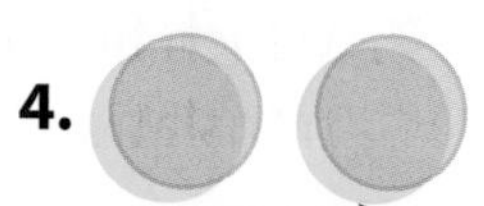

Set B, pages 328–329

Which pair of letters are related by a reflection?

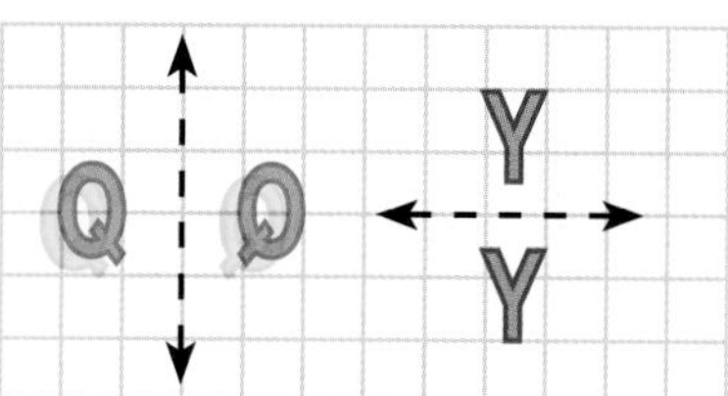

A reflection of a figure gives its mirror image.

The pair of Qs are related by a reflection. The pair of Ys are not.

Remember, when you fold along the dashed line, reflected figures will fit one on top of the other.

Tell if the figures are related by a reflection.

1. 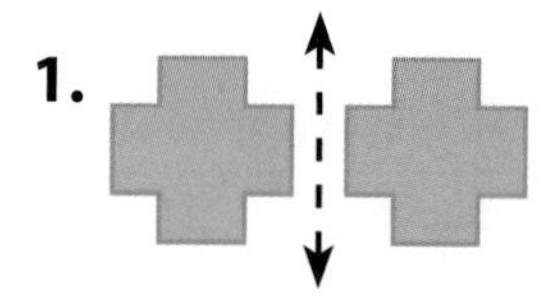
2. 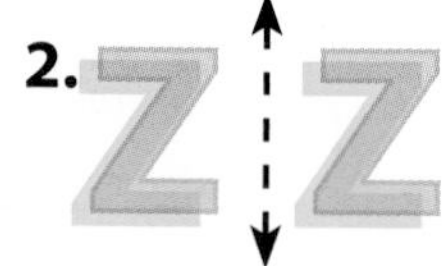

3. 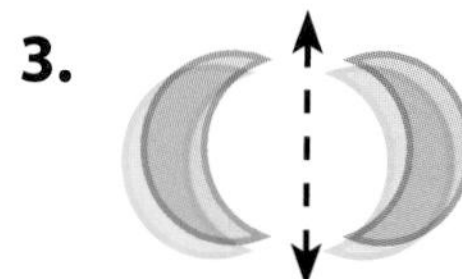
4. 

Set C, pages 330–331

Which figure is rotated $\frac{1}{4}$ turn? Which is rotated $\frac{1}{2}$ turn?

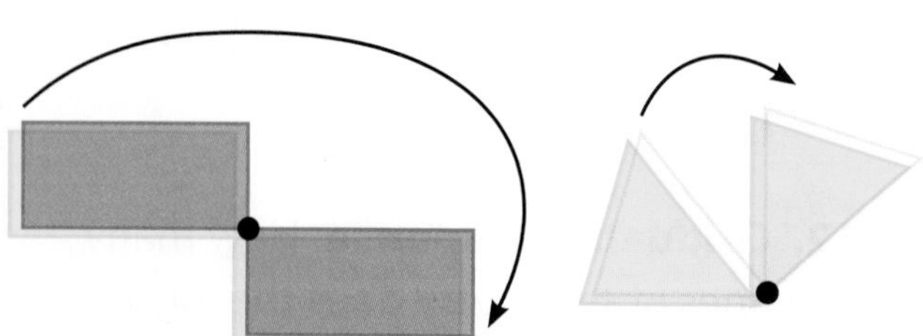

A rotation moves a figure about a point.

The triangle is rotated $\frac{1}{4}$ turn. The rectangle is rotated $\frac{1}{2}$ turn.

Remember, you can trace a figure and rotate it by using a pencil to hold the fixed point in place.

Tell if the figures are rotated $\frac{1}{4}$ turn or $\frac{1}{2}$ turn.

1. 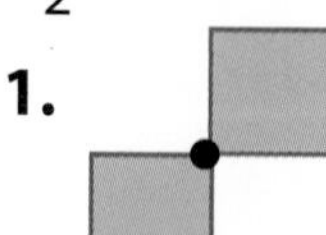
2. 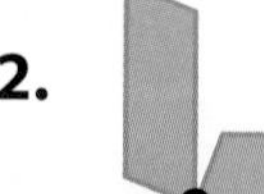
3. 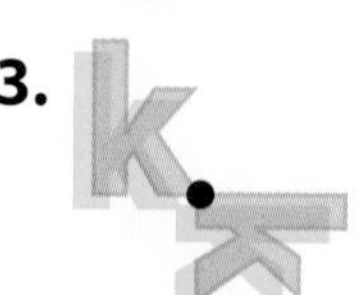
4. 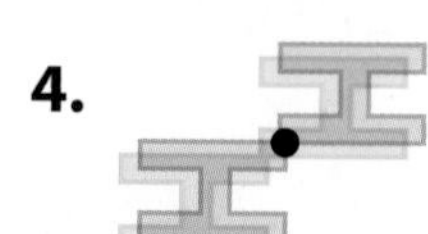

Reteaching

Set D, pages 332–333

Are the figures congruent? If so, tell if they are related by a reflection, translation, or rotation.

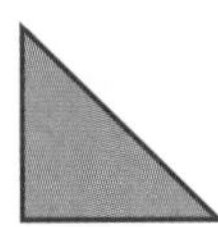
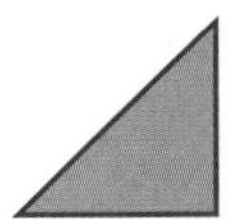

The triangles are the same size and shape, so they are congruent. They are related by a reflection.

The circles are not the same size, so they are not congruent.

Remember that you can use translations, reflections, and rotations to test if two figures are congruent.

Are the figures in each pair congruent?

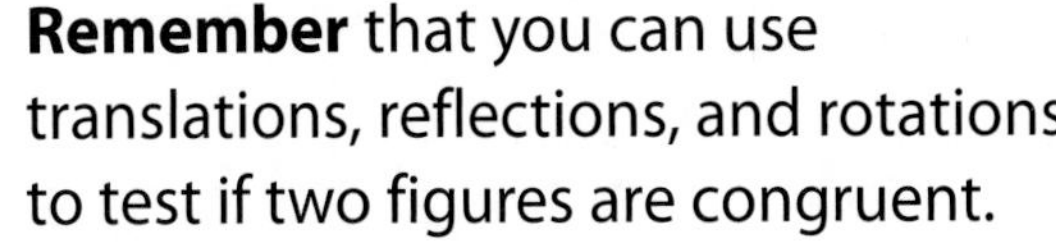

1. 
2. 
3. 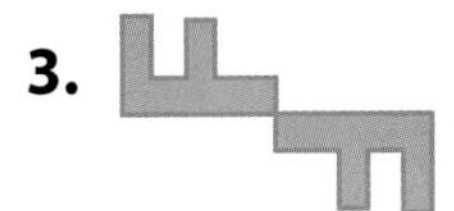
4. 

Set E, pages 334–335

How many lines of symmetry does the figure have?

Fold the figure along the dashed line. The two halves are congruent and fit one on top of the other. It has 1 line of symmetry.

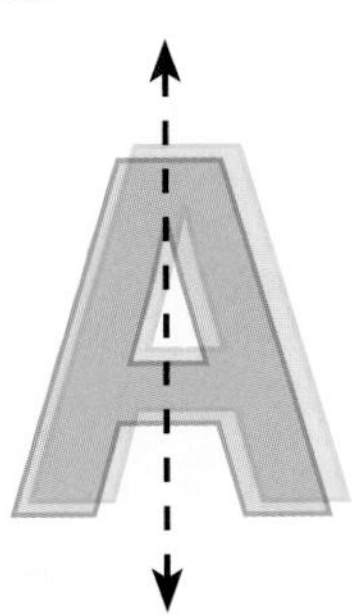

Remember that figures can have many lines of symmetry.

Draw the lines of symmetry for each figure.

1. 
2. 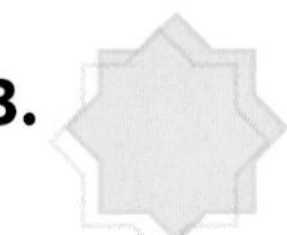
3.

Set F, pages 336–367

Make a letter "T" that is exactly the same shape. Explain how you know it is the same shape.

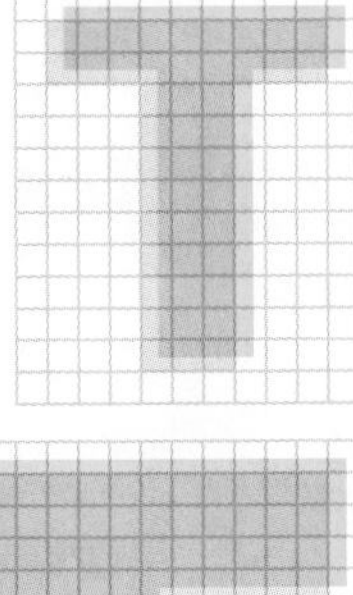

Double the dimensions of this figure. The letter is 11 units in vertical height and spans 9 units horizontally.

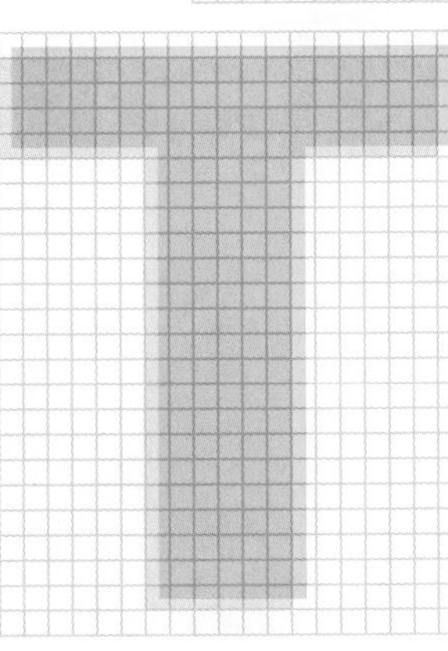

The shapes are the same because the length of each side was doubled.

Remember to find the dimensions of the figure before you draw it.

1. Draw this figure. Explain how you know it is the same shape.

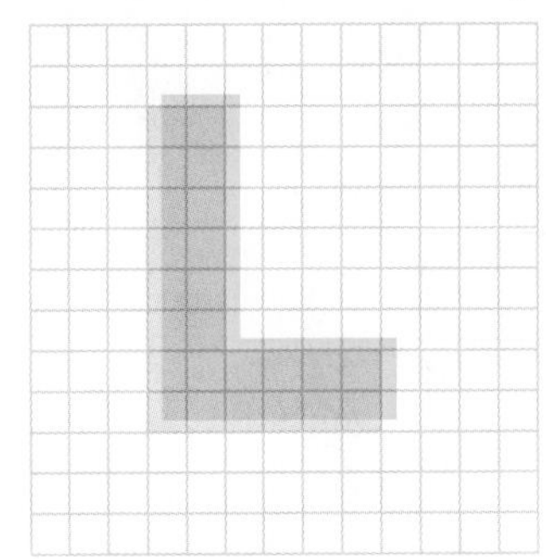

Topic 16
Estimating and Measuring Length, Perimeter, and Area
1
What is the area of this playground map? You will find out in Lesson 16-4.
2
How long is this dragon? You will find out in Lesson 16-2.

3 How tall is the largest model of an ear of corn? Find out in Lesson 16-1.

4 You can use triangles, squares, and rectangles to estimate the perimeter of the State of Texas. You will find out how in Lesson 16-3.

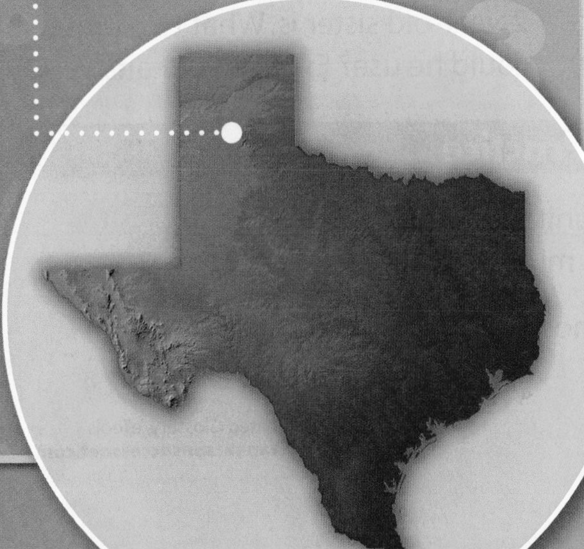

Review What You Know!

Vocabulary

Choose the best term from the box.

- addition
- mile
- multiplication
- perimeter

1. The _?_ is the distance around a figure.
2. A customary unit used to measure long distances is the _?_.
3. _?_ is the operation you use to find the area of a region.

Multiplication Facts

Find each product.

4. 6×5	**5.** 7×9	**6.** 8×8
7. 7×4	**8.** 3×6	**9.** 5×4
10. 4×9	**11.** 8×5	**12.** 9×6
13. 8×4	**14.** 3×9	**15.** 8×7

Measurement

Choose the best unit to measure each length. Write inch, foot, yard, or mile.

16. book	**17.** football field
18. road	**19.** classroom
20. leaf	**21.** marathon race

22. **Writing to Explain** What are two ways you can find the total number of boxes in the array below?

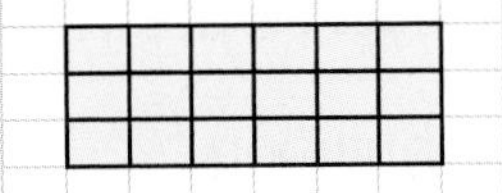

Lesson

16-1

TEKS 4.11A: Estimate and use measurement tools to determine length (including perimeter), area, capacity, and weight/mass using standard units SI (metric) and customary.

Using Customary Units of Length

Hands-On
inch ruler

How do you estimate and measure length?

The United States uses customary units of measure. About how long is Greg's toy car?

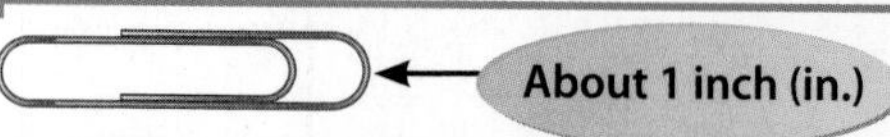

About 1 inch (in.)

Other Examples

A notebook is about 1 foot (ft).

Almost 1 foot

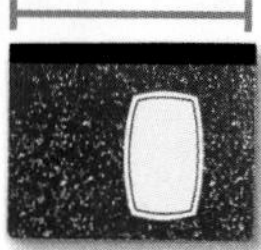

1 ft = 12 in.

A baseball bat is about 1 yard (yd).

1 yd = 36 in.   1 yd = 3 ft

One mile (mi) is about twice around the track.

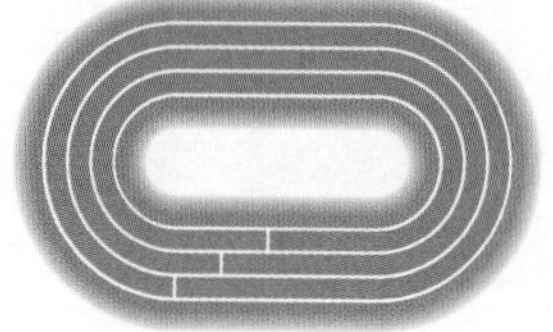

1 mi = 5,280 ft   1 mi = 1,760 yd

Guided Practice*

Do you know HOW?

For **1** through **4**, choose the most appropriate unit to measure the length of each. Write in., ft, yd, or mi.

1. highway   **2.** CD case

3. football field   **4.** room

Do you UNDERSTAND?

5. How long is your textbook to the nearest inch? Explain how you measured.

6. Greg wants to measure how tall his 2-year-old sister is. What two units could he use? Explain your answer.

Independent Practice

For **7** through **10**, choose the most appropriate unit to measure the length of each. Write in., ft, yd, or mi.

7. pencil   **8.** building   **9.** mountain   **10.** spool of ribbon

*For another example, see Set A on page 364.

The toy car is shorter than a foot. So, the best unit to use would be inches.

The car is about 3 inches long.

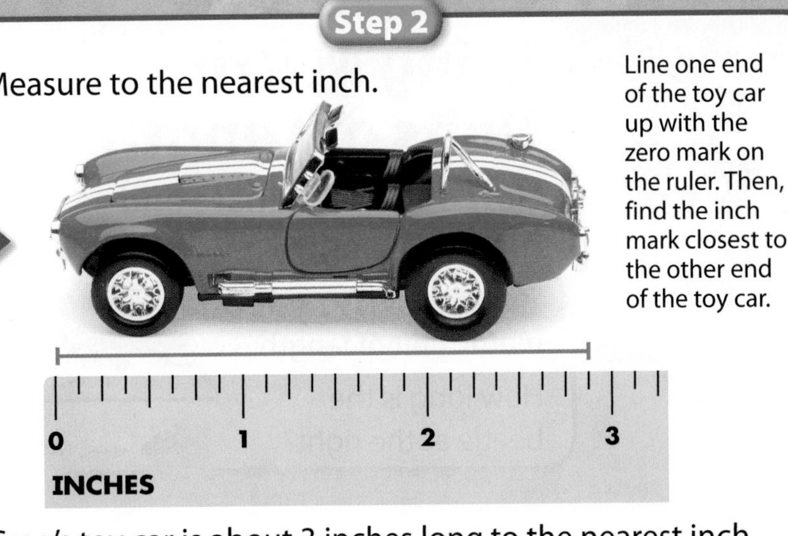

Step 2
Measure to the nearest inch.
Line one end of the toy car up with the zero mark on the ruler. Then, find the inch mark closest to the other end of the toy car.
0
1
2
3
INCHES

Greg's toy car is about 3 inches long to the nearest inch.

For **11** through **13**, estimate and then measure each length to the nearest inch.

11. 

12.

13. 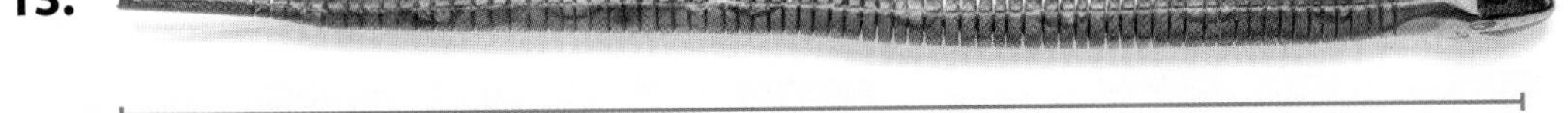

TAKS Problem Solving

14. Geometry If the perimeter of the triangle at the right is 14 yards, what is the length of the third side?

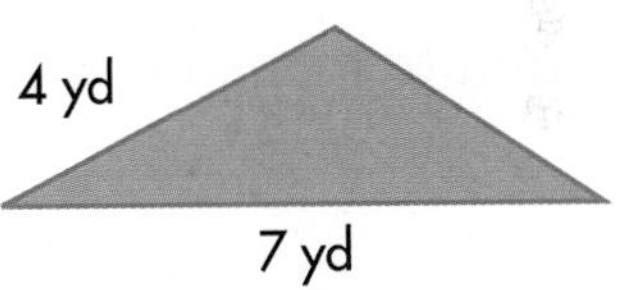

15. Writing to Explain Lionel is building a tree house. The materials list tells the length of the floorboards that are needed. Which would be the best unit of measure to describe the length of the floorboards?

16. Reasoning Trini took some photos. The number of photos she took is a two-digit number. The sum of the digits is 11. The tens digit is 3 more than the ones digit. How many photos did Trini take?

17. In Olivia, Minnesota, there is a giant ear of corn standing over a roadside gazebo. Using the image to the right, which do you think is the actual height of the corn?

A 25 miles

B 25 feet

C 25 inches

D 25 centimeters

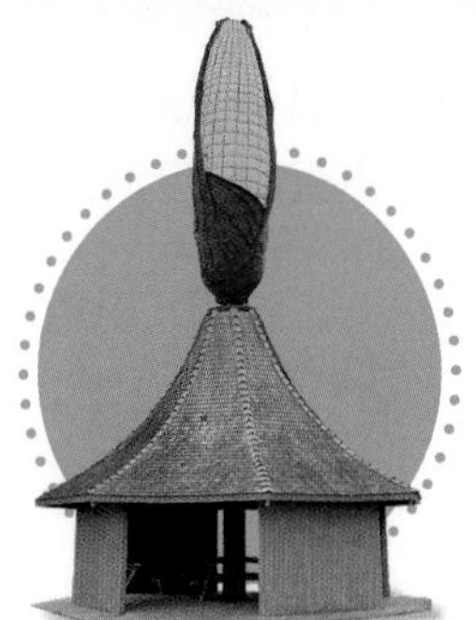

Lesson

16-2

TEKS 4.11A: Estimate and use measurement tools to determine length (including perimeter), area, capacity, and weight/mass using standard units SI (metric) and customary.

Using Metric Units of Length

Hands-On
metric ruler

How do you estimate and measure length?

The meter is the basic metric unit of length.

How long is the beetle at the right?

About 1 cm

Metric Units of Length
1 centimeter (cm) = 10 millimeters (mm)
1 decimeter (dm) = 10 centimeters (cm)
1 meter (m) = 100 centimeters (cm)
1 kilometer (km) = 1,000 meters (m)

Other Examples

1 millimeter (mm) is about the thickness of a dime.

1 meter (m) is about the length of this snake.

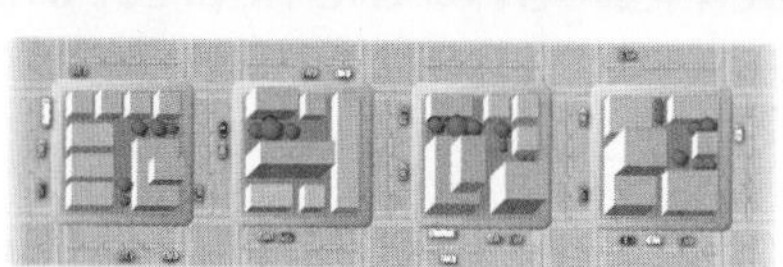

1 kilometer (km) is about the length of 4 city blocks.

Guided Practice*

Do you know HOW?

For **1** through **4**, choose the most appropriate unit to measure each. Write mm, cm, dm, m, or km.

1. height of a house

2. length of a cat

3. width of a sunflower seed

4. distance traveled by plane

Do you UNDERSTAND?

5. How wide is your textbook to the nearest centimeter? Explain how you measured.

6. Joni wants to measure the width of a narrow ribbon she is using to tie around the pinecone. Which metric unit should she use? Explain.

Independent Practice

For **7** through **9**, choose the most appropriate unit to measure the length of each. Write mm, cm, dm, m, or km.

7. length of a shoe

8. height of a tree

9. width of a strand of yarn

*For another example, see Set B on page 364.

Step 1

The beetle is shorter than a decimeter, but longer than a millimeter. So the best unit would be centimeters.

The beetle's length is about 4 centimeters long.

Step 2

Measure to the nearest centimeter.

Line one end of the beetle up with the zero mark on the ruler. Then find the centimeter mark closest to the other end of the beetle.

1 2 3 4 5 6 7 8
CENTIMETERS

The beetle is 4 centimeters long to the nearest centimeter.

For **10** through **12**, estimate, and then measure each length to the nearest centimeter.

10.

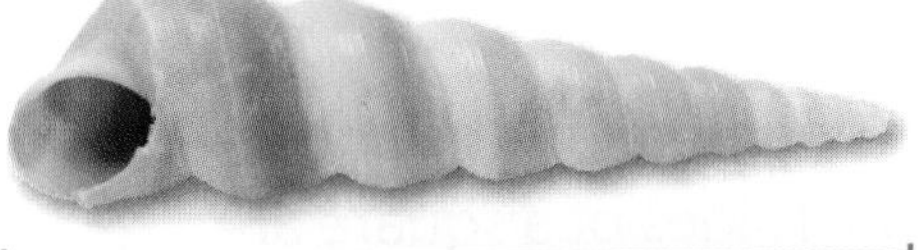

11.

12.

TAKS Problem Solving

13. The fourth grade teachers are planning a pizza party. Each pizza has 8 slices. The teachers want enough pizza so that each student can have 2 slices. If there are 22 students in each of the 3 fourth grade classes, how many pizzas must be ordered?

14. **Writing to Explain** June measured the height from the top of her window to the floor and wrote 3. She forgot to write the unit. Which metric unit of measure did June most likely use?

15. In the year 2000, the world's largest Chinese dancing dragon was part of a celebration at the Great Wall of China. It took 3,200 people working inside the dragon to move it. Which is the best estimate of the length of the dragon?

A 3,048 mm
B 3,048 dm
C 3,048 cm
D 3,048 m

16. Measure to find the length of the bead shown below. What is the length of 32 of these beads on a necklace?

F 30 cm
G 32 cm
H 64 cm
J 100 cm

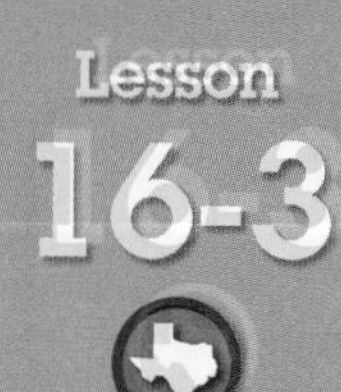

TEKS 4.11A: Estimate and use measurement tools to determine length (including perimeter), area, capacity, and weight/mass using standard units SI (metric) and customary.

Perimeter

Hands-On
metric ruler

How do you find the distance around an object?

Fred wants to put a border around the bulletin board in his room. How much border will he need?

Perimeter is the distance around a figure.

Another Example How do you estimate and find the perimeter of different figures?

Estimate and find the perimeter of the hexagon below.

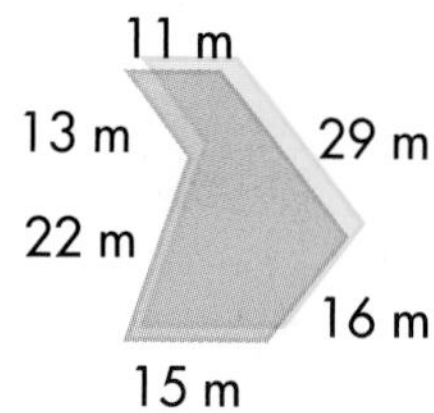

Use rounding to estimate:
$30 + 20 + 20 + 20 + 10 + 10 = 110$

Add the actual numbers:
$29 + 16 + 15 + 22 + 13 + 11 = 106$

The perimeter of the hexagon is 106 m.

Find the perimeter of the square below. All 4 sides of a square are the same length. So, the formula is:
$P = s + s + s + s$
or, $P = 4 \times s$

9 cm

$s = 9$
$P = 4 \times 9$
$P = 36$

The perimeter of the square is 36 cm.

Explain It

1. How can you use addition to find the perimeter of a square? How can you use multiplication?

2. Why couldn't you use a formula to find the perimeter of the hexagon? Could you ever use a formula to find the perimeter of a hexagon? Explain.

One Way

Measure to find the length of each side. Then add to find the perimeter.

36 + 22 + 36 + 22 = 116

The perimeter of the bulletin board is 116 inches.

Another Way

Use a formula.

Perimeter = (2 × length) + (2 × width)

$P = (2 \times \ell) + (2 \times w)$

$P = (2 \times 22) + (2 \times 36)$

$P = 44 + 72$

$P = 116$

The perimeter of the bulletin board is 116 inches.

width

length

Guided Practice*

Do you know HOW?

For **1** through **4**, estimate, and then find the perimeter of each figure.

1. 16 in. 11 in. 13 in.

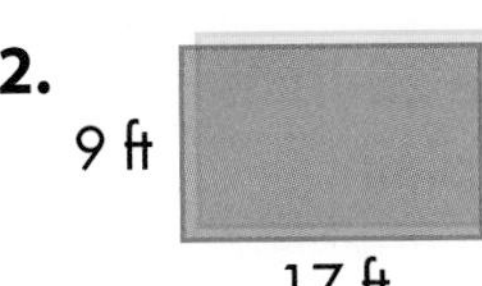

2. 9 ft 17 ft

3. 12 mm 6 mm 15 mm 17 mm 21 mm

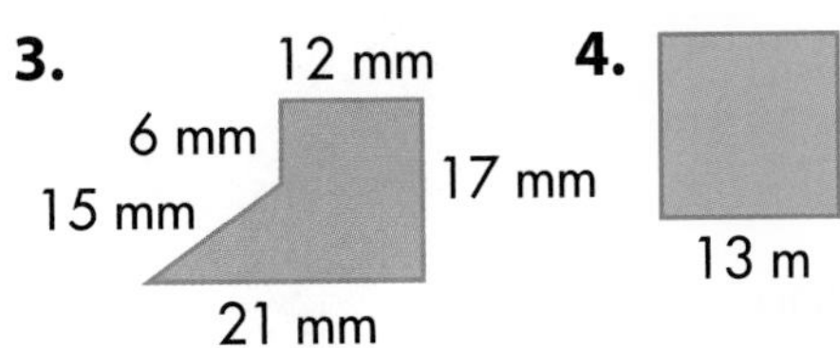

4. 13 m

Do you UNDERSTAND?

5. How can you use a formula to find the perimeter of a polygon that has sides of equal length?

6. How can you estimate to see if the value you found for the perimeter of Fred's bulletin board is reasonable?

7. Fred is making a frame for an autographed photo of his favorite soccer player. If the picture is 8 inches by 10 inches, how much wood will Fred need for the frame?

Independent Practice

Leveled Practice For **8** through **10**, measure the sides and find the perimeter of each figure.

8.

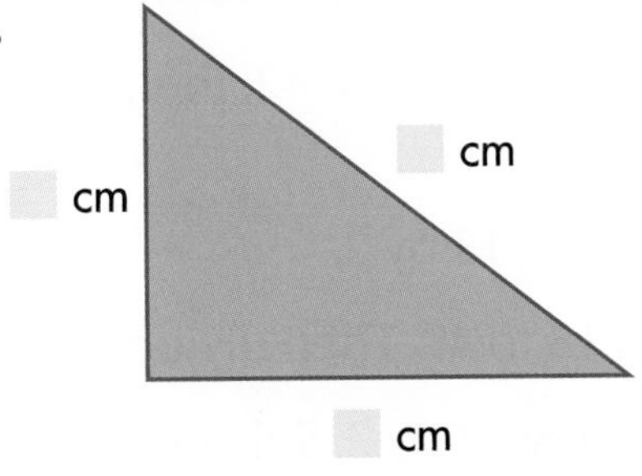

9.

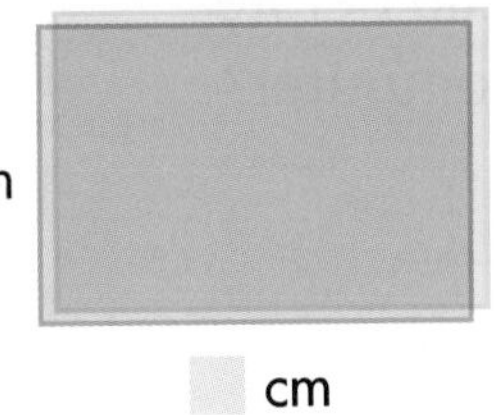

10.

*For another example, see Set C on page 364.

Independent Practice

For **11** through **18**, estimate, and then find the perimeter of each figure.

11. 

12.

13. 

14. 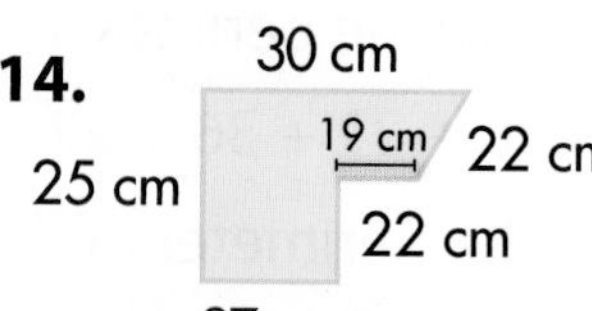

15. 

16. 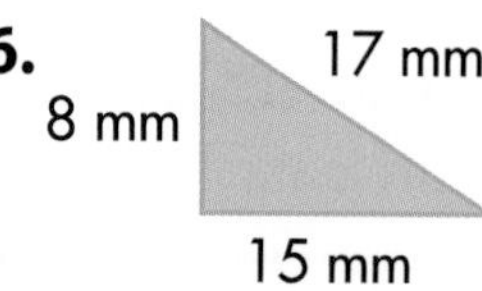

17. 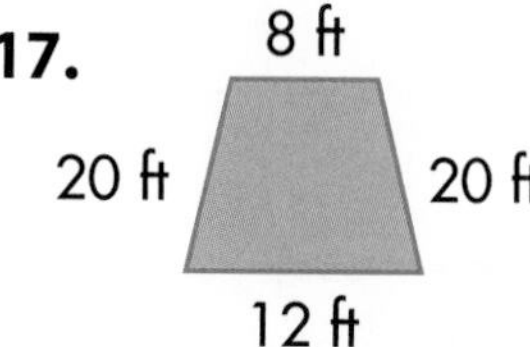

18. 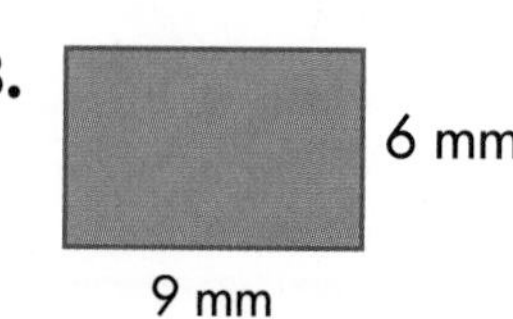

TAKS Problem Solving

19. Tom drew the 2 rectangles at the right. What is the difference between the perimeter of Rectangle A and the perimeter of Rectangle B?

A 3 cm **B** 6 cm **C** 12 cm **D** 54 cm

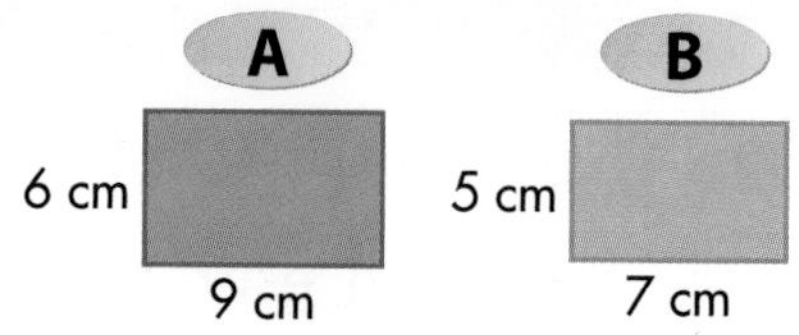

20. **Reasoning** Which has a greater perimeter, a 28-inch square or a 21-inch by 31-inch rectangle? Explain.

21. Charles wanted to estimate the perimeter of Texas, so he drew several polygons and placed them over a map of the state. Estimate the perimeter of Texas to the nearest hundred.

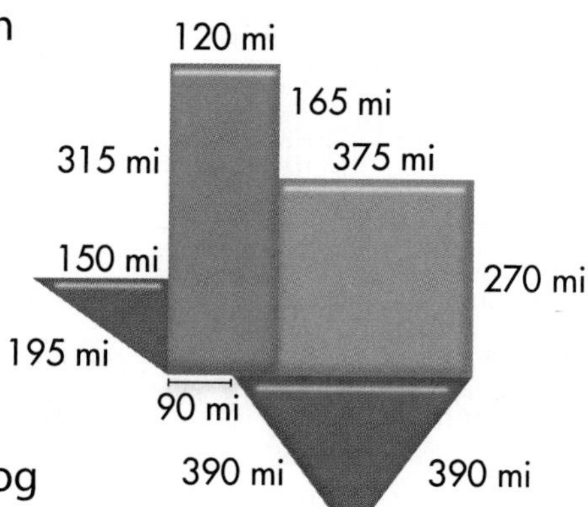

22. **Writing to Explain** Paula built a play area for her dog in the shape of a regular pentagon. If the perimeter is 35 feet, what is the length of each side of the play area?

23. Myles gets to play on the computer every time he reads 120 pages. If he reads 10 pages a night, how many nights will he have to read before he gets to play on the computer?

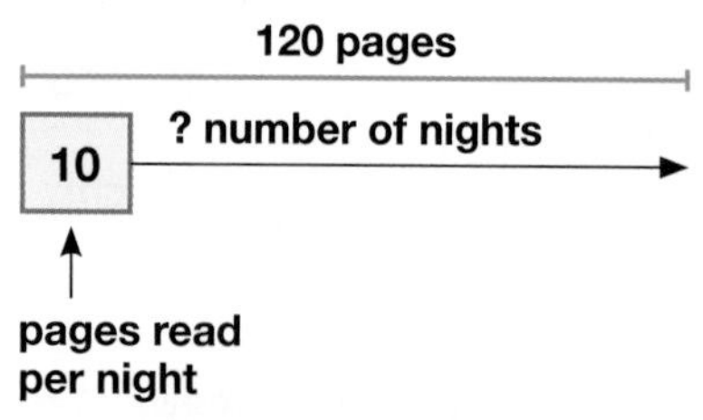

24. Think About the Process James wants to draw a rectangle with a perimeter of 42 units and a length of 13 units. How can he determine the width?

F Subtract 13 from 42, then divide by 2.

G Multiply 13 by 2.

H Add 13 to 42. Then divide by 2.

J Multiply 13 by 2. Subtract the product from 42. Divide the difference by 2.

Algebra Connections

Missing Numbers and Operations

Often there is more than one way to connect two numbers when a number and the operation is missing.

Here are some rules:

- If the number that appears first is less than the second number, try using addition and multiplication.
- If the number that appears first is greater than the second number, try using subtraction and division.

Example: 2 ☐ ▢ = 6

Use addition:

Think *2 plus what number equals 6?*

$2 + 4 = 6$

Use multiplication:

Think *2 times what number equals 6?*

$2 \times 3 = 6$

Find the missing operation for each ☐ and the missing number for each ▢.

1. 4 ☐ ▢ = 8
4 ☐ ▢ = 8

2. 45 ☐ ▢ = 9
45 ☐ ▢ = 9

3. 80 ☐ ▢ = 8
80 ☐ ▢ = 8

4. 6 ☐ ▢ = 30
6 ☐ ▢ = 30

5. 8 ☐ ▢ = 56
8 ☐ ▢ = 56

6. 54 ☐ ▢ = 6
54 ☐ ▢ = 6

7. 3 ☐ ▢ = 21
3 ☐ ▢ = 21

8. 64 ☐ ▢ = 8
64 ☐ ▢ = 8

9. 28 ☐ ▢ = 4
28 ☐ ▢ = 4

10. 6 ☐ ▢ = 36
6 ☐ ▢ = 36

11. 5 ☐ ▢ = 40
5 ☐ ▢ = 40

12. 34 ☐ ▢ = 17
34 ☐ ▢ = 17

For **13** through **16**, find the missing operation and number. Then find the answer.

13. Cassie has \$4. She wants to buy a blouse that costs \$16. How much more money does Cassie need?

\$4 ☐ \$▢ = \$16

14. Doug had 42 patio blocks. He stacked them in equal groups of 7 blocks. How many stacks were there?

42 ☐ ▢ = 7

15. Lesley had 37 postcards. She mailed some to her friends. If 25 postcards were left, how many stamps did she use?

37 ☐ ▢ = 25

16. There were 4 rabbits in each litter. Gerta's pet rabbit was mother to 20 rabbits. How many litters of rabbits were there?

4 ☐ ▢ = 20

Lesson

16-4

TEKS 4.11A . . . use measurement tools to determine length (including perimeter), area, capacity, and weight/mass using standard units SI (metric) and customary.

Area of Squares and Rectangles

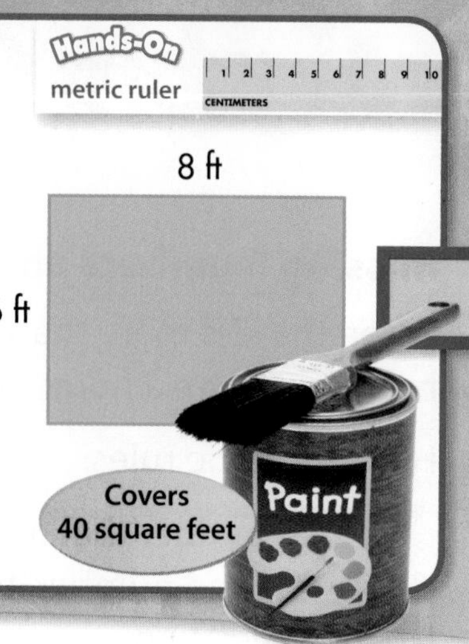

How can you find the area of a figure?

A small can of chalkboard paint covers 40 square feet. Does Mike need more than one small can to paint one wall of his room?

Area is the number of square units needed to cover a figure.

Guided Practice*

Do you know HOW?

For **1** through **4**, find the area of each figure.

1. 7 in, 3 in

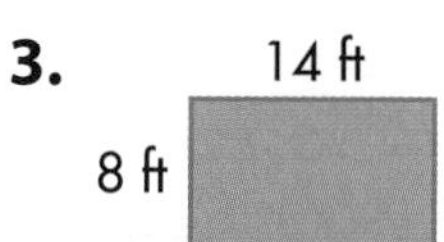

2. 5 m, 4 m

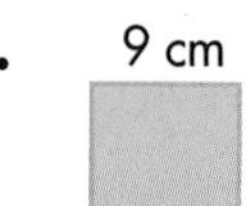

3. 14 ft, 8 ft

4. 9 cm

Do you UNDERSTAND?

5. What is the formula for the area of a square? Explain how you know.

6. Mike plans to paint another wall in his room blue. That wall measures 12 feet by 8 feet. How much area does Mike need to paint?

Independent Practice

Leveled Practice In **7** and **8**, measure the sides and find the area of each figure.

7. ▭ cm, ▭ cm

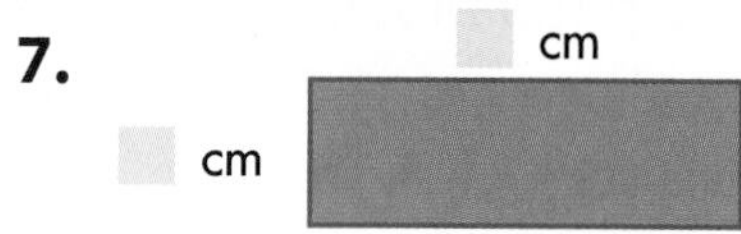

8. ▭ cm, ▭ cm

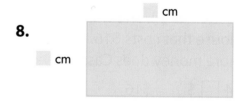

In **9** through **16**, find the area of each figure.

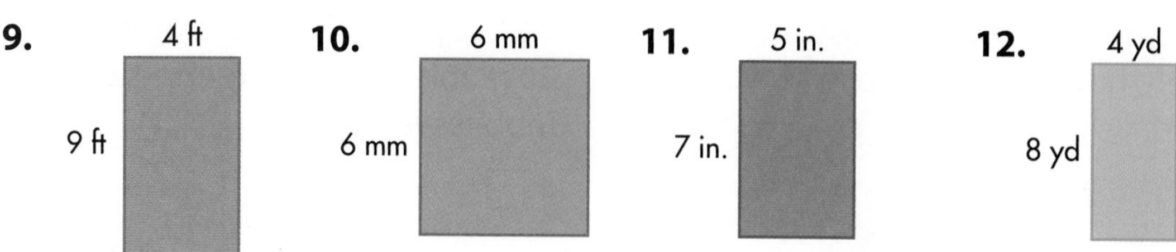

9. 4 ft, 9 ft

10. 6 mm, 6 mm

11. 5 in., 7 in.

12. 4 yd, 8 yd

*For another example, see Set D on page 365.

One Way

You can count the square units to find area.

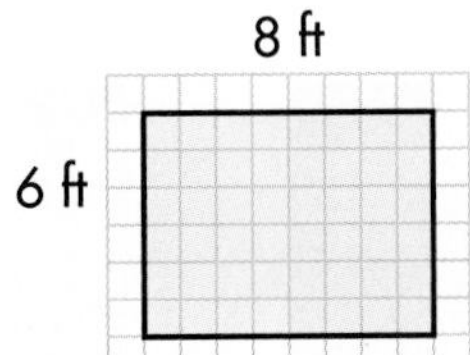

There are 48 square units.

The area of Mike's wall is 48 square feet.

Another Way

You can measure to find the length of each side and use a formula to find area.

Area = length × width

$A = \ell \times w$

$A = 8 \times 6$

$A = 48$

The area of Mike's wall is 48 square feet. He will need more than one small can of paint.

13. 14 m, 3m

14. 13 mm, 9 mm

15. 11 cm, 9 cm

16. 4 yd

TAKS Problem Solving

17. Reasoning Jen's garden is 4 feet wide and has an area of 28 square feet. What is the length of the garden?

18. Diane drew a polygon with 4 sides and 1 set of parallel sides. What type of polygon did Diane draw?

19. Writing to Explain Leah says the area of a rectangle is always greater than its perimeter. Jules says the perimeter of a rectangle is always greater. Who is correct?

20. Mr. Chen is putting tile down in his kitchen. The kitchen is 16 feet long and 8 feet wide. The tile costs $5 per square foot. How much will it cost Mr. Chen to tile his kitchen?

21. Helen's sandbox is 6 feet long and 5 feet wide. What is the area of the sandbox?

A 11 sq ft

B 22 sq ft

C 30 sq ft

D 36 sq ft

22. Number Sense At the first bus stop 18 people got on. At the next stop, 12 people got off and half as many people got on. At the third stop 6 people got off and 2 got on. At the fourth stop, half the people on the bus got off. How many people are left on the bus?

23. The playground map of the United States is a rectangle with a width of 25 feet. Its length is 10 feet longer than its width. Find the area of the map.

DIGITAL Animated Glossary, eTools **www.pearsonsuccessnet.com**

Lesson

16-5

TEKS 4.11A: Estimate and use measurement tools to determine length (including perimeter), area, capacity, and weight/mass using standard units SI (metric) and customary.

Area of Irregular Shapes

Hands-On

metric ruler

How can you find the area of an irregular figure?

Mr. Fox is covering a miniature golf course hole with artificial grass. How many 1-foot squares of carpet will Mr. Fox need to cover the miniature golf course hole?

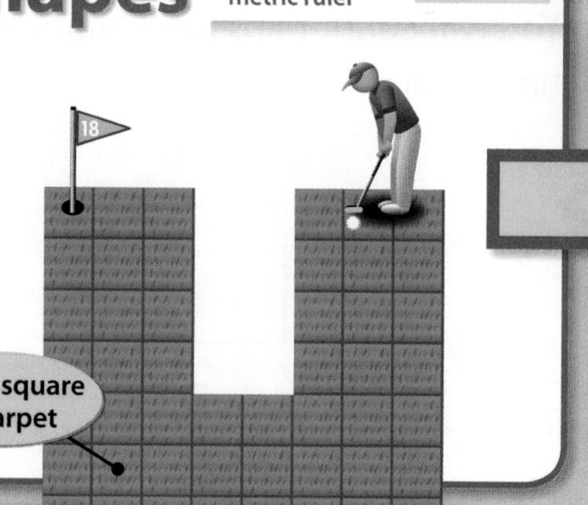

Another Example How can you estimate area?

Some shapes contain partial square units.

Estimate the area of the trapezoid to the right.

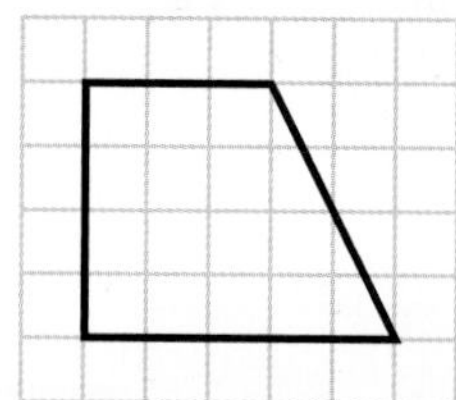

One Way

Count the whole square units. Then estimate the number of units made from combining partial squares.

There are 14 whole square units. The partial square units make about 2 more square units.

$14 + 2 = 16$

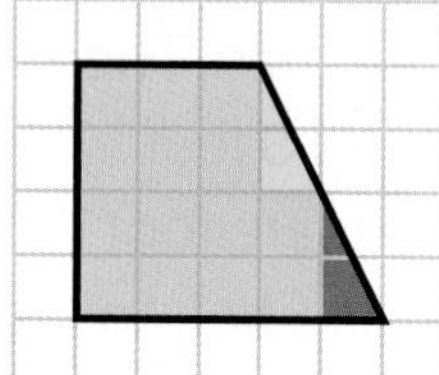

The trapezoid has an area of about 16 square units.

Another Way

Draw a rectangle around the trapezoid and find the rectangle's area.

$A = 4 \times 5 = 20$

Find the area outside the trapezoid but inside the rectangle.

There are about 4 square units not in the trapezoid.

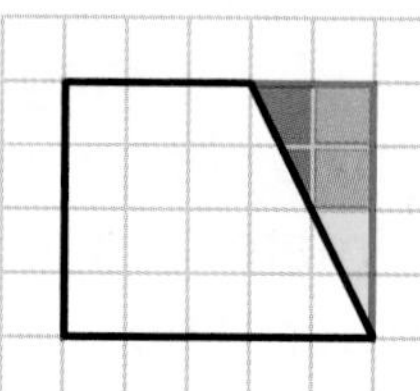

Subtract to find the difference between the two areas.

$20 - 4 = 16$

The trapezoid has an area of about 16 square units.

Explain It

1. Why is the answer of 16 square units considered an estimate?
2. Can the trapezoid be divided into rectangles to find the area?

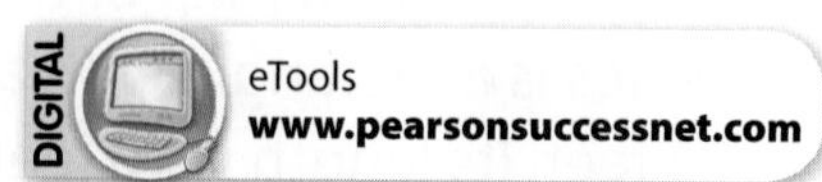

One Way

Count the square units to find the area.

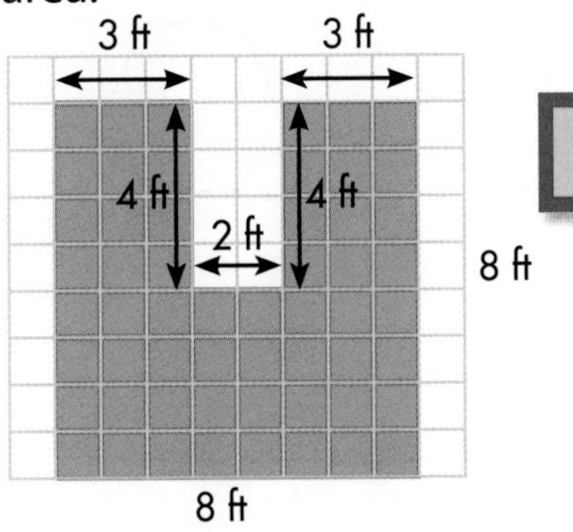

The area of the golf course hole is 56 square feet.

Another Way

Divide the hole into rectangles. Find the area of each rectangle and add.

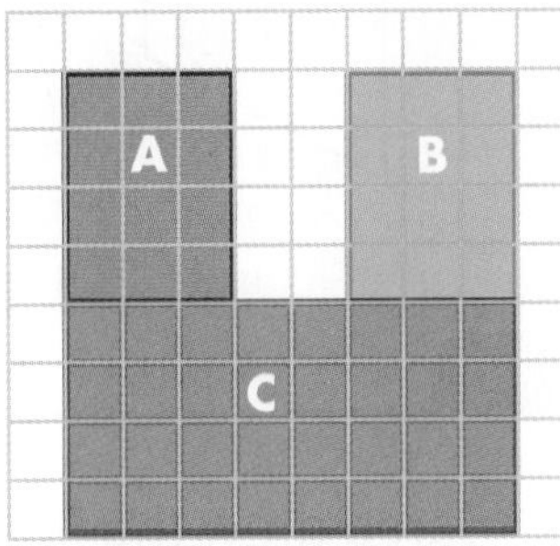

Rectangle A
$A = 4 \times 3 = 12$

Rectangle B
$A = 4 \times 3 = 12$

Rectangle C
$A = 4 \times 8 = 32$

Add the areas: $12 + 12 + 32 = 56$
The area of the golf course hole is 56 square feet.

Guided Practice*

Do you know HOW?

For **1** and **2**, find the area of each figure.

1.

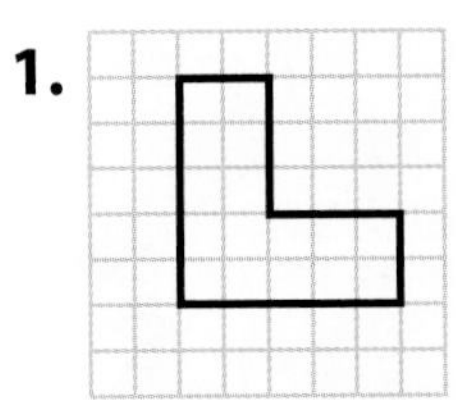

2.

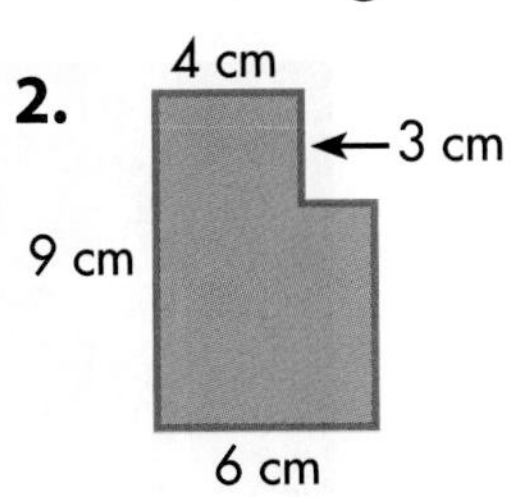

For **3** and **4**, estimate the area of each figure.

3.

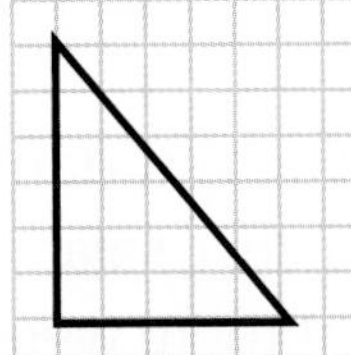

4.

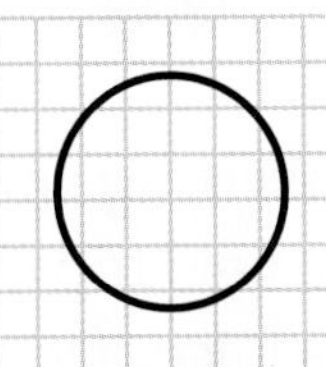

Do you UNDERSTAND?

5. **Writing to Explain** Could the golf course hole be divided into any other set of rectangles?

6. Suppose Mr. Fox bought 75 square feet of artificial grass. How much artificial grass will be left over?

7. Mr. Fox decided the area of the hole was too large. What would the new area of the hole be if he only uses rectangles A and C in the example above?

Independent Practice

For **8** and **9**, measure and find the area of each figure.

8.

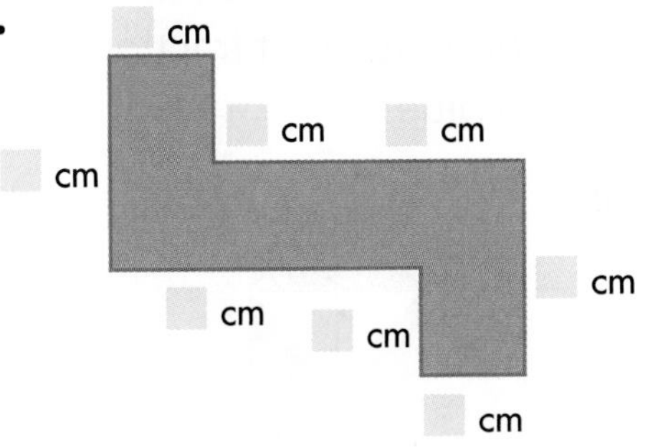

9.

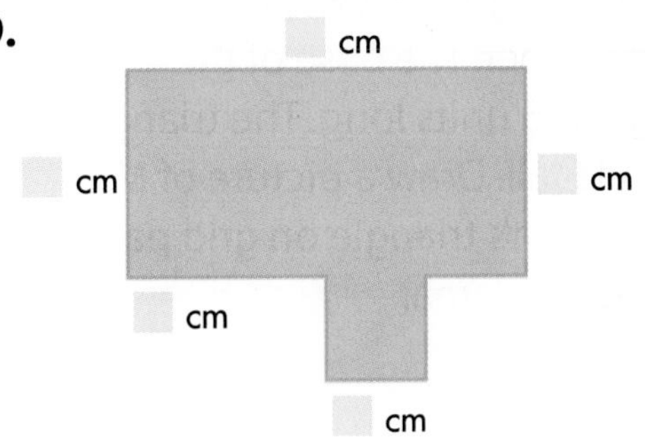

For another example, see Set E on page 365.

For **10** through **13**, estimate the area of each figure. Each □ = 1 square inch.

10. 

11. 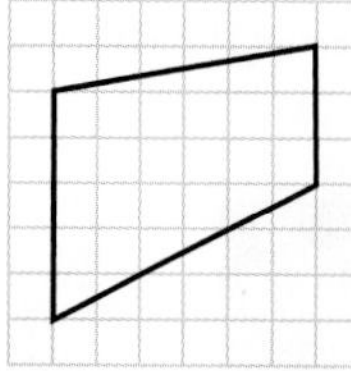

12. 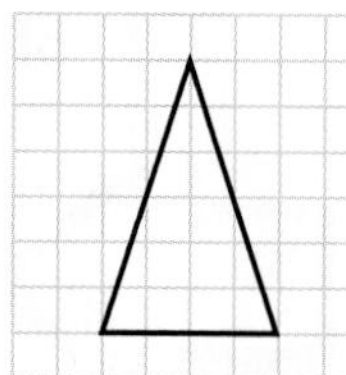

13. 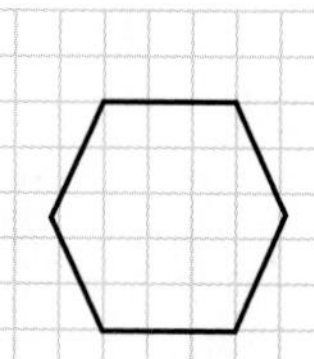

TAKS Problem Solving

14. Think About the Process Jared drew the figure to the right on grid paper. Which is **NOT** a way in which the figure could be divided to find the total area?

A $(4 \times 6) + (3 \times 3)$

B $(3 \times 7) + (4 \times 2) + (4 \times 1)$

C $(4 \times 6) + (3 \times 7)$

D $(2 \times 4) + (3 \times 3) + (4 \times 1) + (4 \times 3)$

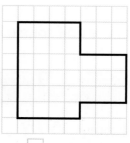

Each □ = 1 square inch.

15. Writing to Explain Laurie's family is building a new house. The design for the house is shown to the right. What is the area of the new house? How big will their yard be?

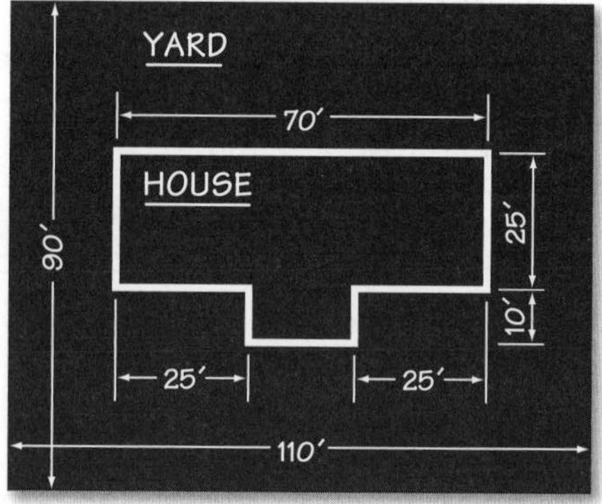

16. Algebra Write an algebraic expression to represent the phrase "six times a number is 24." Solve the expression

17. Writing to Explain Each student on a field trip got a sandwich, a salad, and a juice. If you know that there were 10 students on the field trip, would you be able to tell how much they paid for lunch in all? Why or why not?

18. Mrs. Washington drew a triangle on grid paper. The base of the triangle is 6 units long. The triangle is 8 units tall. Draw a picture of Mrs. Washington's triangle on grid paper. Estimate the area.

19. Mandy designed a patch to add to her quilt. What fraction is colored blue?

F $\frac{2}{8}$

G $\frac{4}{8}$

H $\frac{8}{8}$

J $\frac{8}{4}$

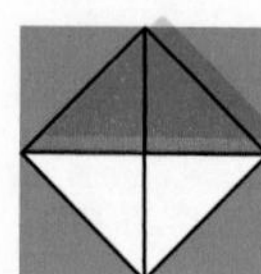

Algebra Connections

Changing Patterns

Algebra is a language of patterns, rules, and symbols. Sometimes the patterns stay the same, but sometimes the patterns change. To identify a changing number pattern, first look at the pattern of numbers.

Ask Yourself:

How is each number related to the number to the left and to the right of it?

Example: Look at this pattern of numbers.

8, 10, 14, 20, 28, 38, 50, 64

What is the next number in the pattern?

Think *What is the difference between each number in the pattern and the following number?*

+2, +4, +6, +8, +10...

64 + 16 = 80

80 is the next number in the pattern.

For exercises **1** through **4**, find the next two numbers.

1. 2, 2, 4, 4, 8, 8, 16, 16, ▢, ▢

2. 5, 10, 9, 18, 17, 34, 33, 66, ▢, ▢

3. 14, 12, 16, 14, 18, 16, 20, 18, ▢, ▢

4. 6, 9, 8, 11, 10, 13, 12, 15, ▢, ▢

For exercises **5** through **10**, find the pattern.

5. 1, 2, 4, 7, 11, 16

6. 2, 7, 9, 15, 17, 24

7. 4, 5, 8, 9, 12, 13

8. 7, 9, 10, 12, 13, 15

9. 2, 4, 12, 48, 240

10. 8, 13, 23, 21, 26, 36, 34

11. It takes 40 minutes to bake a batch of muffins. Two batches of muffins takes 1 hour 20 minutes, 3 batches take 2 hours. How long will it take to make 4 batches of muffins?

12. Linda has three houseplants. She buys two more, then gives one away to her friend, Jayne. If Linda repeats this process five more times, how many house plants will she have?

Lesson
16-6

TEKS 4.14C: Select or develop an appropriate problem-solving plan or strategy, including drawing a picture, looking for a pattern, systematic guessing and checking, acting it out, making a table, working a simpler problem, or working backwards to solve a problem.

Problem Solving

Solve a Simpler Problem and Make a Table

Each side of a triangle cracker below is one inch long. If there are 12 triangle crackers in a row, what is the perimeter of the figure?

1 inch

Guided Practice*

Do you know HOW?

1. Cora is cutting a piece of paper to get equal sized pieces. After the first cut she stacks the two pieces and makes another cut. After she makes the second cut she stacks the pieces again. If this pattern continues how many pieces will she have after the fourth cut?

Do you UNDERSTAND?

2. How was the problem above broken into simpler problems?

3. **Write a Problem** Write a problem that you can solve by making a table.

Independent Practice

Solve.

4. Troy is helping his father build a fence. Each section of the fence has a post at each end. Make a table showing how many posts will be needed if there are 1, 3, 5, 10, 15, or 20 sections of the fence. Look for a pattern.

5. How many posts will be needed if the fence has 47 sections?

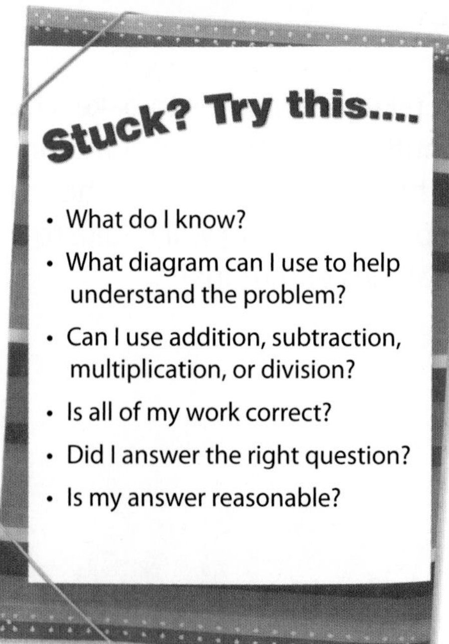
Stuck? Try this....
• What do I know?
• What diagram can I use to help understand the problem?
• Can I use addition, subtraction, multiplication, or division?
• Is all of my work correct?
• Did I answer the right question?
• Is my answer reasonable?

 *For another example, see Set F on page 365.

Plan

Change the problem into problems that are simpler to solve.

Look at 1 triangle, then 2 triangles, then 3 triangles.

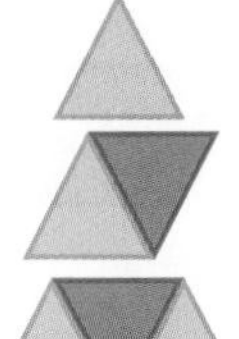

perimeter = 3 inches

perimeter = 4 inches

perimeter = 5 inches

Solve

The perimeter is 2 more than the number of triangles.

Number of triangles	1	2	3
Perimeter (inches)	3	4	5

So, for 12 triangles the perimeter is 14 inches.

---

6. Helen is part of a 32-player one-on-one basketball tournament. As soon as a player loses, she is out of the tournament. The winners will continue to play until there is one champion. How many games are there in all in this tournament?

7. The figure below is a square. If sides A and B are doubled, will this figure still be a square?

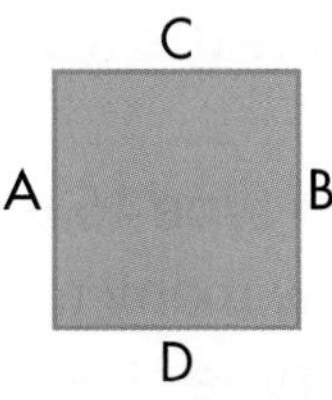

For **8** through **10**, use the table at the right.

8. The missing classes in the schedule to the right are Math, Science, Reading, Spelling, and Social Studies. Math is after morning break. Spelling is at 9:40. Reading and Science are the two afternoon classes. At what time is Math class?

9. What class is at 8:45?

10. Science class is before Reading. What time is Science class?

Data

Class Schedule

Morning	Afternoon
8:30: Opening	12:15:
8:45:	1:00: Break
9:30: Break	1:30:
9:40:	1:55: Recess
10:25: Recess	2:05: Art, Music or P.E.
10:55:	2:40: Pack Up
11:30: Lunch	2:45: School's Out

11. Six friends are playing checkers. If each friend plays against every other friend once, how many games of checkers will they play all together?

12. Mr. McNulty's classroom library has 286 books. If he buys 12 books each month for five months, how many books will he have in all?

13. Jolene, Timmy, Nicholas, Paul, and Kathryn are all planting in a community garden. If each of their plots holds 7 rows and 13 columns, how many plants will they be able to grow all together?

14. Thomas is training for a marathon. He runs for 2 miles and then he walks for a half a mile. If he trains by running 22 miles every day, how many miles would he walk?

15. Every day James spends $\frac{5}{10}$ of an hour on the phone, $\frac{6}{12}$ of an hour reading, and $\frac{3}{6}$ of an hour on the computer. Use the fraction strips to the right to tell which activity James spends the most time doing.

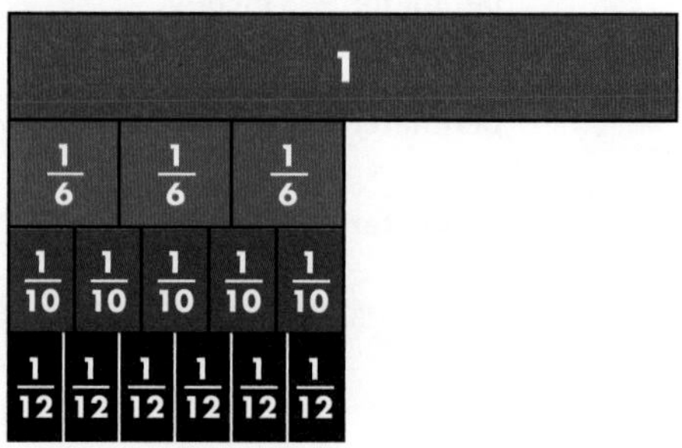

16. Maya is putting 3 ice cubes in each red cup and 4 ice cubes in each blue cup. The cups alternate colors starting with red. How many ice cubes will she use if she has 15 cups?

17. Shaina has a 30-inch necklace she wants to have cut into five 6-inch bracelets for her friends. The jeweler chargers $3 for each cut. How much does Shaina need to pay for the cuts?

18. Danielle can type 15 words per minute. How many minutes will it take her to type 105 words?

Minutes	1	2	3
Words typed	15	30	45

Think About the Process

19. It takes a plumber 4 minutes to cut a pipe. Which expression would you use to find how long it took the plumber to cut a pipe into 7 pieces?

A $4 + 7$

B 4×4

C 7×4

D 7×7

20. On every train car there are two connectors, one at the front and one at the back. These connectors are there so each car can be linked with another car. If a train has 30 cars, how would you find out the number of connections made?

F The number of cars minus 1

G The number of connectors on all the cars minus 1

H Same as the number of cars

J The number of cars plus 1

Finding Area with a Calculator

One Way Find the area of the figure shown at the right:

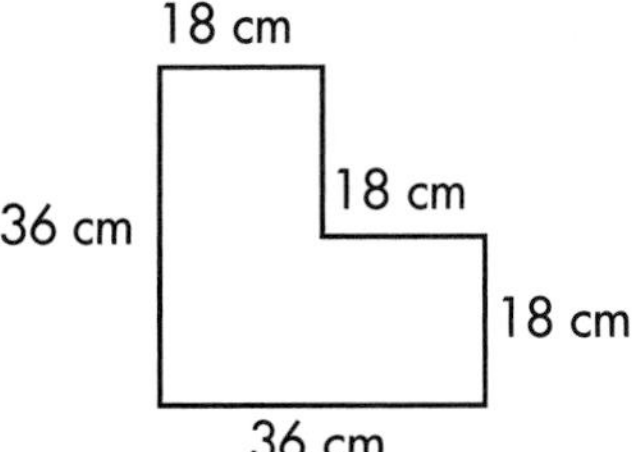

Divide the figure into two rectangles.
Rectangle A is 18 cm by 18 cm.
Rectangle B is 18 cm by 36 cm.

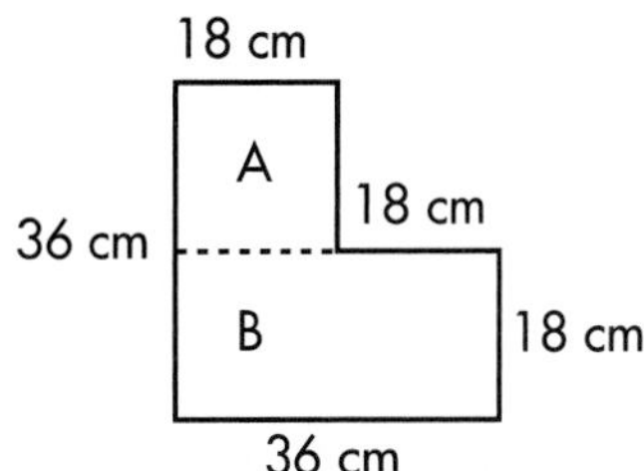

Find the area of each rectangle and add.

Press: 18 [×] 18 [ENTER =] 18 [×] 36 [ENTER =] 324 [+] 648 [ENTER =]

Display: 324 648 972

Another Way Find the area of all at once.

Press: 18 [×] 18 [+] 18 [×] 36 [ENTER =]

Display: 972

The area of the figure is 972 square centimeters.

Practice

Use a calculator to find the area of each figure.

1.

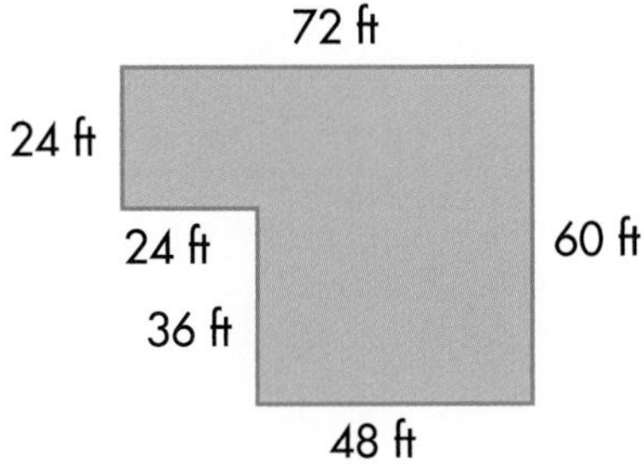

2.

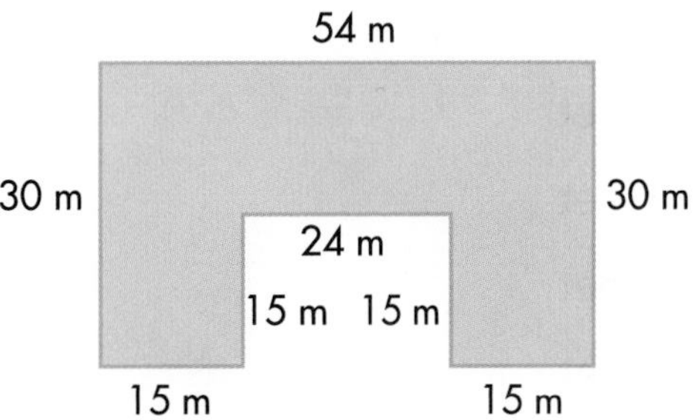

1. Which is the best estimate for the length of an earthworm? (16-1)

A 3 feet

B 3 yards

C 3 miles

D 3 inches

2. Maggie's ping pong table is 9 feet long and 5 feet wide. What is the area of the rectangular playing surface of the ping pong table? (16-4)

F 28 square feet

G 36 square feet

H 45 square feet

J 54 square feet

3. The measurements of the United States flag flying in front of Eugene's school is shown below. What is the perimeter of the flag? (16-3)

A 96 feet

B 40 feet

C 28 feet

D 20 feet

4. What is the difference in the areas of garden plots shown below? (16-4)

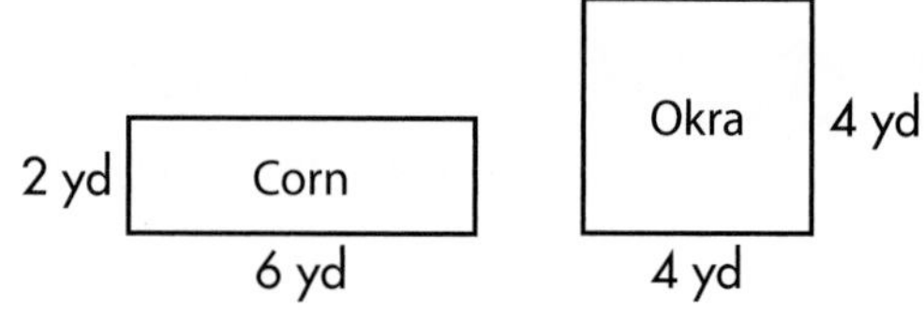

F 2 square yards

G 4 square yards

H 12 square yards

J 16 square yards

5. Which of the following is about 19 centimeters long? (16-2)

A the length of a new pencil

B the width of a school desk

C the width of your pinky finger

D the distance you live from school

6. Each cube has 6 faces. If Tandra stacks 2 cubes on top of each other, she can see 10 faces. If Tandra stacks 7 cubes one on top of the other, how many faces of the cubes will she be able to see? (16-6)

F 42

G 32

H 30

J 28

7. Which is the best estimate of the area of the shape shown below? (16-5)

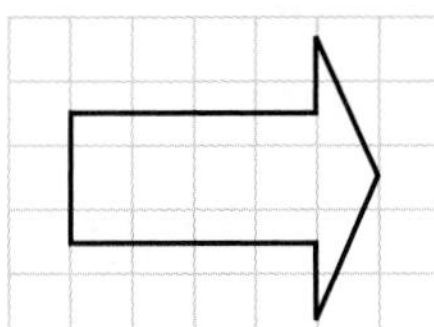

A 19 square units

B 17 square units

C 11 square units

D 5 square units

8. Grayson caught a Woolly Bear caterpillar. It measured 2 inches long. Which caterpillar did Grayson catch? (16-1)

F

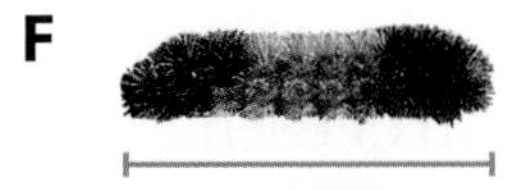

G

H

J

9. Pepper's dog pen measures 4 meters wide and 5 meters long. What is the perimeter of the pen? (16-3)

A 11 meters

B 14 meters

C 18 meters

D 20 meters

10. Which is the appropriate unit to measure the length of a school hallway? (16-2)

F meters

G millimeters

H centimeters

J kilometers

11. A diagram of Izzi's bedroom is shown below. What is the area of her room? (16-5)

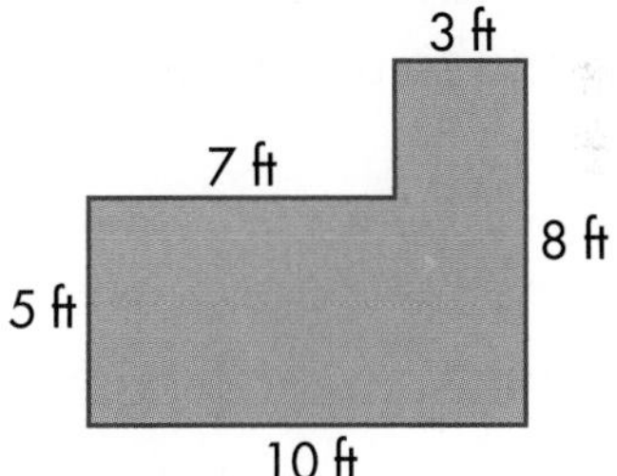

A 44 square feet

B 59 square feet

C 74 square feet

D 80 square feet

12. **Gridded Response** As Devon counted the number of Kennedy half dollar coins he had, he placed the half dollars in one long line. He counted 32 coins. About how many centimeters long was the line of coins? Use a ruler to measure. Then solve. (16-2)

Set A, pages 344–345

Estimate and measure the length of the piece of ribbon.

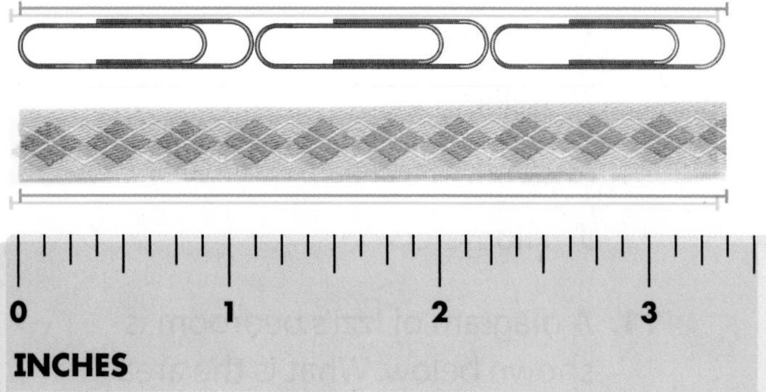

The ribbon's length is about 3 small paper clips. It is 3 inches long to the nearest inch.

Remember to add when combining measurements.

Choose the most appropriate unit to measure the length of each.

1. airport runway **2.** bridge

Estimate and measure the length of the eraser below to the nearest inch.

3.

Set B, pages 346–347

Estimate and measure the length of the crayon.

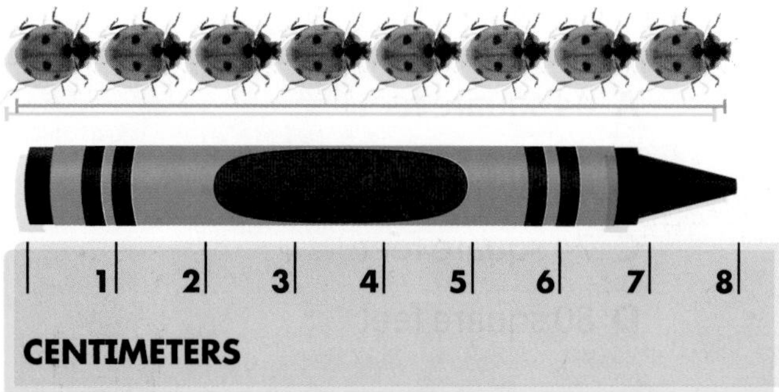

The crayon's length is about 8 ladybugs. It is 8 centimeters long to the nearest centimeter.

Remember you can use objects to help you estimate length.

Choose the most appropriate unit to measure the length of each.

1. baseball bat **2.** penny

Estimate and measure the length of the magnet below to the nearest centimeter.

3.

Set C, pages 348–349

Add to find the perimeter of this rectangle.

$14 + 14 + 6 + 6 = 40$ m

You can use a formula to find the perimeter.

$P = (2 \times \ell) + (2 \times w)$
$P = (2 \times 14) + (2 \times 6)$
$P = 28 + 12$
$P = 40$ m

The perimeter of the rectangle is 40 m.

Remember you can use a formula to find perimeter. Find the perimeter of each figure.

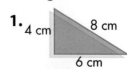

1. 4 cm, 8 cm, 6 cm

2. 9 ft, 26 ft

3.

4.

Reteaching

Set D, pages 352–353

You can count square units to find area.

Use a formula to calculate area.

$A = \ell \times w$
$A = 7 \times 6$
$= 42$

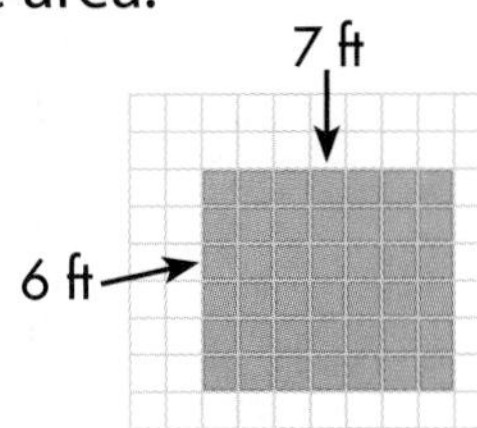

The area of the rectangle is 42 square feet.

Remember you can draw a diagram to help visualize the problem.

Find the area of each figure.

1.

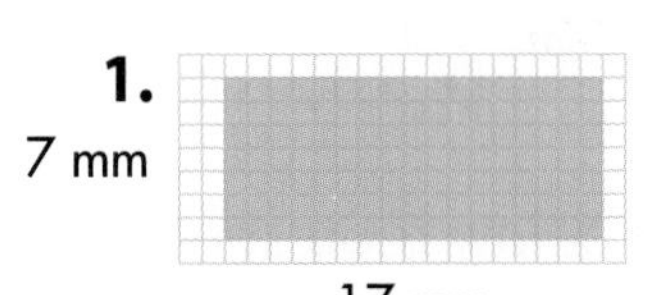

2.

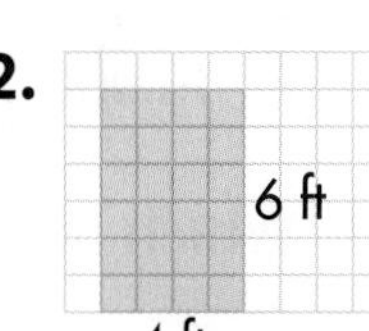

3.

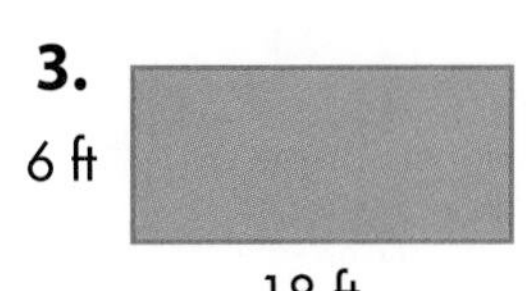

4.

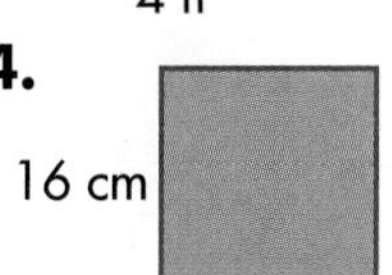

Set E, pages 354–356

You can divide a figure into rectangles to find the area.

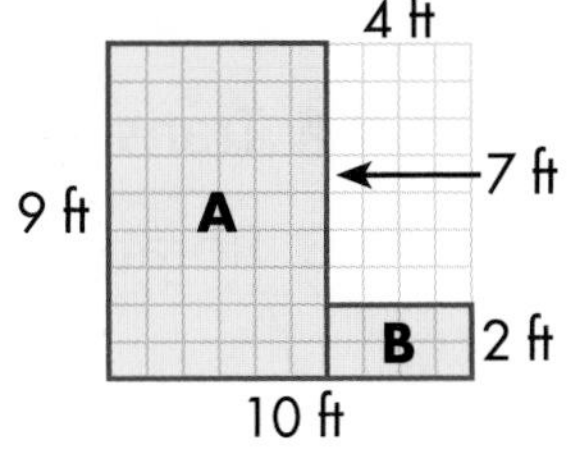

Find the area of each rectangle.

Rectangle A	Rectangle B
$A = 9 \times 6$	$A = 2 \times 4$
$= 54$	$= 8$

Add the partial areas:
54 ft + 8 ft = 62 square feet

Remember you can count the units to find the area.

Find the area of each figure.

1.

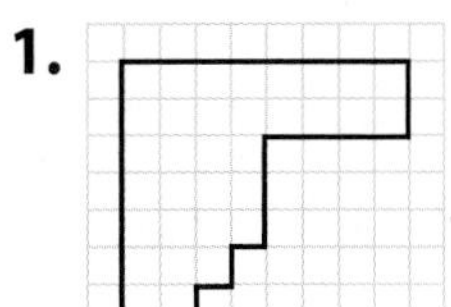

2.

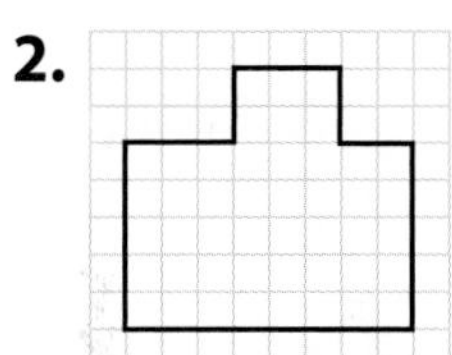

Set F, pages 358–360

Each side of each triangle is two inches. What is the perimeter of the figure with 5 triangles?

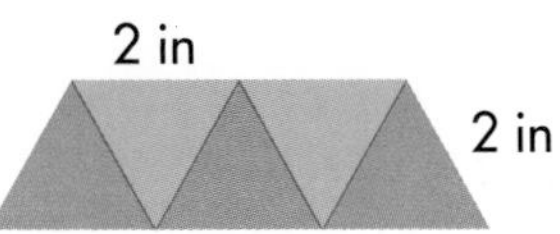

The perimeter increases by 2.

Number of Triangles	1	2	3	4	5
Perimeter	6 in.	8 in.	10 in.	12 in.	14 in.

The perimeter of 5 triangles is 14 inches.

Remember you can break the problem apart and solve.

1. Each side of a square in the figure is one inch. If there are 14 squares in a row, what is the perimeter of the figure?

Topics 1–16

Spiral Review

Number and Operations

1. Which number shows half of ten million?

A 5,000 **C** 500,000

B 50,000 **D** 5,000,000

2. Which model below represents $\frac{1}{2}$?

F 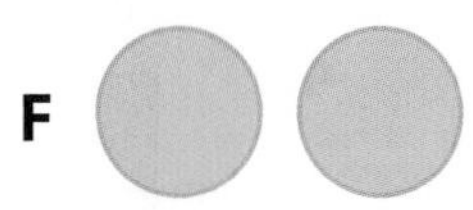

H 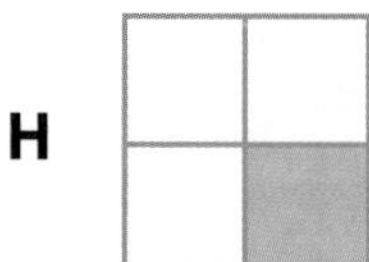

G 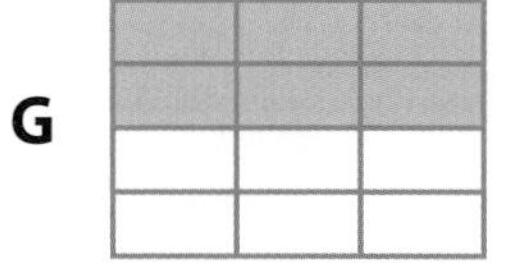

J 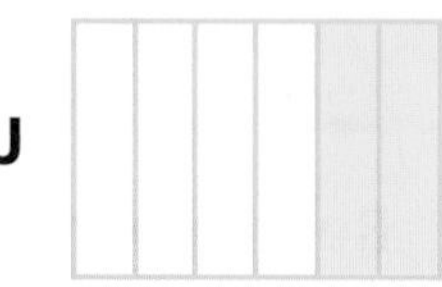

3. Which is the most reasonable estimate for 312×37?

A 10,000 **C** 12,000

B 11,000 **D** 13,000

4. The number line below shows fractions from 0 to 1 divided into eighths. Which point represents $\frac{5}{8}$?

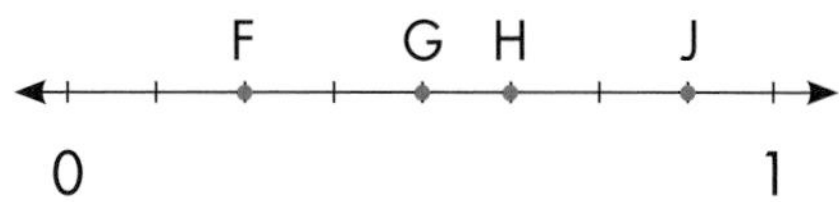

5. Thandie bought a book for $15.95 and a pen for $5.75. She had to borrow two dollars from a friend to pay for her $7.50 movie ticket. How much money did Thandie start with?

6. Writing to Explain Use an array to find 3×18. Explain why this method is like solving two simpler problems.

Geometry and Measurement

7. What kind of angle is shown below?

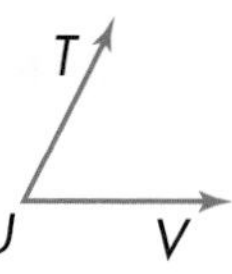

F Acute **H** Obtuse

G Right **J** Straight

8. What transformation was applied to triangle A to get triangle B?

A Translation **C** Reflection

B Rotation **D** Slide

9. I have an odd number of sides. I have more sides than a rectangle but fewer sides than a hexagon. What type of polygon am I?

F Triangle **H** Quadrilateral

G Octagon **J** Pentagon

10. How many lines of symmetry does a pentagon have?

11. Are circles always congruent? Why or why not?

12. Writing to Explain Why can't two lines be both intersecting and parallel?

Probability and Statistics

13. On which color is the spinner most likely to land?

A Blue

B Red

C Green

D Yellow

14. A number cube labeled 1–6 is rolled. What is the probability that the cube will show a number greater than 6?

F Likely **H** Certain

G Impossible **J** Unlikely

Use the bar graph for problems **15** and **16**.

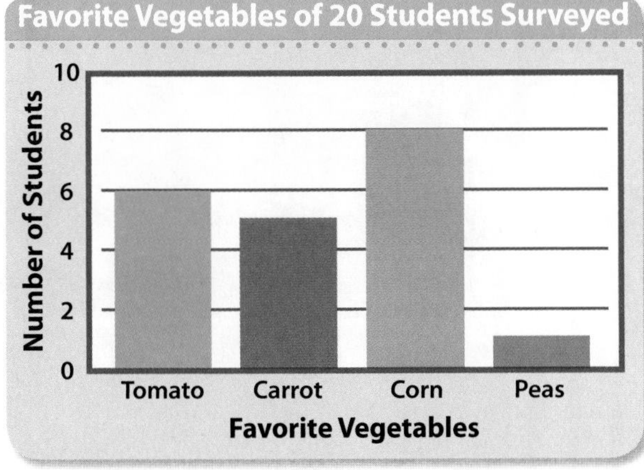

15. What fraction of the people chose carrots?

16. Did more people choose corn or tomatoes as their favorite vegetables?

17. **Writing to Explain** If the probability of spinning yellow is $\frac{2}{8}$, does this mean that you will always spin yellow 2 out of 8 times?

Algebraic Thinking

18. What is the next number in the pattern?

300, 400, 500, 600, ▢

A 650 **C** 750

B 700 **D** 800

19. Solve. $(11 - 7) \times 8$

F 20 **H** 28

G 24 **J** 32

20. The sum of 6 and n is 78. Which number sentence matches the words?

A $6 + 6 = n$

B $n + 78 = 6$

C $78 + n = 6$

D $6 + n = 78$

21. Complete the table.

t	1	2	3	4
$3 \times t$	▢	▢	▢	▢

22. Write an expression for the phrase "j less than 11."

23. Simplify. $(24 \times 8) + r$.

F $30 + r$ **H** $192 + r$

G $32 + r$ **J** $240 + r$

24. **Writing to Explain** How do you use patterns to find $3{,}000 \div 6$ and $3{,}000 \div 60$?

Topic 17

Estimating and Measuring Volume, Capacity, Weight, and Mass

1 The ENIAC was built in 1946 and is known as the first computer ever built. It weighed 30 tons. What units of weight are used to weigh most computers today? You will find out in Lesson 17-6.

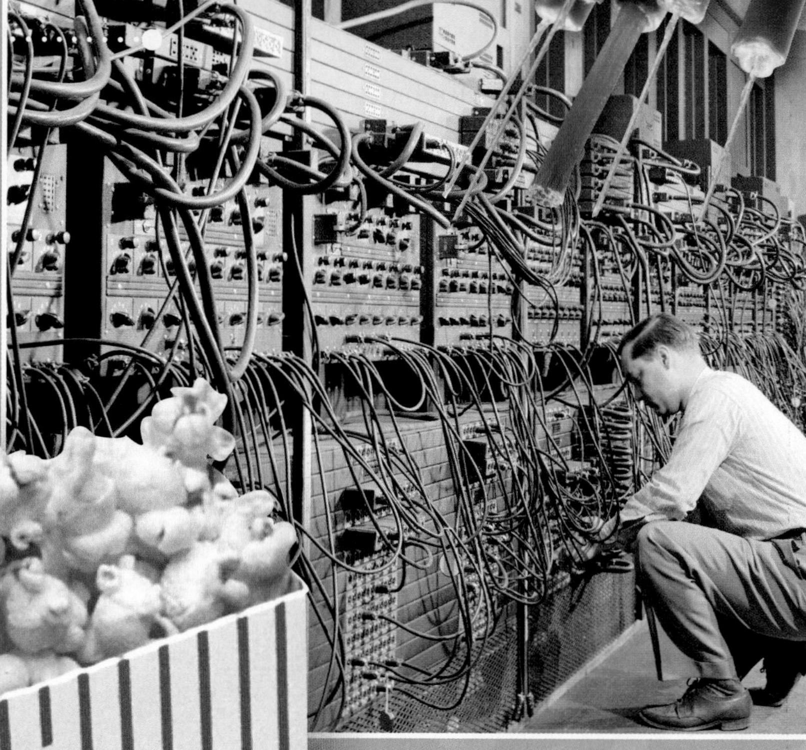

fresh
POP CORN
DELICIOUS CRISP

2 In December 2005, a movie theater in Garland, Texas, broke a world record by filling the largest box of popcorn. It contained over 2,200 pounds of popcorn. How many cubic feet was the box? You will find out in Lesson 17-2.

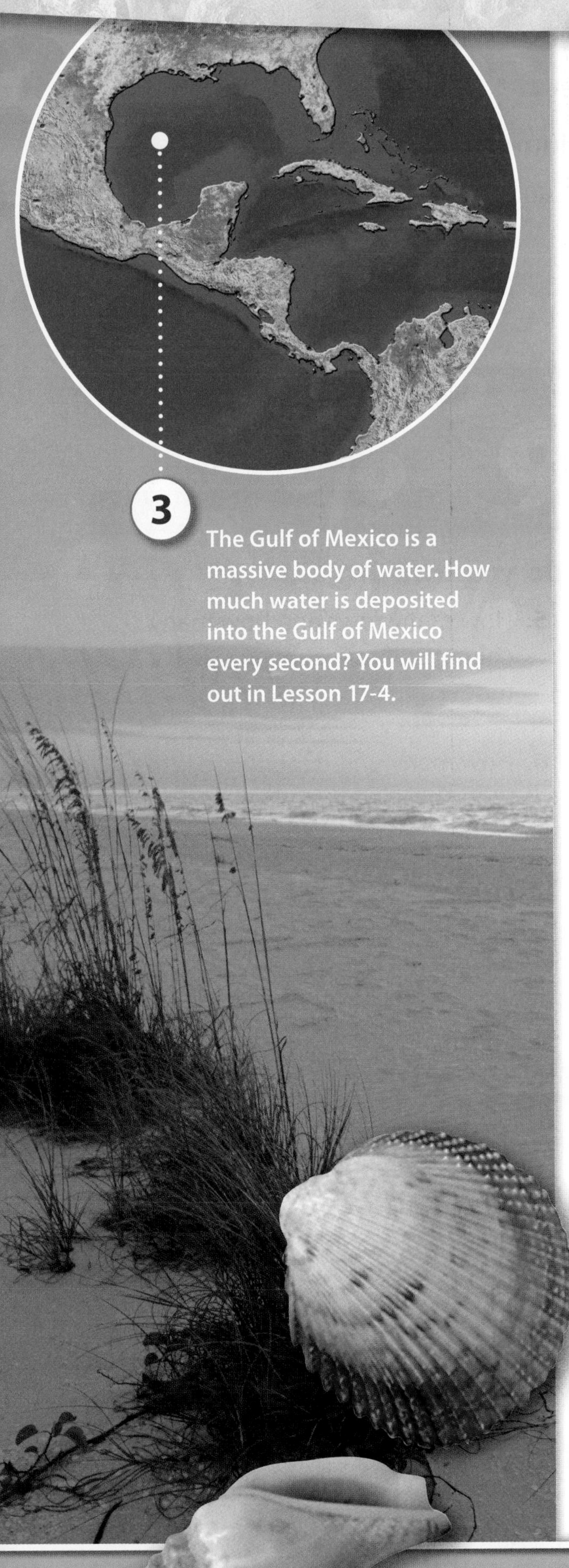

3
The Gulf of Mexico is a massive body of water. How much water is deposited into the Gulf of Mexico every second? You will find out in Lesson 17-4.

Review What You Know!

Vocabulary

Choose the best term from the box.

- cup
- liter
- ounce
- ton

1. A ? is a customary unit of measurement used to find capacity.
2. A ? is equal to 2,000 pounds.
3. A ? is a metric unit of measurement used to find capacity.

Metric Units of Measure

Choose the best estimate for each measurement.

4. Mass of a dog	**A.** 2 kilograms
5. Mass of a bag of flour	**B.** 2 grams
6. Mass of a dime	**C.** 20 kilograms

7. Capacity of a spoon	**A.** 5 liters
8. Capacity of a bathtub	**B.** 5 milliliters
9. Capacity of a pot	**C.** 500 liters

Multiplying Three Factors

10. $3 \times 5 \times 5$	**11.** $6 \times 2 \times 4$	**12.** $1 \times 15 \times 2$
13. $8 \times 8 \times 6$	**14.** $4 \times 10 \times 9$	**15.** $20 \times 7 \times 3$
16. $2 \times 5 \times 4$	**17.** $3 \times 3 \times 3$	**18.** $4 \times 10 \times 2$

19. Writing to Explain Leo can make 3 dozen bagels an hour. If he makes bagels for 8 hours, how many bagels will be made?

Lesson
17-1

TEKS 4.11C: Use concrete models of standard cubic units to measure volume.
Also TEKS 4.14D

Using Models to Measure Volume

Hands-On
unit cubes

How can you measure volume?

Volume is the number of cubic units needed to fill a solid figure.

How many cubes are needed to fill the cereal box to the right?

Guided Practice*

Do you know HOW?

Find the volume of each figure. Write your answer in cubic units.

1.

2. 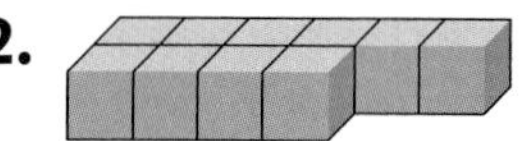

3. 

4. 

Do you UNDERSTAND?

5. How many rows and how many columns of unit cubes are in the model above?

6. How many unit cubes wide is the model in the example above?

7. A model is 2 more cubic units long than it is wide and tall. It is 4 units long. Use unit cubes to find the volume of the model.

Independent Practice

In **8** through **19**, use cubes to find the volume of each figure.

8. 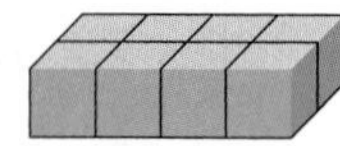

9. 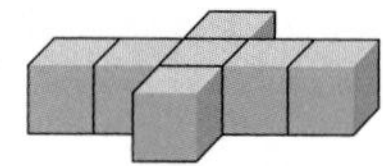

10. 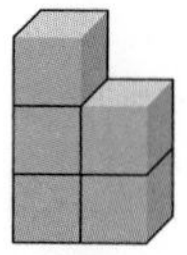

11. 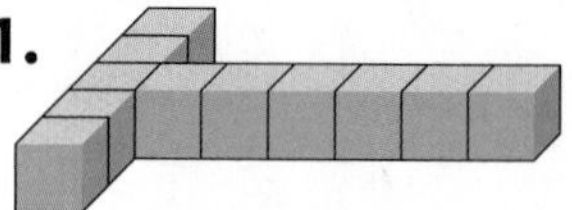

12. 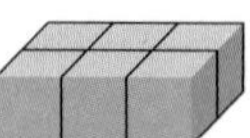

13. 

14. 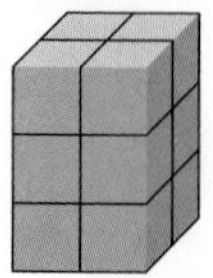

15. 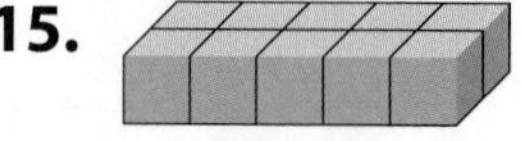

*For another example, see Set A on page 388.

Build a model of the cereal box using unit cubes.

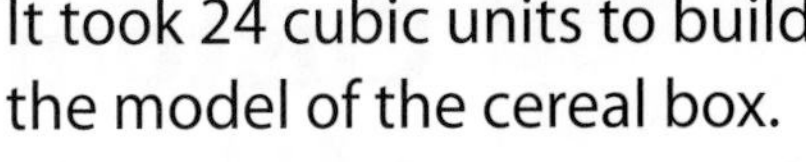

It took 24 cubic units to build the model of the cereal box.

The volume of the cereal box is 24 cubic units.

16. 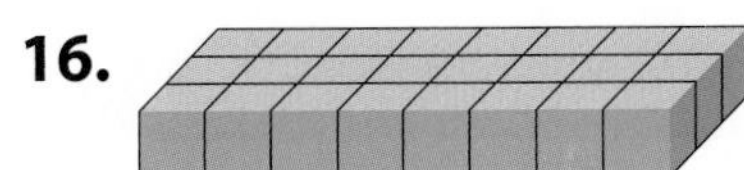

17. 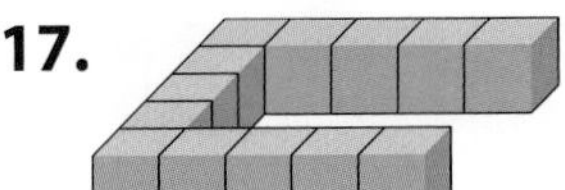

18. 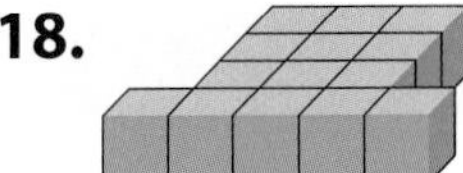

19. 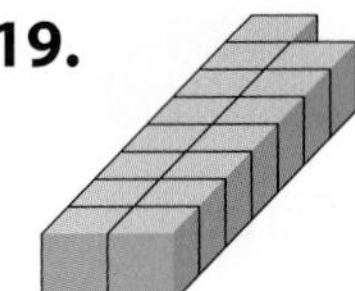

TAKS Problem Solving

20. Writing to Explain Grant drew a triangle where all three sides were 6 inches long. Doreen drew a triangle where two sides were 6 inches and one side was 4 inches long. Are the two figures congruent? Explain.

21. Stella is playing with stacking cubes. She puts 6 cubes in the bottom layer, 4 cubes in the next layer, and 2 cubes in the top layer. Use cubes to find the volume of the stacking cubes.

22. Brenda built a solid figure that has 8 cubes in the bottom layer, 5 cubes in the middle layer, and 3 cubes in the top layer. Use cubes to find the volume of her figure.

23. Use unit cubes to build two different solids each with a volume of 8 cubic units.

24. A baseball team has 7 pitchers. If each pitcher has 3 baseball gloves, how many gloves do they have in all?

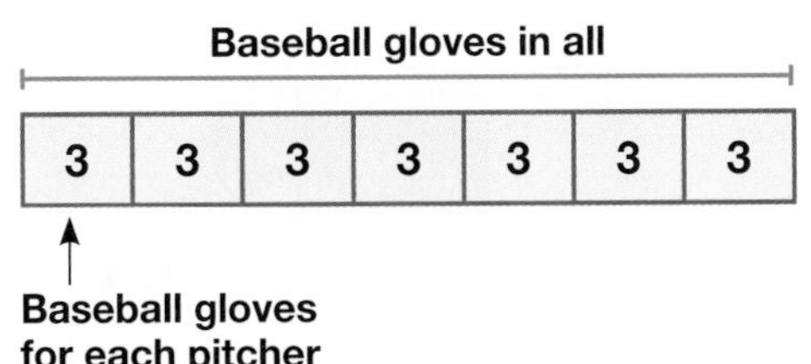

25. Find the volume of the figure. Use cubes to help you.

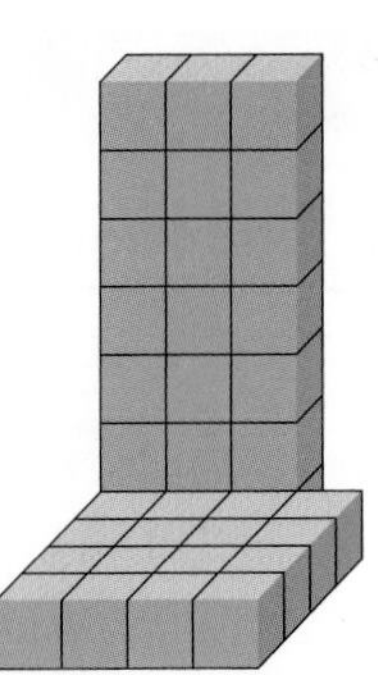

A 35 cubic units

B 37 cubic units

C 40 cubic units

D 42 cubic units

Lesson
17-2

TEKS 4.11C: Use concrete models of standard cubic units to measure volume.
TEKS 4.11D: Estimate volume in cubic units.
Also TEKS 4.14A

Customary Units of Volume

Hands-On
unit cubes

How can you estimate and find the volume of a rectangular prism in customary units?

Stu's family uses a yard cart to haul dirt and mulch. How many cubic feet of dirt can the cart hold without overflowing?

Other Examples

Estimate the volume of this figure.

V = 4 × 2 × 3

V = 24

The volume is about 24 cubic feet.

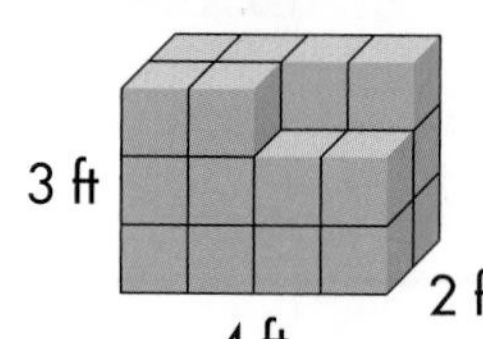

Guided Practice*

Do you know HOW?

For **1** and **2**, find the volume of each figure. Write your answer in cubic units.

1.

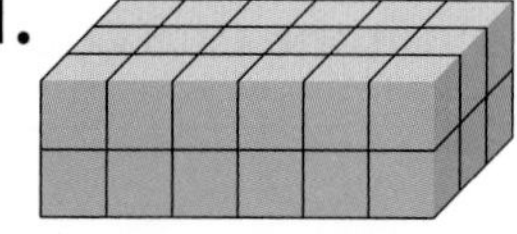

1 cube = 1 cubic yard

2.

Do you UNDERSTAND?

3. A cube has a length of 3 inches. What is the volume of the cube?

Tip Each side of a cube has the same length.

4. Find the volume of the yard cart if it was 2 feet deep.

Independent Practice

For **5** through **7**, estimate the volume of each figure.

5.

1 cube = 1 cubic inch

6.

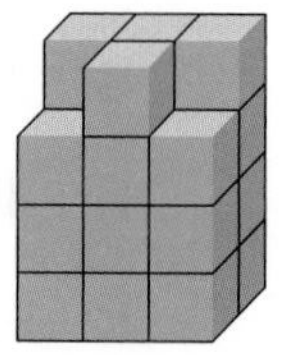

1 cube = 1 cubic inch

7.

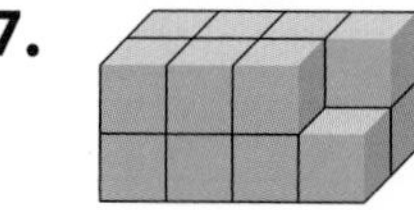

1 cube = 1 cubic foot

*For another example, see Set B on page 388.

Count the cubes.

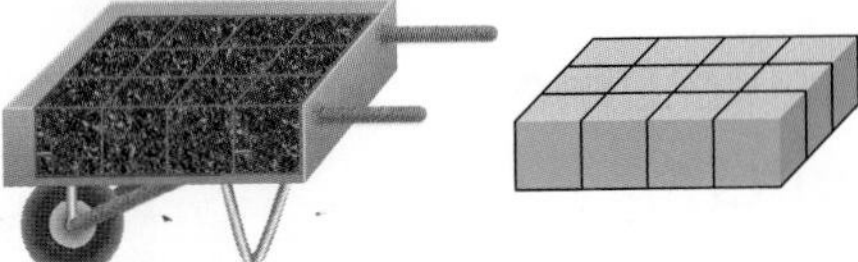

Each cube is 1 cubic foot.
There are 12 cubes in all.

The volume of the cart is 12 cubic feet. The cart can hold 12 cubic feet of dirt.

Use a formula:

Volume = length × width × height

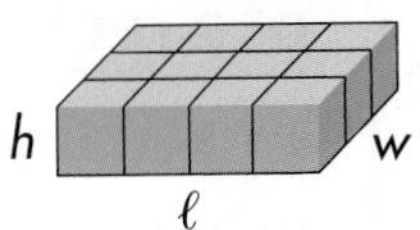

$V = \ell \times w \times h$

$V = 4 \times 3 \times 1 = 12$ cubic feet

The volume is 12 cubic feet.

For **8** through **10**, find the volume of each figure.

8.

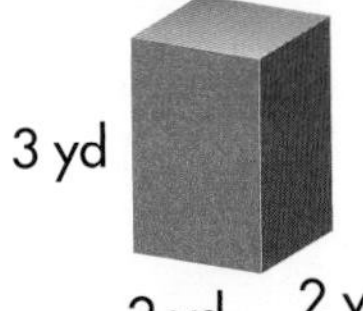

9.

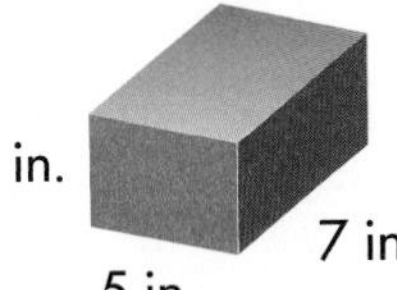

10.

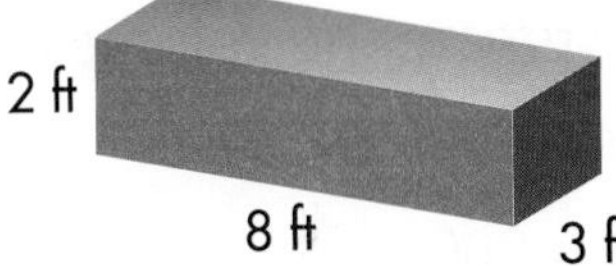

TAKS Problem Solving

11. Reasoning A box with dimensions 2 feet by 2 feet by 2 feet is placed inside a box with the dimensions 4 feet by 4 feet by 4 feet. How much space is not filled inside the larger box after the smaller box is put inside?

12. Writing to Explain The volume of a toy box is 28 cubic feet. Its length is 7 feet and its width is 4 feet. What is the height? Explain how you found your answer.

13. Estimation A crate is 20 inches wide, 20 inches long, and 12 inches high. Which estimate of the crate's volume is true?

A The volume is less than 400 cubic inches.

B The volume is between 400 and 600 cubic inches.

C The volume is between 600 and 800 cubic inches.

D The volume is greater than 800 cubic inches.

14. The world's largest box of popcorn is in Garland, Texas and is 18 feet tall. The box has a square base. One side is 10 feet. What is the volume of the box?

Lesson
17-3

TEKS 4.11C: Use concrete models of standard cubic units to measure volume. TEKS 4.11D: Estimate volume in cubic units. Also TEKS 4.14A

Metric Units of Volume

Hands-On
unit cubes

How can you estimate and find the volume of a rectangular prism in metric units?

What is the volume of the dump-truck trailer?

You can count cubes or multiply to find the volume of a rectangular prism in metric units.

Other Examples

Estimate the volume of this figure.

$V = 10 \times 3 \times 30$

$V = 900$

The volume is about 900 cubic meters.

Guided Practice*

Do you know HOW?

For **1** and **2**, find the volume of each figure. Write your answer in cubic units.

1.

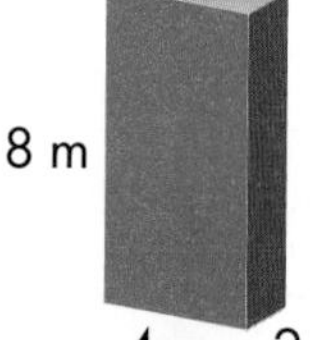

2.

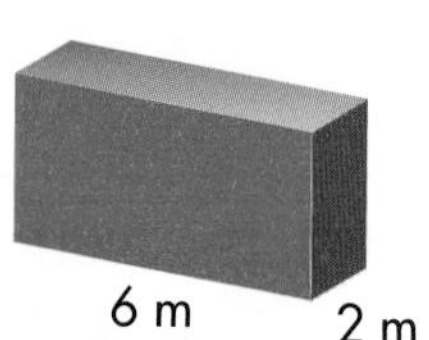

Do you UNDERSTAND?

3. Writing to Explain Find the volume of the figure in Exercise 1 if the height was doubled.

4. Juanita has a box that measures 12 centimeters by 8 centimeters by 3 centimeters. What is the volume of the box?

Independent Practice

For **5** through **7**, find the volume of each figure. Write the answer in cubic units.

5.

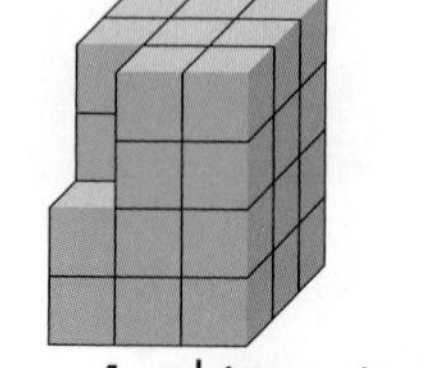

1 cube = 1 cubic centimeter

6.

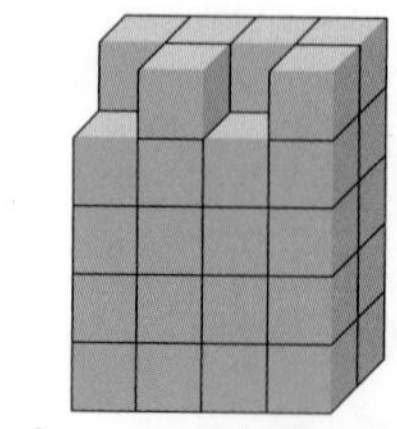

1 cube = 1 cubic centimeter

7.

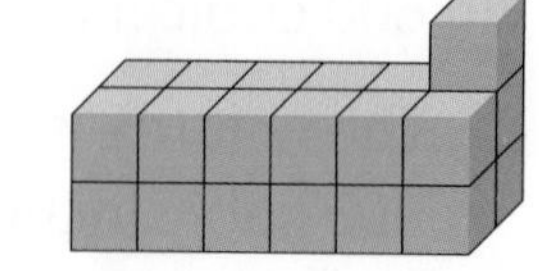

1 cube = 1 cubic centimeter

*For another example, see Set C on page 389.

Count the cubes.

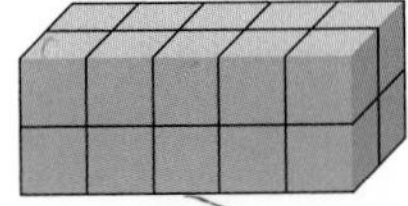

Each cube is 1 cubic meter.
There are 20 cubes in all.

The volume of the trailer is 20 cubic meters.

Use a formula:

$V = \ell \times w \times h$

$V = 5 \times 2 \times 2$

$V = 20$

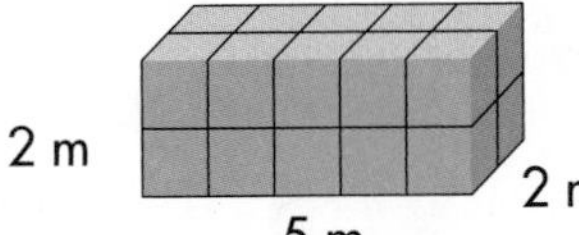

The volume of the trailer is 20 cubic meters.

For **8** through **10**, estimate and then find the volume of each figure.

8.

9.

10.

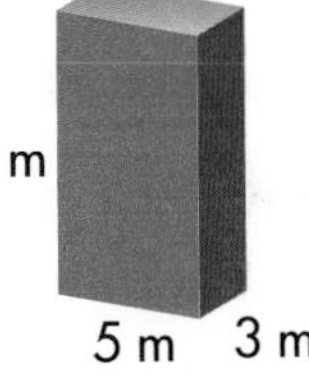

TAKS Problem Solving

11. The volume of the rectangular prism at the right is 72 cubic meters. If the top layer of cubes is removed, what is the new volume?

A 18 cubic meters **C** 69 cubic meters

B 54 cubic meters **D** 75 cubic meters

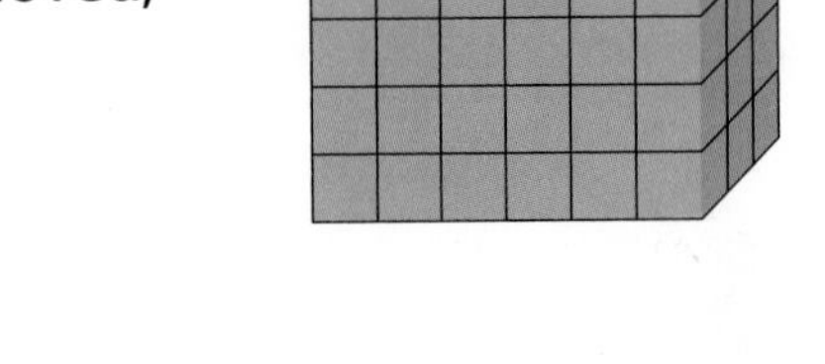

12. A crate is 14 meters in length, 6 meters wide, and by 3 meters high. What is the volume of the crate?

13. The volume of a rectangular prism is 80 cubic centimeters. The length is 4 centimeters and the height is 10 centimeters. What is the width?

14. Estimation Estimate the volume of a gift box that is 12 centimeters long, 31 centimeters wide, and 9 centimeters high.

15. What is the volume of a jewelry box that measures 12 centimeters by 5 centimeters by 20 centimeters?

16. Diana has $18 to spend. How many roses can she buy if they are $2 each?

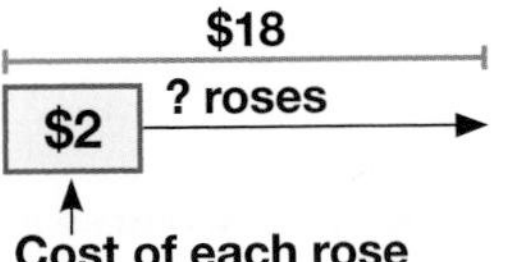

17. Reasoning The base of a pyramid is a rectangle but not a square. Can all four triangular faces be congruent? Why or why not?

Lesson
17-4

TEKS 4.11A: Estimate and use measurement tools to determine length (including perimeter), area, capacity, and weight/mass using standard units SI (metric) and customary.
Also TEKS 4.14A

Customary Units of Capacity

How do you measure capacity in customary units?

Capacity is volume of a container measured in liquid units. Here are some customary units for measuring capacity.

How much water can a kitchen sink hold?

Guided Practice*

Do you know HOW?

Which is the best estimate for the capacity of each item?

1. 
3 gallons or 30 gallons?

2. 
2 cups or 2 quarts?

3. 
1 pint or 4 gallons?

4. 
1 gallon or 1 quart?

Do you UNDERSTAND?

5. Look at the quart and gallon containers above. Estimate how many quarts are in 1 gallon.

6. Estimate how many quarts it would take to fill the kitchen sink.

7. Which is greater, a cup or a quart?

8. Which is greater, a cup or a pint?

Independent Practice

In **9** through **20**, choose the most appropriate unit to measure the capacity of each item. Write c, pt, qt, or gal.

9. juice carton
10. bucket
11. gasoline tank
12. paper cup
13. fish bowl
14. bathtub
15. snow globe
16. cat's water dish
17. spray bottle
18. aquarium
19. soup bowl
20. pond

*For another example, see Set D on page 389.

Step 1

Choose the most appropriate unit to measure:

It would take too long to fill the sink with the cup, pint, or quart.

The best unit would be the gallon.

Step 2

Estimate:

Visualize how many gallons of water it would take to fill the sink.

The sink has a capacity of about 4 gallons.

Step 3

Measure:

Fill the gallon jug with water and pour it into the sink. Do this until the sink is full, and count how many gallon jugs were used to fill the sink.

The sink has a capacity of about 5 gallons.

In **21** through **24**, choose the best estimate for the capacity of each item.

21. 

1 gallon or 10 gallons?

22. 

1 gallon or 1 quart?

23. 

20 quarts or 200 quarts?

24. 

2 quarts or 2 pints?

TAKS Problem Solving

25. In one second, 3,300,000 gallons of water from the Mississippi River enters the Gulf of Mexico. In one day, Houston's water system can carry 900,000 gallons. Which is greater, 3,300,000 gallons or 900,000 gallons?

26. Number Sense A lemonade recipe calls for 1 cup of sugar and 1 quart of water. This recipe makes 4 servings. If you want to make 12 servings, how many cups of sugar will you need?

27. You need 1 teaspoon of bubble bath for every 25 gallons of water. How much bubble bath is needed for a 50-gallon bathtub?

28 The lines on the measuring cup below show fluid ounces (oz) and cups (c). Which is greater, one fluid ounce or one cup?

29. Reasoning Which would be the better unit to measure the water in a swimming pool, the number of juice glasses or the number of bathtubs?

Lesson
17-5

TEKS 4.11A: Estimate and use measurement tools to determine length (including perimeter), area, capacity, and weight/mass using standard units SI (metric) and customary. Also TEKS 4.14A

Metric Units of Capacity

How do you measure capacity with metric units?

Below are two metric units for measuring capacity. How much liquid can the bottle to the right hold?

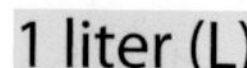

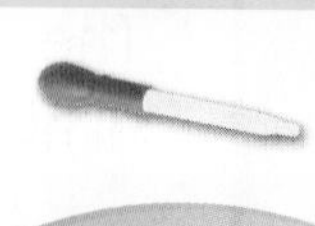

An eyedropper can be used to measure 1 milliliter.

Some water bottles hold 1 liter.

Guided Practice*

Do you know HOW?

Which is the best estimate for the capacity of each item?

1. 

5 liters or 500 liters?

2. 

10 liters or 100 liters?

3. 

100 milliliters or 10 liters?

4. 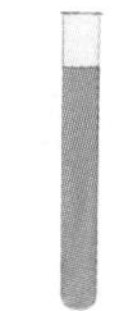

10 milliliters or 1 liter?

Do you UNDERSTAND?

5. Which unit of measure is greater, a liter or a milliliter?

6. Which would be the best unit of measure to use to measure the amount of gasoline in a car's gas tank, a milliliter or a liter?

7. About how many liters would you need to fill 2 milk bottles?

Independent Practice

In **8** through **15**, choose the most appropriate unit to measure the capacity of each item. Write L or mL.

8. bucket **9.** ink pen **10.** juice glass **11.** washing machine

12. soup pot **13.** coffee mug **14.** medicine cup **15.** pitcher

*For another example, see Set E on page 390.

Step 1

Choose the most appropriate unit to measure:

The milliliter is a very small amount. A larger unit would be more appropriate to measure with.

The best unit would be the liter.

Step 2

Estimate:

Visualize how many liter bottles it would take to fill the bottle.

The bottle has a capacity of about 2 liters.

Step 3

Measure:

Fill the liter bottle with water and pour it into the bottle. Do this until the bottle is full, and count how many liter bottles were used.

The bottle has a capacity of about 2 liters.

In **16** through **19**, choose the best estimate for the capacity of each.

16. 

200 milliliters or 200 liters?

17. 

4 liters or 14 liters?

18. 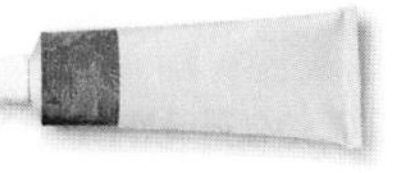

20 milliliters or 200 milliliters?

19. 

3 liters or 300 liters?

TAKS Problem Solving

20. Number Sense Which number would be greater, the number of liters of juice in a pitcher or the number of milliliters of juice in the same pitcher?

21. Reasonableness Zack said he poured lemonade from a 300-liter pitcher into a 20-milliliter glass. Are these numbers reasonable? Why or why not?

22. Which capacities are written in order from greatest to least?

A 5 milliliters, 2 liters, 1 liter

B 2 liters, 5 milliliters, 1 liter

C 1 liter, 2 liters, 5 milliliters

D 2 liters, 1 liter, 5 milliliters

23. Marcus filled a bottle with 1,000 milliliters of water to take with him on his jog. After his jog, he had about 450 milliliters left in his bottle. How much water did he drink while he jogged?

1,000 mL of water	
450	?

24. Geometry What is the perimeter of the triangle?

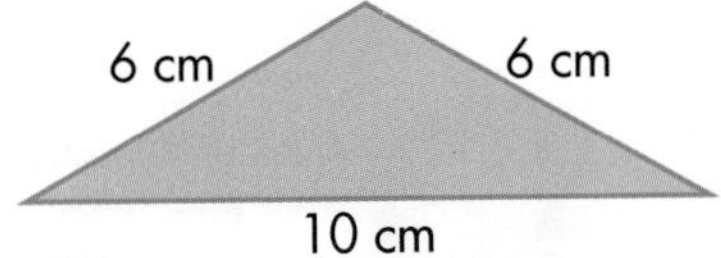

25. How much more water does a 0.75-liter sports bottle hold than a 0.6-liter bottle?

Lesson
17-6

TEKS 4.11A: Estimate and use measurement tools to determine length (including perimeter), area, capacity, and weight/mass using standard units SI (metric) and customary.
Also TEKS 4.14A

Units of Weight

How do you measure weight?

Weight is how heavy an object is. Below are some customary units for measuring weight.

How much does a peach weigh?

1 ounce (oz)

A key weighs about 1 ounce.

1 pound (lb)

A kitten weighs about 1 pound.

1 ton (T)

A giraffe weighs about 1 ton.

Guided Practice*

Do you know HOW?

For **1** through **4**, give the best unit to measure the weight of each item.

1.

a slice of bread

2.

a sheep

3.

a helicopter

4.

a bicycle

Do you UNDERSTAND?

5. **Writing to Explain** How can you tell that the weight of the peach is **NOT** 8 ounces?

6. If you placed 3 keys on the same pan with the peach, how many ounces would be needed to balance the keys and the peach?

Independent Practice

For **7** through **18**, choose the most appropriate unit to measure the weight of each item.

Think of a familiar object that weighs one pound, one ounce, or one ton. Use that object to estimate the weight of other objects measured with the same unit.

7. sea lion **8.** orange **9.** nail polish **10.** greeting card

11. paper clip **12.** canoe **13.** ocean liner **14.** football player

15. telephone **16.** car **17.** fork **18.** bag of potatoes

*For another example, see Set F on page 390.

Step 1

Choose the appropriate unit to measure:

A peach weighs less than a pound.

So, the best unit would be the ounce.

Step 2

Estimate:

A key weighs about one ounce. How many keys would weigh the same as a peach?

About 8 keys would weigh the same.

A peach weighs about 8 ounces.

Step 3

Measure:

Place the peach on one pan of the balance. Place an ounce weight on the other pan. Add ounce weights until the balance is level, and count the ounce weights.

The peach weighs 7 ounces.

TAKS Problem Solving

19. One of the first computers built weighed 30 tons. What would be an appropriate unit of weight to measure the weight of most desktop computers today?

20. Reasoning Name 3 things about the box below that you can measure. Give a reasonable estimate for each measure.

21. Which is a greater number, the number of pounds a rooster weighs, or the number of ounces the same rooster weighs?

For **22** through **25**, use the chart at the right.

22. About how many ounces do two dozen medium apples weigh?

23. Estimate the weight of one apple.

24. Do five dozen large watermelons weigh more or less than 1,000 pounds?

25. About how many pounds do three dozen bananas weigh?

Fruit	Weight of one dozen
	72 ounces
	3 pounds
	264 pounds

26. What is a good estimate for the weight of a bicycle?

A 30 ounces **C** 30 pounds

B 3 pounds **D** 3,000 ounces

Lesson
17-7

TEKS 4.11A: Estimate and use measurement tools to determine length (including perimeter), area, capacity, and weight/mass using standard units SI (metric) and customary.
TEKS 4.11E: Explain the difference between weight and mass.
Also TEKS 4.14A

Units of Mass

What are metric units of mass?

Mass is the amount of matter that something contains.

What is the mass of a red brick?

1 gram (g)

A dollar bill has a mass of about 1 gram (g).

1 kilogram (kg)

A cantaloupe has a mass of about 1 kilogram (kg).

The mass of a red brick is ?

Other Examples

Weight and Mass are different.

The **weight** of an object changes depending on the location.

The weight of a red brick on the moon is not the same as its weight on Earth.

The **mass** of an object always stays the same.

The mass of the red brick on the moon is the same as its mass on Earth.

Guided Practice*

Do you know HOW?

For **1** and **2**, choose the most appropriate unit to measure the mass of each item.

1.

hamster

2.

gorilla

Do you UNDERSTAND?

3. Which number would be less, the mass of grapefruit in grams or the mass of the same grapefruit in kilograms?

4. How many cantaloupes would be needed to have the same mass as one red brick?

Independent Practice

For **5** through **12**, choose the most appropriate unit to measure the mass of each item.

5. pencil

6. baseball player

7. baseball

8. honeydew melon

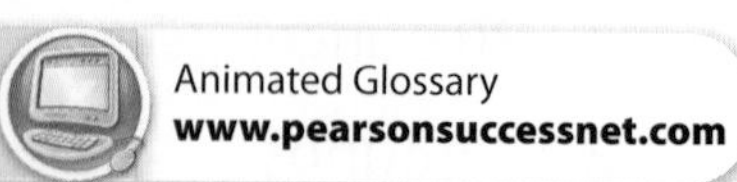

*For another example, see Set G on page 391.

Step 1

Choose the appropriate unit to measure:

A brick has a greater mass than a cantaloupe.

So, the best unit would be the kilogram.

Step 2

Estimate:

A cantaloupe has a mass of about one kilogram. How many cantaloupes would have the same mass as a red brick?

About 3 cantaloupes would have the same mass.

The brick has a mass of about 3 kilograms.

Step 3

Measure:

Place the brick on one pan of the balance. Add kilograms to the other pan until the balance is level. Count the kilograms.

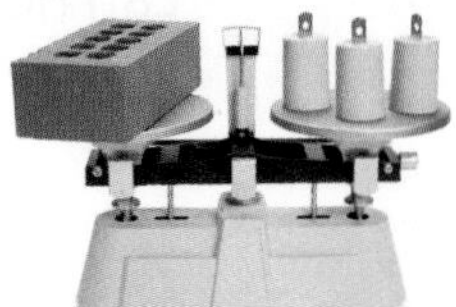

The brick has a mass of 3 kilograms.

9. strawberry

10. penguin

11. sailboat

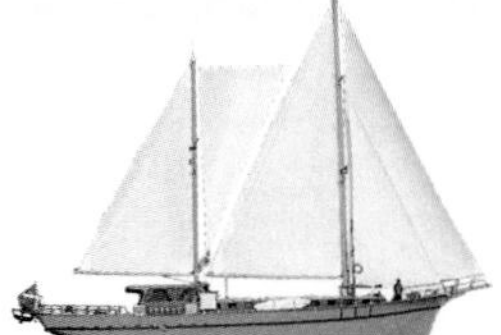

12. dragonfly

TAKS Problem Solving

For **13** through **15**, use the table at the right.

Coin	Mass
	2.500 grams
	5.000 grams
	2.268 grams
	5.670 grams

13. Order the coins from least mass to greatest mass.

14. A dollar bill has a mass of about 1 gram. About how many dollar bills have the same mass as a nickel?

15. There are 40 nickels in a roll of nickels. What is the total mass of the nickels in one roll?

Tip *Find the mass of 4 nickels and multiply by 10.*

16. **Writing to Explain** Mandy says that she has a mass of 32 kg on the Earth. What is her mass on the moon?

17. Which number is greater, the mass of a carrot in grams, or the mass of the same carrot in kilograms?

18. Use the bar diagram below. José needs $78 for a present. He has already saved $33. How much more does he need to save?

$78 in all

?	$33

19. What is a good estimate for the mass of a Texas longhorn steer?

A 15 kg **C** 100 kg

B 50 kg **D** 1,500 kg

Lesson

17-8

TEKS 4.14C: Select or develop an appropriate problem-solving plan or strategy, including drawing a picture, looking for a pattern, systematic guessing and checking, acting it out, making a table, working a simpler problem, or working backwards to solve a problem.
Also **TEKS 4.15A**

Problem Solving

Try, Check, and Revise

Mr. Donovan is stacking 16 plastic crates in his store. How many different ways can he stack the crates?

Guided Practice*

Do you know HOW?

Solve.

1. Brandon uses a 5-milliliter cap to fill a 1-liter plastic bottle with water. How many capfuls of water will Brandon need until the bottle is filled half way?

Tip *Remember 1 liter = 1,000 milliliters*

Do you UNDERSTAND?

2. In Exercise 1, how many milliliters of water are contained in the bottle after Brandon has filled it halfway?

3. How many more capfuls of water will it take until the water bottle is filled to 750 milliliters?

Independent Practice

Solve each problem.

4. Using 36 cubes, how many different ways can you make a rectangular prism if the height is 3 cubes?

5. Using 36 cubes, how many different ways can you make a rectangular prism if the height is 4 cubes?

6. Using 36 cubes, how many different ways can you make a rectangular prism if the height is 5 cubes?

- What do I know?
- What am I asked to find?
- What diagram can I use to help understand the problem?
- Can I use addition, subtraction, multiplication, or division?
- Is all of my work correct?
- Did I answer the right question?
- Is my answer reasonable?

*For another example, see Set H on page 391.

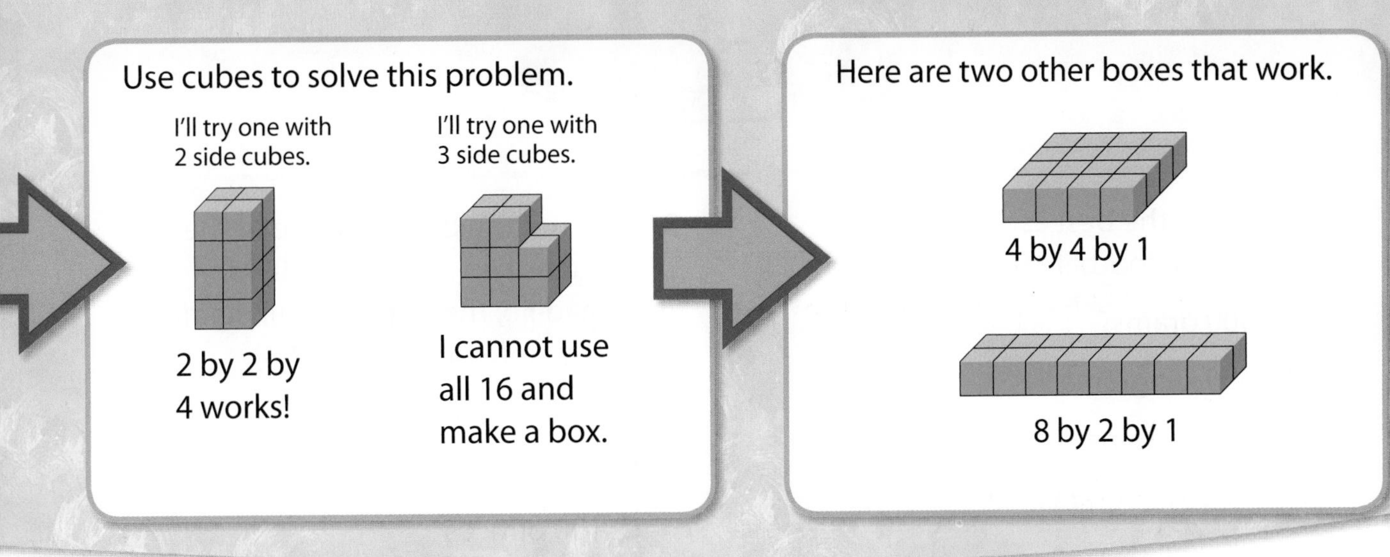

Use cubes to solve this problem.
I'll try one with 2 side cubes.
I'll try one with 3 side cubes.
2 by 2 by 4 works!
I cannot use all 16 and make a box.
Here are two other boxes that work.
4 by 4 by 1
8 by 2 by 1

7. Which of the figures below is **NOT** another way of looking at the figure at the right?

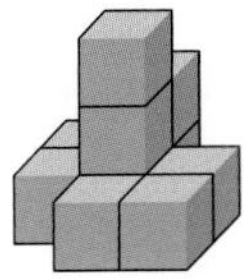

A 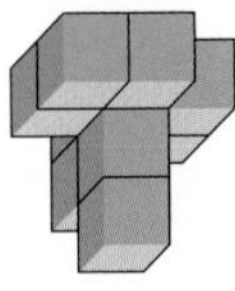 **B** 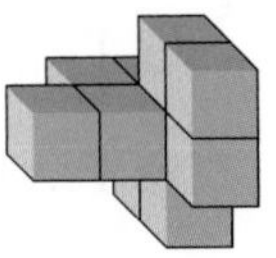 **C** 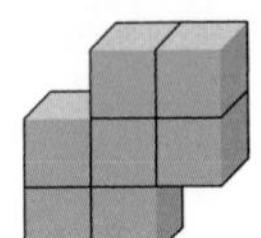 **D** 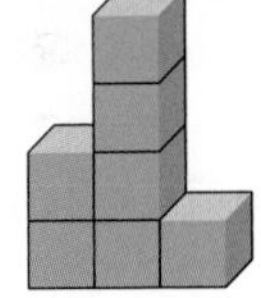

8. **Writing to Explain** If the perimeter of a parallelogram is 56 inches, and you know one side is 8 inches, will you be able to find the length of the other 3 sides? Why or why not?

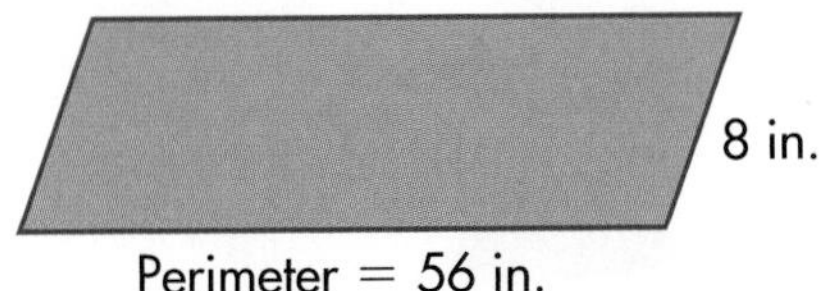

9. Mrs. Bolt drinks 56 glasses of water each week. How many glasses of water is that each day?

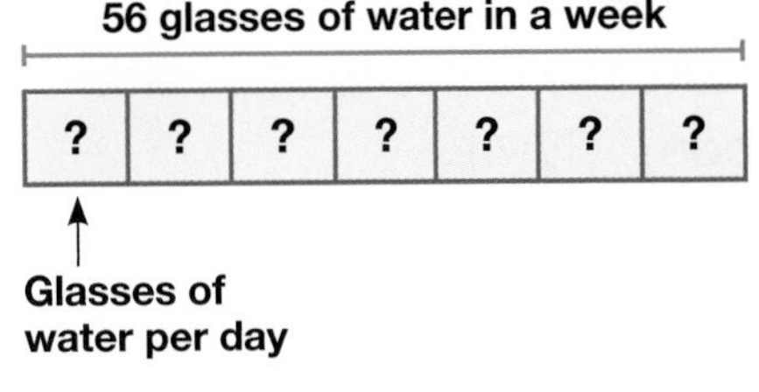

10. **Writing to Explain** If you are making a rectangular prism using 28 cubes, why is it **NOT** possible for a length to be 8 cubes?

11. What possible heights can there be if you use 40 cubes to make a rectangular prism?

12. Victor is growing peppers and tomatoes in different sections of his garden. He planted 8 rows of 5 peppers. If he wants to plant the same number of tomatoes, what array can Victor make with the tomatoes?

13. Look at the figure below. How many cubes were used to make it?

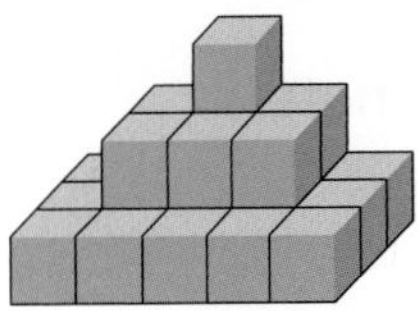

TAKS Test Prep

1. Which is the best estimate of the mass of a football? (17-7)

 A 400 grams

 B 400 kilograms

 C 4,000 grams

 D 4,000 kilograms

2. Fionna used cubes to build a model of the tissue box. What is the volume of the tissue box? (17-1)

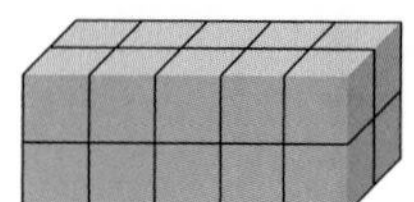

 F 10 cubic units

 G 15 cubic units

 H 20 cubic units

 J 24 cubic units

3. Which of these units would best measure the capacity of a water balloon? (17-4)

 A Quarts

 B Gallons

 C Cups

 D Pounds

4. Which is the best estimate of the capacity of a bottle of shampoo? (17-5)

 F 444 kilograms

 G 444 milliliters

 H 444 centimeters

 J 444 liters

5. Which is the best estimate of the weight of an adult Nine-Banded Armadillo, the official small mammal of the state of Texas? (17-6)

 A 10 ounces

 B 10 pounds

 C 100 ounces

 D 100 pounds

6. Which of the following holds about 2 liters of water? (17-5)

 F Bathtub

 G Drinking glass

 H Pitcher

 J Eye dropper

7. Which of the following has a mass closest to 1 kilogram? (17-7)

 A 

 B 

 C 

 D 

8. Which is the best estimate of the capacity of a bathroom sink? (17-4)

F 3 gallons

G 3 cups

H 300 cups

J 300 pints

9. Which is the best estimate of the volume of the figure? (17-3)

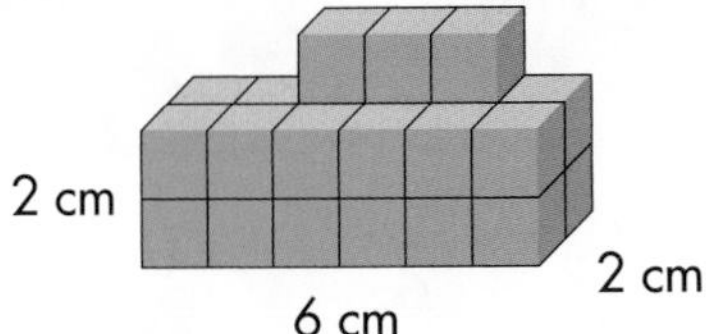

A 12 cubic centimeters

B 18 cubic centimeters

C 24 cubic centimeters

D 36 cubic centimeters

10. The box Mrs. Lawry's porcelain doll was shipped in is shown below. What is the volume of the box? (17-2)

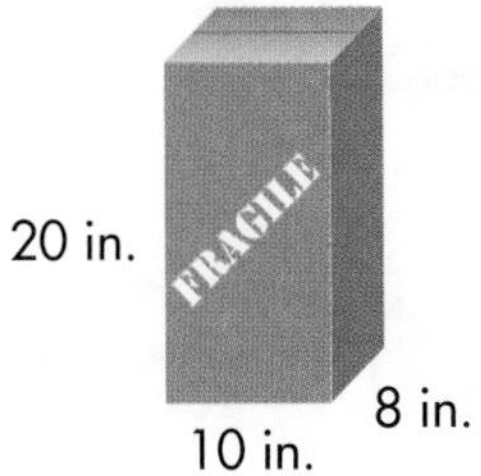

F 200 cubic inches

G 800 cubic inches

H 1,200 cubic inches

J 1,600 cubic inches

11. Which unit would best measure the weight of a pair of scissors? (17-6)

A Pounds

B Ounces

C Tons

D Kilograms

12. Which is the best estimate of the volume of the figure? (17-2)

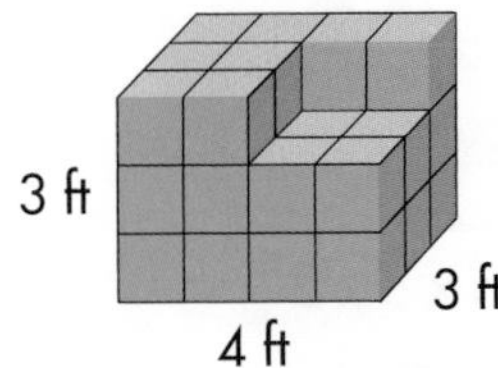

F 12 cubic feet

G 24 cubic feet

H 28 cubic feet

J 36 cubic feet

13. A model of the box that Ben's dune buggy was delivered in is shown. What is the volume of the box? (17-3)

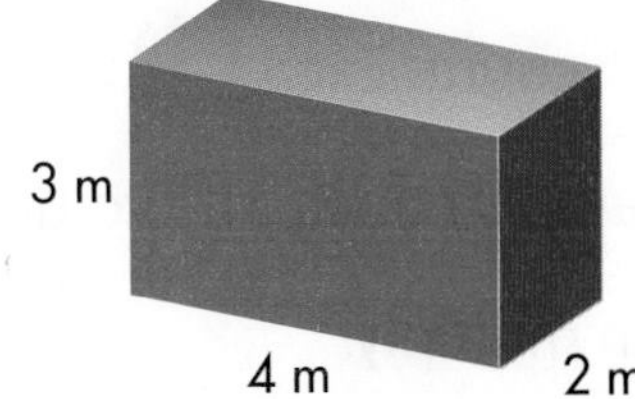

A 6 cubic meters

B 8 cubic meters

C 12 cubic meters

D 24 cubic meters

14. **Griddable Response** How many different rectangular prisms can be made using exactly 12 cubes? (17-8)

Set A, pages 370–371

What is the volume of the box?

Build a model of the puzzle with base-ten blocks. Count the number of cubes. There are 36 cubic units.

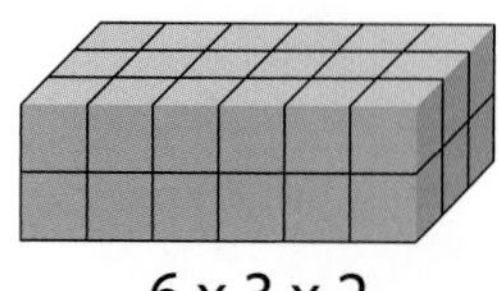

6 x 3 x 2

The volume of the box is 36 cubic units.

Remember that volume is measured in cubic units, not square units.

Find the volume of each figure. Write your answer in cubic units.

1. 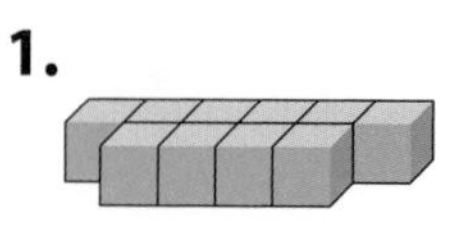

2. 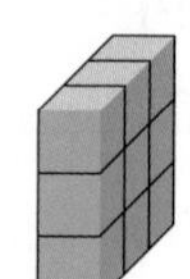

3. 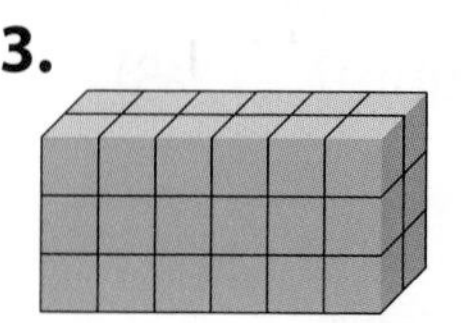

4. 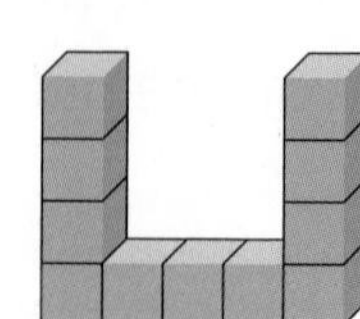

5. 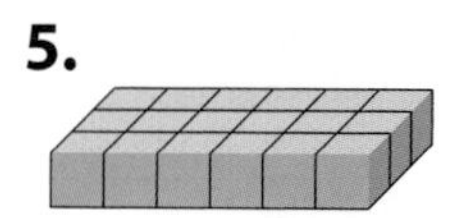

6. 

Set B, pages 372–373

What is the volume of the figure below?

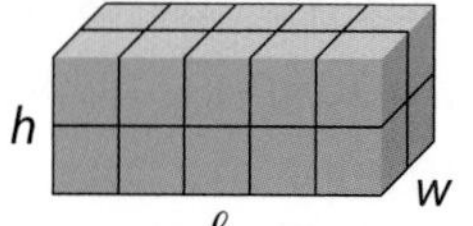

1 cube = 1 cubic foot

You can count. Each  is 1 cubic foot.

There are 20 cubes. The volume is 20 cubic feet.

You can multiply.
Volume = length × width × height

$\ell \times w \times h$
$5 \times 2 \times 2 = 20$ cubic feet

Estimate the volume.

The volume is about 32 cubic feet.

$4 \times 4 \times 2 = 32$.

Remember to use customary cubic units.

Find the volume of each figure.

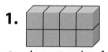

1. 1 cube = 1 cubic foot

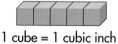

2. 1 cube = 1 cubic inch

3. 1 cube = 1 cubic yard

4. 

5. 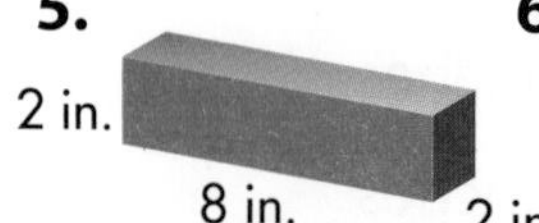

6. 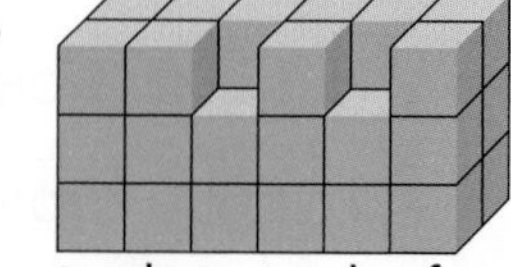

1 cube = 1 cubic foot

Set C, pages 374–375

What is the volume of the figure below?

You can count.
Each ▢ is
1 cubic meter.

There are 60 cubes.
The volume is
60 cubic meters.

You can multiply.

Volume = length × width × height
$V = \ell \times w \times h$
$V = 5 \times 3 \times 4$
$= 60$ cubic meters

Estimate the volume.

$4 \times 2 \times 3 = 24$

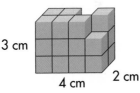

The volume is about
24 cubic centimeters.

Remember to write your answer using metric cubic units.

Find the volume of each figure.

1.

2.

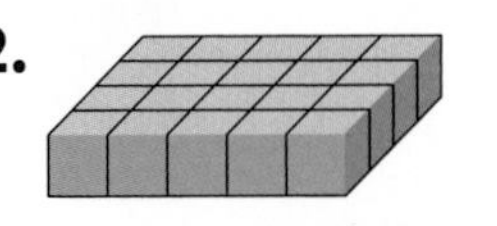

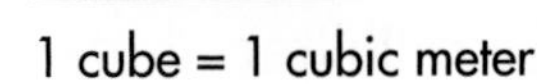

3.

1 cube = 1 cubic meter

4.

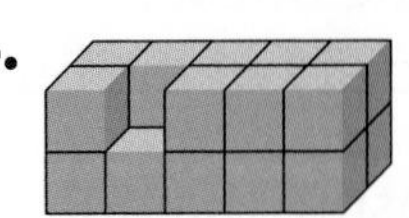

1 cube = 1 cubic cm

5.

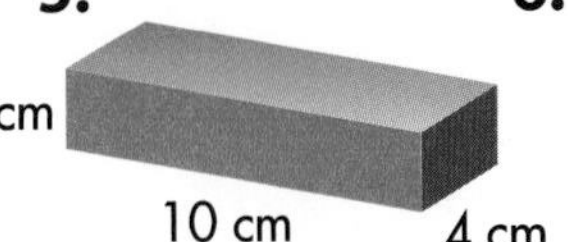

6.

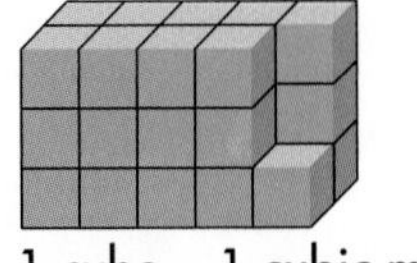

1 cube = 1 cubic meter

Set D, pages 376–377

How much water will this green bucket hold?

1 cup 1 pint 1 quart 1 gallon

The cup, pint and quart are too small.
The best unit to use is the gallon.

Estimate how many gallons it would take to fill the bucket. The bucket has a capacity of about 2 gallons.

Measure the bucket's capacity by pouring one gallon at a time into the bucket.

The bucket will hold 2 gallons of water.

Remember that a cup is a smaller measure than a pint.

Which is the best estimate for the capacity of each item?

1.

2 cups or 20 cups?

2.

1 gallon or 8 gallons?

3.

2 quarts of 12 quarts?

4.

5 gallons or 15 gallons?

Set E, pages 378–379

How much liquid will the bucket hold?

1 milliliter 1 liter

The bucket is larger than 1 liter. The liter is the best unit to use.

Estimate how many liters it would take to fill the bucket. It might take 8 liters, so the capacity of the bucket is about 8 liters.

Measure the bucket's capacity by pouring 1 liter at a time into the bucket.

The bucket holds 8 liters of water.

Remember that a liter is a greater measure than a milliliter.

Which is the best estimate for the capacity of each item?

1.  

5 liters or 15 liters?

2. 

2 liters or 10 liters?

3. 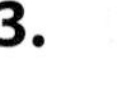 

3 mL or 30 mL?

4. 

10 milliliters or 100 milliliters?

Set F, pages 380–381

How much does a pear weigh?

The pear weighs less than a pound. So, the best unit to use would be the ounce.

A key weighs about one ounce. Estimate how many keys would weigh the same as the pear. About 10 keys would weigh the same. The pear weighs about 10 ounces.

Place the pear on one pan of a balance. Place an ounce weight on the other pan. Keep adding ounce weights until the balance is level. Count the ounce weights.

The pear weighs 10 ounces.

Remember to use benchmark weights to compare.

Give the best unit to measure the weight of each item. Write oz, lb, or T.

1. a whale **2.** an apple

3. a puppy **4.** a baseball

5. a box of books **6.** a house

7. a CD **8.** a baby

9. an 18-wheel truck **10.** a large boat

11. a spoonful of medicine **12.** a bag of oranges

Set G, pages 382–383

What is the mass of a cell phone?

1 kilogram is too large for a cell phone. So, a gram would be a better unit to use.

A dollar bill has a mass of about 1 gram. Estimate how many one-dollar bills have the same mass as a cell phone. About 20 one-dollar bills would have the same mass. So, the mass of a cell phone is about 20 grams.

Measure the mass of a cell phone on a balance. Place the cell phone on one pan of the balance. Add 1 gram masses to the other side, and count the number of grams.

The cell phone has a mass of 17 grams.

Remember that weight depends on location. Mass always stays the same.

Choose the most appropriate unit, a gram or kilogram, to measure the mass of each item.

1. crayon
2. watermelon
3. carrot
4. wallet
5. bicycle
6. table
7. penny
8. paper clip

9. If you had a mass of 25 kg on Earth, what would your mass be on the planet Mars? Explain.

Set H, pages 384–385

This box was built using 18 cubes.

How many different boxes can you build where each box uses 18 cubes?

Here are two other boxes that work:

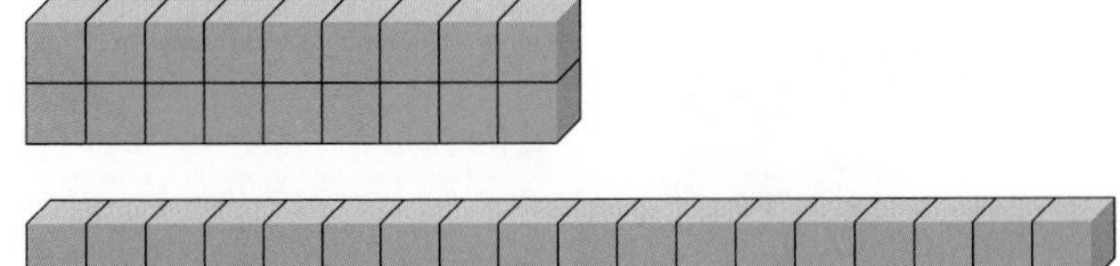

Remember to list the factors of 48.

Jerald uses 48 cubes to make a cube building. How many different buildings can he make if the height is

1. 4 cubes
2. 8 cubes
3. 12 cubes
4. 14 cubes

Topic 18

Converting Measurements

1

The Trevi Fountain in Rome, Italy, is a famous landmark. How many gallons of water flow through the fountain each day? You will find out in Lesson 18-2.

2

The Crested Argus Pheasant has the longest tail feathers of any bird. How many inches long are the feathers? You will find out in Lesson 18-1.

3

This air tanker, built in Texas, is used all over the world to fight forest fires. How many tons of water can this plane carry? You will find out in Lesson 18-3.

Review What You Know!

Vocabulary

Choose the best term from the box.

- capacity
- foot
- length
- volume

1. A ? is a unit of length equal to 12 inches.
2. ? represents the amount a container can hold in liquid units.
3. The ? of a solid figure is the number of cubic units needed to fill it.

Capacity

Choose the best unit to measure the capacity of each. Write cups or gallons.

4. bathtub
5. fish tank
6. soup bowl
7. mug
8. gasoline tank
9. sugar in a recipe

Weight

Choose the best unit to measure the weight of each. Write ounces or pounds.

10. bicycle
11. slice of bread
12. pencil
13. bag of wood chips
14. bowling ball
15. bunch of bananas

Area and Volume

16. What is the width of a rectangle if its area is 16 square feet, and its length is 8 feet?
17. **Writing to Explain** The length of the edge of a cube is 4 feet. Find the volume.

Lesson

18-1

TEKS 4.11B: Perform simple conversions between different units of length, between different units of capacity, and between different units of weight within the customary measurement system.

Converting Units of Length

How can you change customary units of length?

Cheryl is shopping for a bench for the school playground. There is exactly 7 feet of space for the bench. Which bench will fit?

Change the lengths of both benches to feet to find which bench will fit.

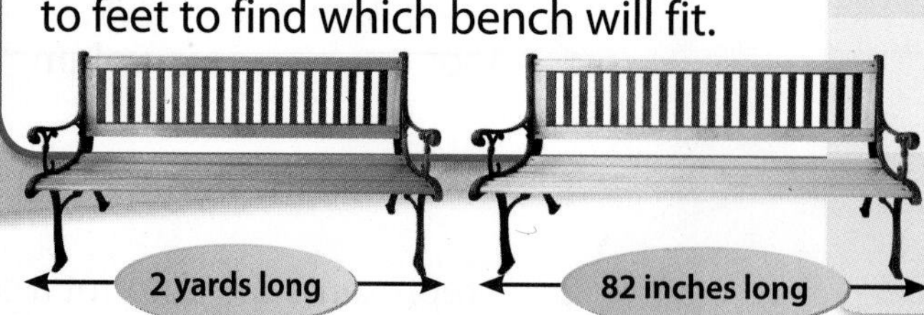

Customary Units of Length
1 foot = 12 inches
1 yard = 36 inches 1 yard = 3 feet
1 mile = 5,280 feet 1 mile = 1,760 yards

Guided Practice*

Do you know HOW?

For **1** through **8**, find each missing number.

1. 4 yd = ____ ft **2.** 2 mi = ____ ft

3. 27 ft = ____ yd **4.** 144 in. = ____ yd

5. 8 mi = ____ ft **6.** 6 yd = ____ in.

7. 60 in. = ____ ft **8.** 9 ft = ____ yd

Do you UNDERSTAND?

9. Do you multiply or divide to convert from feet to yards?

10. Do you multiply or divide to change feet to inches?

11. **Writing to Explain** The student council finds another bench that is 86 inches. Will this bench fit?

Independent Practice

Leveled Practice For **12** through **27**, find each missing number.

12. 12 ft = ____ yd
12 ÷ 3 = ____ yd

13. 108 in. = ____ ft
108 ÷ 12 = ____ ft

14. 84 in. = ____ ft
84 ÷ 12 = ____ ft

15. 4 mi = ____ ft
4 × 5,280 = ____ ft

16. 11 ft = ____ in.
11 × 12 = ____ in.

17. 6 yd = ____ ft
6 × 3 = ____ ft

18. 96 in. = ____ ft
96 ÷ 12= ____ ft

19. 3 mi = ____ yd
3 × 1,760 = ____ yd

20. 33 ft = ____ yd **21.** 90 yd = ____ ft **22.** 24 in. = ____ ft **23.** 15 yd = ____ ft

24. 1 mi = ____ yd **25.** 72 in. = ____ ft **26.** 12 in. = ____ ft **27.** 10,560 ft = ____ mi

*For another example, see Set A on page 404.

To change smaller units to larger ones, divide.

82 inches = ☐ feet

12 inches = 1 foot. So, divide 82 inches by 12.

$$\begin{array}{r} 6 \text{ R}10 \\ 12\overline{)82} \\ -72 \\ \hline 10 \end{array}$$

82 inches = 6 feet 10 inches

Since this is less than 7 feet, this bench will fit.

To change larger units to smaller ones, multiply.

2 yards = ☐ feet

1 yard = 3 feet. So, multiply 2 yards by 3.

$2 \times 3 = 6$

2 yards = 6 feet

Since 6 feet is less than 7 feet, this bench will also fit.

TAKS Problem Solving

28. A super-stretch limousine is 240 inches long. A pickup truck is 19 feet long. Which is longer?

29. **Geometry** If one side of a square measures 5 inches long, what is the area of the square?

30. **Reasonableness** A magazine reports that a giraffe's height is 180 inches, or 15 yards. What mistake was made?

31. A marathon is about 26 miles long. How many yards is this?

A 4,576 yd **C** 45,760 yd

B 13,728 yd **D** 137,280 yd

32. The longest tail feathers of any bird are those of the Argus Pheasant. The feathers measure 5 feet 7 inches in length. How many inches long are these feathers?

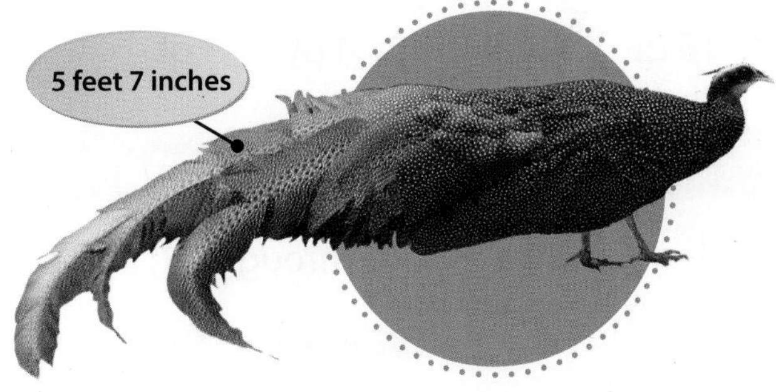

Use the information and the table at the right for **33** through **35**.

33. Will 6 finch cages fit side by side in the birdhouse if it is 10 feet wide?

34. Will 5 parakeet cages fit side by side in the birdhouse if it is 3 yards wide?

35. Suppose that 10 cages fit side by side in the finch birdhouse. Will 5 macaw cages fit in this same space?

Data

Type of Bird	Width of Cage
Finch	18 inches
Parakeet	24 inches
Macaw	36 inches

Lesson
18-2

TEKS 4.11B: Perform simple conversions between different units of length, between different units of capacity, and between different units of weight within the customary measurement system.

Converting Units of Capacity

How can you change customary units of capacity?

Alicia has 7 one-pint bottles of water. How many quarts of water does Alicia have?

How many one-cup glasses can she fill?

1 tablespoon (tbsp) = 3 teaspoons (tsp)
1 fluid ounce (fl oz) = 2 tablespoons
1 cup = 8 fluid ounces
1 pint = 2 cups
1 quart = 2 pints
1 gallon = 4 quarts

Guided Practice*

Do you know HOW?

For **1** through **8**, find each missing number.

1. 8 qt = ☐ gal **2.** 3 c = ☐ fl oz

3. 7 gal= ☐ qt **4.** 5 pt = ☐ c

5. 16 fl oz = ☐ c **6.** 9 gal = ☐ qt

7. 16 qt = ☐ gal **8.** 4 pt = ☐ qt

Do you UNDERSTAND?

9. Do you multiply or divide to convert fluid ounces to cups?

10. **Writing to Explain** In the first example above, why do you multiply?

11. Tom has 2 quarts of water. How many pints is this?

Independent Practice

Leveled Practice For **12** through **27**, find each missing number.

12. 4 pt = ☐ c
$4 \times 2 =$ ☐ c

13. 6 gal = ☐ qt
$6 \times 4 =$ ☐ qt

14. 32 fl oz = ☐ c
$32 \div 8 =$ ☐ c

15. 6 tsp = ☐ tbsp
$6 \div 3 =$ ☐ tbsp

16. 16 pt = ☐ qt
$16 \div 2 =$ ☐ qt

17. 12 pt = ☐ qt
$12 \div 2 =$ ☐ qt

18. 12 c = ☐ fl oz
$12 \times 8 =$ ☐ fl oz

19. 40 qt = ☐ pt
$40 \times 2 =$ ☐ pt

20. 13 qt = ☐ pt **21.** 80 fl oz = ☐ c **22.** 32 pt = ☐ qt **23.** 15 c = ☐ fl oz

24. 8 tbsp = ☐ tsp **25.** 18 c = ☐ pt **26.** 20 gal = ☐ qt **27.** 56 fl oz = ☐ c

For another example, see Set B on page 404.

To change smaller units to larger ones, divide.

7 pints = ☐ quarts

2 pints = 1 quart. So, divide 7 pints by 2.

$$\begin{array}{r} 3\text{ R1} \\ 2\overline{)7} \\ -\ 6 \\ \hline 1 \end{array}$$

Alicia has 3 quarts and 1 pint of water.

To change larger units to smaller units, multiply.

7 pints = ☐ cups

1 pint = 2 cups. So, multiply 7 pints by 2.

pt		pt		pt		pt		pt		pt		pt	
c	c	c	c	c	c	c	c	c	c	c	c	c	c

$7 \times 2 = 14$ cups

Alicia can fill 14 one-cup glasses.

TAKS Problem Solving

28. Laura is making a soup that calls for 8 cups of water. Can she mix the soup in a 1-quart pot? Explain.

qt				qt			
pt		pt		pt		pt	
c	c	c	c	c	c	c	c

29. Every day more than 17,000,000 gallons of water flow through the Trevi Fountain. How many quarts of water is this?

A 68 qt **C** 68,000 qt

B 6,800 qt **D** 68,000,000 qt

30. **Writing to Explain** Which unit of measure would you use to measure the length of your shoe?

31. **Number Sense** Without using a calendar, find the date three weeks after April 3rd.

32. **Writing to Explain** A recipe calls for 3 quarts of milk. How many pints is this?

33. **Geometry** What is the perimeter of a rectangle that is 6 inches long and 2 inches wide?

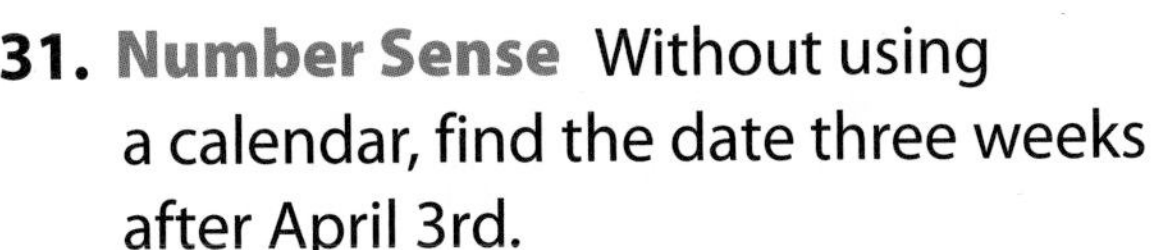

34. Raymond poured 8 cups of punch. Madison poured 5 pints of punch. Ryan poured 2 quarts of punch. Who poured the most punch?

Lesson
18-3

TEKS 4.11B: Perform simple conversions between different units of length, between different units of capacity, and between different units of weight within the customary measurement system.

Converting Units of Weight

How can you change units of weight?

A fruit company is shipping 30,000 pounds of peaches across the country. Each box in the shipment weighs 20 pounds.

How many tons of peaches are being shipped? How many ounces of peaches are in each box?

1 pound (lb) = 16 ounces (oz)

1 ton (T) = 2,000 pounds

semi truck of peaches = 30,000 pounds

box of peaches = 20 pounds

PEACHES

Guided Practice*

Do you know HOW?

For **1** through **8**, find each missing number.

1. 4 T = ☐ lb

2. 80 oz = ☐ lb

3. 48 oz = ☐ lb

4. 16,000 lb = ☐ T

5. 3,000 lb = ☐ oz

6. 85 lb = ☐ oz

7. 6,000 lb = ☐ T

8. 160 lb = ☐ oz

Do you UNDERSTAND?

9. Do you multiply or divide to convert from pounds to ounces?

10. **Writing to Explain** In the first example above, why do you divide?

11. The average peach weighs 8 ounces. If a small box holds 20 peaches, about how many pounds of peaches are in a small box?

Independent Practice

Leveled Practice For **12** through **27**, find each missing number.

12. 45 T = ☐ lb
$45 \times 2{,}000$ = ☐ T

13. 6 lb = ☐ oz
6×16 = ☐ oz

14. 64 oz = ☐ lb
$64 \div 16$ = ☐ lb

15. 22,000 lb = ☐ T
$22{,}000 \div 2{,}000$ = ☐ T

16. 20 lb = ☐ oz
20×16 = ☐ T

17. 112 lb = ☐ oz
112×16 = ☐ oz

18. 32 oz = ☐ lb
$32 \div 16$ = ☐ lb

19. 24 T= ☐ lb
$24 \times 2{,}000$ = ☐ lb

20. 6 T = ☐ lb

21. 160 oz = ☐ lb

22. 16 oz = ☐ lb

23. 14,000 lb = ☐ T

24. 3 lb = ☐ oz

25. 19 T = ☐ lb

26. 7 lb = ☐ oz

27. 60,000 lb = ☐ T

*For another example, see Set C on page 405.

To change smaller units to larger ones, divide.

30,000 pounds = ▢ tons

2,000 pounds = 1 ton
Divide 30,000 pounds by 2,000.

Think $30 \div 2 = 15$
So, $30{,}000 \div 2{,}000 = 15$.

The shipment weighs 15 tons.

To change larger units to smaller ones, multiply.

20 pounds = ▢ ounces

1 pound = 16 ounces
Multiply 20 pounds by 16.

$20 \times 16 = 320$ ounces

There are 320 ounces of peaches in each box.

TAKS Problem Solving

28. Suppose there are 56 penguins in a colony, and each penguin eats 12 pounds of krill and 18 pounds of squid each day. How much food does the colony eat each day?

29. Mr. Kunkle uses a bowling ball that weighs 14 pounds. How many ounces does the bowling ball weigh?

A 116 oz **C** 180 oz
B 140 oz **D** 224 oz

Use the table at the right for **30** through **32**.

The weight of objects on other planets and the Moon is different than it is on Earth.

Approximate Weight of a 4th-Grader

Earth	Jupiter	Venus	Moon
85 lb	215 lb	77 lb	14 lb

30. What is the approximate weight in ounces of a fourth grader on Venus?

31. What is the approximate weight in ounces of a fourth grader on the Moon?

32. **Writing to Explain** Would an adult weigh more on Earth or on Venus? Explain your reasoning.

33. Jeremiah bought 2 pounds of lettuce and 3 pounds of tomatoes for a salad. How many ounces of each did he purchase?

34. This air tanker fights fires using lake water. It refills its tanks by skimming the surface of a lake. If the plane can scoop up 4,000 pounds of water, how many tons of water can it carry?

82
CONAIR
C-FLSI
Each tank holds 2,000 lb of water.

Lesson

18-4

TEKS 4.11B: Perform simple conversions between different units of length, . . . within the customary measurement system.

Problem Solving

Writing to Explain

Three students individually measured the width of their classroom. They recorded their data in the chart. Which student made a mistake?

Data

Student	Measurement
Nancy	44 ft.
Matt	19 ft 6 in.
Mike	6 yds 1 ft 6 in.

Guided Practice*

Do you know HOW?

Solve. Write to explain.

1. A bald eagle can have a wingspan of up to 7 feet 6 inches. A mallard duck can have a wingspan of about 32 inches. How much longer is the bald eagle's wingspan than the mallard duck's wingspan?

Do you UNDERSTAND?

2. How can you explain that one yard is equal to 36 inches?

3. **Write a Problem** Write a problem in which measurements are compared. Write to explain which measurement is correct.

Independent Practice

Solve each problem. Explain your answer.

4. Julia and her brother went deep-sea fishing. They caught a spotted seatrout weighing 5 pounds 10 ounces, a snook weighing 8 pounds 4 ounces, and a redfish weighing 176 ounces. Which was the largest fish they caught?

5. When converting ounces to pounds, you would have to divide the number of ounces by 16 to get the number of pounds. If you get a remainder when converting ounces to pounds, what does the remainder mean?

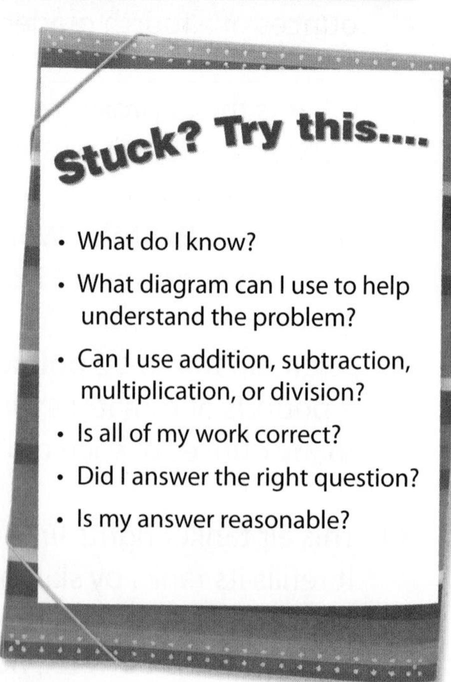
Stuck? Try this....
• What do I know?
• What diagram can I use to help understand the problem?
• Can I use addition, subtraction, multiplication, or division?
• Is all of my work correct?
• Did I answer the right question?
• Is my answer reasonable?

*For another example, see Set D on page 405.

Convert the students' measurements to inches and compare.

Nancy's measurement:

1 foot = 12 inches
44 × 12 = 528 inches

Matt's measurement:

1 foot = 12 inches
19 × 12 = 228 inches

19 feet = 228 inches
+ 6 inches
234 inches

Mike's measurement:

1 yard = 36 inches
6 × 36 = 216 inches

6 yards = 216 inches
1 foot = 12 inches
+ 6 inches
234 inches

Mike's and Matt's measurements are both 234 inches.
Nancy's measurement is 528 inches.

Nancy made a mistake. Her calculation is correct, but she may have measured the length of the classroom not the width.

For **6** and **7**, use the data to the right.

Derek, Kitty, Eva, and Mercedes are measuring planks of wood to build a tree house.

Data

Names	Measurements
Derek	2 yds – 2 in.
Kitty	1 yd 34 in.
Eva	70 in.
Mercedes	60 in.

6. Each plank of wood needs to measure 5 feet and 10 inches. Derek said his planks measure 2 inches less than 2 yards. Did Derek measure correctly?

7. Whose measurement is incorrect? Explain.

For **8** and **9**, use the drawing to the right.

8. What information would you need in order to find the length of the fourth side of the quadrilateral?

9. If the perimeter of the quadrilateral is 25 inches, how long is the final side of the quadrilateral?

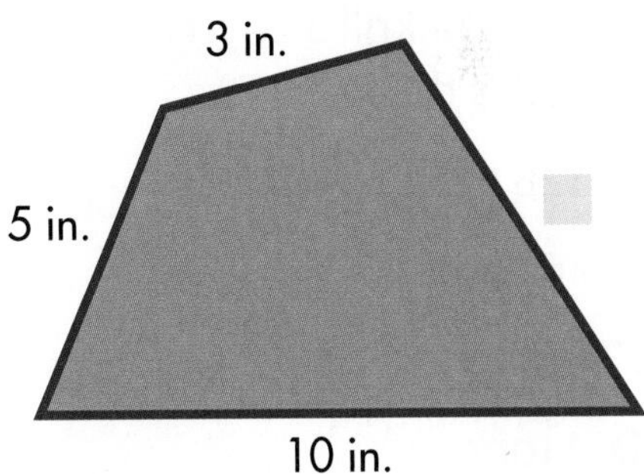

10. Below is a drawing of a race track. How many feet would you run if you went around the inner track twice? Explain.

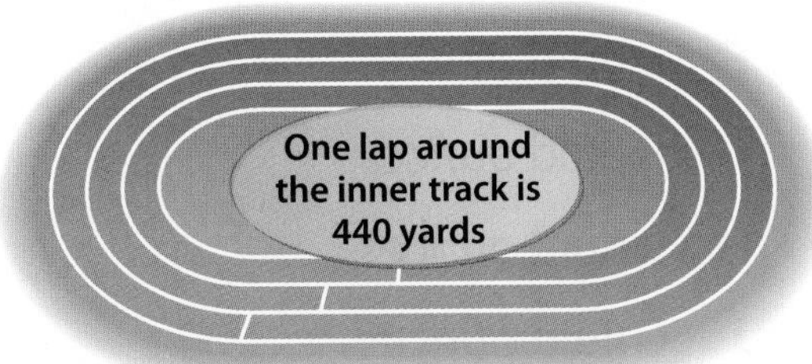

11. Reasoning A milligram is related to a gram in the same way a millimeter is related to a meter. How many milligrams are in one gram?

Tip *1 meter = 1,000 millimeters*

1. Mary bought a trial size of new dental floss. The container had 12 yards of floss. How many feet of floss is this? (18-1)

   A 24 feet

   B 32 feet

   C 36 feet

   D 144 feet

2. On a hiking trip, Mae drank 12 pints of water. Which of the following can be used to find how many quarts of water Mae drank? (18-2)

   F Multiply 12 by 2

   G Multiply 12 by 4

   H Divide 12 by 2

   J Divide 12 by 4

3. A blue whale can eat up to 8,000 pounds of krill a day. How many tons of krill is this? (18-3)

   A 128 tons

   B 16 tons

   C 8 tons

   D 4 tons

4. The mouth on the Statue of Liberty is 36 inches wide. How many feet wide is the Statue of Liberty's mouth? (18-1)

   F 3 feet

   G 4 feet

   H 108 feet

   J 432 feet

5. Melody bought a 1-gallon container of mustard for the concession stand. After the tournament, there was about 1 quart of mustard left in the container. About how much mustard was used? (18-2)

   A 1 quart

   B 2 quarts

   C 3 quarts

   D 4 quarts

6. The African elephant, can weigh up to 7 tons. How many pounds are in 7 tons? (18-3)

   F 3 pounds

   G 700 pounds

   H 7,000 pounds

   J 14,000 pounds

7. Mustang Island State Park has about 5 miles of beach along the Gulf of Mexico. How many yards are in 5 miles? (18-1)

   A 26,400 yards

   B 8,800 yards

   C 8,350 yards

   D 180 yards

8. A science experiment used 7 cups of water. How many fluid ounces is 7 cups?

   F 15 fluid ounces

   G 28 fluid ounces

   H 49 fluid ounces

   J 56 fluid ounces

8. Kendra's puppy, Shamrock, weighs 64 ounces. How many pounds does Shamrock weigh? (18-3)

A 4 pounds

B 52 pounds

C 768 pounds

D 1,024 pounds

9. Three friends individually measured the capacity of a goldfish bowl. Which friend do you think measured incorrectly? (18-4)

Data

Student	Measurement
Janell	28 cups
Leah	10 pints
Kathleen	5 quarts

F Janell, because the other girls' measurements equal 1 gallon 1 quart.

G Leah, because the other girls' measurements equal 1 gallon 1 quart.

H Kathleen, because the other girls' measurements equal 1 gallon 1 quart.

J All 3 girls got the same measure.

10. This weekend, Mr. Scott canned 24 quarts of salsa. How many gallons of salsa did he make? (18-2)

A 4 gallons

B 6 gallons

C 8 gallons

D 12 gallons

11. A bald eagle's nest can weigh up to 2 tons. How many pounds can a bald eagle's nest weigh? (18-3)

F 4,000 pounds

G 6,000 pounds

H 8,000 pounds

J 32,000 pounds

12. The average size of an ostrich egg is 3 pounds. How many ounces does an average ostrich egg weigh? (18-3)

A 6,000 ounces

B 48 ounces

C 42 ounces

D 36 ounces

13. Sea Lion Cave, found along the Pacific coast of Oregon, is the world's largest sea cave. It is about 360 feet long. Which of the following can be used to find how many yards long Sea Lion Cave is? (18-1)

F Multiply 360 by 12

G Multiply 360 by 3

H Divide 360 by 12

J Divide 360 by 3

14. **Griddable Response** Mrs. Gould's pudding recipe calls for 3 cups cold milk. How many fluid ounces are in 3 cups? (18-2)

15. **Griddable Response** One of the largest bears in the world is the Kodiak bear. A male Kodiak bear can stand over 10 feet tall. How many inches are in 10 feet? (18-1)

Reteaching

Set A, pages 394–395

To change smaller units to larger units, divide.

56 inches = ☐ feet

12 inches = 1 foot

56 ÷ 12 = 4 R 8

56 inches = 4 feet 8 inches

To change larger units to smaller units, multiply.

3 yards = ☐ feet

1 yard = 3 feet

3 × 3 = 9

3 yards = 9 feet

Remember that there are 5,280 feet in 1 mile and 1,760 yards in 1 mile.

Find the missing number.

1. 5 yd = ☐ ft

2. 6 mi = ☐ ft

3. 42 ft = ☐ yd

4. 8 yd = ☐ in.

5. 10 mi = ☐ ft

6. 6 mi = ☐ yd

7. 36 in. = ☐ yd

8. 120 in. = ☐ ft

9. 10 yd = ☐ in.

10. 132 in. = ☐ ft

11. 144 in. = ☐ ft

12. 3,520 yd = ☐ mi

Set B, pages 396–397

To change smaller units to larger units, divide.

5 pints = ☐ quarts

2 pints = 1 quart

5 ÷ 2 = 2 R 1

5 pints = 2 quarts 1 pint

To change larger units to smaller units, multiply.

4 pints = ☐ cups

1 pint = 2 cups

4 × 2 = 8

4 pints = 8 cups

Remember to convert units, compare the size of units to decide whether to multiply or divide.

Find the missing number.

1. 36 qt = ☐ gal

2. 6 c = ☐ fl oz

3. 9 tsp= ☐ tbsp

4. 20 pt = ☐ c

5. 16 fl oz = ☐ tbsp

6. 18 gal = ☐ qt

7. 22 c = ☐ pt

8. 24 fl oz = ☐ c

9. 25 pt = ☐ c

10. 8 c = ☐ fl oz

11. 30 qt = ☐ pt

12. 12 gal = ☐ qt

Reteaching

Set C, pages 398–399

To change smaller units to larger units, divide.

6,000 pounds = ▢ tons

2,000 pounds = 1 ton

6,000 ÷ 2,000 = 3

6,000 pounds = 3 tons

To change larger units to smaller units, multiply.

5 lb = ▢ ounces

1 pound = 16 ounces

5 × 16 = 80

5 pounds = 80 ounces

Remember that one pound is equal to 16 ounces.

Find the missing number.

1. 5 T = ▢ lb
2. 64 oz = ▢ lb
3. 6 lb = ▢ oz
4. 16 T = ▢ lb
5. 10 lb = ▢ oz
6. 100 lb = ▢ oz
7. 3,000 lb = ▢ oz
8. 12,000 lb = ▢ T
9. 7 T = ▢ lb
10. 50 lb = ▢ oz
11. 20,000 lb = ▢ T
12. 480 oz = ▢ lb

Set D, pages 400–401

Jenna, Barbara, and Christina measured the width of their playground. Which measurement is not correct? Why?

Data

Student	Measurement
Jenna	12 yds 1 ft 3 in.
Barbara	400 ft
Christina	37 ft 3 in.

Convert each measurement to feet and compare.

Jenna = 36 ft + 1 ft + 3 in.= 37 ft 3 in.

Barbara = 400 ft

Christina = 37 ft 3 in.

Barbara's measurement is incorrect because the other two measurements are equal.

Remember to explain your answer.

1. One hundred people are surveyed about their favorite flower. Of these, 20 people say their favorite flower is the tulip. What fraction of the people say their favorite flower is **NOT** the tulip? Explain your answer.

2. Mr. Gibson wants to make his driveway longer for more cars to park. It is currently 8 yards long. If the maximum length of a driveway is 30 feet long, how many more yards can he add to his driveway? Explain your answer.

Spiral Review

Number and Operations

1. Which is the most reasonable estimate for 7,134 − 2, 923?

A 2,000 **C** 4,000

B 3,000 **D** 5,000

2. Which model below shows $\frac{1}{3} = \frac{2}{6}$?

F
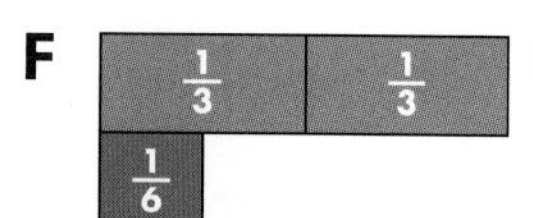

H
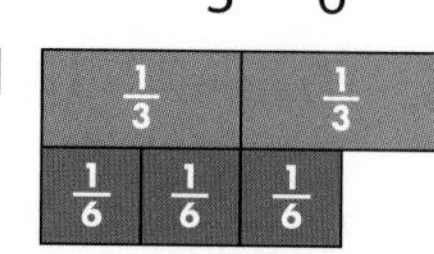

G
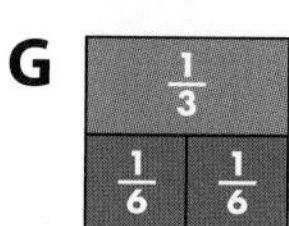

J
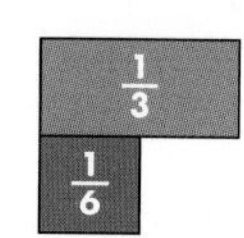

3. Which number is divisible by 4?

A 46 **C** 68

B 51 **D** 85

4. This model is shaded to represent $1\frac{37}{100}$.

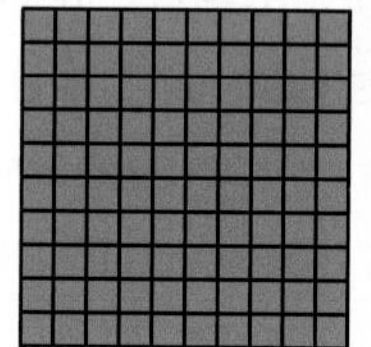
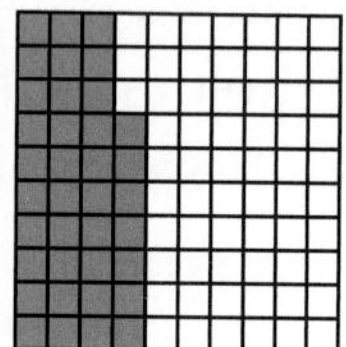

What decimal does the model represent?

F 137.0 **H** 1.37

G 13.7 **J** 0.137

5. Round 423,725 to the nearest thousand.

6. **Writing to Explain** Describe an array of drinking glasses using the product of 3 × 12.

Geometry and Measurement

7. Which two figures are the same size and shape?

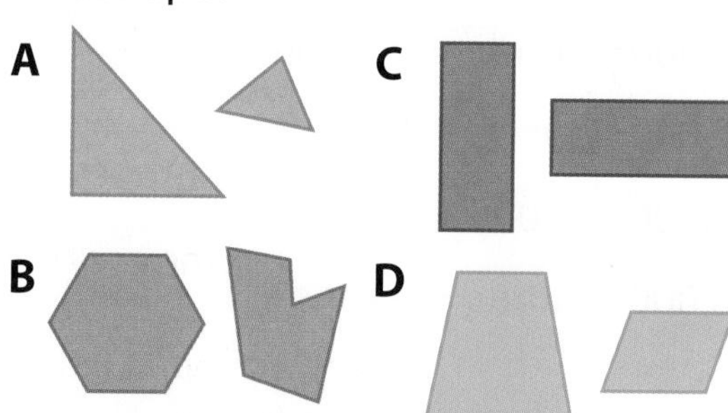

8. What is the area of a rectangle with a length of 12 inches and a width of 27 inches?

F 127 sq. in. **H** 324 sq. in.

G 272 sq. in. **J** 429 sq. in.

9. Which figure is not a quadrilateral?

A
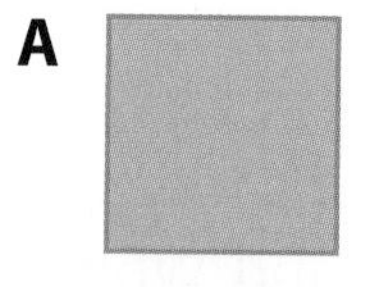

C

B
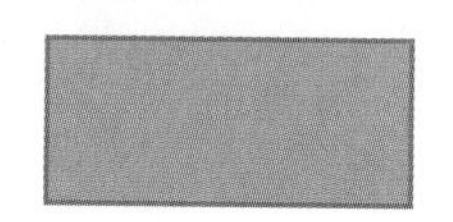

D

10. How many angles does a regular octagon have?

11. Nicole bought 6 pounds of oranges. How many ounces did the oranges weigh?

12. **Writing to Explain** What is the difference between the weight and mass of an object?

Probability and Statistics

13. There are 4 marbles in a bag. Two marbles are blue, one is orange, and one is green. What is the likelihood of picking a yellow marble?

F Certain
G Likely
H Unlikely
J Impossible

14. Twenty-four students were asked to pick their favorite color from a list of four colors. The results are displayed in the bar graph below.

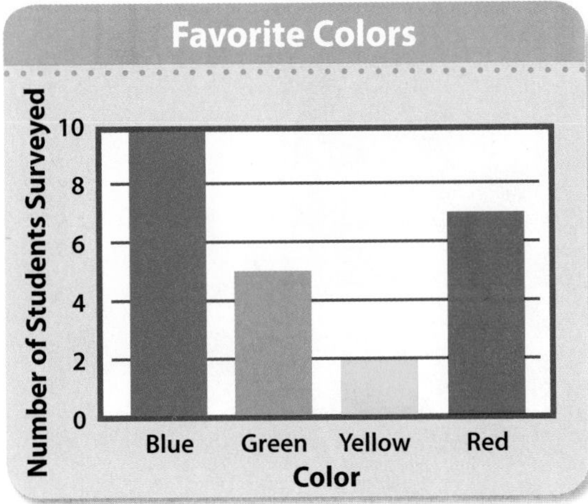

How many students chose green as their favorite color?

A 2 students
B 5 students
C 6 students
D 7 students

15. Is it certain or impossible for a 4th grader to be 20 feet tall?

16. **Writing to Explain** In the data table below, between what two hours did the number of cars change the least?

Time	3 P.M.	4 P.M.	5 P.M.	6 P.M.
Cars in lot	5	2	6	16

Algebraic Thinking

17. Which pair of numbers best completes the equation?

$\square \times 50 = \square$

F 20 and 1,000
G 40 and 1,000
H 40 and 1,500
J 50 and 2,000

18. Which expression shows 3 less than a number?

A $3 - n$
B $n - 3$
C $3 + n$
D $n + 3$

19. If $k = 5$, evaluate the expression $k + 17$.

F 5
G 12
H 22
J 85

20. Is the solution to $m + 24 = 75$ more or less than 50?

21. Fill in the table with the missing number. Then write the rule.

n	6	8	10	12
rule: _____	2		6	8

22. **Writing to Explain** Complete the table. Then explain the pattern you used to find the missing number.

Time	1 h	2 h	3 h	4 h
Distance	70 mi	140 mi	210 mi	mi

Topic 19

Time and Temperature

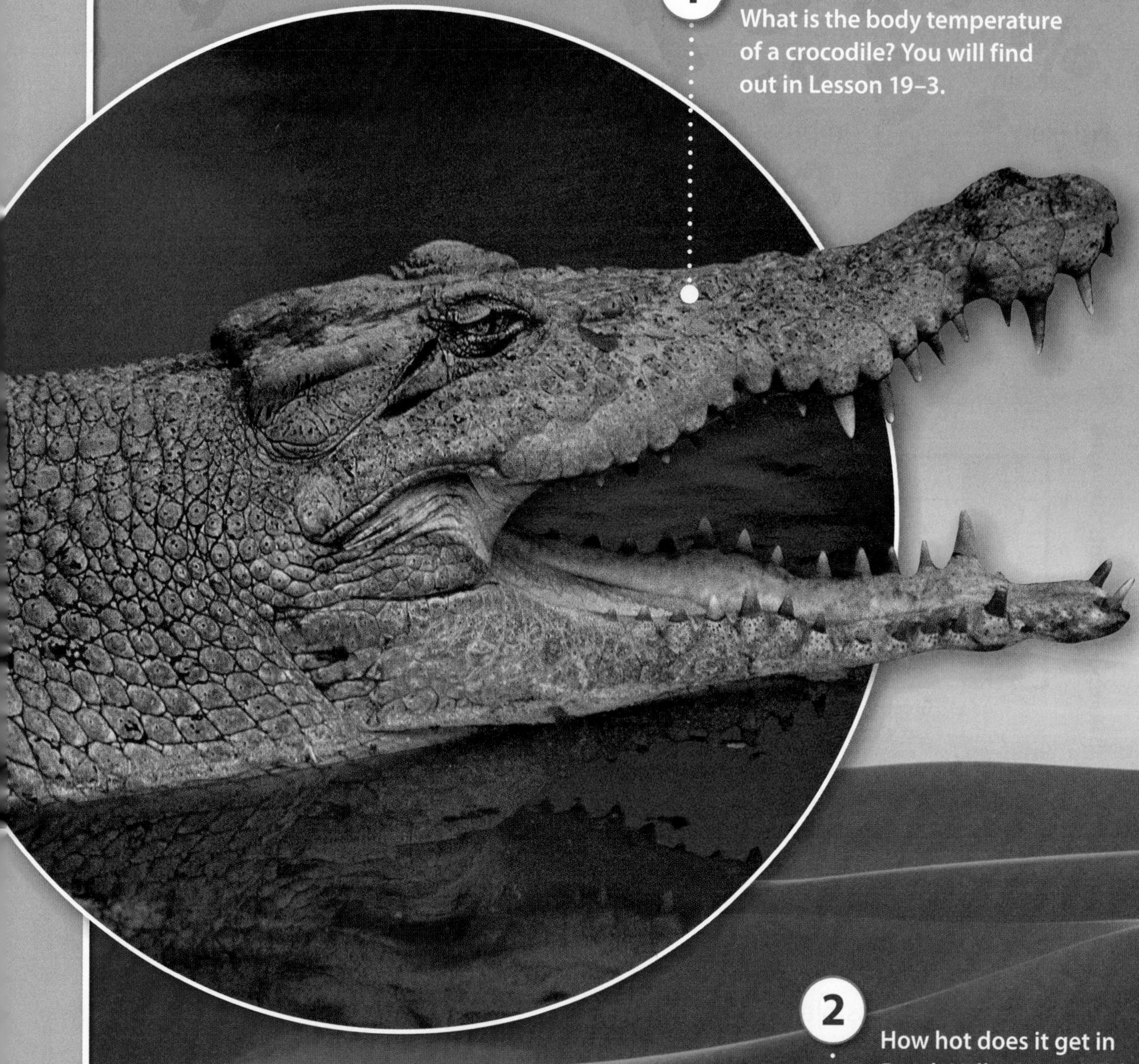

1 What is the body temperature of a crocodile? You will find out in Lesson 19–3.

2 How hot does it get in Death Valley? You will find out in Lesson 19–3.

3

How could an ancient Mayan pyramid be a type of calendar? You will find out in Lesson 19-1.

4

How many days will it take for a cyclist in "Trek Across Texas" to ride from Texline to Houston? You will find out in Lesson 19-2.

Review What You Know!

Vocabulary

Choose the best term from the box.

- minute
- seconds
- negative
- thermometer

1. A _?_ is used to measure temperature.
2. Temperatures below 0 are _?_ temperatures.
3. There are 60 _?_ in one minute.

Telling Time

Find the time.

4. 

5. 

6. 

7. 

Reading a Thermometer

Find the temperature in Fahrenheit and Celsius.

8. 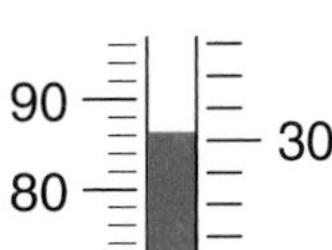

9. 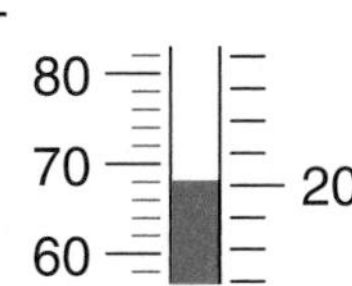

10. **Writing to Explain** Yolanda practices piano 2 hours a week. Pete practices piano 120 minutes a week. They both think that they spend more time practicing. Who is correct?

Lesson
19-1

TEKS 4.12: Apply measurement concepts. The student measures time . . .

Time

How do you compare units of time?

On her birthday, Kara calculated that she was 108 months old. Her friend Jordan has the same birthday. If Jordan turned 8 years old, who is older, Kara or Jordan?

You can convert different units of time in order to compare them.

Data

Units of Time
1 minute = 60 seconds
1 hour = 60 minutes
1 day = 24 hours
1 week = 7 days
1 month = about 4 weeks
1 year = 52 weeks
1 year = 12 months
1 year = 365 days
1 leap year = 366 days
1 decade = 10 years
1 century = 100 years
1 millennium = 1,000 years

Guided Practice*

Do you know HOW?

For **1** through **4**, write >, <, or = for each ◯. Use the chart above to help.

1. 9 months ◯ 27 weeks

2. 17 years ◯ 2 decades

3. 5 minutes ◯ 300 seconds

4. 44 months ◯ 3 years

Do you UNDERSTAND?

5. Writing to Explain How can you tell which is longer, 63 hours or 3 days?

6. Do you multiply or divide if you want to change months to years?

7. How many years old is Kara?

Independent Practice

For **8** through **13**, write >, <, or = for each ◯.

8. 35 weeks ◯ 340 days

9. 7 days ◯ 120 hours

10. 2 years ◯ 730 days

11. 40 hours ◯ 2 days

12. 8 weeks ◯ 56 days

13. 12 months ◯ 40 weeks

For **14** through **22**, complete each number sentence.

14. 6 days = ▢ hours

15. 2 years = ▢ months

16. 6 minutes = ▢ seconds

17. 3 decades = ▢ years

18. 4 hours = ▢ minutes

19. 4 centuries = ▢ years

20. 36 months = ▢ years

21. 104 weeks = ▢ years

22. 5,000 years = ▢ millennia

*For another example, see Set A on page 424.

Step 1

Change 8 years to months.

1 year = 12 months

To find the number of months in 8 years, multiply.

$8 \times 12 = 96$

So, 8 years = 96 months.

Step 2

Compare the amounts.

Kara's age		Jordan's age
108 months	◯	**8 years**
108 months	(>)	**96 months**

So, Kara is older than Jordan.

TAKS Problem Solving

23. **Estimation** About how many minutes does it take you to do your homework? How many seconds is this?

24. Trish is going to camp for 2 months. Which is greater than 2 months?

A 35 days **C** 6 weeks

B 40 days **D** 10 weeks

25. **Reasoning** Gina has 3 yards of fabric. She needs to cut 8 pieces, each 1 foot long. Does she have enough fabric? Explain.

26. A girl from England set a world record by sneezing 978 days in a row. About how many weeks did she sneeze in a row?

27. **Estimation** If you brush your teeth 10 minutes a day, about how many hours do you brush in a year?

28. A theater has 358 seats on the main level and 122 seats in the balcony. How many people can see 6 shows in one day?

29. It is believed that the Mayan pyramid of Kukulkan in Mexico was used as a calendar. It has 4 stairways leading to the top platform. Including the one extra step at the top, it has a total of 365 steps. How many steps are in each stairway?

Tip *Subtract 1 from the total number of steps before you divide.*

Each stairway has the same number of steps.

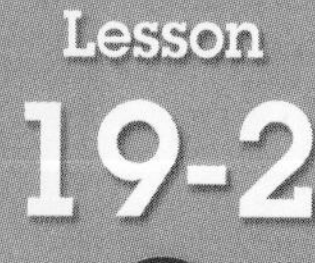

Lesson 19-2

TEKS 4.12B: Use tools such as a clock with gears or a stopwatch to solve problems involving elapsed time.

Elapsed Time

Hands-On
clock

How can you find and use elapsed time?

The dress rehearsal for the school play started at 8:15 A.M. It ended at 10:25 A.M. How long was the rehearsal?

Elapsed time is the amount of time that passes between the beginning and the end of an event.

Another Example **How can you use elapsed time to find when an event began or ended?**

At 11:50 A.M., Kerry's father dropped Kerry off at a Saturday rehearsal for the school play. He was told the rehearsal would last 1 hour and 30 minutes. At what time should he pick her up?

Rehearsal starts at 11:50 A.M.

One Way

The rehearsal started at 11:50 A.M.

Count 1 hour to 12:50 P.M.

Count 10 minutes to 1:00 P.M.

Count another 20 minutes to 1:20 P.M.

Kerry's father should pick her up at 1:20 P.M.

Another Way

From 11:50 A.M. to 12:00 P.M. is 10 minutes.

From 12:00 P.M. to 12:20 P.M. is 20 minutes.

From 12:20 P.M. to 1:20 P.M. is 1 hour.

Kerry's father should pick her up at 1:20 P.M.

Explain It

1. On Sunday, rehearsal starts at 10:30 A.M. When will rehearsal end if it lasts 1 hour and 30 minutes?

2. **Reasonableness** Is the elapsed time from 5:35 P.M. to 8:52 P.M. more or less than three hours?

One Way

From 8:15 A.M. to 10:15 A.M. is 2 hours.

From 10:15 A.M. to 10:25 A.M. is 10 minutes.

So, the dress rehearsal lasted 2 hours and 10 minutes.

Another Way

From 8:15 A.M. to 9:00 A.M. is 45 minutes.

From 9:00 A.M. to 10:00 A.M. is 1 hour.

From 10:00 A.M. to 10:25 A.M. is 25 minutes.

45 minutes + 1 hour + 25 minutes is 1 hour and 70 minutes, or 2 hours and 10 minutes.

The dress rehearsal lasted 2 hours and 10 minutes.

Guided Practice*

Do you know HOW?

Find the elapsed time.

1. Start: 9:00 P.M. Finish: 11:10 P.M.
2. Start: 6:10 A.M. Finish: 10:25 A.M.
3. Start: 1:11 A.M. Finish: 3:26 A.M.
4. Start: 2:37 P.M. Finish: 4:05 P.M.

Do you UNDERSTAND?

5. Is the elapsed time between 4:40 P.M. and 6:20 P.M. more or less than 2 hours? Explain.
6. Based on the rehearsal time, if the play begins at 7:15 P.M., at what time will it end?

Independent Practice

For **7** through **12**, find the elapsed time. Use a clock or stopwatch to help.

7. Start: 5:00 A.M. Finish: 9:20 A.M.
8. Start: 7:15 P.M. Finish: 11:00 P.M.
9. Start: 4:55 A.M. Finish: 5:37 A.M.
10. Start: 4:25 P.M. Finish: 6:41 P.M.
11. Start: 3:07 P.M. Finish: 10:12 P.M.
12. Start: 11:44 A.M. Finish: 1:05 P.M.

In **13** through **16**, write the time each clock will show in 2 hours and 15 minutes.

13. 

14. 

15. 

16. 

DIGITAL Animated Glossary, eTools **www.pearsonsuccessnet.com**

For another example, see Set B on page 424.

Independent Practice

For **17** through **22**, find each start or finish time. Use a clock or stopwatch to help.

17. Start: 9:00 A.M.
Elapsed time: 2 hours and 35 minutes
Finish: ▢

18. Start: 5:25 P.M.
Elapsed time: 3 hours and 23 minutes
Finish: ▢

19. Start: ▢
Elapsed time: 2 hours and 20 minutes
Finish: 3:40 A.M.

20. Start: ▢
Elapsed time: 6 hours and 13 minutes
Finish: 8:27 P.M.

21. Start: 3:16 P.M.
Elapsed time: 2 hours and 51 minutes
Finish: ▢

22. Start: ▢
Elapsed time: 5 hours and 9 minutes
Finish: 11:21 A.M.

TAKS Problem Solving

For **23** and **24**, use the table at the right.

23. Which activities are scheduled to last more than 1 hour and 30 minutes?

24. Paulo's family arrived at the reunion at 8:30 A.M. How long do they have before the trip to Scenic Lake Park?

Data

Suarez Family Reunion Schedule

Activity	Time
Trip to Scenic Lake Park	10:15 A.M. to 2:30 P.M.
Slide show	4:15 P.M. to 5:10 P.M.
Dinner	5:30 P.M. to 7:00 P.M.
Campfire	7:55 P.M. to 9:30 P.M.

25. **Algebra** Thomas saved $256. He used the money to buy 4 model trains. Each train cost the same amount. Write and solve an equation to find the cost of each train.

26. The "Trek Across Texas" bike ride is about 800 miles long. If the average cyclist bikes 50 miles per day, how many days will it take to complete the trek?

27. Which is greater, 13,400 seconds or 2,000 minutes?

28. Which is greater, 104 weeks or 3 years?

29. In 1999, a chain of 2,751,518 dominoes was toppled in Beijing, China. It took a total of 32 minutes and 22 seconds for the dominoes to fall. If the first domino fell at 11:22 P.M., at what time did the last domino fall? Round your answer to the nearest minute.

30. In April, Julie's puppy weighed 14 ounces. In July, the puppy weighed 4 times this much. How much did the puppy weigh in July?

A 2 pounds 10 ounces

B 3 pounds 8 ounces

C 4 pounds 8 ounces

D 7 pounds

Time

Use eTools Time

Jessica gets to play video games from 7:35 P.M. until 8:15 P.M. each evening. She sleeps from 9:40 P.M. until 6:25 A.M. How long does she play video games? How long does she sleep?

Step 1 Go to the Time eTool. Select Elapsed Time from the pull-down menu at the top of the page. Move the minute hand on the clock until it shows 7:35. The digital clock should change to match. Click the + button under starting time to change the time to 7:35. Hold down the button to change the time faster.

Step 2 Change the ending time to 8:15. Push Go to start the elapsed time animation.

Jessica gets to play video games for 40 minutes.

Step 3 Move the hands of the analog clock to show 9:40. Change the Starting time to 9:40 by holding down the + button. Change the ending time to 6:25 by holding down the − button. Push Go to see the animation.

Jessica sleeps 8 hours and 45 minutes.

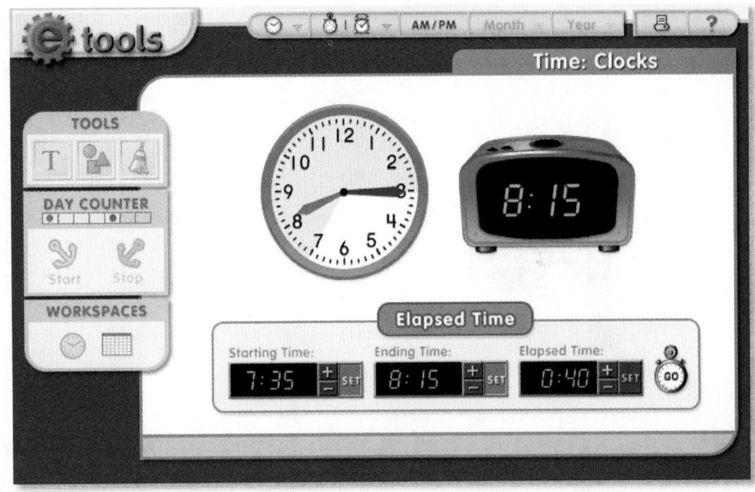

Practice

Use the Time eTool to find each elapsed time.

1. 1:25 P.M. to 3:15 P.M.
2. 5:45 A.M. to 8:05 A.M.
3. 12:45 P.M. to 7:20 P.M.
4. 11:52 A.M. to 2:19 P.M.
5. 3:31 P.M. to 6:46 P.M.
6. 11:43 A.M. to 4:39 P.M.
7. 2:12 P.M. to 3:09 P.M.
8. 7:28 A.M. to 5:30 P.M.
9. 7:30 A.M. TO 11:45 A.M.

TEKS 4.12A: Use a thermometer to measure temperature and changes in temperature.

Temperature °F

Hands-On: thermometer

How can you solve problems involving changes in temperature?

On Saturday how many degrees did the temperature rise between 6:00 A.M. and noon?

Degrees Fahrenheit (°F) are customary units used to measure temperature.

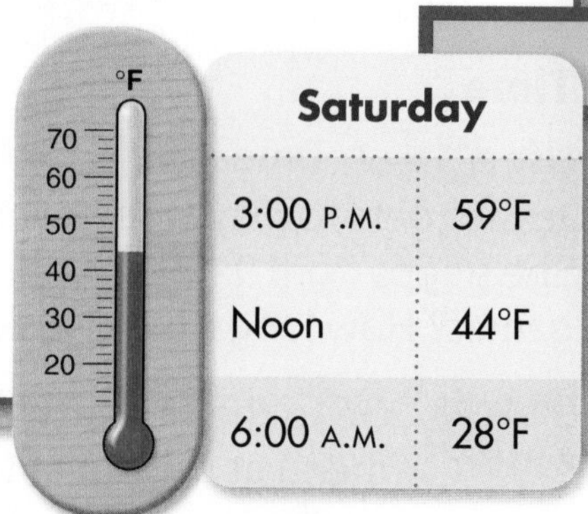

Saturday	
3:00 P.M.	59°F
Noon	44°F
6:00 A.M.	28°F

Guided Practice*

Do you know HOW?

For **1** and **2**, read each temperature. Then tell what the temperature would be after each change described.

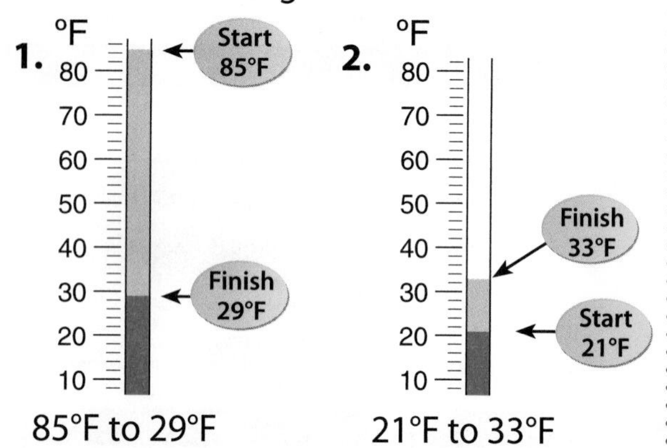

85°F to 29°F

21°F to 33°F

Do you UNDERSTAND?

3. Use the chart above. The temperature at 6:00 P.M. was 31°F. How you can find the change in temperature between 3:00 P.M. and 6:00 P.M.?

4. On Sunday the temperature at 6:00 A.M. was 14° colder than it was at that time on Saturday. What was the temperature at 6:00 A.M. on Sunday?

Independent Practice

For **5** through **8**, find each change in temperature. Tell whether each change is an increase or decrease.

5. 79°F to 38°F **6.** 40°F to 15°F **7.** 44°F to 61°F **8.** 17°F to 52°F

For **9** through **12**, read each temperature. Then tell what the temperature would be after each change described.

9.

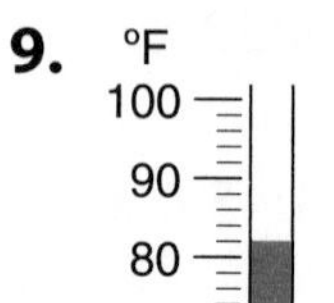

Increase of 9°F

10. °F 50 40 30

Decrease of 21°F

11.

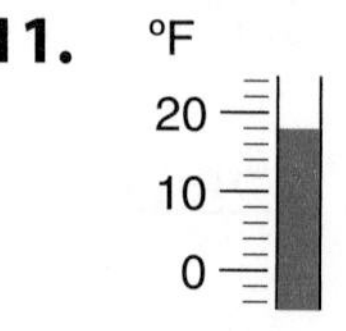

Decrease of 17°F

12.

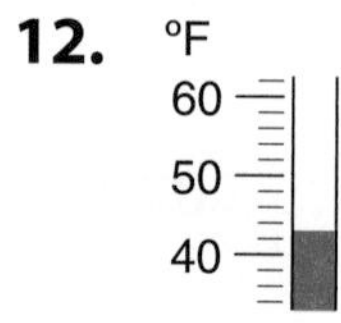

Increase of 26°F

*For another example, see Set C on page 425.

One Way

Add to find the change in temperature between 6:00 A.M. and noon.

You can count between two temperatures to find the change in temperature.

28 + 10 = 38

38 + 6 = 44

10 + 6 = 16

°F
60
50
40
30
20
Noon
6:00 A.M.

Between 6:00 A.M. and noon, the temperature increased by 16°F.

Another Way

Subtract to find the change in temperature between 6:00 A.M. and noon.

Subtract the temperature at 6:00 A.M. from the temperature at noon.

44 − 28 = 16

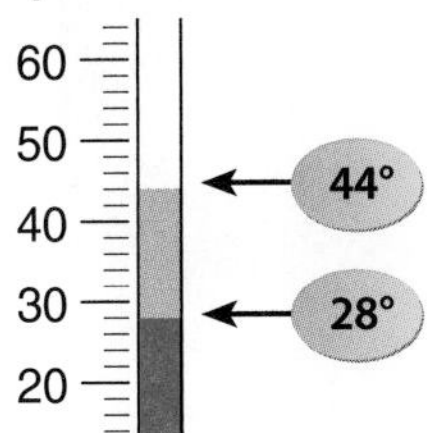

Between 6:00 A.M. and noon, the temperature increased by 16°F.

TAKS Problem Solving

13. Death Valley is the hottest place in the United States. The highest temperature ever recorded there was 134°F. The lowest temperature was 15°F. What is the difference between the highest and lowest temperatures?

14. Writing to Explain At 6:00 A.M. the temperature was 14°F. Between 6:00 A.M. and 6:00 P.M., the temperature rose 25°F and then dropped 9°F. What was the change in temperature between 6:00 A.M. and 6:00 P.M.?

15. On the Fahrenheit scale, water boils at 212°F and freezes at 32°F. What is the temperature difference between boiling and freezing?

16. Geometry Jason drew a rectangle with an area of 24 square inches. One side of the rectangle is 8 inches. What is the perimeter of the rectangle?

17. The temperature at 9:00 A.M. was 29°F. By noon the temperature had risen 17°F. From noon to 7:00 P.M., the temperature fell 9°F. What was the temperature at 7:00 P.M.?

A 20°F **B** 37°F **C** 46°F **D** 55°F

18. The high temperature for a day in June was 68°F. The low temperature that day was 29°F less. What was the low temperature?

F 39°F **H** 87°F

G 40°F **J** 97°F

19. Crocodiles are cold-blooded animals with body temperatures from 86° to 89°F. Crocodiles control their body temperature by moving to warmer or cooler environments. What is the difference between the highest normal body temperature and the lowest normal body temperature?

DIGITAL Animated Glossary, eTools **www.pearsonsuccessnet.com**

Lesson
19-4

TEKS 4.12A: Use a thermometer to measure temperature and changes in temperature.

Temperature °C

Hands-On
thermometer

How can you solve problems involving changes in temperature?

By how much does the Arctic squirrel's temperature drop during hibernation?

Degrees Celsius (°C) are metric units used to measure temperature.

The Arctic squirrel's core body temperature drops from 36°C to 2°C when it hibernates.

Guided Practice*

Do you know HOW?

For **1** and **2**, find each temperature change. Tell whether each change is an increase or decrease.

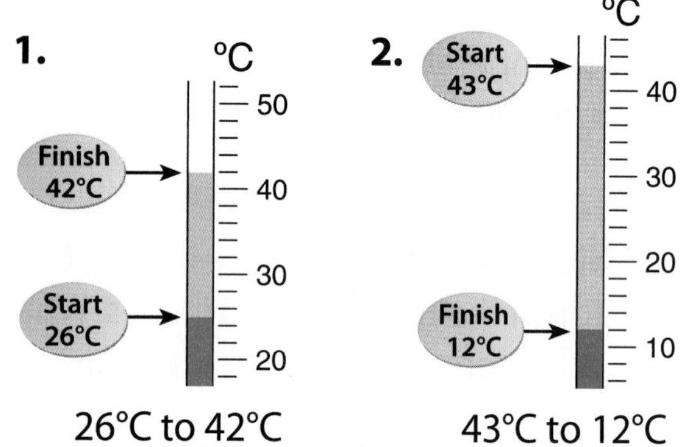

26°C to 42°C

43°C to 12°C

Do you UNDERSTAND?

3. On the Celsius thermometers above, there are 5 tick marks between 20°C and 30°C. What does each tick mark represent?

4. During hibernation, an arctic ground squirrel's body temperature rises to 35°C every 3 weeks. If the squirrel's temperature is 8°C, how much does it need to rise to get to 35°C?

Independent Practice

For **5** through **8**, find each temperature change. Tell whether each change is an increase or decrease.

5. 24°C to 58°C **6.** 31°C to 17°C **7.** 42°C to 14°C **8.** 40°C to 27°C

For **9** through **12**, tell what the temperature would be after each change described below.

9.

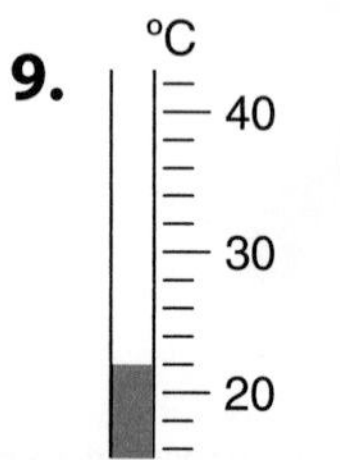

Increase of 13°C

10.

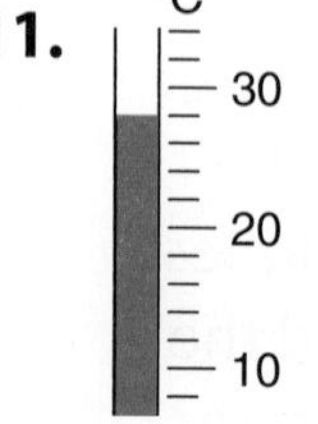

Decrease of 12°C

11.

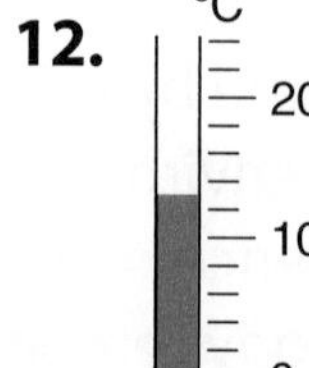

Decrease of 11°C

12.

°C
20
10
0

Increase of 7°C

*For another example, see Set C on page 425.

One Way

Add to find the change in the squirrel's core temperature during hibernation.

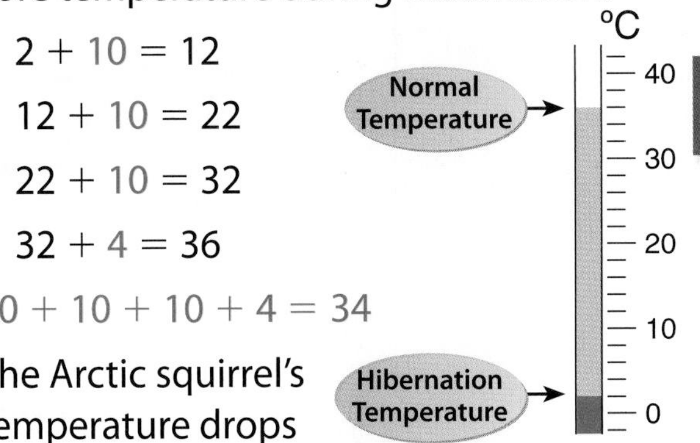

2 + 10 = 12

12 + 10 = 22

22 + 10 = 32

32 + 4 = 36

10 + 10 + 10 + 4 = 34

The Arctic squirrel's temperature drops about 34°C during hibernation.

Another Way

Subtract to find the change in the squirrel's core temperature during hibernation.

°C: 40, 30, 20, 10, 0

Normal Temperature

Hibernation Temperature

36 − 2 = 34

The Arctic squirrel's temperature drops about 34°C during hibernation.

TAKS Problem Solving

13. Rose has 3 times as many pennies as Laurie. If Laurie has 96 pennies, how many pennies does Rose have?

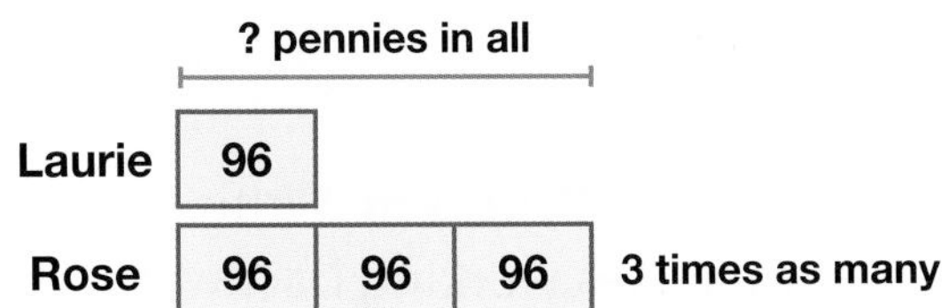

14. **Reasoning** Annie, Bart, and Consuela live in three different cities. One day, the high temperature in Bart's city was 9°C less than in Annie's city. The high temperature in Consuela's city was 14°C more than in Bart's city. Which city was warmer, Consuela's city or Annie's city?

15. Heather and Irene are reading the same 439-page book. Heather read 393 pages. Irene read 121 fewer pages than Heather. How many pages does Irene have left to read?

16. As a general rule, the air temperature drops about 7°C for every 1,000 meters of elevation. If the temperature at sea level is 33°C, what is the temperature at 4,000 meters?

17. The low temperature was 4°C in February. The high temperature was 12°C higher. What was the high temperature?

A 8°C **C** 14°C

B 10°C **D** 16°C

18. **Algebra** Find the next number in the pattern below.

3, 6, 9, 12, 15, ▢

19. On the Celsius scale, water boils at 100°C and freezes at 0°C. What is the temperature difference between boiling and freezing?

DIGITAL eTools **www.pearsonsuccessnet.com**

Lesson

19-5

TEKS 4.14C: Select or develop an appropriate problem-solving plan or strategy, including drawing a picture, looking for a pattern, systematic guessing and checking, acting it out, making a table, working a simpler problem, or working backwards to solve a problem.

Problem Solving

Work Backward

Between 6:00 A.M. and 7:00 A.M., the temperature rose 2 degrees. Every hour after that the temperature rose 4 degrees. At 1:00 P.M., the temperature was 62°F. What was the temperature at 6:00 A.M.?

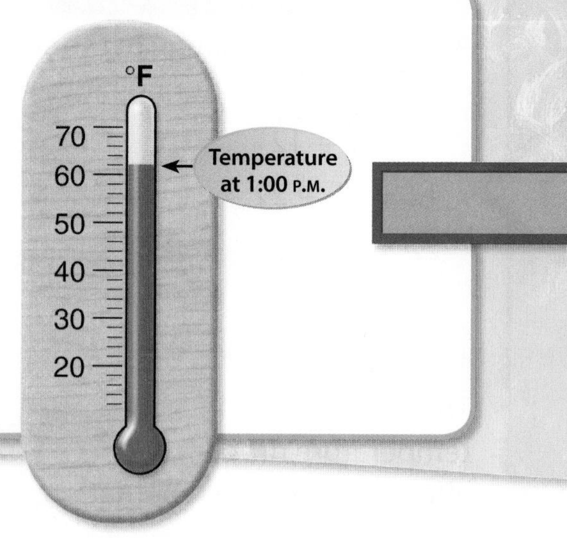

Guided Practice*

Do you know HOW?

Solve.

1. School starts at 7:45 A.M. It takes Fran 30 minutes to walk to school, 15 minutes to eat, and 20 minutes to get ready. What time should Fran get up?

Do you UNDERSTAND?

2. **Reasonableness** Is the answer to the problem above reasonable? Explain.

3. **Write a Problem** Write a problem that uses working backward. Then answer your question.

Independent Practice

Solve. Write the answer in a complete sentence.

4. Wanda walked for 25 minutes from the mall to the train station. She waited 20 minutes for the train, and then had a 20 minute ride. Her train arrived at 12:20 P.M. What time did she leave the mall?

5. Art rode his bike from his house to Jay's house. The boys rode their bikes 3 miles to the park and then 4 miles to the mall. Art rode 9 miles in all. How many miles is Art's house from Jay's house?

Stuck? Try this....

- What do I know?
- What diagram can I use to help understand the problem?
- Can I use addition, subtraction, multiplication, or division?
- Is all of my work correct?
- Did I answer the right question?
- Is my answer reasonable?

*For another example, see Set E on page 425.

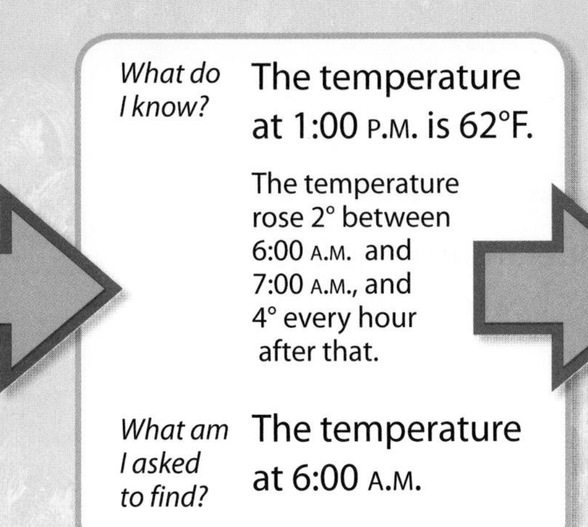

What do I know?
The temperature at 1:00 P.M. is 62°F.
The temperature rose 2° between 6:00 A.M. and 7:00 A.M., and 4° every hour after that.
What am I asked to find?
The temperature at 6:00 A.M.

Work backward:

Draw a picture to show each change.
Work backward starting at 1:00 P.M.

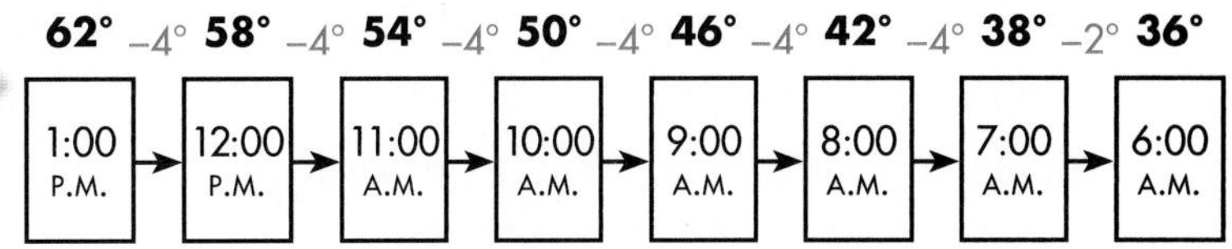

The temperature at 6:00 A.M. was 36°F.

6. Nina walked 1 mile on Monday. She walked twice as far on Tuesday. On Wednesday, she walked three more miles than she did on Monday. On Thursday, she walked a mile less than she had walked on Wednesday. How many miles did Nina walk on Thursday? Explain.

7. Georgette bought some craft items. The silk flowers cost three times as much as the ribbon. The ribbon cost double what the foam cost. The vase cost $12, which was three times as much as the foam. How much did the silk flowers cost?

8. Sylvia had $43 after she went shopping. She spent $9 on pet food, $6 on salad items, $12 on soup, and $24 on vegetables. How much money did Sylvia start with?

? money Sylvia started with

$6	$9	$12	$24	$43

9. Mrs. Harris is planning to drive the twins to a soccer game at 6:00 P.M. They need to arrive 20 minutes early to warm up for the game. It takes 25 minutes to get to the soccer field. What time does Mrs. Harris need to leave her house?

10. Leslie has 3 boxes of tea in her cupboard. Each box contains 11 tea bags. Each tea bag uses 3 cups of hot water to make a mug of hot tea. How many cups of water will Leslie use if she makes all of the tea?

11. The Declaration of Independence was signed in 1776. Three years earlier, the Boston Tea Party took place. Boston was settled 143 years before the Boston Tea Party. What year was Boston settled?

12. **Number Sense** Use the digits 7, 1, 5, 9, and 3 to write the largest number possible. Use each digit exactly once.

13. **Number Sense** Use the digits 6, 2, 5, and 4 to write 2 numbers less than 6,000 but greater than 5,500. Use each digit exactly once.

1. The next total solar eclipse can be seen in Dallas on April 8, 2024. It will last 268 seconds. Which symbol makes the comparison true? (19-1)

268 seconds ◯ 5 minutes

A ×

B =

C <

D >

2. Hayrides leave every 35 minutes. The clock shows the time the last hayride left. What time does the next hayride leave? (19-2)

F 4:20 P.M.

G 5:15 P.M.

H 5:20 P.M.

J 5:25 P.M.

3. The temperature was 81°F when Harvey left for school. By morning recess, it had gone up 8°F. However, by the time school was out, the temperature went down 15°F. What was the temperature at the end of school? (19-3)

A 58°F

B 74°F

C 76°F

D 104°F

4. The temperature of the liquid in Ranaldo's beaker is shown below.

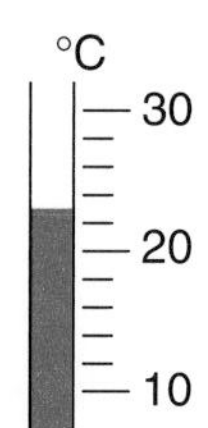

Ranaldo needs to raise the temperature an additional 4°C. What temperature does the liquid need to reach? (19-4)

F 4°C

G 20°C

H 27°C

J 37°C

5. A flight departs Dallas/Fort Worth International Airport at 9:56 A.M. It arrives in Madison, Wisconsin 2 hours and 15 minutes later. What time does it arrive in Madison? (19-2)

A 12:11 P.M.

B 12:11 A.M.

C 11:11 P.M.

D 11:11 A.M.

6. In 2007, Oklahoma celebrated its 100th birthday. How many months are in 100 years? (19-1)

F 600 months

G 1,200 months

H 1,800 months

J 2,400 months

Topic 19

TAKS Test Prep

7. The Hutson family arrived at the Plano Balloon Festival at 7:15 P.M. They left the festival at 9:30 P.M. How long did the family stay at the Balloon Festival? (19-2)

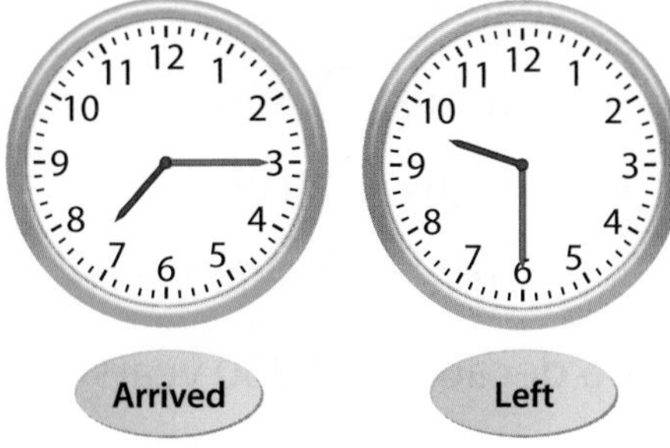

A 2 hours and 30 minutes

B 2 hours and 15 minutes

C 1 hour and 30 minutes

D 1 hour and 15 minutes

8. At 4:30 P.M., the thermometer outside of Yasmine's window read 40°C. It had risen 8° between noon and 4:30 P.M. and 5° between 7:00 A.M. and noon. What was the temperature at 7:00 A.M.? (19-5)

F 27°C

G 32°C

H 35 °C

J 53°C

9. It takes a guinea pig about 68 days to develop completely before it is born. Which of these is greater than 68 days? (19-1)

A 1 month

B 1,200 hours

C 9 weeks

D 10 weeks

10. If the temperature was 12°C at 6:00A.M. and 31°C at 2:00P.M., how did the temperature change? (19-4)

F A decrease of 21°C

G A decrease of 19°C

H An increase of 21°C

J An increase of 19°C

11. Mr. Nettlesport arrived at his office at 8:05 A.M. It took him 15 minutes to get from home to the Dart station, 7 minutes to wait for the train, 34 minutes on the train, and then 9 minutes to walk to his office. What time did Mr. Nettlesport leave his house? (19-5)

A 7:10 A.M.

B 7:09 A.M.

C 7:00 A.M.

D 6:50 A.M.

12. **Griddable Response** What would the temperature be if it decreased by 8°F? (19-3)

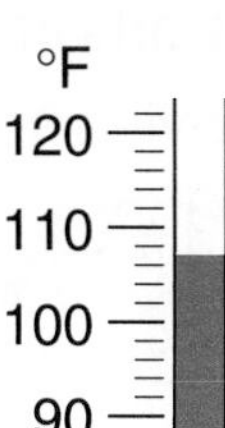

Reteaching

Set A, pages 410–411

Which is greater,12 years or 120 months?

Change 12 years to months.

Since 1 year = 12 months, multiply the number of years by 12.

12 years × 12 = 144 months

144 months > 120 months

So, 12 years > 120 months.

Remember first convert the measurements to the same unit. Then compare the measurements.

1. 36 months ◯ 104 weeks
2. 33 years ◯ 3 decades
3. 90 minutes ◯ 540 seconds
4. 96 months ◯ 8 years
5. 5 centuries ◯ 5,000 years
6. 46 decades ◯ 260 years

Set B, pages 412–414

Find the time that has elapsed between 8:45 A.M. and 1:25 P.M.

From 8:45 A.M. to 9:00 A.M. is 15 minutes.
From 9:00 A.M. to 1:00 P.M. is 4 hours.
From 1:00 P.M. to 1:25 P.M. is 25 minutes.

15 minutes + 4 hours + 25 minutes = 4 hours and 40 minutes.

A $2\frac{1}{2}$ hour movie starts at 7:15 P.M. When does the movie end?

Count 2 hours to 9:15 P.M.

$\frac{1}{2}$ hour = 30 minutes

Count 30 minutes to 9:45 P.M.

The movie ends at 9:45 P.M.

Remember to check whether you are asked to find elapsed time or the finish time.

Find each elapsed time.

1. Start: 8:00 A.M.
   Finish: 10:50 A.M.
2. Start: 3:20 P.M.
   Finish: 9:35 P.M.
3. Start: 2:39 P.M.
   Finish: 4:06 P.M.
4. Start: 3:45 P.M.
   Finish: 5:15 P.M.

Find the time each bus trip ends.

	Bus Trip Starts	Elapsed Time	Bus Trip Ends
5.		2 hours and 10 minutes	
6.		4 hours and 30 minutes	
7.		1 hour and 45 minutes	

Set C, pages 416–419

Find the change in temperature.

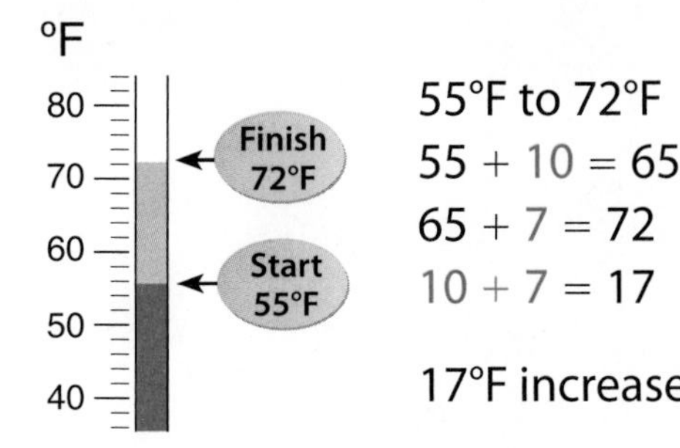

55°F to 72°F
55 + 10 = 65
65 + 7 = 72
10 + 7 = 17

17°F increase

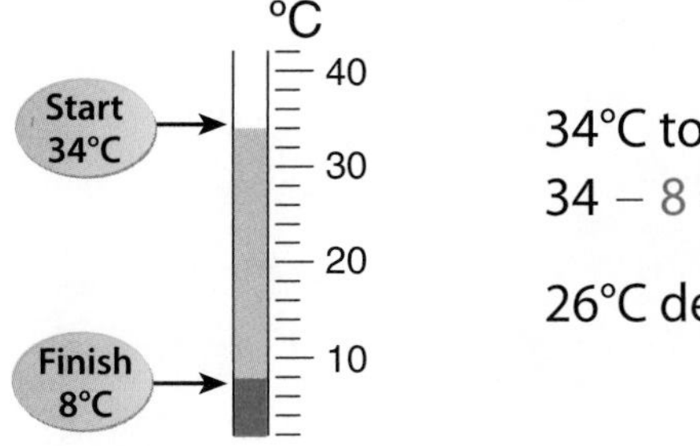

34°C to 8 °C
34 − 8 = 26

26°C decrease

Remember to check whether you are asked to find an answer in Fahrenheit or Celsius degrees.

Find the change in temperature. Tell whether the change is an increase or decrease.

1. 85°F to 29°F
2. 28°C to15°C
3. 38°F to 62°F
4. 3°C to 22°C
5. 40°C to 19°C
6. 96°F to 67°F
7. 2°C to 35°C
8. 84°F to 91°F

Set D, pages 420–421

Solve by working backward.

Jerrold checks the thermometer every hour between 12:00 P.M. and 7:00 P.M.. He noticed the the temperature decreased 3° each hour from 12:00 P.M. to 4:00 P.M. Then from 4:00 P.M. to 7:00 P.M., the temperature decreased 4° each hour. At 7:00 P.M., the temperature was 57°F. What was the temperature at 12:00 P.M.?

Work backward using the opposite of each change.

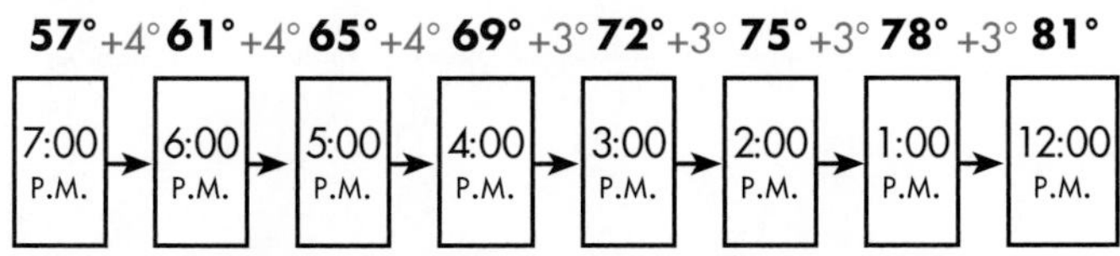

The temperature at 12:00 P.M. was 81°F.

Remember a picture can help you work backward.

1. Brad has trumpet practice at 10:45 A.M. It takes him 15 minutes to get from home to practice and 10 minutes to warm up. What time should he leave home to get to practice on time?

2. In one year, Alex bought half as many movie DVDs as Ashley. Ashley bought 3 times as many movie DVDs as Adam. Adam bought 6 movie DVDs. How many movie DVDs did Alex buy?

Topic 20 Probability and Statistics

1

Texas has more tornados each year than any other state. Radar dishes are used to predict where a tornado will touch down. How many times a year do tornados touch down in Texas? You will find out in Lesson 20-4.

2

When people race model boats, each person uses a different radio signal to control their boat. How do the racers make sure no one uses the same radio signal? You will find out in Lesson 20-1.

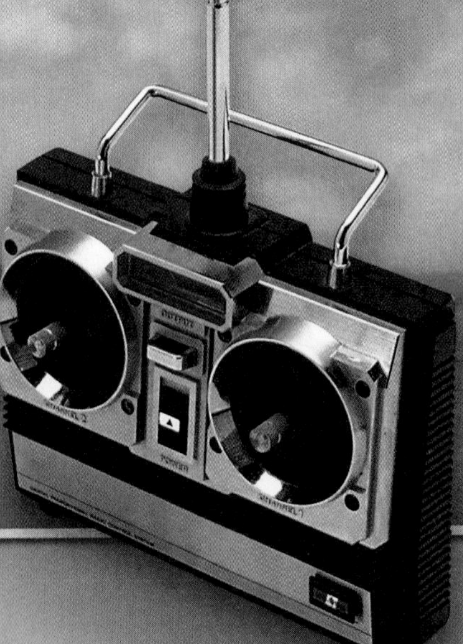

3

The Akashi Kaikyo Bridge in Japan, shown at the top, is the longest suspension bridge in the world. How does this bridge compare in length to the Golden Gate Bridge? You will find out in Lesson 20-5.

Review What You Know!

Vocabulary

Choose the best term from the box.

- data
- survey
- scale
- tree diagram

1. A _?_ is a series of numbers along the axis of a graph.
2. Collected information is called _?_
3. A _?_ is used to list the outcomes of an experiment.

Comparing Units of Time

Copy and complete. Write >, <, or = in the ◯.

4. 3 years ◯ 365 days
5. 4 weeks ◯ 40 days
6. 48 hours ◯ 2 days

Subtract Whole Numbers

Use the bar graph. How much higher is

7. Peak 1 than Peak 3?
8. Peak 3 than Peak 4?
9. **Writing to Explain** Why is this statement incorrect? The heights of Peak 2 and Peak 4 have the greatest difference.

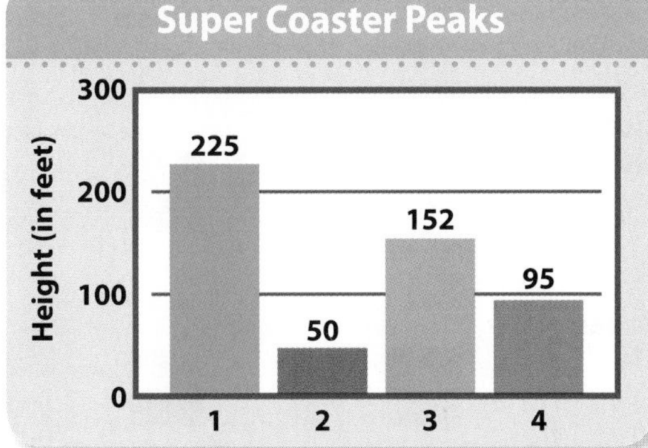

Lesson

20-1

TEKS 4.13A: Use concrete objects or pictures to make generalizations about determining all possible combinations of a given set of data or of objects in a problem situation.

Finding Combinations

Hands-On 2-color counters and color tiles

How can you find all the possible combinations?

Jay's dentist is giving out dental floss and toothbrushes. Jay will get one toothbrush and one kind of floss. How many different combinations can Jay choose?

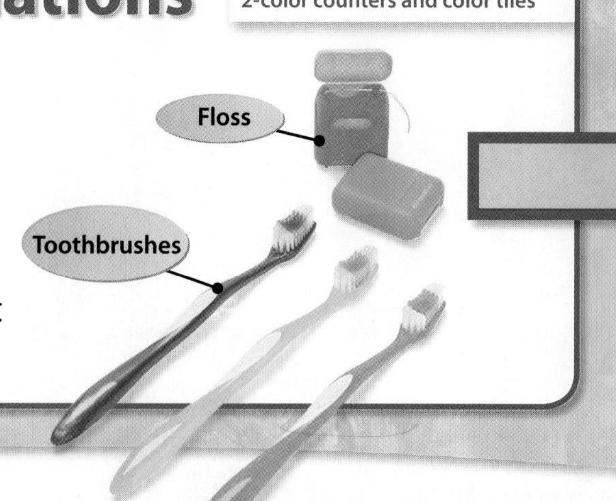

Guided Practice*

Do you know HOW?

For **1** and **2**, find the number of possible combinations. Use counters or tiles to help.

1. Choose one of the letters A or B and one of the numbers 1 or 2.

2. Choose one of the letters A, B, C, or D and one of the numbers 1 or 2.

Do you UNDERSTAND?

3. **Writing to Explain** In Exercises 1 and 2, does it matter whether you choose the letter first or the number first? Explain.

4. In the example above, if a third kind of dental floss is offered, how many combinations can Jay choose?

Independent Practice

For **5** and **6**, copy and complete the table to find the number of possible combinations. Use counters or tiles to help.

5. Choose one color counter and one color tile.

	Red Counter	Yellow Counter
Blue tile		
Green tile		

6. Choose a coin and a bill.

	Quarter	Dime	Nickel	Penny
1-Dollar bill				
5-Dollar bill				

*For another example, see Set A on page 446.

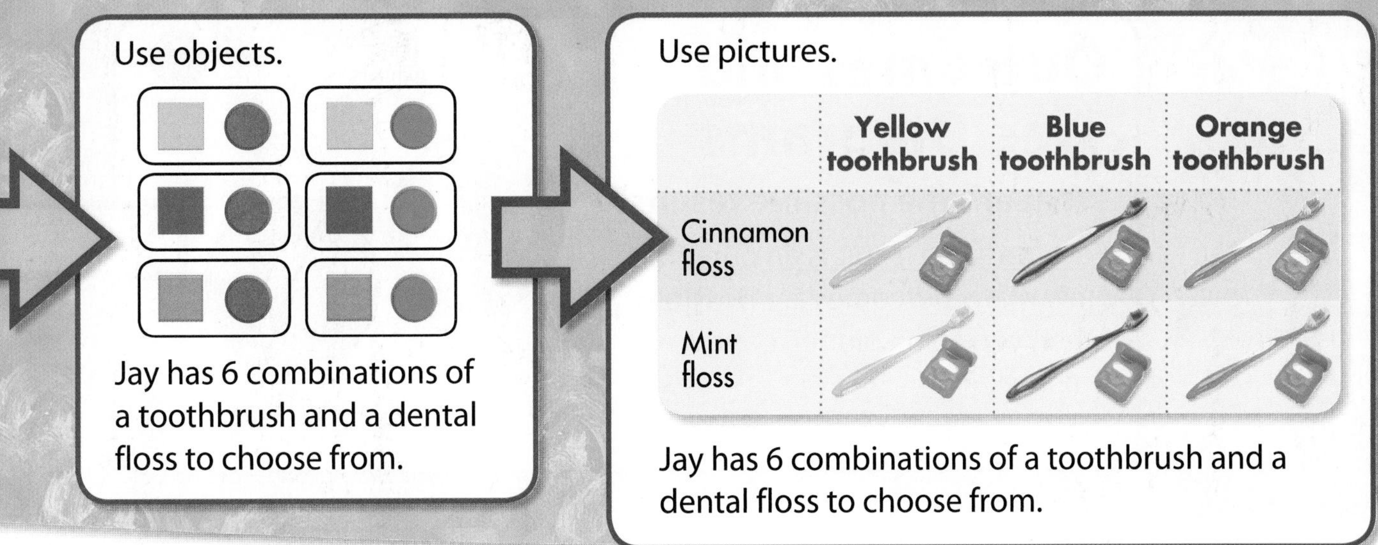

Use objects.
Jay has 6 combinations of a toothbrush and a dental floss to choose from.
Use pictures.
Yellow toothbrush
Blue toothbrush
Orange toothbrush
Cinnamon floss
Mint floss
Jay has 6 combinations of a toothbrush and a dental floss to choose from.

For **7** and **8**, use objects or pictures to find the number of possible combinations.

7. Choose one pet dog, cat, or rabbit and one pet sitter Jill, Marta, or Dave.

8. Choose one of 3 books and one of 8 CDs to bring on a bus trip.

TAKS Problem Solving

9. In a model boat race, each person uses a different radio signal. The radio signal is changed using switches on the radio controller. Each switch can be "on" or "off." If there are 4 switches, one combination could be off-on-on-on-off. How many combinations are possible with 4 switches?

If there are 2 switches, there are 2×2, or 4 combinations. If there are 3 switches, there are $2 \times 2 \times 2 = 8$ combinations.

10. Jane made 19 silver dollar pancakes. She took 7 and then gave an equal number to each of her two sisters. How many silver dollar pancakes did each sister get?

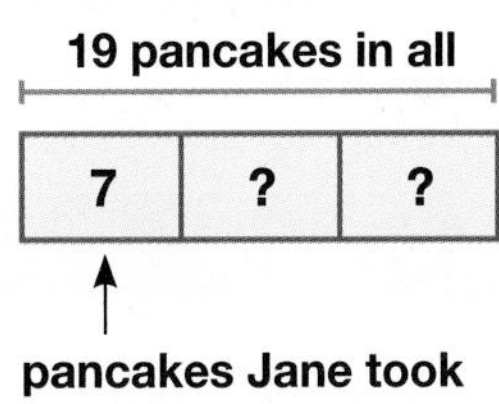

11. Reasoning Mr. Fines needed to buy numbers for an address plaque for his new store. He ordered the numbers 1, 3, and 5. If he could arrange the numbers in any order, what are the possible combinations for his store's address?

12. Tommy had a doctor's appointment at 4:45. He needs 15 minutes to get ready and 20 minutes to drive. At what time does Tommy need to get ready?

Lesson

20-2

TEKS 4.13A: Use concrete objects or pictures to make generalizations about determining all possible combinations of a given set of data or of objects in a problem situation.

Outcomes and Tree Diagrams

Hands-On
spinners

What are the possible results?

Each possible result is an outcome. How many outcomes are possible when you spin Spinner 1 and Spinner 2?

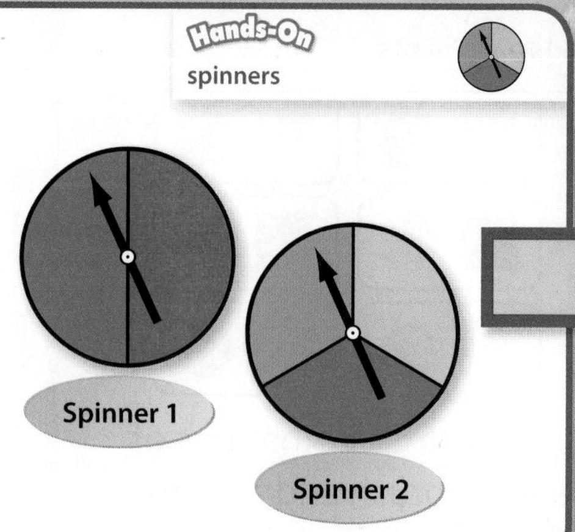

Guided Practice*

Do you know HOW?

For **1** and **2**, use the diagrams below.

1. List all the possible outcomes for picking one card from Bag 2.

2. Make a tree diagram to show all the possible outcomes for picking one card from Bag 1 followed by a card from Bag 2.

Do you UNDERSTAND?

3. What number sentence can you use to find the number of possible outcomes in Exercise 2?

4. **Writing to Explain** In the example at the top, why is Blue Blue an outcome but Red Red is not?

5. A board game uses Spinner 1. On each turn, you must spin Spinner 1 twice. How many outcomes are possible for each turn?

Independent Practice

For **6** through **8**, make a tree diagram to list all the possible outcomes for each situation.

When you make a tree diagram, you can list the outcomes in any order you like.

6. Spin Spinner 3 once and toss the number cube once.

7. Pick one card from Bag 3 and toss the number cube once.

8. Pick one card from Bag 3 and spin Spinner 3 once.

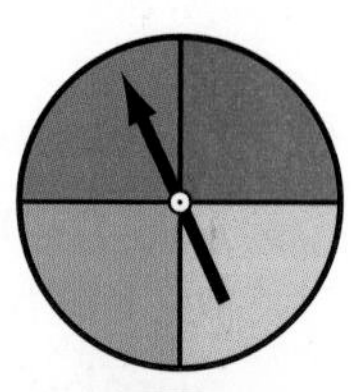

*For another example, see Set B on page 446.

Make a tree diagram. A tree diagram is a display that shows all possible outcomes.

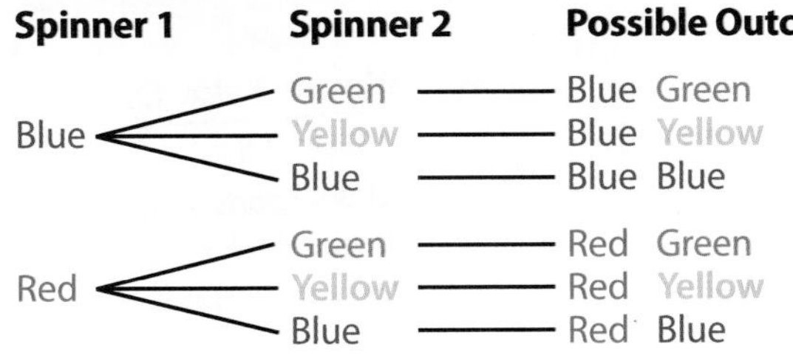

There are 6 possible outcomes.

Multiply.

There are 2 outcomes for Spinner 1 and 3 outcomes for Spinner 2.

$3 \times 2 = 6$

There are 6 possible outcomes.

For **9** and **10**, multiply to find the number of possible outcomes.

9. Flip a coin and toss a number cube that is numbered 1 through 6.

10. Pick one card from each of two piles. One pile has the cards labeled F, I, T, P, N, C, and O. The other has the cards labeled A, R, S, and Q.

TAKS Problem Solving

For **11** and **12**, use the diagram at the right.

Some games use shapes other than a cube to allow for more outcomes.

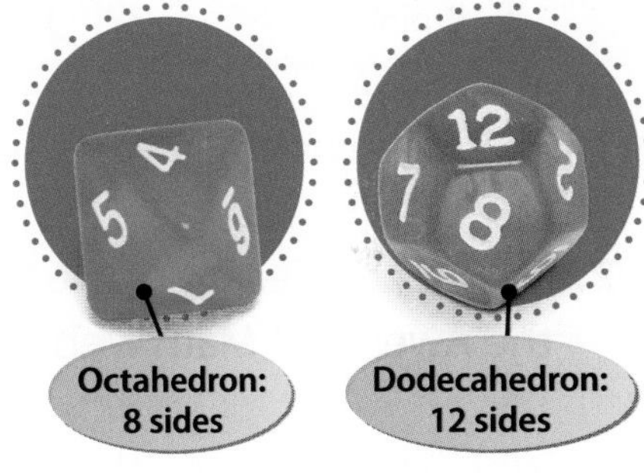

11. How many outcomes are there for one toss of the octahedron and one toss of the dodecahedron?

12. **Reasoning** You toss the octahedron and dodecahedron and add the two numbers. What is the least possible total? The greatest possible total?

For **13** and **14**, use the diagram at the right.

13. Wearing a blindfold, you toss two rings. Both tosses land on a bottle. List all the possible outcomes.

14. **Writing to Explain** Would the number of possible outcomes change if there were more blue bottles than red and white bottles?

15. How many windows are in a 9-story building if there are 28 windows per story?

A 19 **B** 37 **C** 182 **D** 252

Lesson

20-3

TEKS 4.13: Solve problems by collecting, organizing, displaying, and interpreting sets of data.

Data from Surveys

How do you take a survey and record the results?

Pizza Plus took a survey to decide which high school team they should sponsor.

In a survey, information is collected by asking different people the same question and recording their answers.

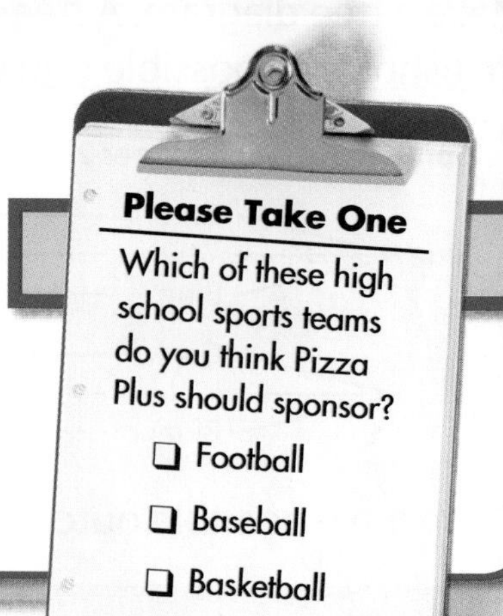

Please Take One
Which of these high school sports teams do you think Pizza Plus should sponsor?
❑ Football
❑ Baseball
❑ Basketball

Guided Practice*

Do you know HOW?

For **1** through **3**, use the tally chart below.

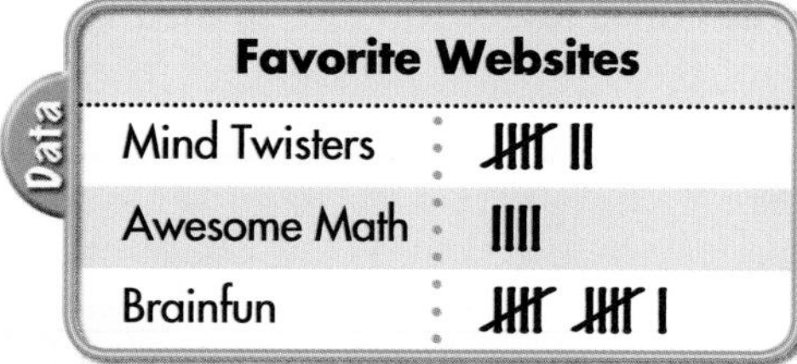

Favorite Websites	
Mind Twisters	𝍸 II
Awesome Math	IIII
Brainfun	𝍸 𝍸 I

1. How many people were surveyed?

2. How many people in the survey liked the Awesome Math website best?

3. Which website was the favorite of more people than any other?

Do you UNDERSTAND?

4. In the survey at the top, do you know whether people thought Pizza Plus should sponsor the soccer team? Why or why not?

5. What question do you think was asked for the survey below?

High School Games Attended Last Year	
Football	𝍸 𝍸 II
Basketball	𝍸
Soccer	𝍸 𝍸 IIII
Baseball	𝍸 III

Independent Practice

For **6** through **8**, use the tally chart at the right.

6. How many people liked using a pencil the best?

7. How many people were surveyed?

8. Which type of project was the favorite of more people than any other?

Tip

Before answering the questions, add up all of the tallies.

Favorite Type of Drawing Project	
Pencil	𝍸 II
Ink	𝍸 II
Paint	𝍸 IIII
Charcoal	IIII

For another example, see Set C on page 446.

Step 1

Write a survey question.

"Which of these high school sports teams do you think Pizza Plus should sponsor: football, baseball, or basketball?"

Step 2

Make a tally chart and record the data.

Count the tallies and record the results.

Team to Sponsor

Football	卌 卌 III	13
Basketball	卌 III	8
Baseball	卌 卌 I	11

Step 3

Explain the results of the survey.

Football was chosen by the most people. So, Pizza Plus should sponsor the football team.

TAKS Problem Solving

For **9** through **12**, use the tally chart at the right.

Pets Owned

Dog	卌 卌
Cat	卌 IIII
Fish	卌 III
Hamster	III
Snake	III

9. How many of the people surveyed have pet fish?

10. Which type of pet was owned by the most people?

11. Reasoning Can you tell how many people were surveyed? Why or why not?

12. Reasoning Can you tell how many of the people surveyed have no pets? Why or why not?

13. Elisa bought a camera for \$29.50 and 2 rolls of film for \$3.50 each. How much did Elisa spend in all?

For **14** and **15**, use the tally chart at the right.

Favorite Type of TV Show

Action	IIII
Animated	III
Comedy	卌 III
Sports	卌

14. What was the total count for each type of show?

15. How many people were surveyed?

16. Think About the Process At a barbeque, 8 out of 10 people ate hot dogs and 4 out of 5 people ate hamburgers. Which number sentence shows that the same fraction of people ate hot dogs and hamburgers?

A $10 - 8 = (5 - 4) + 1$

B $10 + 8 = 2 \times (5 + 4)$

C $\frac{10}{8} = \frac{5}{4}$

D $\frac{8}{10} = \frac{4}{5}$

Lesson
20-4

TEKS 4.13B: Interpret bar graphs.

Interpreting Graphs

How can you read a bar graph?

A bar graph uses bars to show data.

About how many more species of animals are in the Minnesota Zoo than the Phoenix Zoo?

The scale consists of numbers that show the units used on a graph.

The interval is the amount between tick marks on the scale.

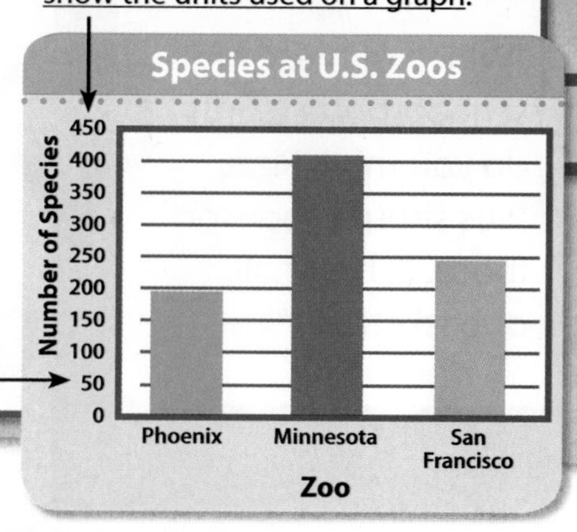

Guided Practice*

Do you know HOW?

For **1** and **2**, use the bar graph below.

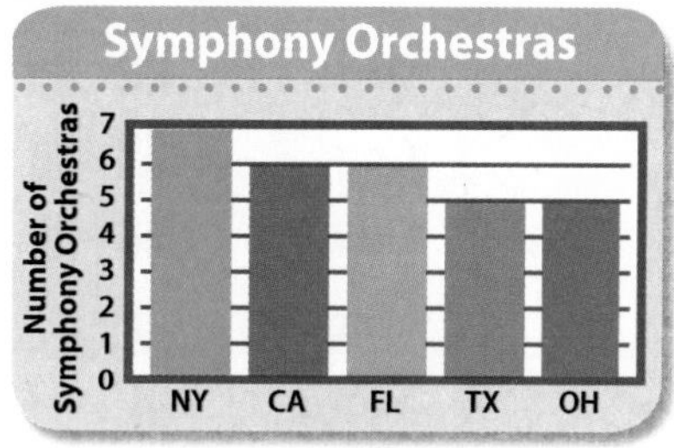

1. Which state shown on the graph has the most symphony orchestras?
2. Which state has the same number of symphony orchestras as Texas?

Do you UNDERSTAND?

3. What is the interval of the scale for the bar graph above?
4. The Miami Metro Zoo has 300 species of animals. Which zoos have a fewer number of species than the Miami Metro Zoo?
5. **Writing to Explain** Explain how you find the difference between the number of species at the San Francisco Zoo and the Phoenix Zoo.

Independent Practice

For **6** through **8**, use the bar graph at the right.

6. About how much longer does a lion live than a giraffe?
7. Which animals have the same average lifespan?
8. The average lifespan of a gorilla is 20 years. How would you change the graph to add a bar for gorillas?

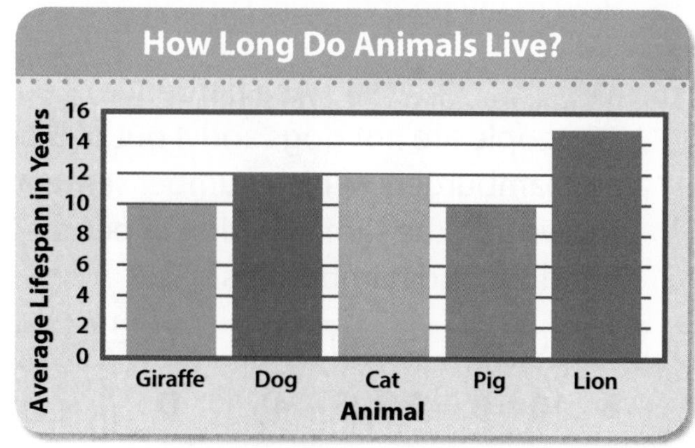

*For another example, see Set D on page 447.

The purple bar is just above the number 400. The Minnesota Zoo has about 400 species of animals.

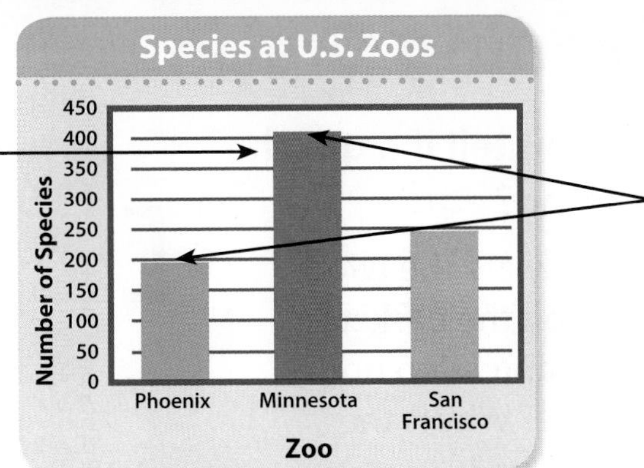

Skip count by 50s from the top of the green bar (Phoenix Zoo) until you are even with the top of the purple bar (Minnesota Zoo). Count: 50, 100.

The Minnesota Zoo has about 200 more species than the Phoenix Zoo.

TAKS Problem Solving

For **9** and **10**, use the bar graph below.

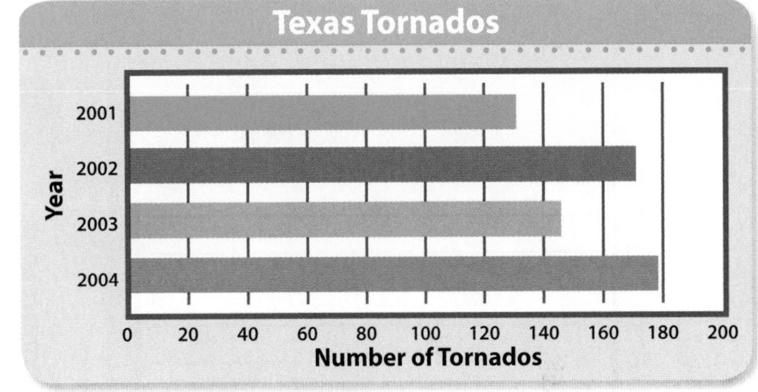

9. Texas has an average of 124 tornados each year, more than any other state. Which year had closest to the average number of tornados?

10. Which year had the most tornados? About how many tornados were there?

For **11** and **12**, use the chart below showing the results of a survey about hours of sleep.

Hours of Sleep Each Night (Data)

8 hours	卌 II
9 hours	卌 IIII
10 hours	III

11. How many people were surveyed?

12. According to the survey, how many hours do most people sleep?

13. There are 12 months in one calendar year. Which fraction shows the number of months that do **NOT** begin with a vowel?

A $\frac{3}{12}$

B $\frac{3}{4}$

C $\frac{12}{12}$

D $\frac{4}{3}$

14. Writing to Explain Debra bought a yard of fabric to use for a costume she was making for her school play. If she used 20 inches of fabric, how much was left? Explain your answer.

DIGITAL Animated Glossary **www.pearsonsuccessnet.com**

Lesson
20-5

TEKS 4.13B: Interpret bar graphs.

Misleading Graphs

How can you tell if a graph is misleading?

Juan and Vinny are the two high scorers on the basketball team. What impression does the graph give? Why is the graph misleading?

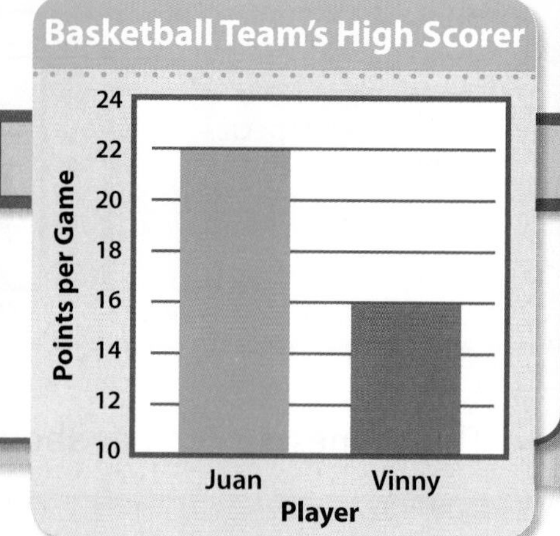

Another Example How can graphs give different impressions?

The two graphs below represent the same data.
What impression does each graph give?

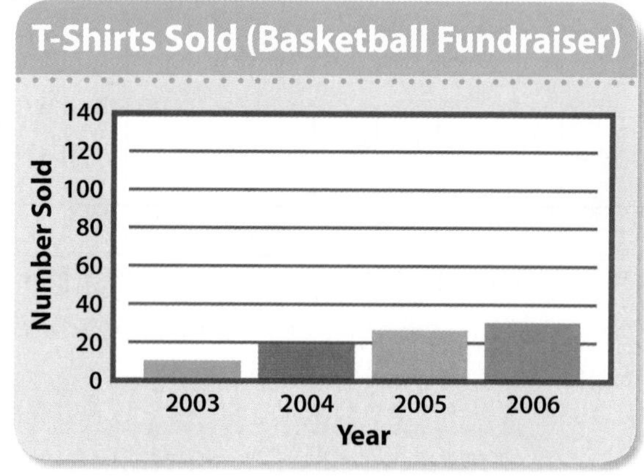

This graph seems to show a small increase in T-shirts sold each year.

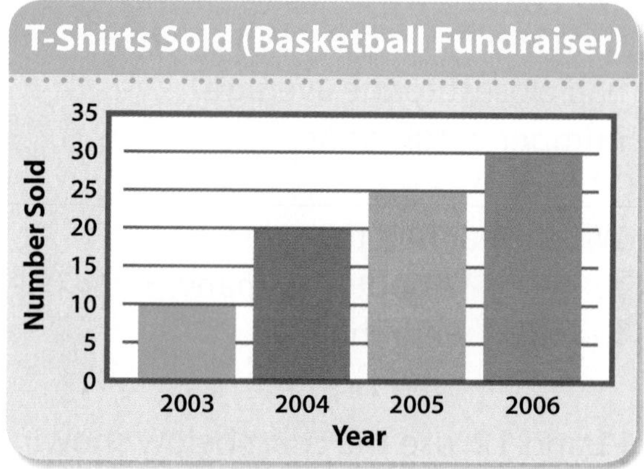

This graph seems to show a greater increase in T-shirt sales each year.

One scale goes to 35 and the other scale goes to 140.
Using a smaller scale makes the changes seem greater.

Explain It

1. What impression would you get from the graph of T-shirts sold if it used a scale of 0 to 200?

2. Which graph do you think gives a more accurate impression of the data? Why?

Misleading impression:

The graph shows one bar twice as tall as the other bar. So, it seems that Juan scores twice as many points as Vinny.

Why it is misleading:

The scale does not start at zero. Juan averages 22 points. That is not twice as many points as 16 points per game.

Here is what the graph looks like with a scale that starts at zero.

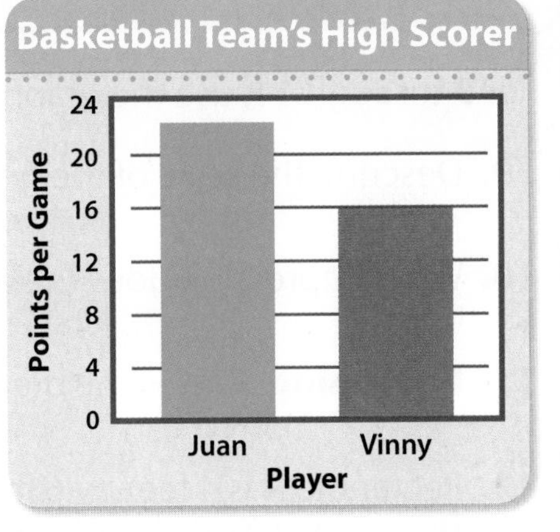

Guided Practice*

Do you know HOW?

For **1** and **2**, use the bar graph below.

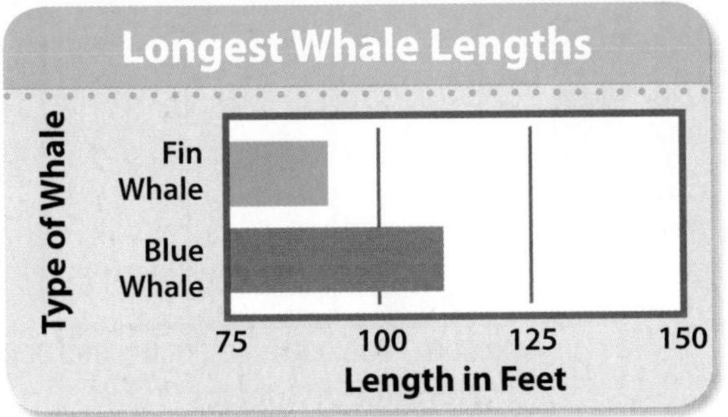

1. About how long is the blue whale? How long is the fin whale?

2. Why is the graph misleading?

Do you UNDERSTAND?

3. What is the difference between Juan's high score and Vinny's high score?

4. What impression does the bar graph above give about the high scorers?

5. What impression would you get if the graph above used a scale with intervals counting by 1?

Independent Practice

For **6** through **8**, use the bar graph at the right.

6. Based on the length of the bars, how many times larger is the number of students attending Middle School than in the Elementary School?

7. About how many children are in the Middle School? The Elementary School?

8. How could you make the graph less misleading?

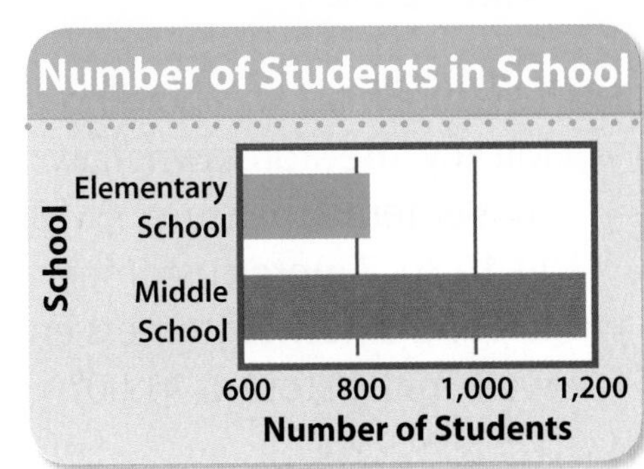

*For another example, see Set E on page 447.

TAKS Problem Solving

For **9** through **11**, use the graph at the right.

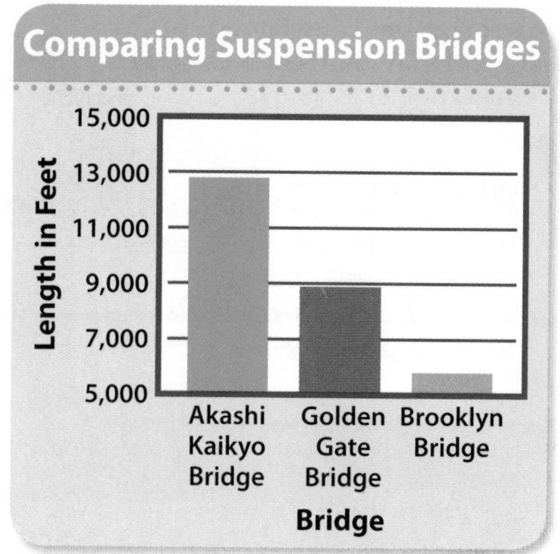

9. Describe the scale of the graph.

10. What impression does the graph give?

11. **Reasoning** Why is the graph misleading?

12. Rectangle A is 4 feet by 6 feet. Rectangle B is 1 yard by 2 yards. Which rectangle has a greater perimeter?

For **13** through **15**, use the graph at the right.

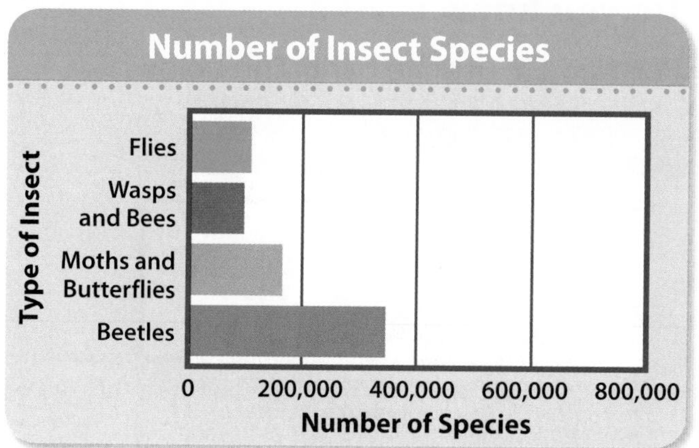

13. There are over 350,000 species of beetles. How does this compare to the number of species shown for moths and butterflies?

14. Which two types of insects have about the same number of species?

15. **Reasoning** How is the graph misleading?

16. A cook at a restaurant makes $15 an hour. How much money would the cook make in an eight-hour day?

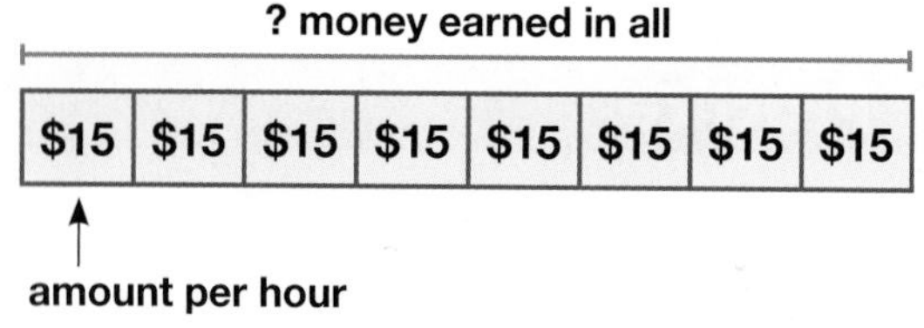

17. Steve wants to estimate the number of marbles in a jar for a prize. He counts 34 marbles in the top layer and he counts 28 layers. Which expression gives the best estimate?

A 34×28

B 30×30

C $34 \div 28$

D $30 \div 30$

18. Treasure Mart was holding their grand opening event. Mickey, the store owner, wanted to count all the customers that entered the store. At 10:00, there were 33 customers. At 10:30, 7 more customers entered. By 11:00, 15 customers left and 3 new customers entered. How many customers were in the store at 11:00?

Mixed Problem Solving

1. Hurricanes are classified by their wind speed. If hurricane winds reach 120 miles per hour, what category of hurricane is it?

Data

Category of hurricane	Maximum wind speed
Category 1	74 to 95 mph
Category 2	96 to 110 mph
Category 3	111 to 130 mph
Category 4	131 to 155 mph
Category 5	Greater than 155 mph

2. Five hurricanes made landfall in one season. Suppose two hurricanes had wind speeds of up to 99 miles per hour. The rest had maximum wind speeds less than 93 miles per hour. How many storms were Category 2? How many were Category 3?

3. At sea, a hurricane had wind speeds up to 152 miles per hour. After making landfall, the wind speed was half as great. What was the wind speed after landfall?

4. What is the difference between the fastest Category 4 speed and the slowest Category 4 speed?

5. A hurricane had a maximum wind speed of 86 miles per hour. Would you expect the storm surge to be 7 feet above normal tides? Why or why not?

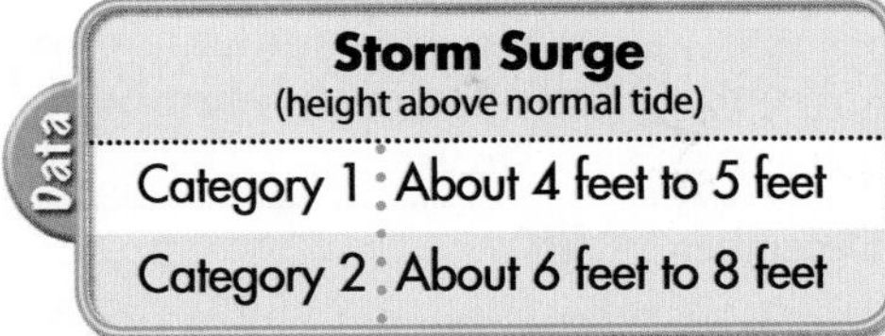

Data

Storm Surge (height above normal tide)	
Category 1	About 4 feet to 5 feet
Category 2	About 6 feet to 8 feet

6. **Writing to Explain** A tropical storm had maximum wind speeds of 45 miles per hour. One week later, the wind speeds were 3 times greater and the storm had become a hurricane. What category was the hurricane?

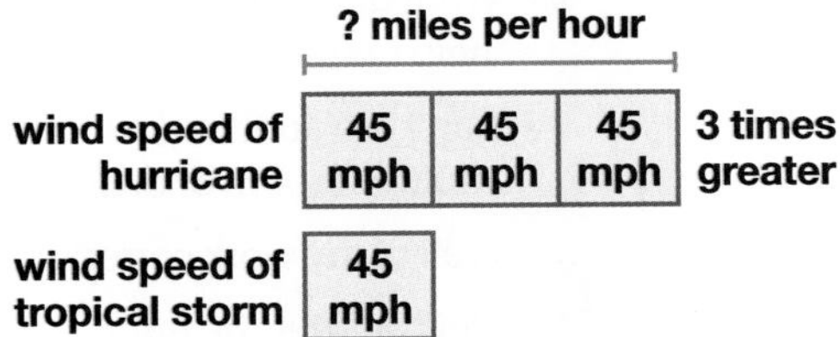

7. Names of hurricanes alternate between male and female names. In one season, 15 hurricanes were named. If the first hurricane was given a female name, how many hurricanes were given male names?

Lesson
20-6

TEKS 4.13: Solve problems by collecting, organizing, displaying, and interpreting sets of data.

Problem Solving

Make a Graph

Students in two fourth-grade classes completed a survey about their favorite hobbies. How were the two classes similar? How were they different?

Data

Mr. Foster's Class

Favorite Hobby	Tally
Swimming	𝍸 𝍸 𝍸
Cycling	𝍸 𝍸
Art	𝍸

Data

Mrs. Lopez's Class

Favorite Hobby	Tally
Swimming	𝍸 𝍸 |
Cycling	𝍸 𝍸 |||
Art	𝍸

Guided Practice*

Do you know HOW?

Solve. Make a graph.

1. Jo recorded the number of snowy days for three months in a tally chart. Make a bar graph using this data. Which month had the most snowy days?

Data

Month	Tally Snowy Days	Number
December	𝍸	5
January	𝍸 𝍸 |	11
February	𝍸 |||	8

Do you UNDERSTAND?

2. How could you make different bar graphs to display the same data from the tally charts above?

3. Suppose you added the numbers from both classes to make one data table. Which hobby was most popular overall?

4. **Write a Problem** Write a problem that uses the data charts above. Then answer your question.

Independent Practice

For **5** and **6**, use the table below.

Data

	Morning	Afternoon	Evening
Cars	142	263	120
Trucks	42	181	64

5. Make two graphs of this data, one for cars and one for trucks.

6. Why is it useful to use the same scale for both graphs?

Stuck? Try this....

- What do I know?
- What diagram can I use to help understand the problem?
- Can I use addition, subtraction, multiplication, or division?
- Is all of my work correct?
- Did I answer the right question?
- Is my answer reasonable?

*For another example, see Set F on page 447.

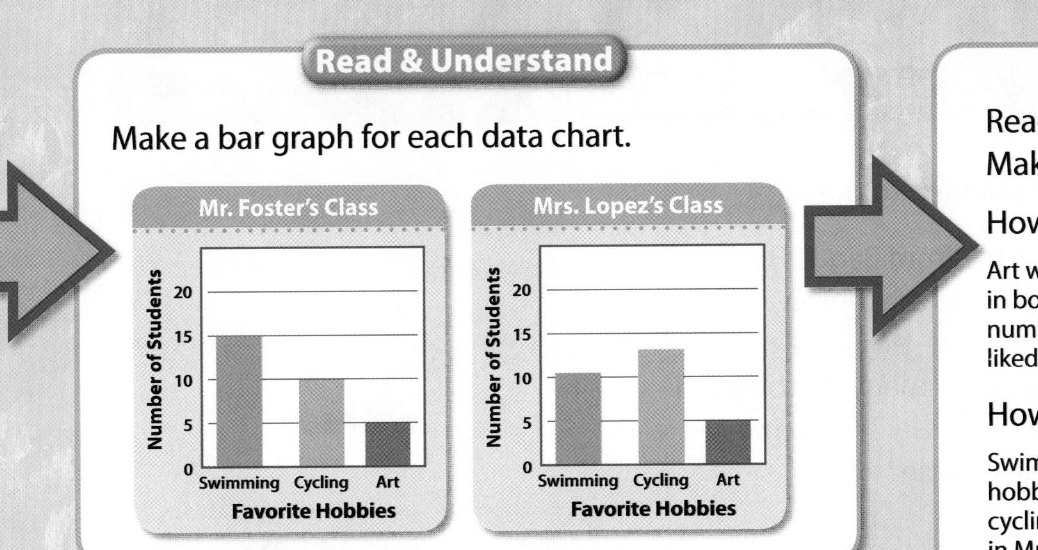

Plan

Read the graphs.
Make comparisons.

How are they similar:

Art was the least popular hobby in both classes, and the same number of students in each class liked art.

How are they different:

Swimming was the favorite hobby in Mr. Foster's class, and cycling was the favorite hobby in Mrs. Lopez's class.

For **7** through **10**, use the tally chart below.

Data

Activity	2008	2009
Newspaper	𝍸 𝍸	𝍸 𝍸
Dance Troupe	𝍸	𝍸 |
Book Club	𝍸	𝍸
Marching Band	||||	𝍸 |

7. The fourth grade students chose which of four activities they wanted to join. Make a bar graph for 2008 and another bar graph for 2009.

8. If 3 people in 2009 left the book club to join the dance troupe, which club would have the most students?

9. Identify two clubs in 2009 that together were chosen by more than half of the fourth grade students.

10. How many more students joined a club in 2009 than in 2008?

For **11** through **13**, use the table to the right.

11. Who rode 15 miles less than Sherry in Week 1?

12. Which person biked fewer miles in Week 2 than in Week 1?

13. **Reasoning** Use the table to compare the total miles ridden in Week 1 to the total miles ridden in Week 2. Which was greater?

Data

Name	Week 1	Week 2
Peter	17 miles	26 miles
Sherry	25 miles	29 miles
Jorgé	22 miles	20 miles
Carla	10 miles	20 miles

Independent Practice

For **14** and **15**, use the diagram to the right.

Bag 1

Bag 2

Bag 3

14. Stella picks one marble from Bag 1. How many possible outcomes are there?

15. **Writing to Explain** How many marbles will Stella have to take from Bag 3 to guarantee she will draw a blue marble?

For **16** and **17**, use the table at the right.

16. Marcia recorded the number of sit-ups and push-ups she did last week. Make two graphs using the data in the table.

17. Compare the number of sit-ups each day to the number of push-ups. What pattern do you notice? What can you conclude?

Marcia's Sit-ups and Push-ups

Day	Sit-ups	Push-ups
Monday	25	12
Tuesday	21	16
Thursday	55	24
Friday	32	12
Sunday	68	28

For **18** and **19**, use the diagram at the right.

18. Ms. Michael planted the flowers in her garden in an array. After she fills in the fifth row, how many flowers will her garden have?

19. If Ms. Michael continues to plant using the same pattern of colors, what will be the colors of the next three flowers that she plants?

Think About the Process

20. There are 14 park benches in the park. Each bench holds 4 people. Which number sentence shows the greatest number of people who can sit on park benches at one time?

A $14 \times 4 = \square$

B $14 + 4 = \square$

C $14 \times 14 = \square$

D $4 \times 4 = \square$

21. Hanna walked to and from school on Monday, Wednesday, and Friday. What information is needed to find how far she walked?

F The distance from home to school

G Who she walked with

H The number of streets she crossed

J The time school starts

Misleading Graphs

Use e tools Spreadsheet/Data/Grapher.
In the United States, 26 states have no coastline along an ocean. 15 states have less than 200 miles of coastline, and 9 states have more than 200 miles.

Step 1 Go to the Spreadsheet/Data/Grapher eTool. Enter the data as shown below.

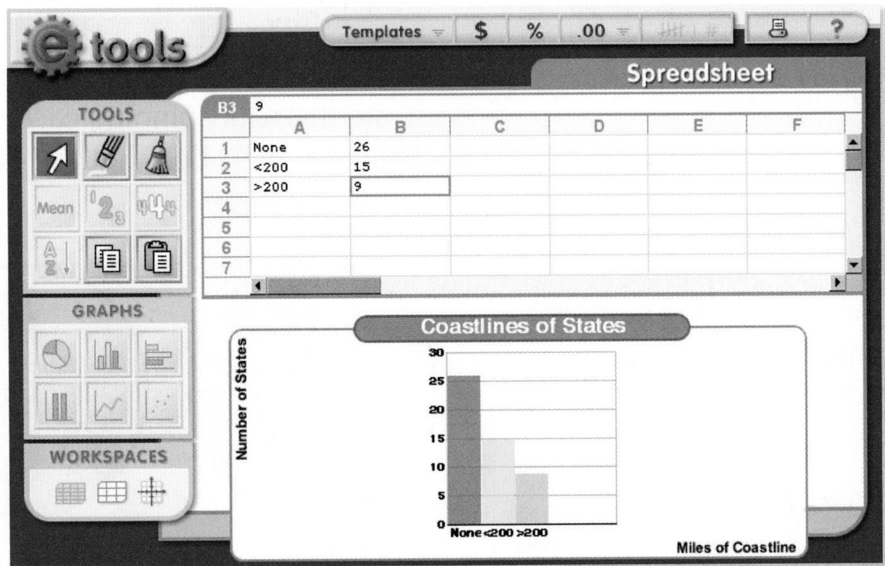

Step 2 Use the arrow tool to select the 2 columns and 3 rows with information. Click on the bar graph icon. Enter the graph title and label the x- and y- axes. Make the interval 5, the minimum 0, and the maximum 30. Click OK.

Step 3 Click in the graph area. Change the minimum to 5 and click OK.

Compare the graphs. The second graph is misleading.

Practice

1. Alaska has 19 mountain peaks that are more than 14,000 feet high and Colorado has 54. Graph the data. First, use a scale from 0 to 60 by 10. Then change the minimum to 10. Describe the different impressions each graph gives.

1. Which subject was the favorite of more students than any other? (20-3)

Data

Favorite Subject	
Social Studies	𝍸 II
Math	𝍸 IIII
Language Arts	I
Science	𝍸

A Social Studies

B Math

C Language Arts

D Science

2. The graphs below show the number of times an answer choice was used on two different tests. Which conclusion can be made? (20-6)

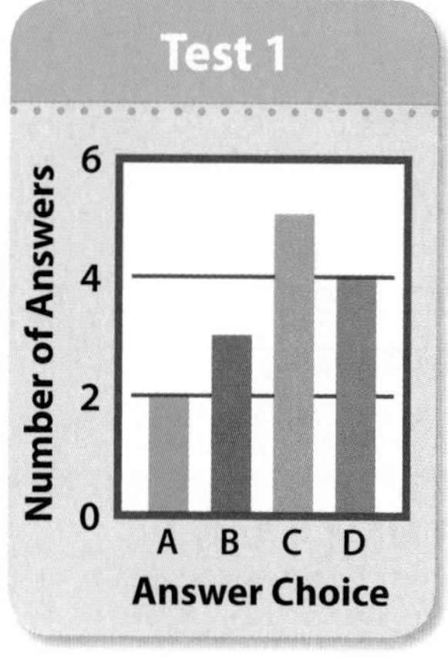

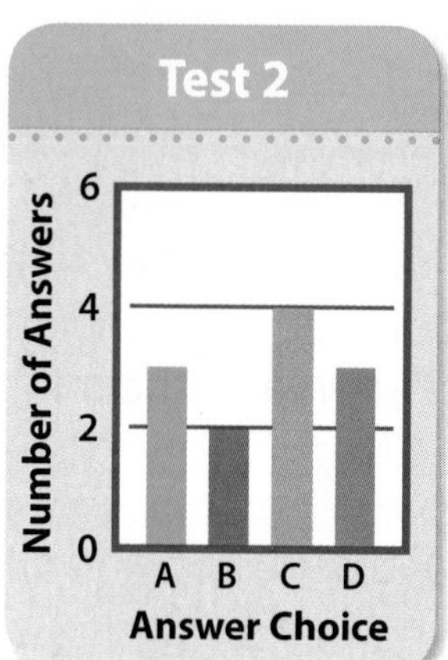

F Answer C was used most often in both tests.

G Answer B was used least often in both tests.

H Answer D was used the same number of times in both tests.

J No conclusions can be made.

3. Find the number of possible combinations if you choose one of the letters M, A, T, H, and one of the numbers 1 or 2. (20-1)

A 4

B 6

C 8

D 10

4. How many possible outcomes are there for spinning each of the spinners below at the same time? (20-2)

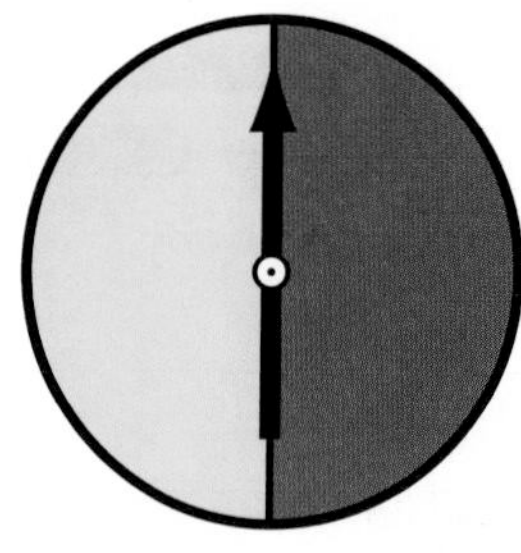

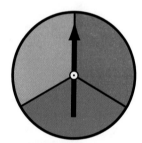

Spinner 1

Spinner 2

F 2

G 3

H 5

J 6

5. What is the number of possible combinations if you toss a number cube numbered 1 to 6, and you flip a coin? (20-1)

A 2

B 6

C 12

D 18

6. Mrs. Chi made a bar graph of the number of books students read over summer break.

How many students read fewer than 3 books during summer break? (20-4)

F 4

G 5

H 6

J 11

7. Neil and Matt are playing a transportation game. The spinner for the game is shown below.

If Matt spins the spinner twice, what are all the possible outcomes? (20-2)

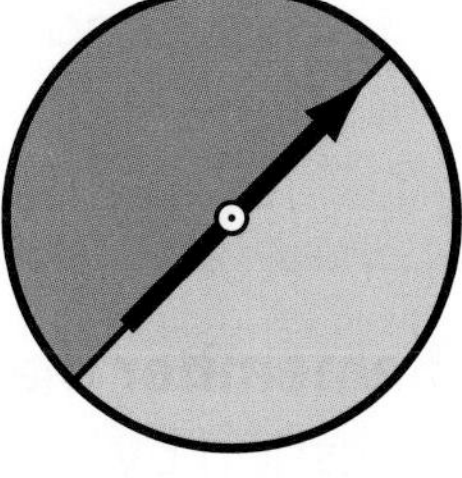

A 2 pinks or 2 yellows

B 2 yellows or 1 pink and 1 yellow

C 2 pinks or 1 pink and 1 yellow

D 2 pinks or 2 yellows or 1 pink and 1 yellow

8. How is the bar graph misleading? (20-5)

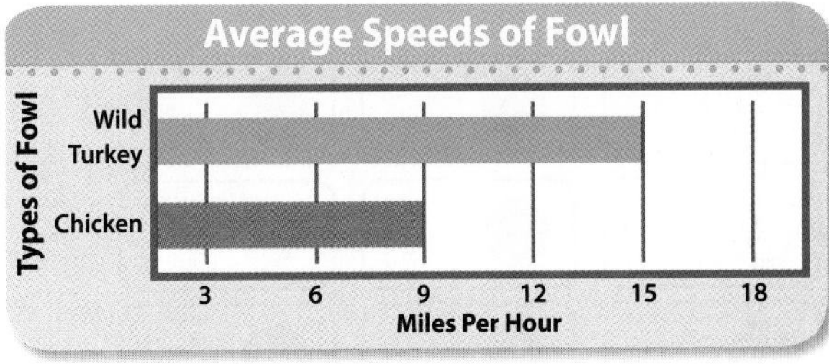

F It appears that the chicken runs twice as fast as the wild turkey.

G It appears that the wild turkey runs twice as fast as the chicken.

H It appears that the difference in the speeds is smaller than it is.

J The bar graph is not misleading.

9. **Griddable Response** Each student picked an individual activity during Fun Day.

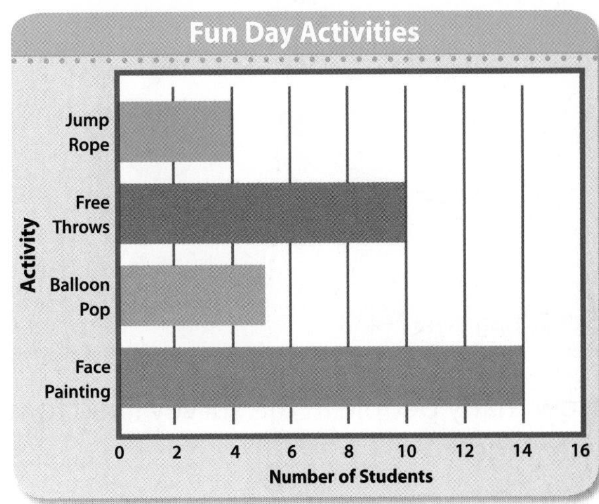

How many more students chose face painting than jump rope? (20-4)

10. **Griddable Response** Alyssa can buy one of 4 jewelry kits and one of 4 dolls. How many different combinations can she buy? (20-1)

Reteaching

Set A, pages 428–429

Choose one color and one shape.
How many combinations are there?

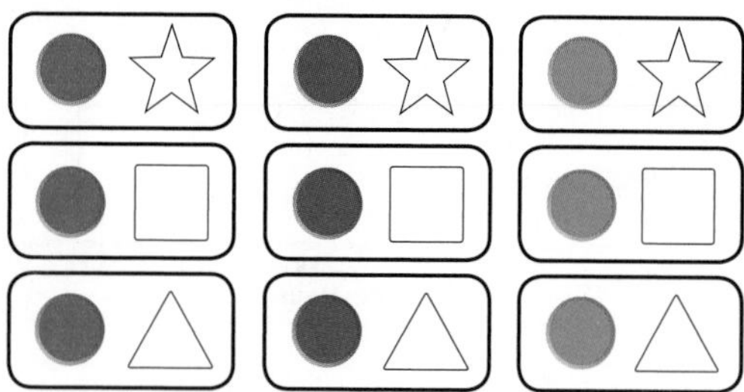

In all, there are 9 combinations.

Remember that the order does not matter when you count combinations.

Find the number of possible combinations.

1. Choose milk or juice plus a side of mashed potatoes, a baked potato, or green beans.
2. Choose a backpack, soft suitcase, or hard suitcase, and then choose one of 5 colors.

Set B, pages 430–431

List the outcomes for picking a square or oval from Box 1 and a diamond or pentagon from Box 2.

You can make a tree diagram.

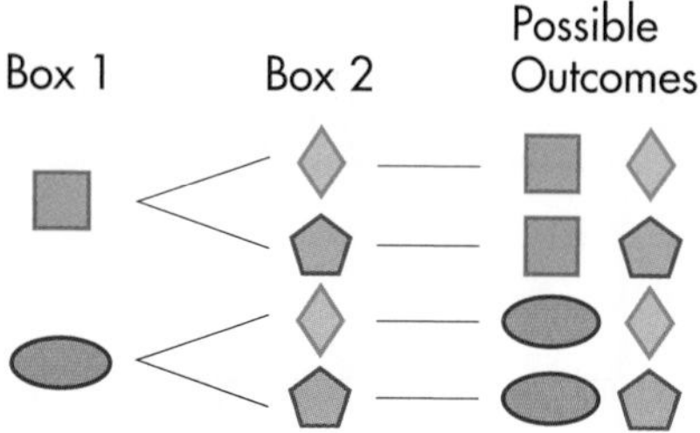

Remember you can use a tree diagram or multiply to find the number of possible outcomes.

Find the number of possible outcomes for picking a shape from:

1. Bag 1
2. Bag 2
3. Bag 1 and Bag 2
4. Bag 2 and Bag 3

Set C, pages 432–433

How many people in the survey liked to watch the rings?

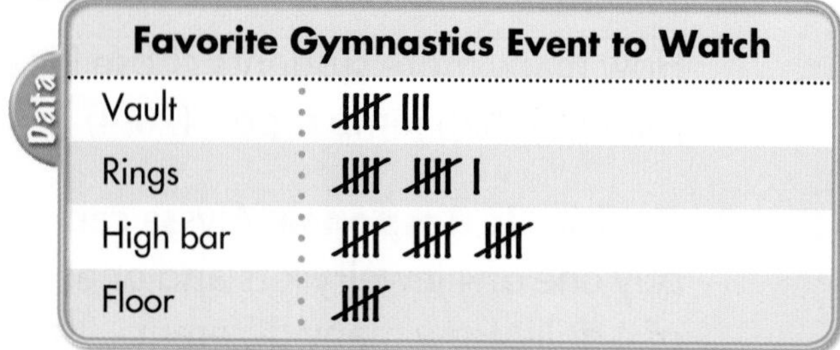

Favorite Gymnastics Event to Watch	
Vault	𝍸 III
Rings	𝍸 𝍸 I
High bar	𝍸 𝍸 𝍸
Floor	𝍸

Eleven people liked to watch the rings best.

Remember that you can answer a question by taking a survey.

1. How many people in the survey liked to watch the vault best?
2. Which event was named by more people than any other event?
3. Can you tell from the survey whether people liked to watch the uneven bars? Explain.

Set D, pages 434–435

Which animal has about 34 teeth?

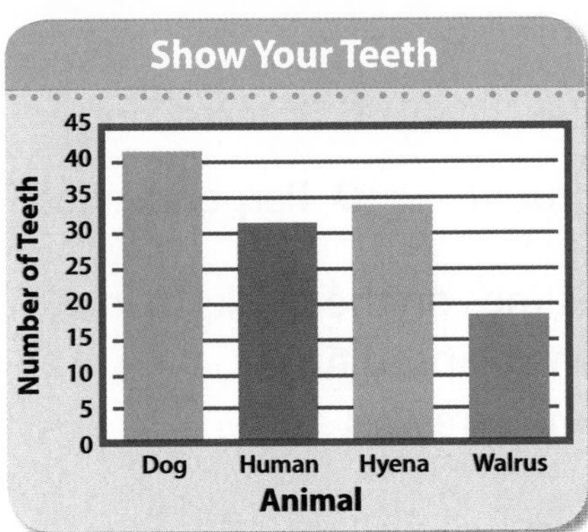

The bar that is just below the line for 35 is the one for hyenas.

Hyenas have about 34 teeth.

Remember looking at the scale can help you interpret the data.

1. What is the graph about?
2. What is the scale of the graph? What is the interval?
3. Which animal has 32 teeth?
4. About how many more teeth does a dog have than a human?

Set E, pages 436–438

What impression does the graph give about how many times faster a cheetah runs than a cat?

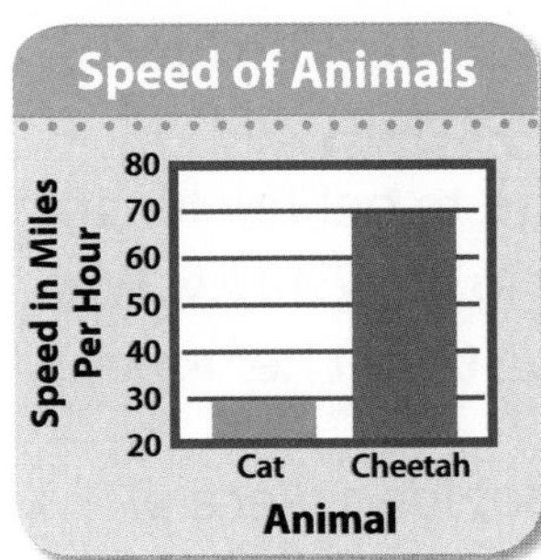

The graph seems to show that a cheetah runs 5 times faster than a cat.

Remember the scale of a graph can make a graph misleading.

1. What is the speed of a cheetah?
2. What is the speed of a cat?
3. Why is the graph misleading?
4. How could you change the graph so that it is not misleading?

Set F, pages 440–442

How can you use a bar graph to find which team is in second place in the standings?

Data

Volleyball Wins	
Hawks	10
Lions	14
Falcons	12
Bears	7

Choose a scale. Choose an interval. Make a bar for each team. Label the axis and give the graph a title.

The Falcons are in second place.

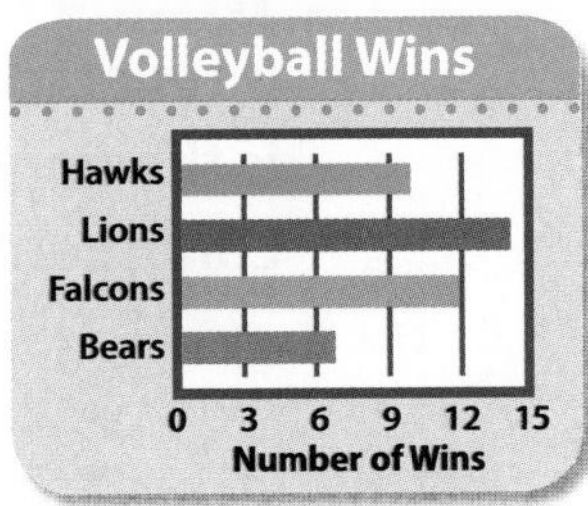

Remember to use a scale that starts at 0 and goes beyond the highest number in the data when you draw a bar graph.

1. How can you check whether the bars on the graph are correctly drawn?
2. What is the interval of the graph?
3. Which team came in third place?

Spiral Review

Number and Operations

1. Which of the following is in order from greatest to least?

   A 3,422 3,419 3,409 1,998

   B 3,42 3,409 3,419 1,998

   C 1,998 3,422 3,419 3,409

   D 3,419 3,409 1,998 3,422

2. A penny is 0.75 inches wide. A Susan B. Anthony dollar is 1.04 inches wide. Use the grids to find how much wider the dollar is.

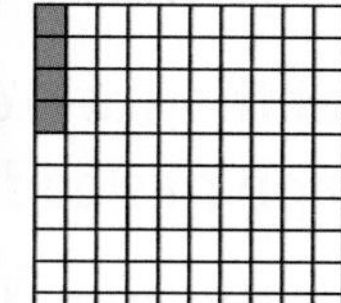

   F 0.04 inches **H** 0.29 inches

   G 0.25 inches **J** 0.79 inches

3. Find the product of 23 and 14.

   A 222 **C** 322

   B 312 **D** 422

4. What fraction should be written at point *P* on the number line?

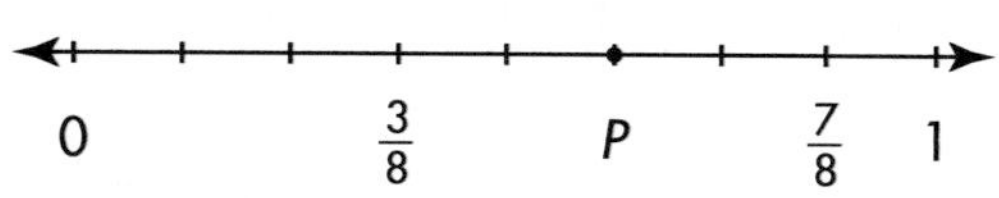

   F $\frac{3}{8}$ **H** $\frac{1}{2}$

   G $\frac{4}{8}$ **J** $\frac{5}{8}$

5. **Writing to Explain** How can you break numbers apart to find the product of 14×9? What is the product?

Geometry and Measurement

6. Which pairs of lines always form a right angle?

   A Parallel **C** Intersecting

   B Congruent **D** Perpendicular

7. Use the times on the clocks below to find the elapsed time. (Both times are A.M.)

   F 1 h 20 min **H** 2 h 15 min

   G 1 h 35 min **J** 2 h 45 min

8. Kay spent 20 minutes eating lunch, 5 minutes waiting in line, and 10 minutes driving to get her lunch. She finished eating at 12:40 P.M. What time did Kay leave to get her lunch?

9. Alex needs a 2-foot long piece of wood to repair a chair. He cuts two pieces of wood. One is 23 inches long and the other is 27 inches long. Which piece can he use, and how much must he cut off to use it?

10. Which unit would best measure the weight of a calculator—ton, pound, or ounce?

11. **Writing to Explain** Triangle *XYZ* is reflected across a horizontal line. Is the figure that results always congruent to triangle *XYZ*?

Probability and Statistics

12. Hank tosses a number cube and spins a spinner. The number cube has the numbers 1 through 6 on its sides. If the spinner has 6 different colors, how many possible outcomes are there?

A 6 **B** 12 **C** 24 **D** 36

13. Tina picked shapes from two bags. She then drew this tree diagram. What is wrong with the outcomes shown?

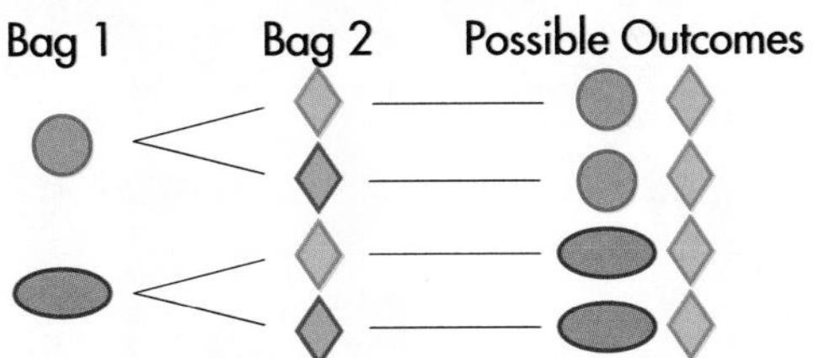

F There should be no red circles.

G The blue diamonds are missing.

H There are too many outcomes

J There are too few outcomes.

For **14** through **16**, use the data table below.

Data

Candidate	Votes
Cam	12
Trina	16
Jason	34
Randy	11

The class voted for class president. Jason made a bar graph of the results shown in the table.

14. What scale should be used for the graph?

15. Who won the election?

16. **Writing to Explain** If 12 missing votes were added to Cam's total, would his bar be taller or shorter than Trina's? Explain.

Algebraic Thinking

17. Which expression models the phrase "15 greater than a number?"

A $n + 15$ **C** $n - 15$

B $15 \div n$ **D** $15 \times n$

18. Which rule can be used to describe the table below?

Month	1	2	3	4
Money saved	$45	$90	$135	$180

F Add 45 **H** Multiply by 45

G Add 90 **J** Multiply by 90

For **19** and **20**, use the table below.

e	36	15	99	51
	12	5		17

19. Write the rule for the table using the variable *e*.

20. What is the missing value in the table?

21. How do you evaluate the expression $(20 + 4) \div 6$?

22. **Writing to Explain** When Val mows lawns for money, it takes her 20 minutes to get the tools out and 40 minutes to clean up. If it takes her 2 hours to mow each lawn, how much time does it take to mow 5 lawns? Explain.

Step Up to Grade 5

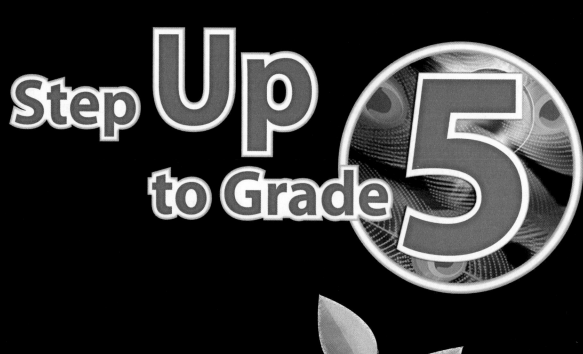

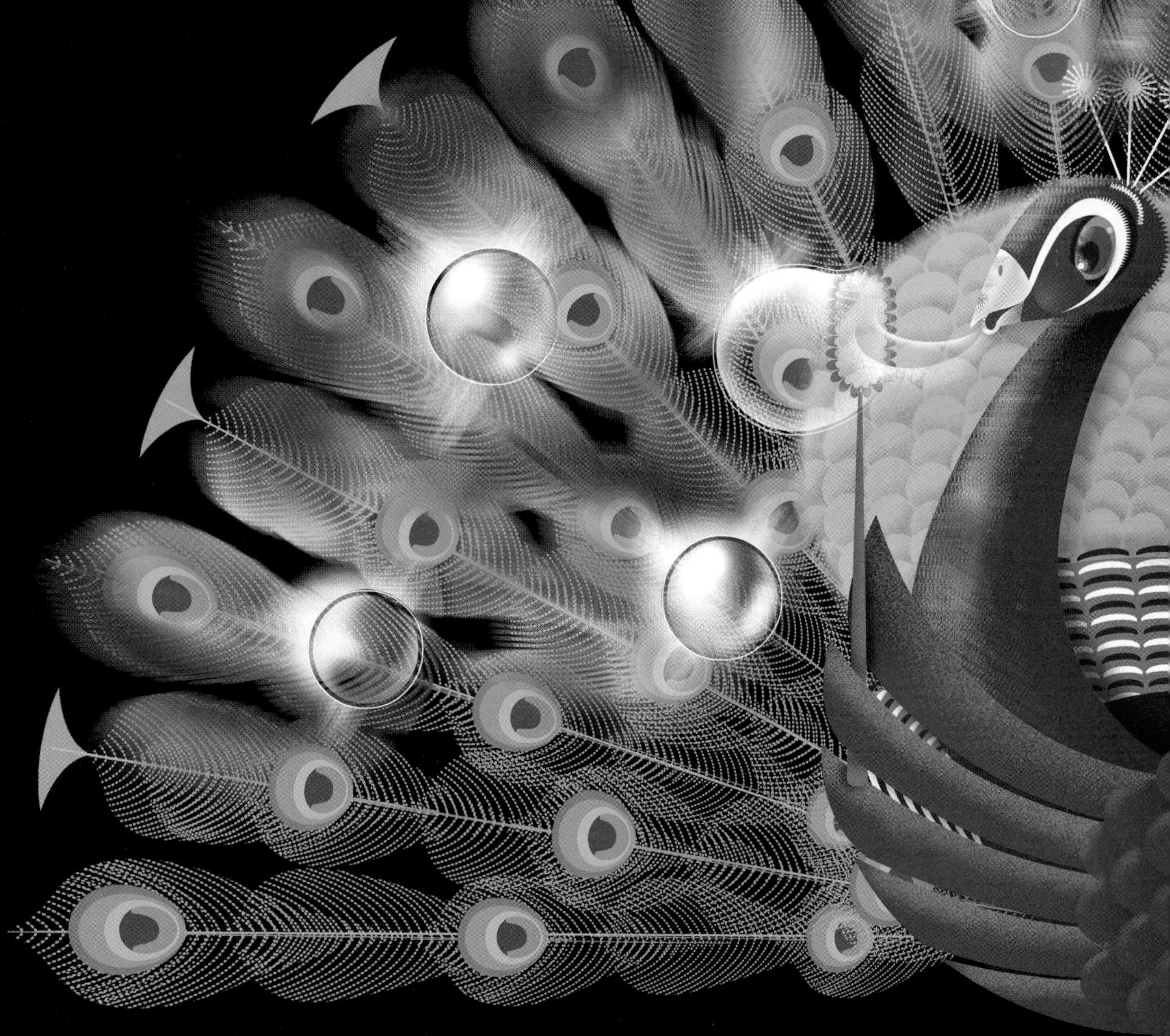

TEKS 5.3B: Use multiplication to solve problems involving whole numbers.

Multiplying by 1-Digit Numbers

How do you multiply by 1-digit numbers?

How many beads are in 7 containers?

Choose an Operation

Multiply to join equal groups.

36 Beads

Another Example How do you multiply a 1-digit number by a 3-digit number?

A theater has 5 sections with 347 seats in each section. What is the total number of seats in the theater?

A 1,505 seats

B 1,535 seats

C 1,705 seats

D 1,735 seats

? seats in theater

347	347	347	347	347

Choose an Operation Multiply to join equal groups.

Step 1

Multiply the ones, and regroup if necessary.

$$\begin{array}{r} {\scriptstyle 3} \\ 347 \\ \times \quad 5 \\ \hline 5 \end{array}$$

5 × 7 ones = 35 ones
Regroup 35 ones as
3 tens 5 ones.

Step 2

Multiply the tens.
Add any extra tens.
Regroup if necessary.

$$\begin{array}{r} {\scriptstyle 2\,3} \\ 347 \\ \times \quad 5 \\ \hline 35 \end{array}$$

5 × 4 tens = 20 tens
20 tens + 3 tens = 23 tens
Regroup as 2 hundreds
3 tens.

Step 3

Multiply the hundreds.
Add any extra hundreds.
Regroup if necessary.

$$\begin{array}{r} {\scriptstyle 2\,3} \\ 347 \\ \times \quad 5 \\ \hline 1{,}735 \end{array}$$

5 × 3 hundreds = 15 hundreds
15 hundreds + 2 hundreds =
17 hundreds
Regroup as 1 thousand 7 hundreds.

The theater has 1,735 seats. The correct choice is D.

Explain It

1. In Step 1, how do you know that 35 ones is 3 tens and 5 ones?
2. In Step 3, why are 2 hundreds added to the 15 hundreds?

One Way

Remember how to multiply using partial products.

```
   36
×   7
   42  ← 7 × 6
+ 210  ← 7 × 30
  252
```

The partial products are 42 and 210. You add them to find the product.

Another Way

Step 1 Multiply the ones. Regroup if necessary.

```
  4
 36
× 7
  2
```

7 × 6 ones = 42 ones
Regroup 42 ones as 4 tens 2 ones.

Step 2 Multiply the tens. Add any extra tens. Regroup if necessary.

```
  4
 36
× 7
252
```

7 × 3 tens = 21 tens
21 tens + 4 tens = 25 tens
Regroup 25 tens as 2 hundreds 5 tens.

There are 252 beads in 7 containers.

Guided Practice

Do you know HOW?

In **1** and **2**, find each product. Estimate to check that your answer is reasonable.

1. 57 × 8

2. 268 × 3

Do you UNDERSTAND?

3. Writing to Explain In Step 2 of Another Example, why is it necessary to regroup the 23 tens?

4. In the example above, how many beads would be in 8 containers?

Independent Practice

In **5** through **14**, find each product. Estimate to check that your answer is reasonable.

5. 122 × 3

6. 783 × 6

7. 645 × 5

8. 221 × 7

9. 259 × 4

10. 35 × 9

11. 533 × 9

12. 21 × 8

13. 752 × 6

14. 59 × 7

15. How do you know if the actual product of 23 × 46 is between 800 and 1,500?

16. Estimation Estimate the product of 83 and 8. Do you have an underestimate or overestimate?

Step-Up Lesson 2

TEKS 5.3B: Use multiplication to solve problems involving whole numbers.

Multiplying 2-Digit by 2-Digit Numbers

How do you multiply by 2-digit numbers?

Sammy's Car Wash had 38 full-service car washes in one day. How much money did Sammy's Car Wash make in one day from full-service car washes?

Choose an Operation
Multiply to join equal groups.

SERVICE	COST
EXTERIOR ONLY	$8.00
FULL SERVICE	$12.00
VACUUM	$5.00

CAR WASH

Guided Practice

Do you know HOW?

In **1** through **4**, find each product. Estimate to check that your answer is reasonable.

1. 82 × 16

2. 74 × 21

3. 25 × 22

4. 34 × 12

Do you UNDERSTAND?

5. In the example at the top, what would the car wash make if it charged $11 for each full-service wash?

6. **Writing to Explain** How can you use estimation to decide if your answer in **5** is reasonable?

Independent Practice

Leveled Practice In **7** through **23**, find each product. Estimate to check that your answer is reasonable.

	7.	8.	9.	10.	11.	12.
	44	79	87	96	18	55
×	25	11	57	45	12	71
	□□0	7□	□09	□8□	3□	□5
	8□0	□□0	□350	3□40	1□0	3□5□
	□□0□	8□□	4□5□	□3□0	□□6	3□0□

	13.	14.	15.	16.	17.	18.
	26	45	73	18	82	35
×	17	29	51	15	47	16
	□□□	□□□	□□	□□	□□□	□□□
	□□□	□□□	□□□□	□□□	□□□□	□□□
	□□□	□□□□	□□□□	□□□	□□□□	□□□

19. 53 × 36 **20.** 77 × 19 **21.** 24 × 31 **22.** 64 × 42 **23.** 96 × 22

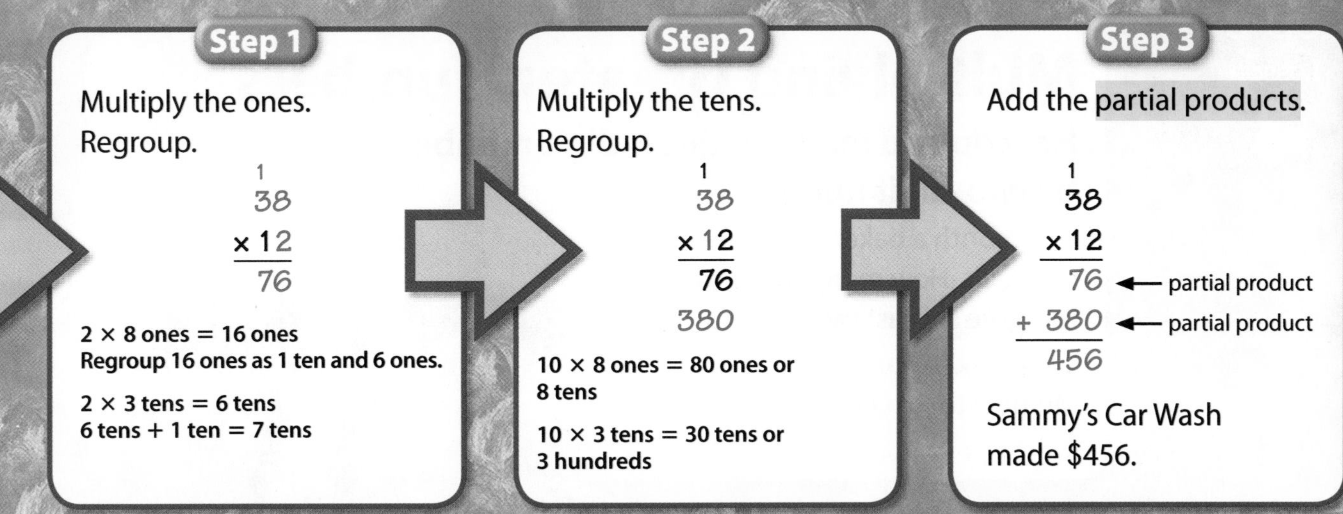

Step 1
Multiply the ones.
Regroup.
1
38
× 12
76
2 × 8 ones = 16 ones
Regroup 16 ones as 1 ten and 6 ones.
2 × 3 tens = 6 tens
6 tens + 1 ten = 7 tens
Step 2
Multiply the tens.
Regroup.
1
38
× 12
76
380
10 × 8 ones = 80 ones or
8 tens
10 × 3 tens = 30 tens or
3 hundreds
Step 3
Add the partial products.
1
38
× 12
76 ← partial product
+ 380 ← partial product
456
Sammy's Car Wash
made $456.

TAKS Problem Solving

24. There are 35 glasses in a case. If each glass holds 20 ounces, how many total ounces would the glasses in a case hold?

25. The principal of a school is buying 2 computers at $900 each. She can pay $98 per month instead of paying the full price at the time of purchase. Will she have paid for them by the end of 12 months?

26. **Writing to Explain** How can finding the product of 5×800 help you check the product of 5×789?

27. The label on a jigsaw puzzle said it has more than 500 pieces. After Julie put the puzzle together, she counted 31 pieces across the top and 23 pieces down the side. Estimate to determine if the label was correct.

28. There are 41 classrooms at Maple School. There are between 27 and 33 students per room. Which is the best estimate of the total number of students in the school?

A 300 **B** 400 **C** 900 **D** 1,200

29. The Explorer Hiking Club has 53 members. How much will it cost for all members to buy new Terrain backpacks?

30. The club also needs to buy 15 dome tents and 15 propane stoves. Will they spend more or less on these items than on the backpacks? How much more or less?

Data: Camping Gear Prices

Gear	Price
Dome Tent	$99
Propane Stove	$28
Terrain Backpack	$87

Step-Up Lesson 3

TEKS 5.3B: Use multiplication to solve problems involving whole numbers.

Multiplying Greater Numbers

How do you multiply three-digit numbers by two-digit numbers?

Last month a bakery sold 389 trays of bagels. How many bagels did the store sell last month?

Choose an Operation
Multiply to join equal groups.

Guided Practice

Do you know HOW?

In **1** through **4**, find each product. Estimate to check that your answer is reasonable.

1. 417×34

2. 243×51

3. 827 × 23

4. 745 × 13

Do you UNDERSTAND?

5. In Step 2 of the example at the top, do you multiply 1 × 9 or 10 × 9?

6. **Writing to Explain** Is 300 × 10 a good estimate for the number of bagels sold at the bakery?

Independent Practice

In **7** through **31**, find each product. Estimate to check that your answer is reasonable.

7. 739×10

8. 892×18

9. 453×95

10. 132×47

11. 611×24

12. 901×62

13. 325×43

14. 227×87

15. 164×22

16. 735×41

17. 35 × 100 **18.** 529 × 47 **19.** 14 × 560 **20.** 498 × 42 **21.** 271 × 22

22. 205 × 72 **23.** 150 × 25 **24.** 35 × 515 **25.** 81 × 11 **26.** 853 × 10

27. 15 × 723 **28.** 602 × 14 **29.** 30 × 902 **30.** 500 × 62 **31.** 99 × 199

Step 1

Multiply the ones, and regroup if necessary.

```
  1 1
  389
×  12
  778
```

2 × 9 ones = 18 ones or 1 ten and 8 ones

2 × 8 tens = 16 tens
16 tens + 1 ten = 17 tens
17 tens = 1 hundred 7 tens

2 × 3 hundreds = 6 hundreds
6 hundreds + 1 hundred = 7 hundreds

Step 2

Multiply the tens, and regroup if necessary.

```
   389
×   12
   778
+ 3890
```

10 × 9 ones = 90 ones
10 × 8 tens = 80 tens or 8 hundreds
10 × 3 hundreds = 30 hundreds or 3 thousand

Step 3

Add the partial products.

```
   389
×   12
   778
+ 3890
 4,668
```

The store sold 4,668 bagels last month.

TAKS Problem Solving

For **32** through **34**, use the data chart.

32. How many times does a gerbil's heart beat in 30 minutes?

33. In 15 minutes, how many more times does a rabbit's heart beat than a dog's?

Data

Animal	Heart Rate (beats per minute)
dog	100
gerbil	360
rabbit	212

34. Think About the Process Which expression shows how to find the total number of heartbeats in 1 hour for a gerbil and a rabbit?

A (360 × 1) + (212 × 1)

B 60 × 360 × 212

C (60 × 360) + (60 × 212)

D (212 × 360) + 60

35. The length of the Nile River in Africa is about 14 times the length of Lake Michigan. About how many miles long is the Nile River?

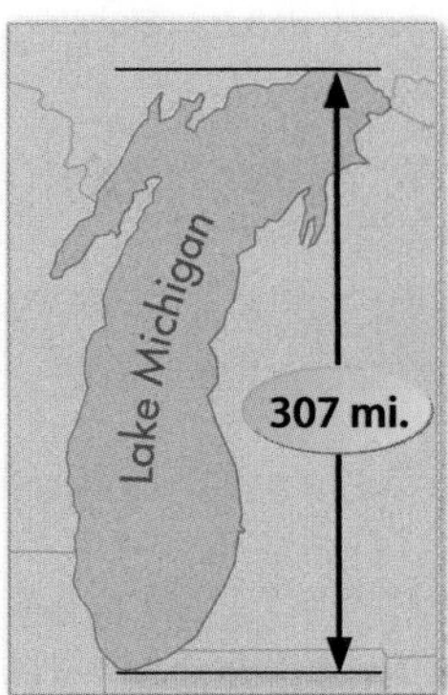

36. The fourth-grade class at South School sold more bags of popcorn than any other class. They ordered 17 cases of popcorn. Each case had 242 bags. How many bags of popcorn did the class sell?

37. A nursery sells plants in flats. There are 6 plants in each tray. Each flat has 8 trays. The nursery sold 25 flats on Saturday and 23 flats on Sunday. How many plants did the nursery sell in all?

38. **Writing to Explain** Is 3,198 a reasonable product for 727 × 44? Why or why not?

39. The theater in Darling Harbour, Australia can seat 540 people. How many tickets can be sold if the theater sells out every seat for 15 performances?

Step-Up Lesson 4

TEKS 5.3C: Use division to solve problems involving whole numbers . . . , including interpreting the remainder within a given context.

Using Patterns to Divide

How can patterns help you divide large multiples of 10?

A jet carries 18,000 passengers in 90 trips. The plane is full for each trip. How many passengers does the plane hold?

Choose an Operation Divide to find how many people were on each trip.

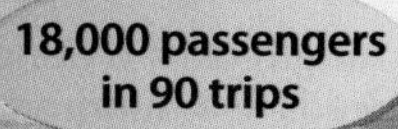

18,000 passengers in 90 trips

Guided Practice

Do you know HOW?

In **1** through **4**, find each quotient. Use mental math.

1. 210 ÷ 30 = 21 tens ÷ 3 tens = ▢

2. 300 ÷ 60 = 30 tens ÷ 6 tens = ▢

3. 7,200 ÷ 90 = ▢

4. 2,800 ÷ 40 = ▢

Do you UNDERSTAND?

5. In Exercise 1, why is 210 ÷ 30 the same as 21 tens ÷ 3 tens?

6. In the example at the top, if the jet carried 10,000 people in 40 trips, how many people did it carry for each trip?

Independent Practice

In **7** through **22**, use mental math to find the missing number.

7. 540 ÷ 90 = 54 tens ÷ 9 tens = ▢

8. 480 ÷ 60 = 48 tens ÷ 6 tens = ▢

9. 3,500 ÷ 50 = 350 tens ÷ 5 tens = ▢

10. 24,000 ÷ 40 = 2,400 tens ÷ 4 tens = ▢

11. 3,000 ÷ 30 = ▢

12. 6,300 ÷ 70 = ▢

13. 230 ÷ 10 = ▢

14. 28,000 ÷ ▢ = 700

15. 810 ÷ 90 = ▢

16. 36,000 ÷ ▢ = 600

17. 30,000 ÷ ▢ = 500

18. 1,600 ÷ ▢ = 20

19. 56,000 ÷ ▢ = 700

20. 1,000 ÷ 10 = ▢

21. 2,500 ÷ 50 = ▢

22. 40,000 ÷ 80 = ▢

Think of a basic fact to help you solve.

18 ÷ 9 = 2

Think about multiples of 10:

180 ÷ 90 = 18 tens ÷ 9 tens = 2

1,800 ÷ 90 = 180 tens ÷ 9 tens = 20

18,000 ÷ 90 = 1,800 tens ÷ 9 tens = 200

The pattern shows us that 18,000 ÷ 90 = 200.

So, the jet can hold 200 people during each trip.

You can multiply to check your answer.

200 × 90 = 18,000

TAKS Problem Solving

For **23** and **24**, use the information at the right.

Data	
Total passengers	3,000
Flights per day	20
Bottles of water	6,000

23. If each flight was stocked with the same number of bottles of water, how many bottles were on each flight?

24. If all the flights were full and all planes carried the same number of passengers, how many people were on each flight?

25. There are 9 schools in the district. Each school receives a $200 donation. What is the total amount of the donation?

26. Leah bowled 5 games. Her scores were 95, 104, 112, 98, and 100. What was the total of her scores?

27. **Think About the Process** Dividing 420 by 70 is the same as

A dividing 42 ones by 7 ones.

B dividing 42 tens by 7 ones.

C dividing 42 tens by 7 tens.

D dividing 42 hundreds by 7 tens.

28. Suppose there are 1,250 pencils in 25 bins. You want to put the same number of pencils in each bin. Which expression shows how to find the number of pencils in each bin?

F 1,250 − 25 **H** 1,250 ÷ 25

G 1,250 + 25 **J** 1,250 × 25

29. One dozen eggs is 12 eggs. A farmer harvested 1,824 eggs from the hen house. Which expression shows how to find how many dozen eggs the farmer harvested?

A 1,824 + 12 **C** 1,824 × 12

B 1,824 − 12 **D** 1,824 ÷ 12

30. It takes 1,500 kg of sand to fill 50 school sandboxes. How much sand will a construction company need to put in each of the 50 sandboxes to get ready for the new school year?

TEKS 5.4: Use strategies, including rounding and compatible numbers, to estimate solutions to addition, subtraction, multiplication, and division problems.

Estimating Quotients with 2-Digit Divisors

How can you use compatible numbers to estimate quotients?

Betty made $159 by selling 75 bracelets. Each bracelet cost the same. About how much did each bracelet cost?

Choose an Operation We know the total amount made and the number of bracelets. Divide to find the price.

Guided Practice

Do you know HOW?

In **1** through **6**, estimate using compatible numbers.

1. 167 ÷ 42 **2.** 298 ÷ 11

3. 255 ÷ 49 **4.** 473 ÷ 62

5. 1,220 ÷ 61 **6.** 2,874 ÷ 42

Do you UNDERSTAND?

7. In the example above, find another way to estimate the cost of each bracelet.

8. Reasonableness Betty has 425 more bracelets to sell. She wants to store these in plastic bags that hold 20 bracelets each. She estimates she will need about 25 bags. Is she right? Why or why not?

Independent Practice

In **9** through **26**, estimate using compatible numbers.

9. 412 ÷ 11 **10.** 282 ÷ 37 **11.** 2,964 ÷ 61

12. 208 ÷ 19 **13.** 1,784 ÷ 34 **14.** 4,620 ÷ 53

15. 1,179 ÷ 12 **16.** 455 ÷ 92 **17.** 542 ÷ 61

18. 2,090 ÷ 32 **19.** 2,910 ÷ 67 **20.** 532 ÷ 11

21. 5,900 ÷ 58 **22.** 8,100 ÷ 44 **23.** 6,395 ÷ 84

24. 4,953 ÷ 74 **25.** 2,495 ÷ 49 **26.** 6,284 ÷ 73

The question asks, "About how much?" So, an estimate is enough.

Use compatible numbers to estimate 159 ÷ 75.

Find compatible numbers for 159 and 75.

Think 16 can be divided evenly by 8.

160 and 80 are close to 159 and 75.

So, 160 and 80 are compatible numbers.

Divide.

160 ÷ 80 = 2.

So, Betty charged *about* $2 for each bracelet.

Check for reasonableness:

2 × 80 = 160

TAKS Problem Solving

27. A high school volleyball team has made it to the state tournament. There are 256 students who want to go, and 34 students can fit on each bus. How many buses are needed?

28. Each player contributed $4 for a gift for the head coach. The two assistant coaches each donated $10. If there were 24 players on the team, how much money did the team raise in all?

29. There are 135 comets that are visible from Earth every 20 years or less. What is an estimate of how many of these comets are seen each year?

30. Josh bought 6 CDs on sale for $78. The regular price for 6 CDs is $90. How much did Josh save per CD by buying them on sale?

31. Which is the best estimate of the product for the following expression?

    611 × 53

    A 3,000

    B 30,000

    C 36,000

    D 300,000

32. Which property does the following equation illustrate?

    36 + 72 = 72 + 36

    F Commutative Property of Addition

    G Associative Property of Addition

    H Identity Property of Addition

    J Commutative Property of Multiplication

33. Dorian bought a clock radio. She paid $15 less than the regular price. If the regular price was $43, how much did Dorian spend on the radio?

34. **Writing to Explain** Skylar needs to estimate the quotient of 725 ÷ 92. Explain how she can use compatible numbers to make a reasonable estimate.

Step-Up Lesson 6

TEKS 5.3C: Use division to solve problems involving whole numbers (no more than two-digit divisors and three-digit dividends without technology), including interpreting the remainder within a given context.

Dividing by Multiples of Ten

What are the steps in dividing by a multiple of ten?

This year a group of 249 students are taking a field trip. One bus is needed for every 20 students. How many buses are needed?

Choose an Operation Divide to find the number of buses.

20 students per bus

Guided Practice

Do you know HOW?

In **1** through **6**, divide.

1. $10\overline{)345}$ **2.** $20\overline{)255}$

3. $50\overline{)452}$ **4.** $40\overline{)841}$

5. $30\overline{)313}$ **6.** $80\overline{)798}$

Do you UNDERSTAND?

7. In the example above, if only 137 students were going on the trip, how many buses would be needed?

8. **Reasonableness** In the example above, why is 12 buses a reasonable estimate?

Independent Practice

Leveled Practice Copy and complete.

9.
```
     ▢5 R1▢
 20)317
    2▢
    ──
    ▢1▢
    1▢▢
    ───
     1▢
```

10.
```
     1▢ R 0
 60)710
    6▢
    ──
    1▢▢
     6▢
    ───
    ▢0
```

11.
```
     3▢ R▢
 10)328
    ▢▢
    ──
    ▢▢
    20
    ──
     ▢
```

12. $40\overline{)169}$ **13.** $70\overline{)480}$ **14.** $80\overline{)641}$

15. 557 ÷ 90 **16.** 119 ÷ 30 **17.** 512 ÷ 50

18. 724 ÷ 10 **19.** 841 ÷ 40 **20.** 222 ÷ 70

21. 245 ÷ 40 **22.** 295 ÷ 30 **23.** 479 ÷ 20

Step 1

Find 249 ÷ 20.

Estimate: 240 ÷ 20 = 12

Divide the tens.

$$\begin{array}{r} 1 \\ 20\overline{)249} \\ -\,20 \\ \hline 4 \end{array}$$

Divide 24 ÷ 20 = 1
Multiply 1 × 20 = 20
Subtract 24 − 20 = 4
Compare 4 < 20

Step 2

Bring down the ones. Divide the ones.

$$\begin{array}{r} 12\text{ R9} \\ 20\overline{)249} \\ -\,20\downarrow \\ \hline 49 \\ -\,40 \\ \hline 9 \end{array}$$

Divide 49 ÷ 20 = 2
Multiply 2 × 20 = 40
Subtract 49 − 40 = 9
Compare 9 < 20

Since the remainder is 9, one more bus is needed. A total of 13 buses are needed.

The answer is reasonable since 13 is close to the estimate, 12.

TAKS Problem Solving

Use the chart to answer **24** through **26**.

24. Ray's family is moving from Little Rock to Chicago. The van that is moving them averages 60 miles an hour. About how many hours does it take the family to reach their new home in Chicago?

Data

Dallas, TX, to Grand Junction, CO	980 miles
Nashville, TN, to Norfolk, VA	670 miles
Charleston, SC, to Atlanta, GA	290 miles
Denver, CO, to Minneapolis, MN	920 miles
Little Rock, AR, to Chicago, IL	660 miles

25. A van driver ran into construction delays on her trip from Grand Junction to Dallas. She averaged 50 miles an hour. About how long did the trip take?

26. Sherry has to pay a toll of $3 for every 30 miles on her trip from Charleston to Atlanta. About how much money does Sherry pay in tolls?

27. Central High School has 2,402 students, while West High School has 2,593 students. How many more students are there in West High than in Central High?

28. The Port Lavaca fishing pier is 3,200 feet long. If there is one person fishing every twenty feet, how many people could fish from the pier at once?

29. Each person on a boat ride pays $32 for a ticket. There are 50 passengers. How much money is collected from all the passengers?

A $85

B $160

C $1,500

D $1,600

30. *Think About the Process* What is the first step in finding 652 ÷ 30?

F Regroup 5 tens as 50 ones

G Regroup 6 hundreds as 60 tens

H Find the remainder

J Multiply 3 by 65

Step-Up Lesson 7

TEKS 5.3C: Use division to solve problems involving whole numbers (no more than two-digit divisors and three-digit dividends without technology), including interpreting the remainder within a given context.

1-Digit Quotients

What are the steps for dividing by 2-digit numbers?

A theater sold 428 tickets for a show. A section in this theater has 64 seats. How many sections must there be to seat all the ticket holders?

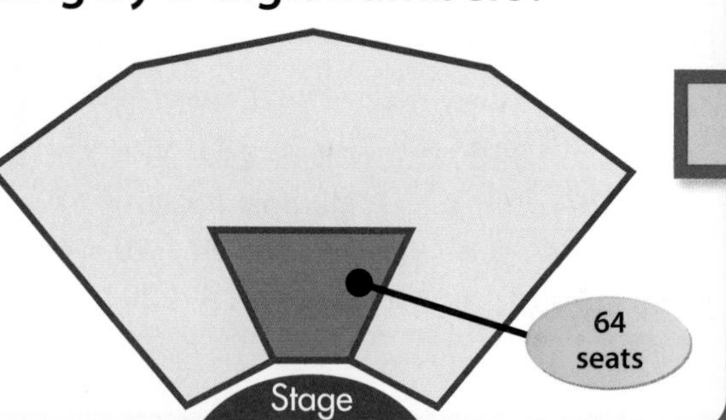

Choose an Operation Divide to find the total number of sections.

Another Example How can estimation help you find 330 ÷ 42?

Step 1

Estimate first.

330 ÷ 42 is about 320 ÷ 40, or 8.

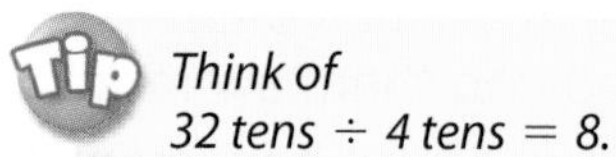

Step 2

Divide the ones. Multiply and subtract.

8 groups of 42 or 8 × 42 = 336.

Since 336 > 330, my estimate is too high.

$$\begin{array}{r} 8 \\ 42\overline{)330} \\ -\ 336 \\ \hline \end{array}$$

Oops!

Step 3

Revise your estimate. Since 8 was too high, try 7 and divide.

7 groups of 42 or 7 × 42 = 294

330 − 294 = 36

36 < 42, so I do not have to divide again.

$$\begin{array}{r} 7 \\ 42\overline{)330} \\ -\ 294 \\ \hline 36 \end{array}$$

Answer: 7 R36

Step 4

Check your work.

7 × 42 = 294

294 + 36 = 330

Explain It

1. In Step 1, how did the estimate tell you to start dividing ones?
2. In Step 2, how did you know that your first estimate of 8 was too high?

Step 1

Estimate to help decide where to place the first digit in the quotient.

428 ÷ 64 is about 420 ÷ 70, or 6.

Start dividing ones.

Step 2

Divide the ones. Multiply and subtract.

$$\begin{array}{r} 6 \text{ R44} \\ 64\overline{)428} \\ -\ 384 \\ \hline 44 \end{array}$$

428 ÷ 64 = 6 R44

Step 3

Check:

$$\begin{array}{r} 64 \\ \times\ \ 6 \\ \hline 384 \\ +\ \ 44 \\ \hline 428 \end{array}$$

So, the theater must have 7 sections.

Guided Practice

Do you know HOW?

Copy and complete.

1. $21\overline{)195}$ with quotient ▢ R ▢, subtract ▢▢▢, remainder ▢

2. $31\overline{)239}$ with quotient ▢ R ▢▢, subtract ▢▢▢, remainder ▢▢

Do you UNDERSTAND?

3. Can the remainder in either example be greater than the divisor? Why or why not?

Independent Practice

Leveled Practice Copy and complete.

4. $16\overline{)143}$ with quotient ▢ R1▢; − 1▢▢; remainder 1▢

5. $52\overline{)402}$ with quotient 7 R ▢8; − ▢▢4; remainder ▢8

6. $74\overline{)739}$ with quotient ▢ R ▢3; − 66▢; remainder ▢3

7. $30\overline{)275}$ with quotient ▢ R ▢; − ▢▢▢; remainder ▢

In **8** through **11** divide.

8. $56\overline{)550}$

9. $29\overline{)248}$

10. $56\overline{)360}$

11. $58\overline{)528}$

12. There are 30 members in a photography club. The club members took a total of 728 pictures. If they use memory cards that hold 85 pictures per card, how many cards will they use?

13. Megan wanted to get 8 hours of sleep before a test. She went to bed at 9:00 P.M. and woke up at 7:00 A.M. How many more hours of sleep did Megan get than the 8 hours she wanted?

A 10

B 3

C 2

D 1

Step-Up Lesson 8

TEKS 5.3C: Use division to solve problems involving whole numbers (no more than two-digit divisors and three-digit dividends without technology), including interpreting the remainder within a given context.

2-Digit Quotients

How can you divide larger numbers?

So far, 467 tortillas have been made. These tortillas will be placed in packages of 15. How many complete packages will be filled?

Choose an Operation Divide to find the number of packages of tortillas.

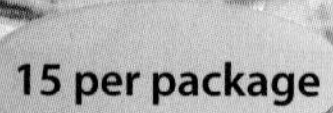

15 per package

Guided Practice

Do you know HOW?

Copy and complete.

1. 47)955 R, − ,
2. 34)358 R, − ,

For **3** and **4**, divide.

3. 17)298
4. 23)315

Do you UNDERSTAND?

5. **Writing to Explain** In the problem above, why will 31 packages be filled instead of 32?
6. How many packages will 627 tortillas fill?
7. How do you decide where to place the first digit in the quotient for Exercises 1–4?

Independent Practice

Leveled Practice Copy and complete.

8. 36)582 R; − ; − 1; 6
9. 45)963 R; − 0; 3; −
10. 53)645 R; − ; −

In **11** through **22**, divide.

11. 76)852
12. 21)389
13. 63)640
14. 18)633
15. 47)582
16. 25)784
17. 13)976
18. 72)2,530
19. 4,338 ÷ 93
20. 679 ÷ 27
21. 980 ÷ 44
22. 719 ÷ 31

Step 1

Estimate to help decide where to place the first digit in the quotient.

Use compatible numbers.

$450 \div 15 = 30$

Start dividing tens.

Step 2

Divide the tens. Multiply and subtract. Continue the process.

```
    31 R2
15)467
  - 45
    17
  - 15
     2
```

Step 3

Check:

$$\begin{array}{r} 31 \\ \times\ 15 \\ \hline 155 \\ +\ 310 \\ \hline 465 \end{array}$$

$465 + 2 = 467$

So far, 31 packages of tortillas will be filled.

TAKS Problem Solving

23. **Writing to Explain** If you are asked to find $496 \div 48$, how do you know the quotient will be greater than 10 before you actually divide?

24. Erin bought a sandwich for $4.75 and a glass of juice for $1.50. The tax was $0.38. She paid with a $10 bill. How much change did she get?

25. Luis spends about $\frac{1}{2}$ hour reading every night. Luis owns 13 science fiction books, 9 mystery books, and 9 history books. He wants to add enough books to his collection to have 50 books. How many more books does he need?

26. An outdoor concert company is putting on 9 concerts this summer. Each concert is sold out. The company sold a total of 945 seats for all performances. How many people will attend each performance?

A 10 **C** 105

B 45 **D** 106

27. There are 60 minutes in 1 hour. How many minutes are there in 24 hours?

28. What compatible numbers can you use to estimate $709 \div 73$?

29. One of the Thorny Devil lizard's favorite foods is ants. It can eat up to 45 ants per minute. How long would it take it to eat 675 ants?

F 9 minutes

G 10 minutes

H 12 minutes

J 15 minutes

30. **Number Sense** Decide if each statement is true or false. Explain.

a $655 \div 20$ is greater than 30.

b $400 \div 25$ is exactly 16.

c $902 \div 40$ is less than 20.

Step-Up Lesson 9

TEKS 5.6: Describe relationships mathematically. Select from and use diagrams and equations such as $y = 5 + 3$ to represent meaningful problem situations.

Addition and Subtraction Patterns

How can you use an expression to write an equation?

What expression tells how to find the total height of a person on 14-inch stilts when you know the person's height without stilts?

An equation is a number sentence that uses an equal sign to show that two expressions have the same value.

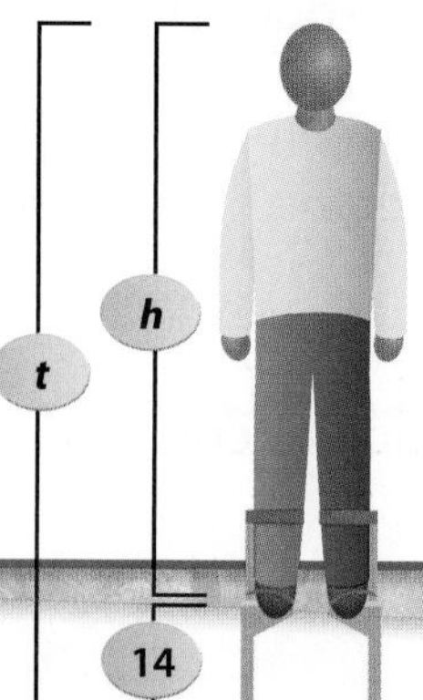

Guided Practice

Do you know HOW?

Write an equation for each table.

1.

a	8	19	22
b	29	40	43

2.

c	25	30	41
d	4	9	20

Do you UNDERSTAND?

3. In the example above, what does the variable t represent?

4. **Writing to Explain** In the example above, does $h + 14 = t$ express the same relationship as $t - 14 = h$?

5. **Writing to Explain** In the example above, does $h + 14 = 70$ have the same value as $14 + h = 70$?

Independent Practice

In **6** through **8**, write an equation for each table.

6.

m	9	16	20
n	34	41	45

7.

x	30	42	57
y	3	15	30

8.

r	9	18	29
s	21	30	41

In **9** through **11**, complete each table.

9.

a	2	3.5	
$a + 4.5$			12

10.

d	18	14	
$18 - d$			9

11.

w	8	23	
$w - 3.7$			34.7

DIGITAL Animated Glossary www.pearsonsuccessnet.com

Height of person in inches (*h*)	Total height on stilts in inches (*t*)
53	67
56	70
61	75
65	79
72	■
■	70

Pattern: Add 14 to the person's height

Expression: $h + 14$

$72 + 14 = t$ so, $t = 86$

$h + 14 = 70$ so, $h = 56$

The equation $h + 14 = t$ tells the relationship between the height of a person and the total height of that person on stilts.

TAKS Problem Solving

12. Number Sense What is the value of the underlined digit in 253.8<u>9</u>2?

13. Write a Problem Write an equation that has a solution of $y = 15$.

14. Which fraction is equivalent to $\frac{2}{3}$?

A $\frac{4}{5}$

B $\frac{4}{6}$

C $\frac{6}{10}$

D $\frac{3}{2}$

15. Find the value of a represented by this diagram.

35				
a	*a*	*a*	*a*	*a*

16. Kate wants to buy a new computer that costs $899. She can save $25 every month and thinks that in 3 years she'll have enough money. Will Kate have enough money?

a Solve the equation $3 \times 12 = w$ to find the number of months in 3 years.

b Using the answer from **a**, write and solve an equation to find how much money Kate will save in 3 years. Will she be able to buy the computer?

17. Which of the following equations describes the pattern in the table below?

x	3	12	21	27
y	1	10	19	25

F $y = x + 2$

G $y = x - 2$

H $y = x + 3$

J $y = x - 3$

18. Writing to Explain Camille says the value of v in the equation $v - 9 = 17$ is 8. Is she correct? Explain.

19. A newly hatched Egyptian tortoise is 5 mm long. It will grow approximately 20 mm each year until it reaches its full size. How many years will it take the tortoise to reach a size of about 126 mm?

TEKS 5.6: Describe relationships mathematically. Select from and use diagrams and equations such as $y = 5 + 3$ to represent meaningful problem situations.

Multiplication and Division Patterns

How can you use an expression to write an equation?

What expression tells how to find the amount Sally would get paid for babysitting when you know how many hours she babysat?

Guided Practice

Do you know HOW?

Write an equation for each table.

1.

x	54	66	72
y	9	11	12

2.

n	15	25	35
m	45	75	105

Do you UNDERSTAND?

3. In the example above, what does the variable d represent?

4. In the example above, how many hours would Sally have to babysit to earn $36?

5. **Writing to Explain** For the example above, does $d \div 4 = h$ express the same relationship as $h \times 4 = d$?

Independent Practice

In **6** and **7**, write an equation for each table.

6.

x	5	7	10
y	60	84	120

7.

m	30	75	90
n	2	5	6

Data

Roses (r)	Cost (c) (in dollars)
12	48
24	96
36	144

8. Find a pattern for the table. Write the pattern as an equation.

9. How much would 48 roses cost?

10. Shayna wants to save $50 to buy a new video game. She earns $5.00 an hour for taking care of the neighbors' dogs. Write an algebraic expression to describe how much Shayna would earn if she worked h hours.

Hours babysitting (h)	Amount paid in dollars (d)
2	8
3	12
4	16
5	▢
▢	24

Pattern: Multiply the hours by 4

Expression: $h \times 4$

$3 \times 4 = d$ so, $d = 12$

$h \times 4 = 24$ so, $h = 6$

The equation $h \times 4 = d$ tells the relationship between the number of hours Sally babysits and the amount of money she is paid.

TAKS Problem Solving

11. Which numbers are equivalent?

A $\frac{1}{5}$ and 0.25

B $\frac{3}{10}$ and 0.3

C $\frac{3}{10}$ and 0.03

D $\frac{1}{3}$ and 0.3

12. If there are 8 crayons in a box, how many boxes are needed for each student to have 3 crayons if there are 20 students?

13. Writing to Explain Dylan said that the value of n in the equation $n \times 5 = 35$ is 30. What is Dylan's mistake?

14. How would you use mental math to evaluate $6 + b = 15$?

15. Larry can type 55 words per minute with errors. He can type 40 words per minute without errors.

a Write a rule to find how many words Larry can type in m minutes with errors. How many words can Larry type in 10 minutes with errors?

b Write a rule to find how many words Larry can type in n minutes without errors. How many words can Larry type in 5 minutes without errors?

16. Think About the Process Amy has 7 more pieces of paper than Holly. Let p equal the number of pieces of paper Amy has. Holly has a total of 50 pieces of paper. Which equation represents the number of pieces of paper Amy has?

F $p + 7 = 50$

G $p - 7 = 50$

H $p \times 7 = 50$

J $p \div 7 = 50$

17. Writing to Explain The local newspaper sells advertising space for $15 per half-page and $30 per full-page. The school wants to buy 4 half-page ads and 1 full-page ad. In addition, they want to buy 1 radio ad for $100. The school has $200 to spend on advertising. Do they have enough money to buy all the ads?

TEKS 5.9: Locate and name points on a coordinate grid using ordered pairs of whole numbers.

Ordered Pairs

Hands-On
grid paper

How do you name a point on a coordinate grid?

A map shows the location of landmarks and has guides for finding the landmarks. In a similar way, a coordinate grid is used to graph and name the locations of points in a plane.

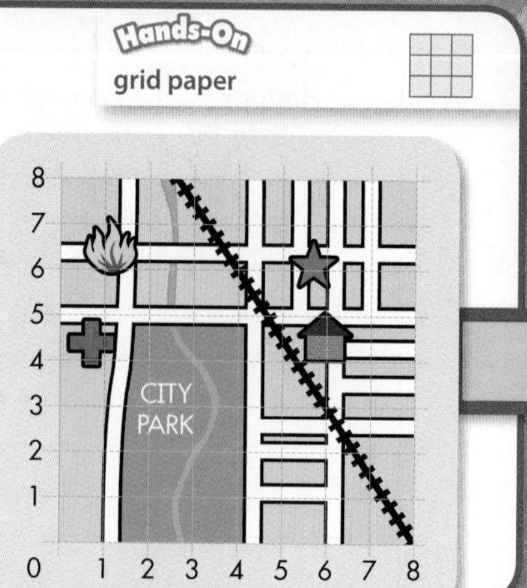

Another Example How do you graph a point on a coordinate grid?

Graph Point *R* at (4, 5).

Step 1

Draw and number the *x*-axis and *y*-axis on grid paper.

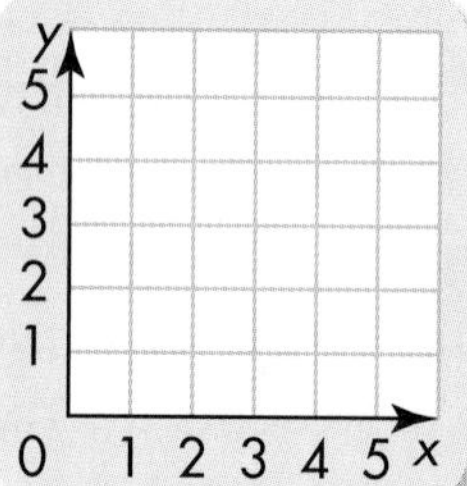

Step 2

Move 4 units to the right from 0. Then move 5 units up.

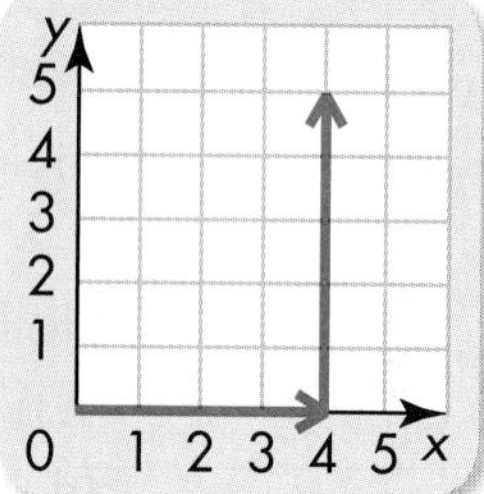

Step 3

Mark a point and label it *R*.

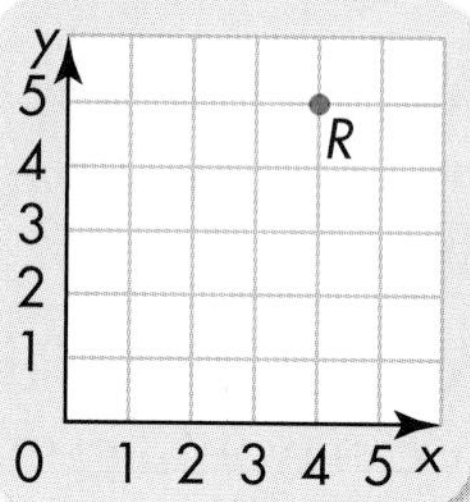

Explain It

1. Why is the order important when naming and graphing the coordinates of a point?
2. If the location of Point *R* changed to (6, 5), would it be to the right or to the left of its current position?
3. You have labeled the *x*-axis and *y*-axis on grid paper. You want to graph Point *D* at (0, 5). Do you move right zero units or move up zero units? Explain.

A coordinate grid has a horizontal *x*-axis and a vertical *y*-axis. The point at which the *x*-axis and *y*-axis intersect is called the origin.

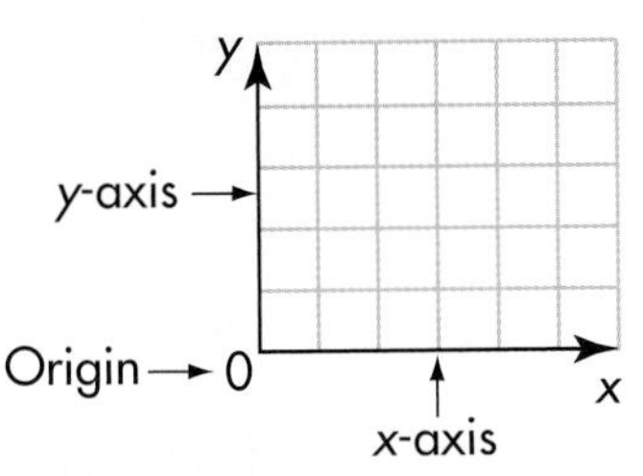

A point in a plane is named using an ordered pair of numbers. The first number, the *x*-coordinate, names the distance to the right from the origin along the *x*-axis. The second number, the *y*-coordinate, names the distance up from the origin along the *y*-axis.

A (1, 3)

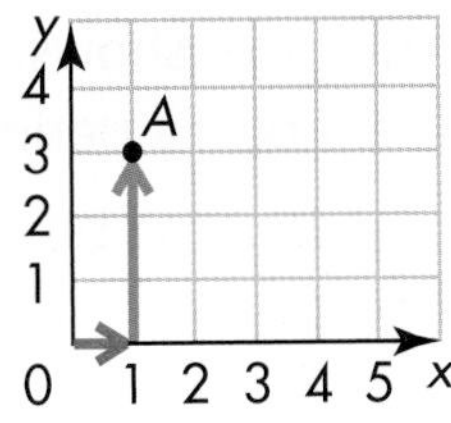

Guided Practice

Do you know HOW?

In **1** and **2**, write each ordered pair. Use the grid at the right.

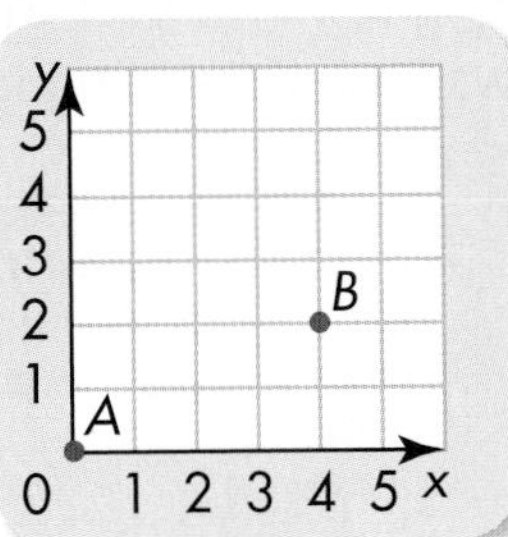

1. *B*

2. *A*

Graph and label each point on a grid.

3. *C* (1, 4)

4. *D* (5, 3)

Do you UNDERSTAND?

5. Using the example above, name the ordered pair for Point *B* if it is 3 units to the right of Point *A*.

6. What ordered pair names the origin of any coordinate grid?

7. **Writing to Explain** Describe how to locate Point *K* at (5, 3).

Independent Practice

In **8** through **11**, write the ordered pair. Use the grid at the right.

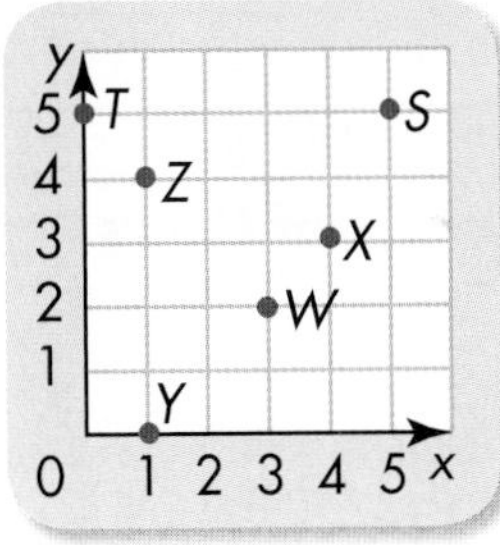

8. *W*

9. *S*

10. *Y*

11. *T*

In **12** and **13**, graph and label each point on a grid.

12. *N* (1, 5)

13. *M* (0, 3)

14. **Writing to Explain** The streets on maps of many cities in the United States are laid out like a coordinate grid. How is this helpful when finding locations in cities such as Austin, Texas.

DIGITAL Animated Glossary, eTools **www.pearsonsuccessnet.com**

Step-Up Lesson 12

TEKS 5.13A: Use tables of related number pairs to make line graphs. Also **TEKS 5.9**

Line Graphs

Hands-On
metric ruler
grid paper

How can data be represented?

A line graph is often used to show a trend or general direction in data.

This table shows the growth of a plant over a period of several days.

The data can be displayed in a line graph.

Plant Growth

Day	Height (cm)
1	4
3	8
5	10
7	11
9	14

Another Example How can you read data from line graphs?

To use data from a graph, locate a point on the graph, and read the values on both axes. To estimate a value not on a graph, interpret the data to determine a trend. The graph below shows Sasha's reading log.

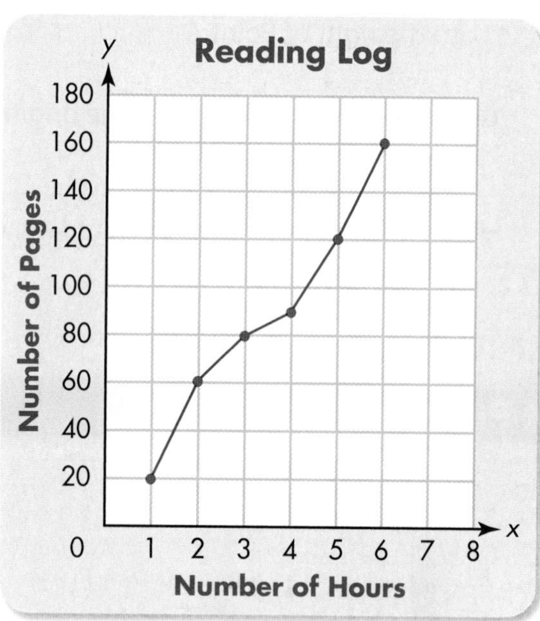

Reading Log

Hours	Pages Read
1	20
2	60
3	80
4	90
5	120
6	160

Explain It

1. Based on the data, how many pages had Sasha read after 2 hours? After 4 hours?
2. If the trend continues, about how many hours will Sasha take to finish a 190-page book?
3. Using the graph, between what two hours was Sasha reading page 140?

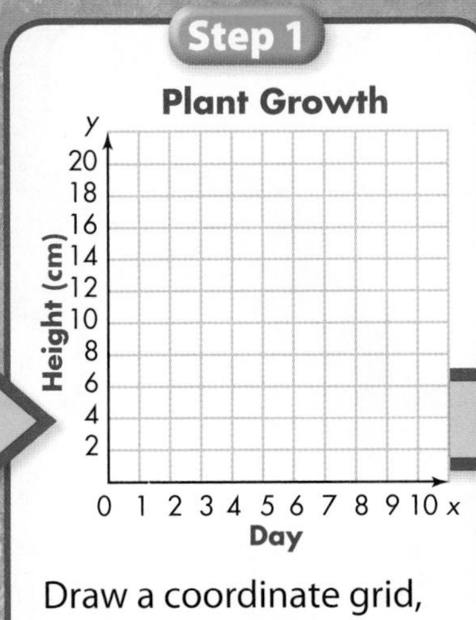

Draw a coordinate grid, use an appropriate scale, and label each axis. Title the graph.

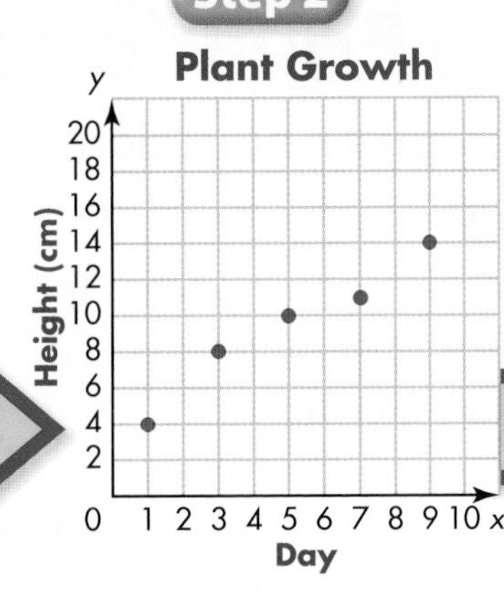

Plot each ordered pair from the table.

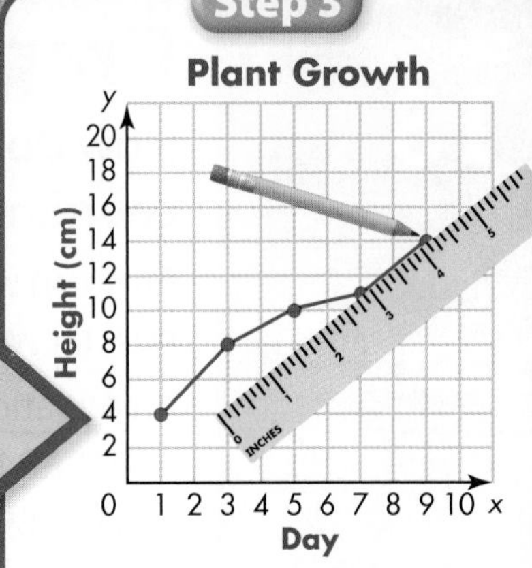

Use a ruler to connect the points.

Guided Practice

Do you know HOW?

1. Use grid paper to make a line graph. Plot the ordered pairs from the table of values. Use an interval of 2, and a ruler to connect each point.

Sam's Reading Log

Minutes	Pages
2	4
4	6
6	10
8	10

Do you UNDERSTAND?

2. In the problem above, between which two days was the plant growth the greatest?

3. If the line connecting the points for several days in a row is horizontal, how much taller did the plant grow during those days?

4. **Writing to Explain** How can you determine information from a line graph for a point that is not plotted?

Independent Practice

For **5** through **7**, use the information from the line graph at the right.

5. When were the least DVDs sold?

6. How many more DVDs were sold during Week 2 than Week 5?

7. Based on the trend, estimate the number of DVDs sold during Week 7.

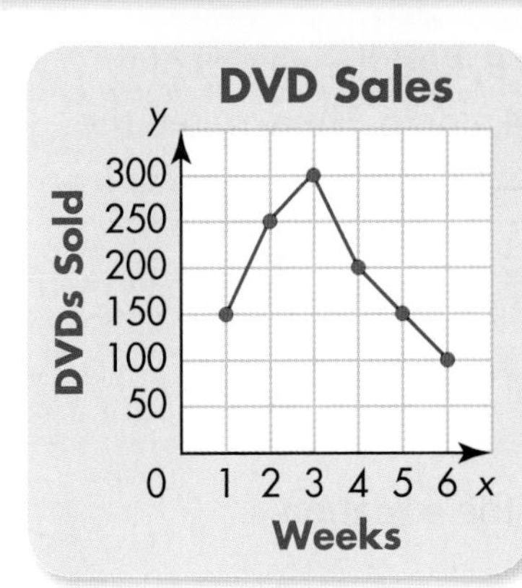

TEKS 5.13A: Use tables of related number pairs to make line graphs.
Also **TEKS 5.9**

Graphing Equations

Hands-On: grid paper

How do you graph an equation on a coordinate grid?

Amy can walk 3 miles in 1 hour. At that speed, how far would she walk in 7 hours?

An equation whose graph is a straight line is called a linear equation.

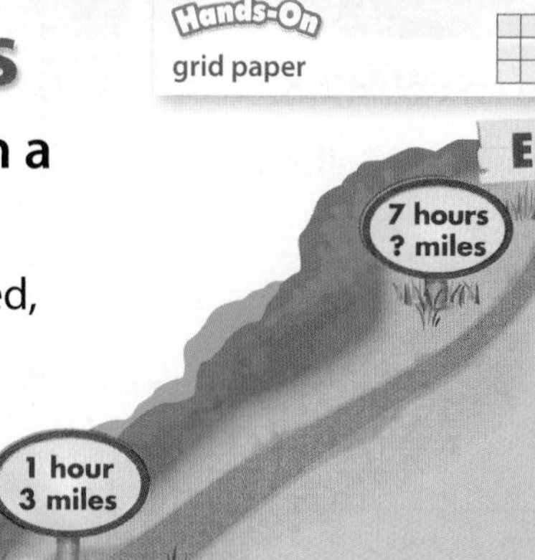

Another Example How do you graph linear equations?

Carl is four years older than Jamal. How can you graph this situation?

Step 1

Write an equation.

Carl is four years older than Jamal.

Carl's age = Jamal's age + 4

$y = x + 4$

When making a table of values for a linear equation, use at least three values for x.

Step 2

Make a table of values.

Jamal x (years)	Carl y (years)
2	6
4	8
6	10

Step 3

Plot the ordered pairs and connect the points.

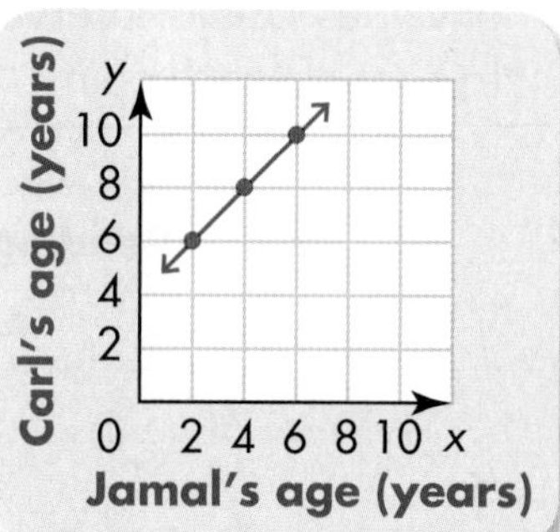

Guided Practice

Do you know HOW?

In **1** through **4**, find the values of y when $x = 2, 4$, and 6. Then, name the ordered pairs.

1. $y = x + 2$

2. $y = 5x$

3. $y = x - 1$

4. $y = 4x$

For **5**, graph the equation.

5. $y = x + 4$

Do you UNDERSTAND?

6. Reasonableness Does the line for $y = x - 4$ include the point (4, 0)?

7. A lion can run about four times faster than a squirrel. What equation represents that relationship? How would you graph it?

Step 1

Write an equation.

Amy walks 3 miles each hour.

miles = 3 × hours

Let y be the number of miles and x be the number of hours.

$y = 3x$

Step 2

Make a table of x- and y- values to show how x and y relate and satisfy the equation.

$y = 3x$

x	y
1	3
3	9
5	15

Step 3

Label the axes on a coordinate grid. Plot the ordered pairs and connect the points to graph the equation.

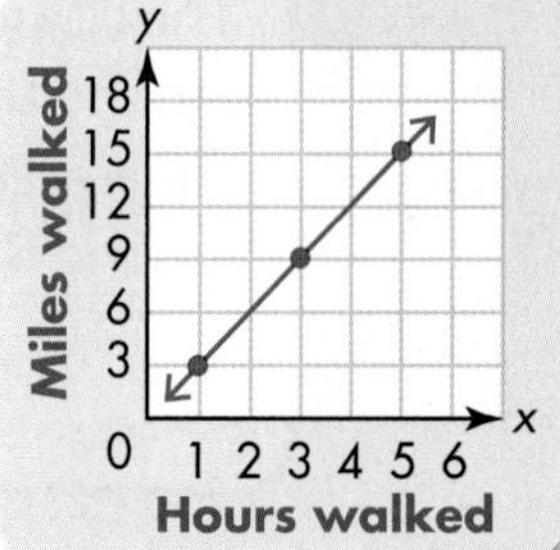

Extend the y-axis. The y value when $x = 7$ shows that Amy walked 21 miles.

Independent Practice

In **8** through **11**, name the ordered pairs. Let $x = 3, 4,$ and 5.

8. $y = 8x$ **9.** $y = x + 5$ **10.** $y = x + 7$ **11.** $y = x - 2$

In **12** through **15**, make a table of values for each equation and then graph each equation. Use $x = 1, 2,$ and 3.

12. $y = x - 1$ **13.** $y = 2x$ **14.** $y = x + 1$ **15.** $y = x$

TAKS Problem Solving

16. Reasoning If the points (0, 1), (7, 1), (10, 1), and (18, 1) were graphed, they would form a horizontal line. Do you think the equation for this line would be $x = 1$ or $y = 1$? Explain.

17. Writing to Explain How do you know that the point (4, 12) will appear on graphs for both of the equations $y = 3x$ and $y = x + 8$?

18. Complete the table of values for the equation: $y = x - 6$.

x	6	7		11
y	0		2	

19. Reasoning Will the point (25, 50) be included on a graph for the equation $y = 2x$? Explain your answer.

20. Which ordered pair will be included on the graph for $y = 3 + x$?

A (6, 3) **C** (1, 3)

B (3, 6) **D** (9, 3)

Step-Up Lesson 14

TEKS 5.10B: Connect models for perimeter, area, and volume with their respective formulas. Also **TEKS 5.10C**

Perimeter

How can you find the distance around a polygon?

The city wants to build a new fence around the rose garden in the town square. Perimeter is the distance around the outside of any polygon.

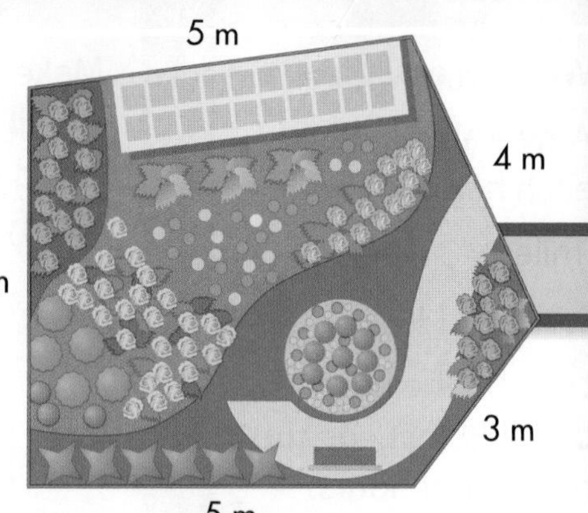

Another Example

How can you use a formula to find the perimeter of a square and a rectangle?

A formula is a rule that uses symbols.

Use a formula to find the perimeter of the square.

Perimeter = 4 × side

$P = 4 \times s$

$P = 4 \times 29 = 116$ cm

Tip s = side

29 cm
29 cm 29 cm
29 cm

Use either of these formulas to find the perimeter of the rectangle.

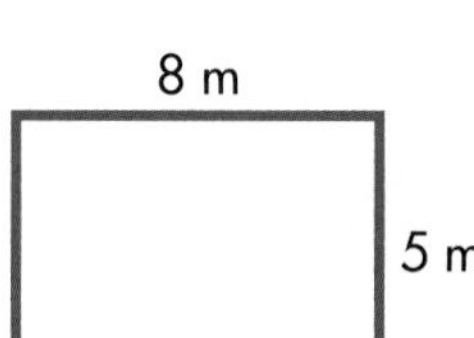

One Way

Perimeter = (2 × length) + (2 × width)

$P = (2 \times \ell) + (2 \times w)$

$P = (2 \times 8) + (2 \times 5)$

$P = 16 + 10 = 26$ m

Tip ℓ = length
w = width

Another Way

Perimeter = 2 × (length + width)

$P = 2 \times (\ell + w)$

$P = 2 \times (8 + 5)$

$P = 2 \times 13 = 26$ m

Explain It

1. Will the formula for finding the perimeter of a square work for finding the perimeter of a rectangle?

Find the perimeter of the rose garden to find the total length of the new fence needed.

Perimeter is equal to the sum of the side lengths of a polygon.

One Way

Add the lengths of the sides.

$P = 5 + 5 + 4 + 3 + 5$
$P = 22$ m

The perimeter of the rose garden is 22 m.

Another Way

Since the longest side lengths are the same, multiplication can be used in the equation.

$P = 5 + 5 + 4 + 3 + 5$
$P = (3 \times 5) + 4 + 3$
$P = 15 + 7$
$P = 22$ m

The perimeter of the rose garden is 22 m.

Guided Practice

Do you know HOW?

Find the perimeter of the figure.

1. 12 in., 12 in., 10 in.

Do you UNDERSTAND?

2. Look at the dimensions of the garden above. If the longest sides of the garden were 9 m, how long would the fence need to be?

Independent Practice

For **3** through **8**, find the perimeter of each figure.

3.

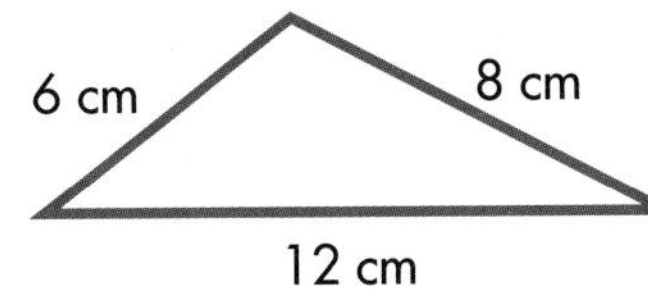

4.

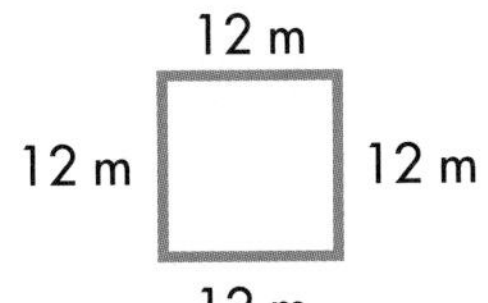

5.

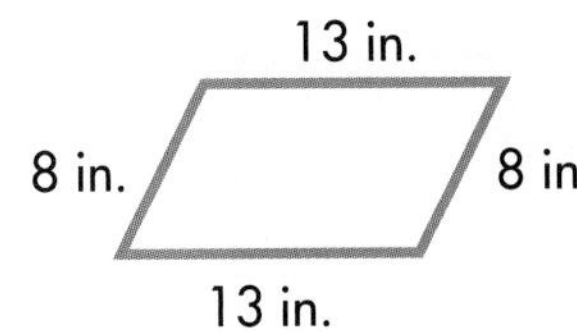

6.

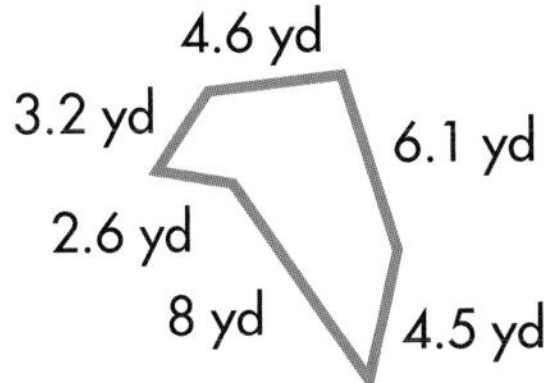

7.

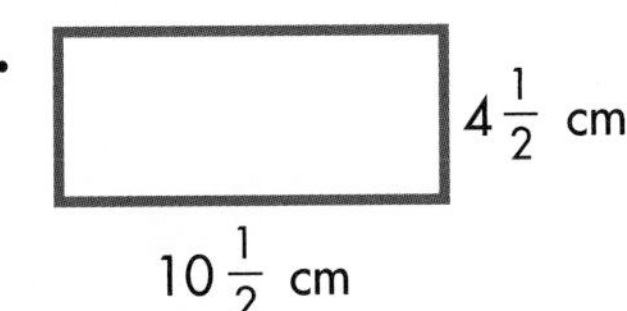

8.

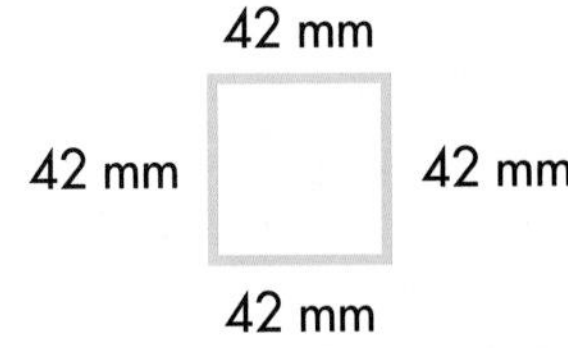

9. **Number Sense** The perimeter of an equilateral triangle is 27 feet. What is the length of each of its sides?

10. **Reasoning** Maria says her pencil is 1.7 meters long. Is this measurement reasonable? Explain.

DIGITAL Animated Glossary **www.pearsonsuccessnet.com**

Step-Up Lesson 15

TEKS 5.10B: Connect models for perimeter, area, and volume with their respective formulas. Also **TEKS 5.10C**

Area of Squares and Rectangles

How can a formula be used to find area?

The area of a figure is the amount of surface it covers. What are the areas of the baseball infield and the tennis court?

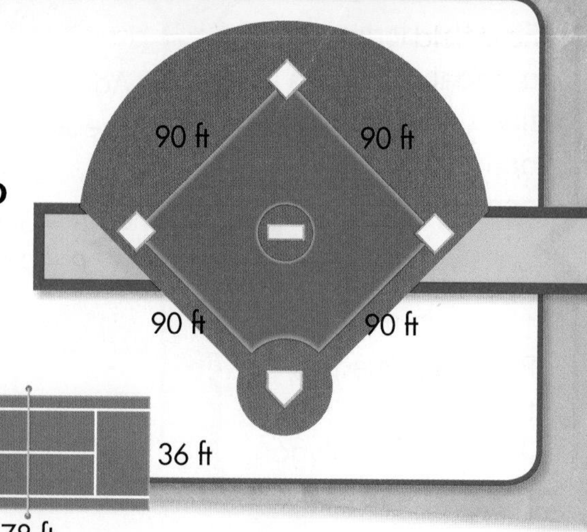

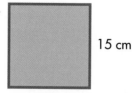

Guided Practice

Do you know HOW?

In **1** and **2**, find the area of each figure.

1. Find the area of a square with a side that measures 11 cm.

2. Find the area of a rectangle with length 17 m and width 9 m.

Do you UNDERSTAND?

3. Which two dimensions are multiplied when finding the area of a rectangle?

4. **Writing to Explain** In the example above, how can you decide which figure has the greater area, without using the formula?

Independent Practice

For **5** through **10**, find the area of each figure.

5. 12 in., 18 in.

6. 9 ft, 9 ft

7. 23 m, 45 m

8. 15 cm, 15 cm

9. A rectangle with length 300 in. and width 60 in.

10. A square with a side that measures 30 yd

The infield is a square, so all of its sides are equal.

Use the formula below to find the area of a square. Area is measured in square units.

Area = side $\times$ side

$A = s \times s$

$A = 90$ feet $\times$ 90 feet

$A = 8{,}100$ square feet

s

s

The area of the infield is 8,100 square feet.

The tennis court is a rectangle, so its opposite sides are equal.

Use the formula below to find the area of a rectangle.

Area = length $\times$ width

$A = \ell \times w$

$A = 78$ feet $\times$ 36 feet

$A = 2{,}808$ square feet

The area of the tennis court is 2,808 square feet.

TAKS Problem Solving

11. The East Room of the White House is 79 feet long by 36 feet wide. What is the area of the room?

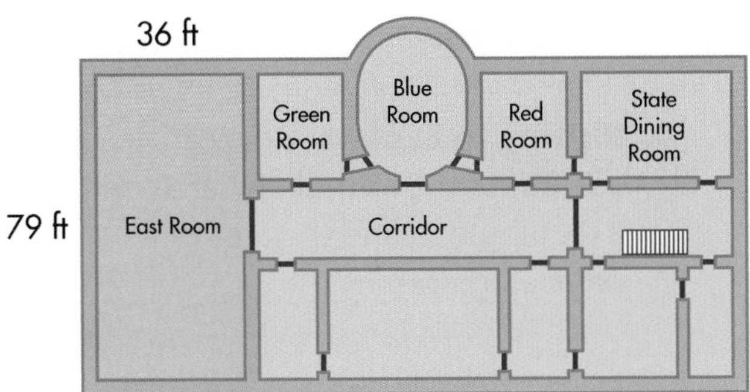

12. Ben's mom wants to buy new carpet for the family room that measures 15 feet by 12 feet. She can purchase the carpet on sale for $6 per square foot including installation. How much will Ben's mom spend to carpet the family room?

A $108

B $801

C $1,008

D $1,080

13. **Number Sense** A set of four postcards cost $1.00. Single postcards cost $0.50. What is the least amount of money you can spend to buy exactly 15 postcards?

14. Which has the greater area: a square with a side that measures 8 meters, or a 7-by-9-meter rectangle? What is the area?

For **15** through **17**, use the drawing at the right of an Olympic-size swimming pool.

15. What is the perimeter of the swimming pool?

16. What is the area of the swimming pool?

17. What is the perimeter of each lane?

18. What is the perimeter and area of a square with a side that measures 20 m?

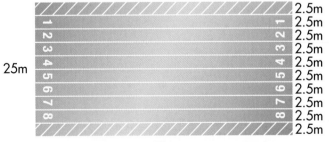

Step-Up Lesson 16

TEKS 5.10B: Connect models for perimeter, area, and volume with their respective formulas. Also **TEKS 5.10C**

Area of Parallelograms

How can finding the area of a rectangle help you find the area of a parallelogram?

Southwestern rugs often have parallelograms as part of the design. The base of this parallelogram is 8 cm. The height is 4 cm. What is its area?

Guided Practice

Do you know HOW?

in **1** and **2**, find the area of each parallelogram.

1.

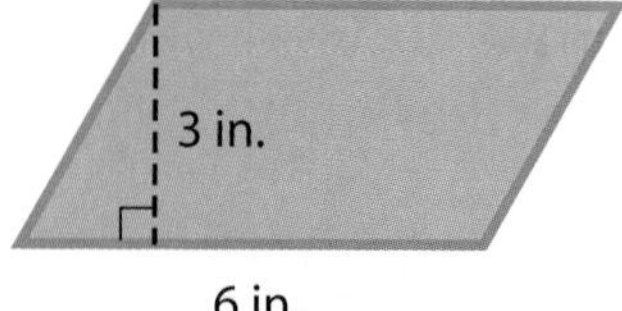

2.

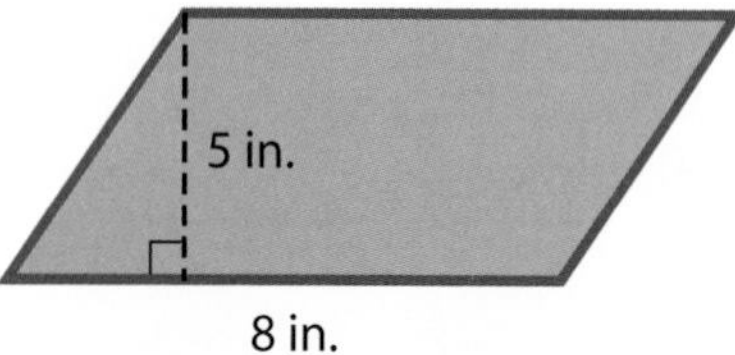

Do you UNDERSTAND?

3. In the example above, which dimensions of the parallelogram correspond to the dimensions of the rectangle?

4. **Writing to Explain** How can you adapt the formula for area of a rectangle to find the area of a parallelogram?

Independent Practice

For **5** through **11**, find the area of each parallelogram.

5.

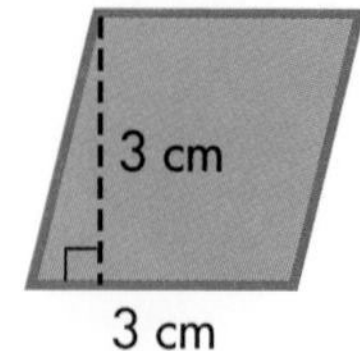

6.

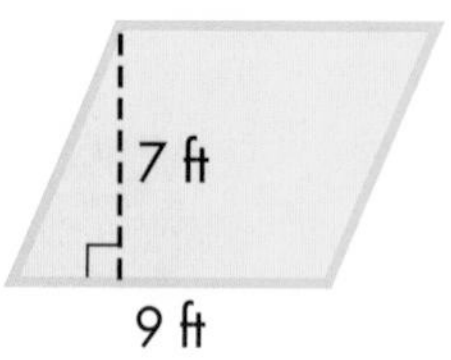

7.

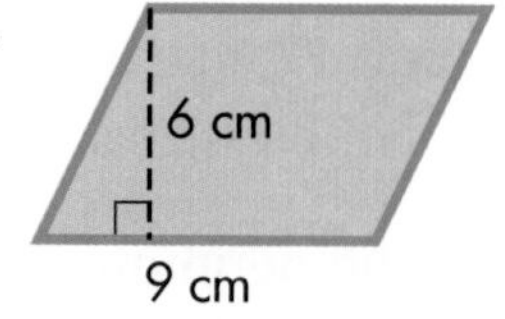

8.

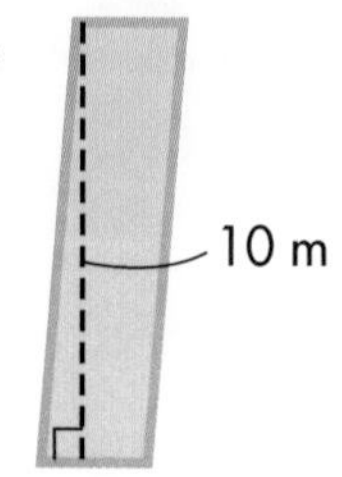

9.

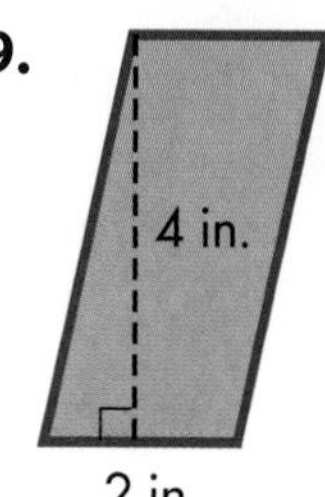

10.

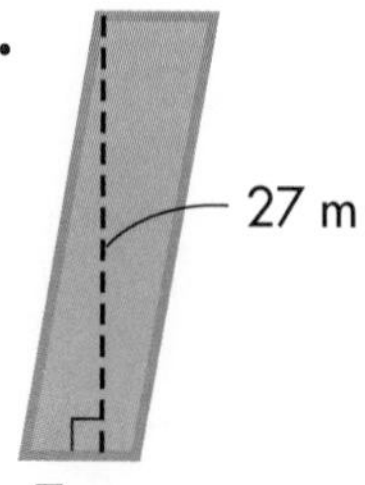

11.

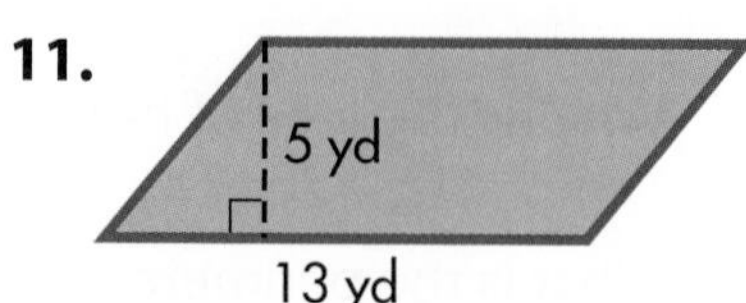

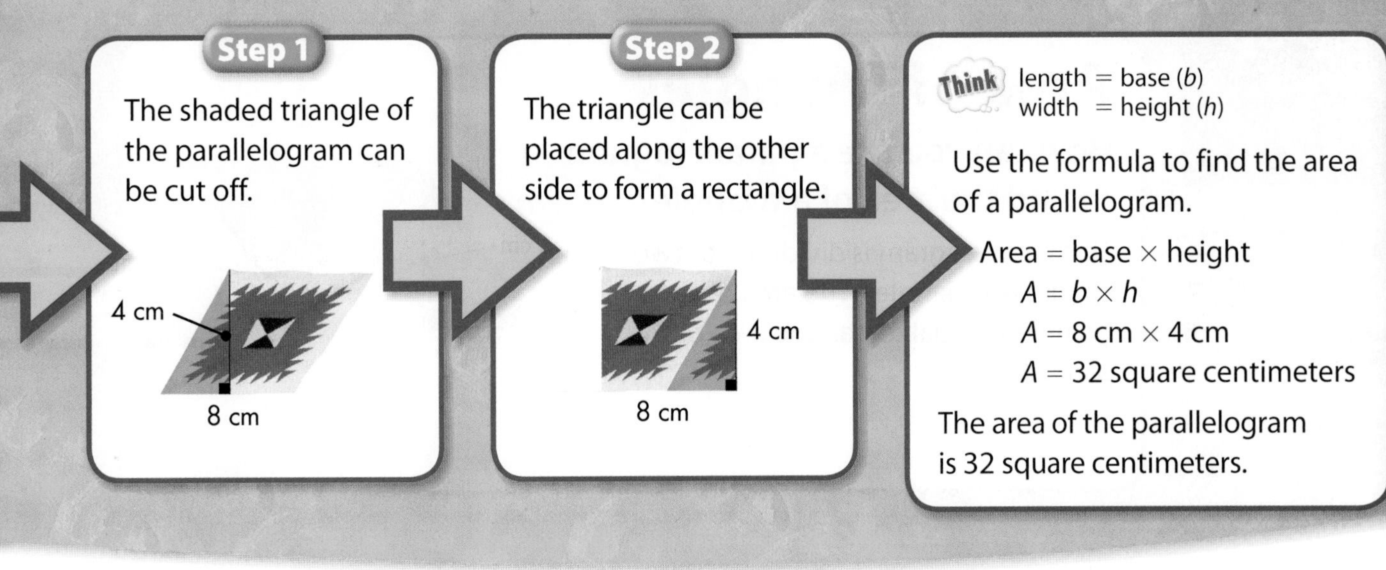

Step 1
The shaded triangle of the parallelogram can be cut off.
4 cm
8 cm
Step 2
The triangle can be placed along the other side to form a rectangle.
4 cm
8 cm
Think
length = base (b)
width = height (h)
Use the formula to find the area of a parallelogram.
Area = base × height
A = b × h
A = 8 cm × 4 cm
A = 32 square centimeters
The area of the parallelogram is 32 square centimeters.

TAKS Problem Solving

12. Parallelogram *A* has a base of 11 ft and a height of 9 ft. Parallelogram *B* has a base of 12 ft and a height of 8 ft. Which parallelogram has the greater area? How much greater is the area?

13. Each morning, Kelly rides the train 15 km to work. The train takes 10 minutes to travel $7\frac{1}{2}$ km. How much time does he spend on the train each day going to and from work?

14. Which of these figures has the least area?

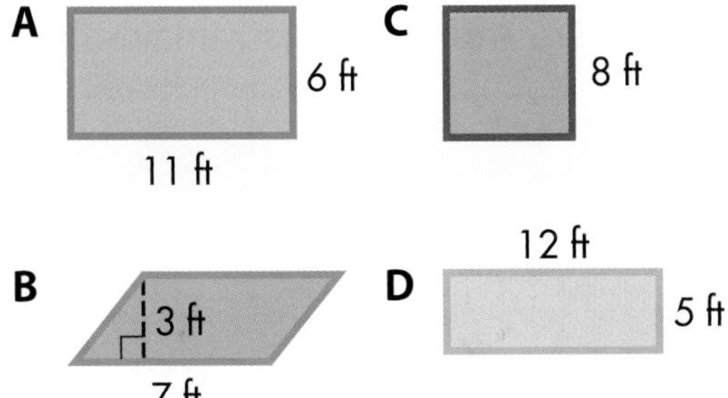

15. A store display has 36 bottles of shampoo on the bottom shelf, 30 bottles on the shelf above that, and 24 on the shelf above that. If this pattern continues, how many bottles will be on the next shelf above?

16. What is the area of the parallelogram lift shown below?

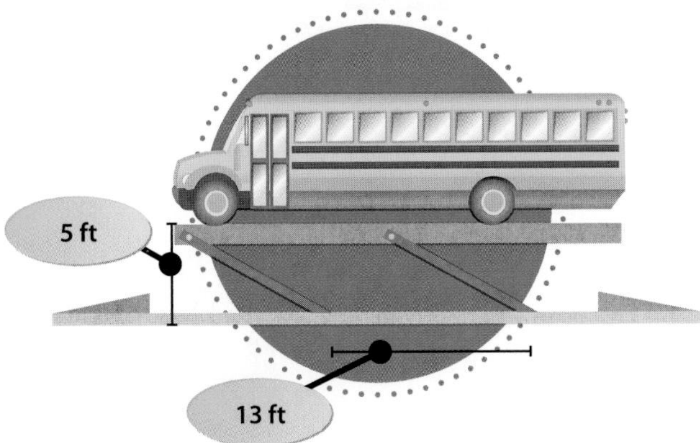

17. **Writing to Explain** Don bought two items that cost a total of $100. One item cost $10 more than the other. What was the cost of each item? Explain your reasoning.

18. **Algebra** Libby knows the area of a parallelogram is 48 square inches. The base of this parallelogram is 8 inches, and the height is *h* inches. What is the measure for the height of this parallelogram?

Step-Up Lesson 17

TEKS 5.10B: Connect models for perimeter, area, and volume with their respective formulas. Also TEKS 5.10C

Area of Triangles

How can you use a parallelogram to find the area of a triangle?

This parallelogram is divided into two congruent triangles. The area of each triangle is equal to half the area of the parallelogram.

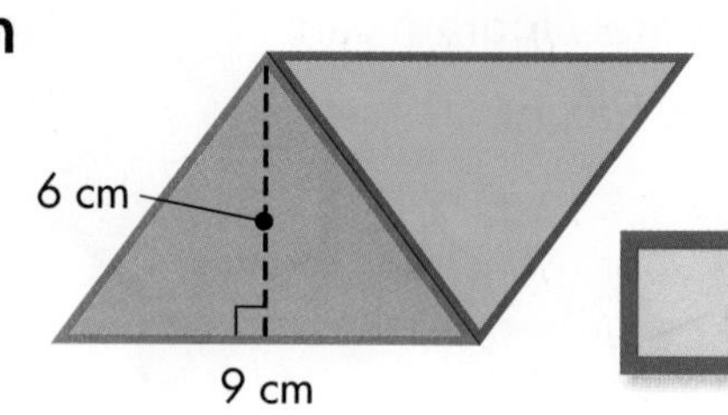

Guided Practice

Do you know HOW?

In **1** and **2**, find the area of each triangle.

1.

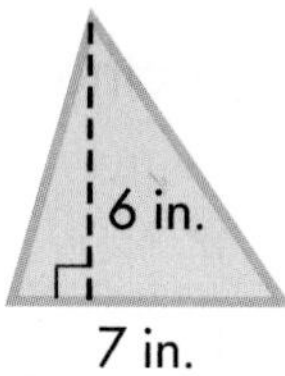

2.

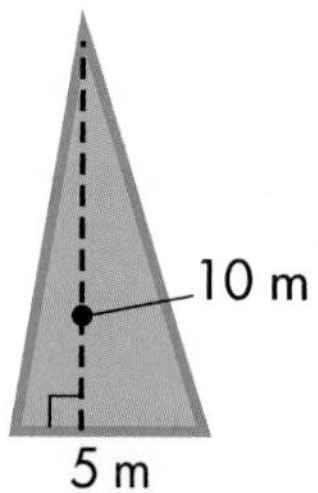

Do you UNDERSTAND?

3. Writing to Explain In the example above, how do you know the area of the triangle is equal to half the area of the parallelogram?

4. In the example above, find the area of the red triangle if the base measures 12 cm and the height remains the same.

Independent Practice

In **5** through **10**, find the area of each triangle.

5.

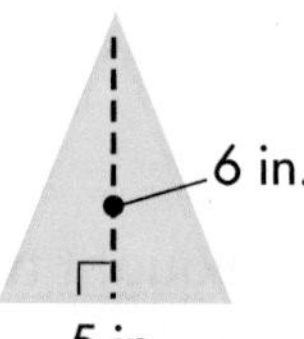

6.

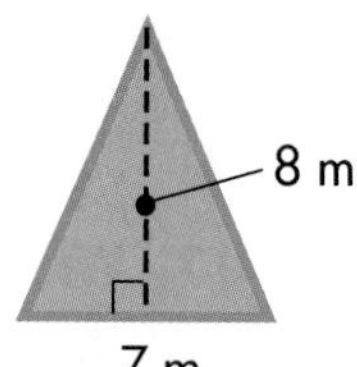

7.

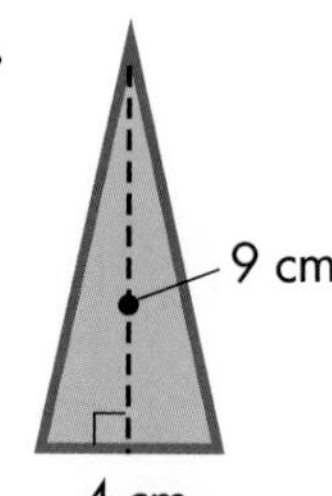

8.

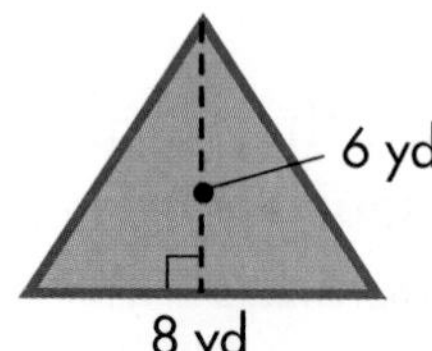

9.

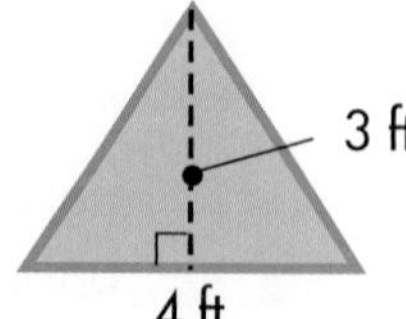

10.

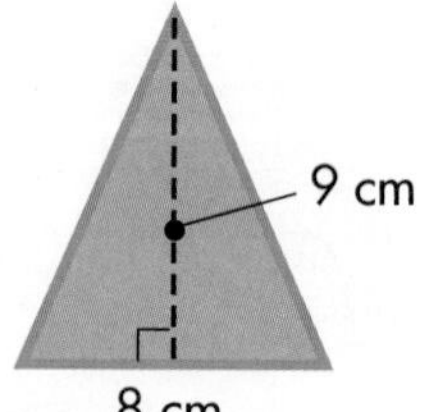

Step 1

Find the area of the red triangle.

Identify the measures of the base and height of the triangle.

base (b) = 9 cm
height (h) = 6 cm

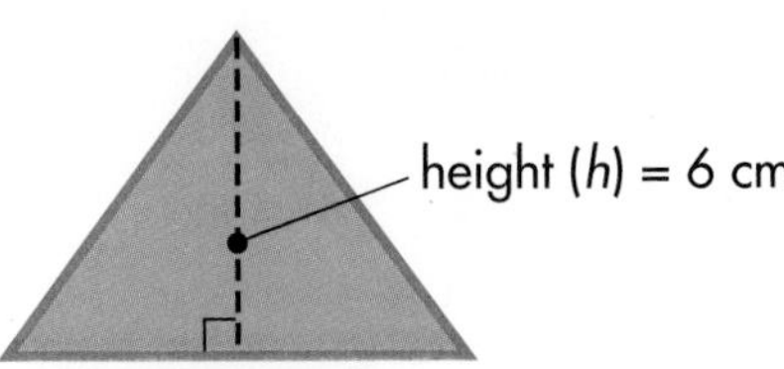

Step 2

To find the area of a triangle, adapt the formula for the area of a parallelogram—just multiply by $\frac{1}{2}$.

Substitute the values into the formula.

Area $= \frac{1}{2} \times$ base $\times$ height

$A = \frac{1}{2} \times b \times h$

$A = \frac{1}{2} \times 9 \times 6$

$A = 27$ square centimeters

The area of the red triangle is 27 square centimeters.

TAKS Problem Solving

11. Writing to Explain Ian says that this triangle has an area of 3,000 square inches. Is Ian correct? Explain.

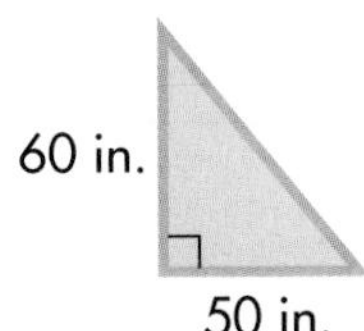

12. Marna wants to buy one pair of gloves. She can choose from some that cost \$22.50, \$27.00, \$20.95, and \$24.75. How much will Marna save if she buys the least expensive instead of the most expensive pair?

13. Reasoning The difference between the prices of two CDs is \$5. The sum of the prices is \$33. How much does each CD cost?

14. What is the area of a triangle with a base of 9 inches and a height of 6 inches?

A 15 sq. in.
B 27 sq. in.
C 54 sq. in.
D 56 sq. in.

15. Which of the following numbers is a prime number?

F 12
G 14
H 15
J 17

16. Ann is going to wallpaper her room. Each wall in her room measures 10 ft by 8 ft. How much wallpaper will Ann need to cover 3 of the walls?

17. Algebra A lunar module has triangular-shaped windows. The base of each window is 60 cm. The height is h cm. The area of each window is 1,200 square centimeters. Find the height of each window.

18. What is the area of the dinner bell shown at the right?

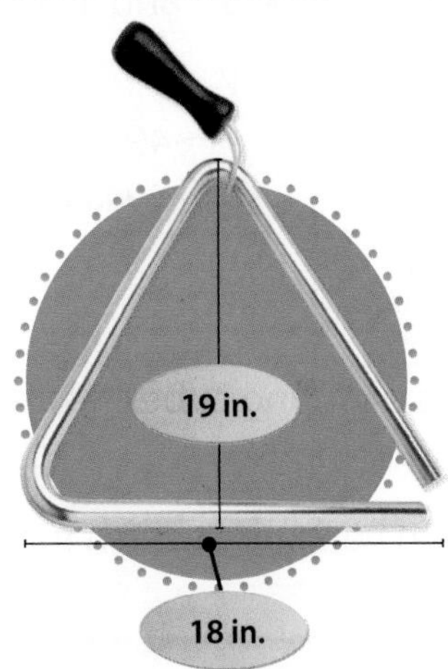

Step-Up Lesson 18

TEKS 5.10B: Connect models for perimeter, area, and volume with their respective formulas. Also TEKS 5.10C

Volume

How do you find the volume of a prism?

Volume is the number of cubic units needed to fill a solid figure.

A cubic unit is the volume of a cube 1 unit on each edge. Each cube = 1 cubic unit

Find the volume of the rectangular prism.

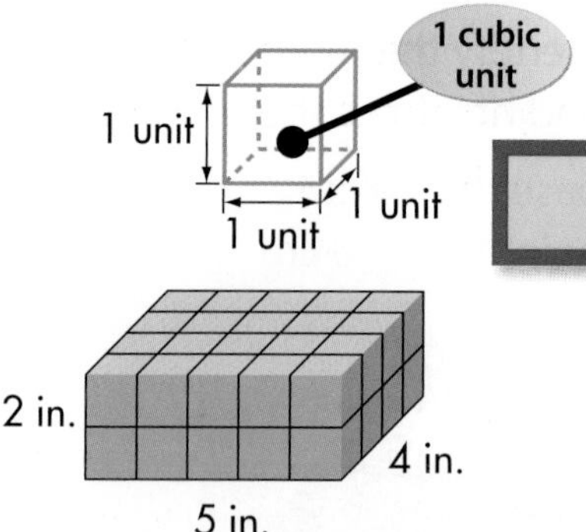

Another Example How do you use a formula to find volume?

If the measurements of a prism are given in length ℓ, width w, and height h, then use this formula to find volume V:

$$\text{Volume} = (\text{length} \times \text{width}) \times \text{height}$$
$$V = (\ell \times w) \times h$$

Use a formula to find the volume of the prism.

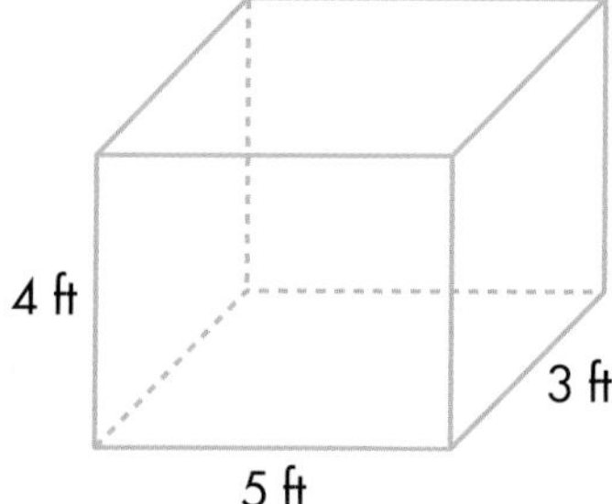

$$V = (\ell \times w) \times h$$
$$V = (5 \times 3) \times 4$$
$$V = 60 \text{ cubic feet}$$

The volume of the prism is 60 cubic feet.

Sometimes the area of the base will be given.

If a rectangular prism has a base area B and a height h, use this formula:

$$\text{Volume} = \text{base} \times \text{height}$$
$$V = B \times h$$

Tip *Base area is the same as $\ell \times w$.*

Find the volume of a rectangular prism with a base area of 49 square centimeters and a height of 6 cm.

$$V = B \times h$$
$$V = 49 \times 6$$
$$V = 294 \text{ cubic centimeters}$$

Explain It

1. How is counting cubes related to the formulas for finding volume?
2. How do you know which formula for volume to use?

Count cubes to find volume.

If the cubic units are shown, you can count the cubes inside the rectangular prism. Begin with the base layer of the prism. It has 5 cubes each in 4 rows.

There are 20 cubic units in the base layer of the prism.

There are two layers.

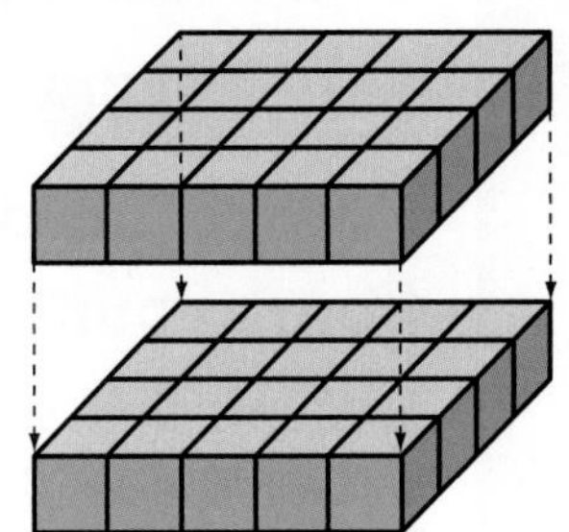

20 cubes × 2 layers = 40 cubic units.

The measures are in inches, so the volume of the rectangular prism is 40 cubic inches.

Guided Practice

Do you know HOW?

In **1** and **2**, find the volume of each rectangular prism.

1.

2.

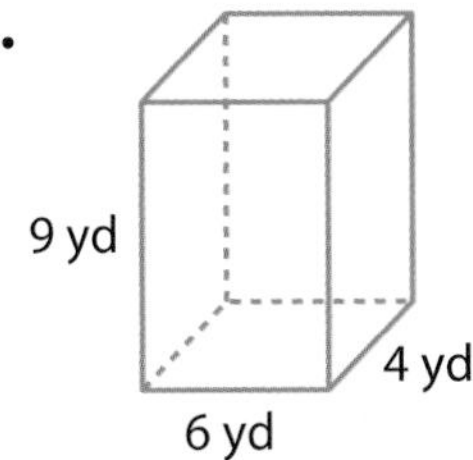

Do you UNDERSTAND?

3. In the example above, how do you know both of the layers are the same?

4. A cereal box measures 6 in. by 10 in. by 2 in. Draw a rectangular prism and label it. What is the volume of the figure you drew?

Independent Practice

In **5** through **10**, find the volume of each rectangular prism.

5.

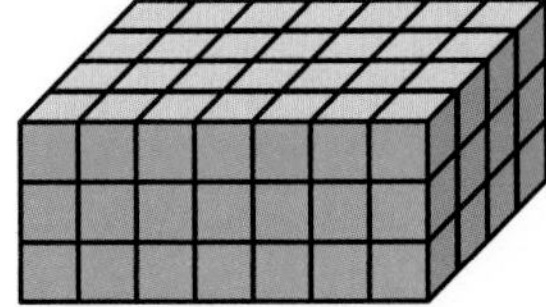

6.

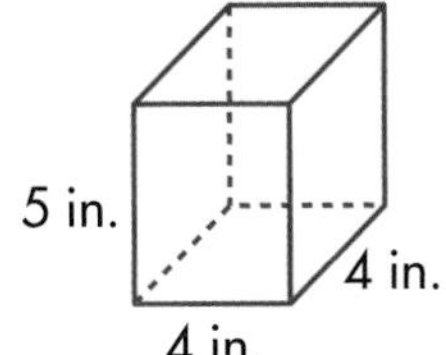

7.

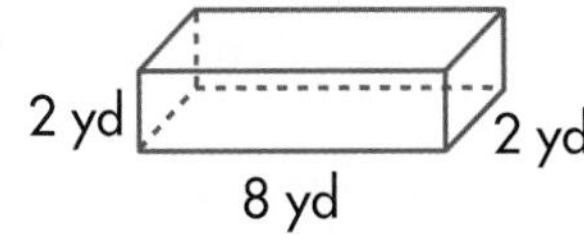

8. Base area: 40 square inches
height: 9 in

9. Base area: 100 square feet
height: 21 ft

10. Base area: 64 square yards
height: 8 yds

11. What is the perimeter of this figure?

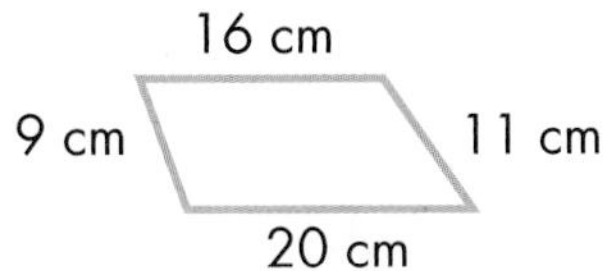

12. A refrigerator measures about 6 feet tall, 4 feet wide, and 3 feet deep. Estimate the volume of the refrigerator.

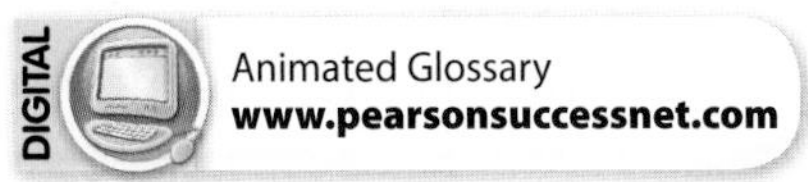

Step-Up Lesson 19

TEKS 5.13: Solve problems by collecting, organizing, displaying, and interpreting sets of data.
Also TEKS 5.13C.

Bar Graphs and Picture Graphs

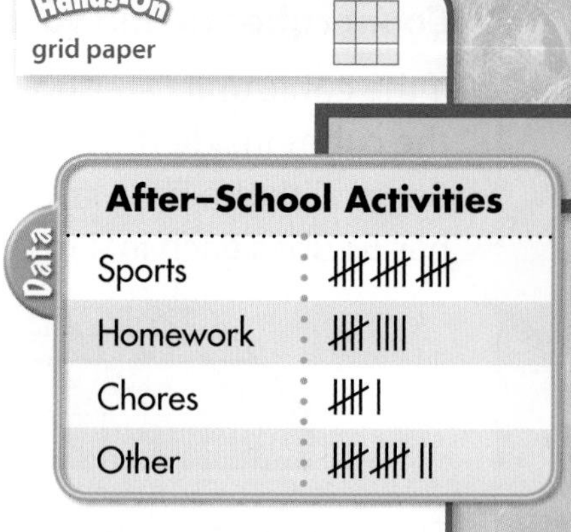

After-School Activities	
Sports	𝍸 𝍸 𝍸
Homework	𝍸 ||||
Chores	𝍸 |
Other	𝍸 𝍸 ||

How do you display data collected from a count or measure?

Students were surveyed about what they do after school. The results were displayed in a bar graph.

A bar graph uses rectangles (bars) to show and compare data that tells how many or how much.

Another Example How can you make and interpret picture graphs?

Sonya gathered data about the number of ducks in some of the 2006 rubber duck derbies. Sonya listed the data in a frequency table. Then she drew a picture graph to display the data.

Rubber Duck Derbies, 2006				
Location	*Congaree River, SC*	*Lake Lanier, GA*	*St. Louis Riverfront, MO*	*Meinig Memorial Park, OR*
Number of Rubber Ducks	5,000	13,000	15,000	1,000

A picture graph uses pictures or symbols to represent data. Each picture represents a certain amount in the data.

Rubber Duck Derbies, 2006

Location	Number of Rubber Ducks
Congaree River, SC	🦆🦆🦆🦆🦆
Lake Lanier, GA	🦆🦆🦆🦆🦆🦆🦆🦆🦆🦆🦆🦆🦆
St. Louis Riverfront, MO	🦆🦆🦆🦆🦆🦆🦆🦆🦆🦆🦆🦆🦆🦆🦆
Meinig Memorial Park, OR	🦆

Key: 🦆 = 1,000 ducks

Explain It

1. Which is easier to interpret, a pictograph or a frequency table? Explain.

Step 1 List the survey answers along one axis.

Choose an interval, the difference between adjoining numbers on an axis. Label both axes.

Step 2 Along the other axis mark the scale, the series of numbers at equal distances. Include the least and greatest numbers in the survey results.

Step 3 Graph the data by drawing bars of the correct length or height.

Step 4 Title the graph.

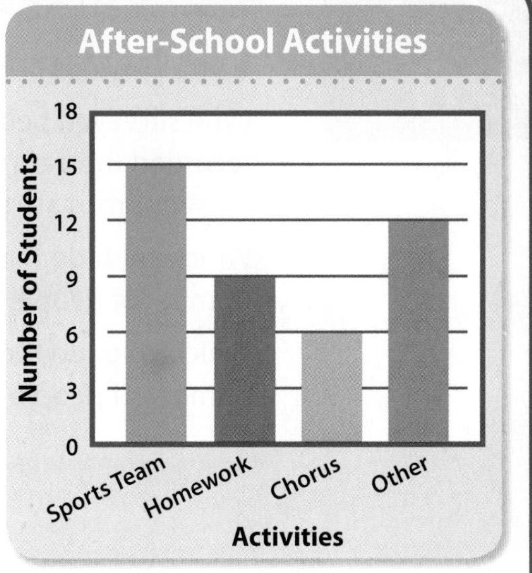

Interpret the Graph

Most students play sports. The fewest number of students sing in the chorus.

Guided Practice

Do you know HOW?

In **1** and **2**, decide if a bar graph or picture graph would better present the data.

1. The number of cats, dogs, and hamsters in a neighborhood.

2. The number of parks in three cities.

Do you UNDERSTAND?

3. Could the data in the example of the bar graph above be presented in a picture graph? Explain.

4. How are bar graphs and picture graphs similar? How are they different?

Independent Practice

In **5** through **8**, answer the questions about the picture graph shown to the right.

5. How many people are represented by each picture?

6. What is the population of the second least populated city?

7. About how many more people live in New York than in Los Angeles?

8. Can this data be presented in a bar graph? Explain.

Top 5 U.S. Cities by Population

New York	
Los Angeles	
Chicago	
Houston	
Philadelphia	

Key: = 1 million people

DIGITAL Animated Glossary, eTools **www.pearsonsuccessnet.com**

TEKS 5.13: Solve problems by collecting, organizing, displaying, and interpreting sets of data.
Also TEKS 5.13C.

Problem Solving

Choose an Appropriate Graph

Lynn surveyed people to ask them their favorite color. She recorded the data in a spreadsheet. What type of graph is most appropriate to answer these questions? Explain.

Which color do the greatest number of people like?

Which color do the least number of people like?

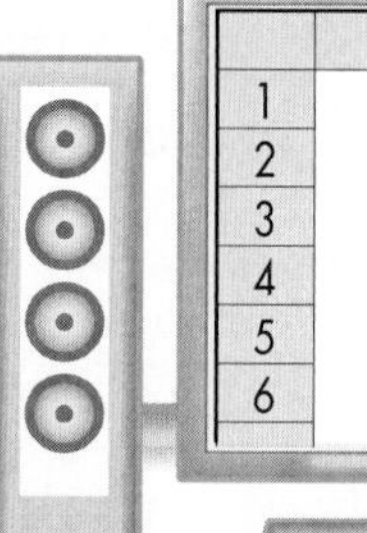

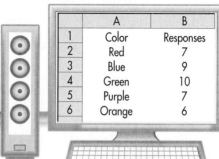

	A	B
1	Color	Responses
2	Red	7
3	Blue	9
4	Green	10
5	Purple	7
6	Orange	6

Guided Practice

Do you know HOW?

Tell what type of graph would be most appropriate to represent the following data.

1. Number of calories burned throughout your day
2. Comparing the number of soccer players to baseball players

Do you UNDERSTAND?

3. In the example above, why is a line graph not appropriate?
4. When is a line graph appropriate?
5. **Write a Problem** Write a real-life problem in which you have to choose an appropriate graph.

Independent Practice

Tell what type of graph would be most appropriate to represent the following data.

6. Number of books checked out from a library throughout a day
7. Number of different types of apples picked in a day
8. Hourly temperature readings throughout a day
9. A student's growth from birth to 10 years old
10. Students' favorite pet results from a class survey

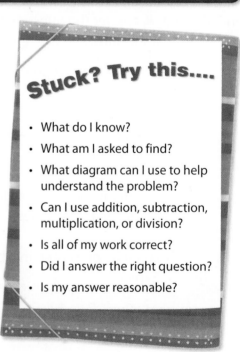

Stuck? Try this....

- What do I know?
- What am I asked to find?
- What diagram can I use to help understand the problem?
- Can I use addition, subtraction, multiplication, or division?
- Is all of my work correct?
- Did I answer the right question?
- Is my answer reasonable?

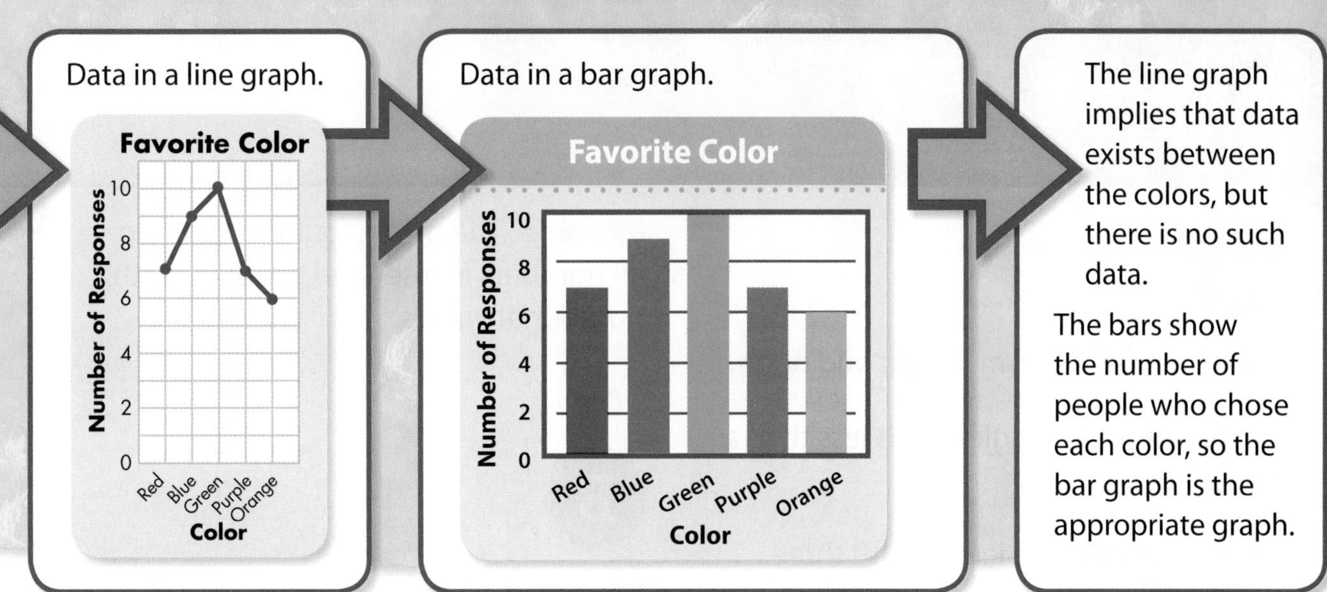

Manuel and Kara's class took a survey of the number of siblings per student. Use their graphs of the data to answer **11** through **13**.

11. What type of graph did each of the students make?

12. Which number of siblings do most students have?

13. **Writing to Explain** Which graph is more appropriate? Explain.

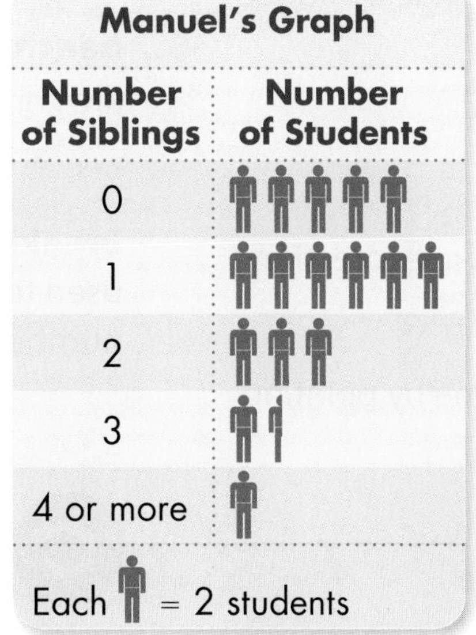

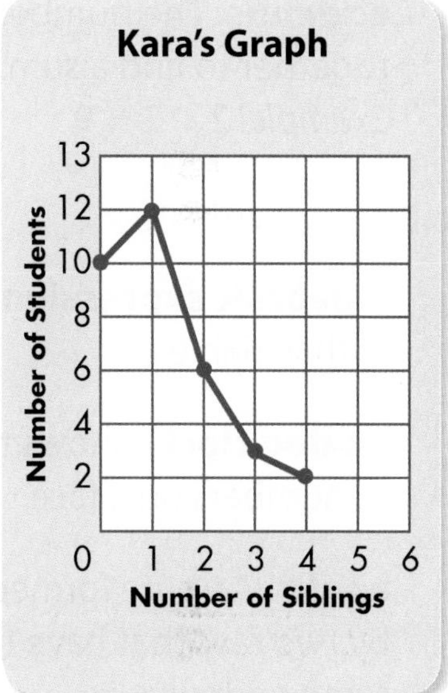

Use the line graph at the right to answer **14** through **17**.

14. During which week did the least growth occur?

15. Describe the trend in plant growth for the four weeks.

16. How tall did the plants grow in the 4 week period?

17. **Writing to Explain** Is the line graph appropriate for this data? Explain.

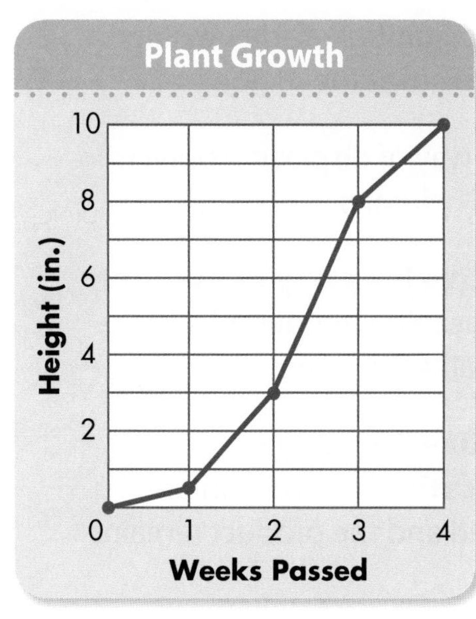

Glossary

A.M. Time between midnight and noon.

acute angle An angle that is less than a right angle.

acute triangle A triangle with three acute angles.

addends The numbers that are added together to find a sum.
Example: 2 + 7 = 9
addend

algebraic expression An expression with variables.

analog clock Shows time by pointing to numbers on a face.

angle A figure formed by two rays that have the same endpoint.

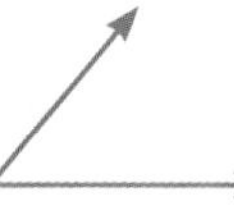

area The number of square units needed to cover the region.

array A way of displaying objects in rows and columns.

Associative Property of Addition Addends can be regrouped and the sum remains the same.

Associative Property of Multiplication Factors can be regrouped and the product remains the same.

average The mean, found by adding all numbers in a set and dividing by the number of values.

bar graph A graph using bars to show data.

benchmark fractions Fractions that are commonly used for estimation: $\frac{1}{4}$, $\frac{1}{3}$, $\frac{1}{2}$, $\frac{2}{3}$, and $\frac{3}{4}$.

breaking apart Mental math method used to rewrite a number as the sum of numbers to form an easier problem.

capacity The volume of a container measured in liquid units.

center A point within a circle that is the same distance from all points on a circle.

centimeter (cm) A metric unit of length. 100 centimeters = 1 meter.

century A unit of time equal to 100 years.

certain (event) An event that is sure to occur.

chord Any line segment that connects any two points on the circle.

circle A closed plane figure in which all the points are the same distance from a point called the center.

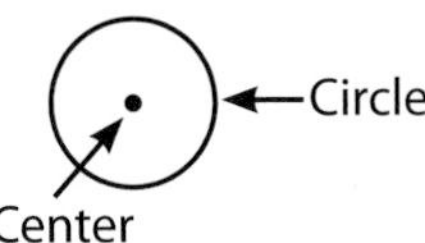

circle graph A graph in the shape of a circle that shows how the whole is broken into parts.

common factor A factor that two or more numbers have in common.

Commutative Property of Addition Numbers can be added in any order and the sum remains the same.

Commutative Property of Multiplication Factors can be multiplied in any order and the product remains the same.

compatible numbers Numbers that are easy to compute mentally.

compensation Adding and subtracting the same number to make the sum or difference easier to find.

cone A solid figure with a base that is a circle and a curved surface that meets at a point.

congruent figures Figures that have the same shape and size.

coordinate grid A grid used to show ordered pairs.

cube A solid figure with six congruent squares as its faces.

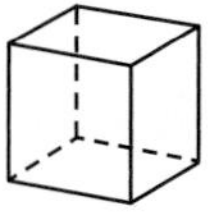

cup (c) A customary unit of capacity.

customary units of measure Units of measure that are used in the United States.

cylinder A solid figure with two congruent circular bases.

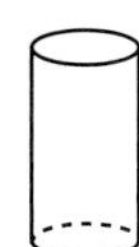

D

data Pieces of collected information.

day A unit of time equal to 24 hours.

decade A unit of time equal to 10 years.

decimal point A dot used to separate dollars from cents or ones from tenths in a number.

decimeter (dm) Metric unit of length equal to 10 centimeters.

degrees Celsius (°C) Metric unit of temperature.

degrees Fahrenheit (°F) Standard unit of temperature.

denominator The number below the fraction bar in a fraction; The total number of equal parts in all.

diameter A line segment that connects two points on a circle and passes through the center.

difference The answer when subtracting two numbers.

digital clock Shows time with numbers. Hours are separated from minutes with a colon.

digits The symbols used to write a number: 0, 1, 2, 3, 4, 5, 6, 7, 8, and 9.

Distributive Property Breaking apart problems into two simpler problems. *Example*: $(3 \times 21) = (3 \times 20) + (3 \times 1)$

divide An operation to find the number in each group or the number of equal groups.

dividend The number to be divided.

divisibility rules The rules that state when a number is divisible by another number.

divisible Can be divided by another number without leaving a remainder. *Example*: 10 is divisible by 2.

divisor The number by which another number is divided. *Example*: $32 \div 4 = 8$

↑ Divisor

E

edge A line segment where two faces of a solid figure meet.

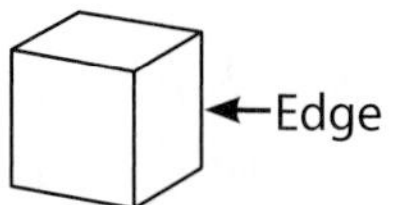

elapsed time The amount of time between the beginning of an event and the end of the event.

equally likely (event) Just as likely to happen as not to happen.

equation A number sentence that uses the equal sign (=) to show that two expressions have the same value.

equilateral triangle A triangle in which all sides are the same length.

equivalent Numbers that name the same amount.

equivalent fractions Fractions that name the same region, part of a set, or part of a segment.

expanded form A number written as the sum of the values of its digits. *Example*: 2,000 + 400 + 70 + 6

F

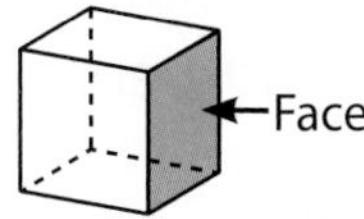

face A flat surface of a solid that does not roll.

fact family A group of related facts using the same set of numbers.

factors The numbers multiplied together to find a product.
Example: $3 \times 6 = 18$

Factor

fair game A game in which each player is equally likely to win.

fluid ounce (fl oz) A customary unit of capacity.
1 fluid ounce = 2 tablespoons

foot (ft) A customary unit of length.
1 foot = 12 inches

fraction A fraction is a symbol, such as $\frac{2}{3}$, $\frac{5}{1}$, or $\frac{8}{5}$, used to name a part of a whole, a part of a set, a location on a number line, or a division of whole numbers.

front-end estimation A way to estimate a sum by adding the first digit of each addend and adjusting the result based on the remaining digits.

G

gallon (gal) A customary unit of capacity. 1 gallon = 4 quarts

gram (g) A metric unit of mass.

H

hexagon A polygon with 6 sides.

hour Unit of time equal to 60 minutes.

hundredth One part of 100 equal parts of a whole.

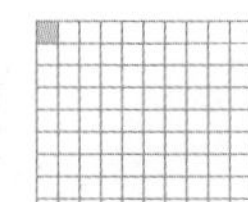

I

Identity Property of Addition The sum of any number and zero is that number.

Identity Property of Multiplication The product of any number and one is that number.

impossible (event) An event that cannot occur.

improper fractions A fraction in which the numerator is greater than or equal to the denominator.

inch (in.) A customary unit of length.

inequality A number sentence that uses the greater than sign (>) or the less than sign (<) to show that two expressions do not have the same value.

intersecting lines Lines that cross at one point.

interval A number which is the difference between two consecutive numbers on the scale of a graph.

inverse operations Two operations that undo each other.
Examples: Adding 6 and subtracting 6 are inverse operations. Multiplying by 4 and dividing by 4 are inverse operations.

isosceles triangle A triangle that has at least two equal sides.

key Part of a pictograph that tells what each symbol stands for.

kilogram (kg) A metric unit of mass.
1 kilogram = 1,000 grams

kilometer (km) A metric unit of length.
1 kilometer = 1,000 meters

leap year Unit of time equal to 366 days.

likely (event) An event that probably will happen.

line A straight path of points that goes on and on in two directions.

line graph A graph that connects points to show how data changes over time.

line of symmetry A line on which a figure can be folded so that both halves are congruent.

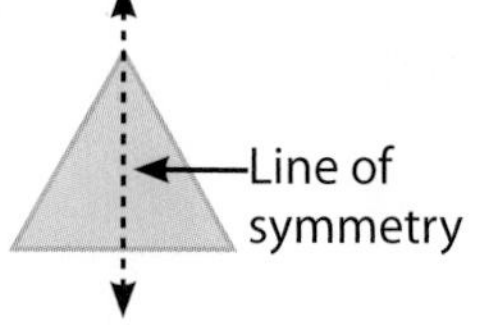

line plot A display of data along a number line.

line segment A part of a line that has two endpoints.

liter (L) A metric unit of capacity.

mass The amount of matter that something contains.

mean An average, found by adding all numbers in a set and dividing by the number of values.

median The middle number in an ordered data set.

meter (m) A metric unit of length.

mile (mi) A customary unit of length.
1 mile = 5,280 feet.

millennium A unit for measuring time equal to 1,000 years.

milliliter (mL) A metric unit of capacity.

millimeter (mm) A metric unit of length.

minute A unit of time equal to 60 seconds.

mixed number A number that has a whole number and a fraction.

mixed number A number that has a whole number and a fraction.

mode The number or numbers that occur most often in a data set.

month One of the 12 parts into which a year is divided.

multiple The product of any two whole numbers.

net A pattern used to make a solid.

Example: 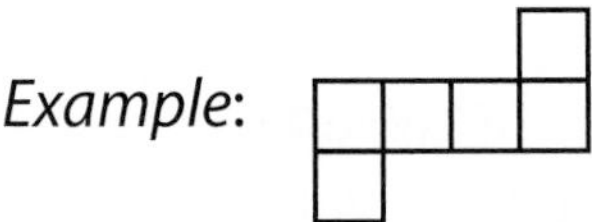

number expression An expression that contains numbers and at least one operation. A number expression is also called a numerical expression.

numerator The number above the fraction bar in a fraction.

obtuse angle An angle that is greater than a right angle.

obtuse triangle A triangle in which there is one obtuse angle.

octagon A polygon with 8 sides.

ordered pair A pair of numbers that names a point on a coordinate grid.

ordinal numbers Numbers used to tell order.

ounce (oz) A customary unit of weight.

outcome A possible result of a game or experiment.

outlier A number in a data set that is very different from the rest of the numbers.

overestimate An estimate that is greater than the exact answer.

P.M. Time between noon and midnight.

parallel lines In a plane, lines that never intersect.
Example: 

parallelogram A quadrilateral in which opposite sides are parallel.

partial products Products found by breaking one factor in a multiplication problem into ones, tens, hundreds, and so on and then multiplying each of these by the other factor.

pentagon A plane figure with 5 sides.

perimeter The distance around a figure.

period In a number, a group of three digits, separated by commas, starting from the right.

perpendicular lines Two intersecting lines that form right angles. *Example*:

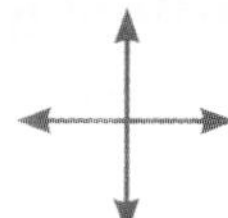

pictograph A graph using pictures or symbols to show data.

pint (pt) A customary unit of capacity. 1 pint = 2 cups

plane figure An endless flat surface.

plot To locate and mark a point named by an ordered pair on a grid.

point An exact location in space.

polygon A closed plane figure made up of line segments.

pound (lb) A customary unit of weight. 1 pound = 16 ounces

prediction An informed guess about what will happen.

probability A number telling the likelihood an event will happen.

product The answer to a multiplication problem.

pyramid A solid figure whose base is a polygon and whose faces are triangles with a common vertex.

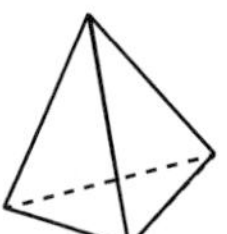

quadrilateral A polygon with 4 sides.

quart (qt) A customary unit of capacity. 1 quart = 2 pints

quotient The answer to a division problem

radius Any line segment that connects the center to a point on the circle.

range The difference between the greatest value and the least value in a data set.

ray A part of a line that has one endpoint and continues endlessly in one direction.

rectangle A quadrilateral with 4 right angles.

rectangular prism A solid figure whose faces are all rectangles.

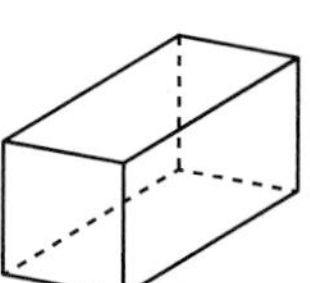

rectangular pyramid A solid figure with a rectangle for its base and triangles for all other faces.

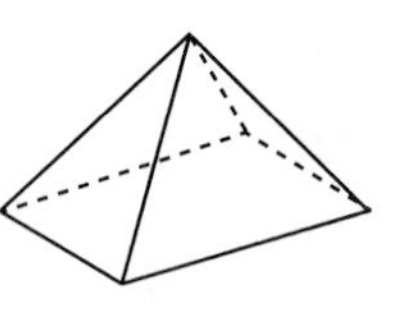

reflection Gives its mirror image.

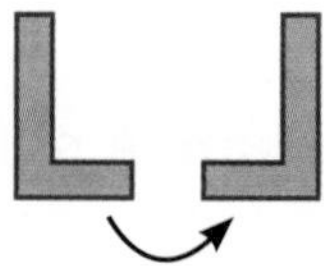

remainder The number that remains after the division is complete.

rhombus A quadrilateral in which opposite sides are parallel and all sides are the same length.

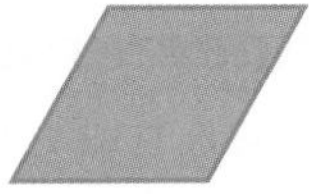

right angle An angle that forms a square corner.

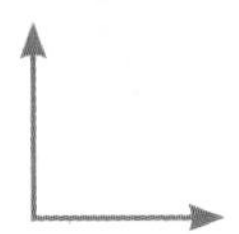

right triangle A triangle in which there is one right angle.

rotation Moves a figure about a point.

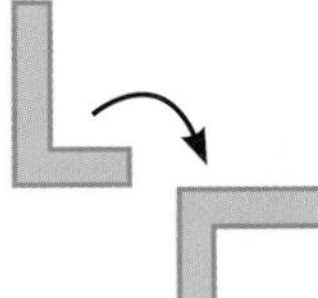

rounding Replacing a number with a number that tells about how many or how much to the nearest 10, 100, 1,000, and so on.

S

scale Numbers that show the units used on a graph.

scalene triangle A triangle in which no sides are the same length.

second A unit of time.
60 seconds = 1 minute

side Each of the line segments of a polygon.

similar figures Figures that have the same shape and may or may not have the same size.

simplest form A fraction in which the numerator and denominator have no common factors other than 1.

solid figure A figure that has length, width, and height.

solution The value of the variable that makes an equation true.

solve Find a solution to an equation.

sphere A solid figure which include all points the same distance from a point.

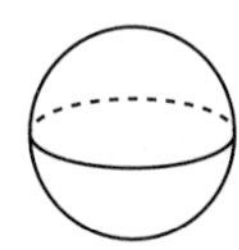

square A quadrilateral with 4 right angles and all sides the same length.

square pyramid A solid figure with a square base and four faces that are triangles.

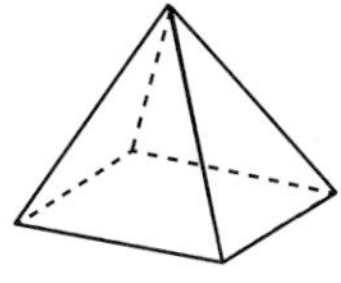

standard form A way to write a number showing only its digits.
Example: 2,613

straight angle An angle that forms a straight line.

sum The result of adding numbers together.

survey Collecting information by asking a number of people the same question and recording their answers.

symmetric A figure is symmetric if it can be folded into two congruent halves that fit on top of each other.

tablespoon (tbsp) A customary unit of capacity. 1 tablespoon = 3 teaspoons

teaspoon (tsp) A customary unit of capacity. 3 teaspoons = 1 tablespoon

tenth One of ten equal parts of a whole.

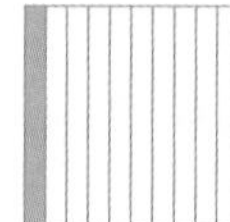

ton (T) A customary unit of weight. 1 ton = 2,000 pounds

translation A change in the position of a figure that moves it up, down, or sideways.

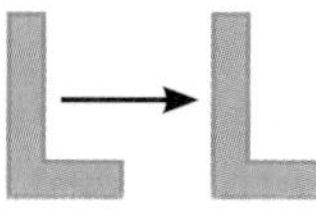

trapezoid A quadrilateral with only one pair of parallel sides.

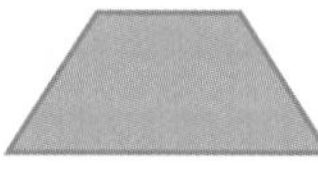

tree diagram A display to show all possible outcomes.

trend A pattern in the data on a line graph, shown by an increase or decrease.

triangle A polygon with 3 sides.

triangular prism A solid figure with two bases that are triangles and the other three faces are rectangles.

underestimate An estimate that is less than the exact answer.

unfair game A game in which each player doesn't have the same chance of winning.

unlikely (event) An event that probably will not happen.

variable A symbol or letter that stands for a number.

vertex (plural, vertices) The point where two rays meet to form an angle. The points where the sides of a polygon meet. The points where three or more edges meet in a solid figure that does not roll. The pointed part of a cone.

volume The number of cubic units needed to fill a solid figure.

week A unit of time equal to 7 days.

weight How heavy an object is.

word form A number written in words. *Example*: Four thousand, six hundred, thirty-two.

yard (yd) A customary unit of length.
1 yard = 3 feet

year A unit of time equal to 365 days or 52 weeks or 12 months.

Zero Property of Multiplication The product of any number and zero is zero.

Scott Foresman • Addison Wesley

enVisionMATH™ Texas

Cover

Luciana Navarro Powell

Photographs

Every effort has been made to secure permission and provide appropriate credit for photographic material. The publisher deeply regrets any omission and pledges to correct errors called to its attention in subsequent editions.

Unless otherwise acknowledged, all photographs are the property of Scott Foresman, a division of Pearson Education.

Photo locators denoted as follows: Top (T), Center (C), Bottom (B), Left (L), Right (R), Background (Bkgd).

Front Matter: xvi ©Bob Mitchell/Corbis

2 ©Merlin D. Tuttle/Bat Conservation International; 3 (TL) ©Tom Van Sant/Geosphere Project-Santa Monica/Photo Researchers, Inc., (BL) ©Bettmann/Corbis, (BC) Getty Images; 9 Getty Images; 13 ©Rexford Lord/Photo Researchers, Inc.; 16 ©VStock/Index Open; 28 (L) ©Jill Stephenson/Alamy Images, (B) Brand X Pictures; 29 (TL) ©Nicholas Veasey/Getty Images, (BL) NASA; 32 (BL) ©Nicholas Veasey/Getty Images; 34 ©Cameron Laird/Rex Features, Limited; 39 (BC) Corbis, (CL, C, TC) ©photolibrary/Index Open; 47 ©Ulrich Doering/Alamy Images; 54 ©Mark Sykes/Alamy; 66 (Bkgd) ©Marc Muench/Corbis, (C) Imaginary recreation of an Aztec Sun Stone calendar, Late post classic period, Aztec/Jean-Pierre Courau, Private Collection/Bridgeman Art Library; 67 ©Worth Canoy/Corbis; 71 ©Garold W. Sneegas; 73 (CL) ©Amos Nachoum/Corbis, (L) ©AGE Fotostock/SuperStock; 90 ©Royalty-Free/Corbis; 91 ©Labat J.M./Peter Arnold, Inc.; 112 (TL) ©Roger Harris/Photo Researchers, Inc., (B) ©Purestock/Getty Images; 113 ©Joe McDonald/Animals Animals/Earth Scenes; 117 Richard Lewis/©DK Images; 128 (L) ©Witold Skrypczak/Lonely Planet Images, (TR) ©Nils Jorgensen/Rex USA; 129 ©Alex Steedman/Corbis; 131 ©Steve Vidler/SuperStock; 141 (CL, C, R) ©Royalty-Free/Corbis; 143 (BR) ©Yann Arthus-Bertrand/Corbis, (BR) Tracy Morgan/©DK Images; 152 (C) Andy Holligan/©DK Images, (TL) ©Drawhorn's Classic Images; 153 (TL) ©Daniel Joubert/Reuters/Corbis, (C) ©SSPL/The Image Works, Inc.; 156 GSFC/NASA; 165 ©Daniel Joubert/Reuters/Corbis; 174 (T) ©AP Images, (B) ©Stefano Paltera/Reuters/Landov LLC; 175 ©JSC/NASA; 184 ©AP Images; 196 ©AP Images; 197 (T) ©Richard D. Fisher, (BL) ©Panoramic Images/Getty Images; 200 ©Panoramic Images/Getty Images; 211 (C, CL) Digital Vision, (CR) Getty Images; 218 (B) ©Keren Su/Corbis, (TR) Courtesy of New Bremen Giant Pumpkin Growers; 219 (TL) ©Geosphere/Planetary Visions/Photo Researchers, Inc., (BL) ©Kent Kostka; 230 Courtesy of New Bremen Giant Pumpkin Growers; 233 Rex USA; 242 Corbis; 244 (B) ©Momatiuk - Eastcott/Corbis, (TL) ©Charles E. Rotkin/Corbis; 245 (TL) ©Millard H. Sharp/Photo Researchers, Inc., (C) ©D. Hurst/Alamy Images; 259 ©Charles E. Rotkin/Corbis; 260 ©Phyllis Greenberg/Animals Animals/Earth Scenes; 268 (B) ©Don Klumpp/Getty Images, (TL) ©Pablo Martinez Monsivais/AP Images; 269 ©Mehau Kulyk/Photo Researchers, Inc.; 276 Jupiter Images; 284 (B) ©Louie Psihoyos/Getty Images, (CL) Getty Images; 285 (TL) The Granger Collection, NY, (B) Getty Images; 291 Hemera Technologies; 300 Getty Images; 301 (C) Jupiter Images, (C) ©photolibrary /Index Open, (TL) Getty Images, (BL) ©3D4Medical/Getty Images; 306 Getty Images; 307 Getty Images; 309 Netter medical illustration used with permission of Elsevier. All rights reserved.; 315 (TL) Getty Images, (TR) ©Goodshoot/Jupiter Images; 319 ©Royalty-Free/Corbis; 324 (B) ©D. Boone/Corbis, (B) Max Alexander/©DK Images; 325 (CR) Getty Images, (C) Hemera Technologies, (TL) M. C. Escher's "Symmetry Drawing E78"/©2007 The M. C. Escher Company, Baarn, Holland. All rights reserved.; 326 (TR) Jupiter Images, (TR) Getty Images; 327 M. C. Escher's "Symmetry Drawing E78"/©2007 The M. C. Escher Company, Baarn, Holland. All rights reserved.; 328 Jupiter Images; 331 Jupiter Images; 335 ©Dean Fox/SuperStock; 342 (TL, CC) Courtesy of TelecomPioneers, (B) ©AP Images; 343 (TL) ©AP Images, (BL) Getty Images; 344 Jupiter Images; 345 ©AP Images; 346 (TC) Jerry Young/©DK Images, (C) ©Jonathan Blair/Corbis; 362 ©BIOS Gilson François/Peter Arnold, Inc.; 363 ©Scott Camazine/Photo Researchers, Inc.; 368 (CR) ©Jerry Cooke/Corbis, (BL, TR) Getty Images; 369 (TL) ©AGE Fotostock/SuperStock, (B) ©Fraser Hall/Robert Harding World Imagery/Getty Images, (BL) Getty Images; 373 Linda Jeresh/©The Garland News, LLC.; 376 ©Royalty-Free/Corbis; 377 (CL, BR) ©photolibrary/Index Open, (CR) ©GK & Vicki Hart/Getty Images; 378 Getty Images; 379 Stockdisc; 380 (C, TC) Getty Images, (CL) Hemera Technologies, (CL) ©photolibrary/Index Open, (TR) Jupiter Images; 381 Getty Images; 382 (BL) Getty Images, (C) ©Face to Face Bildagentur GMBH/Alamy; 383 (CL) Corbis, (C) Ingram Publishing, (CR) ©Goodshoot/Jupiter Images, (CR) ©DK Images; 386 (C, BR) Jupiter Images; 390 Stockdisc; 392 (CL) ©Guy Vanderelst/Getty Images, (B) ©Fletcher & Baylis/Photo Researchers, Inc.; 393 ©A. T. Willett/Alamy Images; 394 Jupiter Images; 395 ©Dr. John Corder; 397 ©Royalty-Free/Corbis; 399 (BR) Courtesy of Air Tractor, Inc., (C) ©Royalty-Free/Corbis, (CR) Digital Vision, (CR) Jupiter Images, (CR) Getty Images; 408 (CL) ©Bill Varie/Corbis, (Bkgd) ©Harald Sund/Getty Images; 409 (TL) ©Norman Tomalin/Alamy Images, (BL) ©Blend Images/Getty Images; 411 ©Jose Fuste Raga/Corbis; 417 Jerry Young/©DK Images; 418 Design Pics; 426 (TL) ©Gene Rhoden/Visuals Unlimited, (B) ©Alexander Walter/Getty Images, (BR) ©Dorling Kindersley/Getty Images; 427 (TL) ©DAJ/Getty Images, (CR) ©Rubberball/Jupiter Images; 462 ©Visions of America. LLC/Alamy; 467 (B) ©DANI/JESKE/Animals Animals/Earth Scenes, (B) ©IT Stock Free/Jupiter Images

Index

L

M